POLSKA
ČESKÁ
REPUBLIKA
SLOVENSKO

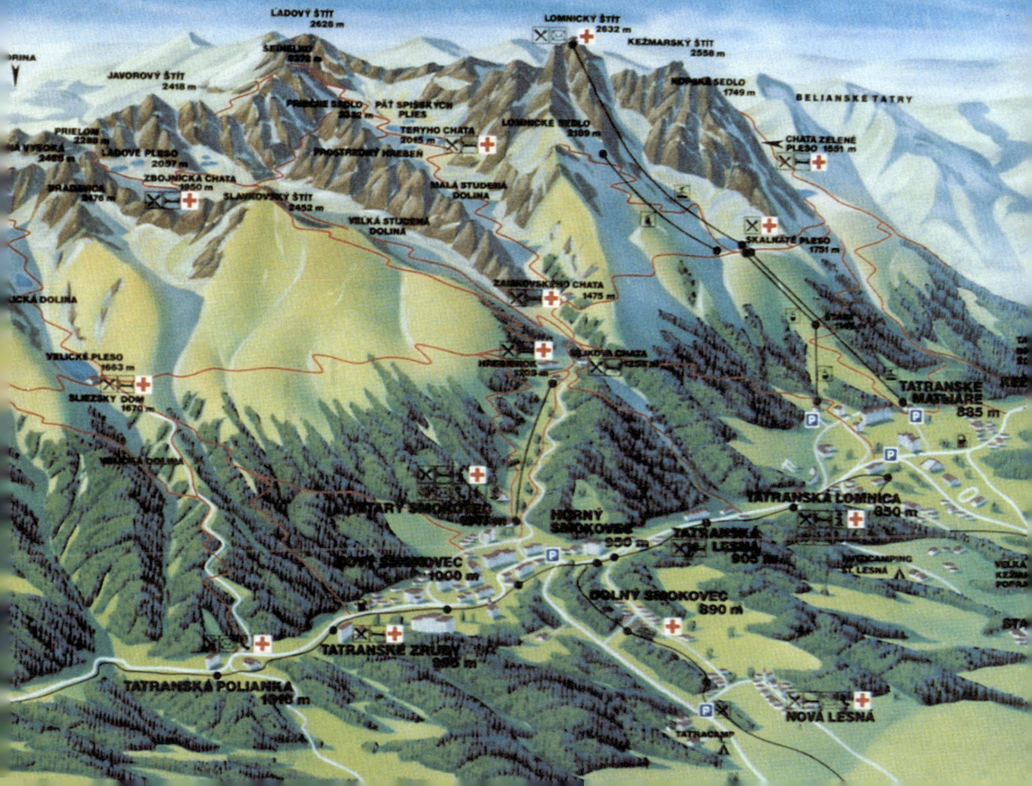
LADOVÝ ŠTÍT
2628 m
LOMNICKÝ ŠTÍT
2632 m
KEŽMARSKÝ ŠTÍT
2558 m
JAVOROVÝ ŠTÍT
2418 m
BELIANSKE TATRY
PÄŤ SPIŠSKÝCH
PLIES
TERYHO CHATA
LOMNICKÉ SEDLO
2189 m
CHATA ZELENÉ
PLESO 1551 m
PRIELOM
LADOVÉ PLESO
2057 m
PROSTREDNÝ HREBEŇ
ZBOJNÍCKA CHATA
1950 m
SLAVKOVSKÝ ŠTÍT
2452 m
MALÁ STUDENÁ
DOLINA
VEĽKÁ STUDENÁ
DOLINA
SKALNATÉ PLESO
1751 m
1475 m
VELICKÉ PLESO
1663 m
SLIEZSKY DOM
1670 m
TATRANSKÉ
MATLIARE
885 m
TATRANSKÁ LOMNICA
850 m
HORNÝ
SMOKOVEC
950 m
NOVÝ SMOKOVEC
1000 m
DOLNÝ SMOKOVEC
890 m
TATRANSKÉ ZRUBY
TATRANSKÁ POLIANKA
NOVÁ LESNÁ

DANIEL KOLLÁR
JÁN LACIKA
ROMAN MALARZ

THE SLOVAK-POLISH TATRAS

DAJAMA
VYDAVATEĽSTVO

Partners of media

DENNÍK SME TIE PRAVÉ NOVINY

gratex international

THE SLOVAK-POLISH TATRAS

1st edition, 1998

Published by: DAJAMA, Klimkovičova 1, 841 01 Bratislava

Authors: Daniel Kollár, Ján Lacika, Roman Malarz

Editor: Daniel Kollár

Technical editor: Daniel Kollár, Ján Lacika

Translation: Hana Contrerasová

Language editor: Alan Jones

Photographs: Ladislav Deneš, Mikuláš Huba, Ladislav Janiga, Daniel Kollár, Ján Lacika, Jaromír Sýkora, Miroslav Vážny

Cartography: Vojenský kartografický ústav, š. p., Harmanec
Kartanova, spol. s r. o., Bratislava

Design and layout: Peter Blaho and Ján Hladík

Lithographs: RESSPRINT, a. s., Senica

Print: adut FORTUNA PRINT

This guide book is available also in the Slovak, German, Polish, Hungarian, Russian languages.

ISBN 80-967547-4-2

INTRODUCTION

DAJAMA publications is pleased to present another title from its series "Regions without frontiers" which traditionally promotes the idea of the coexistence of two nations in the boundary areas of Slovakia. The territories on both sides of the border have many common features and strong historical links. The contemporary frontiers are no longer barriers between the respective countries, moreover, the opposite is true, as they represent a bond between the nations and their cultures. The geographical, historical and cultural kinship of the boundary regions of Slovakia offers an ideal opportunity to present natural and cultural landmarks and the unique characteristics of the territories, with numerous traces of important historical events and traditions.

The first book to appear in the series was "The Slovak-Austrian basin of the river Morava" published in the Slovak and German languages. This particular book, however, "The Slovak - Polish Tatras" appears in six languages. The fundamental aim of the authors is to present to the reader the territory of the Slovak and Polish Tatras. The territory around the Tatras overlaps with almost the whole of the Orava, Liptov, Spiš and Podhale regions, while only the remotest corners of the regions have been omitted herein. As the main subject of the book is the High Tatra mountains only the most important travel and tourist centres have been included.

The introductory chapters of the Slovak part of the territory of the Tatra region contain basic and general geographical characteristics, its history, historical links with the Polish side, its population and settlements. The second section is dedicated to the settlements of the Tatra region of the Slovak part of the Západné and the Východné Tatry mountains (from Zuberec to Tatranská Javorina) highlighting their natural beauty, with descriptions of the most beautiful tourist tracks and trips, as well as the characteristics of the historical and cultural monuments of the Tatra communities. The third chapter deals with the towns and villages of the sub Tatra region of Orava, Liptov and Spiš (including Zamagurie), again presenting its history, monuments and nature. The Polish part of the Tatras is structured in the same way, beginning with a general introduction, followed by the characteristics of the Polish part of the mountains and concluding with the areas of Polish Orawa, Podhale, Spisz, and Pieniny.

The text is refreshed by various legends, stories, myths and some interesting details which complement the general picture of the mentality, customs, nature and cultural affinity of both the Slovaks and the Poles. The Tatras in fact do not separate these nationalities, instead they represent the common setting and bond of a centuries-long coexistence of the members of the various ethnic groups. I trust that this book will be a tribute to the wonderful nature of the Slovak and Polish Tatras and it is our aspiration to convey a colourful picture of the people who created, and still create, its history. I am convinced that the book will be a good and interesting guide to the attractive territory of the Tatras and will pay homage to the common Slovak-Polish cultural traditions and the friendly co-operation between these two Slavic nations.

The Editor

ACKNOWLEDGEMENT

First of all I should like to express my gratitude to the co-authors Ján Lacika and Roman Malarz. I am equally indebted to the historian Ivan Chalupecký, mountaineer Marián Šajnoha, ecologist Milan Koreň and the team of the employees of the Museum of Janko Kráľ in Liptovský Mikuláš who provided indispensable guidance and suggestions. The preparation of six language versions would not have been possible without the co-operating translators, proof-readers, and a team of technicians lead by Erika Mészárosová. Also, the information and finances provided by the mayors of the towns and villages in the sub Tatra region represent an important contribution to our publications. My thanks go to all of them.

But the greatest share of gratitude goes to my closest collaborators, Danica and Peter Augustini and my wife Zuzka. Without their help this big six-language project would have been an impossible venture. Let this book motivate our children Peťka, Kamilka, Miško and Danielka to frequently visit the Tatra valleys and its peaks.

The Editor

CONTENTS:

THE SLOVAK TATRAS

SITUATION

The southernmost and larger part of the Tatras is a region which belongs to the Slovak Republic. It is situated in the northern boundary, on the frontier with Poland and occupies almost a central position, slightly displaced to the east. Its prolonged shape traces the geographical parallel. The distance between the edge of the region and the westernmost point of the Republic is approximately 190 km, whilst from its easternmost point it is about 160 km in a straight line.

Three sides of the Slovak part of the Tatra and sub Tatra regions are limited by the geographical co-ordinates and the remaining fourth side constitutes the state border line. The western fringe corresponds to the meridian of 19° and 30′ of eastern longitude, the southern border traces the parallel of 49° northern latitude. The eastern limit shifts about 10 km eastward of the meridian 20° 30′ of eastern longitude. The northern border follows the Slovak-Polish state border line.

The inner division of the region is, depending on criteria applied, administrative or official, or the natural division. The borders of the land forms agree with the ones of the geographical units. The Tatra mountains are a compact territorial unit representing an independent region. Another seven geographical units entering with their larger parts in the Tatras are: the Podtatranská kotlina basin, Oravská kotlina basin, Podtatranská brázda furrow, and the mountain ranges: Oravská Magura, Pieniny, Skorušinské vrchy, and Kozie chrbty. The Low Tatras, the Chočské vrchy, Levočské vrchy mountains, Ľubovnianska vrchovina highlands, Spiš-Šariš intermediate mass, Oravská Magura mountains, Oravská vrchovina mountains, and the Hornádska kotlina basin come in to the Tatras only on their outskirts.

On the Slovak side of the Tatras three distinct historical provinces were originally formed: Orava in the north-west, Liptov in the south-west of the region and Spiš in the east. The Tatras represent their natural borders. The changes brought about by the new territorial and administrative division of the Slovak Republic in 1996 have divided the Tatra region into two new provinces, those of Žilina and

Above: Kolový štít peak in the High Tatras

Prešov. The province of Žilina corresponds with the districts of Liptovský Mikuláš in the west and Tvrdošín in the north-west, and Prešov province contributes by the districts of Poprad, Kežmarok and the western parts of the districts of Stará Ľubovňa and Spišská Nová Ves.

NATURAL SETTING

GEOLOGY AND RELIEF

The Tatra mountains occupies an area of 786 square kilometres of which 550 are in Slovakia. The Tatra mountains consist of the higher Východné Tatry or the eastern Tatras and the lower Západné Tatry or the western Tatras. The border between them passes from the Ľaliové sedlo saddle over the Tichá dolina valley to the Závory saddle in the lateral ridge of Liptovské kopy mountains. It descends from the Závory saddle to the bottom of the Kôprová dolina valley and continues along its axis up to Podbanské.

The eastern Tatras are further divided into the High Tatras and the Belianske Tatry. The two mountain ranges are separate from each other by two opposite valley systems heading to the Kopské sedlo saddle. West of the saddle the border follows the axis of the Zadné Meďodoly valley and the lower reaches of the Javorová dolina valley. On the eastern side of the Kopské sedlo saddle it runs down the Predné Meďodoly valley. At the point of reaching the valley of Kežmarská Biela voda it turns north below the slope of the Bujačí vrch mountain to the neighbouring valley dolina Siedmich prameňov.

The High Tatra mountains are set like a gem in the centre of a ring formed by basins and mountains. A distinctly lower surrounding landscape offers a complete panoramic view of this most precious Slovak mountain range. The typical jagged silhouette of the Tatras appears on the horizon even from a distance of several tens of kilometres, providing the weather is favourable.

Left: The group of Lomnický štít peak

Rivals of the Tatras:

The basins and furrows in the Tatra region are significantly lower than the highest Carpathian mountain range and the surrounding lower mountains cannot compare with the rocky giants of the Tatras. The highest summits of the surrounding mountain ranges are lower than the Tatra peaks by 800 to 1,400 metres. Only some more distant Carpathian mountains, such as Veľký Choč (1,611 m) lying more than 20 kilometres further west or the Low Tatras most dominant peaks, Ďumbier (2,046 m) and Kráľova hoľa (1,946 m) about 30 km south, can compete with the Tatra peaks. North and east of the Tatras there are no rivals, if we do not take into consideration the Babia hora mountain (1,723 m) north-west of the Roháče mountains.

The twenty five highest Tatra peaks

(in metres above sea level)

1.	Gerlachovský štít	2 655
2.	Gerlachovská veža	2 642
3.	Lomnický štít	2 632
4.	Ľadový štít	2 627
5.	Pyšný štít	2 623
6.	Zadný Gerlach	2 616
7.	Malý Ľadový štít	2 611
8.	Lavínový štít	2 606
9.	Kotlový štít	2 601
10.	Lavínová veža	2 600
11.	Malý Pyšný štít	2 591
12.	Veľká Litvorová veža	2 581
13.	Strapatá veža	2 565
14.	Vysoká	2 560
15.	Kežmarský štít	2 558
16.	Supia veža	2 540
17.	Končistá	2 535
18.	Malá Litvorová veža	2 533
19.	Baranie rohy	2 526
20.	Dračí štít	2 523
21.	Veľká Vidlová veža	2 522
22.	Český štít	2 520
23.	Veterný štít	2 515
24.	Malý Kežmarský štít	2 513
25.	Zadný Ľadový štít	2 507

The Tatra peaks rise above the southern basins by an entire two kilometres and are the highest of all the mountain ranges of the 1,200 km long Carpathian Arch. A glance at an atlas will show that, north of Alps in Europe, there is no mountain range higher than the High Tatras. Ten Tatra peaks extend beyond 2,600 metres above sea level and another fifteen are higher than 2,500 metres above sea level. The Moldoveanu mountain, in the second highest mountain range in the Carpathians, Fagaraš (Rumania), would occupy with its altitude of 2,543 m only the sixteenth position in the scale of the highest Tatra peaks. The second highest mountain range of Slovakia, the Low Tatras, is lower by more than 600 metres than the High Tatras and its highest peak, Ďumbier, would reach some place in the second hundred of the altitude scale of the Slovak peaks.

School children are taught that, geologically, the Tatras are of granite. The term is not altogether correct as the Tatra granites, taking into account their mineral composition, are actually biotic granodiorites. They are by far the greatest geological composition of the Tatras, amounting to approximately four fifths of the entire mountain range. Among the granodiorites, positions of other rocks, like gneiss, mica schist, composite gneiss and other sorts of schist only sporadically occur. North of the mountain range is a consistent belt of folded Mesozoic sediments. In the west the territory of the Tatras enters into the massif of the Sivý vrch mountain, and cuts across the Roháčska dolina valley and below the Osobitá mountain proceeding east of the Polish Western Tatras. The rock composition of the northern sedimentary fringe of the Tatras is highly variegated, consisting of limestone and dolomites, quartzite, sandstone, and Werfenian shale. Limestone rock is rich in karstic phenomena. In the Belianske Tatry mountains we find caves, lapies-fields, and dolines, and in the high mountain environment of the Červené vrchy mountains, in the Západné Tatry mountains, there are also deep karst abysses.

Tatra granite:

Tatra granite is different to the compact Czech or Scandinavian granites. The dominating rock of the Tatras is heavily cracked as a result of alpine orogenic forces. If we climb to any of the Tatra peaks we shall not find a single granite block suitable for sculpture. This property of Tatra granite is of great concern, especially to mountaineers. Erosion and avalanches, as well as sudden weather changes are the most frequent causes of accidents in the Tatras. In the granite face of the Kostolík mountain in Batizovská dolina valley such an expe-

rienced mountaineer as the Pole Wieslaw Stanisławski fell to his death. Despite these dangers, however, committed climbers still challenge the rocky walls of these granite mountains.

The Tatras are a comparably young mountain range. Of the same age as the whole of the Carpathians, the Alps and the Balkan mountain ranges, they belong to the group known as Alpine Europe. The appearance of the pre-Tertiary Tatra landscape is now irrevocably lost, destroyed forever by the dramatic events of the younger geological periods. Perhaps the only passive witnesses of these past orogenic events, during the Palaeozoic and Mesozoic periods, are the rocks of the highest Carpathian mountain range. The hidden secrets buried in rock formations can only be disclosed by the patient hands of geologists. They are trying to reconstruct the face of the Mesozoic Tatras which first succumbed to the folding process and later submerged under the waves of the tropic sea during the Tertiary period. Sediments from the sea can be found in the filling of the contiguous embedded sub Tatra basins.

A dinosaur in the Tatras:

In the autumn of 1995 fortune smiled on a pair of Slovak geologists. On a plain surface of a piece of Mesozoic rock, picked up in the Tichá dolina valley, they noticed some unusual little hollows. Laboratory analysis revealed a surprising find: The hollows in the rock were simply the footprints of a large three-digit creature that once walked in the ancient Tatras. Experts in ancient fauna tried to decipher the mystery, in a manner not unlike a detective investigation. Finally they found out that the creature treading the prehistoric Tichá dolina valley was a species of dinosaur with the scientific name Coelurosaurichus tatricus. *The footprints of the dinosaur had been miraculously preserved on the surface of a limestone fragment which was once, some 195 million years before, an area of soft mud. The area of the contemporary Tichá dolina valley was then a wasteland with dispersed tropical vegetation of prehistoric shrubby horsetails and ferns. Then the sandy mud dried up and became solid, and later turned into limestone.*

The present form of the Tatras started to emerge only in the Tertiary period, about 15-20 million years ago. It is supposed that at the beginning they were lower, medium high mountains free of cliffs, rocky ridges, deep valleys and mountain lakes. A good example what the Tatras looked like in the Tertiary period is the Lúčne sedlo saddle over the Popradské pleso lake. The most significant geological changes in the Tatras occurred in the last two million years, a period which endowed them with their present, dramatic appearance, the product of tectonic and glacial movement. The inner forces beneath the Tatras contributed to the uplifting of the mountain range over the surrounding basins and furrows to such an extent that in parts surpassed even the snow line.

In the Quaternary period the Tatra valleys were repeatedly filled with glaciers and the mountain ridges changed to a harsh unfriendly tundra and chilly rocky desert.

The Tatras were presumably covered by ice at least three times. In the course of the third and last of the glaciations, that started about 70 thousand years ago and lasted 60 thousand years, an enormous Scandinavian continental glacier came about

Left: Jahňací štít peak and the Belianske Tatry mountains

250 kilometres close to the Tatras. The snow line at the region of Central Europe dropped below 1,700 m above sea level and 33 Tatra valleys (in the Slovak part of the mountain range) were filled by valley glaciers, and also a number of kettle-like fields filled with hardened snow. During the ice expansion the glaciers covered the relief over an area of 15 thousand hectares. The southern part of the mountain range, higher as a result of the symmetrical uplifting of the mountain range, was more covered by ice. The southern glaciers occupied an area of 8,470 ha and the northern glaciers covered a total area of 6,530 ha. The longest glacier at the northern side of the Tatras filled the Bielovodská dolina valley. Its glacial tongue ends at distance of 14 km from the glacial cirque (a deep, steep-walled basin on a mountain shaped like a half a bowl) under the main ridge. It is estimated that the icy filling of the valleys was 330 m thick. The biggest glaciers on its southern side were in the Kôprová (12.5 km) and Mengusovská (10.7 km) valleys.

The last Glacial period finished about 10 thousand years ago. In an increasingly warm climate the glaciers disappeared from the Tatra valleys in the course of several centuries. First the heads of the glaciers were rapidly retreating upwards to colder and more sheltered cirques only to succumb later to the effect of ever warmer sunshine. The last of the small cirque glaciers thawed about 8 thousand years ago.

Ten thousand years in the history of the Tatras is too short a period for substantial changes in the appearance endowed to them by the glaciers of the last Glacial period. The only notable manifestation of the changes of glacial relief is the gradual filling of the valleys by rocky debris. The steep cliffs lost their icy shield against the destructive climatic effects following the ice period. The denuded rocky faces, steep troughs and sharp ribs release large amounts of eroded blocks and stones. The process is slow though continuous and the stony fragments roll down over the surface of large convex debris cones. Occasionally huge rocky blocks suddenly tumble down into the valley. The testimony of such dramatic events is represented by the heaps of unclassified stones found in some of the Tatra valleys, which are called fault fields. Under the massive debris cones and fault fields, at the bottom of glacial cirques, the most beautiful mountain lakes are also disappearing.

The **High Tatras** or Vysoké Tatry represent in Europe a unique concentration of natural beauty deserving their attribute of "the miniature Alps". In an area of 341 square kilometres (of which the Slovak part makes for 260 km^2) there is everything that may be offered by its bigger counterpart, the Alps, failing perhaps only in glaciers and capricorns. High mountain beauty dispersed in the Alps over a much larger area is here in the Tatras neatly confined to a small space. The main ridge of the High Tatras is 26 km long. It runs from the Ľaliové sedlo saddle (1,947 m) in the west, to the Kopské sedlo saddle (1,749 m) in the east. Its westernmost mountain is Svinica (2,300 m) and the last mountain in the east is Jahňací štít peak (2,229 m). The shape of the main ridge is that of a convex arch. The main ridge almost never drops below 2,000 m above sea level and culminates at Ľadový štít peak (2,627 m). The majority of the peaks of the main ridge are from 2,400 to 2,500 m high.

The main ridge of the High Tatras has several lateral ridges, five of which turn towards the south. Looking from the west to the east they are: the forks of Kriváň Mt. (2,494 m), Končistá Mt. (2,535 m), Gerlachovský štít peak (2,655 m), Slavkovský štít peak (2,452 m) and Lomnický štít peak (2,632 m). Due to the asymmetrical uplifting of the Tatras the peaks of the southern lateral ridges are higher than those in the principal ridge and northern lateral ridges. The highest peak of the Tatras is the Gerlachovský štít (2,655 m) in the central fork. The longest and most dissected is the fork of Kriváň. The northern forks of the High Tatras are lower and longer. In the Slovak part of the mountain range there are two main forks which jut out: the fork of the Vyšší Žabí štít peak (2,259 m) and the fork of the Široká peak (2,210 m).

The Tatra valleys represent a natural contrast to the mountain ridges and forks, the largest of which are situated at the southern region: Kôprová, Furkotská, Mlynická, Mengusovská, Batizovská, Velická, Veľká Studená, Malá Studená and Kežmarská Biela voda. The north has less valleys. More dissected valley systems are here connected into two large valleys: the Bielovodská and the Javorová.

The majority of the Tatra valleys was glaciated during the Glacial Age, which profoundly influenced their appearance. In the upper parts there are deep cirques, the central parts are mostly troughs (typical U-shaped glacial valleys) while the lower parts are covered by moraines. (moraine is a term for accumulation of earth and stones carried and finally deposited by a moving glacier – the result of a geological process in the remote past). The valleys descend in a step-like manner of plateaus with lakes, alternating with high rocky thresholds. The lateral valleys often end in the hanging part, high above the bottom of the principal valley. The majority of the valleys are adorned by numerous glacial lakes, in Slovak they are called *plesá*.

The peaks of the High Tatras:

The dissected relief of the High Tatras consists of 97 important mountains. A closer look at the network of fissured rocky ridges, forks and ribs reveals that it is formed by approximately one thousand peaks, towers, bastions and needles, each bearing its own distinctive name. The nomenclature of the Tatra peaks contains numerous evocative names like Baranie rohy (Ram Horns), Mlynár (The Miller), Satan, Dračí štít (Dragon Peak), Jastrabia veža (Goshawk Tower), derived from their strange shapes or some old folk tale.

The **Belianske Tatry mountais** is much smaller than the High Tatras and because of different geological factors their relief is also quite different. They extend over an area of 67.5 square kilometres and comprise a massive series of layers of Mesozoic sediments. Alternation of resistant limestone and dolomites, with softer shales and marlites, creates a typical terraced appearance of the slopes. The form of the Belianske Tatry is that of a straight line along the principal ridge almost tracing the geographical parallel. The ridge, 14 km long, is perpendicular to the eastern end of the High Tatras. In the north the Belianske Tatry are sharply limited by the Podtatranská brázda furrow. The southern border, with the High Tatras, consists of a series of valleys connected by the Kopské sedlo saddle (1,749 m).

There are nine mountains in the main ridge, six of them are more than 2,000 m above sea level (the mean altitude of the peaks is 2,038 m). The dominant mountains – Havran (2,125 m) and Ždiarska vidla (2,146 m) – are of exceptional beauty and create an original background to the village of Ždiar. The main ridge ends in the west by the lowest, but imposing mountain of Muráň (1,890 m) towering over the Javorina community. There are no large valleys in the Belianske Tatry such as there are in the High Tatras. Several short valleys are located north of Ždiar and the largest of them is the Monkova dolina valley. In the east the valley dolina Siedmich prameňov attracts lovers of romantic landscapes. There are several steep troughs cut into the southern flanks of the mountain range. During the Glacial periods in the Belianske Tatry there were only some minor slope and cirque glaciers not longer than 2.5 km.

The Tatra karst:

The limestone of the Tatras proved favourable for the origin of remarkable high-mountain caves. The karst area reaches over the timber line i.e. above 2,000 m above sea level. There are numerous karstic phenomena in the limestone ridge of the Belianske Tatry, namely the underground world of caves hidden in the limestone slope over the Tatra basin, which is variegated and quite fascinating. There are several caves (the Belianska jaskyňa cave, Alabastrová jaskyňa cave, and Ľadový sklep cave). The Belianska cave is the largest and the only one open to the public in the Slovak part of the Tatras. The Červené vrchy Mts. shelter the most beautiful alpine karst forms in the western Tatras. Besides the sinkholes in the Rozpadlá dolina valley and on the slòpe of the Kresanica Mt. there are some chimney abysses, typical for the region. The abyss of Zadný úplaz is 82 m deep. Vyšná Kresanica, at 2,081 m above sea level is the highest abyss in Slovakia. Also the limestone rock of the Sivý vrch Mt. and Osobitá Mt. with contiguous Juráňova dolina valley are karstificated. Deep in the ridge of the Sivý vrch mountain there is the deepest Tatra abyss with its bottom lying at a depth of 88 m. Near the forester's house in the Roháčska dolina valley there is an entrance to the Brestovská jaskyňa cave, the largest cave in the Belianske Tatry mountains. The Medvedia jaskyňa cave in the Suchá dolina valley is known for the discovery of bones of a long extinct cave bear.

The **Západné Tatry** or the Western Tatra mountains lie between the Eastern Tatras in the east and the Chočské vrchy mountains in the west. In the past they were called Liptovské hole or simply Hole. The older names suited them better (holý means naked) because they differ from the cliffs prevailing in eastern Tatras. The alpine meadows often reach as far as the tips of the peaks. Only the Roháče Mt, or the limestone-dolomite massif of the Sivý vrch mountain (1,806 m), the Osobitá (1,687 m) and the Červené vrchy mountains are actually cliffs.

Right: Západné Tatry mountains

The main ridge of Západné Tatry mountains proceeds roughly in the same direction as the geographical parallel. It is 32 km long and winding. Its westernmost peak is the Biela skala Mt. (1,316 m) above the Hutianske sedlo saddle. In the east it ends by the often visited Kasprový vrch Mt. (1,985 m), on the Polish side of the mountain range. In the central ridge of the Western Tatras there are 27 mountains, twenty of them are higher than 2,000 m. Their mean altitude is 2,035 m. The highest peak of the main ridge is the Baníkov Mt. (2,187 m) in the Roháče Mts. In the eastern side it culminates in Kresanica (2,122 m). The most conspicuous depressions in the main ridge of the western Tatras are the saddles of Pálenica (1,574 m) and Tomanová (1,680 m). The remaining saddles seldom drop below 1,900 m.

The main ridge has several lateral ridges in both northern and southern directions. Looking from the west they are: Babky (1,565 m), Ráztoky (1,948 m), Baranec (2,184 m), Jakubina (2,194 m), Bystrá (2,248 m) and Liptovské kopy (2,052 m). Again in the southern lateral ridges we find the highest peaks of the mountain range. The Bystrá Mt. (2,248 m) is the highest peak in the fork of the same name. Likewise, Jakubina (2,194 m) and Baranec (2,184 m) are higher than all the mountains of the main ridge. The southern forks abruptly descend by 1,000 to 1,500 m to the Liptovská kotlina basin.

A separate mountain group is formed by the Liptovské kopy Mts. in the east of the southern hill slope of the Západné Tatry mountain range, separated from the rest by a ring of the Tichá and Kôprová dolina valleys. The massif covered by alpine meadows sharply contrasts with the neighbouring lofty Kriváň mountain in the High Tatras.

The northern forks are lower and longer. The group of Osobitá (1,678 m), the lateral branch of the most bulky and divided fork of the High Tatras, called Dlhý úplaz, stands out for its robustness. The second branch traces the Slovak-Polish frontier and culminates in the Bobrovec Mt. (1,663 m). The remaining northern forks east of the Volovec Mt. (2,068 m) incline to the Polish side of the Západné Tatry mountains.

On the southern side of Západné Tatry mountain range the ridges regularly alternate with valleys. The following valleys point to the Liptovská kotlina basin: Suchá (border of the Západné Tatry and Chočské vrchy Mts.), Jalovecká, Žiarska, the

twins Jamnícka and Račkova, and the Bystrá dolina valley is the only one that does not reach the main ridge. In the east there are the two largest and most beautiful valleys, Tichá and Kôprová. The northern valleys of the Slovak part of the Západné Tatry mountains are arranged in a different way. We find here one large and branched Roháčska dolina valley. Beneath the lateral ridge are the attractive Bobrovecká and Juráňová dolina valleys oriented to the north, towards the Podtatranská brázda furrow. The Juráňov potok brook has carved a spectacular gorge into the resistant limestone and dolomite of the valley.

The **Roháče mountains** are often and justly praised as the most beautiful part of the western Tatras. The extensive Roháčska dolina valley is surrounded by a crown of wonderful peaks dominated by the majestic Baníkov Mt. In turn, the Ostrý Roháč and Volovec Mts. are the princes of the Roháče Mts. They form an indivisible couple of slender rocky mountains in the principal ridge, and look like two devil's horns, as expressed in their names (Ostrý Roháč = sharp horn and Volovec = the ox).

North from the western Tatras behind the Zuberecká brázda furrow lies a long ridge of the **Skorušinské vrchy mountains**. Their area is 176 km^2. The relief of the Skorušinské vrchy is rather monotonous, because of the geological process, with prevailing sandstone. It consists of a ridge about 30 km long with plateaus. The central ridge descends by steeper and shorter slopes to the Podtatranská brázda furrow, losing height of between 300 and 400 m on every 2 or 3 km. The northern and longer less steep slopes descend to the Oravská kotlina basin. Before reaching the basin they also descend by between 300 to 400 m but over almost twice the distance. The height of the ridge of the Skorušinské vrchy Mts. oscillates over one thousand meters and the highest mountain, Skorušiná, reaches 1,314 m above sea level. The ridge is interrupted only at two points by the valleys. The mountain range is cut between the mountain groups of Kopec and Skorušiná by a fault of the Oravica brook. The Skorušinské vrchy Mts. continue into Poland where they are called Gubalowka.

Left: Roháče mountains

In the region of Orava, the Oravská Magura Mts. and the Oravská vrchovina upland marginally come into the region of the Tatras. The **Oravská vrchovina upland**, in the picturesque landscape of the Orava region, even though called an upland it is actually a depression embraced by higher situated ridges of the Oravská Magura Mts. in the north-west and the Skrušinské vrchy Mts. in the south-east. The relief of the upland is composed of a network of moderately high round ridges and rather shallow branching valleys. The ridges which are between 700 to 900 metres above sea level, alternate with valleys and form the winding valley of the Orava river. The stream of the river meanders wonderfully on its way to the river Váh.

The high ridge of the **Oravská Magura mauntains** cloaked by forests, enters the region of the Tatras by its easternmost extreme. The continuous mountain barrier does not drop under the thousand meter contour line. It loses height only at the eastern end, where beyond the Magurka Mt. (1,112 m) it suddenly drops by 500 m in a distance of almost two kilometres directly into the water of the Orava dam.

The magic of the cliffs:

No natural line drawn on the map of Slovakia is as long as the cliff belt. Not even the blue ribbon of the river Váh equals it in length. The westernmost cliffs emerge from the Vienna basin and their massive arch reaches up to the region of upper Zemplín. This narrow cliff belt contributes an unusual magic to the landscape of some of the regions in Slovakia. Millions of years of active erosion disclosed the soft marlites and resistant limestone, moulding them into cliffs and small rocks which are pleasant to the eye. The forms of these huge cliffs acquire special dramatic features in the area of the Pieniny Mts. In contrast to them the river Orava in the Oravská vrchovina upland is bordered by a very narrow belt of limestone cliffs, some of which are very imposing, such as the slender cliff with the Orava Castle on top.

The south of the Oravian part of the Tatra region also represents the eastern part of the **Chočské vrchy mountains**, and consists of limestones and dolomites. It is transversally cut by narrow fault valleys of the streams springing in the Orava region and with an outlet to the river Váh in Liptov. The valleys Prosiecka and Kvačianska have a form of deep rocky gorges.

The twelve highest peaks of the Western Tatras *(in metres above sea level)*

1.	Bystrá	2 248
2.	Jakubina	2 194
3.	Baranec	2 184
4.	Baníkov	2 178
5.	Klin	2 176
6.	Blyšť	2 169
7.-8.	Pachoľa	2 166
7.-8.	Hrubá kopa	2 166
9.	Tri kopy	2 154
10.	Nižná Bystrá	2 153
11.	Príslop	2 145
12.	Hrubý vrch	2 137

The mountain ranges of the Orava region are much like those in Spiš. Both mountainous groups are as if a mirror reflection of the erect Tatra walls. The Spišská Magura Mts. are similar to the Skorušinské vrchy Mts. The Orava upland with its cliffs finds its parallel in the Pieniny Mts. and the Ľubovnianska upland. At the Orava end of the Tatra region there is a massive barrier of the Oravská Magura Mts., similar to the Spiš edge, where there are the equally massive and high Levočské vrchy Mts. And just as the Orava Mts. form a mountainous background to the Oravská kotlina basin, in the same way the Spišské vrchy Mts. surround the Popradská kotlina basin.

The **Spišská Magura mountains** neighbour with the Belianske Tatry. The two mountain ranges are so close that in winter the Havran and Ždiarska vidla Mts. cast their long shadows over the southern slopes of their neighbour, rising to the north, right behind the back of the Ždiar region.

The realm of the Maguras:

The Carpathians are full of Maguras. This name, which is common in the Carpathian Mts. and mountain ranges, occurs not only in the territory of Slovakia, but practically in all countries of the huge Carpathian Arch. They do not exist in Hungary, but in Slovakia there are 60 of them, 40 in Poland, 70 in Ukraine, and 25 derivations of the word Magura, such as Mahura, Megura, Megora, Migora or Magurka are found in Romania. As Fedorowicz asserts, the word magura has spread from Rumania. It was probably propagated by the

shepherds who together with their sheep were the protagonists of the Wallachian colonisation. The Romanian root of the word and the meaning of "hill" has presumably originated from an older Slavic word known in the 6th century in the form of magula. Its contemporary Slovak and Polish forms are mohyľa and mogila respectively, meaning a barrow.

The Spišká Magura mountain range has a 35 km long central ridge shaped like a vast boomerang. Its top is located north of the community of Lendak. One arm is oriented to the west with mount Repisko (1,259 m) at the end, the highest of the mountain range. The opposite arm of this mountain range is a central ridge running towards the north-east and again culminating at the end by the mountain Veterný vrch (1,101 m). The crosswise asymmetry of the Spišská Magura Mts. is even more conspicuous than in the Skorušinské vrchy Mts. The central ridge descends on its steeper and shorter side to the south and into the Ždiarska brázda furrow. The southern slopes are bordered by a row of isolated mountains, almost as high as the main ridge. The Vojnianska hora mountain (930 m) towering over the Vojňany community is the most remarkable of them. The country behind and north of the Spišská Magura Mts. is called Zamagurie. The relief and the whole landscape behind the Magura Mts. look different from the landscape situated in front of it. A complex system of long lateral ridges and valleys alternate with terrace fields and picturesque Zamagurian villages.

Left: Levočské vrchy mountains

The **Levočské vrchy mountains** are the limits of the Tatra region in the east. It is a massive mountain range built mostly of blocks. In thick coniferous forests of the short central ridge the Čierna hora mountain (1,289 m), the highest peak of the mountain range, is hidden. From the centre several long and terraced lateral ridges with deeply embedded valleys run outwards. Mineral water springs are frequent at the fault bordering the Levočské vrchy mountains. In the north-east the Levočské vrchy Mts. connect with a short section of the Spišská Magura Mts. Both mountain ranges are divided by the Ružbašská brána with the river Poprad. The river connects the Popradská kotlina basin above the community of Podolínec with the Ľubovnianska kotlina basin under the community Forbasy.

The Ľubovnianska basin belongs to the **Spiš-Šariš intermediate mass**. In the north-east there is a small protuberance of the **Ľubovnianska vrchovina uplands**. The north of the low mountain range is cut by ten embedded meanders of the river Poprad.

Zamagurie can boast of one of the most beautiful mountain ranges in Slovakia – the **Pieniny mountains**, which occupy an area of more than 100 square kilometres. Half of them are situated in the territory of Slovakia, the other half belongs to Poland.

The canyon of the Dunajec river:

The main protagonists in the Pieniny landscape are the river Dunajec and the cliffs. In the western part of the mountain range the two powerful natural rivals run up against each other: The swift waters of the Tatra river and the massive limestone cliffs. The final winner is the mighty Dunajec that subdues the hard rocks created here a deep canyon. On its way through the cliffs the Dunajec bends several times. The beginning and the end of the nine kilometre long canyon are only 2.5 kilometres distant from each other in a straight line. The canyon is up to 500 m deep in some places, its perpendicular walls are set directly in the river bed with numerous rock thresholds and rapids.

The Pieniny Mts. are not, especially their western part, exceptionally high. However, the fact is somewhat disguised by the extreme dissection of the land forms in the canyon of the Dunajec. The group of the Trzy Korony mountains on the Polish side does not reach a height of 1,000 m, falling 18 m short. The Holica mountain, the highest on the Slovak side is 156 m lower. It is paradoxical that the highest part of the mountain range is called Malé Pieniny (The Little Pieniny). The highest part in the boundary ridge, consisting of several smaller cliffs is Vysoké skalky (1,050 m). Farther to the south-east the relief is again lower and smooth land forms contrast with the cliffs of Litmanová. One of them is cut by the wonderful Jarabiná with cascades and giant pots.

The Aksamitka cave:

The valley of Lipnik is bordered in the north by a huge stone wall of the Haligovské skaly. These limestone cliffs, 400 m high, enshrine the well-known Aksamitka cave, 330 m long, named after the commander of the Hussite troops, Peter Aksamit, who fought in the territory of Old Hungary and who allegedly found refuge in the cave. Moreover, in 1874 the discovery of human remains in the same cave aroused a great deal of archaeological and public interest and confirmed the existence of a Stone Age settlement (Aurignacien) in Central Europe.

The region of the High Tatras is limited in the south by the high faces of the Low Tatras which, as they head towards the east, drop to the substantially lower Kozie chrbty mountains. The Low Tatras, which extend in the direction of the geographical parallels, have a central ridge which is 95 km long and presents a formidable obstacle when travelling from the south to the north of Slovakia. The highest peak of the mountain range, Ďumbier (2,034 m), is situated within the central ridge.

A much lower natural barrier are the Kozie chrbty Mts. Their highest peak Kozí kameň (1,255 m) offers tourists a privileged view of other Tatra peaks.

Piracy at the Kozie chrbty mountains:

Kozie chrbty became the setting of the "conflict" between the contiguous river basins of the rivers Hornád and Poprad. The river network of the Hornád, lying in the lower Hornád Basin, "attacks" the network of valleys draining the higher situated Poprad basin. The Hornád river was luckier as it seized the Gánovský potok brook which should in fact drain the basin of the river Poprad. Piracy, as this phenomenon is called, proceeded over the canyon in the easternmost promontory of the Kozie chrbty mountains. The "struggle" between these river basins is not yet over, favouring the aggressive Hornád over its rival Poprad.

The contrast between the sub Tatra depressions and the Tatras intensifies the overall impression of the mountains. The crown of basins and furrows enhances its majestic altitude. In the sub Tatra region are located the **Podtatranská kotlina**, **Oravská kotlina**, and **Hornádska kotlina basins**. The Podtatranská kotlina splits to the Liptovská kotlina and Popradská kotlina basins. The border between them represents a comparably low gravel threshold lying in the lowest section of the main European water divide in the region. The relief of the sub Tatra basin was formed on huge alluvial cones brought up to the basin by the wild water of the rivers fed by the Tatra glaciers in the Glacial period. The monotonous relief of the basins relief is interrupted by isolated mountains rising about 100 m over the surrounding plains. A good example is the Bôrik Mt (992 m) situated between the settlements of Mengusovce and Svit. The northern slopes of the Tatras drop to the Podtatranská brázda furrow. A narrow depression prolonged in the direction of the parallel consists of the Zuberec and Ždiar furrows connected across southern Poland in the region of Zakopane.

The sub Tatra travertine:

An interesting surface formation can also be found in the basins and furrows around the Tatras. Certainly the most fascinating are the travertine hills and cascades around the mineral water springs. The region of Liptov has its travertine formations near Bešeňová, Sliače and the Lúčky spa. The water of the Lúčanský vodopád waterfall flows on a travertine cascade. The Spiš region is rich in travertine. In Vyšné Ružbachy at the top of a sunken travertine hill a well-known circular lake, called the Kráter, has been formed. The travertine hills in the region of Gánovce and Hôrka became famous for significant archaeological finds documenting the oldest period of settlement in the territory of Slovakia. In the past travertine was extracted here and used for sculpture and stone-masonry.

WATER

The main European water divide between the Black and Baltic sea passes the Tatra mountains. Water from the Tatras is drained by forty streams that unite beyond the mountains into four principal rivers. The Czarny Dunajec and Poprad rivers head to the north and end as the Visla river in the Baltic sea. The water of the Biely Váh and Orava is carried by the Váh and Danube to the Black sea. High precipitation totals i.e. the overall amount of rain and snow, low evaporation and dissection of relief are the agents contributing to the Tatras' high specific runoff surpassing 50 litres per second of one square kilometre. The mountains have an extraordinary capacity to attract the atmospheric precipitations and to slow down their runoff. Great amounts of water accumulate in the debris cones, moraines and dwarf pine forests, however, the circulation of this water is rather shallow and consequently it is low in mineral content.

The water regime typical for high mountain ranges is preserved by the Tatra streams even far from the boundaries of the mountain range. The least discharge takes place during winter when a great part of water is bound by snow and ice, but an abrupt rise in the water levels comes with the first April snow thaw, culminating in early summer. The regime of the streams which do not spring up in the Tatras is different and their discharge culminates in the spring months.

The slope curves of the river network of the Tatras are uneven. There are numerous water falls at the rocky thresholds and overhanging lateral valleys at the point or their contact with the principal valleys.

The Tatra waterfalls:

The presence of waterfalls in the Tatra valleys contributes to their attraction. The most frequently visited are the Studenovodské waterfalls easily accessible from the Tatras' main tourist path, called the "magistrála". In the Nefcerka valley, one of the best preserved Tatra valleys there is one waterfall hidden in a spruce forest. At 80 metres it is the highest waterfall, not only in the Tatras, but probably in Slovakia. The waterfall bears the name of Slovakia's most important botanist – Andrej Kmeť. Below the Temnosmrečinské plesá lakes resounds the thundering of the Vajanského waterfall. The Skok waterfall in Mlynická dolina valley is visible from the ski resort – Areál snov – at Štrbské pleso. The biggest waterfall in the western Tatras is the Roháčsky measuring 18 m in height.

Bearing in mind that Slovakia, in general, is a country not rich in natural lakes, the Tatra region is an exception. The data available on the number of mountain lakes in the Tatras differ considerably. The reason for this is that the high-mountain lakes are gradually disappearing and so estimates vary over the criteria of what actually constitutes a lake. Consequently, the figures range from 121 to 189. The majority of them are in the High Tatras, where on the Slovak side of the mountain range there are approximately 100 with a water area of 3 square kilometres. Fewer lakes are in the Low Tatras (about 20), the largest being the Prvé

Right: Hincovo pleso lake

Roháčske pleso lake in Roháčska dolina valley extending over 2.22 hectares. There are no lakes in the Belianske Tatry mountains. There are several natural lakes outside the territory of the Tatras. In Spišská Magura there are the Jezerské (0.6 ha) and Osturnianske lakes that originated after the valley was blocked by a landslide. A small crater lake, 12 m diameter, can also be found in Vyšné Ružbachy, which originated because of the sinking of the travertine hill.

On the edge of the region two of the five largest artificial water reservoirs in Slovakia have been constructed. The earliest of these, the Orava Dam, was constructed in the 1950's and has a total reservoir area of 35.4 square kilometres and a volume of 346 million m^3 of water. Two decades later another dam was constructed on the river Váh in Liptovská Mara with an area of 21 km^2 and a volume of 360 million m^3 together with a smaller reservoir called Bešeňová (area 1.9 square kilometres). Two smaller artificial lakes were also constructed to meet the needs of a re-pumping water power station in Čierny Váh. The upper reservoir is situated on a high plain and the lower in the bed of the river Čierny Váh.

The **Tatra lakes** (called plesá) are the result of glacial activity during the last Glacial period. The water resulting from the thawed glaciers filled vari-

	Ten of the highest waterfalls in the High Tatras	*high (m)*
1.	Kmeťov vodopád *(Nefcerský potok brook)*	80
2.	Vajanského vodopád *(Temnosmrečinský potok brook)*	30
3.	Vodopád Skok *(Mlynický potok brook)*	25
4.	Katarakty (Studený potok brook)	22
5.	Obrovský vodopád (Studený potok brook)	20
6.	Roháčsky vodopád *(a brook in Spálená dolina valley)*	18
7.	Dlhý vodopád *(Studený potok brook)*	16
8.	Hviezdoslavov vodopád (Biela voda brook)	15
9.	Velický vodopád *(Velický potok brook)*	15
10.	Český vodopád *(a brook in Česká dolina valley)*	12

ous depressions, some of which are situated in bowl-like holes at the bottom of glacial cirques. The largest and the deepest of these cirque lakes in the Slovak Tatras is the Veľké Hincovo pleso lake and the highest is the Modré pliesko lake (2,192 m) in the Malá Studená dolina valley. Many lakes are in the lower parts of the valleys, close to their outlets to the land mass of the mountain range. They originated by blocking by a terminal moraine, such as the Popradské pleso lake in the Mengusovská dolina valley.

Of a partially different origin is that of the Štrbské pleso lake, where the water filled a depression on the surface of a thawing moraine. Cirque lakes have a clear and transparent water in places where they are more than 12 m deep. Their eventual disappearance was caused by the gradual infilling of stone debris. Dammed lakes are situated in a lower, biologically richer environment, hence their water is not as clear. However, they are also doomed to disappear as they become progressively covered by earth and subsequently turned to peat bogs. Numerous Tatra peat bogs are proof that this was the fate of the lower lying lakes. The total water volume of the Tatra lakes is about 50 million m^3 and only one fifth of the amount corresponds to the lakes on the Slovak side of the mountain range. The water of the lakes is, of course, not the original water of the thawed Tatra glaciers, but the accumulation of precipitation water over the course of ten thousand years.

The Tatras and the sea:

In the past an idea spread that the Tatra lakes were connected underground to the sea, which was propagated not only by common people. This hypothesis was investigated by some respectable 18th century scientists. For example, in 1751 the Imperial Commission of Mineralogy was ordered to research whether sea water manifested in the Tatra lakes. According to a rumour at the time, on the surface of the Zelené pleso lake, at the point where the Brnčalova chata cottage stands today, the remains of a sail were discovered. Also the alleged remains of a sea vessel found in the Morskie Oko lake were even displayed at the royal palace in

Left: Štrbské pleso lake

Warsaw. The presumed connection of the lakes and the sea is expressed in the name of the largest Tatra lake – Morskie Oko (The Sea Eye).

One of the great riches of the Tatra region is represented by the mineral and thermal water springs. Their occurrence is linked to the tectonically "alive" dislocation belts. In a massive fault at the southern edge of the Tatras several springs exist which according to their chemical composition are simple acidulous waters. Five of them are in the Starý Smokovec community (the best known is the Csáky's spring), whereas another three are located in the environs of Dolný Smokovec. Cold acidulous springs can be found in the communities of Tatranské Matliare, Kežmarské Žľaby and Lendak. A big sub Tatra fault heads further out to the east and to the southern borders of the Spišská Magura mountains. Here, in Vyšné Ružbachy some mineral springs can be found, such as in the faults of the northern slopes which also contain several mineral springs (for example, in the Oravice community). In the south-eastern margin of the region mineral springs can be found in Gánovce and Hôrka and in Červený Kláštor and Tvrdošín there are cold hydrogen monosulphate springs.

Ten largest lakes in the Slovak part of the Tatras *(ha)*

1.	Veľké Hincovo pleso	20.1
2.	Štrbské pleso	19.8
3.	Nižné Temnosmrečinské pleso	12.0
4.	Vyšné Bielovodské žabie pleso	9.6
5.	Popradské pleso	6.9
6.	Vyšné Temnosmrečinské pleso	5.6
7.	Nižné Terianske pleso	5.4
8.	Vyšné Wahlenbergovo pleso	5.2
9.	Krivánske Zelené pleso	5.2
10.	Nižné Bielovodské Žabie pleso	4.7

The five largest Tatra lakes

Lake	*Altitude above sea*	*Area in hectares*
1. Morskie Oko	1,393	34.9
2. Wielki Staw	1,664	34.3
3. Czarny Staw	1,580	20.6
4. Veľké Hincovo pleso	1,965	20.1
5. Štrbské pleso	1,350	19.8

CLIMATE

Regular weather reports often forecast that the coldest weather can be expected in the Orava, Liptov or Spiš regions, which affirms the fact that the Tatra region is the coldest in Slovakia. The most general and typical aspect of the climate, and not only of the Tatras, is the reduction in air temperature with rising altitude. Naturally then, the coldest places to be found are on the Tatra peaks and the warmest are the bottoms of the basins. On average each 100 metres of altitude means a drop in temperature by about 0.6 °C.

From among 87 weather stations the Lomnický štít peak (2,635 m) records the lowest mean annual temperature –3.8 °C. The highest mean annual temperature was taken in the town of Liptovský Mikuláš (573 m above the sea level) 7,0 °C, a difference of more than 10 °C. According to the monthly mean temperatures there are variations on the Lomnický peak between the coldest and the warmest months (February and July) of 16.2 °C, while in Liptovský Mikuláš it is 21.1 °C. The climatic contrasts rise in the basins as a consequence of the autumn and winter inversions that cool down the depressed parts of the Earth's surface in winter time. The difference in altitude between the community of Tatranská Lomnica and the higher situated Skalnaté pleso is 938 m, but the difference in the mean January temperatures is only 1.2 °C. There are incidences during some winter months when the sunny Skalnaté pleso lake is up to 10 °C warmer than the town of Poprad, submerged below in a frosty fog.

Meteorological research in the Tatras:

The oldest documents commenting the meteorological events in the Tatras are from the 18th century. However, regular meteorological observations began only in the 1860's when the first observation stations were founded over the entire territory of the Austrian-Old Hungarian Empire. The first weather stations in the Tatras were opened on the Polish side in 1867, in the areas of Poronin and Zakopane. In the southern side of the Tatras there are the oldest preserved records of meteorological observations kept by Dr. M. Szontagh between June 1875 and December 1891. Significant

weather stations originated at the time when a suspended cabin lift to the Lomnický peak was under construction, during the Second World War. Its lower station at the Skalnaté pleso lake has been in operation since 1939 and the upper station at Lomnický peak opened in October 1940. At 2,635 metres above sea level it is the highest situated weather station in Slovakia.

The Tatra region experiences many extremes also in snow and rain fall, with great variations throughout the region. Their amount can change from place to place depending on sea levels and slope exposure. Generally speaking, the higher the altitude the greater the increase in annual precipitation. For example, the difference in altitude between Tatranská Lomnica and the Skalnaté pleso lake (938 m) manifests in an increase of the mean annual precipitation total by 547 mm.

But there is another important factor to take into account, which is that the high barrier of the Tatras, almost 2,000 metres, obstructs the main rain bearing currents coming from the west and north-west. Consequently, the other side of the mountains is in a rain shadow ensuring that the Popradská kotlina and Hornádska kotlina basins do not receive as much rain as they should according to their altitudes. Poland's Zakopane, however, annually receives 300 milimetres more rain. The mean annual precipitation total in Poprad is 608 mm, and in Levoča it even drops to below 600 mm.

The largest amount of rain is recorded in the High Tatras: the mean annual total at Lomnický štít peak is 1,561 milimetres. Some rainfall stations in the Tatra valleys record values over 2,000 mm and the localities in Veľká Studená dolina valley, under the Svišťový štít peak (2,710 mm) and the Zbojnícka chata cottage (2,455 mm) experience most rain. The most humid month of the year is July (approximately 16% of the annual rainfall), and the least rain falls in February (about 4.5 % of the annual total). In the higher reaches of the Tatras a "double pace" of rainfall occurs with a principal summer maximum and a secondary one in December. Between these periods comes the main autumn precipitation minimum, and the secondary one occurs in March.

Left: The weather station at Lomnický štít peak
Right: Temperature inversion

Mean air temperatures *(in °C)*

station and its altitude	*I*	*II*	*III*	*IV*	*V*	*VI*	*VII*	*VIII*	*IX*	*X*	*XI*	*XII*	*Rok*
Liptovský Mikuláš (573 m)	-4,0	-3,4	1,4	6,4	11,7	15,6	17,1	16,3	12,2	7,6	2,7	-0,2	7,0
Poprad (703 m)	-4,8	-4,2	-0,6	5,0	10,2	14,2	15,8	15,0	11,0	6,3	1,3	-1,2	5,5
Tatranská Lomnica (840 m)	-4,9	-4,4	-0,8	4,4	9,7	13,6	15,2	14,6	10,5	5,8	0,9	-1,6	5,2
Štrbské Pleso (1 330 m)	-5,7	-5,6	-2,5	1,8	6,8	10,8	12,7	12,4	8,6	4,4	-0,4	-2,6	3,4
Skalnaté pleso (1 778 m)	-6,1	-6,6	-4,4	-0,8	4,0	8,1	10,0	9,7	6,3	3,2	-0,9	-3,2	1,6
Lomnický štít (2 635 m)	-11,6	-12,0	-9,5	-6,5	-1,6	2,5	4,2	3,9	0,8	-1,9	-6,0	-8,5	-3,8

Precipitation totals - snow and rain *(in mm)*

station and its altitude	*I*	*II*	*III*	*IV*	*V*	*VI*	*VII*	*VIII*	*IX*	*X*	*XI*	*XII*	*Rok*
Liptovský Mikuláš (573 m)	39	32	46	46	64	103	110	72	62	43	35	44	696
Poprad (703 m)	29	23	32	36	71	86	88	74	56	40	40	33	600
Tatranská Lomnica (840 m)	44	38	47	51	87	114	117	105	71	58	53	48	833
Štrbské Pleso (1 330 m)	60	58	60	64	95	122	125	103	78	67	69	63	964
Skalnaté pleso (1 778 m)	82	70	81	103	128	194	208	159	96	84	88	87	1380
Lomnický štít (2 635 m)	118	120	99	126	120	187	188	142	91	93	129	148	1561

The Tatras were denoted in the old maps by a German word *Schneeberg* meaning the Snow Mountain. The name was an appropriate one, as the snow cover exists in the Tatras longer than anywhere else. The Podtatranská kotlina basin maintains its typical autumn colours until the end of October, by which time the peaks are often dusted by the first snow falls. In May the basin landscape is fresh green but the Tatras are still covered by a white blanket of snow. In the Lomnické sedlo saddle the ski season usually ends late in May and in the Tatra valleys the snow lasts until late summer. The Veľká Zmrzlá dolina valley over the Brnčalova chata cottage is the focal point for summer ski enthusiasts.

The weather in the Tatras is characterised by instability, where the situation can completely change in a few minutes. In the summer this instability manifests in an intense storm activity, especially from June to August. At that time of year morning sunshine can often degenerate into a violent summer storm around midday accompanied by sweeping rain. Lightning is especially dangerous for tourists in open high-mountain country. The most stable weather can be expected in the Tatras in autumn during the time of an "Indian summer", which falls practically always at the end of September and through October although its length is, again, unpredictable. This period is remarkable for its stable, dry and comparably cool weather.

The weather in the Tatra regions is also influenced by the amount of sun radiation in the mountain ranges and basins. During the winter inversions the Tatra peaks get more sun than the depressed basins. For example, in January the Lomnický štít peak has a mean 137 hours of sunshine compared to the city of Poprad where it is only 95 hours. The Tatra valleys receive less winter sunshine than any other area in the region: the Zbojnícka chata cottage lacks sun almost throughout the whole of December because of low clouds and the long shadows of the surrounding ridges. The opposite is true during the summer, when the summer air currents often wrap the Tatra peaks in cloud, while below in Poprad or Štrba the sun is more likely to be shining. Tourists may not see the Tatras from Štrbské pleso lake for a whole week, Lomnický štít peak has a mean 199 hours of sunshine in July, but Poprad enjoys sun for 257 hours.

A typical feature of the Tatra climate is its windiness. Winds, near gale force, often spoil the stay of tourists over the upper timber line, whereupon it can change to violent storms. The notorious local wind, called in the Tatras the "fall wind" can especially cause a great deal of damage, as even the strongest trees can break under its impact.

SOILS, VEGETATION AND ANIMALS

The soil composition of the Tatra and sub Tatra regions is extremely variegated. The mountain, prevailingly forest soils, are in general shallow and a little fertile. Rendzinas, developed on limestone substrate, the silicate rocks generate more diversified soil types. In the lower parts of the mountain ranges there are brown forest soils which change to various types of Podzol soils according to rising altitude. Above the timber line in the Tatras shallow alpine soils are typical, whereas in the wet spots gleyic and peat soils predominate. More fertile basin and furrow soils are intensively used for agricultural purposes.

As far as vegetation is concerned, the Tatras belong to one of the most rich and variegated territories. More than 1,300 species of rare plants can be found here. The basic component of vegetation is represented by the alpine-Central European species spread over all the European mountain ranges, from the Pyrenees to the Caucasus since the Tertiary period. Numerous arctic-alpine species occurred in Central Europe in the Glacial period, and warmer inter-glacial epochs, surviving only in the cool positions of high mountains in the contemporary warmer period. *Dryas octopetala* grows in the Tatra alpine meadows in the same way it does in the arctic tundra. Botanists found in the Tatras about twenty of the Tatra and West Carpathians endemits (plants native to and growing only in the Tatras or West Carpathians).

A characteristic trait of the Tatras is the distribution of the vegetation into several altitudinal vegetation tiers. The beech belt is situated up to an altitude of approximately 1,250 metres. Man-made reforestation on the slopes of the medium high mountains has replaced the beech trees with rapidly growing spruce trees. Before deforestation the basins and furrows were also covered by beech forests. Now the beech does not grow in the Tatras with the exception of the remaining beech forests in the north of the Belianske Tatry Mts. Between 800 to 1,550 m above sea level in the Tatras there is an extensive and little differentiated spruce belt. The spruce forests locally alternate with fir-spruce forests. Natural spruce forests in the medium high mountains can be found only in the highest parts of the Chočské vrchy Mts., the Skorušinské vrchy Mts., the Oravská Magura Mts., the Spišská Magura Mts., the Levočské vrchy Mts., and on the northern slopes of the Low Tatras.

The upper timber line in the Tatras represents a significant landscape dividing line. Depending on the orientation of the slopes it oscillates between 1,550 and 1,650 metres above sea level and runs continuously along the entire circumference of the Tatras, entering some valleys and also into the interior of the mountain range. The upper timber line has in some places been artificially lowered, especially in the alpine parts of the Západné and Belianske Tatry mountains. In the past the shepherds cleared the spruce growths in the upper part of the forest vegetation tier to widen the pastures for ever larger sheep flocks and herds of cattle.

Unfavourable climate beyond the upper timber line is the reason why only solitary spruce trees and larches with flag-like crowns, and limba pines grow here, having been cut by violent winds. A dwarf pine belt reaches an altitude of between 1,800-1,850 metres above sea level. It is followed by subalpine and alpine vegetation belts. In extreme conditions of the alpine meadows about 300 species of tiny and assiduous plants grow and about 40 of them are even capable of surviving an altitude of 2,600 m above sea level. The richest in flora are the alpine meadows growing on the limestone base rock of the Belianske and Západné Tatry mountains.

The Limba pine:

*The Limba pine (*Pinus cembra *L.) is a high mountain type of pine, indeed an adornment of the Tatra nature. It grows next to the upper timber line, often in the steepest parts of the rocky hills. A poet described the limba pine as follows: "It breathes the blue of the sky and dreams the fairy dark of the starry nights..." The limbas of the Tatras are very stocky trees. In spite of it, there are not many of them left. The foresters estimate that the total area of the Tatra limba forests is not larger than 200 hectares. The largest limba forest is in the Furkotská dolina valley.*

The numbers of single animal species vary. One can meet them in the fields near the Gerlachov community just as on top of the Gerlachovský štít peak. Birds especially accompany Tatra visitors everywhere. In the foothills of the Tatras storks (*Ciconia ciconia*) make their nests, in the environs of Podspády in the Ždiarska brázda furrow the rare black stork (*Ciconia nigra*) can be observed. Thick woods are inhabited by red deer, boar, fox, badger, wild cat and minor rodents. Some of these rare animal species are unique to the region, having long since become extinct in Western Europe, such as

Right: The limba pine tree

varieties of bear, wolf, lynx, and river otter. Many of these forest animals, the bear for example, also roam in the territory above the upper timber line that shelters rare animals preserved from the last Glacial period. This is especially the terrain of the chamois (*Rupicapra rupicapra tatrica*) – a small goatlike antelope of Europe, the mountain marmot, as well as less known mammals such as the *Microtus nivalis, Pytimys tatricus, Sorex alpinus*. The rocky cliffs of the High Tatras are also the domain of the eagle (*Aquila chrysaetos*) nesting in inaccessible places on the cliff face. A typical high mountain bird which moves around the upper timber line is the timid *Nucifraga caryocatactes* nourishing on the limba cone seeds. In summer the Tatras only high altitude reptile, the viper, lies on the sunlit rocks, while in the brooks trout, grayling, and goby thrive. Fish live only in the lower situated lakes, the highest of which is the Popradské pleso lake, the natural environment for trout and the unique inhabitant of the cold water of the Furkotské lakes is the transparent crustacean *Branchinecta padulosa*. Fish stocks in the Štrbské pleso lake have been introduced there mostly by artificial means.

Chamois – the symbol of the Tatras:

The Tatras provide home for approximately 900 chamois, whose scientific name is Rupicapra rupicapra tatrica. *According to the renowned French scientist, C. Coututier, the Tatra chamois does not belong to the eleven breeds of mountain goat, but is a unique subspecies which developed in complete isolation following the last Glacial period. This is the reason why the Tatra chamois differs from its relatives in the Alps, the Apennines, the Balkans and it even possesses many different traits from the chamois living in other Carpathian mountain ranges. Accordingly, we can say then that there are only 900 Tatra chamois in existence on Earth.*

NATURE CONSERVATION

The unique natural wealth of the Slovak part of the Tatras is an object of conservation represented by three national parks, one protected landscape area and thirty small protected areas (national nature reserves and nature reserves). The first protected area, the Tatra National Park (TANAP) was founded by an Act of the Slovak Parliament on the Tatra National Park as approved in December 18, 1948, which came into force on January 1, 1949. Five years later a national park was also created on the Polish side of the Tatras.

The TANAP is an area consisting of the national park itself and an additional protective belt. The original area of the TANAP was 510 square kilometres with the protective belt consisting of the Západné Tatry Mts. and a part of the Zamagurie region with an area of 700 km^2. In 1978 TANAP was extended by the Západné Tatry and its area was then 730 km^2. Included in the protective belt of 390 km^2 is the Zuberec region, the picturesque meadow landscape of the upper Liptov region, and an edge of the Popradská kotlina basin neighbouring with the High Tatras. The administrative headquarters of the national park is located in Tatranská Lomnica.

The territory of the attractive Zamagurie region was already declared a protected territory in 1932, being the first protected large-area region in Europe. On the Polish side it is called Pieninski Park Narodowy, while the Slovak part of the Pieniny Mts. was a Slovak National Reservation. In 1967 The Pieniny National Park (PIENAP) seat-

ed in Červený Kláštor was established. According to the 1994 Act of the Slovak Parliament, concerning nature and landscape protection, its name was changed to the National Park Pieniny Mts. The total area of the National Park is 2,125 hectares and is surrounded by a protective belt of a much larger area than the National Park itself. It comprises Spišká Magura and the Malé Pieniny Mts., the western part of the Spiš-Šariš intermediate mass and the Ľubovnianska vrchovina Upland. In the south and south-west, bordering the TANAP, the protective belt of the National Park Pieniny reaches the Popradská kotlina basin and the Ždiarska brázda furrow.

Of the three national parks in the Low Tatras, the National Park of the Low Tatras (NAPANT), is the most recent, being officially declared in 1978. With its parkland area of 810 km², and an area of protective belt, 1,240 km², it is the largest national park in Slovakia, but it enters our territory only with its northern margin. The seat of NAPANT's administration is in the city of Banská Bystrica. Similar to NAPANT the Protected Landscape Region (CHKO), Horná Orava, enters the region of the Tatras only partially and marginally. CHKO was officially declared in 1978 and takes in an unspoilt area of the Orava landscape, in total 700 km². The CHKO Horná Orava also includes the Orava dam.

Left: Tatra chamois
Right: A typical Tatra flower (*Pulsatilla slavica)*

HISTORY

The origin of the name "the Tatras":

The origin of the word Tatras is most frequently attributed to the Ukrainian word "toltry" meaning stones or gravel. A less probable origin of the word is associated with the Greek "terdr" (peak, tip) or the Basque word "tutur" which has a similar meaning. Both theories are unlikely given that there is no evidence of a Greek or Basque presence in the region. The word Tatry appeared for the first time in the writings of the Czech chronicler Cosmas. His chronicle interprets the words of the dying king Boleslav II, remembering the days when he extended his realm up to the Triti montes mountains.

The history of the settlement of the sub Tatra region dates back to a very remote past, at least to the last interglacial period. Over the years archaeologists have gathered numerous pieces of evidence about the Tatras being settled by Neanderthal people, and it is interesting that all findings are bound to the Spiš and Liptov travertine. In a travertine hill in Gánovce, near to Poprad, a famous cast of the scull bone of a Gánovce man was found, traces of another Spiš Neanderthal man were also found in the travertine in Bešeňová, in the Liptov region. Scientists assume that these people, probably the oldest inhabitants of the sub Tatra region, lived in climatically comparably favourable environment of the last Glacial period, between 90,000 to 120,000 years ago.

The Gánovce man:

In 1926 a stone cutter from Gánovce discovered in a local travertine hill an unusual oval stone of unknown origin. After being indelicately cut it was sent to the National Museum of Prague, where for twenty years it remained in the depository before ending up in the hands of a distinguished specialist in ancient history, Dr. Emanuel Vlček. He came to the surprising conclusion that the fragment was in fact a piece of skull bone of an ancient Neanderthal man, one of the oldest inhabitants of ancient Slovakia. The Gánovce man lived near a thermal spring approximately 120,000 years ago, and it is supposed that he drowned after being stupefied by carbon gasses escaping from the spring. The stage of this tragic event was covered by a travertine hill that also buried the skeleton of the dead Neanderthal man. The braincase was filled with a limestone sinter. The filling hardened and the result was a sinter cast which can be seen today at an exposition of the Slovak National Museum in Bratislava Castle.

The ancient peoples of the Tatras did not leave the region even during the last Glacial period, in spite of a bitterly cold climate. Fragmentary archaeological findings confirm their presence next to thermal springs, which provided some protection against the harsh tundra, in the same way that an oasis functions in a desert. This was also the case in Hôrka near Poprad, where various stone tools belonging to ancient hunters were found, estimated to be approximately 20,000 years old.

The profound changes in the landscape of the Tatra region, by the end of the last Glacial period, took place without the active participation of man. After several thousand years, however, a transformation of the natural landscape of the sub Tatra basins was caused by its inhabitants. In the Stone Age the migrating hunters were substituted by more settled and civilised shepherds and farmers, who worked on the natural landscape of the basins and valleys of lower mountain ranges, turning the terrain into agricultural fields. These new inhabitants cleared and burned the forests, marked out fields, creating pastures and settlements. The mountains, however remained intact for a much longer period of time...

In the first wave of migration, about 4,000 years B.C., people of what is called by the experts the beech-mountain and channelled cultures entered the Poprad kotlina basin. They, like their predecessors also found the region of Gánovce and Hôrka more attractive and built their settlements there. Among the numerous archaeological discoveries the specimens of stone axes with bone handles are exceptional. About the same time the people of the Upper Stone Age settled the travertine hills around Bešeňová in the Liptov region. The Upper Stone Age is also the period when Orava steps into the history of the settlements of the Tatras. It is highly probable that previous civilisations lived there before, because the Orava region provided at least as good living conditions as the Liptov or Spiš regions. In Oravský Podzámok various stone tools were found, as well as a copper wedge.

An ancient city under the Tatra mountains:

One of the most remarkable discoveries in Slovakia was made by archaeologists on Myšia Hôrka mountain near the community of Spišský Štvrtok: An ancient settlement occupying an area of 6,600 square metres which bore numerous signs of a high level of development among its ancient inhabitants. The settlement was enclosed within a bulky fortification system with ditches, mounds, stone walls and bastions. A part of the discovered settlement on Myšia Hôrka was an acropolis which may have served as a centre of cult practices. The religious ceremonies probably included some kind of worship of the Tatra mountains, as the location of the acropolis offers the best possible view of the Tatra peaks. This would enable priests to turn to the mountains in supplication like the ancient Greeks turned their faces to Olympus. The nature of the settlement was undoubtedly urban. Its ground plan suggests that it was easily comparable to the developed settlements of the Aegean type in the eastern Mediterranean, culminating approximately in the same period. The stone city under the Tatras was inhabited by people of the Ottoman culture who lived in the territory of Slovakia about 3,500 years ago. Strategically, the city guarded the ancient merchant route which connected the Spiš region and the Baltic with the Mediterranean. Its existence was abruptly ended by some kind of, as yet, unspecified disaster. Under the ruins of the Spiš "Pompeii" everything was found just as it was left providing us with a vivid idea on the life and culture of the people living at the beginning of the Bronze Age.

In the Lower Iron Age the sub Tatra region became the place where the people of Lusatian culture arrived, bringing with them a mostly developed agriculture system and cattle raising. Traces of their existence were found in the basins of the rivers Váh and Orava. The last century B.C., however, belonged to the Celts. Their expansion throughout Europe also manifested itself by settling the Tatra region. Around the year 300 B.C. the first nation we are able to attach a name to, arrived and subdued the local people. The Rhineland Celts were equipped with numerous civilising elements of the Iron Age, such as iron, glass and an advanced type of ceramics. Metallurgy flourished in centres near Važec, Gerlachov, Veľký Slavkov, and in Stráne pod Tatrami. Traces of the Celts were found even in the Tatra mountains, where they extracted wood for their smelting plants and mined for ore.

The smelters under Slavkovský štít peak:

In 1875 while digging out the foundations for a building in the Tatra community of Nový Smokovec workers found a silver coin portraying a Roman emperor. Until then archaeologists never thought of having to explore even the territory of a virgin Tatra nature. Nine years later, on the bank of the Slavkovský potok brook, they discovered the remains of a smelting plant with a fragment of smelted iron. Nearby they also found loaves of malleable iron and a worked granite block that was used as a forging stand. Later on, the Tatra collection of Celtic artefacts was enriched by the remains of ancient metallurgy discovered in the Žltá stena rock in the vicinity of Tatranská Polianka. We also must attribute local geographical names to the Celtic heritage, such as Orava, Pieniny, the Carpathians or the Dunajec. The name Arva quoted in the annals of 1267 developed through Oravia to the contemporary form of Orava.

The Roman civilisation touched the sub Tatra region only through its merchants, as evidenced by the discovery of Roman coins in Poprad, Nový Smokovec and Spišská Belá. The Celtic and Germanic population of the early centuries dominated the Tatra region and only in the 8th to 9th century merged with a new Slavic ethnicity penetrating along the river Váh. The discoveries of Slavic sites under the Tatras are rather poor and the Slavic presence here in the 8th-9th centuries is not abundantly documented. For many centuries the Tatras were a *res nulius* – a no man's land. The population of the neighbouring regions were not interested in property claims and concentrated only to the fields

Right: Slavkovský štít peak

and pastures next to their settlements. The Slavs, characterised by free and unlimited exploitation of the resources offered by the Tatra's nature, behaved in the same way.

In the 11th and 12th centuries the Tatra region was conquered by the cavalry of the Old Hungarians. The territory and its indigenous population became the hereditary property of the Old Hungarian kings. At the beginning of the Old Hungarian state, in the country surrounding the Tatras, the competing interests of the Polish and the Slovak settlers came into conflict. The Old Hungarian Arpads resolved the situation by driving a wedge of German colonists between the disputing parties. In this way they invited the first German farmers, craftsmen, merchants, and miners to the Spiš region.

The 13th century meant great changes for the Tatra region. The local population survived the Tartar invasion by easily hiding themselves in the deep Tatra forests. After the invasion king Belo IV decided to strengthen the boundaries of Old Hungary with new colonists. More people also needed more agricultural land which was possible only through clearing the forests. Deforestation was rather dramatic and did not stop in higher reaches either, which meant that precious woodland disappeared from the slopes of the Tatras.

The first thing the king and the nobility decided was to guarantee the safety of the northern frontier of Old Hungary by building several castles. The most important of them were the Oravský hrad castle in the valley of the river Orava, the Likavský hrad castle near Ružomberok, the Liptovský hrad castle at the Sestrč Mt. in the Chočské vrchy Mts., the Liptovský hrádok castle in the Liptovská kotlina basin, the Nedecký hrad castle at the western edge of the Pieniny Mts., and the Ľubovniansky hrad castle in the valley of the river Poprad. Also, the administration of the Tatra region was gradually completed between the 11th and 13th centuries. Independent administrative and economic units called comitates, were created. In the second half of the 13th century the western part of the region belonged to Zvolen and the eastern part was attached to the Spiš region. Parallel to secular administration the church also established its own system. The western and eastern parts of the sub Tatra region belonged to the Hont and Spiš church administrative units respectively.

Portioning of the Tatras:

A process that meant some kind of medieval "privatisation" of the Tatras started at the beginning of the 13th century and lasted approximately two centuries. King Ondrej II donated in 1209 a large piece of land around the Lomnický štít peak to the presbyter Adolf of Spiš and his sister. In 1294 count Botyz had as reward for his military merits an "unsettled forest Chetene under the mountain range of Tortol" in Mengusovská, Batizovská and the Velická dolina valleys with their corresponding peaks. The heirs of Botyz administered the territory until the 19th century. Count Bogomel became the owner of an extensive area of the Tatras on the boundary of Spiš and Liptov, including the Štrbské pleso lake. Gradually the Slovak part of the Vysoké and Belianske Tatry Mts. was portioned to eight principal territorial units and the western Tatras or Západné Tatry mountains were, with the exception of the easternmost part, broken down into twelve ownerships.

In the 14th century the administrative division was completed and survived in its original form until the 19th century. Adjustments, as compared to the 13th century, were made in the western part of

the territory when it was divided between the Orava (in the north-west) and Liptov (in the south-west) counties. Development of the area received a stimulus with the arrival of the German colonists who were granted considerable economic privileges and rights. The communities with a privileged population grew and became townships. In Liptov it was Nemecká Ľupča (1263) Hybe (1265), and Ružomberok (1318). In the 14th century they were followed by Liptovský Mikuláš and Liptovský Hrádok. The towns on the Orava side of the Tatras originated in stages. The first one to obtain municipal privileges was Trstená (1424). Neighbouring Tvrdošín was gradually developing from a tributary community, benefiting by having the custom office (1265) to a town granted the right to run fairs (1640). Dolný Kubín obtained its municipal privileges only in 1633 and in 1683 became the seat of the Orava county. Námestovo was the last community to obtain the status of a town.

The most intense medieval urbanisation took place in Spiš. On the Spiš side of the Tatras the towns of Poprad, Veľká, Stráže pod Tatrami, Matejovce, Spišský Štvrtok, Levoča, Kežmarok, Spišská Belá, Podolínec, Hniezdne, and Stará Ľubovňa originated, forming a Union of 16 Spiš towns. Several of them were promoted to free royal cities (Levoča in 1323, Stará Ľubovňa in 1364, Kežmarok in 1380, Podolínec in 1412, and Hniezdne in 1566).

Trade with towns:

In 1412 the towns of Spiš became a part of a big trade transaction between two European rulers. Because of financial problems the Old Hungarian King Sigismond of Luxembourg traded 16 rich towns in the Spiš region to the Polish king Vladislav Jagiełło, for a loan of 37 thousand kopas of silver Prague groschen (1 kopa equaled 60 groschen). The trade was allegedly agreed at the Nedecký hrad castle situated at the border, which at that time belonged to Old Hungary (today it is on the Polish side of the frontier). The duties of the towns in Spiš were limited only to the delivery of fees and earnings. In 1769 they were annexed by queen Maria Theresa. Annexation came into force only three years later during Poland's first division. Sixteen Spiš towns passed under the administration of the Old Hungarian bureaucracy, but they preserved a comparably high degree of autonomy as a separate province of the Spiš towns. After losing the status of a province, they were included into the Spiš county.

The Tatras were a frequent subject of numerous ghostly tales about dragons and other monsters narrated by the common people. In spite of this there were brave individuals who dared to enter the territory of the wild Tatras. They had a variety of motivations, but the majority went there for purely pragmatic reasons: They went as colliers, gold miners, hunters, fruit and mushroom pickers; and, of course, shepherds climbed the rocks and high valleys. In the thick Tatra woods outlaws, deserters, persecuted free-thinkers and runaway serfs, who wanted to escape the bailiff's whip, found their refuge. Even today there are people who believe that in some unknown hiding place a legendary treasure of the most famous Slovak forest robber, Juraj Jánošík, remains hidden. A special group of visitors was that of the smugglers who made their living out of the fact that the Tatras constituted a frontier between Poland and Old Hungary.

Left: Orava castle

The seekers of ore and other minerals climbed high indeed. The mining shafts are still to be seen close below the very top of the Kriváň mountain, as well as in other elevated and sometimes fairly exposed places. The miners who had no luck in prospecting often joined the forest robbers. Courageous hunters, who chased the chamois and mountain marmots, climbed the rocky Tatra mountains, along with poachers. Originally, they were mostly shepherds who went up to the mountains in pursuit of their prey, which provided extra food and resources through trading hides. As they drove their flocks as high as the Liptovské hole mountains or to the Skalnatá dolina valley, under the steep walls of the Lomnický štít peak, they got quite near to the habitat of the chamois.

Between the mountains and their inhabitants existed an emotional, as well as a pragmatic relationship. The practical component had a specific form that cannot be simply described as property. The actual owners of the Tatra plots were the nobility, the ruler and the towns. A better expression of the relation is the right of the occupant of each particular sub Tatra community to a particular Tatra valley or ridge. Externally this right was expressed by the nomenclature of the Tatras. For instance, the community of Batizovce used the Batizovská dolina valley, the Batizovský peak, the Batizovský brook and the Batizovské pleso lake. The people of Gerlachov who occupied the Gerlachov forest and the area of the highest Tatra peak also bore the name of the community. The same occurred with Tatra names linked with Veľká (Velická dolina valley) Štrba (Štrbský štít peak) Mengusovce (Mengusovská dolina valley), Kežmarok (Kežmarský štít peak), Veľká Lomnica (Lomnický štít peak), and Spišská Belá which has rendered the name to the whole mountain range (Belianske Tatry).

The oldest written reports on visitors who were attracted to the Tatras, for other than economic reasons, date back to the 16th century. As they surveyed the glorious Tatra peaks a group of educated Tatra personalities felt a spiritual need to go and discover the world looking down on them. This was the day when tourism was born! The first known tourist trip to the Tatras was undertaken by an enlightened lady from Kežmarský hrad castle by the name of Beata Laská (1515-1576). In the spring of 1566, together with several companions, she climbed to the valley of Biela voda, probably reaching the Zelené pleso lake. At the end of the century her exploits were imitated by the students and professors of Kežmarok and Prešov. The first ascent to a Tatra peak was described by the mathematician and astronomer David Fröhlich of Kežmarok (1595-1648). As a twelve-year old boy he set out, accompanied by two friends, to one of the peaks of the Lomnický massive and probably climbed up to the Kežmarský štít peak.

Kežmarok – the town of the Tatra discoverers:

The town of Kežmarok has been the birth place of many discoverers and experts of the highest Carpathian mountains. This picturesque town with perhaps the most famous vista of the wonderful Tatra peaks was the starting point of trips undertaken to the Tatras by local priests, teachers and students of the Evangelic college. Sometime in the mid-17th century an anonymous student set out, together with five schoolmates and a teacher, for a three-day trip to the valley of Biela voda. Their aim was to climb one of the peaks near the Lomnický štít peak (perhaps the Kežmarský štít peak), whereupon the student chronicled the experience in the now famous book "Simplicissimus hungaricus seu dacianus". An engaging work, edited in Levoča in 1683, it is written in a style imitating German adventure novels of the time and presents an exciting story of how the boy with five other students wandered around the mountains. The descriptions give a truly authentic impression of the landscape with remarkable precision describing, for instance, the flora and fauna of the Tatras, shepherding and an interesting description of the basic mountaineering equipment in use at the time.

The first half of the 17th century was a period of successful exploration of the Tatras, above all by the members of the Buchholtz family. Matej Bel (1684-1723), a Slovak intellectual of European significance, the pride of Old Hungary, also participated in the exploration of the Tatras. The geography and history of the Liptov Tatras is described in the second volume of the magnificent work *Notitia Hungariae novae historico-geographica*. Besides the text, which was jointly written by Juraj Buchholtz junior of Kežmarok, the volume contains a valuable map compiled by the famous Slovak cartographer Samuel Mikovíny. This scientific work of Bel, the Buchholtz family, Bohuš and other national authors made its way beyond the frontiers of Old Hungary allowing the world to discover the Tatras for

the first time. Many European scholars, inspired by Rousseau's ideas of man's return to nature, visited the largely unknown Carpathian mountain range. Most notable among these were: B. Hacquet, R. Townson, S. Staszic, G. Wahlenberg, and F. S. Beudant.

Tourism came to the Tatras much later than to the Alps. It practically did not exist before the 18th century, mainly because the cumbersome mode of travel made them so inaccessible. Uncomfortable and tedious transport and bad roads discouraged many a tourist who would have liked to have seen the attractive landscape of the Tatras.

The hardships of the first tourists:

The experiences of the first tourists in the Tatras were not all fun. Unlike today, there were no roads, hotels or cottages or restaurants, or indeed any lifts. Experienced poachers substituted for maps and the passage through the thick dwarf-pines called for a sharp axe. Juraj Buchholtz senior needed three days for a risky ascent to the Slavkovský štít peak in June 1664 and another three days for a tiresome descent. Today the average tourist needs only about half a day to ascend this little demanding Tatra peak. Taking the bus to Kežmarok in the morning, by noon he can be in Smokovec drinking to a successful venture.

Left: Kežmarok

The series of anti-Hapsburg rebellions in the 17th and 18th centuries did not avoid the Tatra region, where fighting took place also under the Tatras. The people of the sub Tatra area were living in such abject poverty at the time that many of them fled to Poland or to the southern regions abandoned by the Turks. At the beginning of the 18th century the region was occupied by imperial troops who burnt down many sub Tatra communities. The plague and hunger in the years 1710-1711 also took its toll when 20 thousand people died.

After the Szatmár armistice was signed in 1711 a period of consolidation and economic development began. New guilds were founded and the number of organised craftsmen grew. In the sub Tatra regions the guilds of the furriers, tailors, cloth-makers, hatters, shoe-makers or boot-makers were common. Liptov, for instance, became an important centre of cheese making and the Liptov sheep's cheese called bryndza became known, at home and abroad, as early as the mid-18th century. The most significant centres of the crafts and economic life were Kežmarok, Spišská Sobota, and Hybe.

However, the majority of the Tatra population still made their living through agriculture, raising and keeping cattle and sheep. Flax and flaxen products made the traders of the Liptov and Spiš regions famous. The local population was also occupied in logging, transporting timber on the river Váh to the Danubian regions. The development of woodworking also brought about the opening of numerous sawmills in Štrba, Poprad, Kežmarok, and Važec and paper producing plants in Poprad and Veľká. Agriculture was also dominant in the 19th century, and with the exception of the local plants, there was no comparable industry.

The upper reaches of the Tatra region were still largely uninhabited, visited only by shepherds and loggers. The oldest Tatra community was Starý Smokovec, founded near a spring of mineral water which was believed to possess magic properties, and where people used to gather at the time of the summer solstice, a custom preserved from remote heathen times. Count Štefan Csáky built a little hunting cottage there in 1793. Four years later a chapel was constructed along with additional wooden buildings to accommodate summer guests. The development of the Tatra communities was bolstered considerably by the construction of the Košice-Bohumín railway. In the last quarter of the 19th century the number of the visitors to the Tatras grew six-fold.

Progress was brought to Tatras by train:

It was a big event for the sub Tatra people when on December 8, 1871 the first train whirled into Poprad station. It was the start of many which would bring masses of tourists and spa visitors to the region, stimulating the development of the towns and communities along the track, Poprad and Spišská Nová Ves among them. Both towns rapidly overgrew Levoča, traditionally the more important and renowned centre as the railway bypassed it, whilst Važec, on the other hand, became a typical railway men's community.

The second community to be founded in the Tatras was one on the shore of lake Štrbské pleso. The origin of Štrbské Pleso was triggered off by the construction of a hunting cottage in 1872, followed by other communities: Nový Smokovec (1875),), Dolný Smokovec (1881), Kežmarské Žľaby (1885), Tatranské Mlynčeky (1884), Tatranská Polianka (1888), Vyšné Hágy (1890), and Tatranská Lomnica (1892). In 1900 there was a total of 2,300 accommodation beds available in the High Tatras. The first page of the history of the Tatra spa activities was written in Starý Smokovec in 1839, but the main centre, from the balneological point of view, became Nový Smokovec where the first therapeutical pavilion was built in 1875.

Its origin was assisted by the pioneer of Slovak climatotherapy, Dr. Mikuláš Szontagh senior, who acquired vast experience in the cure of respiratory diseases in the famous sanatoriums in Switzerland. Among Dr. Szontagh's famous patients was the Czech poet Jiří Wolker. Other centres gradually appeared, in Štrbské Pleso, Tatranská Polianka and in Vyšné Hágy, the latter becoming the main centre for curing tuberculosis. In 1941 the sanatorium under the Gerlachovský štít mountain became the largest therapeutical institution of tuberculosis in Central Europe.

In the 1880's a new transversal road, now called the Road of Freedom, connecting the Tatra communities, began construction and in 1900 the first car travelled along it to Starý Smokovec. Six years later the event was repeated to Tatranská Lomnica. In 1912 the first coaches began to commute between Starý Smokovec and Spišská Nová Ves. However, the most important means of transport in the Tatras became the Tatra railway, firstly the track between Veľká Lomnica and Tatranská Lomnica (1895) and a year later the narrow-gauged rack railway connecting the Tatranská Štrba and Štrbské Pleso communities. The railway network was completed by electric traction between Poprad and Starý Smokovec (1908), Starý Smokovec and Tatranská Lomnica (1911) and Starý Smokovec and Štrbské Pleso (1912). In 1908 access to the mountains was improved by the opening of a terrestrial funicular from Starý Smokovec to Hrebienok and from 1940 visitors could comfortably travel from Tatranská Lomnica up to the summit of Lomnický štít.

To the Tatras by plane:

The last form of transport to come to the Tatras was by air. The first attempt to establish an airline, between the spas of the inter-war Czechoslovakia of 1922 failed to materialise because of a dispute between the towns of Poprad and Liptovský Mikuláš over airport privileges. Eventually, the businessman Baťa, who owned a factory in Svit, west of Poprad, intervened and supported the candidature of Poprad. In 1940 the first ever plane landed in the meadows near Veľká, the site of the present day international airport of Poprad-Tatry. Efforts to use the water table of the lake at Štrbské pleso for the landing of hydroplanes were, of course, in vain.

Even before 1900 there was a growing number of people who enjoyed hiking in the wonderful mountain environment of the Tatras. And with the constantly growing popularity of the mountains came the need to prepare tourist paths and construct mountain cottages, a task that was undertaken by the Carpathian Union, the oldest tourist organisation in Old Hungary. Besides creating the infrastructure the Union also organised the mountain guide and rescue service.

The Tatra mountain guides:

Most people visiting the Tatras in the past, for whatever reason, had no maps and knowledge whatsoever of the mountain range, having to rely almost entirely on the local mountain guides. The most knowledgeable mountain guides were usually the poachers, hunting for chamois and marmots, shepherds and treasure seekers. History has recorded entire dynasties of the Tatra mountain guides, famous amongst them being the families of Gasienic, Sieczko, Tatar and Walo. Two of the most popular tourist guides were the shepherds Ján Ruman Driečny senior and junior. Another respected mountain guide was the legendary poacher Jonek Lysý of Javorina. The guide service was provided and protected by the tourist organisations, and as early as the end of the 19th century the Old Hungarian Royal Association began a training scheme for mountain guides. This scheme was later maintained by the Club of the Czechoslovak Tourists creating, in 1923, the Corps of the Tatra Guides as a professional association. Today the use of mountain guides is obligatory if hikers or climbing groups attempt to scale areas outside the officially marked paths. Such restrictions are in the interests of safety, for example, it is forbidden to ascend the highest peak of the Tatras, Gerlachovský štít, without a guide.

Left: A mountain guide
Right: Chata pod Rysmi cottage

In order to promote tourism in the mountains accommodation shelters were constructed. The first of these was a stone cottage, known as Rainer's shelter, built in 1863 near the Kamzík hotel in Hrebienok. Later these stone cottages were built in much higher places in the mountain range: In 1876 Egid's hut in Rakúska Poľana, below lake Zelené pleso, as well as other dwellings beside the lakes of Velické pleso and Popradské pleso. Edmund Téry (1856-1917) a physician from Banská Bystrica constructed a mountain cottage in the valley of Malá Studená dolina, which, bearing the name of its founder, is still the highest located cottage in the Tatras which is open all year round. Another cottage, even higher, is located below the Rysy mountain but is only open during the summer season.

New tourist paths and mountain cottages facilitated access to the lofty peaks of the High Tatras, where the most courageous visitors climbed one virgin peak after another. By 1913 there remained practically no peak unscaled by human being who sought ever more challenging ascents. Inspired by their colleagues from the Alps they began competing for the privilege of achieving the first ascent by various routes up the Tatra rock faces. After the first World War the Slovak mountaineers joined together in an Association of Slovak Mountaineers to be joined later by a similar tourist organisation founded in 1919. It was the Tatra Tourist Association which later merged with the Club of Czech Tourists which became the national Club of Czechoslovak Tourists. In 1921 Miloš Janoška, an outstanding representative of the club, founded a tourist monthly publication called Krásy Slovenska (The Charms of Slovakia). This was followed in 1931 with the periodical Vysoké Tatry (The High Tatras) both of which still exist today.

The duel of the giants:

The people of Liptov always asserted that there was no higher peak in the Tatras than the Kriváň peak. This claim was countered by the citizens of Spiš who never doubted that primacy belonged to the peak of Lomnický štít, and seen from the north the peak of Ľadový štít appeared to be the highest. The people living below the Tatra mountains disputed for many years which of the three mountains was the highest. The first of them to

leave the ring was the Kriváň peak when the Englishman Robert Townson barometrically measured its height and found it lower than Lomnický peak, which left the two remaining peaks to contest supremacy. This decision was finally made by Ľudovít Greiner, the director of the Coburg-owned woods in Jelšava. Equipped with measuring apparatuses he climbed to the summit of Lomnický štít and began comparing the height of the surrounding peaks using a protractor and libela. The results of the measurements were surprising, revealing the highest of the Tatra mountains to be the peak of Gerlachovský štít! However, it took a long time before the locals got used to the idea and for many years it was still believed that the highest peak of the High Tatras was Lomnický štít.

The sub Tatra towns and communities also revived with the arrival of the railway. New factories of wood, textiles and food industries emerged (Kežmarok, Poprad, Liptovský Hrádok, Spišská Belá) and provided the population with new jobs. The desintegration of the Austro-Hungarian Empire and the origin of the First Czechoslovak Republic meant for Slovaks the end of oppression, but the position of the wider strata of the population had not improved and unemployment still remained high. The most important development, from the point of view of new opportunities, was the founding in 1934 of the Baťa's factory producing artificial fibre. The plant was constructed near the community of Batizovce, practically on a "green meadow", and later when it acquired the status of an independent community it was called Svit.

The Second World War caused considerable damage in the region. Numerous industrial buildings were damaged and destroyed resulting in a very slow return to something like normality. The power in individual communities passed to the members of the revolutionary committees who were not democratically elected by the citizens, but had secured their positions through resistance to the former regime in the Slovak state and developments in the rejuvenation of the Czechoslovak state. In the autumn of 1945 currency and land reforms were realised, whereupon large estates were confiscated and prosperous farmers were obliged to hand over often unrealistic levies in kind, called contingencies. The 1946 general elections were won by the Democratic Party by almost two thirds of the vote, but the Communist party attacked the results and initiated a campaign, culminating in 1948, by seizing power. Thus, the period of socialism had begun. The basic aim of the period was the collectivisation of agricultural production, the nationalisation of industry, of trade and crafts and the total liquidation of medium and small enterprises. In the majority of the sub Tatra villages co-operatives and state property farms were founded operating in large fields, and industry was promoted in Poprad, Kežmarok, Svit, Liptovský Hrádok and Spišská Belá. During this period the population grew rapidly, especially in urban areas.

The second half of the 1960's brought some relaxation in the social and political order. Many existing barriers to personal and religious freedom were removed and new possibilities for enterprise emerged. But the process of democratisation was soon interrupted by the troops of the Warsaw Pact who occupied Czechoslovakia on August 21, 1968. Not until November 1989, twenty one years later, did the communist regime finally collapse in the events of the "Velvet Revolution". In January 1993, following the division of the Czech and Slovak Federal Republic, the Slovak Republic was finally established and a new phase in the economic and social life of the country became a reality.

Sport in the Tatras:

Economy and tourism have not been the only forces at work in the Tatras and the sub Tatra region, but also sport and culture. The natural attributes of the region have proved to be an ideal resort for winter sport, which have been fully developed in the local centres. The first pair of skis were brought to the Tatras by the pharmacist Karol Cornidesz of Smokovec in 1865 as a souvenir from Norway. And the first actual skier in the Tatras was another scientist from Smokovec, a physician by the name of Mikuláš Szontagh who used his skis for winter hunting. In 1899 the first ski training course was given in the environs of Štrbské Pleso, and in 1911 ski competitions were first introduced to the Tatras when a down-hill race was ran on the 6 kilometres long track from the cottage of Sliezsky dom to Tatranská Polianka. Two years later runners on cross-country skis took part in a debut race, and the first ski jumpers used a wooden ski-jump in Tatranská Polianka. On a nearby ski-jump in Velická dolina valley jumpers reached the unbelievable distance of 24 metres. As well as these traditional winter sports also some typically summer sports like lawn tennis and volley ball have found popularity in the Tatras. After the Second World War two important events in modern Tatra history took place. The first was the foundation of the Tatra National Park in 1947, formally identifying the natural assets of the region. And in 1970 the World Championship in cross-country ski disciplines took place in the High Tatras. This latter event not only had a sport dimension but it also made a considerable impact on the social and economic life of the region. Extensive reconstruction and the creation of modern sport facilities also brought new opportunities with the development of hotels, restaurants and shops. The infrastructure also benefited through improved transport and the overall enhancement of the resort.

The Tatras after 1945 acquired a more "plebeian" character, caused by a mass trade union recreation of workers and various forms of collective travel. Immediately after the war about 20,000 tourists visited the Tatras annually. In the mid 1980's the number of tourists grew to 4 million. The huge influx of domestic and foreign visitors to the Tatras subsided only after 1989. The new political and economic situation influenced the number of visitors because of the transformation of their social and nationalistic structures. However, following the initial drop in visitors at the beginning of the 1990's, the number of visitors again increased and the candidature for staging the Winter Olympic Games in 2006 will certainly make the Tatras a winter sport resort with a world reputation.

HISTORICAL COMMUNICATIONS

The natural assets of the central part of the Western Carpathians were more favourable to the development of communication passages, oriented in a parallel direction which made better use of the basins and valleys arranged in the west-east direction. On the other hand, in the direction of the meridians there are numerous natural obstacles like massive mountain ridges that only rarely

Right: Areál snov

drop to lower and more easily passable mountain saddles. This is especially so for the Low Tatras with their unavoidable long massive central ridge. Yet high and difficult passable Tatra ridges can be easily bypassed on the western and eastern sides. The barrier of the boundary mountain ranges, in the neighbourhood of the Tatra massive, can be easily overcome at two points: in the valleys of the Orava and Poprad rivers.

Important trade routes ran across these two valleys for at least three thousand years. Both of them connected the north of Slovakia with neighbouring southern Poland, but in some periods also fulfilled the function of alternative roads, including the famous Amber Road, mediating contact between the Baltic and the Mediterranean. This is documented by the findings of Bronze Age objects in the fortified settlement of Myšia hôrka, near Spišský Štvrtok, undoubtedly of Aegean origin. They were probably brought to the Spiš region of Slovakia by merchants travelling from southern Europe who used the Poprad branch of the old Transeuropean trade route.

These trade roads were preserved during the expansion of the Celts in La Téne period and the merchants probably also used them in the Roman period. In the times of the Great Moravia the roads crossing the Kysuce region and the Low Beskydy mountains were more frequently used. Traditional trade roads across the Orava and Upper Spiš regions revived again during the early Old Hungarian State. The Orava road to Poland ran up the Orava river valley, past the customs office in Tvrdošín, where it headed to Kraków passing the Suchá Hora mountain. In the 15th century the merchants travelling to Tvrdošín could also use the road from Liptovská Sielnica across the Chočské vrchy mountains. Spiš, in medieval times, even offered three options on getting to Poland's Kraków or Nowy Sącz. In the 15th century three trade roads were crossing Spišská Belá. The westernmost road made use of the furrow Ždiarska brázda, a depression between the Tatras and Spišská Magura. Passing Ždiar it easily traversed the valley of Bialka and brought the merchants to the valley of the river Dunajec. The central branch of the Spiš trade road to Poland crossed the ridge of the Spišská Magura in the Magurské sedlo, continued to the river Dunajec and along the river to Kraków. The most important was the eastern branch of the Polish road reproducing the old road along the river Poprad. Once beyond Stará Ľubovňa travellers had two possibilities of how to get to the royal city of Kraków. The shorter way was to go directly to Mníšek nad Popradom and the longer option was keeping its course along the big bends of the river Poprad.

The Slovak-Polish frontier was set down in the second half of the 11th century in the time of establishing the early Old Hungarian state. Territorial raids, led by the Polish ruler Boleslav the Valiant, over the ridges of the Carpathians against the Old Hungary of the Arpads, were the last conflicts at this, perhaps the quietest European frontier at that time, in a region shaken by incessant wars. Since then the coexistence of the sub Tatra Poles and Slovaks has been positive and peaceful, filled with exclusively economic, social and cultural links.

The Slovak-Polish frontier was subject to little change throughout the nine centuries of its existence, and at the point between the Volovec mountan in the Roháče mountains and the Rysy mountain in the High Tatras, has practically remained stable during all that time. Historians do not consider the "leasing" of the Spiš towns to the Polish ruler by Sigismond, for almost three centuries an actual change of the Polish-Old Hungarian frontier. These surrendered towns kept their cultural and religious appurtenance to Spiš whilst being under Polish financial and economic administration.

The greatest changes of the Polish-Slovak frontier took place in the 20th century. The succession states of the disintegrated Austro-Hungarian monarchy had to tackle numerous problems while drawing their state frontiers. The disputes between the contiguous Central European countries concerning borders contaminated the Slovak-Polish relationship, which until then was free of problems. The most serious situation arose in Spiš when the Germans living there declared an independent republic of Spiš on December 9, 1919. Armies encamped on the Slovak-Polish border though fortunately they did not have to intervene. Tensions were calmed by signing the peace treaty between Czechoslovakia and Poland on July 28, 1920. The treaty also provided for the questionable sector between the Orava and Zamagurie regions. Unsolved issues, such as the claims of both states over the territory of Suchá Hora in Orava and Javorina. were finally adjoined to Czechoslovakia in the years 1923-1924.

The question of the Slovak-Polish frontier emerged again in 1938. In October of that year the Poles occupied the area of Suchá Hora and Javorina but precisely a year later were given back to the Slovak state established on March 14, 1939, whereupon Poland surrendered to Slovakia 374 square kilometres, and a population of 16,000 in Upper Orava and in Zamagurie. The Slovak-Polish frontier never obstructed mutual influences, which enriched the cultures on both sides of the frontier. The result of this close historical coexistence is a specific ethnicity, living north of the Tatras. The country between the Upper Orava and Zamagurie is populated by the Gorals who speak their special dialect. Even the name "Goral" means a mountain man, which aptly expresses the life in the hard mountain environment under the Tatras.

Right: Levoča town hall

POPULATION AND SETTLEMENTS

The history of the settlement of the sub Tatra region goes back to a very remote past and it was also influenced by the harsh natural conditions and marginal position of the important civilisations who lived there. Even though several settlements are mentioned in remote historical records we can actually talk only about a sporadically settled territory, where the majority of the settlements (contemporary archaeological localities) were concentrated in the valleys of the rivers Váh, Orava and Poprad. The Tatras, in the Celtic, Germanic and Slavic periods, were always on the periphery of geopolitical interests, and so the settlements corresponded to this fact.

After the establishment of the Old Hungarian state the region became a boundary area and this is the period when the first written references to settlements below the Tatras are dated. The Popradská kotlina and Liptovská kotlina basins, eventually the valleys across which the trade routes to Poland passed (the Orava valley, some valleys of Zamagurie and the valley of Poprad) are characterised by the most rapid development of the structured settlement. The Sholtys (sholtys means mayor) colonisation in the 13th and 14th centuries contributed to the basic formation of the settlement structure in the basins. Communities

arose either as serf communes of the local aristocracy or they were founded by colonists invited from the German lands, and even Walloonia (Vlachy in the Liptov region). The majority of the villages founded in the period exist today, the earliest recorded being Veľký Slavkov, Ľubica, Vrbov and Matejovce. The most important market centres were Kežmarok and Spišská Sobota. The oldest communities in Liptov are Bobrovec, Okoličné, Hybe and Liptovská Mara and are often referred to in the old records as the most important market towns under the Tatra mountains.

One of the most significant events in the Zamagurie region was the foundation of the Carthusian monastery in Červený Kláštor in 1319, before which originated the community of Spišská Stará Ves in 1308, and by the end of the 13th century Spišské Hanušovce was founded. The origins of the communities of Lechnica, Lesnica, Veľký Lipník, Reľov, Kamienka, and Havka falls into the period of the first wave of colonisation. The oldest communities in the Orava side of the Tatras are actually located in the valley of Orava, around the trade road leading to the customs point in Tvrdošín. They came into being somewhat later, in the 15th and 16th centuries, though some communities existed as early as the mid-13th century (Istebné, Dolný Kubín, Nižná, Tvrdošín). The more remote parts of Orava and Zamagurie waited longer for their colonists, and were settled by the Wallachian colonists in the 16th and 17th centuries. Also during this period the first Ruthenians arrived, and settled in the north-east of the region where they still live today. This was also the period when Osturňa originated (1594), and Ždiar and Jezerska at the beginning of the 17th century. The family of Thurzo founded in the Orava region 24 new communities inhabited by the Goral population, among them, for instance, Oravský Biely Potok, Habovka, and Zuberec.

Many of these invited colonists were able to found strong roots because of the privileges bestowed upon them, which helped some of the communities to change into towns and cities. In the second half of the 18th century 24 towns in the sub Tatra region are referred to.

The boom in the towns and villages was connected with the construction of the Košice-Bohumín railway track in 1871, mentioned earlier, and after the disintegration of the Austro-Old Hungarian empire the process of urbanisation stopped for a while, reviving after the Second World War.

The historical development and natural setting of the Tatras has ensured it to be the least populated area in Slovakia. A census of January 1, 1996 recorded 468,000 inhabitants living in the territory of the present districts of Tvrdošín, Liptovský Mikuláš, Poprad, Kežmarok and a part of the district of Stará Ľubovňa. The population density is 53 per km^2, while the Slovak average reaches a value of up to 108 inhabitants per km^2. At the present time more than half of the population live in the towns (56%). There are eleven towns in the territory of the High Tatras: Poprad, Liptovský Mikuláš, Kežmarok, Tvrdošín, Liptovský Hrádok, Svit, Trstená, Spišská Belá, Starý Smokovec, Podolínec, and Spišská Stará Ves. From the point of view of population numbers, Poprad (55,000) followed by Spišská Nová Ves (39,000) and Liptovský Mikuláš (34,000) are the largest towns. Among the remaining district towns, according to the most recent territorial and administrative divisions, are Ružomberok (31,000), Dolný Kubín (20,000), Kežmarok (17,000), and Tvrdošín (10,000 inhabitants).

The character of the sub Tatra region is a combination of the industrial and the agricultural. Employment is concentrated above all in the food industry, with regional variations in the machinery industry (Poprad), the chemical industry (Svit), tannery (Liptovský Mikuláš) electro-technical industry (Liptovský Hrádok, Trstená), textile industry (Liptovský Mikuláš, Svit) and sporadic wood processing. In agriculture, operating in specific conditions of the Tatra region, plant production i.e. foodstuffs, grains and potato growing are predominant, with light concentrations of cattle rearing and sheep keeping. In the service industries, especially in the realm of travel and tourism, there is continued expansion. Jobs are concentrated in the larger cities to which more than two thirds of the economically active population commutes from the nearby villages. More recently, however, a drop in commuting related to jobs is observed, while the number of the people working abroad or in other Slovak regions is increasing.

THE SLOVAK TATRAS

Zuberec and its environs

The region of Zuberec is spread out in the north-western part of the Tatra region occupying the Orava part of the Západné Tatry mountains, the Podtatranská brázda furrow and the Skorušinské vrchy mountains. In the south it is bordered by the ridge of the Západné Tatry mountains, in the west and north by the ridge of the Skorušinské vrchy mountains and in the east by the Slovak-Polish state border.

ZUBEREC (743 m, population 1,700) is 12 km from Podbiel lying on the main road from Dolný Kubín to the Polish border. It is situated in the furrow of Podtatranská brázda at the foothills of the Západné Tatry mountains, in an area called Roháče.

The Roháče mountains:

The name Roháče (horned animals) is derived from the name denoting the tops of the main ridge in the central part of the mountain range – the Ostrý Roháč and Plačlivý mountains (originally also called Plačlivý Roháč). In the past the local people, above all the shepherds and hunters, called the higher south-western peak (2,126 m) Roháč and the lower north-eastern peak (2,084 m) Šuta (hornless animal). Roháč *was a simplified expression denoting the horned animals and* šutá *was used for the hornless ones. At present the name Ostrý Roháč refers to Roháč and the names Plačlivý Roháč or Plačlivý correspond to what was formerly called Šutá. Both peaks are usually the final aims of the visitors of the Západné Tatry mountains and provide a superb view of the surrounding mountains which bear the same name. The experience can be heightened by the possible incidental encounter, swift though it may be, with the rare Tatra endemite – the chamois, symbolising the "horned" tops of the Západné Tatry mountains.*

The community was mentioned for the first time in the historical acts of 1593 under the name *Zwberczyc* as a serf community of the Orava castle. The name is derived from the European bison that

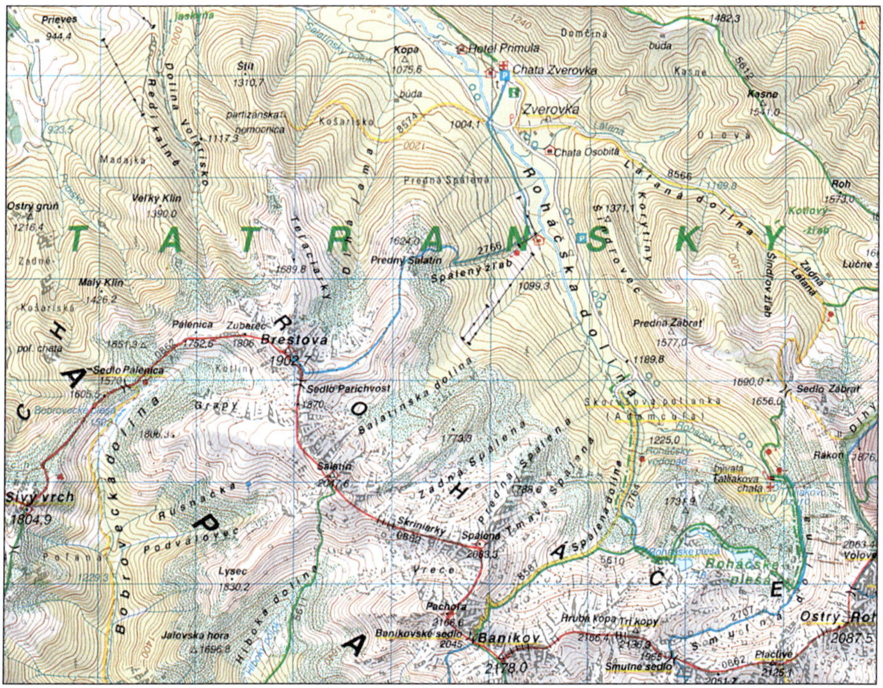

used to live in abundant numbers all over the Orava region in the Middle Ages. Similar to the rest of the communities under the Roháče mountains, Zuberec was founded by the Wallachian right. The settlers came from the villages along the river Orava and their obligation was to protect the territory of the Orava castle and to render duties in kind to the landlords. The original Wallachian communities of the 15th century did not have to comply with the then current obligations of serfs as they fulfilled the function of guarding the roads and borders. In the 16th century these privileges were gradually forgotten under the pressure of the noble family of Thurzo (the owners of the castle at that time) and the population living in the villages assumed similar tasks as the rest of the serfs.

The Wallachians:

There exists diverse opinions on the ethnic origin of the Wallachian population. Some historians assert that the Wallachians were of Rumanian nationality who came from the Eastern Carpathians. Others in turn maintain that when the shepherd people, originally of Rumanian nationality, penetrated the Western Carpathians they found it already "Slavicised" by the Ukrainian, Polish and Slovak population. However, at present many of them believe that the shepherd population of East-Roman origin, who came from Balkans to Central Europe, with the aim of settling the territory by pursuing the Wallachian right, were of Rumanian provenance only in Transcarpathian Ukraine, while the settlement in Eastern Slovakia was Ruthenian and in north-western Slovakia it was Slovak. The original denomination of the ethnic term "Wallachian" lost its ethnic meaning in the Western Carpathians and assumed the meaning of a shepherd – it denotes economic activity.

At the very beginning of the 17th century, in the time of Bocskay's rebellion, the community of Zuberec was completely abandoned, but life returned in 1609. In 1612 the village mayor Jakub Baran received a donation act quoting all the rights and duties of the settlers. The act was issued by the Old Hungarian paladin Juraj Thurzo, owner of Orava Castle and its estate, including Zuberec. In the first quarter of the 17th century there lived in Zuberec approximately twelve families and in total about 60 people. The community was later sacked by Lithuanian troops and only at the beginning of the 18th century repopulated again. The new settlers made their living from raising cattle and forestry. Agricultural activities were not so frequent because of unfavourable climatic conditions and poor soil quality. The harsh climate and infertile soil compelled the population to emigrate to other districts and even abroad. Those who stayed also bred sheep and felled trees. Lime burning and the pressing of a thin-wound wool cloth (using a fulling mill) were other common activities. In the 20th century new jobs became available in weaving and in the sawmills. The population at the beginning of the 18th century was 150, rising at the end of the century to 350 and at the beginning of the 20th it dropped as a consequence of intense emigration, not only to bigger Austro-Hungarian cities, but also to America and Australia. Only after the Second World War this diminishing trend was stopped with the newly emerging work opportunities. Zuberec is today a tourist centre in the Orava part of the Západné Tatry mountains and a point of departure for the Sivý vrch mountain or otherwise to the region of the Roháče mountains.

Sacral cultural, historical monuments are represented by the Roman-Catholic **church of St. Valentín** built in 1933 and designed by the architect M. M. Harminc. The intense spiritual life of the people in Zuberec is manifested by 14 **crosses** dispersed all over the community's environs. Especially valuable are the stone crosses and **tombstones** adorned with relieves in the local cemeteries, from the turn of the 19th and 20th centuries (the work of the local stone masons) and a stone cross near the church bearing a picture of the life of St. Andrej and St. Florián from 1839. Folk architecture, characteristic of the mountain region of Central Slovakia, is represented by the few houses at the lower end of the village.

However, three kilometers from Zuberec, at Brestová, a unique **open-air museum of the Orava village** can be visited. It is located in impressive mountain scenery overlooked by the peaks of the Pálenica, Sivý vrch and Brestová mountains in the south, the Osobitá mountain in the east and the massive Mních mountain in the west. Over an area of about 20 hectares, and on both sides of the Studený potok brook, is a village containing the typical folk buildings of the individual regions of Orava. Styles of all regions are represented here – the south-western part of the lower, central and up-

---

Right: The open-air museum in Zuberec

per Orava regions, the north-eastern Tatras, the Goral area and the north-western Beskydy region. The first example is a **forester's house** from the Zákamenné region with a typical village tavern, which was built in 1970, and the first part of the museum was opened to the public in 1975. A visitor can see here **all kinds of buildings** – peasant houses, larders, lumber rooms, farmsteads, shepherd's huts, haylofts, etc.); **sacral buildings** (a wooden church, cemetery and belfry) and the **craftsman's** and **linen-maker's houses** (a Wallachian mill and sawmill, a potter's furnace and fulling mill, etc.). The Museum is thematically divided into five sections regarding each individual region. **The Market Place of the Dolná Orava Region** exemplifies the richer side of the region with rather large, ostentatious houses. **The Mill** near the brook includes a water mill, sawmill and fulling mill with their common water-driven mechanism. **The Lane of the Zamagurie Region**, with houses and farmsteads of rich and medium rich farmers, represents the typical structure of an Orava village. The house of the Slovík family from Rabčice contains the living rooms and bedrooms and also a hall for communal council sessions which isparticularly interesting. **The Goral Settlement** represents the poorest part of Orava lying on south-eastern slopes of the Oravské Beskydy mountains. Here can be seen the poor loggers', shepherds' and peasants' houses, and the house from Oravské Veselé with log walls, a clay floor and a open fire place, stands out. The **cemetery** with the Late-Gothic **wooden church** from Zábrež from the 15th century, standing on an elevated location, dominates the area and symbolises the place where a man is nearer to God.

The museum regularly organises ethnological expositions and the **Podroháčsky Folk Festival** is held in the local amphitheatre in August.

Múzeum oravskej dediny (Museum of Orava Village)
tel.: 8847/395 149
Opening hours: January 1- April 30 Monday to Friday 8:00–15:00 h, May 1 – October 31 daily 8:00–16:00h, November, December closed.
Group visits notified in advance can be admitted outside regular opening hours.

Not far from the museum, at the foothills of Madajka mountain in the Studená dolina valley there is an interesting **protected landscape – the**

cave of Brestovská jaskyňa. It is the largest cave in the Orava region and also the most important one in the Západné Tatry mountains. The length of its underground space reaches up to 1.8 km. With its unique underground water labyrinth the cave is planned to be opened to public in the near future.

Going southeastward across the Studená dolina valley, the longest and most dissected valley of the Roháče mountains, we can see the **protected landscape formation of the rocky Mačie diery** (Cat Holes) on the left hand side, with extremely rare vegetation growing on a limestone basement.

At the upper end of the Studená dolina valley at an altitude of 1,037 m above sea level extends a sunny mountain alpine meadow called **Zverovka**, the principal centre and natural starting point to all parts of the Roháče mountains. Originally there was only a **gamekeeper's lodge** here and in 1928 a **tourist cottage** was built next to it. In 1944 the Roháče mountains became the centre of north Slovakian and south Polish anti-Nazi resistance, and a group of partisans operated in Zverovka.

Left: Roháče mountains

The partisan field hospital:

In December 1944 the German Nazis attacked Zverovka with the final aim to eliminate the partisan units hidden in the Roháče mountains. The partisans moved their wounded to a hunting log hut under the Brestová mountain, two kilometres from Zverovka. The Nazis burnt down and destroyed the whole area and the hunting hut was transformed into a provisional field hospital. A young physician called Juraj Bernát and two nurses worked in primitive conditions and bitter cold weather, without medicine (all they had was disinfectant, a little wood saw and a pocket knife) and food consisting of several kilograms of lentils and about 150 grams of horse meat per person and day. For more than two months they looked after 17 seriously wounded and sick partisans. On several occasions, when enemy troops got close to the hut, all patients and staff had to abandon the hut for the thick forest, until it was relatively safe to return. In this critical situation the physician Bernát decided to go and seek help in the Polish community of Zakopane, which was, as intelligence services reported, already liberated. In harsh climatic conditions Dr. Bernát crossed the ridges of the Západ-

né Tatry mountains to Zakopane (it took him more than 60 hours) and brought the assistance of the Polish mountain rescue service. In spite of unimaginable difficulties the Polish rescuers finally salvaged the partisans and took them over to Zakopane. In commemoration of the event a trip to the hut is organised every year in September (it follows a yellow-marked path).

At the present time there are numerous options for accommodation in Zverovka available for the tourists, with well accessible high mountain hiking tours. One of them (the yellow marked path) leads across the **Látaná dolina valley**, an eastern prolongation of the the Studená valley. On the left side of the path there is the **nature reserve of Osobitá** bearing the same name as the cliff peak Osobitá (1,687 m) among the the most beautiful mountains of the Orava region. For the sake of protecting the rare flora at the summit, the Osobitá mountain is not accessible to visitors. In the Látaná dolina valley iron ore was extracted in the past and the surrounding slopes were used as pastures in the mid-19th century, but today such activities have stopped in favour of nature conservation. At the end of the Látaná dolina valley, another favourite family walk is to the **national nature reserve of Kotlový žľab**, a trough with original forestation in steep mountain terrain. Tourists who continue higher will get to **Zábrad saddle** (1,660 m) which separates the valleys of Látaná and Roháčska dolina, with the additional possibility to ascend even higher to the easiest accessible mountain of all the Roháče – **Rákoň** (1,879 m). Its peak is situated in the main ridge which forms a part of the Slovak-Polish state border and offers wonderful views of the Roháčska kotlina basin and the Chocholowska valley in Poland. South-east of Zverovka is the long **Roháčska dolina valley** with a paved road leading across it. As far as the scenery is concerned this valley is the most remarkable in the region. There are high quality elevated cross-country skiing tracks, excellent opportunities for walking and an abundance of snow. The glacial origin of the Roháčska dolina valley is obvious for its numerous glacier relief manifestations.

The glacier in the Roháče mountains:

In the period of the last glaciation the glacier in the Roháče mountains was about nine kilometres long and was one of the longest glaciers in the Západné and Východné Tatry mountains. Its shape was regular and it left numerous traces of its activity. At the conclusion of the Roháčska dolina valley there is a glacier kettle of enormous dimensions (it is called a glacier amphitheatre) with small kettles hollowed in its surface, giving origin to the lakes. They are called the Roháčske plesá lakes and the unusual thing about them is that they are situated 300-400 m lower than the lakes in the High Tatras. The size and the lower sea level altitude of the surface relief forms, originating from glacier activity in the valley makes Roháčska dolina a European rarity.

The southern side of the Roháčska dolina valley has several projections which branch out into smaller valleys. The best known are the **Salatínska dolina valley** and the trough of **Spálený žľab**. They are popular as centres of winter sports and downhill skiing with excellently treated tracks and artificial snow available when necessary. The **ski resort** in the Salatínska dolina valley has become a favoured and much frequented destination for all lovers of skiing, which is possible in late spring time, therefore one is able to prolong its magnificent experience. Five ski lifts, daily treated ski slopes, areas for cross-country skiing, hiring agencies and service centres will satisfy the most fastidious visitor.

Parallel to the Salatínska dolina valley are the valleys of **Zadná Spálená dolina** and **Spálená dolina** situated higher in the Roháčska dolina valley. The valley Spálená dolina (alternatively called Zelená dolina or Green Valley, a reference to the deep green colour of its vegetation in spring time) is particularly attractive for tourists because of its bizarre relief and rather wild nature. There are two routes for hiking, a yellow path (leading to the Baníkovské sedlo saddle – 2,045 m) and a blue-marked one (which leads to the Roháčske plesá lakes). The Spálená dolina valley, together with the higher situated **Smutná dolina valley**, in the upper part of the Roháčska dolina valley, and the contiguous peaks, form the **national nature reserve of the Roháčské plesá lakes**. It extends over an area of almost 452 hectares, which from a scenic and a scientific point of view, is one of the most valuable landscapes, not only in the Roháče mountains, but throughout the Západné Tatry mountains. Visitors can familiarise themselves with it by using the **tourist path with information boards,** leading from the conclusion of the Roháčska dolina valley to the Spálená dolina valley, which passes the lower part of the valley Smutná dolina beside the Ro-

háčske plesá lakes and ends in the alpine meadow of Adamcuľa. The tour is not exacting and passes the most interesting and most beautiful parts of the reserve. The instruction boards display the geomorphologic, climatologic, hydrological, botanical, zoologic and historical characteristics of the territory of Roháče mountains. The route begins at the point where the cottage Ťatliakova chata used to stand (it burnt down in 1963) and where the Roháčska dolina valley passes over to the Smutná dolina valley. From here it continues along the Ťatliakovo jazierko lake (1,370 m above sea level, covering an area 0.28 ha, at a depth of 1.2 m, and colloquially called The Black Pond) to the Roháčske plesá lakes, remnants of the Glacial period in the Tatra territory. The **first Roháčske pleso** lake lies at an altitude of 1,563 m above sea level, its area is 2.22 ha, and its depth is 6.5 m. The **second** and the **third** Roháčske pleso lakes are at an altitude of 1,650 m and 1,653 m, above sea level, their areas are 0.21 and 0.61 ha, and are 1.3 m and 3.7 m deep respectively. The **fourth** Roháčske pleso lake is the highest at an altitude of 1,718 m, above sea level with an area of 1.45 ha, and it is 8.1 m deep. All lakes, partially silted by the remains of the moraines are situated in a kettle hollowed by the glacier.

More sturdy tourists usually continue to follow the blue path up the Smutná dolina valley to the **Smutné sedlo saddle** (1,955 m) in the main ridge of the Západné Tatry mountains. The saddle provides the best possible passage between north and south. Excellent skiers like to ski in upper part of the Smutná dolina valley, but they have to carry their equipment on their backs. A tour tracing the ridge is possible in a north-easterly direction to the Volovec mountain or by taking the north-western route to the Baníkov mountain and the Baníkovské sedlo saddle.

The first peak of the main ridge of Roháče mountains, east of Smutné sedlo saddle, is the **Plačlivé mountain** (2,126 m). It is a sharp and cliffy peak which was once also called Plačlivô or Plačlivý Roháč. Together with the **Ostrý Roháč mountain** (2,084 m) they form the typical mountain silhouette of the Roháče mountains and the Zá-

Left: A trip to the Roháče mountains
Right: Sivý vrch mountain

padné Tatry mountains. The view from Plačlivé is broader than from Ostrý Roháč and especially the vista over the Smutná dolina valley, which is a captivating experience of beautiful natural scenery. The Ostrý Roháč mountain is a double-top cliff peak, although its crumbling surface makes climbing possible only from the saddles of the Smutné sedlo or the Jamnické sedlo (1,905 m). For the majority of visitors this is the final destination to the Roháče mountains, even though some sections of the track are rather exposed and secured by chains. But the rare prospect of seeing chamois and mountain marmot make the experience worthwhile.The third mountain of the Roháče triplet is the **Volovec mountain** (2,063 m), a massive mountain which spreads over the Slovak-Polish border. It is, for the most part, a deforested, steep, dome-shaped mountain rendering perhaps the most exquisite view when compared to the rest of peaks in the Západné Tatry mountains, and where one can see the valleys of Roháčska dolina, Jamnícka dolina and Chocholowska dolina. The descent is possible by the Rákoň and sedlo Zábrad saddles to the valleys of Roháčska dolina or Látaná dolina continuing on to Zverovka.

Departing from the Smutné sedlo saddle some sturdy tourists can undertake a very exacting tour with several exposed points, secured by chains, to the **Baníkovské sedlo saddle**. The first ascent is to the tripple topped expanded rock formation (Prvá, Druhá and Tretia kopa) called the **Tri kopy mountain** (2,154 m). In the north-east a rocky projection called Zelené separates the kettle of the Roháčske plesá lakes from the Smutná dolina valley. The passage over the ridge from Tri kopy is demanding and not suitable for the casual and ill-equipped hiker. Alternately, the passage to the neighbouring **Hrubá kopa mountain** (2,166 m) is easier and leads mostly through grassy slopes. Somewhat more difficult is the tour to **Baníkov** (2,178 m), the highest peak of this part of the Západné Tatry mountains ascending over awkward scales, which in places are secured by chains. From the point of view of landscape the Baníkov mountain is one of the most attractive peaks of the mountain range having on its slopes numerous well preserved surface formations of glacial activity and some rare plant species, such as *Ranunculus glacialis*. There is a panoramic view from the top of the mountain to all the surrounding cardinal points. Below, in the west is the Baníkovské sedlo saddle (2,054 m) with the majority of ascending and descending routes

oriented towards either the summit or to the valley. The Baníkovské sedlo saddle is often used for travelling from the Orava part of the mountain range (from Spálená dolina valley) to the Liptov region (passing the valley of Parichvost).

The best start for the tour to the westernmost part of the Západné Tatry mountains is the gamekeeper's lodge, Biela Skala, situated several kilometres south of Zuberec, near the paved road to the city of Liptovský Mikuláš. The red marked path leads from the lodge to the forest, ascending to a steep slope and ending in a grassy saddle under the **Biela skala mountain** (1,316 m). The location offers a wonderful view of the Biela skala cliffs the highest peak of the mountain range. The people living in Zuberec also called it Jánošík's rock after an old legend of the Slovak folk hero – the forest robber Juraj Jánošík who hid his treasure under Biela skala. Its almost two kilometres long ridge astonishes the eye with a variation of bizarre limestone rocks and grassy alpine meadows containing a plethora of protected flora. A well-maintained path leads from Biela skala along a mountain ridge providing a magnificent view over the valleys of the

Orava and Váh rivers and practically all of the Orava and Liptov regions. Some parts of the path are more exposed encountering various dolomite towers and fissures. This part of the tour is called "Skalné mesto" (Rocky City) and opens the way to the **Sivý vrch mountain** (1,805 m). The ridge including its forks covering an area of almost 113 hectares nature reserve of Sivý vrch. It is a protected area because of its bizarre formations (cliffs, karst forms, rock sites, etc.) with exceptionally variegated calciphilous high mountain flora. The vegetation looks like a botanical garden with some species not found anywhere else in the Tatras (such as, *Dianthus nitidus*) especially visible in spring time. It is precisely because of the diversity of its vegetation that the Sivý vrch mountain is considered one of the most remarkable mountains in Slovakia.

In this same north-estern region is another **nature reserve** called **Úplazíky**, covering an area of approximately 31 hectares to 150 m in height of geomorphologically variegated dolomitic, limestone cliffs with numerous rare species of plants. Advancing along the ridge of the Západné Tatry mountains over the sedlo Pálenica saddle (1,570 m, an old historical route from Orava to Liptov, which is seldom used today) the red-marked path leads to the **Zuberec mountain** (1,746 m) and further to the **Brestová mountain** (1,902 m). From here one can descend from its summit following the blue marked path to Zverovka, or for the more fitter hiker, there is the alternative treck south-east over the **Parichvost saddle** (1,870 m), along the ridge. There is also a more moderately difficult ascent to the top of the **Salatín mountain** (2,047 m) with steep faces on the northern and southern sides, followed by a pass over the **Skriniarky ridge**. This tour is considered the most exposed though also the most beautiful in the Západné Tatry mountains, especially the parts over what is called Zvon (the Bell) – distinct rocky formations hanging over the valley Predná Spálená dolina and around Červená skala which are among the most exposed parts of the main ridge. In the following peak of the **Spálená mountain** (2,083 m) the main ridge bends from the east to the south-west towards the **Pachoľa peak** (2,166 m) which has a regular pyramidal shape and offers a splendid view of the surrounding landscape. The descent is comfortable and ends in the Baníkovské sedlo saddle or further on into the valleys of Orava or Liptov.

Right: The thermal swimming pool in Oravice

The deep valleys, bizarre peaks and gloomy forests of the Roháče mountains inspired the people living here to invent and narrate horror stories, legends and tales full of supernatural beings, such as the goddesses of Roháče...

The goddesses of Roháče:

They were either very beautiful or unattractive women but they always had large bosoms. They lived near the Žabie pliesko lake in Zverovka and everybody knew that their favourite pastime was stealing children, replacing them with their own. Usually they changed their weak and deformed offspring for healthy children from Zuberec and Habovka. People say that they even stole adult women to care for the children. One such woman was seen by a man from Zuberec near the lake and she begged him to carry a message to her husband. Her husband was supposed to bring her some eggs laid by a black hen to entertain the children of the goddesses and some peas to throw under the feet of the pursuers whilst she would escape. But her husband left behind the two things he was supposed to bring.

HABOVKA (725 m, population 1,200) is situated only one kilometre south-west of Zuberec on the way to Podbiel, eleven kilometres distant. It is situated on the confluence of the Blatná brook and the Studený potok brook beside the Skorušinské vrchy mountains and the Podtatranská brázda furrow.

The same as the nearby community Zuberec Habovka was mentioned for the first time in 1593 under the name *Habowka* when it was founded and colonised by settlers from the villages around the Orava river who took advantage of the Wallachian privilege. It belonged to Orava Castle and was administered by hereditary village mayors and later by elected mayors. In 1625 there were only five houses in the village. The hard and infertile soil compelled the people to dedicate themselves to sheep breeding, the production of cloth, linen, shingles and the extraction of iron ore. As the soil was not capable to sustain the local population, many of them emigrated in pursuit of other work. In the 17th century Habovka was completely burnt down by the troops of rebellious nobility and in 1683 it was also sacked by Lithuanian troops crossing the Orava region to Vienna. Further devastation was also caused by floods in 1813 which destroyed a wood-

en church built in 1715. In the mid-19th century the community had about 800 inhabitants and in 1900 it increased to 913. But they still had to migrate in search of sustenance (especially the bricklayers of Habovka who were known for their excellent skills in the southern counties of Old Hungary) and emigrated to America. Although at the time of the First Czechoslovak Republic there existed in the community a sawmill, fullmil and numerous weaving workshops and mills, the population dropped to 747, but soon after the Second World War the population progressively grew. At present the local people are employed in industry, forestry and private farming.

Among the most important sacral monuments is the Roman-Catholic **church of the Virgin Mary** built in the Classicist style in the years 1817-1820 and reconstructed in 1952. Besides the two baptisteries from the 17th and 18th centuries, there are also the stained glass window panes of 1951 designed by the renown artist V. Hložník which are exceptionally interesting. Let us mention also the chapel of 1812, standing above the community with a folk sculpture of Madonna, and a Baroque organ of the second half of the 18th century.

In the southern part of the community's territory there is a **nature reserve** called **Medzi borami**, which consists of two localities with occurrences of important plant life growing on a sub-mountainous peat bog.

North-east of Habovka lies the holiday community of **Oravice** (790 m). Its precise location is in the furrow Podtatranská brázda 10 km from Habovka and 6 km south of Vitanová in the valley of the Oravica brook and is a part of the territory of the town of Tvrdošín.

The community Bystrá, or Oravická Bystrá (in the territory of the contemporary Oravice community), which again was founded by the Wallachian privilege was colonised in the first half of the 17th century by the inhabitants of Trstená who received the area from Juraj Thurzo in 1608. In the past the word "oravice" was locally used to denote an expanded territory of mountains, hamlets and pastures. The community itself consisted of 16 colonists and their families. A harsh climate and barren soil caused difficult living conditions for the subjects of the landlords seated in the Orava Castle, who continuously rebelled against their duties. After one rebellion the landlord of Orava castle,

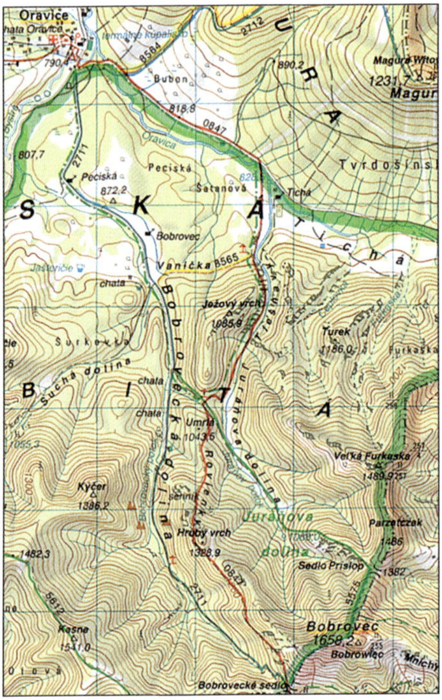

Štefan Thököly, liquidated the community in 1659 and donated the territory of Oravice to Tvrdošín, after which Oravice served the citizens of Tvrdošín as a resource for wood and pasture land. In the Bobrovecká dolina and Juráňová dolina valleys, lying south-east of the contemporary community, the extraction of iron ore was introduced in the 17th and 18th centuries and the ore was transported to a furnace in Hámričky near Trstená and from 1837 to a new metallurgical works in Podbiel. Iron ore was extracted in Oravice up until 1860. In the years between 1817-1820 the citizens of Tvrdošín built in Oravice a Roman-Catholic **church of St. Anna** which was restored in 1864.

By the end of the 19th and beginning of the 20th century Oravice was also discovered by the tourists. Hunters and scientists were the first visitors, who especially in the years 1870-1887 visited the virgin environment of Oravice, which was abundant with game and numerous unique communities of fauna and flora. Several very interesting natural specimens from the territory are included in the collections in museums in Budapest, Kraków and Poprad. During the First Czechoslovak Republic the first tourist footpath was made which led from Vitanová, passing Oravice to the Juráňová dolina valley and in 1931 the more enthusiastic tourists from Tvrdošín constructed here the first cottage housing 15 beds. The most attractive feature about Oravice is its geo-thermal water spring (the temperature of the water is 54°C and its yield is 120 l/sec). Progressively additional cottages, a swimming pool with thermal water, open all the year round, a ski lift, car-camping, and playgrounds now make of Oravice a favourite holiday and tourist resort.

For lovers of hiking Oravice represents a starting point to the picturesque and secluded corners of the Tichá, Juráňova, Bobrovecká, Suchá and Mihulčia dolina valleys offering wonderful scenery full of multifarious gorges. The yellow-marked footpath from Oravice to the north-east and the state border with Poland, continuing by a field road to the border crossing in Suchá hora, is not an exacting tour. Along the route, especially in May, tourists can admire a lovely view of the snow-capped Tatra mountains contrasting with the green colour of the surrounding meadows. A walk to the **Magura mountain** (1,232 m) located on the Slovak-Polish state border, east from Oravice, is also not exacting.

However, a more demanding tour is from Oravice to the **Juráňova dolina valley** and the **Bobrovec mountain** (1,666 m). It is marked in red and starts at the Oravice chata cottage, heading to the Tichá dolina valley, bending towards the Šatanová alpine meadow, which continues further southward to the Juráňova dolina valley and ends in the one-kilometre long gorge of **Tiesňavy**. The path here is interrupted by numerous bridges. Tiesňava in the Juráňova dolina valley is a narrow canyon with hollowed basins known among the local people as "giant pots" which have little waterfalls. It is considered to be one of the most beautiful gorges in Slovakia. The path leading over the right slope of the gorge is carved in the rock face and is secured by banisters and in places also by ladders. In the past the gorge was used for transporting wood, by means of rolling it down the slopes, over a kilometre-long wooden bridge, the remains of which still exist. Diverse calciphilous plant communities grow here at an altitude of 900 m, though they are rather typical for much higher

Right:A gorge in the Juráňova dolina valley

locations, and are well worth a mention, which exist here because of the cold micro-climate of the gorge where snow lasts longer and less sunshine enters in summer. Beyond the gorge the Juráňova dolina valley broadens and meadows alternate with forests. The green-marked path leads to the Príslop saddle on the Slovak-Polish state border and continues across a thin forest, alpine meadows, and dwarf pine trees to the top of the Bobrovec mountain. The second path leads below the Hrubý vrch mountain (1,327 m) to the grassy **Bobrovské sedlo saddle** (1,355 m) from where there is the possibility to continue either to the north-east arriving to Bobrovec or to the south-west ending in Lúčna (1,652 m).

Also the blue-marked route across the **Bobrovská dolina valley** leads from Oravice to the Bobrovské sedlo saddle. Its length is about five kilometres. Again the gorges formed by the rock Skalka and its cliffs are among the most beautiful parts of the valley. In its upper part the valley broadens and the path continues across the forest and clearings to the Bobrovské sedlo saddle. At the end of the Bobrovská dolina valley the path divides and turns to the neighbouring **national nature reserve Tichá dolina valley** with a path leading along the rocks called Cigánka and over the grassy trough of Široký žľab up to the top of the Osobitá mountain. The last of the valleys around Oravice is the **valley of Mihulčie** dividing the Západné Tatry mountains from the Skorušinské vrchy mountains. Together with the Blatná dolina valley it connects Oravice with Habovka. Here there is a paved road used mostly by cyclists. There are several cyclist routes in the environs of Oravice, Habovka and Zuberec (for instance in the Roháčska, Tichá dolina valleys, below the Skorušiná mountain) and more and more visitors from the Orava part of the Západné Tatry mountains dedicate themselves to this particular sport. Its wonderful natural setting and numerous quiet corners offer abundant and impressive experiences for the ardent cyclist.

ORAVSKÝ BIELY POTOK (644 m, population 570) situated six kilometers north-west of Zuberec and six kilometres east of Podbiel also belongs to the communities lying below the Roháče mountains. It is situated in the valley of the Studený potok brook, in the Skorušinské mountains.

Its history goes back to 1567 when it was for the first time quoted in the list of communities belonging to Orava Castle (it remained in its ownership until 1848) under the name Biely Potok. It was founded on the basis of the Wallachian privilege and the name is derives from the former name of the Studený potok brook. The first settlers dedicated themselves to rearing sheep and to agriculture. The local people suffered considerably during the wars in the 17th century, which caused a dramatic drop in the number of population, but after the turn of the century, in 1715, there lived about 300 inhabitants in the village. Since the 18th century the community became renown for its stone-masons who manufactured mill stones, hewed ashlars, and carved various stone ornamental objects. In the 19th century the family of Belopotocký became especially famous for figural works of white sandstone, extracted near the community, crafted in the Late-Baroque style. Statues and other works of art made in their workshops can be found even today in several cities and communities, both on the Slovak and Polish sides of the Orava region. Besides masonry the local population was active in glass manufacture, offering their products throughout the region, as well as pottery and weaving. A paper mill also existed here in the 19th century. At the beginning of the 20th century many of the local people emigrated abroad and at the time of the First Czechoslovak Republic the extraction of minerals and masonry gradually declined. After the Second World War the population grew again and at the present time they are employed mainly in industrial firms existing in the vicinity or are otherwise involved in farming.

As a consequence of frequent fires there are no folk architectural objects left in the village. However, the most important cultural and historical monument of Oravský Biely Potok is the Classicist Roman-Catholic **church of St. Štefan the King** built in 1800, reconstructed in 1892 and again after the Second World War. In its interior a Baroque altar from the 18th century and a painting of St. Vojtech by J. Hanula are the two objects of main interest. The local **cemetery**, on an elevated location, surrounded by walls, is also worth a visit.

Žiar and its environs

Žiar and its environs spreads out into the south-western region of the Tatras and includes the Liptov part of the Západné Tatry mountains. In the north it is restricted by the ridge of the Západné Tatry mountains, in the west by the fork of the Sivý vrch mountain and in the east by the massive mountain of Baranec. In the south the territory includes the communities representing the starting points for the tours to the best known valleys of this part of the territory.

ŽIAR (765 m, population 420) lies 10 kilometres north-east of Liptovský Mikuláš, not far away from of its namesake valley which opens out into the Liptovská kotlina basin.

The community was founded as early as the 13th century on a clearing made by tree felling and burning. As the name Žiar means glow its origin is obviously connected with the burning and clearing of forest. The community was mentioned for the first time in 1349 under the name *Zar*, later *Ziar* (1535) or *Zjár* (1808). In the 18th century the population was about 250. They subsisted on sheep keeping and pasturing in the Žiar valley and the surrounding sub Tatra meadows and since the 18th century also the production and sale of charcoal. The population number reached almost its present level in the 19th century. The first half of the 20th century is characterised by scarce opportunities of employment other than in agriculture or forestry. The local people were obliged to migrate in pursuit of work out of their native district. Traditional female work besides the weaving of linen and simple carpets was the making of bobbin laces, a product that made Žiar famous all over the region. During the Second World War (October 1944) the community was burnt down by the Nazi troops for its active help to the partisans operating in the surrounding forests. The Monument of the Slovak National Uprising placed at the edge of the village near the point where the Žiarska dolina valley opens up to the Liptovská kotlina basin commemorates this sad event. The community was gradually reconstructed after the Second World War. Its inhabitants work mainly in industrial firms in the city of Liptovský Mikuláš or in agriculture and services in the village.

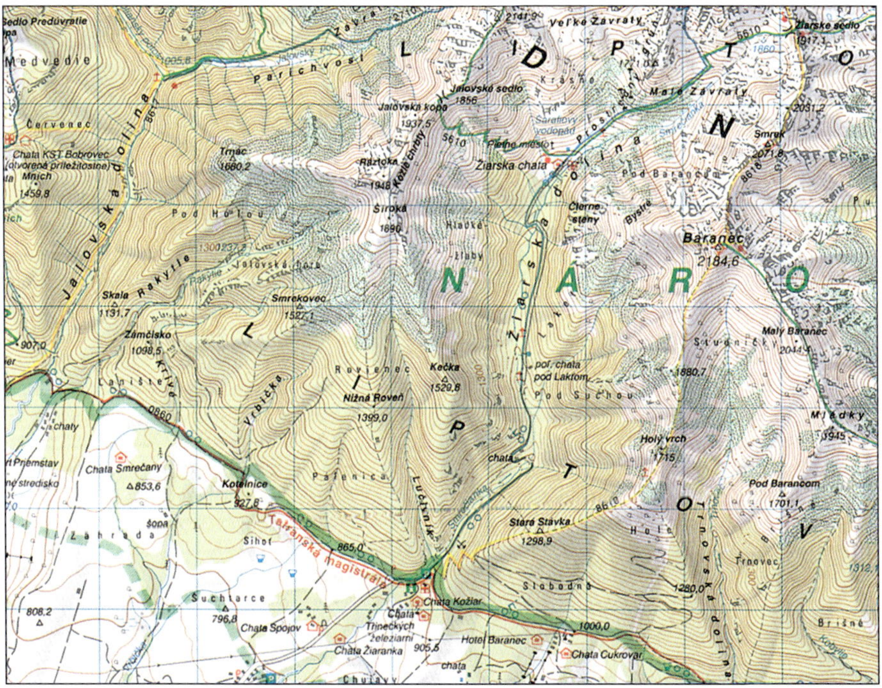

SMREČANY (704 m, population 600) forming practically a common settlement with Žiar, stretches on both banks of the Smrečianka brook, five kilometres north-east from Liptovský Mikuláš.

Although the first written document mentioning the community dates to the end of the 13th century, its territory was settled long before in pre-historic times. On a nearby hill the remains of an ancient hill fort with distinct rampart and a ditch, and some objects of older Iron period (6th-5th century B.C) were found. They belonged to the farming and cattle keeping people of Lusatian culture (mainly axes, sickles, pins and decorating items). The fort was undoubtedly settled also at the turn of the era by the people of Púchov culture. Existence of the community was for the first time mentioned in 1299 under the name *Zemerchen*, as land belonging to count Bohumír. Later, called *Szmercen* (1349) then *Smrezcany* (1460) it was owned by the squire family Szmrecsány. Bohumír's descendants' name was derived from that of the community. In the 18th century iron ore was extracted near the community. But as the population's possibilities of sustenance were scarce, (almost 530 by the end of the 18th century) many were forced to leave and take up seasonal jobs, mostly in Budapest.

The bricklayers of Liptov:

They say that the city of Budapest was built by the bricklayers of Liptov. It indeed sounds likely as the farmers from Smrečany and other Liptov villages often left in search of bricklaying jobs to Budapest after finishing their spring work in the fields. Multitudes of Liptov men moved to the capital of Old Hungary with the expectation of good earnings. The bricklayers were accompanied by auxiliary hands and even women, who also helped at the sites. It was not easy at all to become a bricklayer. Good bricklayer had to pass three years of apprenticeship, later another three years as a journeyman and only then was he eligible to become a properly qualified bricklayer. An experienced and reliable bricklayer could earn 200-300 guldens in a season depending on his effort and saving abilities. Thus the Liptov bricklayers worked from dawn to dusk on modest meals, saving a lot of money either to buy later a piece of land or a cow, sheep, or for the reconstruction of their own houses. At the end of the autumn they returned home exhausted but happy with their earnings and proud of "averting the poverty from the thresholds of their houses."

The local population was also active in various additional handicrafts like linen weaving, masonry and basket making. Baskets of unstripped wicker were made, and there also existed a wool comber and a wool cloth fulling mill in the village. At the time of the First Czechoslovak Republic a modern sawmill and small power station were also built there. The most dramatic period lived by Smrečany was during the Slovak National Uprising. In October 1944 the Nazi troops undertook to Smrečany a punitive campaign and a part of the community was burnt down. At the beginning of 1945 there were other tough battles for Smrečany. The local people remember especially the battle for the elevation point no 746 between the First Czechoslovak Military Corps and the Germans. After the Second World War life in Smrečany regained its normal pace and today the village is along with Žiar a tourist centre. Both of them are departing points to the Roháče mountains on the southern side of the mountain range.

As for the interesting cultural and historical monuments, an original Baroque **manor house** from the mid-18th century progressively altered in 1810 and 1955, which is today a home for the elderly, is worth mentioning. Tourists can also visit the **commemorative room of Fraňo Kráľ**, an important Slovak poet and writer of the first half of the 20th century. A valuable sacral buidling in the community is a Gothic Roman-Catholic **church of Purification of the Virgin Mary** of the 13th century. It was reconstructed in the 14th and 15th centuries and again in the 20th. In the interior of the church the Gothic-Renaissance wooden painted ceiling and wall paintings of the 14th century are of interest. The Late-Gothic main altar with a triptych of Madonna, St. Barbara and St. Katarína are from the second half of the 15th century. The side Late-Gothic altars of St. Martin and St. Mikuláš, and of the Holy Family originate from the beginning of the 16th century. A Gothic baptistery with pulpit, Baroque pews and organ supplement the objects in the interior of the church, and because of its wall paintings it is among the most valuable sacral monuments of the sub Tatra region. The spiritual life of Smrečany is also evidenced in the Evangelical church of 1880 standing nearby, interesting for its ground plan in a form of a cross.

Right: Žiarska dolina valley

Visitors to Smrečany and Žiar usually pass through the communities in pursuit of snow or undertaking walks to higher situated places on the southern slopes of the Západné Tatry mountains. Immediately beyond the community Žiar is a **group of holiday cottages** with two ski lifts and downhill skiing tracks for less demanding skiers. By taking a red-marked path towards Podbanské one gets to two short ski lifts placed two kilometres from the end of the **Žiarska dolina valley** at the point where it opens up to the Liptovská kotlina basin. However, the main aim of the tourists and skiers in the area is a seven kilometres long valley bordered in the west by the mountain fork consisting of the Baníkov-Ráztoka-Kečka mountains and in the east by the fork at the Plačlivé-Baranec-Holý vrch mountains. The end of the valley with the Smrečianka brook is at a sea level altitude of 900 m and its highest parts reach an altitude of as much as 1,870 m (Baníkovský kotol). The lower part of the valley is comparably narrow. It widens only in the central positions where there the alpine meadows open to the sunshine. Its ending is formed by a massive amphitheatre with glacier kettles called Veľké and Malé Závraty separated from each other by the rocky crest of the Prostredný grúň mountain. The valley was glaciated up to an altitude of 1,000 m above sea level during the last Glacial period. Its glacial past is well visible, especially in the glacier kettle and near the Šarafiov vodopád waterfall.

A favourite and sought-after resting place in the upper part of the valley is the **tourist cottage of Žiarska chata** (1,300 m). It was built in 1949-1950 on the site of an old cottage of the thirties, burnt down by the Nazis in 1944. Its position amid the mountains represents an excellent departing point for high-mountain tours to the surrounding peaks or passages over the saddles to the neighbouring valleys. It has a ski lift that enhances its attractiveness for winter skiing. North of the cottage and passing the dwarf pines are green and blue marked footpaths which lead up to the bottom of the Prostredný grúň mountain. The ascent is not too demanding and tourists enjoy the lovely silhouette of the surrounding peaks, especially Baranec. The blue track continues further up to the Smutné sedlo saddle (1,965 m) while the green-marked path deviates north-east up to a small wooden shelter about 450 m below the rocky Žiarske sedlo saddle (1,917 m) right below the top of Plačlivý mountain. It is possible to continue along the saddle observing the green mark to the Jamnícka dolina valley or the yellow one over a grassy ridge leading to the top of Smrek mountain (2,089 m). Smrek is usually only a stop on the ridge tour to the top of **Baranec mountain** (2,184 m) also called the Veľký vrch mountain. It is the third highest peak of the Západné Tatry mountains and offers a grandiose vista to all cardinal points. From the point of view of high-mountain flora it is interesting for its diversity, above all in northern and north-eastern parts of the summit, as well as on the south-eastern forks with the most dense growth of dwarf pine preserved in the Západné Tatry mountains. The descent from the top of the Baranec mountain leads along the green-marked track south-eastward to the conclusion of Račková valley. But the descent south-westward is also popular. The path following the yellow mark leads across the dwarf pine forest to the Holý vrch mountain (1,715 m), further on along a rocky ridge and a forest to Stará stávka mountain (1,299 m) ending in the outlet of Žiarska valley.

Another favourite, initially comfortable, but later a bit demanding is the tour from the Žiarska chata cottage to Baníkov which leads along the green-marked path. It passes below the Šarafiov vodopád waterfall, along the serpentines across the dwarf pines up to the grassy Jalovecké sedlo saddle, separating the Žiarska dolina valley from the Parichvost valley. But it is not advisable to continue from the north-western slopes of the saddle to the Parichvost valley as it is better accessible from the Baníkovské sedlo saddle. On the way it is necessary to pass the **rocky mountain Príslop** (2,145 m). Its grassy top provides a lovely view of the Žiarska dolina valley. The final aim for the majority of the tourists is one of the most attractive summits of the Západné Tatry mountains, Baníkov (see page 49) which continues along the rocky ridge of the fork and is very close to the Baníkovské sedlo saddle. Then it is possible to start the descent along the blue-signed route to about three kilometres along the **valley of Parichvost**. This particular valley is a deviation from the Jalovecká dolina valley parallel to the Žiarska dolina valley. Parichvost starts in its upper rocky and comparably steep incline by a trough called Závraty, and progressively descends in a more moderate manner. Nevertheless, the descent and ascent to the valley is demanding, and among the most difficult ones in the Západné Tatry mountains. The impression of the valley is enhanced by the cleft forms of the relief in its upper part and the deep forests in the lower. After two kilometres of descent there is the Hlboká dolina valley deviating to the north with a green-marked route heading for the Salatín mountain. The length of the valley is about 2.5 km and its upper part is at a height of 1,800 m. It is a typical glacier valley and at its end there is an interesting rocky kettle called Vrece (Bag). The name of the valley (hlboká = deep) illustrates its mysteriousness and gloominess ascribed to it in the past by the shepherds. About a kilometre west of the outlet of the **Hlboká dolina valley**, the principal branch of the longest valley of this part of the Západné Tatry mountains is situated – the Jalovecká dolina valley.

The starting point for the Jalovecká valley and the northerly Bobrovecká valleys are the communities of Jalovec and Bobrovec.

BOBROVEC (640 m, population 1,820) is the largest community and a centre of this part of the Západné Tatry mountain range. It lies in the Liptov basin near the Jalovecký potok brook, only several kilometres north of the city of Liptovský Mikuláš.

It is one of the oldest settlements of the Liptov region. It was first mentioned in old acts under the name of *Bobrouch* as early as 1231. The name is without doubt derived from that of the beaver (bobor = beaver) which lived in Jalovecký potok brook in ancient times. One of the first owners of this territory were count Behar, son of Semel and count Bohumír in the 13th century. Later when the communities Bobrovček, Beharovce and Jalovec separated from Bobrovec, the land belonged to the landlords of the Likava Castle. From the 15th century on Bobrovec developed into a town, with privileges which were recorded in an act of 1482 issued by the Old Hungarian king Matej Korvín. The privileges were expanded in the 16th century when they were, for instance, exempt from paying the toll. Although the Likava landlords tried incessantly to reduce the rights of Bobrovec, at the end of the 18th century the town still enjoyed the right to weekly markets and also owned the expanded privilege to fairs. There existed in the town numerous guilds (those of the bricklayers, shoemakers, musicians, carpenters). The production of linen, lace-making, blue-and-white printed textile also prospered. In the last quarter of the 18th century the community was purchased by the family of Okolicsányi, who owned it until the mid-19th century. Bobrovec counted 1,367 inhabitants in 1784 in spite of the fact that at the beginning of the 18th century about 50 families moved to the Lower Land (the southern part of the Austro-Hungarian Empire) liberated from the Turks in search of better living conditions. The population continued to grow and in 1828 it surpassed the contemporary number. During the 19th century the community's population manifested a strong patriotic enthusiasm as a response to the attempts of Magyarization, preserving its lively activities in various associations and amateur theatre.

The Sobriety Association:

Among the most interesting activities of the local population in the mid-19th century was the one called the Sobriety Association founded in 1840 by the local priest Peter Árvay. The idea and aim of the Association was to distract the local men from the pubs, and above all from the excessive consumption of alcoholic beverages (a

Right: A sheep dairy farm near Bobrovec

problem for a great part of the Slovak nation) and to open up other options for leisure. The foundation of associations (there were various types in the region of Liptov) was accompanied by the opening of libraries with the final aim to support the promotion of reading and further education. Considering that the common Liptov people were used to spending a considerable part of their low earnings on spirits, the activity of the associations was justified and a very important one. But further development showed that alcohol remained the true companion of the farmers, tradesmen, loggers, shepherds, rafters... and as a matter of fact it is until the present time. Even so, the similar efforts of the local priests or teachers deserves admiration and respect although it might be characterised as a vain "fight against the windmills".

The community was not capable of offering any decent means of subsistence by the beginning of the 20th century, so many locals emigrated to America. Bobrovec became famous for the heavy battle between the 1st Czechoslovak Military Corps and the 320th German division in the spring of 1945. The victory of the Czechoslovak troops in the battle for Bobrovec meant a principal break in the German defences and opened the way to the city of Ružomberok and finally liberation of the entire Liptov region. The character of the community today is agricultural but most of the local people work in industry and services in the nearby city of Liptovský Mikuláš.

The most significant cultural-historical monument in the community is the Roman-Catholic **church of St. Juraj**. Originally a Gothic building of a church from the 14th century it was rebuilt in 16th in Renaissance style and in 1723 expanded into Baroque style. In the interior, painted by J. B. Klemens in the years 1852 to 1854, the painting of St. Juraj placed in the main altar and a Renaissance stone baptistery of the 16th century are of interest. Then there are the Late-Baroque **chapel** of the 18th century, built in the centre of the community and surrounded by a wall, as well as the stone **pillar** with a sculpture of St. Jozef from 1818.

JALOVEC (700 m, population 260) is much smaller in comparison to Bobrovec and lies near the Jalovecký potok brook, two kilometres north of Bobrovec.

Even though the community was mentioned in 1391 under the name *Ilochfeu*, it was probably founded in the first half of the 14th century, when it was donated to count Martin, son of Panest. Among its owners was the family of landlords Baan of Trstená who owned the community until 1848. A story from the past proclaims that the name of the community was derived from juniper (jalovec = juniper) a tree growing abundantly around the area. The local population was engaged besides farming in the extraction and processing of wood, sheep, horse and cattle keeping and pasturing in the Jalovecká dolina valley. In addition they produced shingles, and were also busy in coopery, weaving, and the wheelwright's trade. Brass buckles, dishes and tools for the shepherds (above all the wooden mugs of the Liptov type) are characteristic of the region. The shepherds' traditions and patterns were preserved up until the 20th century in the work of the local folk artisans. The population in Jalovec remained more or less stable throughout its history, oscillating between 200 and 300. Similar to Bobrovec the hard times for the community were those of the last years of war, above all in the spring of 1945. It found itself in the front line of the fighting and the German troops burnt down great part of it. The events are commemorated by a monument to the **Slovak National Uprising**. The community was reconstructed after the Second World War and today it is a tourist starting point for the Jalovecká and Bobrovecká dolina valleys.

In the west, several kilometres from Jalovec, there are communities similar in size, namely Pavlova Ves, Liptovské Beharovce, and Bobrovček.

The existence of **PAVLOVA VES** (620 m, population 280) lying six kilometres north-west of Liptovský Mikuláš is documented by the acts of 1469 under the name Pawlowa vieska. It belonged to the estate of Likava and after it was transferred as a form of advance payment to the families of Pongrácz and Kubíny in the 17th and 18th centuries. Its people lived of agriculture and were recognised as skilled carpenters, shingle, wooden trough and basket producers. They brewed beer and distilled spirits and sold them around the neighbourhood. Tragic events befell the community in the Second World War when the retreating German army burnt it down.

Right: On the crest of the Západné Tatry mountains

LIPTOVSKÉ BEHAROVCE (635 m, population 50) is an even smaller community, for the first time mentioned in historical sources as *curia Behar*. The community developed within the administrative territory of Bobrovec bearing the name of its past owner Behar who recieved it in 1231 from the Old Hungarian king Ondrej II. The ownership of the community passed from one noble family to another in the course of time and its population, besides agriculture, lived of sheep keeping, carpentry and some of them, by the 18th century, worked in the local brewery and distillery. The community used to be famous in the past for violin manufacturing. Regarding the cultural and historical monuments two 19th century rural Classicist curias and several shingle covered **log huts** have been preserved in the community.

Situated in the north-east **BOBROVČEK**, also called Malý Bobrovec, (660 m, population 225) is much alike the neighbouring communities and originated by separation from Bobrovec in the 13th century (first mentioned in 1231). The local population found its source of living in the surrounding forests as they provided wood for the carpenters, shingle-makers and producers of wooden dishes and for the production of pitch. In 1948 the community was destroyed by fire which engulfed almost all the original buildings.

In this part of the Západné Tatry mountains the **Jalovecká dolina valley** is extraordinarily attractive from the point of view of tourists and visitors. Near its outlet to the Liptovská kotlina basin there is a **holiday area called Bobrovecká vápenica** where besides numerous cottages, there is also a short ski lift available. But nature lovers usually go deeper in the valley bordered by the forks of the Sivý vrch mountain in the west, the massive mountain of Salatín in the north and the mountain fork of Baníkov in the east. There is a yellow-marked path up to the Pálenica saddle on the main ridge of the Západné Tatry mountains. At the entrance to the saddle there are the **national natural reserves of Mních and Sokol** with rock walls and an interesting rocky needle called Kamenná Mara. The cliff walls of Mních and Sokol separate the lower part of the Jalovecká dolina valley from the undulating plain Červenec situated in the west, a prolongation of the grassy peak of **Babky** (1,566 m). The route which passes it is marked in green, starting at the end of the Jalovecká dolina valley, continuing across pleasant alpine meadows and a broad grassy ridge up to

the foothills of the Ostrá mountain (1,763 m), the top of which is by-passed by the path on its eastern side and crossing the patches of dwarf pine trees. Later it becomes steeper leading over a stony surface up to the top of the Sivý vrch mountain.

But most tourists going to the main ridge of the Západné Tatry mountains prefer the route leading across the Jalovecká and Bobrovecká dolina valleys. This path continues in a northerly direction along the Jalovecký potok brook up to the steep slopes of **Lysec** (1,827 m). Its massive body represents the south-western fork of the Salatín mountain. It is called so because its summit is bare (lysý = bold). The valley under Lysec divides into two branches: the Bobrovecká dolina and Parichvost valleys. The **Bobrovecká dolina valley** stretches under the Sivý vrch mountain up to Brestová. Its lower part is covered by forests and in its upper part combines dwarf pines and alpine meadows. The glacial activity left here distinctive forms of a modelled surface, as well as two glacier lakes – Bobrovecké plesá. As the lower situated **Čierne Bobrovecké pliesko lake** has water only occasionally it is not quoted among the lakes of the Západné Tatry mountains. The **Biele Bobrovecké pliesko lake**, at an altitude of 1,503 metres above sea level is larger and its parameters are somewhat more significant. It occupies an area of 0.1 ha, its length is 77 m, max. width is 21m and the depth is 1.5 m. The path goes on over the two lakes into a slope covered by dwarf pine trees and after a steep ascent it reaches the Pálenica saddle. From there one can continue north-east or south-west along the main ridge of the Západné Tatry mountains.

PRIBYLINA (765 m, population 1,350) lies ten kilometres south-westward from Podbanské on the road from Liptovský Hrádok near the confluence of the Račkov potok brook and the river Belá.

Its history dates back to 1286 when it existed under the name of *Perbenye* as the property of Ondrej, founder of the family of Pongrácz who owned the community until 1848 when serfdom was abolished. The original community was situated closer to the Belá river, a part of Kostolec, but because of frequent floods the inhabitants gradually moved to a nearby hill where they felt safer, which is its location today. The contiguous Račková dolina valley was a rich source of pasture for sheep and cattle. In the 15th century the settlers arrived from the east,

also mostly shepherds who besides keeping sheep and cattle processed the hides of the animals manufacturing fur coats and shoes. The also wove linen and wool, and manufactured the wooden dishes and tools used by the shepherds (for instance their wooden mugs and sticks). A burnt lime of excellent quality was made here and the first sawmill was established in the 17th century. The population grew rapidly especially during the 18th century, ultimately reaching approximately 1,000. This growth continued also in the following century and in 1869 the number surpassed its present level. For a time Pribylina was considered a big community with numerous well-developed trades. The most typical trade carried out in Pribylina, however, was rafting.

The rafters of Pribylina:

Rafting developed in Pribylina thanks to the enormous reserves of wood in the Tatra forests and good navigating conditions offered by the Liptov rivers. Another such river was the Belá allowing the transportation of wood not only to Pribylina but mainly to Hrádok and further on down the river Váh. The rafters in Pribylina fastened together what was called half-rafts (approximately 10 m^3 of wood) on the bank of the river near Podbanské. Then they conveyed the rafts on the fast flowing Belá up to Hrádok. The rafters had to be strong, skilled and dexterous men if they wanted to transport the raft unharmed and successfully to Hrádok in one hour (walking distance, three hours). If necessary they also knew how to stop and anchor the raft. At the end of the journey they usually partook of hearty refreshment and returned on foot. Rafting was a seasonal job starting from the beginning of April to the end of June. After Easter the raw material was transported for the manufacture of wooden boards. This transportation process on the river was supervised from the bank by skilled man ready to intervene if some pieces got stuck. In May and June longer pieces of wood were floated down river. At the end of the rafting season all rafters with their wives met at the main contractor's who prepared the final clearing and set a banquet. However, there was not too much time

Left: Christmas in Pribylina
Right: Sunday of Compatriots

available for feasting as the people of Pribylina had to start with their other seasonal work – hay-making.

However, these occupations did not provide sufficient sustenance and the people of Pribylina had to migrate to the southern territories of Old Hungary in pursuit of other seasonal jobs. Along with their fellow compatriots the bricklayers of Pribylina built various mansions in Budapest. In the second half of the 19th century the "guest workers" of Pribylina were active in revolutionary workers' movements. Among the prominent turn-of-the-century members of the movement was also the bricklayer Matej Šuňavec, organiser and founder of the local workers' trade union, editor of the first Slovak socialist newspaper and the journals *Nová doba, Zora* and *Robotnícke noviny*. He was also chairman of the Building Workers Union in building, stonemasonry, and ceramics in time of the First Czechoslovak Republic. During the Slovak National Uprising Pribylina and its population were among the most active supporters of the partisan group Vysoké Tatry which liberated the community as early as January 1945. The rich tradition of associative life in Pribylina has been preserved until the present day and the community, as far as the organisation of cultural events and travel and tourism are concerned, is one of the principal leisure and holiday centres in the Liptov region of the Západné Tatry mountains.

The community has also several cultural and historical sights, namely the Roman-Catholic Neo-Baroque **church of St. Katarína**, built in 1910 on the site of the old wooden church is one of the sacral monuments. Likewise, the Evangelical church in Neo-Romanesque style was built also on the site of an old wooden church in 1901-02 following the design of architect M. M. Harminc. Secular sights are represented by the **commemorative room of Matej Šuňavec** containing an exposition presenting the life and work of this prominent Slovak revolutionary and organiser of the workers' movement in the first half of the 20th century.

The most attractive sight, however, is the **Museum of Liptov Village**, documenting the folk architecture of the Liptov region. The impetus behind the establishing the museum arose out of extensive flooding west of Liptovský Mikuláš caused by the construction of the Liptovská Mara dam, whereupon the main task of the Museum was to save the most valuable monuments of the

flooded area. The most important cultural monuments were moved from the eleven flooded communities which constitute the main exhibits in the museum. Original and even entire buildings were dismantled and moved to the museum which was opened to public in 1991. But the construction is going on project and at the present not even the first stage has yet been completed. The public now can see 14 exhibits reflecting the simple and modest style of living of the poor rural people in the Liptov region, as well as that of the well-to-do farmers or tradesmen's families. A classic example is represented by five houses of the community of Liptovská Sielnica characterising a poor family, the house of a middle class farmer and shoemaker in one, and a house of wealthy wheelwright. The house of the village mayor of Liptovský Trnovec and a village school comprising also the teacher's apartment of Valaská Dubová will also intrigue the visitor. Precious samples of sacral and secular folk architecture are the Gothic-Renaissance **manor house** of Parížovce and an Early-Gothic **church of the Virgin Mary** from Liptovská Mara. The manor house is a fine

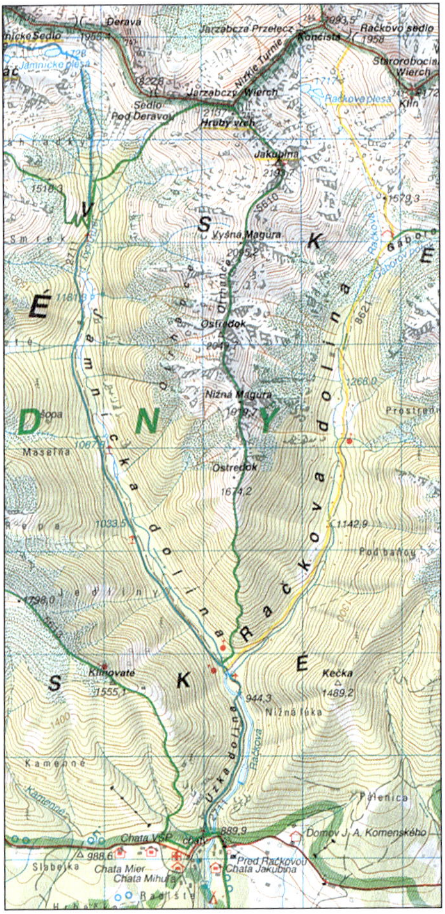

example of some of the oldest landowners' architecture of the Liptov region and various architectural details including the Late-Gothic wall paintings will certainly attract the attention of the tourist. The church itself is much older, its foundations were constructed in Romanesque style and laid down probably in the 12th century. It was rebuilt in the second half of the 13th century, later expanded, and in the 17th century the tower was added to it. Both buildings are true copies of the two most valuable monuments from the deluged territory. The nature and appearance of the Liptov village in the past is finally recreated by the

Right: Gáborova dolina valley

smith's furnace, a fire station, belfry and farmsteads.

Within the museum complex there is a training centre for folk crafts offering visitors samples of folk craft and arts (weaving, bobbin-lacing, wood, metal and leather-working, the manufacturing of wicker or straw baskets, etc). as well as Liptov folk and customs. Regular events are the **Sunday of Children** held in June, the **Sunday of Compatriots** in July, the **Sunday of Bee-Keepers** in August, the **Day of St. Hubert** in September, and **Harvest Thanksgiving** in October, as well as **Liptov Christmas** in December. The museum also has a zoo where horse-riding is possible.

Múzeum liptovskej dediny
(Museum of the Liptov Village) tel.: 0844/293 163
Opening hours: November 1 to May 14, Mon-Fri 9:00-15:00h, May 15 to October 30 daily except Mon 9:00-17:00h. Visits announced in advance also provide the opportunity to participate in various cultural events.

The lively cultural activities of Pribylina include a festival of amateur films on natural history, usually held in autumn under the title *Tatranský kamzík* and a cross-country ski race called *Po stopách partizánskeho oddielu Vysoké Tatry*.

Tourists know Pribylina mainly as a departing point to the **Račkova** and **Jamnícka dolina valleys**. A road starting near the museum leads to the Račkova dolina valley. At its end opening up into the Liptovská kotlina basin there is a group of tourist cottages and a caravan camping regularly visited by natives and foreigners. Winter is the time for the fans of cross-country and downhill skiing as there are three ski lifts and well-maintained running tracks in the Račkova dolina valley. At the end of the valley there is an intersection of tourist routes. The red one leads along the borderline of the Tatra National park starting at Žiarska valley up to Podbanské which is not too demanding and affords comfortable walk and offering some lovely views of the Liptovská kotlina basin. The ascent by the green route leading north-west to the top of Mládky mountain and further to Baranec mountain is more tiresome, mainly in the early stages. Tourist prefer the blue-marked path leading deeper into the Račkova dolina valley. The first two kilometres, common for both the Račkova and Jamnícka dolina valleys are called the Úzka dolina valley. It starts at 885 m above sea level and branches to the Račkova and Jamnícka valleys which are 960 m above sea level. In both valleys, separated from each other by the fork of Jakubiná traces of glacial activity are evident. From the point where the valley branches a yellow-market footpath leads along the Račkova dolina valley. The first two thirds of the ascent up the valley is comparably easy. The route continues across ever thickening woods to a large, almost flat alpine meadow called Prostredná poľana with an old log hut, testimony that there used to be pastures here in the past. Even further the remains of what was once the highest situated sheep dairy farm in Slovakia (1,600 m) can be found. Past this landmark one can turn to the **Gáborova dolina valley**.

Sheep dairy-farming:

Numerous sheep dairy-farms existed around Pribylina in the past. The sheep were an inseparable part of the life of the local people. They provided milk, a first class cheese, meat, and fleece at minimum outlay. Mixed flocks of sheep and rams grazed outdoors from early spring. Every farmer kept a record of how many animals went off to pasture. In the autumn the sheep returned home and were recorded. The sheep dairy farm or shieling, in Slovak "salaš " was administered by a warden, called "salašník" and the organiser of the life in the farm was "bača". He seldom went out with the flocks staying most of the time in the farm where he cooked and processed the cheese, moved the fences on the meadows and prepared the food for the men. His hands called "valasi" cared after and milked the sheep. They had their salary called "salár" paid in money and in kind. The grazing sheep and their supervision was assisted by the men called "honelníci" who were temporarily contracted as the need arose. White sheep dogs were the best assistants to the bača and the men. The most feared enemy of the sheep dairy-farmer was the bear. The men defended the sheep as best they could by setting fires around the fences, by shouting, accompanied by the barking dogs. But the occasional attacks by the bears were difficult to prevent and consequently the farm lost one or two sheep, usually the fattest and biggest ones.

Ascending up the Gáborova dolina valley one can get to the main ridge and further to the Gáborovo sedlo (1,890 m) or the Bystré (1,960 m) saddles. But the most attractive destination for the tourists is the upper part of the Račkova dolina valley via the yellow-marked path. The stony path, crossing the dwarf pine forest is comparably steep making the ascent difficult and straining, but the reward comes in the form of excellent sights of the surrounding peaks of Bystrá, Klin, Jakubiná and above all the romantic mountain scenery of **Račkove plesá lakes** at an altitude of 1,697 m above sea level which are set in a distinct glacier kettle. There is a lower situated Dolné Račkovo pleso lake, the area of which is 1.19 ha with a maximum depth 1.5 m. What is interesting about this lake is that during dry spells its water table drops and then a prolongated elevation separating the lake in two emerges in its centre. The Horné Račkovo pleso lake is smaller but deeper, reaching a maximum depth of 10 m. A winding path above the lakes leads further to the **Račkovo sedlo saddle** (1,956 m) situated in the main ridge of the Západné Tatry mountains over which the top of **Končistá peak** (1,993 m) towers. From here one can ascend by a stony path (tracing the Slovak-Polish state borderline) to the very top of **Hrubý vrch mountain** (2,137 m) and enjoy the fine view of the Roháče mountains, the massive body of Bystrá mountain and the furthermost parts of the Račkova and Jamnícka dolina valleys. South of it is Jakubiná

mountain (2,194 m), the second highest top of Západné Tatry mountains. Ascent to Jakubina is very difficult. It is a high-mountain tour by green mark passing its rocky crest recommended only in good weather. This goes for both, the northern and southern access tracks.

But the most favourite track in this part of Západné Tatry is the ascent along Jamnícka dolina valley following the blue mark. It starts at an approximate altitude 960 m and ends in the conclusion of the valley in the height 1,860 m. Jamnícka dolina valley is 6.5 km long and narrow. It widens in its end under the Ostrý Roháč mountain and Žiarske sedlo saddle, called **Záhrady**. It is actually a kettle and the green mark leading to Žiarske sedlo saddle proceeds along its rim crossing the blue route across Jamnícka dolina valley. This is the most beautiful part of the valley. It is full of variegated high-mountain plants and provides some wonderful sights of Ostrý Roháč, massive Hrubý vrch and Jakubiná mountains. The area belongs to the ones with the highest rate of rain in Slovakia (mean annual totals of precipitation is 2,200 mm). The blue mark continues along the Jamnícky potok brook up to the **Jamnícke plesá lakes**. Nižné Jamnícke pleso lake is in the altitude 1,728 m, its area is 1.13 ha and depth is 4 m. Vyšné Jamnícke pleso lake is situated higher, 1,834 m, it is smaller (0.41 ha) and deeper (8 m). Above, along the main ridge of Roháče mountains, a winding footpath leads up to Jamnícke sedlo saddle (1,908 m) which is situated between Ostrý Roháč and Volovec mountains. In upper part of the valley under Žiarske sedlo saddle, in the altitude 1,835 m another little lake is hidden. It is **Žiarske pleso lake**. Its area is 0.11 hectares and depth only 0.8 m.

Left: Žiarske pleso lake

Podbanské and its environs

The area of Podbanské extends in the easternmost part of the Západné Tatry mountains and the westernmost part of the High Tatras. In the north it reaches a mountain ridge which marks the frontier with Poland, the eastern extreme is closed in by the ridge of Ostrá mountain and the western border is actually coincides with the fork of Baranec mountain. In the south the area opens up into the Liptovská kotlina basin.

PODBANSKÉ (940 m, population 50) is the most westerly located of all the Tatra communities, which lies at the cross-roads of the Cesta Slobody (Road of Freedom) and the torrential river Belá. It is 16 km from Štrbské Pleso and 15 km from Liptovský Hrádok.

The history of Podbanské was closely connected with gold mining as expressed by its name (baňa = mine) until the 19th century. The first miners arrived as early as the first half of the 15th century, at the time of the Old Hungarian king Sigismond of Luxembourg, and by the following century the Tatras were in the grip of gold fever which had seized Old Hungary. The perpetrator was the Old Hungarian king Ferdinand I whose legal provisions practically nationalised the Old Hungarian mining industry in expectation of a generous revenue, money which should have been used to expand the imperial army in the fight against the Turks and the rebellious Old Hungarian nobility. Mining rights in the area below the Kriváň mountain, then under the administration of Liptovský Hrádok, were fully exploited only at the time of the emperor Maximilián. However, the value of the golden grains extracted from the quartzose veins of the Tatra granites did not even cover the cost of labour in the high-mountain environment. In a short time also the local hammer-mills in Liptovský Hrádok ran short of material as the local deposits of antimony did not render enough ore. This was the reason why the miners, under the command of experienced mining experts from the Špania dolina valley near the city of Banská Bystrica, had to ascend higher and higher in their search for an ore. The remains of their dwellings have been preserved up to the present day, in a locality under Priehyby, at an altitude of

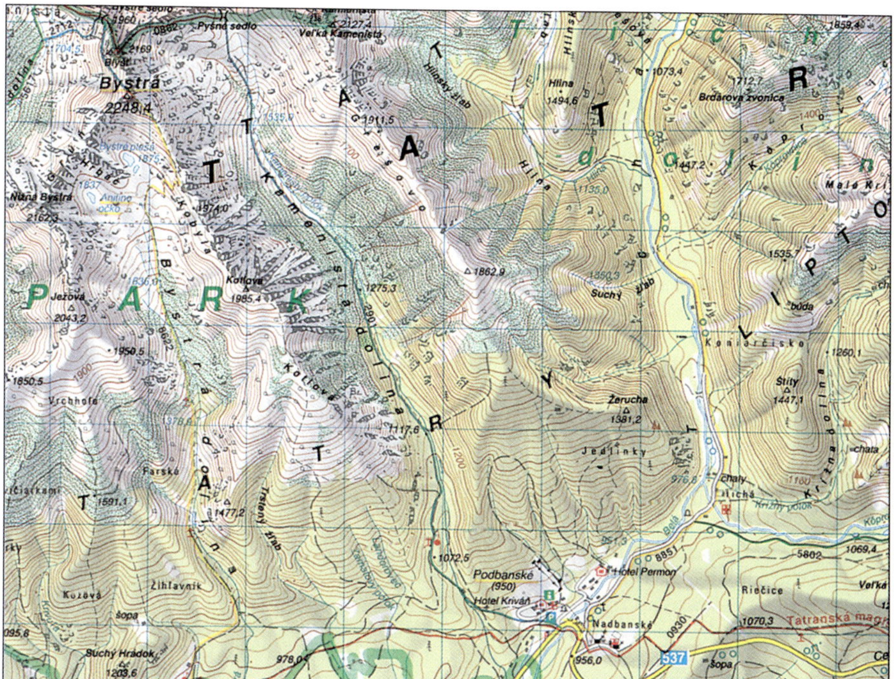

about 2,000 m above sea level. The highest shaft called Terézia was hardly 50 m below the top of the Kriváň mountain. The disappointed Hapsburgs sold the poorly yielding mines to the squire family of Szentiványi who were not successful in the search for precious ores either.

The angry ghost of the Kriváň mountain:

People living under the Tatras interpreted the failure of the miners on the slopes of the Kriváň mountain in a more superstitious way. They invented a strange legend, the story of which narrates how the miners working underground were frightened by a thundering voice coming out of the bowels of the mountain. The voice threatened to flood the whole region if they did not stop disturbing his sleep with their hatchets. So petrified were the miners that they ran away from this ghost of Kriváň and never returned to the mines.

For a long time the territory of the present day Podbanské was a deep forest thinned in places by the axes of the Liptov colliers. In the forest clearings at the end of the Tichá and Kôprová dolina valleys, sheep, horses and cattle of the farmers living in Pribylina grazed. The shepherds' huts provided an occasional shelter to the few tourists who started to appear below the Kriváň mountain during the 18th century. The beauty of this future Tatra community was the state owned forester's cottage with a room reserved for tourists and built above the left bank of the river Belá in 1871. Later it gained the name Harmanova, immortalising the local forester Ján Harman, a reliable mountain guide and recognised expert of the Tatras. Near the cottage a water driven saw mill for cutting and shredding the spruce bark needed by the Liptov tanners was founded. By the late 19th century Podbanské had the first opportunity to establish itself as a Tatra community. It had aroused the interest of the tourists of the town Mikuláš who included it in a project called the Liptov spa. This interesting idea was finally not realised and so the first community buildings did not take place until 1923. The main stimulus was the widening of the forest road from Štrbské Pleso passing by Tri studničky. The first modest hotel was opened for tourists in 1925, and in the 1930's Podbanské could have become an important traffic cross-roads. Luckily this ambitious, environmentally unfriendly project, of a road across the valleys of Tichá and Tomanova dolina, was never realised.

Right: Podbanské

During the Second World War a group of partisans operated in the area under the command of Štefan Morávek. In the first years after the war the community below Kriváň rapidly expanded with the construction of ten wooden houses belonging to the Youth Forest Works. 1968 was another important year for the local community as they prepared for the World Championship in cross-country skiing. In 1970 the Road of Freedom was prolonged from Podbanské to Liptovský Hrádok and the winter visitors had their new ski lift built on the slope of Hlina. A year later the **hotel Kriváň** was opened and in 1981, in a somewhat higher location, a big **Trade union hotel** called **Permon** was built. In recent decades, in the forest around Podbanské, numerous private cottages have been built and on the left bank of the Belá river there are several buildings that sprang up around the original forester's cottage. This area is colloquially called **Nadbanské**.

Podbanské is frequently used as a base for trips to the valleys of Tichá and Kôprová dolina and to the Bystrá mountain. The **Tichá dolina valley** is today indeed worthy of its name (tichá = silent). It is preferred above all by the tourists searching for a quiet natural environment. In its softer landscape, cloaked by rich meadows, the visitor is more likely to meet a herd of chamois than a group of noisy day trippers. The Tichá dolina valley with its length of 13.8 km and a total area of 52 square kilometres is the largest of its kind in the Tatras. The hiking route traces its whole length from the point where it opens into the Liptovská kotlina basin up to its conclusion below the majestic Svinica mountain (2,301 m) in a boundary mountain ridge. The noise of Podbanské disappears with the growing distance from the Permon hotel. Only the solemn silence of Tatra nature remains along the yellow-marked footpath beyond the confluence of the brooks of Tichý and Kôprovský potok. However, the Tichá dolina valley was not always so quiet. In the past there used to be the lively and busy activity of the loggers and colliers who disturbed its tranquillity by the strokes of their axes, the excited hubbub of the gold miners, as well as the bells of freely grazing cattle and sheep. The name of the valley derives from the local brook of Tichý potok, an unusually calm stream for the Tatras. Older and less eager

walkers will certainly appreciate the moderately ascending path (the lower eight kilometre section of the path inclines up to only 250 m), which is the obvious reason why the Tichý potok brook is so calm. Looking from the Liptovské kopy mountains there are another three lateral valleys ending in the Tichá dolina valley, the highest one being the **Špania dolina valley**. It was given its name by the miners from a community of the same name, near Banská Bystrica, to remind them of their native home. In the bottom of the Špania dolina valley is the longest of the 339 registered avalanche tracks in the territory of the TANAP, which can experience enormous masses of fast moving snow moving dangerously down the valley to a distance up to 3,100 m. Under the big curve of the valley the cross-road board points the tourist to the direction of the **Tomanovská dolina valley** the name of which is related to the miner Toman. A red-marked footpath crossing the valley ends in Tomanovské sedlo saddle a deep, grassy saddle, which with its altitude of 1,680 m above sea level is the second lowest depression of the main Tatra mountain ridge. In the past it was frequently exploited by poachers, and from the path under the saddle the **Tomanovské plesá lakes** can be seen. Two small lakes are the only ones in an extensive system of the Tichá dolina valley. Above the cross-roads under the outlet of the Tomanovská dolina valley to Tichá dolina the valley turns in the direction of the geographic parallel. Both the Tomanovská dolina and the Tichá dolina valleys are closed to the public in the winter season.

White death in the Tichá dolina valley:

Many and frequent snow avalanches occur in the Tichá dolina valley, more than anywhere else in the Tatras, the heaviest being in 1924 under the saddle of Ľaliové sedlo, which decimated the trees and the dwarf pines growing on the slopes of the valley over an area of 4 kilometres. In 1956 there were 29 avalanches in one month, when three and a half million m³ snow was recorded in the Tichá dolina valley. The avalanches not only destroyed the vegetation but claimed several lives as well. This "white death" began as early as 1868, and the first victims killed by an avalanche in the Tichá dolina valley were three Polish tourists. Unfortunately they were not to be the last.

The upper section of the massive Tichá dolina valley has an unusual aspect. The bend of the valley ensures that tourists loose their visual contact with the Liptovská kotlina basin and find themselves as if in the bottom of some volcanic crater, surrounded by high slopes covered by stones, meadows and dwarf pines. The view to the north is particularly interesting, where above the tops of the spruce trees one can see the silhouette of the **Červené vrchy mountains**. This part of the main ridge of the Tatras, between the saddles of Tomanovo and Ľaliové sedlo, is of limestone and got its name (červený = red) because of the typical autumn hue of the grass. The Červené vrchy Mts., along with the Belianske Tatry Mts., are the most important high mountain karst areas in Slovakia with large lapies-fields and deep karst abysses.

These karstificated slopes are not accessible to tourists and there is only one route to the boundary ridge of the Červené vrchy Mts. and then only in summer. Anyone who ascends along the serpentines of the yellow-marked footpath as far as the Suché sedlo saddle (1,955 m) must expect the possibility of leaving behind the calm and silent Tichá dolina valley for the bustle of civilisation in the environs of the Kasprový vrch mountain. Here you will find yourself among the numbers of tourists brought up the mountain by cabin lift from Poland, in both the summer and winter seasons. The end of the valley is called the **Zadná Tichá dolina valley**. In the past it was often frequented by the shepherds who crossed the Červené hory Mts. of Poland's Podhale. The initial slightly ascending footpath becomes steeper nearer to the tops of the westernmost part of the High Tatras, and leads to the **Závory saddle** (1,876 m). An additional 15 minute walk is needed to arrive to higher location of the **Hladké sedlo saddle** in the main mountain range. After the return to the Závory saddle tourists can take the same route to Podbanské or go back to the neighbouring Kôprová dolina valley.

The origin of the name of the **national nature reserve Kôprová dolina valley** is probably connected to the German word for copper, the subject of intense interest to the local miners. The German miners called the valley *Koppertal*. A trip to the Kôprová dolina valley starts at the same point as the one to the Tichá dolina valley. At the crossroads near the forester's cottage one has to turn to a green-marked path leading along the noisy Kôprovský potok brook. The footpath, without any intense ascent, heads on to another cross-roads and then it continues in a similar comfortable manner. Already the first few kilometres of one of the longest Tatra valleys, will reveal its greatest asset – the distinct natural contrasts of the Západné Tatry mountains with those of the High Tatras. Looking west there is the wonderful view of the Liptovské kopy mountains, while the opposite side of the valley is adorned with substantially more dramatic curves of the cliff massif of Kriváň. Alpine dimensions are reached, above all, by the jagged Rameno Kriváňa (Arm of Kriváň). One of the jutting ridges has the same name as the giant K2 mountain in the Caracoram range. Behind it the **Nefcerka valley** opens out into the main valley.

The valley of count Neftzer:

After count Neftzer was driven out of Germany he came to the Tatras, where he lived in exile with his daughter Agnesa in a secluded forest near Štôla, where his uncle was an abbot of the

Left: Červené vrchy mountains
Right: A sheep dairy farm at Podbanské

Benedictine monastery. Count Neftzer's involuntary separation from his country might have been ended with the good news that he was granted grace and repatriation. Unfortunately the messenger, a young man happened to be Agnesa's lover, which infuriated the count. In a fit of high rage Neftzer killed both the young man and his daughter. Driven out by his own guilt people met him aimlessly wandering in an alien country until he froze to death in the valley which now bears his name.

The extraordinary beauty of the waterfall cascades flowing over the high threshold of this strictly protected valley can be observed only from a comparably long distance. This is also the case for the **Kmeťov vodopád waterfall** which is a champion among the Tatra waterfalls with its height of 80 m. It bears the name of an important Slovak scientist and a fellow-founder of the Slovak National Museum, Andrej Kmeť (1841-1908). A real high-mountain climb starts only after the turn on to a green-marked footpath ascending to the Temnosmrečianska dolina valley. On the right side of the path is the **Vajanského vodopád waterfall**, one of the most beautiful Tatra waterfalls commemorating the Slovak writer S. H. Vajanský. (1847-1916). The **Temnosmrečinská dolina valley** looks like a wonderful natural amphitheatre. Its would-be auditorium is a high cliff with the jutting summit of the Čubrina mountain (2,378 m). Where the stage would be is the flat bottom of the valley and its two large lakes, among the largest in the Slovak part of the High Tatras. The footpath ends near the bigger **lake**, called **Nižné Temnosmrečinské pleso**, with an area of 12 ha and 40 m deep. Another **lake, Vyšné Temnosmrečinské pleso** is situated higher and off the tourist path. The name of the valley (Temnosmrečinská = dark spruce trees) expresses the fact that in the past the spruce forest covered the entire area. The remote valley, populated by numerous game, used to be a favourite hunting ground of the poachers of Liptov, as well as from Poland. A legendary mountain guide by the name of Klimek Bachleda used to bring here his clients, as the valley almost certainly provided some encounter with herds of chamois. When this "king" of the Tatra guides accompanied here the Polish poet F. Nowicky in 1887 they saw a herd of chamois consisting of almost 80 animals. The forest was slowly moving to lower positions under the effect of the activities of shepherds. Excessive pasturing lowered the upper timber line of the Tatras before the end of the 19th century by three hundred meters, and in other sections of the forests, which escaped the devastation caused by shepherds and colliers, were stricken by disastrous forest calamities.

The forest calamities in Tatra valleys:

In a single August day in 1925 a violent whirlwind in the Tichá dolina valley caused enough forest destruction to leave behind 52 thousand cubic meters of wood. This damage was compounded by other violent storms, so that after five years a total of 180 thousand cubic meters of smashed timber was carried out of the valley. As many as 500 forest workers on occasion were removing the fallen trees and a large amount of the work required helping hands from as far afield as Maramures in Rumania. The Rumanian loggers built here round log huts called cirkusy. *The spruce trees never "returned" again to the valley and the administrators of TANAP are still today trying to solve the problem of rejuvenation of the spruce trees.*

There are three alternatives how to end the hike, but each of them is quite demanding. The first, relatively the easiest one, is to return to Podbanské retracing the same route. More time and energy is required by the second option: a green-marked path to the **Kobylia dolina valley**. The name of the valley (kobyla = mare) is associated with the tradition of high-mountain horse breeding in this part of the Tatras. The path goes on from the saddle Závory down the Tichá dolina valley to Podbanské. Those who are interested in the third option of descent must go back to the blue-marked footpath and ascend up the **Hlinská dolina valley** to the Vyšné Kôprovské sedlo saddle (2,180 m). The valley is restricted in the south by a massive stone wall of the ridge Hrubé, the high pillars and troughs which are among the most searched after mountaineering terrain in the High Tatras. Leaving the saddle the track goes on down the Mengusovská dolina valley in Štrbské Pleso.

The route to Bystrá starts in Podbanské and goes on following the blue-marked path up the **Kamenistá dolina valley**. This seven kilometre long valley is special for not having any branches. Its slopes remained mostly naked after an extensive fire in 1904. In the upper part of the valley there is a shallow glacier basin and the path ascends from this point to the **Pyšné sedlo saddle** (1,791 m). In this saddle the red-marked mountain ridge track over the Západné Tatry mountains starts or ends the journey, as the case may be. Its route is the most demanding track in the Slovak Carpathians with a total variable elevation of about 2,800 m. The Pyšné sedlo saddle is 24 km from the opposite end of this track – the Hutianske sedlo. The track follows the line of the crest only by a short section from the saddle Pyšné passing Blyšť mountain (2,169 m) to the Bystré sedlo saddle (1,960 m) and goes on by the blue-marked footpath up to the top of the Bystrá mountain. **Bystrá mountain** with an altitude of 2,248 m above sea level is the highest peak of the Západné Tatry Mts. The cone-shaped summit offers a wonderful panoramic view, which in good weather will take in the whole of the Liptov region, a part of Spiš and Podhalie. The shortest return trip to Bystrá is the yellow-marked footpath descending to the small but attractive **Bystrá dolina valley**. In the upper part of the path one can admire a group of four lakes called the Bystré plesá. The largest one of them is the **Vyšné Bystré pleso** lake with an area of 0.86 ha. It is also the deepest lake in the Západné Tatry mountains (12.5 m). At the point where the Bystrá dolina valley opens up into the Liptovská kotlina basin the yellow path crosses with the Tatra main tourist path leading to Podbanské.

Tri studničky (1,140 m) is a landmark near Cesta slobody (the Road of Freedom) between Podbanské and Štrbské Pleso, in the lower edge of Podkrivánska poľana. The place was seasonally settled since the beginning of the 19th century and its name (Three Wells) relates to one of the legends.

The legend of Three Wells:

A local forester remarried after his wife died. The arrival of the step-mother to his house, under the Kriváň mountain meant bad times were ahead for the forester's two daughters Zuzka and Marienka. Their new mother did not care for the girls and instead of giving love and understanding she only offered punishment by continually scolding them. Once she sent Zuzka to a well to bring water. The little girl found a limping little red dear near the well and decided to treat its wounded leg. After a while the step-mother sent Marienka to look for the sister and to hurry her home. Both sisters cared after the animal forgetting that the step-mother was waiting for them. As the children did not return the impatient and angry step-mother pronounced a terrible curse. The children disappeared at the very instant and out of one well there were suddenly three. The people say that the water in them are the tears of the forester's unfortunate little girls.

In 1806 a shelter was built here. Originally it was intended for the archprince Joseph of Hapsburg and his expected trip to the Kriváň mountain which never materialised. The improved shelter was instead used by tourists. In 1907 a forester's house was built in the lower part of the clearing with an extra room for tourists, who later also were able to use a cottage south-east of the forester's house called Važecká chata and built by Jozef Kertész. For a while it was called Kertészova chata or Kertész's cottage, but in August 1944 it was burnt down by the Nazis. Throughout the fighting that took place here a captain by the name of Ján Rašo of Štrbské Pleso was killed and the new **cottage** built in Tri Studničky, in 1961, was named after him: **Chata kapitána Rašu**. Next to the cottage

Right: Kriváň mountain

is also a symbolic cemetery of the partisans who died defending the cottage.

There is another possible trip from Tri Studničky to the Jamské pleso lake – a pleasant and comfortable walk over a well maintained Tatra main footpath called in Slovak *Tatranská magistrála.* The route mostly proceeds through a spruce forest that occasionally retreats to offer an open view of the broad southern slope of the Kriváň mountain. The footpath brings the tourists to the southern shore of the **Jamské pleso lake** (1,447 m), which is surrounded by spruce and pine forests. In 1936 a cottage called Krivánska chata was built here but it burned down seven years later. Near the western shore of the lake is the **limba pine grove** founded in the memory of the heroes and victims of the **Slovak National Uprising**. It is possible to go on from the Jamské pleso lake to Štrbské Pleso or to go back via the blue and green-marked path to Tri Studničky.

The Tatra tourist path – Tatranská magistrála:

This path is the most popular and frequently used of the Tatra footpaths by tourists. The idea of founding such an arterial path over the Tatra mountains originated back in 1903 though its realisation started only three decades later. Its creators used the already existing footpaths and connected them with new ones. When in 1949 the last missing section between the lakes Batizovské and Velické pleso was opened tourists could finally walk the continuous red-marked footpath from Podbanské to Tatranská Kotlina. The original route of the main tourist path was twice readjusted. In 1978 it was reduced by 19 km when a track tracing the crest of the Belianske Tatry mountains was closed. The second adjustment has in turn prolonged it by adding the tourist paths between the resorts on the southern foothill of the Západné Tatry mountains. Its length is 70 kilometres at present. It leads from the end of the Jalovská dolina valley in the Západné Tatry mountains to the Veľké Biele pleso lake in the limits of the High Tatras and Belianske Tatry. The optimum time necessary to pass the complete route is 4 to 5 days. The section in the High Tatras often exceeds the upper timber line offering wonderful vistas of the Tatra peaks and the sub Tatra basin. Some sections are almost like a promenade but there are also some serpentines with an altitude difference equalling 500 m.

In the winter season some of the sections of the main tourist path are closed, or otherwise they are closed to the public in time of avalanches or when covered by ice.

An exceptionally attractive climb is the ascent of the **Kriváň mountain** (2,494 m) a stout peak in the western part of the High Tatras. This multiple winner of competitions for the most beautiful mountain in Slovakia is appropriately named when looking up from Liptov. It is easily recognisable for its conspicuously curved summit, which is the reason why it was called Kriváň (curved mount).

Why Kriváň is a curved mountain?

On the seventh day of Creation God sat down and pondered over the quality of his work. He arrived at the conclusion that something was missing in the world. He summoned his most skilled angel and ordered him to throw over the world another sackful of beauties. The angel adorned one country after another before he arrived to the group of the Tatra peaks. But he underestimated their altitude and ran into one of the peaks, ripping open the sack which contained the bounty. Beautiful peaks, meadows, forests, torrents and lakes fell down around the rocky peaks. Marmots, chamois, red-deer and other animals hurried out of the sack into the mountain landscape. The mountain range, later called by people the Tatras, received in this way so many natural beauties rarely found anywhere else in the world. The tip of the peak which had caused the collision with the inattentive celestial flier was curved, so no wonder it is called Kriváň – the curved mount.

The most comfortable and quick way to reach the top of Kriváň starts in Tri studničky. The first serpentines of the green-marked footpath bring the tourists to a place called **Grúnik**, which witnessed some bitter fighting between the partisans and the Nazi troops at the end of the Second World War. Seven members of the squad called Vysoké Tatry were killed here. The path goes on from Grúnik crossing the slope of the Priehyby mountain to a steep trough covered with falling debris from the Kriváň. Continuing from the cross-roads below the mountain the track joins the path from the Jamské pleso lake. In the **Daxnerovo sedlo** saddle, named after the Slovak writer and revivalist Š. M. Daxner (1823-1892) several dangerous snow fields last until advanced spring. The reward for a rather demanding ascent is a wonderful panoramic vista. The usual way back from the top of mount Kriváň is the one following the blue-marked path leading to the Jamské pleso lake. From there one can get either to Podbanské or to Štrbské Pleso.

Ascents to Kriváň:

When J. A. Czirbesz conquered the Kriváň mountain in 1772 he was certainly not the first to the top. He was undoubtedly preceded by anonymous miners who did not leave any traces at the summit, such as this Evangelical priest from Spišská Nová Ves, who was later followed by many other enthusiastic admirers of the Tatras. Among them were several famous figures, such as R. Townson, B. Hacquet and G. Wahlenberg. Kriváň mountain even seduced some royal personages. In 1840 the Saxon king Fridrich August II accompanied by the Liptov aristocracy looked over the sub Tatra landscape from its curved summit. At the occasion an almost three metres high monument was placed here at the honour of the ruler. The act has deeply touched the feelings of the Slovak patriots who considered Kriváň their national symbol, in the same way Swiss people regard the Matterhorn, the Říp mountain for the Czechs or Olympus for the Greeks. The first protest against the presence of a non-Slavic ruler to the sacred Slovak mountain was the walk to Kriváň organised by Ľ. Štúr and J. M. Hurban, which took place on August 18, 1841. In 1856 the first traces of violence appeared on the monument. As the official report quotes "some unknown perpetrators living nearby" threw down of the top of the metal pyramid the gilded copy of the Saxon royal crown. Later an inscription reading GLORY TO THE SLAVS, HELL FOR THE TRAITORS appeared. Participants of the second national ascent to the mountain in 1861 finished the job of demolition by throwing it into an abyss. The last piece of undesired monument was found in 1967 by a group of Polish mountain guides. In contrast to the monument the tradition of the repeated ascents to the Kriváň mountain is kept until the present days.

Štrbské Pleso
and its environs

The area of Štrbské Pleso is located in the western part of southern foothills of the High Tatras. Its northern border traces the main crest of the mountain range, which corresponds to the state frontier at the point between the Čubrina and Rysy mountains. The western limits of the area is the fork of the Ostrá mountain in the Kriváň massif, whilst the eastern end is the fork of the Gerlachov štít peak. In the south the area borders on the sub Tatra basin.

ŠTRBSKÉ PLESO (1,335 m, population 350) is the highest situated Tatra locality, existing around the lake bearing the same name, a product of the moraine pushed out into the mouth of the Mlynická dolina valley by a glacier in ancient times. Štrbské Pleso is 15 km from Starý Smokovec and 17 km from Podbanské. A 6 km long road connects the community with its southern neighbour Tatranská Štrba whereafter it links-up to the main road from Žilina to Poprad. The western branch of the Tatra electric railway track and the rack-railway linking with Tatranská Štrba terminate at the station.

This thickly wooded landscape at the edge of the Spiš and Liptov regions was a "no man's land" until the second half of the 13th century. Its first owner was a Czech aristocrat count Bogomil who received it as a donation from the Old Hungarian king Belo IV in 1267. It was he who founded in the "cleavage" between the High and the Low Tatra mountains a settlement called Štrba (štrbina = cleft).

A nearby mountain lake hidden in thick forests represented for the people of the community simply a Lake. But as there are many lakes in the Tatras, they started to refer to it as Štrbské pleso lake and the name has passed over to the present. The territory adjacent to the community, along with the lake itself, once belonged to the squire family of Szentiványi, but after the abolition of serfdom a part of the land passed to the Štrba people. The squires kept for themselves the cultivated areas and the peasants received extensive, though economically less productive, areas of forests and mountain pastures.

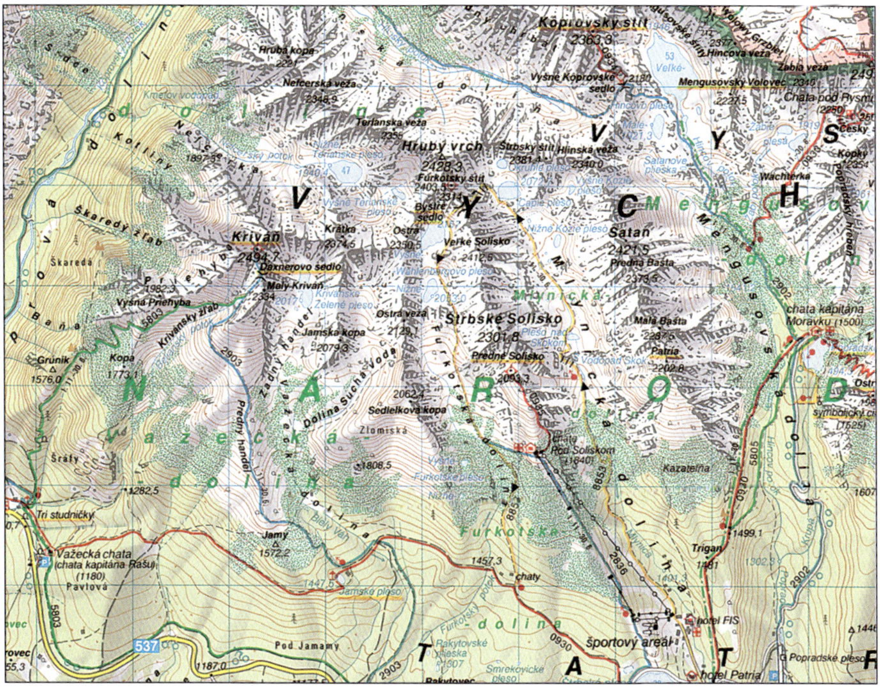

A "useless pool":

The peasants of Štrba were not too enthusiastic about the territory allotted to them by the Szentiványis'. They disliked particularly that the assigned area included the lake. Not knowing anything about its potential as a tourist resort, the lake represented for them a mere "useless pond". They threatened to discharge the water and to use the empty basin as for pasture. Finally, however, they attained the desired pastures from the Szentiványi family and the lake was saved. Štrbské Pleso is today the second largest lake on the Slovak side of the Tatras, with an area of 19.76 hectares. The lake basin has a volume of 1,284,000 m³ is 20 m deep at its lowest point. The depression which originated after the glacial activity in the Mlynická dolina valley, was deepened by the sinking of the moraine's surface. The water temperature in the lake reaches a mean value of about 6°C. In summer it rarely rises above 15°C and during the year Štrbské pleso lake is covered by ice for about 155 days. This ice clad appears towards the end of November and thaws by late April. No brooks flow in the lake and besides minor seepage in the moraine rampart no concentrated discarge is observable. If the water level in the lake changes it is only due to rain or thaw water.

Štrbské Pleso lake provoked interest amongst the first tourists, the "Tatra wanderers", in the 17th century, perhaps due to written material about the lake produced by the scholar David Frölich of Kežmarok in 1644. After the opening of the Bohumín-Košice railway track in 1871 which came within 6 km of the lake, it was only a matter of time before the first tourists would appear. The local landlord Jozef Szentiványi of Liptovský Ján quickly found out that the land so blindly rejected by the earlier peasants was not in the least useless. In the south-eastern end of the lake he built a log hut in 1872 and the following summer he turned this hunting lodge into board and lodge for tourists. Three years later the Old Hungarian Carpathian Association added to the further development of Štrbské Pleso by erecting another building for tourists near the Szentiványi's log hut, named in honour of the landowner Jozefova chata (Jozef's Cottage), and six years later it was granted spa status. Jozef Szentiványi gradually sold or donated several plots of land where summer residences for prominent people were built. Shortly there followed a restaurant, coffee house and a spa building. The best equipped tourist building at the time was the Vila Mária Terézia (later called Detvan). In the beginning the only link the community had with the outside world was one solitary road. But from 1884 cabmen awaited spa patients in railway station Štrba to bring them up to the lake and also a newly constructed road from Starý Smokovec contributed to better communication of the place. By the late 19th century the government showed interest in the administration of Štrbské Pleso and intervened to stop the business activities of the prince of Hohenlohe in the area. The government then invested in the construction of a rack railway, following which the first train set off on the track between Tatranská Štrba and Štrbské Pleso on July 28, 1896. A steam engine pushing two carriages had to climb a differential altitude of 451 m along a distance of 4740 m. Five years later the government bought all land plots from Jozef Szentiványi along with the buildings, later to rent a part of them to the international company Wagons Lits Cook seated in Brussels. The company did not choose the best moment for the start of their business. The beginning of the 1920's was a period of great tourist competition, and so the idea was conceived to build a Grand Hotel on the southern shore of the lake to attract deserting tourists back to the Tatras. After the First World War this still unfinished building passed under the administration of the Czechoslovak Ministry of Health which finalised the project with modifications. Today it has two connected **sanatoriums – the Kriváň** and **the Hviezdoslav**. Prolongation of the Tatra electric railway from Tatranská Polianka to Štrbské Pleso in 1912 meant increased interest in winter holidays and it became quickly the most important ski resort in the Tatras. In 1935 it set the stage for the FIS ski world championship in cross-country disciplines, and in February 1970 the second, even more successful world championship in cross-country skiing disciplines, was held again in Štrbské Pleso. Preparation for this big event meant the construction of numerous sport and tourist facilities for the community. In the Mlynická dolina valley, in the course of two and a half years, Areál snov (Dream Area) centre of winter sports sprang up. The accommodation capacity was enlarged with addition of two new hotels – **the Panoráma** and

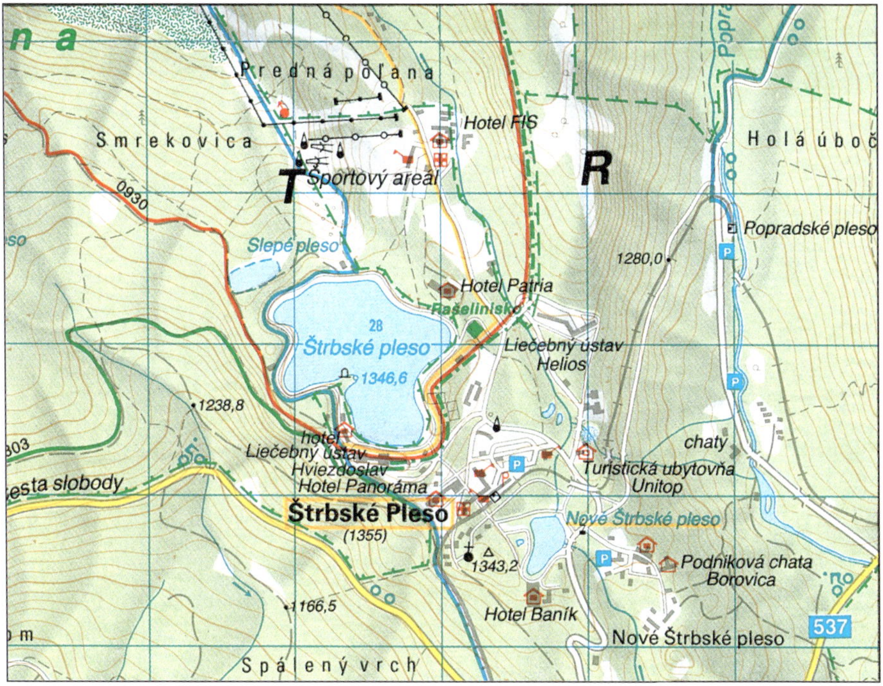

the FIS. And to the existing therapeutical buildings a new sanatorium **Helios**, especially intended for children suffering from the respiratory diseases, was also added. In addition, the local transport underwent great changes. The terminal of the Tatra railways, originally located on the south-western shore of the lake, was moved to a platform under the moraine, next to the post office building, the store and **the hotel Panoráma**. This is also where the station of the rack-railway from Tatranská Štrba, restored in 1970 after a break of thirty seven years, was located. A large capacity parking lot was opened here as well.

The Dream Area dreams for Olympic games:

The people living below the Tatra mountains long to experience the same explosion of joy brought here by the decision of the FIS Congress in 1967, to organise the 1970 world championship in cross-country skiing disciplines in Štrbské Pleso. After the great success of the championship and the abundant experience gained through organising the World Cup, the ambitions of the Tatra people grew to Olympic dimensions. The local people have not given up the idea that one day the Olympic flame will burn below the Tatra peaks, and over Štrbské Pleso the five-ring Olympic banner would flutter.

The community of **Nové Štrbské Pleso** (1,515 m) has totally merged, over the years, with its higher located and much bigger neighbour, Štrbské Pleso. The local plots within the territory of Štrba were bought in 1897 by the architect Karol Móry of Banská Bystrica. In the course of the next three years he changed the natural swamp and old peat bog into an artificial fish pond, and called it Nové Štrbské Pleso. The water table of the lowest situated Tatra lake is covered by ice for about 160 days of the year, primarily because the lake is shadowed by the surrounding spruce trees. Its shallow basin is the reason why it freezes down to the bottom, another factor which keeps it covered with ice until almost the beginning of summer. If not for human intervention the rapidly growing vegetation would have quickly changed the lake again to a swamp. Móry set about the realisation of his business intentions in 1905, by building a hotel and a look-out tower. He simultaneously pre-

pared projects for tourist facilities competing with fashionable Štrbské Pleso, by providing recreation to a middle class clientele. What's more, a new hotel, an old steam rack-railway and even the community itself bore the name of its founder. Between the two World Wars another two pensions were built here, but after nationalisation the name of Móry's community was changed to Nové Štrbské Pleso and his pensions passed to the ownership of the trade union organisation. After 1970 they were substituted by the modern **sanatorium Baník**.

The environs of Štrbské Pleso offer to visitors numerous tourist activities and a variable programme for several days in any season. From spring to autumn it is visited by lovers of high-mountain tracking. Most of them head for the waterfall of Skok in the Mlynická dolina valley or to Popradské pleso lake. For ones who are less inclined to walk there is a chair lift to the Predné Solisko mountain. But for the real physical challenges there are the ascents to the mountains of Kriváň, Predné Solisko, Rysy, the Kôprovský štít peak and Bystré sedlo saddle, or the many serpentines of the main Tatra tourist footpath below the Ostrva mountain. In winter there are available top quality ski tracks on the slopes of the Solisko mountain, with carefully maintained running tracks between 5 and 50 km long.

The initial walk to Štrbské Pleso may just as well start at the south-eastern shore of the lake near **Solisko sanatorium**. Standing at the former railway station one gets the most beautiful view of the indented silhouette of the Tatra peaks, where the fourfold peak of the Vysoká mountain (2,547 m), redolent of a royal crown, stands out. One cannot help noticing also the white slender ski-jump tower on a round hill nearby. In 1976 the triangular shaped hotel **Patria** joined this most frequently photographed Tatra view. There is a comfortable promenade, blue-marked path, around the whole lake and on the western shore the path passes by a "peninsula" with a **monument dedicated to partisans** who died in the war. The peninsula is the place where there is a nice view of the compound of the **Kriváň** and

Left: The Patria Hotel at Štrbské pleso

Hviezdoslav hotel buildings standing on the southern shore. Immediately behind the hotel Patria starts the red-marked main Tatra tourist footpath, or *magistrála*. The forests along the path is the hiding place for the **nature reserve of Rašelinisko** (Peat Bog) which is closed to public to protect some threatened plant species. The mountain type of peat bog is formerly a lake filled with peat, and there are five such dead lakes around Štrbské pleso, called by the local people "mozgroviská". **Slepé pleso** (Blind Lake) lying about 100 m from the north-western shore of the Štrbské pleso lake is also almost dry, as it is progressively covered by peat, and is slowly, as people say, "losing sight". The route of the trip soon leaves the short section of the Tatra main tourist path and goes out to the left tracing the road to **Areál snov**. This ski resort has received its unusual name (Dream Area) when the Chairman of the International Ski Federation noted with satisfaction that the area "is dream-like". It is dominated by two ski-jumps: the standard point of the smaller of them is 70 m and the higher was built for the world championships in 1970 for a 90 m long **ski-jump**. The performances of the courageous ski-jumpers can be watched by audiences of up to 60 thousand. By the final ceremony of the 1970 world championship a record hundred thousand people visited the event. A short ascent to the ski-jumps is rewarding, especially in fine weather, as it offers a wonderful view of the dark-blue water table of the Štrbské Pleso lake. A part of the area is also the **FIS hotel**, with its intriguing design imitating the shape of the Tatra peaks. The hotel is frequently the destination of top sportsmen and they are often around. The slope of the Solisko mountain, behind the Dream Area, is a ski paradise. In the lower part of the down-hill track, called the **Interski** slope, frequent exhibitions and races by acrobatic skiers and snow boarding events are held. A **chair lift** to Solisko exceeds a differential altitude of 438 m at a distance of 2,170 m. A twenty minute ride provides an excellent opportunity for undisturbed contemplation of the Tatra's treasures being right amid them. The sights of the Mlynická dolina valley on the right hand side are particularly splendid, and on the left, the belt of the down-hill skiing tracks on south-eastern slope of Predné Solisko mountain,

can be seen. It is precisely the place where the first ski lift in the Tatras was put into operation in 1943. Next to the upper station of the chair lift, at an altitude of 1,840 m above sea level, is the cottage **chata pod Soliskom**. A red-marked footpath starts near the cottage and leads to the Predné Solisko mountain (2,093 m). The ascent, by a winding path to the last peak of the Solisko crest, takes about one hour. Taking the same path is the quickest return trip, whilst a somewhat longer option is the one leading across Furkotská dolina valley.

The Dream Area is the gateway to the **national nature reserve Mlynická dolina valley**. The valley, squeezed between the crests of the Solisko and Bašty mountains, is accessible by a yellow-marked path. This step-like glacier valley, lacking any lateral valleys, is six kilometres long. For many years in the past there existed no tourist paths to the valleys Furkotská and Mlynická dolina, neighbouring with Štrbské pleso lake, and they were accessible only by the paths made by hunters and shepherds. In 1899, however, the people of the owner of the valley Jozef Szentiványi built a comfortable tourist path ending below the **Skok waterfall** visible from the lake as a narrow white ribbon on the grey rocks. The total height of this cascading waterfall is 25 m and the best time to visit it is between spring and summer when its at it most beautiful. In March barely 54 litres of water per second passes down the rocky threshold of the Mlynická dolina valley, but in July the water discharge in the Skok waterfall rises to 880 litres per second. During the great floods of 1958 an enormous water mass of 30,000 litres of water per second flowed down the rocky step. The veil of mist hovering above the tumbling water not only refreshes the air around the waterfall but enhances the overall impression.

The waterfall of tears:

The origin of the misty veil above the Skok waterfall is the subject of a legend about an unfortunate girl who looked for her dead lover who had died while hunting chamois some place under the Štrbský štít peak. The legend says that the crying young woman is still wandering about in the Mlynická dolina valley and that tears falling from her eyes feed the Skok waterfall. The waterfall certainly resembles a veil, the symbol of mourning for a woman.

The path leading from the Skok waterfall to the Bystré sedlo saddle was built only in 1935 so that the Mlynická dolina valley was long spared the damaging effects of tourism. There was never any tourist hotel or cottage, not even a mill that would give the origin to its name (mlyn = mill). The name of the valley is derived from the Mlynica brook where there used to be some mills in the past, though not in the mountains, but down in the basin. Juraj Buchholtz wrote in 1719 about one such mill, Matej Bel also mentioned two decades later two mills standing near Štrba. There is still a farm near Tatranská Štrba called Stredný Mlyn and next to the railway station in Štrba is a popular folk restaurant called Starý mlyn (An Old Mill). On a terrace in the Mlynická dolina valley above the waterfall is the lake **Pleso nad Skokom** the size of which is continuously reducing. Its is another example of the irreversible process of the disappearance of the Tatra

Left: Skok waterfall

lakes, only in this case somewhat quicker. Over the course of several decades its area has diminished from 3 to less than one hectare. Numerous little lakes are on higher terraces in the Mlynická dolina valley. Small **lakes** like the **Volie plieska** (Ox Lakes) the name of which reminds one of the presence of the shepherds who brought their herds of cattle and sheep up here until the government drove them off the land in 1901. Even higher situated are the numerous small lakes called **Kozie plesá** (Goat Lakes) including the **Capie pleso** (The Billy Goat Lake). As the pasturing of goats was not as common as that of sheep or cattle it was presumably the wild goat or chamois that inspired the unknown author of the above mentioned names. The occurrence of chamois in the Mlynická dolina valley was documented by Matej Bel more than 250 years ago, who characterised the valley called Mlynica as a garden of herbs with therapeutic effects sown here by mother nature, and abundance of mountain goats (chamois) and marmots. At an altitude of 2,105 m above sea level there is the highest situated **Okrúhle pleso lake**. The sight of this undoubtedly round shaped lake clearly explains its name. The most difficult section of the trip starts at the Capie pleso lake. The path climbs up to the Bystré sedlo saddle by numerous serpentines. The demanding ascent is made even more difficult by numerous and dangerous snow fields, the reason why the return trip, using the same route, is not recommended (descent is always more difficult than ascent). The **Bystré sedlo saddle** (2,314 m) is the fourth highest pass of the Tatra crests facilitated by a marked path.

It provides a somewhat limited view of the Mlynická and Furkotská dolina valleys where it descends to the **national nature reserve Furkotská dolina valley** which is one of the five valleys descending southward, down to the Kriváň fork. Its length is about three and a half kilometres and is the easternmost Tatra valley. Its streams flow first into the rivers Váh and Danube which end in the Black Sea, while the streams of the neighbouring Mlynická dolina valley end in the Baltic Sea. The attractiveness of the Furkotská dolina valley is enhanced by its lakes, the largest ones being the **Wahlenbergove plesá lakes**. The name of an important Swedish scientist, Göran Wahlenberg, who won acclaim for his research in botany in the Tatras in 1813 was given to the lakes by the end of the 19th century. Wahlenberg probably never visited the Furkotská dolina valley though he moved around Kriváň. The Vyšné (Upper) Wahlenbergovo pleso lake is, at 2,158 m above sea level, the second highest permanent lake in the Tatras. As far as its area is concerned it occupies the eighth position among the lakes on the Slovak side of the Tatras. What is remarkable about this lake is the fact that its ice cover lasts 300 days a year, while the Nižné (Lower) Wahlenbergovo pleso lake, situated only about 100 m lower, is covered by ice only for 180 days. The path proceeds left of the both Wahlenberg's lakes. On opposite side of the valley the attention of tourists is attracted by the forked crest running out of the Ostrá mountain (2,350 m) south. The shape of the crest is uneven, and slender rocky towers alternate with deep clefts. The deep rift between the Kozí roh and the Ostrá veža mountains is particularly noticeable. Its depth drops below the level of the terrace of the Nižné Wahlenbergovo pleso lake giving an impression that it sinks into the water of this beautiful mountain lake. Passing by the lake terraces the path still keeps to the left side of the Furkotská dolina valley where the noisy waters of the Furkotský potok brook can be heard. The best contemporary connoisseur of the Tatras, Ivan Bohuš, asserts that the sound of this brook gave the origin to its name and consequently the valley itself. The torrential water bounces against the boulders in its bed, splashing and making a strange gurgling sound, in Slovak *fŕka*. The upper timber line at an altitude of about 1,600 m is covered by spruce and limba pine trees, which the Furkotská dolina valley has in abundance. At the end of the valley a cottage used to stand. It was built in 1936 and its name was the Furkotská Cottage, though tourists called it the Lonekova chata which was the surname of its owner. After the Second World War it was nationalised and the name changed to chata kapitána Rašu. In 1956 it was burnt down and the name passed to another newly constructed cottage at Tri studničky. Visitors to the Furkotská dolina valley often go back to the Štrbské Pleso pleso lake using the main Tatra tourist path. There is also another option, using the blue-marked path turning left into a dwarf pine forest in the direction towards the Chata pod Soliskom cottage.

The climb to **Kôprovský štít peak** offers the tourists an opportunity to see the whole of the eight kilometre long **national nature reserve,**

Mengusovská dolina valley. The route starts on the eastern shore of the Štrbské pleso lake and heads north along the main Tatra tourist path – *magistrála*. The moderately steep path leads to the top of the moraine rampart called Trigan (1,481 m). The moraine is the result of two neighbouring glaciers that once filled the Mlynická and Mengusovská dolina valleys. Beyond Trigan the path passes the slope of the Patria mountain (2,203 m), the last peak in the massive Bašty crest. The section of magistrála between the Štrbské and Popradské pleso lakes is also called the Summer Road as it is open only in summer. In winter the Popradské pleso lake is accessible by the Winter Road, tracing the axis of the Mengusovská dolina valley (blue marked) on the last but one stop of the Tatra tram on the route between Starý Smokovec and Štrbské Pleso. The Summer Road is threatened by frequent avalanches in winter that fall down the eastern slopes of the Bašty mountains.

Deadly avalanches:

A black day in history of the Tatras was January 20, 1974. The tranquillity of one afternoon was suddenly shattered by a weird sound, like a low flying aeroplane. The employees of the mountain hotel near Popradské pleso lake immediately recognised that somewhere very near an avalanche had occurred. At twenty minutes to eleven a huge snow drift tore off the saddle above Skok in the Bašty crest and in few seconds an enormous mass of snow tumbled at great speed down to the Mengusovská dolina valley. The avalanche crashed down, crossing the Tatra main tourist path and stopped at the opposite slope where students at the grammar school, with their instructors, were learning to ski. The avalanche buried 24 people in all. Eleven of them came out by themselves but the remaining students and their teacher remained under the snow, in places six meters thick. The mountain rescue service used all accessible means to save the people buried under the avalanche. After five hours of searching one student was found and carried to hospital. The others were not so lucky. The same day, before evening, another two fatal avalanches fell in the Tatras, killing tourists. The sad entry in the chronicle of the mountain rescue service documents three avalanches and fourteen victims.

The **Mengusovská dolina valley** is one of the most frequently visited valleys in the Tatras. Its first owner was count Botyz who obtained it in 1264 as a donation from king Belo IV whom he allegedly saved from a furious bear in the "Snow Mountains". As records do not mention the event at all, the reason for the king's generosity might have been the military service of Botyz to his king. The name of the valley suggests that it used to belong to the sphere of economic interests of the population living in the Mengusovce community. The valley was owned by the Máriássys', the descendants of Botyz until 1897, then a part of it was bought by a Prussian aristocrat, Hohenlohe, who previously had acquired extensive lands in Javorina, in the northern part of the Tatras before. After 1928 the valley was owned by the government. The oldest written reference to the Mengusovská dolina valley is from 1719 by Juraj Buchholtz, the senior. Interest in the valley by tourists rose in the second half of the 19th century when access to it was facilitated by the construction of comfortable footpaths leading to the Popradské pleso lake, starting in Štrbské Pleso and Mengusovská poľana (today the tram stop is called Popradské Pleso). In the years between 1879 to 1904 the tourist paths to the lakes Hincove plesá and Žabie plesá, and to Ostrva and Rysy mountains were built.

The cabman Gallus of Lučivná:

A rich peasant and cabman Gallus of Lučivná opened a profitable business in the Mengusovská dolina valley more than hundred years ago. The community of Štrbské Pleso did not yet exist when he decided to earn money through the travel business. He offered the tourists trips to the Popradské pleso lake. Firstly he brought them in coaches to Mengusovská poľana, where he had a special well equipped coach prepared for the ladies and a young and good-looking mountain guide called Ján Galo of Mengusovce, who was groomed in a folk costume. Tourists then continued on foot from Mengusovská poľana to the Gallus' "travel agency". At Popradské pleso lake a picnic awaited them where a juicy boiled mountain ham, homemade bread, and Liptov sheep cheese were served. The meal was accompanied by excellent wines imported from the Lower Land and cooled in the lake.

Right: Chata pri Popradskom lese cottage

The trip finished with a lavish dinner in a spa tavern in Lučivná accompanied by Gypsy music.

Popradské pleso lies amid a forest at an altitude of 1,494 m. The lake, with an area of 6.88 hectares, contains about 450,000 m^3 of water. As one of the few lakes where fish live it was called Rybie pleso lake (Fish Lake). Its contemporary name is associated with the river flowing out of it. The first tourist facility on the bank of the Popradské pleso lake originated in 1879. The building of a single room log shelter was financed by the Old Hungarian Carpathian Association and named after the deputy of the head of the province Liptov, Vojtech Majláth. But the shelter only existed for a year before it suffered the fate of many such establishments and was burnt down. Allegedly, a collector of herbs set fire to it as he considered the tourists to be intruders threatening his source of living. Another cottage, made of stone, was later built in the Žabia dolina valley in 1881. The building of what was the third cottage, called Popradská, was the work of the local landowner, František Máriássy. The new owner, prince Hohenlohe, made it available to tourists only after a great deal of public pressure. The Popradská chata cottage, later named the chata kapitána Morávka, underwent numerous adjustments. Its wooden structure completely collapsed under the weight of snow and the resultant following reconstruction was the present **Horský hotel pri Popradskom plese** (the moutain hotel near the Popradské pleso lake). The route continues from the Popradské pleso lake along a blue-marked path to the **Hincova dolina valley**. The Hincova dolina valley forms, along with the Zlomiská valley, a giant triangle. The back side of the triangle traces the main Tatra ridge along a 6 km long section between the Čubrina mountain (2,376 m) and the Popradský Ľadový štít peak (2,396 m). The couple of large valleys are separated from each other by the rocky Popradský crest, a barrier preventing the view of the Rysy from Štrbské Pleso lake. The Hincova dolina valley is restricted by the massive crest of the Bašty mountains in the west. The landmarks in these mountains reflect the fertile imagination of the old local shepherds, chamois hunters and treasure seekers, like Pekelník (Hell Dweller), Čertova štrbina (Devil's Cleft) Diablovina (Devil's Business).

The satan legend:

A collier working near Popradské pleso lake once met a strange man with a load on his back who asked him an unusual favour. He begged him to help him carry the heavy bag up to the high saddle at the Bašty crest. The sound of the coins in the pocket of the stranger was the reason why the collier decided to agree and shortly after both of them were slowly ascending the steep trough. However, before they reached the saddle the sun began to set and it got dark, compelling them to stay in a hostile spot. The clear and moonlit night was very cold so the mysterious stranger gathered a heap of stones and spat on them. Red flames of fire sprung out of the heap of stones. The astounded collier immediately realised whom he was passing the night with. His companion was Satan himself, a hell guard of the treasures hidden in the entrails of the Tatras. The poor collier did not sleep the whole night and with the first sunlight he set off back to Mengusovská dolina valley to show the people the golden grains he was given and to tell them how he earned the reward. Many adventurers went to seek treasure in the slopes of the steep peak, known since then as Satan, but the hell guard has always driven them away with big stone avalanches. Who knows whether Satan or his treasure are indeed hidden inside the highest peak of the Bašty crest. The only thing for certain is that the stones fall very often down Satan's trough.

Left: Rysy
Right: Hincova dolina valley

The valley Hincova dolina, allegedly named after the shepherd Hinco (a dialect for the name Ignác), has the largest and also deepest lake on the Slovak side of the Tatra mountains. The area of the lake **Veľké Hincovo pleso** is 20.08 ha and it is 53 meters deep and contains almost 1,800,000 m^3 of water. The lower situated lake, the **Malé Hincovo pleso**, is 9-fold smaller than its neighbour. At the end of the valley Hincova dolina there is a trio of peaks called the **Mengusovské štíty**, shadows of which fall on the opposite side, into a deep valley in Poland. Also the view from the southern, sun bathed faces of this proud Tatra triplet is very impressing. The highest peak is the Veľký Mengusovský štít (2,424 m). The path deviates left near the lake Veľké Hincovo pleso and ascends by serpentines to the saddle **Vyšné Kôprovské sedlo** (2,180 m). The climb continues from the saddle up to the top of the peak **Kôprovský štít** (2,363 m). Here there is a wonderful view of the Hincovo pleso lake, the Rysy and Vysoká mountains. After returning to the saddle the trip can be concluded either by a shorter way down, passing the valleys Hincova and Mengusovská dolina, to Štrbské Pleso using the same path, or there is a much longer option, to continue by the blue-marked path over the valleys Hlinská and Kôprová dolina to Podbanské or to Tri studničky.

One of the most frequently visited Tatra peaks is undoubtedly the **Rysy**. Its popularity is due to the collective ascents by tourists held annually from early August – an event with a 40 year tradition. Participants were imitating V. I. Lenin when he allegedly set off on a trip to the Rysy from Poland's Poronin on August 11, 1913. This particular event very quickly found mass appeal attracting as many as three thousand tourists in a season. After the "Velvet Revolution" the ascents to Rysy lost their political motivation. The route of the ascent is the same as the route to the peak of Kôprovský štít, up to the point of the cross-roads in the lower part of the valley Hincova dolina, where an old Hincova hut used to stand. Then it turns right along a red-marked path ascending by numerous serpentines over a rocky threshold of the valley **Žabia dolina**. In the bottom terrace of the valley there are three lakes, the **Žabie plesá**. Two of the lakes, the Veľké and Malé Žabie pleso, used to be one large lake. The name of the lakes (The Frog Lakes) originated in a folk legend which told of a lonely rock jutting out over the water table of the larger of the two lakes. Its form resembles a frog, a sufficient reason for the anonymous author to take it for a frog turned to stone, guarding a treasure at the bottom of the lake. On the left, above the lake Vyšné žabie pleso, a conspicuous cone of the peak Žabia veža (2,335 m) can be seen. On its right side there is a lower mountain, popular among mountaineers, called Žabí kôň (2,291 m) providing excellent possibilities for climbing an exposed razor sharp ridge. Beyond the resting point at the lower terrace of the valley Žabia dolina the path again ascends to the next steep rocky step where the most exposed sections are secured by iron chains. The path heads to a small valley under the Váha peak where in the middle the cottage called **Chata pod Rysmi** stands. Its construction started in 1933 and it was accompanied by numerous adversities like snow blizzards and stone avalanches. During the Second World War it provided shelter for the Polish mountaineers being hunted by the Nazis. In 1977 it was enlarged by adding a second floor. The cottage is at an altitude of 2,250 m above sea level (the next higher place where a tourist can take a cup of tea is only on the top of the peak Lomnický štít). In spite of technical progress and inventions such as helicopters, this highest situated cottage in the Tatras is supplied only by high-mountain carriers. It is quite common to meet strong men carrying huge loads on their backs on the tourist path between lake Popradské pleso and the cottage. There are numerous tales told in the Tatras concerning these carriers, who compete with one another in terms of weight and speed.

The Sherpa Rallye:

On the Saturday morning October 11, 1985 visitors to the Popradské pleso lake were welcomed with an autumn sun and an unusual activity. After a routine medical examination and the weighing of the bearers' knapsacks a pistol starting shot sent eight participants off on the first year of the Sherpa Ralley competition. The task of these exceptionally strong men was to carry up to the highest Tatra cottage, under the saddle Váha, at an altitude of 2,250 m above sea level, a load of 60 kg in the shortest possible time. This exacting climb has a differential altitude of 756 m. The winner was Viktor Beránek, who reached his goal in a time of 1 hour and thirty one minutes. In 1994, alongside 27 men, 9 courageous women also stood at the start of the competition. The female participants in the first year of the Lady Rallye bore a load of twenty kilograms on their tender backs. The best of them, Majka Brošková of Spišská Nová Ves, reached the fantastic time of one hour and twenty two minutes, four minutes less than the winner of the male category, Oto Janigloš of the cottage Téryho chata.

The **saddle Váha** (2,237 m) is situated on a ridge in the Tatras equal to the top of the contigu-

ous Rysy peak. As there is no path to the opposite valley Česká dolina, visitors must content themselves with the mere sight of the deep and shadowy branch of the valley Bielovodská dolina and the lakes Zmrzlé and České pleso. The Česká (Czech) valley has nothing to do with the Czechs themselves. Its name originated by an erroneous Polish transcription and simultaneously the Goral word *ciezky* translated into Slovak as ťažký or difficult. It was probably invented by the shepherds speaking the Goral dialect expressing the hostile and uninhabitable nature of the place. The view of the broad saddle to the opposite side of the valley, Česká dolina, provides a unique possibility to see the famous **Galéria Ganka** or the Gallery of Ganek. The peak in the main ridge, called **Ganek** (2,459 m) has in its north-western flank a conspicuous scree ramp descending to the bottom of the basin by a perpendicular, and in places overhanging, rocky wall. At three hundred meters high and almost equally wide this rocky formation is a much talked about subject of the mountaineers. There are about thirty climbing tracks in the labyrinth of its crevices and pillars, and conquering some of them requires great mountaineering skill. The difficult north-western face of the Galéria Ganku proved fatal for W. Birkenmajer, one of the best Polish climbers of the inter-war period. Paradoxically, on the day of his tragic death on April 16, 1933 the most important figure in Tatra mountaineering, L. Chalubinský, the first climber who successfully climbed the Galéria Ganka, was buried. The final ascent from the saddle Váha to the top of the **Rysy mountain** (2,499 m) takes less than an hour. The first known ascent to the peak was made by Eduard Blásy, the administrator of Starý Smokovec, accompanied by the famous mountain guide, Ján Ruman-Driečny. Originally the nearby peak of Vyšný Žabí štít (2,259 m) was called Rysy and later the name was attributed to the peak within the main ridge. The name Rysy has probably nothing to do with our biggest predator lynx (in Slovak rys). It is rather more associated with the fact that the slopes of the peak are covered by troughs and grooves and the Gorals characterised it as "grooved" or *porysované*. The top of Rysy is also accessible by a tourist path from the other side of the mountain, but the descent by this path is not possible as it means crossing the Slovak-Polish frontier. The climb can be completed only by descending to Štrbské Pleso using the same path.

A wonderful trip from the Popradské pleso lake is a red-marked footpath to the Batizovské pleso lake. Near the mountain hotel at Popradské pleso the yellow-marked path turns first to **Symbolický cintorín** or the Symbolical Cemetery which is worth visiting.

The Symbolical Cemetery:

The Tatras collect their cruel toll every year. Inexperienced tourists, those poorly prepared for the extreme high-mountain conditions meet their death. But fatalities also occur amongst experienced mountaineers or mountain guides, like Bachleda, Stanisławski, Birkenmajer or Kriššák. The place where the memory of the victims of the High Tatras can be honoured is the Symbolical Cemetery under the western wall of the Ostrva peak. The idea was originated by the painter Oto Štáfl. The cemetery itself was ceremoniously

Left: The usual means of supply in the Tatras
Right: Symbolic cemetery

opened on August 11, 1940 and consists of a small chapel with a shingle roof, carved wooden crosses and numerous commemorative boards. The oldest of them commemorates an Hungarian student and mountaineer, Jenö Wachter, who tragically died while descending the Žabí kôň peak in 1907. There are also boards with the names of Tatra mountaineers who lost their lives abroad, while participating in expeditions to other mountain ranges. Unfortunately, the number of boards in the cemetery is not the final one. Victims accumulate and the boards commemorate sad events with ever more human lives being lost each year. Every visitor should then read very carefully the sentence written on the wall of the chapel: "To commemorate the dead and to warn the living..."

The route of the trip returns to the main Tatra tourist path – *magistrála*. It crosses, via a bridge, the Ľadový potok brook flowing from the valley called **Zlomiská**. This valley more than any other in the Tatras is covered by scree and stones and people have always avoided it. It proved difficult for the shepherds, as the big barren stones did not offer any pasture to the sheep or cattle. Superstitious people living in sub Tatra regions also found it easier to avoid going into the Zlomiská valley and invented various stories about giants and dragons inhabiting this remote valley under the Vysoká peak.

A legend of the lazy dragon:

In one of the basins of the Zlomiská valley a lazy dragon used to live and his servant was the most beautiful girl of the nearby village of Mengusovce. Nobody dared to fight against the monster. Finally though, the mother of the stolen girl decided to free her daughter and so she went to the valley and standing against the furious dragon she pronounced a curse upon it. The curse of the brave old woman worked and the dragon turned to stone. His tail changed to what is today called Dračí hrebeň or the Dragon's crest, and in other places one can discern the Dragon's head and the Dragon's teeth set in granite rock.

The desolate valley of Zlomiská was visited only by some gold miners or the occasional lonely wanderer and it remains equally forlorn and forgotten nowadays. At present no tourist paths lead to this austere but beautiful valley. There is a winding path from Popradské pleso lake ascending to the **saddle under the Ostrva peak** (1,959 m). Similar to other serpentines, climbing from the cottage near the Zelené pleso lake, to the saddle under the Svišťovka peak, one encounters a main path which is very passable but also very exacting. The ascent with a differential altitude of 459 m requires a lot of effort. Luckily, the superb sight of the Poradské pleso lake, surrounding the Tatra valleys, peaks, and crests improves the mood of tourists. The path crosses the massive edges of the slopes of the peaks Tupá and Končistá which were not affected by the activity of glaciers. There are no traces of glaciation in the small Štôlska dolina valley. Everywhere around only huge scree heaps can be seen. The dwarf pine trees are only sporadically seen near magistrála, their upper edge is normally several tens of meters lower. The way to the Batizovské pleso lake is full of enchanting views of the basins and the crests of the Low Tatras.

The **national nature reserve Batizovská dolina valley** is closed to public, as well as the valley Zlomiská. It is squeezed between the

Končistá (2,537 m) and Gerlachovský štít peaks (2,655 m) – a singular rocky setting. In the middle of the valley stands a lonely mountain called Kostolík (2,251 m) or Small Church, reminding one of a little Gothic church. Kostolík mountain is a typical example of an unglaciated mountain surrounded on all sides by a glacier that used to fill the Batizovská dolina valley in the Glacial period. Kostolík has a sad history. A legendary Polish mountaineer by the name of Stanisławski and his companion Wojnar had bad luck while climbing a moderately difficult section of the ascent to Kostolík. A large piece of weathered rock suddenly broke off and carried them both down to the abyss.

Leaving the picturesque Batizovské pleso lake one can continue along the main Tatra tourist path passing the cottage of Sliezsky dom to Starý Smokovec, or turn left on to a yellow-marked path and finish the trip in Vyšné Hágy.

Left: Relaxing in the company of a mountain guide

Starý Smokovec
and its environs

The area of Starý Smokovec is situated on the southern foothills of the Vysoké Tatry mountains, of which three aspects of its relief constitute other areas of Vysoké Tatry mountain range. In the north it comes into contact with the main Tatra ridge between the peak of Popradský Ľadový štít and the Východná Vysoká peak. Its western border is limited by the fork of the Slavkovský štít peak, whilst the southern part borders on the Popradská kotlina basin.

STARÝ SMOKOVEC (1,010 m, population 5,700) is the largest of the four original Tatra communities bearing the name Smokovec. They are all situated on the southern foothills of Slavkovský štít peak and gradually merged into a common settlement with the exception of Dolný Smokovec, which has the statute of a town. Dolný Smokovec is the location of the municipal office administrating all High Tatra community seats, and is the main tourist centre of the Tatras, being an important communication cross-roads. Roads from Štrbské Pleso (15 km), from Poprad (13 km) and Tatranská Lomnica (6 km) meet here. It is also a railway junction where the network of the Tatra tram branches into western, eastern and southern routes.

Archaeological research carried out in the territory of Smokovce in the second half of the 19th century disclosed the remains of an ancient iron smelting plant from the turn of the era. Besides various tools a precious silver coin of the Emperor Marcus Aurelius (120-180) proved the existence of trade contacts of the local smelters. The Celts who once lived in the sub Tatra areas eventually disappeared in the "trap-cellar" of history but their paths leading from the basin to smelting plants were probable never again covered by vegetation. They were used also by younger generations of the sub Tatra populations. Their steps led to the mineral water springs which they believed possessed miraculous curing properties. In the mid-13th century the thick woods around the springs provided shelter and hiding places for the people fleeing

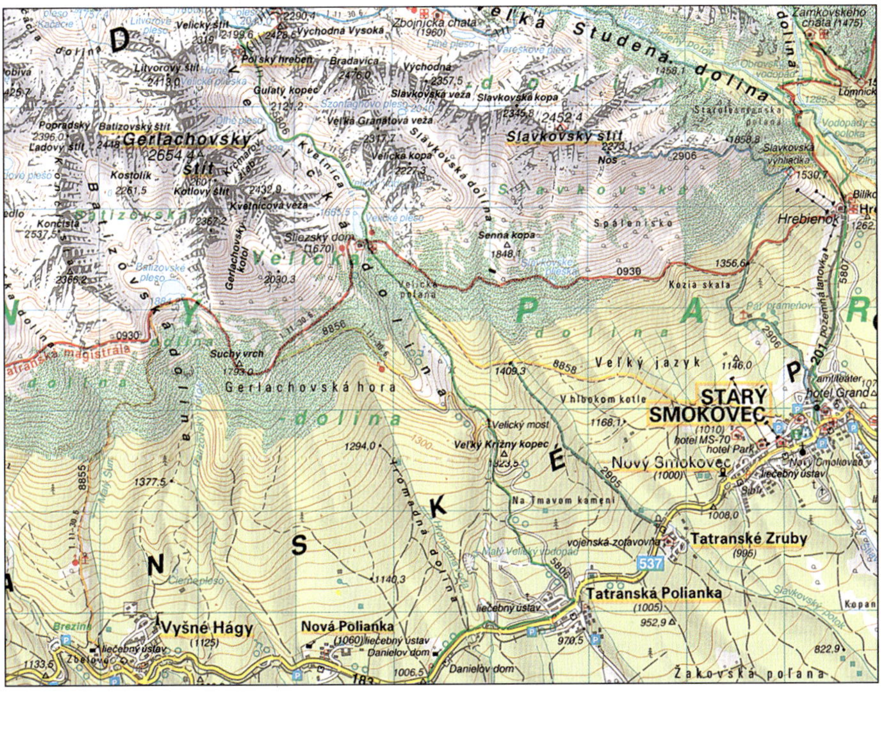

from the Tartar hordes and about two centuries later from the Hussite troops.

Petropavlovian pilgrimage:

What used to be a reliable forest refuge for the shepherds and farmers in the turbulent history of the Spiš region became a scene of traditional folk feasts. Every year on St. Peter and Pavol's day people used to gather near the Smokovec mineral springs. Some assert that the famous Petropavlovian pilgrimage predates medieval times. They maintain that the origins of this tradition are in the pagan cult of the Old Slavic god Zmok, a powerful guardian of the water and the treasures hidden deep underground. It is even purported that the name Smokovec is connected to the god, but it is only one of an existing number of versions explaining the name of the community.

The forests above Veľký Slavkov first belonged to the monastery of Turiec. In 1465 an extensive territory of the community became the property of the Zápoľský family who sold it to count Csáky in the 17th century, one of the hereditary heads of the Spiš province connected to one of the oldest Tatra communities. It is supposed that the spiritual father of the idea to found a summer holiday resort, at the foothills of the Tatra mountains, was the Evangelical pastor Tomáš T. Mauksch who belonged to a group commonly known as "the Tatra wanderers". He often set out to discover trips to his beloved Tatras from his parsonage in Veľký Slavkov in the summer, and then dedicated long winter evenings to the study of the history of the Saxon colonisation of the Spiš region. He shared the idea to found a summer resort in the Tatras with the landowner Štefan Csáky who in turn was a great lover of hunting in the Tatra estate belonging to his sister. After some persuasion the pastor finally convinced the count help construct the first building of the future Smokovec in 1793. It was originally a hunting lodge, a favourite destination for summer trips of the local aristocracy. The owner of the cottage was so much appreciated for having invented this new form of social amusement it encouraged him to continue in the construction of other new buildings and facilities.

Right: The Nový Smokovec spa

The origin of the name Smokovec:

One day count Štefan Csáky set out on an usual hunting trip to the forests near Veľký Slavkov. He saw a young girl drinking water from the mineral spring. He patted her on the shoulder and asked her in German: "Schmeckt est dir?" (Does it taste good?). A corruption of the expression was allegedly the core of the future name of the summer holiday resort near the mineral springs. The older name of the community, Schlandorfer Sauerbrunn, or Slavkov springs was quickly forgotten, and evolved into Šmeks, and later Smokovec. Who knows what Smokovec would be called if the count asked the girl the same question in Slovak "Chutí?"...

The first administrator of the Csáky's summer residence, Tomáš Mauksch, was true to his profession of an Evangelical pastor. Every time after the departure of the noble guests he invited to the house some of his less noble friends, like teachers, pharmacists and students. Among them was also the famous British traveller and scientist Robert Townson. When in 1802 the count learnt about the insolence of the pastor he immediately sacked him. However, the count himself had to leave the same year after having lost a litigation over the property with his sister. The new owner of the estate, Veľký Slavkov, became Karol Csáky who soon got in touch with the disadvantaged pastor and between them they formed a business partnership, that of a wealthy count and an intelligent pastor. Between them they believed in collective tourism as a necessary means of resource for the maintenance of the decaying Csáky's summer residence. But the social changes that might have promoted the more rapid development of tourism and travel in Old Hungary were still absent in the mid-19th century. Count Karol decided then to abolish serfdom, at least in his estate and offered many of his serfs freedom for money. The inhabitants of Mlynica, neighbouring with Veľký Slavkov, became free citizens. The people of Mlynica also obtained with their freedom the lands where Smokovec was situated and started to apply their business activities towards developing the potential of a holiday resort. A hundred years of what was a premature holiday resort, when compared with other Tatra communities, was mainly the result of the mineral water springs. Karol Csáky, upon listening to advice from the pastor Mauksch, provided extensive vis-

its to the curing springs. The local water was used not only as a refreshing beverage but it was applied also in curative spa activities. Smokovec became a spa locality offering diverse varieties of water-curing. Climatic therapy was introduced several decades later. In 1833 a successful businessman by the name of Ján Juraj Rainer visited Smokovec and stayed for 34 years. He and his wife rented an existing business and undertook a grandiose project by constructing an ostentatious spa resort. By 1839 Smokovec acquired another four new buildings called Flóra, Švajčiarsky dom, Rigi and Čarovný dom. The still standing Flora is the oldest tourist building in the Tatras. In 1850 the first two-storeyed brick house called Bellevue (not the present Bellevue Hotel) was built. Until then neglected appearance of the communities was improved by a beautiful park. The new spa facilities attracted a number of new guests and Smokovec became a successful rival to the spa on the shores of lake Balaton in what is present day Hungary. The Hungarian tourists inspired by the name of the Balaton spa, Balatonfüred, attached to Smokovec the derived name of Tatrafüred. The idea to apply water cures in the Tatras was that of Dr. Samuel Posewitz. The cold water cure was used for the improvement of blood circulation, regulation of blood pressure and an overall regeneration, while the hot water baths had no specific function other than a hygienic one. The Reiners' did not neglect the social function of the spa either. A ball held regularly in June was the first social event to open the season. Favourite pastimes were the walks to the Hrebienok or to Studenovodské vodopády waterfalls and to the Velické pleso lake. The interest in Smokovec further increased when the Košice-Bohumín railway track was opened in 1871. A new leaseholder of the community was the credit bank of Spiš which invested in the construction of a new centre, situated below the old one. The buildings of a sanatorium and two hotels were erected along the Klotildina cesta road, today called Cesta Slobody. Csáky's house was given the name of the founder of the community and the other hotel was called after the Latin word for Spiš – *Scepusia.* In the northern part of the road a sumptuous villa called Klotilda, commemorating its owner the archprincess of Hapsburg, was built. By 1872 other Tatra communities sprang up and became rivals to

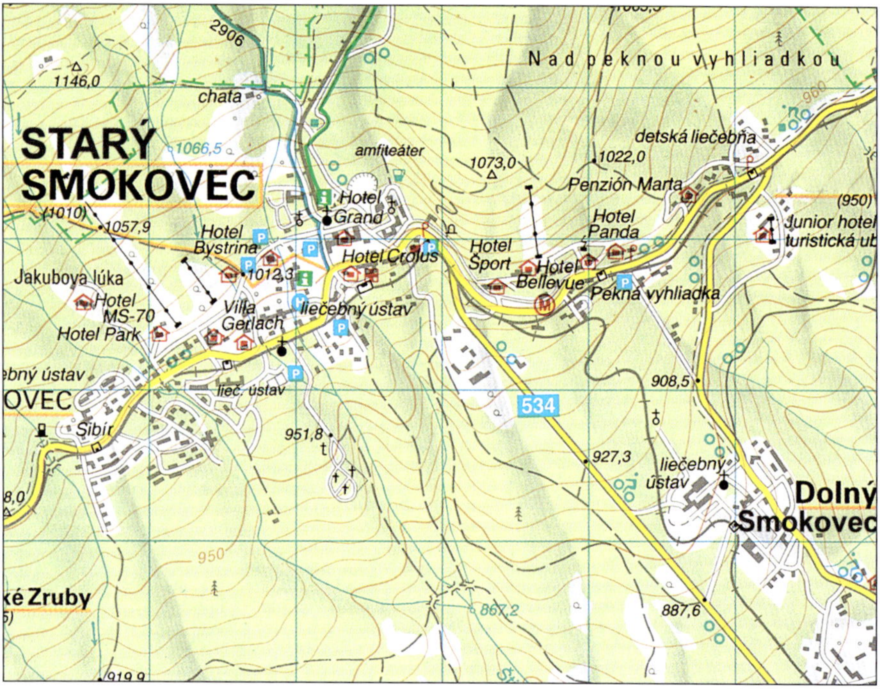

Smokovec. As a result Smokovec lost its battle for the railway connection with Tatranská Lomnica and Štrbské Pleso. After a failed experiment with trolley buses in 1904 the cabmen survived a little longer only to be outmatched by the Tatra tram introduced on December 17, 1908. On that particular day the first tram arrived from Poprad to Starý Smokovec on a 13 kilometre long track and only four days later the first rack railway carriage climbed to Hrebienok. In spite of the pressure from the newer Tatra communities, Starý Smokovec maintained its conservative and old-fashioned character and its leading position as the principal Tatra community. At the present time it is the seat of the municipal office, an all-Tatra authority, and of the mountain rescue service (Horská služba).

This oldest Tatra community was called Smokovec by the Slovaks, *Schmecks* by the Germans and *Tátrafüred* by the Hungarians. But when the dream of Mikuláš Szontagh of building a new modern climatic spa began to materialise in 1875, its name had to be changed to Starý Smokovec (Old Smokovec or *Alt-Schmecks* and *Ó-Tátrafüred*).

The village of **NOVÝ SMOKOVEC** (1,000 m, population 700) west of Starý Smokovec was also a spa centre, which continues up to the present time. Its foundation was a response to the new trends in balneology as a fashionable branch of therapy in the second half of the 19th century. Mikuláš Szontagh brought the desire to own a proper high-mountain sanatorium over from Switzerland. After he married a rich bride his vision acquired more realistic ground and as he signed the lease contract there was nothing to stop it becoming a reality. The new climatic spa of Dr. Szontagh welcomed its first patients in 1876. At the beginning it had to face the jealous rivalry of its older fashionable neighbour. The people of Starý Smokovec were particularly opposed to the presence of tuberculosis infected patients. In 1883 Dr. Szontagh pioneered a previously never heard of experiment, which was to run the sanatorium during the winter season. Luckily the fears of bitter frost and blizzards were not justified. On the contrary, the tourist discovered the charm of the Tatra winter and the winter season became the natural component of the tourists' stay throughout the Tatras.

Szontagh's promotion of the winter season:

Dr. Szontagh advertised the assets of the winter season in Nový Smokovec in a regional periodical called Zipser Bote (The Spiš Messenger) written as follows: "Relying on a many years' experience acquired in medical practice and on an eight-years observation I declare with all responsibility that the position of Nový Smokovec is the most advantageous of all European climatic centres. It is situated on the southern slopes of the High Tatras at an altitude of 3,200 feet above sea level, i.e. in a bacterium-free zone. It is perfectly guarded against the northern winds by the mountains higher than 8,000 feet, and due to open southerly exposure it enjoys an extraordinary abundance of sunshine. Among other climatic assets I can quote scant occurrences of mist, moderate rain, air rich in ozone and a high-mountain position. There are no glaciers, avalanches and the centre is perfectly accessible (one hour's ride from the railway station in Poprad-Veľká). The therapeutic factors are roughly the same as in the Prussian resort of Göbersdorf, hence very suitable for winter stays for patients suffering from lung diseases".

By the late 19th century Mikuláš Szontagh and his son founded a joint stock company supported by the rich businessmen of Liptovský Mikuláš, who consequently realised the construction and modernisation of Nový Smokovec. Besides the operational sanatoriums the first cinema in the Tatras was introduced as early as 1913. The dominant building of the spa community became the large TB sanatorium designed by the famous architect M. M. Harminc of Bratislava. Later another, Harminc's sanatorium Palace, emerged. The former villa of Szontagh, built in 1914 (today the Tokajík Hotel) and another three hotels were acquired by Nový Smokovec thanks to the world championship in cross-country skiing in 1970.

DOLNÝ SMOKOVEC (890 m, population 1,000) is the only one of the communities bearing the name Smokovec which does not lie on the road Cesta Slobody, and which has not yet merged with the existing agglomeration. Its name (Lower Smokovec) implies that it is situated lower than its neighbouring Tatra communities, and lies off the road between Poprad and Starý Smokovec, about 2 kilometres from its junction with the road Cesta Slobody. Dolný Smokovec originated in 1881 as the result of the teacher, Jozef Bohuš's efforts to establish a tourist base for school excursions to the Tatras. This new Tatra community was intended to provide a rather low market alternative to the somewhat snobbish Starý Smokovec with an entirely different clientele. But Bohuš's project ran into much resistance. Lack of financial means forced the teacher to sell the unfinished students' cottage at a mean price to the bank. Thus, instead of benefiting youth short of money, the wealthiest class of the society spent their holiday in these luxurious villas. The families of count Széczényi or count Zichy had their summer residences in Dolný Smokovec. The community acquired the nature of an after-care spa with several sanatoriums specialising since 1919 in children's diseases. In 1931 a modern sanatorium with centres of internal medicine and surgery was built here for the specialised therapy of children's tuberculosis and lung disease patients.

In the opposite direction **HORNÝ SMOKOVEC** (950 m, population 200) merged with Starý Smokovec. Its name meaning "upper" is correct only in relation to Dolný Smokovec, as Starý and Horný Smokovec are situated above it. Horný Smokovec is the youngest of the four communities at the foothills of Slavkovský štít peak. In the second half of the 19th century there was only a wooden look-out tower accessible by a comfortable path frequently used by the spa guests. The view from the look-out tower inspired people to call it Pekná Vyhliadka (Pretty View). In 1926 several family pensions, the names of which immortalised the wives of their owners (Vlasta, Irma, Klára, and Dagmar) were built in this new Tatra community. The name Pekná vyhliadka was preserved until 1938 when it was officially changed to Horný Smokovec. Then the building of a larger pension Helios (today Poľana) and two sanatoriums followed. The former sanatorium of Dr. Opatrný is used today as a pavilion for children suffering from the diseases of upper and lower respiratory system. The villa of Dr. Opatrný was changed to the Home of Slovak Writers. Other sanatorium, founded by Dr. Julius Holzmann-Horný, is a part of the aforementioned therapeutic compound for children suffering from TB and respiratory diseases. The space between Horný and Starý Smokovec was filled by two new hotels, the Bellevue and Šport.

Sightseeing the communities requires about two or three hours, starting in the parking lot near the bus station. Right at the parking lot there is a small wooden arbour with the inscription **Smokovecká kyselka**. It is a mineral water spring, a former Csáky's spring. Nearby, there is another **water spring Hygaea**. Other two **mineral water springs called Castor** and **Pollux** are under a wooden shelter while the last, fifth spring, flows to a small lake in front of the amphitheatre.

The legend of the fairy of Smokovec:

In the past, near the two Smokovec springs of Castor and Pollux a charming voice could be heard singing. It was the voice of a beautiful water fairy who sang of joy when thinking of her lover whose last day of the seven years' service to the Tatra queen was about to come. She was dreaming of the day when he would take her to his house under the Tatras. But the goblin living in the Studený potok waterfalls intervened and tried to court her. Because the fairy refused he decided to kidnap her. The ruler of the Tatra lakes, torrents and wells saved the fairy by making the water of the spring bubble so violently that the goblin believed it was boiling, and so the goblin gave up his intention and fled from the place for ever. Shortly after the fairy left happily with her lover leaving behind the bubbling water of the Smokovec springs.

The oldest part of the Smokovce communities was situated between the amphitheatre and the lower station of the rack railway. Historic testimony, which is an example of the oldest architecture in the area is the villa **Flóra** built in 1839. Originally a log house it is today used for cultural events. Behind the ostentatious building of the **Grand hotel** of 1904, the work of an outstanding architect Guido Hoephner, from Budapest, is that of a wooden Roman-Catholic **church of Immaculate Conception of the Virgin Mary**. The church was designed by the architect Gedeon Majunke of Spišská Sobota and built in 1894. West bound roads and paths lead to the spa area of Nový Smokovec. The buildings of **Szontagh's sanatoriums and the sanatorium Palace** have been restored. The **Tokajík hotel** created from the former Szontagh's villa carries the family coat of arms. Its principal element is the sun, symbolising its curing properties used in climatic balneology. The path along the road Cesta Slobody leads back to Starý Smokovec. The centre of the community is on both sides of a busy road, north of which, beside the Grand Hotel, stands the building of the **municipal office**. In the opposite direction there is the **railway station, Krokus** (formerly Hoephner's house) the shopping centre **Dom potravín** (formerly a spa building) and the **Dom Horskej služby** (the House of the Mountain Rescue Service) as well as a group of buildings that originated by connecting the Csáky's former house and Sepusia. The best way to get from Starý Smokovec to Dolný Smokovec is to take the Tatra tram (the first stop in the direction of Poprad). The most interesting spa building from an architectural point of view is a wooden chapel standing near the road which connects Dolný and Horný Smokovec. Both of them are from 1890 and designed by the architect G. Majunke. Horný Smokovec is connected to Dolný Smokovec by a comfortable footpath which goes past the modern hotels of the **Bellevue** and **Šport**. Also the **Tatranská galéria** (the Tatra Gallery) deserves a visit where the important painters of the Tatra landscapes exhibit their works of art.

Left: The "baby" ski lift at Hrebienok
Right: A rack railway

Tatranská galéria, Tel.: 0969/42 22 18
Opening hours:
Tue-Fri 10:00-17h, Sat-Sun 10:00-16:00h

A favourite half-day trip is the one from Starý Smokovec to the Vodopády Studeného Potoka waterfalls. The trip can begin by using the rack-railway to Hrebienok or by ascending a green-marked path.

The rack-railway to Hrebienok:

In 1908 the community of Starý Smokovec got a Christmas present from the Phoebus company who built here a new rack-railway to Hrebienok. Three days before Christmas the first pair of cars with 45 passengers set off on a track 2,019 m long surmounting the altitude difference of 354 m. The rack-railway was a novelty at the time. The machine room equipped with a modern electric engine set in motion the traction steel wire passing over 442 pulley sheaves. The shuttle cars met half-way at a shunting place where they automatically cleared the way. The cars were modernised in 1951. A more substantial change though was

the general reconstruction in 1970. The new rack-railway to Hrebienok also got new buildings and cars with higher passenger capacity – 800 passengers an hour in one direction.

Hrebienok (1,285 m) situated in the south-eastern end of the crest of Slavkovský štít peak has been one of the best attractions for visitors to the Vysoké Tatry mountains for about one hundred years. The first tourist facility originated in a place called Kanceľ under Hrebienok in 1875. It was built by the Old Hungarian Carpathian Association mainly due to the financial support of a lady singer and pianist called Ružena Graef-Györffyová. This famous artists born in Spiš dedicated the proceeds of one of her concert tours to the building of a cottage. The building was christened Ružena's Cottage. It existed for 18 years before it burnt down. At the time there were several new tourist buildings around Ružena's Cottage. In 1883 Anton Döller of Kežmarok published a generous project of what he called Studenopotocké spa. The project consisted of tourist and spa buildings along the path leading from Hrebienok to the vodopády Studeného potoka waterfalls. The largest and best equipped hotel in the Tatras, called Spiš was planned to be built within this new spa area. Besides expanding Ružena's Cottage the retired officer Döller planned to substitute the Rainerova chata cottage in the Veľká Studená dolina valley with the hotel Kamzík. But the project was completely unrealistic because the land in Hrebienok and Kanceľ was owned by various proprietors. The forest company of Spišská Sobota who owned Kanceľ was the most active of the builders. It built a two-storeyed hotel, Studený potok (in German "Kohlbach") and a spa building in 1884. Ten years later the hotel Spiš, though much smaller and more modest than the planned Grand Hotel, was added. Promotion of the spa was much helped by the construction of a broad road and rack-railway at the turn of the century. Along with the upper station of the rack-railway a restaurant Kiosk also providing accommodation for tourists was opened. But in 1927 a fire finished the short existence of Studenopotocké spa. The abandoned land in Kanceľ, with the ruins of the spa, was bought by Michal Guhr, a physi-

cian from Tatranská Polianka, who almost immediately donated it to the German tourist organisation *Karpathenverein*, which built here a wooden Guhrova Cottage in 1934. After the Second World War the name of the cottage was changed to **Bilíkova chata** cottage honouring Pavol Bilík (1916-1994), a customs officer from Horný Smokovec. This successful racer in cross-country skiing and a participant of the anti-Nazi movement in the Tatras was executed in 1944 at Kežmarok castle.

The owners of the Tatra railway connected the upper station of the rack-railway and Kiosk with the newly built Šport hotel (today called **Hrebienok**) in 1928. The environs of Hrebienok has been a favourite place for skiers since the 1930's. In 1956 beside the ski slalom track under Slavkovská vyhliadka the first 750 metres long ski-lift was built. And after 1970 the steep grassy meadow hosted the participants of several races of the World Cup in downhill skiing disciplines.

Left: Hrebienok
Right: Bilíkova chata cottage

A big winter attraction became the tobogganning on the **bobsled track** from Hrebienok to Starý Smokovec. As a matter of fact it is a steep meandering paved road used in summer for various cyclist events and races, though in opposite directions.

Hrebienok is a traditional starting point for trips to the Studená dolina valley, the Skalnaté pleso lake, the mountain hotel Sliezsky dom, and Slavkovský štít peak. Hrebienok itself offers a superb view of the Lomnický štít peak. The western face of the second highest peak with one of the most popular mountaineering tracks in the Tatras, and the famous "hockey stick" can be seen from here. The closest and at the same time, the most visited landmark is the nearby vodopády Studeného potoka waterfalls. A part of the main Tatra tourist path connecting Hrebienok with Skalnaté pleso leads to it. A red-marked, comfortable path heads to the place where the thundering waters of the torrents flowing from Veľká and Malá Studená dolina valleys join. At the end of the Veľká Studená dolina valley there used to stand the Kamzík chata (cottage) until quite recently, which was built in 1884. In the original

Döller's project of Studenopotocké spa chata Kamzík was to substitute an older tourist building sometime in the 1860's. The tourists visiting the Studené doliny valleys and the Lomnický štít peak called the cottage Rainerova chata. However, chata Kamzík was finally built by its side and Rainerova chata cottage was transformed to a fuel store for its much bigger neighbour. This historical building was successfully reconstructed in 1983. After seeing vodopády Studeného potoka waterfalls (see page 112) the return trip is either possible by the same track to Hrebienok and to Starý Smokovec or by continuing to Zbojnícka chata, the Téryho chata cottages or by *magistrála* to the Skalnaté pleso lake (see page 112).

The starting point of another half-day trip to the Velické pleso lake is again Hrebienok. The main Tatra tourist path ascends moderately then gets steeper. After about two kilometres it ascends to a dwarf pine tier which opens up into beautiful sights of the Slavkovský štít peak (2,452 m) on the right and the basin on the left. The route passes by an elevation behind which is the small **Slavkovské pleso lake** (1,676 m). Originally there were three small lakes in the basin of Slavkovské plesá lakes. Two of them do not exist any more. The Old Hungarian Carpathian Association built a small shelter near the lakes in 1878 for tourists on the way to Slavkovský štít peak which today is a forgotten path. In 1882, however, a huge avalanche demolished it. A group of enthusiasts from Smokovec started to build a new shelter in an apparently safer place, but when, in 1945, an avalanche carried away the provisional store of building material, they gave up on the idea. On the right side of the path is the terrace-shaped **Slavkovská dolina valley** squeezed between the crest of Slavkovský štít peak and Granátové veže peak. In the past it was frequented by shepherds from Veľký Slavkov. At the end of the valley and at a sea level altitude 2,040 m there are two small lakes **Szontaghovo pleso** and **Malé Szontaghovo pliesko** bearing the name of the founder of Starý Smokovec – M. Szontagh senior. Nevertheless, Slavkovská valley is closed to tourists and therefore they must continue to travel over the Senná kopa mountain (1,848 m) beyond which *magistrála* slightly descends to the Velická dolina valley. At the lowest step of the valley, at an altitude of 1,663 m above sea level, is Velické

pleso lake. The area of this elongated lake blocked by a moraine has an area of 2.22 ha and a depth of 5 m. Taking refreshment in the hotel Sliezsky dom (see page 101) tourists can decide on one of three options on how to conclude their trip. The longest route continues on the magistrála over Popradské pleso lake to Štrbské pleso lake. The shortest and most comfortable option is offered by the descent following the green-marked footpath to Tatranská Polianka. A direct return to Starý Smokovec is possible by a yellow-marked path traversing the forests on the southern slope of the foothills of Slavkovský peak štít.

One of the most interesting all day trips from Hrebienok is the tour to Slavkovský štít. Its typical round top is an indivisible part of the mountain scenery around the Smokovce community. In the past the tourist approached it from the south. Maximilián Weisz (1845-1825), a clerk from Smokovec, initiated in the years 1902-1908 a new tourist path leading along the edge of Slavkovský crest up to the top of the peak. A blue-marked path starts by a moderate ascent across the forest. Before it crosses the magistrála or the main Tatra tourist path it passes a place called **Päť prameňov** (Five Springs). The spa and hotel guests visited the springs as early as the second half of the 19th century, made possible by a path made by J.J. Rainer in 1862. Along the path there is also a wooden arbour. At present the springs represent the source of drinking water for the people of Smokovce. The path leaves the forest below **Slavkovská vyhliadka** (1,531 m). It is a plateau in Slavkovský hrebeň adjusted to a look-out platform offering a lovely view of the Veľká Studená dolina valley. It is also called Maximiliánka, commemorating its creator Maximilián Weisz. Leaving this spot, the path ascends by serpentines first to a south slope of the peak and afterwards along the edge of what is called the Štrbavý hrebeň crest. The view to all sides of the path reveals a different character of the slopes of the crest. This conspicuous asymmetry of the Slavkovský crest is observable also from Tatranská Lomnica. An almost smooth slope facing south covered by debris sharply contrasts with the northern steep slopes, cut by numerous rocky troughs, towers, pillars and

Left: Sliezsky dom hotel and Velické pleso lake

walls, perpendicularly descending to the Veľká Studená dolina valley. The asymmetry of Slavkovský crest is the result of glacial activity during the Glacial period. The northerly slopes of Slavkovský peak were undercut by the glacier of the Veľká Studená dolina valley, while the southerly side turned towards the basin was spared the destructive activity of glacial erosion. The fore-top of the Slavkovský štít peak is called **Nos** (The Nose) (2,272 m). According to legend the Old Hungarian king Matej Korvín climbed the summit and consequently it is also called the Royal Nose. The route of the ascending path passes by Nos on the right side and follows serpentines to the top of **Slavkovský štít** (2,452 m). The majestic round peak was one of the first conquered. The oldest document written in 1664 by Juraj Buchholtz senior quotes an ascent to the peak *Schlagendorfer* Spitze i.e. Slavkovský štít peak. The primary Buchholtz's ascent was followed by a winter ascent accomplished in January 1873 by E. Blásy, accompanied by the mountain guide Gellhof, by the same route on the southern side of the mountain. Slavkovský štít peak is relatively accessible, hence popular and the most frequently ascended Tatra peak, especially when the Weisz's path was built in 1908. Descent is possible only by the same route. Both, ascent and descent are much easier when the rack-railway to Hrebienok is used.

The lost top of Slavkovský štít peak:

In the second half of the 19th century people spread a rumour that some kind of natural disaster damaged the top of the peak, lowering it by two or three hundred meters. It was allegedly an earthquake said to take place in Spiš on August 6, 1662. The propagator of this scientifically unproven event learned of the fact that the top of the peak was round, giving the impression of a missing tip. The heaps of rocks and cones covering extensive areas of the southern side of the mountain were taken for the rest of the collapsed peak. They say an enormous boulder called Rozvaliny rolled almost to Starý Smokovec. The credibility of the theory supporting the disaster was much shaken by an excellent connoisseur of the Tatras, Ivan Bohuš. Analysing historical resources he found out that in 1662 only some destructive floods provoked by summer storms occurred in the Tatras. Geomorphic research of Professor Lukniš also failed to support the hypothesis of the seismic destruction of Slavkovský štít peak.

TATRANSKÉ ZRUBY (995 m, population 80) is a small hamlet situated near the road Cesta Slobody about 2 km west of Starý Smokovec.

The community originated in 1923 as a training camp for the mountain troops of the Czechoslovak army consisting of log huts, the reason why it was initially called Vojenské Zruby (Military Log Huts). The trainees of the local military courses often participated in the construction of the Tatra tourist paths and cottages. During the Slovak National Uprising the local military garrison joined the anti-Nazi resistance. After the threat of bombing the Tatra communities by the German air force it moved to the Low Tatras. After the war a military convalescent centre was established in Tatranské Zruby. In 1967 a big and modern central hotel was constructed here.

TATRANSKÁ POLIANKA (1,005 m, population 300), is another hamlet situated on both sides of the road Cesta Slobody between Starý Smokovec (3 km) and Štrbské Pleso (11 km).

It is among one of the oldest Tatra communities. Its origins date back to 1884. Near the local forester's hut a rich farmer and butcher by the name of Pavol Weszter of Veľký Slavkov built a hunting cottage. In 1888 together with his relatives Samuel Nitsch and Michal Guhr he started the building of three mountain hotels under the Gerlachovský štít peak, right beside the hunting cottage. The Marian, Tusculum and Themis hotels soon became favourite resting places of the coaches arriving from the newly opened Klotilda's road (the contemporary road Cesta slobody) between the Smokovce communities and Štrbské Pleso, up to the starting point to the Velická dolina valley. The local restaurant with excellent cuisine was visited also by the spa guests staying in Smokovce. Before the end of the century another three buildings accrued, increasing the accommodation capacity of the new Tatra summer resort to 125 tourist beds. The successful enterprise of three businessmen of Veľký Slavkov was carried on by Weszter's nephew Michal Guhr (1873-1933). He was graduate physician and he founded a climatic sanatorium oriented to the therapy of tuberculosis and asthma in Tatranská Polianka in 1902. Later it focused on patients suffering from Basedow's disease. In 1912 the private pension of Dezider Raichart was built on the eastern edge of the community and in the same year the long expected railway was constructed. In the 1920's the capacity of the spa was enlarged

by two new modern sanatoriums. M. Guhr was not only a good physician but also the founder of the mountain rescue service and an enthusiast in winter sport. He brought over a passion for skiing from his stay in Switzerland. Thanks to him in the conclusion of the nearby Velická dolina valley the first ski-jump was built. The opening ski-jump competition was held in February 1911. The winner, Bruno Weiss, reached a nine and a half meters long jump. Later adjustments to the ski-jump allowed for the possibility to reach jumps up to 60 m long. Untiring Guhr also organised the first skiing competition in the Tatra mountains. Other competitions in bobsled in a newly constructed four kilometre long bobsled track from the mountain hotel Sliezsky dom to Tatranská Polianka followed these earlier ventures.

Jiří Wolker in the Vysoké Tatry mountains:

Among one of the most famous patients of the sanatoriums of Tatranská Polianka was the distinguished Czech poet Jiří Wolker. An extensive correspondence in his legacy describes his stay in the Tatras, which also takes into account Dr. Guhr. He respected him as an physician and as a human being always referring to him with great respect as an excellent physician and art connoisseur. The poet demonstrated his gratitude to Dr Guhr by reciting him in a collection of his poems. Unfortunately, the stay in the Tatras did not help Wolker from a curative aspect and he died of tuberculosis on 3 January 1924 in the Moravian town of Prostějov. He was only twenty four. Tatranská Polianka honoured the memory of the poet in 1949 by placing his bust in one of the sanatoriums and by organising an annual competition in reciting under the name "Wolker's Polianka".

One of the short trips starting in Tatranská Polianka is a walk to a place called **Veľká Žltá stena** (Big Yellow Wall). About a kilometre west of Tatranská Polianka before arriving to the bridge over Velický potok brook a non-marked forest path turns north and after half an hour's walk it arrives under a yellow-coloured wall. It is a remarkable geological and archaeological locality. The wall

Left: Tatranská Polianka sanatorium

was originally about 60 m high representing the highest geological rock exposure in Slovakia disclosing the Quaternary sediments, a more than million year-old sequence of deposition of river or glacier sediments in the Velická dolina valley. In 1894, after Alexander Münich found in Veľká Žltá stena the traces of a fortified settlement of Púchov culture it became a great point of interest for archaeologists. More detailed research proved the existence of a local settlement of inhabitants, about two thousand years old, which were busy in mining and iron smelting.

An all day trip from Tatranská Polianka is an ascent to the **Východná Vysoká mountain**, an opportunity to see the very attractive Velická dolina valley with a singular view of the highest Tatra peak – the Gerlachovský štít. The route starts in Tatranská Polinka leading up to the Poľský hrebeň saddle by a green-marked footpath. Its lower section ending in the mountain hotel Sliezsky dom slightly ascends across a spruce forest. Under the Velický bridge it joins a paved road (accessible only with a permit issued by TANAP) also bound to the mountain hotel Sliezsky dom near the Velické pleso lake. The path twice crosses the noisy Velický potok brook and closely enters the dwarf pine forest before reaching the crossing with a yellow-marked path. An excellent opportunity for a short rest and refreshment is offered by **Sliezsky dom**. This mountain hotel on the western shore of the Velické pleso lake is the largest high-mountain tourist facility in the Tatras. It is situated at an altitude of 1,670 m above sea level. The first tourist shelter was built near Velické pleso lake in 1871. It was called Blásy's cottage after its builder Eduard Blásy (1820-1888) of Veľká, one of the enthusiasts who contributed much to the overall promotion of tourism and mountaineering in the Tatras in the second half of the 19th century. The shelter was destroyed after two years of existence by an avalanche that fell off the Velické Granáty mountains. It was substituted by Hunfalvy's cottage built on an alpine meadow, Vyšná Velická poľana, in 1878. Hunfalvy was an outstanding Old Hungarian geographer born in Veľký Slavkov. After opening Sliezsky dom its use was restricted to the bearers, mountain guides and the service of rich tourists. The firm foundations of an originally wooden cottage can be seen from the main Tatra tourist path. The new tourist facility near Velické pleso lake was opened by the beginning of June of the same year in spite of many adversaries. Due to the fact that it was administered by the Silesian section of the Old Hungarian Carpathian Association seated in Vratislav it got the name Sliezsky dom (Silesian House). The hotel was repeatedly reconstructed. For example when it was reconstructed in the years 1957-1959, a helicopter assisted in the construction of a high saddle roof for the first time in the Tatras. But the renewed building burnt down on the night of November 29 to 30, 1962. After a demanding preparation of projects, a new building of generous proportions was finished in 1968. Immediately above the Velické pleso lake the first step of the terrace-shaped **Velická dolina valley**, with a beautiful 15 m high **Velický vodopád waterfall**, is situated. A five and a half kilometre long glacier valley between Gerlachovský štít peak and the ridge of Velické Granáty mountains has four steps and a short glacial valley. For its botanical diversity the valley terrace above Velický vodopád waterfall won the name Kvetnica (The Flower Garden). David Frölich described it in the first half of the 17th century as a garden of spice plants, meaning medicinal herbs. Also Göran Wahlenberg, an important Swedish botanist and traveller dedicated his attention and study of Kvetnica whilst visiting the Tatras in 1813.

The ascent to Gerlachovský štít peak:

An unmarked footpath near Kvetnica diverges to the left of Kvetnica and heads out to a place called Velická próba, a starting point for the ascent to Gerlachovský štít peak (2,655 m). In turn, the Batizovská próba is the usual route of descent to the opposite side, the Batizovská dolina valley. Tourists interested in the ascent to the highest peak of the Tatras and Carpathians, should know, that it can be accomplished only in the company of a mountain guide. The service of experienced Tatra mountain guides to the visitors of the Tatras is provided, at certain prices, by the mountain rescue service (Tatranská Horská služba) situated in Starý Smokovec. The ascent to Gerlachovský štít is not demanding but it can be dangerous. Especially treacherous are the immediate changes in the weather conditions. Many a tourist has lost his way in a complex mountain setting in poor visibility, and this classic Tatra tour has proved fatal for some them.

Dom horskej služby TANAP-u (The House of Mountain Rescue Service of the TANAP), 062 01 Stary Smokovec tel.: 0969/42 28 20 or 0969/2855

At an altitude of 1,929 m above sea level and located in the valley terraces over Kvetnica is Dlhé pleso lake (The Long Lake) named so because of its shape. The area of this cirque lake is 0.63 ha and it is 5 m deep. In the highest part of the Velická dolina valley there are another two **Vyšné Velické plieska** lakes. However, the lakes in Velická valley are disappearing, being either drained by the seepage of the moraine or silted by debris which have already affected many similar lakes. The Červené jazierko lake painted by the Polish artists Zygmunt Stecynsky (1814-1890) in 1851 is a very lifelike landscape, but by the end of the 19th century only a small swampy pond was all that remained of it. It was gradually buried by the alluvia brought by the Velický potok brook during the flood in 1958. The environs of Dlhé pleso are impressive. The altitude difference between the bottom of the valley and the surrounding crests is 750 m, and in the east there are the rocky faces and towers of the **Velické Granáty** mountains. They are so-called because of the occurrence of crystals of garnet, semi-precious stone, in the rock, here mostly crystalline shales. It was because of it, but above all because of gold and other precious metals, why miners came to the Velická dolina valley. They were none too successful, however, as the garnets of Velická valley were too soft and their sheen insufficient. What was extracted was used for making cheap souvenirs or mashed into a powder as a popular medicine "for all ailments". The dominant peak of the crest is the **Bradavica** mountain (2,476 m) ending in four massive rocky peaks. On the other side of the Dlhé pleso lake a deep Krčmárov žľab trough can be seen. Its length of 800 m makes it the longest in the Tatras and is almost always covered in snow. Skiing down this particular trough is a top skiing achievement. The tourist path over the Dlhé pleso lake by-passes the **Guľatý kopec** mountain (2,125 m). The round rocky elevation lying in the middle of the valley is an excellent example of the abrading and eroding activity of the glacier that once filled the Velická valley up to an altitude of two hundred metres. The path continues ascending by serpentines over debris fields to the saddle of **Poľský hrebeň** (2,220 m) where there is a possibility either to continue to the Bielovodská dolina valley (see page 130) or to ascend to the top of the Východná Vysoká mountain. The name of the saddle expresses the fact that it was used by Polish smugglers trafficking their goods out of and to Poland. The Poľský hrebeň saddle is connected by a jagged section of the main Tatra ridge known among mountaineers as Martinovka. Climbing to Martinovka is one of the traditional mountaineering events in the Vysoké Tatry mountains.

A tragedy on the Zadný Gerlachovský štít:

Zadný Gerlachovský štít peak (2,616 m) with the highest and, simultaneously, the shortest lateral fork of the High Tatras, jutting out southward, was the site of a tragic air accident in the autumn of 1944. A DC-8 aircraft took off from the airport in Polish Krosno. Its mission was to bring a parachute unit to the Slovak

---

Left: A mountaineer in an icefall
Right: A view from Gerlach peak

Donovaly region to take part in the Slovak National Uprising. But the military plane never reached its destination. Bad weather over the Tatras hampered the navigation and the pilot, disoriented due to a broken altimeter, directly ran up against the rocks of the peak. The remains of the wreck were found by Polish tourists only after the war was over. The bodies of the 24 victims of the air accident were carried down on July 28, 1946 and buried with corresponding honours in the cemetery of Gerlachov. The propeller, a wing, and several automatic machine guns from the crashed plane are deposited in the Museum of the Slovak National Uprising in Banská Bystrica.

A short but demanding ascent of the Poľský hrebeň saddle, to the opposite side, along the yellow-marked path to the **Východná Vysoká** mountain provides tourists with a wonderful panoramic sight of the surrounding high-mountain landscape. The shortest conclusion of the tour is possible by descending along the same route to Tatranská Polianka. Longer alternatives are the ones along the tourist paths of the Bielovodská dolina valley (to Lysá Poľana) or the Veľká Studená dolina valley (to Hrebienok).

Danielov dom (1,010 m) is a foresters' building belonging to the administration of TANAP and stands on the Cesta Slobody road about 2 kilometres of Tatranská Polianka. It developed from the original hunting hut of Daniel Roland Diergardt who owned the surrounding forests in the years 1898-1929.

Closer to Vyšné Hágy at the foothills of the Gerlachovský štít peak is the small spa village of **NOVÁ POLIANKA** (1,060 m, population 150). It was founded only after the Second World War. The dominant building here is the one which serves as a military TBS sanatorium. It was designed by the architect M. M. Harminc and opened in 1956.

VYŠNÉ HÁGY (1,125m, population 500) is one of the most important spa villages in the Vysoké Tatry mountains. It is situated close to the point where the Batizovská dolina valley opens to the Popradská kotlina basin, on the Cesta Slobody road between Štrbské Pleso (7 km) and Starý Smokovec (8 km). The origin of this village is largely the accomplishment of the landowner František Mariássy. In 1890 he built a wooden house in Swiss mountain style here, spacious enough to accommodate twelve tourists. His business philosophy was to offer a service equal to the competing hotels in neighbouring Štrbské Pleso though at a lower price. He supplied the cottage with the produce from his cattle and fish farms in Batizovce. After a year a spa house was built near the cottage. The first buildings in Vyšné Hágy were designed by G. Majunke. Máriássy sold his Tatra property to the Prussian prince Kristián Hohenlohe in 1897. The architect Majunke also built for him a nice hunting manor house in Vyšné Hágy. The oldest part of the village was about three hundred metres below the contemporary tram stop. The Prussian aristocrat was not interested in the promotion of tourism in the village and it started to decay, but the situation eventually changed in 1927 when Hohenlohe's property was acquired by the government. The intention of the new owner was to start here a project of a workers' insurance company from Bratislava. As the idea provoked reluctance, the construction of the sanatoriums was postponed. The first patients of then the biggest sanatorium for tuberculosis in Central

Europe were admitted only on June 1, 1941. A 270 metre long modern eight-floor building had 1,950 beds. The facility originally planned for TB therapy later admitted also patients suffering from other respiratory diseases. The equipment of the sanatorium allows for the performance of demanding surgery and scientific research. Vyšné Hágy is known to the public not only as a spa but also as the place where the popular **international volley-ball tournament** is regularly held every year in August. Vyšné Hágy is also the starting point for hiking tours to the Batizovské pleso lake (see page 88).

Between Vyšné Hágy and Štôla is the next village of **NIŽNÉ HÁGY** (901 m). It is situated at the place where one of the oldest forester's houses in the Tatras used to stand which disappeared by the late 19th century. A group of cottages built at the lower end of the village has almost joined it to the nearby village of Štôla. A green-marked tourist path leads from Vyšné Hágy north-eastward through the forest. It passes by **Mraznica, a national nature reserve** protecting since 1991 precious peat bog plant areas with numerous threatened species over an area of 160 hectares.

Tatranská Lomnica
and its environs

The area of Tatranská Lomnica is the easternmost region lying on the southern foothills of the Tatras. Its larger part is situated in the territory of the High Tatras its edges entering also the one of Belianske Tatry mountains. In the north and north-west it stretches up to the main ridge of the High and Belianske Tatra mountains, and in the south it neighbours with Central Spiš region. Its boundary with the area of Starý Smokovec traces the fork of Slavkovký štít peak.

TATRANSKÁ LOMNICA (850-890 m, population 1,650) is the easternmost tourist centre of the three centres located on the southern foothills of the High Tatras. It is situated on the road Cesta slobody (Road of Freedom), 6 km north-east from another small community, Starý Smokovec. It has a good road and railway communication with Poprad, 18 km away.

Tatranská Lomnica originated only at the end of the 19th century, as one of the last Tatra communities, because of government action. It had purchased the forests at the foothill of the Lomnický štít peak in 1892 in order to construct there the first state-owned climatic spa centre in the Tatras. The last owner of the land was Ondrej Spóner, which was the reason why the referred to forests were called "the Spóner's Matliare". As the new spa was founded on the ground belonging to the territory of Veľká Lomnica it acquired the name Tatranská Lomnica which it has kept up to the present time. When this resort was being built neighbouring Starý Smokovec had already been in existence for about hundred years. And at the time of its construction, in the middle of the forest clearing near the Skalnatá dolina valley, only a gamekeeper's lodge and several summer residences existed, while the oldest community near the famous Smokovce springs was already then older than today's Tatranská Lomnica. Tatranská Lomnica established the first state-owned spa in the Tatra region. In trying to promote it the government divided the original forests into 69 building lots and subsequently leased or sold them to people wishing to construct their summer houses there. However, along with the new owners, or tenants, there were

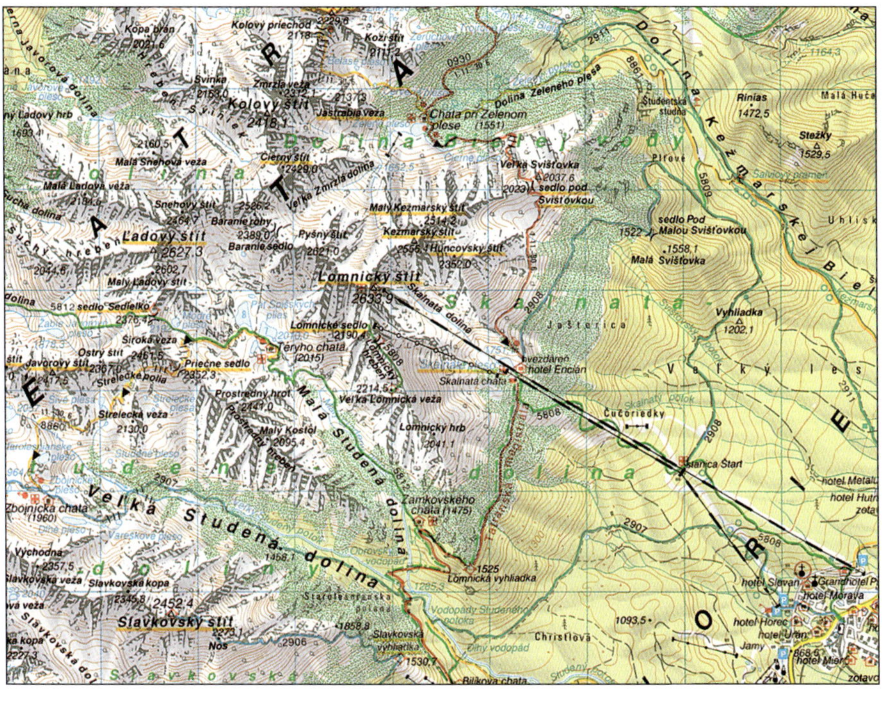

also speculators who were more interested in profit than in promoting this newly founded Tatra community. Instead of the planned luxurious summer residences there remained among the dispersed new buildings extensive unexploited areas of land and the concept of the Tatranská Lomnica development suffered a serious blow. But later it became apparent that the initial chaos paradoxically resulted in the useful further development of the spa. Vacant lots were changed into a forest park and Tatranská Lomnica, vested with green natural parkland easily gained an unusually pleasant chamber atmosphere, still envied by the rest of the Tatra communities.

The turn of the century found the Tatra summer residences in partial decline. A well-to-do clientele discovered the charms of the sea, and the mountain tourist resorts had to share their clients with those seeking sea-side holiday resorts. To combat this situation large luxurious hotels, offering a diversity of services, were constructed to attract more visitors and spa customers. This initiative bolstered Tatranská Lomnica enabling it to compete with its older and more established neighbours at the foothills of the Tatra peaks. In less than a year the inhabitants of Lomnica built the first of the big hotels in the Tatras. With the assistance of the Spiš credit bank in Levoča, and at a cost of 85,000 of zlaté (Austro-Hungarian guldens), the **Hotel Lomnica** (then called Tátra-Lomiczsáloda) was built and remained for several decades without equal in the neighbourhood. The hotel still provides a good level of service for visitors to the Tatras. Together with the hotel the community attained a new restaurant, coffee house with terrace, and a seasonal post office. Besides the Hotel Lomnica other more modest lodging and spa facilities were built. The community of Veľká Lomnica built in 1895 a tourist hotel and another two hotels the **Lomnička** and **Slovenský dom** (called before 1918 Bethlen-ház). Architecturally interesting the **Kúpeľný dom**, with an entrance hall designed in an unconventional Moorish style, provided therapeutical services. Construction of the Hotel Lomnica was a kind of general rehearsal for future ambitious buildings in the Tatra region, culminating in three new ostentatious hotels, built between 1904 to 1906. In 1902 the contract between the Old Hungarian railways and the international society of sleeping and restaurant cars, Wagons Lits Cook, seated in Brussels, expired and some smart representatives of the firm began to think of ways to remain in the attractive Tatra region. Their efforts ended in a successful contract with the government, part of which was also the building of three grand hotels. All three big projects were designed by a renowned Budapest architect, Guido Hoepfner born in Spišské Podhradie and were finally realised in 1944, in Starý Smokovec, a year later in Tatranská Lomnica, and two years later in Štrbské Pleso. For the new Grand Hotel in Lomnica a rather unusual place was chosen: a water logged hill covered by a forest, outside of the main community. It is quite possible these entrepreneurs anticipated the fact that wealthy visitors would reach the hotel in "motor coaches" later called automobiles, just as it was confirmed a year after opening the hotel in 1906. Perhaps the designers were also inspired by the generous intent of the society to build a rack-railway, but the accomplishment of this interesting project was ultimately frustrated by the First World War. However, the attractiveness of the hotel was shortly after enhanced by two local facilities – a bobsled track, as well as the funicular station.

Right: Lomnický štít peak

The Grand Hotel Prague:

The Lomnica Grand Hotel was erected amid a virgin spruce forest in 26 months. From the moment it was opened it was called Palota-Szálló (Palace Hotel). In 1919 it acquired a new name – Grand Hotel Prague – commemorating the occasion of the foundation of the Czechoslovak state. In many respects the technical specifications were ahead of their time, such as electrical installations and iron-concrete building materials, which in 1904, in the Austrian-Hungarian Empire, were the most recent innovations. As were the heating system, lifts and kitchen equipment. The first year of its operation the Grand Hotel, which opened throughout the winter season was extraordinarily successful. An advertising campaign attracted numerous clients, thirty per cent of them from abroad, to this comfortable hotel built in end-of-the-century style. The mainstay of the advertising campaign were, quite besides the beauty of the Tatras, the offer of a luxurious hotel, restaurant for three hundred guests, exclusive "American bar", conference hall, reading room, billiard hall and a charming park around the grounds of the hotel. The staff included a "genuine" Negro steward Dressed in snow-white tails. The view from the closed and open balconies offered a splendid panorama. The guests who lodged in the northern side of the hotel enjoyed the view of the silhouette of the Lomnický and Kežmarský štít peaks.

Tatranská Lomnica received a big present on its birthday. On September 1, 1895 the first train, pulled by a heavily blowing steam locomotive, rushed into the local station in a white cloud of steam bringing the first railway passengers directly to the foothills of the Tatras. The neighbouring Smokovce communities had to wait another thirteen years for a similar event. The ten kilometre long railway track connected the stations of Studený Potok, on route to Poprad, to Podolínec and Tatranská Lomnica. The entire construction took only five months and swallowed an investment of 180,000 zlaté. Initially it was possible to travel by train only in summer, and only after the construction of the Lomnica Grand Hotel was the new railway exploited all the year round. The railway and Grand Hotel have both equally contributed to the rapid promotion of Tatranská Lomnica which soon occupied a privileged position among the Tatra communities. The new Grand Hotel also brought the arrival of sport to the Tatras, opening its own ski and sled hiring service. In summer besides the popular sports of lawn tennis and shooting the hotel also offered the hire of bicycles by the enthusiastic staff.

Skijöring in the Tatras:

Another favourite pastime for the Grand Hotel guests was skijöring, an unusual Scandinavian winter sport. The skiers were pulled by saddled horses and driven over the snow covered roads of the spa, eventually some of them could choose to ride on a sledge also driven by horses. In 1907 there were available twelve pairs of horses, all equipped with fancy harnesses, and additional twelve skijöring sledges were made to a special order in Budapest.

The boom in Tatranská Lomnica's fortunes slowed down because of new lease conditions imposed by the government in 1908. Numerous tenants ended their contracts and before the end of the First World War only three new private villas were constructed, as well as a mechanical lift near the bobsled track above the Grand Hotel and a new railway connection with Starý Smokovec. During the First World War some of the tourist facilities and spa buildings changed to temporary military hospitals of the Red Cross and convalescent centres of the Austro-Hungarian army officers. The inter-war period in Tatranská Lomnica was remarkable for the construction of smaller pensions. One exception to this trend was the building of a big sanatorium of a Moravian insurance company in 1937 named after the native land of its owner: **Morava**. However, before the beginning of the Second World War the development of Tatranská Lomnica received another stimulus, which was the opening of a funicular in 1937, first between Tatranská Lomnica and Skalnaté pleso lake, and in 1940 it was extended to the top of the Lomnický štít peak. The idea to construct the funicular in the Tatras originated on November 20, 1895. At a meeting of the committee of the Old Hungarian Nature-Scientific Society a demand by meteorologists to establish a meteorological station on top of some of the Tatra peaks was pronounced for the first time. This idea was also supported by the astronomers. The first proposal was the Slavkovský štít peak which could be connected with Starý Smokovec or Hrebienok. Also the community Tatranská Polianka entered in this, mockingly

named "the funicular war" claiming that only the highest Tatra peak deserved the funicular – Gerlachovský štít peak. But the favoured choice was finally Lomnický štít peak, in 1932.

By funicular to the Lomnický štít peak:

The Skalnatá dolina valley is the end station of two funiculars starting in Tatranská Lomnica. Each of them has its valley station in a different location. Near the Grand Hotel Prague there starts the older funicular and in a parking lot near Sasanka Pension tourists can take a newer funicular going up to Skalnaté Pleso lake. The funicular surmounting the differential height 1722 m (between the start and end points), has connected Tatranská Lomnica with the Lomnický štít peak for more than half a century. The highest of the nine pylons is 37 m high. The straight line length of the second part of the track (between Skalnaté Pleso lake and the top of the Lomnický štít peak) is 1,655 m and the overall one is 1,870 m long. It is in this part of the track where the funicular reaches the differential height of 856 m. Originally one pylon placed in the southern face of the peak was needed to support the funicular, but after the last reconstruction it goes even without the one. This challenging and daring construction maintained world primacy until 1958, when it was surpassed by the cable railway of Aiguille di Midi in the French Alps. The other funicular has been in operation since August 27, 1973, which is fully used, especially in winter months, carrying hundreds of skiers to their favourite ski tracks below the Lomnické sedlo saddle.

Left: The funicular to Lomnický štít peak
Right: At the summit of Lomnický štít peak

During the inter-war period Tatranská Lomnica began to gradually lose the original purpose it was founded for – that of a climatic spa. The modern development of an expanding community under the Lomnický štít peak activated a preference for sporting and leisure activities. The former sanatoriums and convalescent centres changed to hotels, pensions and hostels and simultaneously various sport and social services were founded. At the western margin of the community a new **sport area Jamy** with two ski-jumps and a downhill ski track was built. Close to the Grand Hotel Prague there arose the first **artificial bobsled track** in the Tatras complying with very exacting technical specifications of international standard. The length of the track is 1,172 m with a differential height of 94 m. Some racers reach speeds here up to 100 km/h.

When in 1948 the Tatra National Park (TANAP) was inaugurated, the head office of its administration was located in Tatranská Lomnica. Gradually a new research centre and a TANAP museum were added. After the war Tatranská Lomnica became the largest centre in the Tatras for trade union recreation activities. Trade union sanatoriums and thousands of trade union members came here for their holidays, making this the most typical feature of the post war years. Originally the trade union organisation, well-known under the abbreviation ROH administered older facilities like Morava, Jánošík, and Volga and built progressively new hotels, the Urán, Odborár, Švermovo, and Dombas. After 1990 the majority of these trade union orientated facilities were transformed into public hotels and pensions, which has also reflected in the changing profile of the visitors. Many buildings in Tatranská Lomnica originated during the last quarter of the century. The forest park shel-

ters new hotels, sanatoriums and pensions like Slovan, Horec, Urán, and Sasanka. Near the railway station there are located services and shops. The community expanded, especially in a south-easterly direction. At the edge of the forest a modern and well-equipped **car camping area Eurocamp** was established, a place where after the first year of its existence a world wide meeting of members of FICC (International Federation of Caravan Camping) was organised. In the southern part of the area there is a more modest **Športcamp**, and the **Tatranec car camping site** is located in the opposite direction.

A walk around the locality, set amidst the forest is a pleasant and relaxing experience. Starting at the **Hotel Lomnica**, on the left hand side there flows a romantic brook passing by a building with a frontage which recreates a Tatra peak. This is the **Museum of the Tatra National Park** or **TANAP**. It replaced the former Tatra Museum when it passed under the administration of TANAP in 1957. Two years later the first expositions were presented to the public in the former Széczényi's summer residence built after the Tudor style. The collections were later moved to a modern building sharing the place with the **TANAP Research Centre**. It was ceremoniously opened on the occasion of the 20th anniversary of the establishment of the Tatra National Park. The architect who designed the new building of the TANAP Museum is Pavol Merjavý who obtained a prestigious award for the design. Seeing the museum may be a good educational start for visitors to the High Tatras to enlighten them for their further encounters with the natural beauties of the Tatras, their history and their present day activities. The collections are classified into nature-scientific, nature-conservation, historical and ethnographic sections. The most valuable items of the historical exposition is the 18th century Herbarium of monk Cyprián from Červený Kláštor.

TANAP Museum, tel.: 0969/46 7951
Opening hours: Mon-Fri 8:00-12:00h, Sat-Sun 13:00-16:30h

A building situated somewhat lower down is the seat of the **TANAP administration** and further down again there is a **cultural centre** with cinema, small gallery and shops. Sight-seeing tours continue in the opposite direction. Passing the Road of

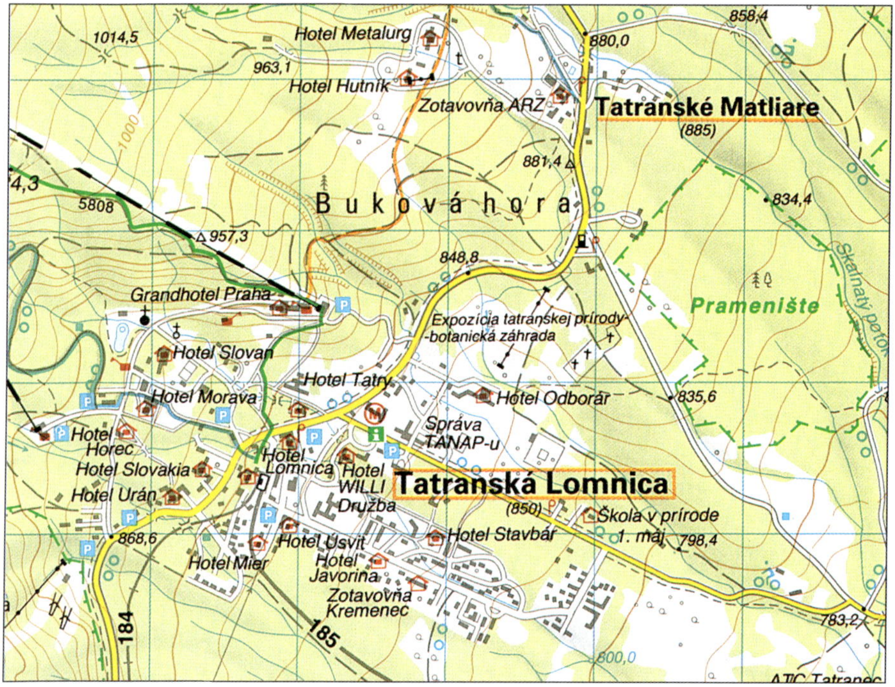

Freedom walkers are still in the vicinity of extensive forest parkland, inviting the tourist to rest under the crowns of huge spruce trees. Encounters with playful squirrels are not uncommon. At the end of the moderately ascending road there is the slender tower of the Evangelical **church** built in 1902. On the right hand side of the road one can pick out the Roman-Catholic **church**, a simple building dating from 1900. The road bending to the right continues in front of the luxurious building of the **Grand Hotel Prague**, behind which is the **lower station of the funicular to Lomnický štít peak**. Returning to the cross-roads in front of the church one can continue south-west. The path beside the **Slovan hotel** and the sanatorium **Morava** leads to the next cross-roads. The road bending between the **pension Sasanka** and a stylish **Fiaker bar** heads to the lower station of the **funicular to the Skalnaté Pleso lake**. The road continues to bend near the **sport area Jamy** and joins the road Cesta slobody. A path behind the Morava hotel heads to one of the most beautiful spots in Tatranská Lomnica. The meadow near the Morava hotel offers a wonderful view of the silhouette of the Lomnický and Kežmarský štít peaks towering above the white building of this trade union sanatorium. This classical landscape motif often appears on postcards. The path carries on across the forest park to the Cesta slobody road, behind which there is the biggest group of buildings gathered around the Lomnica railway station. This pleasant walk can be concluded with a cup of coffee in the friendly atmosphere of the coffee room of the oldest hotel, Lomnica, or in other nearby stylish bars.

Tatranská Lomnica is today the principal centre of winter and summer sport in the eastern part of the High Tatras and offers a wide variety of choice. Besides hiking and mountaineering, there is downhill skiing, cross-country skiing, snowboarding, skating, swimming, tennis, minigolf and cycling.

A trip to **Lomnický štít peak** by chair lift is among the most attractive adventures for tourists and, indeed, enjoys the popularity of the public. It reaches in only a few minutes the differential height 1,700 m and carries tourists to a height of 2,632 m above sea level. The only higher point in the Tatras, even throughout the whole Carpathians, is the Gerlachovský štít peak (2,655 m) situated about 7 km south-east, which can be easily recog-

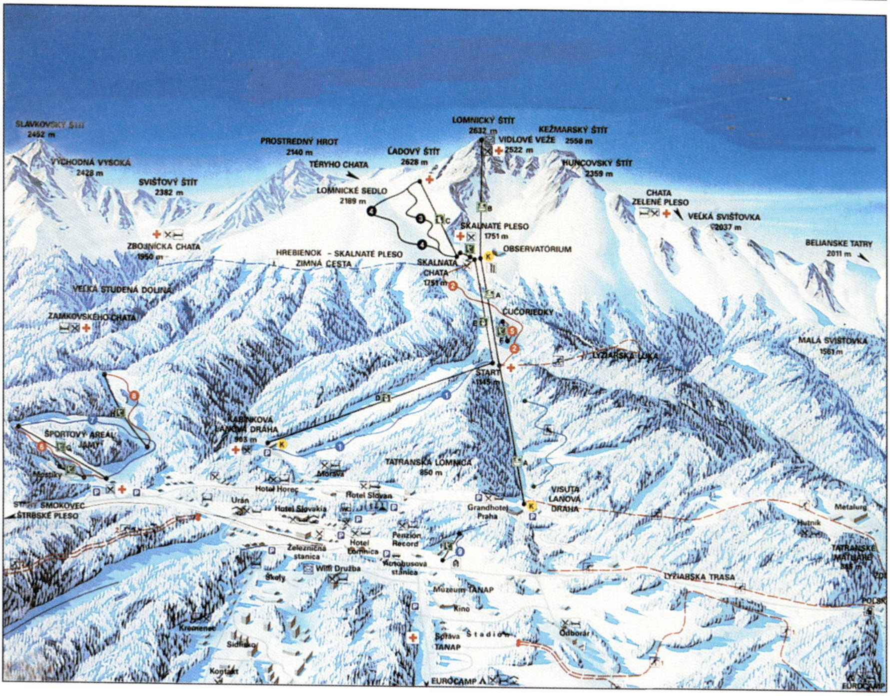

nised for its unusually bevelled summit. In fine weather, from the top of the Lomnický štít peak, you can experience a unique panoramic view over the whole area. If the visibility is good, one can see over the Belianske Tatry mountains, the unending Polish plains, while in the opposite direction the human eye can perceive perhaps a fifth of the Slovak territory. But if the weather is not agreeable, and this is only too often at this altitude, the disappointed tourist will be surrounded by a milk-white mist, obscuring even the meteorological apparatuses placed right below the ledge. Regular meteorological measurements have been carried out at the Lomnický štít peak since 1940. After a short break at the end of the Second World War the work of the station was resumed on January 1, 1947 and the station has supplied valuable data on extreme climatic conditions, in this high-mountain environment, ever since. It is the highest located working place in Slovakia. Since the 1950's the meteorological station has been accompanied by a new building for astronomers, employed at the laboratory of physics of cosmic radiation and a coronal station of the Institute of Astronomy belonging to the Slovak Academy of Sciences.

Dr. Robert Townson and the Lomnický štít peak:

The Lomnický štít peak was long taken to be the highest mountain in the Tatras and the interest in conquering it was ever apparent. Possibly some of the brave chamois hunters scaled its heights in earlier times, but the oldest known testimony about a successful ascent was written by Dr. Robert Townson. He included it in his book Travels to Old Hungary published in London in 1797. The first attempt by this English physician, geographer and traveller made from the valley of Zelené pleso lake failed. However, the relentless scientist returned to Stará Lesná, where he hired a horse and two guides among the local chamois hunters, and on August 14, 1793 the small group made a camp in Ohnisko, in the Malá Studená dolina valley. In the afternoon Dr. Towson left for the Päť Spišských plies (Five Spiš lakes) and came back to the camp in the evening. The next day, as the weather was bad, Dr. Townson devoted his time to botany. The third day saw an improvement in the weather and the group began their ascent. The scholarly foreigner carried a cumbersome barometer, but in spite of this he and his guides reached as far as the Lomnické sedlo saddle, where they encountered

thick cloud. The guides first refused to continue, but Dr. Towson persuaded them to carry on with the ascent. After some more trouble they finally stood on the top of the "Granddad", as the Spiš people familiarly nickname the peak. Townson's barometer recorded 2,882 yards equivalent to 2,644 meters. The measurement was only 12 meters awry!

The spruce forest over Tatranská Lomnica is ideal for agreeable and physically undemanding hiking, along the well maintained and marked footpaths. A blue-marked path points tourists comfortably towards the **waterfalls of the Studený potok**. It continues for about one kilometre from the funicular station over the pension Sasanka, tracing a route which is accompanied by the discrete humming of the lift. Then the path bends to a thick forest passing numerous little clearings. After an hour and half of easy walking the path reaches a crossroads of the marked footpaths, near the central four cascading **waterfalls** of the Studený potok brook. These waterfalls are among the most frequently visited in the Tatras and form a complex system of multi-terraced cascades. The upper, called **Obrovský vodopád** (The Giant waterfall) is well visible from the bridge on the Tatra main tourist path. White-foamed water tumbles down the trough passing between two rocks into a 20 meter profusion. The name of the lower waterfall, **Trojitý vodopád**, in the Hungarian and German languages is rather poetic - "the waterfall of artists". It is hidden deep in the forest and because of this is seldom visited. Under the confluence of the Veľký and Malý Studený potok brooks there are another four waterfalls. The highest of them is the cascade of the **Malý vodopád waterfall**. At an altitude of 1,247 m there is the **Skrytý vodopád waterfall** and somewhat lower at 1,226 m above sea level is the lower end of the cascades of the **Veľký vodopád waterfall**. Its highest cascade is 13 metres. The Dlhý vodopád waterfall is also on the Studený potok brook, immediately opposite the Bilíkova chata cottage in Hrebienok and is accessible by a yellow-marked path leading to the small community of Tatranská Lesná.

The majority of tourists try as quickly as possible to get above the upper timber line and to dedicate themselves to hiking passing the extensive dwarf pine growths and the rocky terrain. In Tatranská Lomnica there are two funiculars to the Skalnaté Pleso lake. The station mid way up the funicular's track, and the end station of the other cabin funicular, coincide on the moraine ridge of the Skalnaté pleso lake at an altitude of 1,751 m above sea level. The first tourists and treasure hunters started to ascent to the Skalnatá dolina valley during the second half of the 17th century. At the beginning they approached from Starý Smokovec, as the path from Tatranská Lomnica originated later in 1894. In the second half of the 1930's the several thousand years' silence, existing under the southern wall of the Lomnický štít peak, was shattered by the noise of the construction of the funicular. Simultaneously, in 1937, at the Skalnaté pleso lake, the building of the highest situated Tatra community was started. Beside the Skalnatá chata cottage, built on the foundations of older tourist shelters, named Skalnaté ohnisko and Kaverna, a group of buildings connected with the funicular stations and the Encián hotel were erected. Inconsiderate activity on sensitive landscape of a moraine, around the Skalnaté pleso

Left: Obrovský vodopád waterfall
Right: Zamkovského chata cottage

lake caused serious damage, resulting in significant water loss and threatening the disappearance of the lake. Despite damage limitation measures the level of the water continues to oscillate.

The **national nature reserve Skalnatá dolina valley** belongs to the smallest of the Tatra valleys, but as far as beauty is concerned it can compete with any of them. Its principal assets are the incomparable peaks of Lomnický štít (left) and Kežmarský štít (right) and in the background the notched top of the Vidly mountain. The highest rock terrace in the valley is called **Cmiter** (Cemetery). Perhaps the shepherds invented this unusual name, associating the silence and solitude of the valley under the Vidly mountain, with that of a rural cemetery. The majestic tranquillity of Cmiter is contrasted today with the noise brought by the "wind" from under the Lomnické sedlo saddle, where every winter there are hundreds of skiers present until the late spring months. After seeing the rather overcrowded environs of the Skalnaté pleso lake one can descend, via the scarcely visited blue-signed path, to the silence of the scree areas, the dwarf pine and spruce forest. The path leads below the **observatory of the Institute of Astronomy of the S.A.S**. with two typical rotating domes of the astronomic telescopes. Then it continues in a north-easterly direction. Short stops offer an occasion to admire the beautiful scenery. A look back reveals the view of the massive Lomnický štít peak from a seldom photographed angle. Equally interesting are the open views to the Popradská kotlina basin, the bottom of which is situated thousand meters below. Passing the **Huncovská dolina valley** the path descends to a shallow **saddle** under the **Malá Svišťovka mountain** (1,525 m) and further on it steeply descends to the forest. Making a large turn it heads over the **Vyhliadka mountain** (1,202 m) to the middle station of the funicular called Štart. Its name reminds us that this was the place where the races on the oldest bobsled track, built in 1908 over the Lomnica Grand Hotel, used to begin. A green-marked path from **Štart** leads the tourists to Tatranská Lomnica, a walk lasting about half an hour.

The hiking part of the trip begins at Skalnaté Pleso lake (1,751 m) which is possible to access by one of the two funiculars from Lomnica. The route of the trip coincides at its first section with the red-marked arterial, or main tourist path magistrála in the direction of Hrebienok. The track first passes the dwarf pine and maintains a south-easterly direction up to **Lomnická vyhliadka** (1,525 m), a spot with a wonderful view of the principal aim of the trip – the Veľká and Malá Studená dolina valleys. Later the path bends to the north-west and moderately descends into the forest. After more than a hour's walk it reaches the cross-roads, where the blue-marked path is to be chosen. After several meters there is the first opportunity to take refreshment in **Zamkovského chata cottage** (1,475 m). The cottage was built by a well-known Tatra climber, a mountain guide, and former administrator of the Téryho chata cottage, Štefan Zamkovský (1908-1961). The cottage was nationalised in 1951 and its name was changed to chata kapitána Nálepku (The Cottage of Captain Nálepka). Nálepka was a partisan commander killed in 1943 near the Ukraine city of Ovruč. In 1993 the cottage was again privatised by Zamkovský's grandson Stanislav Tichý, who restored its original name.

The not too distant **Malá Studená dolina valley** is a typical terrace-like glacial valley of the Tatras. It won the attribute Malá (Small) mainly because it is smaller than its twin, the Veľká Studená dolina valley. The lower threshold of the Malá Studená dolina valley is 130 m high and is

situated under Zamkovského chata cottage and its name is Schodíky, over which flows the Obrovský vodopád waterfall. Above the cottage a low moraine ridge cuts the valley, and over the upper threshold, 200 m high, the winding hiking track leads on. Jazerná stena, which is the name of the upper threshold, is divided into the Malý svah and Veľký svah slopes. Mountaineers know them under the name of the Veľký hang and the Malý hang. Studený potok brook passes the Jazerná steps by the Zlatý vodopád waterfall and over it, at an altitude of more than 2,000 m the valley expands into a system of glacial basins, known under the common name of the basin of the Päť Spišských plies. The path between the cottages of Zamkovský's and Téry's ascends reaching a differential height of 540 m. An averagely fit tourist can make this section in about 2 hours. A typical U-shaped transversal cut in the valley is closed in by two high cleft mountain ridges. On the right side there is the Lomnický hrebeň ridge and on the left the Prostredný hrebeň ridge, forming a separate body between the two Studená valleys. A reward for the tiresome ascent to Jazerná stena is refreshment taken in **Téryho chata cottage** (2,015 m), affording a fascinating view of the natural amphitheatre at the end of Malá Studená dolina valley. The idea to build a tourist cottage at the upper terrace of Malá Studená dolina valley was fathered by the famous pioneer of Tatra mountaineering, Dr. Edmund Téry (1856-1917). In Banská Štiavnica, where he lived, he was known as the "physician of the poor". Dr. Téry founded the Tatra Association which obtained exclusive rights to any building activity in the Malá Studená dolina valley. The designer and builder of the high-mountain cottage was the architect Gedeon Majunke of Spišská Sobota. The cottage was ceremoniously opened on August 21, 1889.

The basin called Kotlina Piatich Spisškých plies is surrounded by a range of Tatra peaks which are amongst the highest in the region. Four of them are higher than 2,600 m. The top point of the Lomnický štít peak turns to the basin by its western wall, which is traversed by a classic climbing route known as "the hockey stick". The highest mountain of the main Tatra ridge, **Ľadový štít peak** (2,627 m), lies north-east. The Žltá stena peak (2,169 m) which is distinctly triangular shaped and covered by an eternal shadow, juts out of the steep sides of the Prostredný hrot Peak (2,440 m) with one of its faces called **Žltá stena** or Yellow Wall (2,169 m). It is not an extremely high face, but is very exposed and a favourite amongst mountaineers. Sitting in front of the Téryho chata cottage with a cup of tea or hot grog one can observe from quite a close distance the mountaineers climbing the rock. Metaphorically speaking the Žltá stena provides some kind of natural stage where the mountaineers represent the actors and onlookers the grateful audience.

A green and yellow-marked path proceeds from the Téryho chata cottage to a little basin under the Sedielko saddle and the Široká veža peak (2,461 m). Resting places along the serpentines provide opportune moments for contemplation and taking in the lakes called **Päť Spišských plies**. The lakes are simply named after their number (Five Spiš Lakes) and their situation, and all of them are typical cirque lakes. The largest is the Veľké Spišské pleso lake with an area of 3.48 ha. In the basin under the Sedielko saddle our route of ascent diverges from the green-marked path to Sedielko,

Left: Kotlina Piatich Spišských plies basin
Right: The mountain rescue service in action

the highest (2,372 m) mountain saddle accessible to tourists in the Tatras. Beyond **Sedielko** the path continues across the Javorová dolina valley to Tatranská Javorina. A yellow-marked path leads over the screes and snow fields to the second highest situated saddle, **Priečne sedlo** (2,352 m). The ascent to the saddle from the Téryho chata cottage takes about one and a half hours. The final section of the path is equipped with safety chains facilitating the passage. The Priečne sedlo saddle offers a good view of the **Modré pleso lake**, the highest situated permanent lake (2,190 m) in the Tatras. It acquired its name because of the deep blue colour of its water and is enhanced by the shadows of the surrounding peaks. Its area is 0.4 ha and the depth of the water is 4.5 m. Under the southern slopes of the **Baranie rohy mountain** (2,526 m) on the opposite side of Malá Studená dolina valley there is an even higher situated lake the small Baranie pleso. However, because it sometimes dries up entirely it is not considered the highest located lake in the Tatras.

A partially limited view of the Priečne sedlo saddle, to the south-west, provides tourists, approaching from the other side, the first opportunity to see the **Veľká Studená dolina valley**. The descent to the **Zbojnícka chata cottage** (1,960 m) takes about one and a half hours. The Zbojnícka chata cottage was built by the government only in 1907 and used as a hunting cottage. This one-room stone building has since been partially rebuilt and after three years opened to tourists. Polish mountaineers called it "the morgue" because of its cold and damp interior. In 1924 it was made more comfortable by the Club of the Czechoslovak Tourists and now there is a permanent warden on duty. The most recent reconstruction of the cottage increased its lodging and catering capacity. The proper name of the cottage (The Robber's Cottage) is set amongst the natural landmarks of the Veľká Studená valley: the Zbojnícke plesá lakes and the Zbojnícka kopa mountain. The highest parts of the Veľká Studená dolina valley are surprisingly spacious. The wide end of the valley is divided into six what the experts call glacial kettles. On their surface numerous traces of intense glacial activity can be seen. The glacier filled the Veľká Studená dolina valley during the last Glacial period and left there numerous glacier trenches, bulging and smoothed by glacial stones and hollowed-out lake basins. Today numerous lakes fill these basins. There are 26 small lakes in the Veľká Studená

dolina valley, representing one sixth of the total number of lakes in the Tatras, a figure which relates to their number and not their volume of water, which is a much lower percentage representation. The area of the largest **Ľadové pleso lake** is 1.72 ha. But in the recent past there was in the Veľká Studená dolina valley probably the largest lake in the Tatras, covering an area of at least 60 ha (three times larger than the Veľké Hincovo pleso lake). It has since disappeared presumably because of the break in the moraine (moraine is an accumulation of earth and stones carried and finally deposited by the glacier) dike by the Studený potok brook. A blue-marked path leads from the Zbojnícka chata cottage to the Tatra main tourist path, or magistrála. The trough section of the valley borders the Prostredný hrebeň ridge and on the opposite side the afternoon shadow of the fork of the Slavkovský štít peak, with the highest mountain of the whole valley, the **Bradavica peak** (2,476 m) falls over the bottom of the Veľká Studená dolina valley. The descent to the rack railway in Hrebienok does not under normal conditions take more than 3 hours.

TATRANSKÉ MATLIARE (885-920 m, population 125) is the first community on the road Cesta slobody, between Tatranská Lomnica and the Tatranská kotlina basin, through which flows the Skalnatý potok brook. It is only 1.5 km away from its larger south-western neighbour Tatranská Lomnica.

Not far from this community there used to be, in the 14th century, an estate called Metler or Maklar belonging to a Veľká Lomnica landowner. The colonists who arrived here from Tyrol, lived in a high-mountain village called Matrei. The historical documents of the town Kežmarok of 1326, mention the community of Martyrumfalua situated on the bank of the Skalnatý potok brook. The estate disappeared in 1360, but the pastures and forests in the region preserved the name reminding the Tyrolese settlers of home. The original name Matreier Laren (mountain pastures of Matreierians) later developed to Matlaren and the Slovakized form "Matliare". The modern history of Tatranské Matliare dates back to the 19th century, when the gamekeeper's lodge of the landowners' association was built here. One of the owners, Matej Loisch, also constructed beside the lodge a hunting cottage. Later it was opened to the public and a new tourist hotel called Skalnatý potok (Steinbach) was added. Before the First World War other buildings, like the villa Tatra, the spa house and villa Ratzenberg emerged. During the war there was a **military sanatorium** established in the provisional wooden barracks, and in 1928 the luxurious Esplanade Hotel was opened, serving also as a sanatorium, and after the war the Esplanade became the central building of military sanatoriums. In 1956 treatment for pulmonary diseases moved to a new sanatorium in Nová Polianka, but Matliare still kept its role of providing therapeutical and medical service to the army. In the years between 1982 and 1985 Tatranské Matliare was expanded by new trade union **convalescent homes, the Metalurg and the Hutník**, administered by the giant metallurgical works in Košice. Both buildings are situated off the Cesta slobody road in a quiet neighbourhood of **Loisch's spring**, a summer holiday resort, more than hundred years old, named after the founder of Tatranské Matliare.

The forests under Tatranské Matliare cover the **national nature reserve, Pramenište** declared so in 1991, on an area of 45.6 ha. The reserve protects the best preserved old pine-birch forests in the Tatra regions. As it contains some critically endangered plant species it is not open to the public.

Tatranské Matliare offers similar possibilities to tourists as neighbouring Tatranská Lomnica, which one can reach on foot in about 20 minutes, beginning near the Hutník Hotel (a yellow-marked path).

The location of this community facilitates easier access to the valley of Kežmarská Biela voda, to the cottage Chata pri Zelenom plese and the Jahňací štít peak (blue marked, see page 118)

KEŽMARSKÉ ŽĽABY (902 m, population 21) is a small holiday resort on the road Cesta slobody, about 4 km away from Tatranská Lomnica and 5 km from the Tatranská kotlina basin.

The name Kežmarské Žľaby is older than the community itself. Before the first buildings appeared the land served as pasture for the communal cattle. The communal land, the property of Kežmarok, originally reached as far as the valley of the Zelené pleso lake. The first building erected here, in 1885, was the gamekeeper's lodge available also for tourists. After three years a simple log hut hostel and several additional houses were built here. The community originated at the place of a former shepherd's hut with a mineral water spring in the lot. The name of Kežmarské Žľaby (Troughs of Kežmarok) derives from the wooden troughs the mineral water was channelled to. However, a part of the community burnt down in 1933 and the preserved houses became a part of a **recreation resort for young people Dukla**. Besides two older gamekeeper's houses two new buildings belonging to the TANAP administration were also built here. The rather remote location of Kežmarské Žľaby is the reason why it has remained such a small community.

About one kilometre before arriving in Kežmarské Žľaby (from Tatranské Matliare) the Cesta Slobody road is cut by the Kežmarská Biela voda brook. A nearby seclusion is called Biela voda where used to stand the private pension of a businessman called Rudolf Parenčár of Kežmarok, but it burnt down in 1948. Near the Cesta Slobody road, at the edge of the **national nature reserve Mokrina**, one comes across the **Kyslý prameň** – a mineral water spring. The reserve was established in 1991 on an area of 160 ha with the purpose of protecting in the past widely extended pea bog vegetation on the foreland of the Tatras. This reserve is

Right: Jastrabia veža peak

among of the most valuable nature localities of Central Europe and is closed to the public.

Biela voda is the best starting point for the **Kežmarská Biela voda valley**. Starting at the bus stop called Biela voda the moderately ascending yellow-marked path leads across a forest. Where the path, or rather road, is wide enough it is used for supplying the Brnčalova chata cottage by horse wagons. After an hour of easy walking one reaches a water spring at **Šalviový prameň**, 1,100 m above sea level. It took its name (Sage Spring) from the abundance of sage plants (*Salvia officinalis*) growing around the spring, which are said to grow only next to "sound" water. The **Tardíkova chata cottage** used to stand near the spring, built by one Július Tardík as a private pension in 1927. Passing the spring a yellow-marked path ascends a moderate slope preceding the **Kovaľčíkova poľana, an alpine meadow**. The stony road ascends up to the dwarf-pine stage and offers a wonderful view over the valley of the Zelené pleso lake, the next stop on the trip. After a three hour walk from Biela voda walkers can relax and enjoy the beauty of high-mountain nature with a cup of hot tea served in the **chata pri Zelenom plese cottage**, which is 1,551m above sea level. Many know the cottage under the name of the Brnčalova chata cottage, which is approximately one hundred years old though it was not the first cottage built in the valley of the Zelené pleso lake. As early as 1888 the Egidova chata cottage used to stand on the northern bank of the Zelené pleso lake, but it burnt down after three years. Another fire also completely destroyed the second Egidova chata cottage. The third cottage near the Zelené pleso lake was walled and was opened on August 27, 1897 bearing the name of Archduke Fridrich. After the First World War it was open all year round and between the wars it was twice reconstructed and expanded. The name of the cottage was changed to Brnčalova. Brnčal was a teacher and mountaineer who died in the Malá Zmrzlá dolina valley and finally in 1992 the cottage resorted to its old name – the Chata pri Zelenom plese cottage. The beautiful landscape around the cottage is enhanced by the picturesque **Zelené pleso lake** (1,545 m). With its area of 1.7 ha it is the largest lake in this easternmost part of the High Tatras and has been enjoyed by visitors since the 17th century. The name of the lake (zelené = green) is associated with the green spots produced by the water springs at the bottom of the lake. The green colour of the lake encouraged the fantasy of brave treasure seekers, who probably invented the legend of the Jastrabia veža peak (The Goshawk Tower).

The Legend of the Goshawk Tower:

In the distant past a valuable stone glowed on the steep peak of the invincible Goshawk Tower. Many brave men longed to reach it but nobody knew how to conquer the steep rocky walls of the peak. Finally one young man who promised to bring the gem to his beloved girl as a wedding present attempted the feat. But at the very moment when he grasped the stone the guardian spirit of Tatra treasures shook the rocky wall and the unfortunate young man fell into the lake below the Goshawk Tower. The water swallowed him up with the green gem still in his hand, which has forever gleamed deep under the water, and is the reason why the lake is called the Green Lake. Some interpreters of the folk legend add that the hero of the legend was the young count Štefan Thököly, son of the landlord of Kežmarok castle.

Any view from Zelené pleso lake is fascinating. Standing with your back turned to the Jastrabia veža peak (2,137 m) you get a view of the huge rock face. Only by bending your head well back can your eyes appreciate the highest perpendicular rock face of the Tatras on the northern side of the **Malý Kežmarský štít peak** (2,513 m). The height of the rock face measured from the bottom to the top is 900 m. A triangle-shaped granite monolith is transversally cut by an oblique rocky ledge called the "German ladder". There are seven very difficult mountaineering tracks at the rock face. The most demanding of them is "superdiretissima", leading across the middle of the rock wall. The first mountaineers to climb it were Pavol Pochylý and Jiří Unger-Zrust in 1967. West of the lake are the **Veľká** and **Malá Zmrzlá dolina valleys**. Both of them belong to the highest situated valleys in the Tatras. Surrounding peaks cast shadows over these valleys for almost the whole day, which is why the snow there thaws more slowly and lasts until deep into summer. Until recently the Veľká Zmrzlá dolina valley was a favourite place for summer skiing. In pursuit of the "firn" snow it was necessary to climb over a high rocky threshold secured by iron chains, but now TANAP strictly forbids skiing off the marked ski tracks and skiing in the Veľká Zmrzlá dolina valley is no longer possible. The cottage at Zelené pleso lake is the best starting point for a high-mountain trek. For those who would like to reach the top of the Jahňací štít peak there still remains about two hours of a tiresome though undemanding ascent. A narrow yellow-marked path rises to the 200 m high threshold of the **Červená dolina valley** covered by dwarf pines, on its way to the **Červené pleso lake** (1,811 m). At 1,865 m the **Belasé pleso lake** is situated somewhat higher with a path transversing several troughs and ribs under the rocky ridge between the **Kolový** (2,418 m) and **Jahňací štít peaks** (2,229 m). The chains installed under the Kolové sedlo saddle help to pass a small rocky wall. The return trip from the top is possible only by the same track and lasts approximately four and half hours.

Jahňací štít peak:

Jahňací štít peak is the easternmost peak in the main High Tatra ridge. It is one of eight mountains accessible to the public in the Slovak part of the High Tatras. If the weather is fine it offers a wonderful panoramic view. Especially beautiful are the Belianske Tatry mountains, a silhouette of which can be seen in the north, behind the Kopské sedlo saddle. Under the Jahňací štít peak the shepherds of the villages, Spišská Belá and Rakúsy, used to graze which suggests that the origin of the name of the peak (jahňací = lamb) was invented by the shepherds themselves, who may have also been the poachers who chased here the lambs of chamois. Old records also quote the German form of the name Gemsenspitze (the Chamois Peak). The first known ascent to the Jahňací štít peak was accomplished by Dr. Robert Townson in 1793.

TATRANSKÁ LESNÁ (915 m, population 50) is a tiny holiday resort situated on the Cesta Slobody road near the point where it crosses the Studený potok brook. It lies about 2 km south-west of Starý Smokovec and 4 km north-east of Tatranská Lomnica.

Tatranská Lesná originated as one of the last Tatra communities in the inter-war period. In 1927 a construction of small family pensions began in the territory of Stará Lesná. For three years these buildings had no geographical denomination, and only when, in 1930, and the first of Dr. Jurecký's children's sanatorium was built did the newly founded community assume the name related to that of the adjacent Tatra village – Stará Lesná. The children's sanatorium recieved in turn the name **The Children's Paradise** and together with some additional buildings, constructed later, it became an **international centre of child recreation**. The older houses existed above the Cesta slobody road, but the new buildings were started below it, near the village of Stará Lesná. A group of cottages and hotels belonging to various firms was constructed at the edge of the forest, close to the limit of the national park. Stará Lesná is a good example of an environmentally friendly development in the Tatra region where the building activities should be concentrated in the sub Tatra area, though connected with the Tatra region by means of efficient and ecological transport.

Very good connections between Tatranská Lesná, Starý Smokovec and Tatranská Lomnica allow the tourists to enjoy the options of hiking and or winter sports.

A yellow-marked path leads directly from Tatranská Lesná along the right bank of the Studený potok brook to the vodopády Studeného potoka waterfalls (1,240 m) (see page 112).

Ždiar and its environs

The Ždiar region is the only one which lies in the northern part of the Východné Tatry mountains. Its northern boundary constitutes the main ridge of the Spišská Magura mountains. In the west it is limited by the state borderline with Poland heading of Lysá Poľana southward up to the Bielovodská dolina valley and along the Žabí hrebeň ridge up to the top of the Rysy Mt. The southern boundary of Ždiar is formed by the main ridge of the High Tatras and the Belianske Tatry mountains between the Rysy Mt. and Tatranská Kotlina.

ŽDIAR (896 m, population 1,300) is a typical Goral community, a living museum of folk architecture. Its beauty is enhanced by its position amid a lovely natural setting between the cliffs of the Belianske Tatry mountains and the Spišská Magura mountains covered by thick woods. Ždiar stretches over the Podtatranská brázda furrow, the Cesta slobody road of Tatranská Kotlina to Lysá Poľana and runs parallel to the axis of the community. The centre of the 6 km long community is about 13 km of the boundary cross point to Poland in Lysá Poľana and the shortest road of Ždiar to the district town of Poprad measures 34 km.

The old acts of 1282 quote the name of the region where much later Ždiar originated as *Stragar*. The origin of this antiquated name is not known. Until 1470 the land belonged to Gallus-Kostroš and his heirs, the family Berzeviczy of Veľká Lomnica. In the second half of the 16th century the Biela brook valley was seasonally inhabited by shepherds and colliers, mostly during the summer. The presence of the colliers is proven by several places which conserve aspects of their activities. The serfs of the Lendak estate expanded their land by burning the forest. The procedure was called žiarenie (glowing) and that is where the community founded by a castle warden František Lužinský sometimes at the beginning of the 17th century, took its name of. A document dated 1773 cites the name *Ždyar*; however, in 1808 the name *Žjár*, closer to the original one, is quoted.

The Goral Zor:

Local folk tradition offers a more romantic explanation of the community's original name. In the

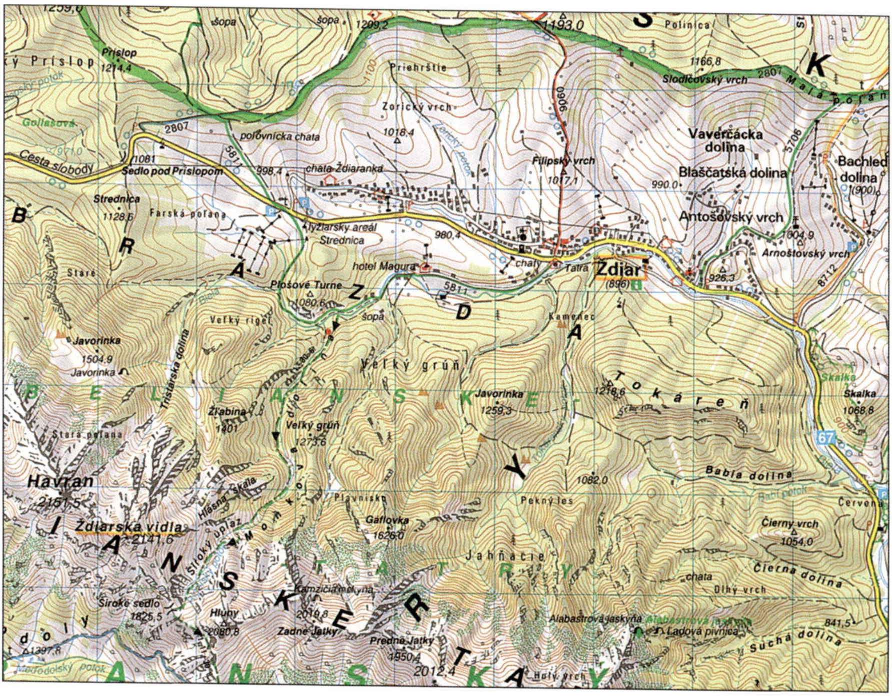

distant past the thick wood in the broad valley of Biela under the Belianske Tatry mountains was frequented by the people of nearby villages to make charcoal. Legend states that one of the colliers built in the middle of the forest a triangle shaped little hut. The only window of the hut was turned so that the light of the morning star entered the room. The star, called in Goral dialect Zor, was the source of inspiration of the name for the community that later sprang around the old collier's hut. The Ždiar people speaking their Goral dialect still refer to their community as Zor.

The community of Ždiar originated during the Sholtys (sholtys = mayor) colonisation based on Wallachian privilege. Initially 13 families arrived to the burnt out forest. The territory chosen for the settlement was divided to 13 equal parts. To mark the division the brook was used as an imaginary axis around which 13 equal clearings called záruby were made and they became the limits of the individual lots. The large area around the village allowed for additional lots and the oldest inhabitants of Ždiar had comparably abundant land. That is how was the community extended to its total length of six kilometres. During the second wave of colonisation the repartition continued and involved the lateral valleys and contiguous hills. In new lots communities like the Bachledova dolina valley, the Antošovský vrch mountain, the Pavlovská dolina valley, the Blasčacká dolina valley, the Bartušovská dolina valley, the Monkova dolina valley, and the Sladičovský vrch mountain originated and are under the administration of the community. Until the end of the 19th century one-roomed wooden houses were built. The oldest buildings were used only seasonally. They were shepherds', loggers' or colliers' log huts with inner fire places, one door, and lacking a ceiling or windows. They were simultaneously used as stables for young cattle or sheep. When their owners started to use them the whole year round, they added a little window or ceiling making the buildings more habitable. The corner where the cattle use to stand later became the basis for a separately built stable. The original buildings were progressively recon-

Left: Ždiar houses
Right: Ždiar costumes

structed and adapted for tourism after the First World War. One-wing buildings were changed to two or more winged houses for the sake of obtaining more space and the possibility to lodge the tourists. The builders of such houses found inspiration of Polish tourist regions, for instance in Zakopane. The original architectural style of the community was partially disturbed only after the Second World War when conservationists actually neglected the preservation of the precious old log houses in Ždiar. In spite of it, the community preserved its prevailing original character with a minimum representation of the modern brick houses. The four most valuable groups of folk buildings were in 1977 declared the **monument reserve of folk architecture**. Three-roomed wooden houses, making together with farmsteads, an enclosed atrium houses with a central courtyard are typical examples. Wooden houses with characteristic joints painted in blue and with folk ornaments can be seen here. Even some more recent buildings observe some elements of the traditional architecture, such as the favourite **stylish restaurant of Ždiarsky dom**. In the 1970's and 1980's Ždiar progressively became one of the largest tourist centres of the Slovak Tatras, as far as the accommodation capacity was concerned, citing "the biggest hotel of the High Tatras". There were seasons when in the houses of Ždiar as many as 3,000 visitors were lodged in summer. Before 1989 the great majority of the Ždiar clientele consisted of tourists coming of the former Eastern Germany. Because of the numerous cars of German provenance, almost exclusively all the famous two-stroke Trabants, parked next to the wooden houses of Ždiar, the community was mockingly called "Trabantovo". German tourists still come to Ždiar nowadays but in other, far more luxurious forms of transport.

Ždiar is famous for its folk arts and traditions. The time when the villagers put on their folk costumes on Sundays or feast days continued until not so long ago. Today they can be seen only at the shows of the folk ensembles or in the **Museum** called **Ždiarska izba.** Opportunities to put on wonderful folk costumes of the Goral people and to take part in a staged traditional wedding are very popular among tourists.

Ždiarska izba, tel.: 0969/49 81 35
Opening hours: Mon – Sun, 9:00-16:00h

The folk costumes of Ždiar:

The Ždiar folk costume belongs to Goral ethnicity. The community benefited of being located on the important trade route between Spišská Belá and Nový Targ in the sense that they could always purchase special fabrics used for the details of their folk costumes that have made them distinct among the poorer costumes of other Goral communities. A typical part of the Ždiar female folk costume is the so called ranťuch – a straight belt of thinly woven linen of very fine flaxen threads with inter-woven patterns of a thick cotton thread. The married women dressed their heads with caps set high on their head crowns inserted with pads around which the hair was pleated. The cap was decorated by glittering and colourful strings. When worn outside it was covered by a scarf giving the women of Ždiar their typical head-dress. Men of Ždiar usually wore trousers called portky, a jacket of home-made roughly woven woolen fabric, a fur vest and a shirt of home-made thick linen. Especially the lamb vests called lambaky are abundantly embroidered by ornaments. The masculine Goral

folk costumes are easily recognisable by a typical Goral hat called kapelušok. It is always dressed with a piece of eagle's feather.

In 1925 the first folk ensemble was founded. Its activities were perpetuated by four men of Ždiar, Matej Pitoňák, Ján Pitoňák, Jozef Pitoňák, and Vojtech Sabanský who founded the **folk group** called **Ždiaran**. Progressively they became one of the outstanding folk groups active in Slovakia. They present original songs, dances, customs and shepherds's plays of sub Tatra provenance in numerous big folk festivals throughout Slovakia and abroad. Also the folk wood-carvers of Ždiar are widely respected for their art. In the same year when the first folk ensemble was founded the famous Czech photographer and expert in folk arts, Karol Plicka visited Ždiar. Besides unique photographs of the simple countrymen in the authentic setting of the charming Ždiar landscape he also made here many images of the lyrical shots for his famous film *The Singing Land*.

Left: The entrance to the Monkova dolina valley

Opportunities for tourists coming to Ždiar are considerably limited at present as many of the marked footpaths in the Belianske Tatry mountains are closed. The reason is the need to revive the disturbed ecological balance in this particular area of the mountain range. In 1991 an area of 5,408 ha of this unique territory was declared a **national nature reserve of the Belianske Tatry mountains**. The only accessible path is the green-marked one tracing the edge of the reserve and continuing by a **educational tourist path, Monkova dolina valley-Kopské sedlo saddle**. The path was opened in the summer of 1993 and crosses the Belianske Tatry mountains over a total length of 6 km reaching an elevation difference of about 900 m. It is accessible only in the summer season, in a one-way direction of the bottom and subject to an entrance fee. There are six stops on the track presenting the sights and places of interests of the Belianske Tatry mountains. Information on the stops is provided by leaflets. However, lovers of hiking do not have to avoid Ždiar. There are some interesting walks to the opposite side, with an easily accessible **mountain range of Spišská Magura**. The ascent to the main ridge of the mountain range is worth it for the

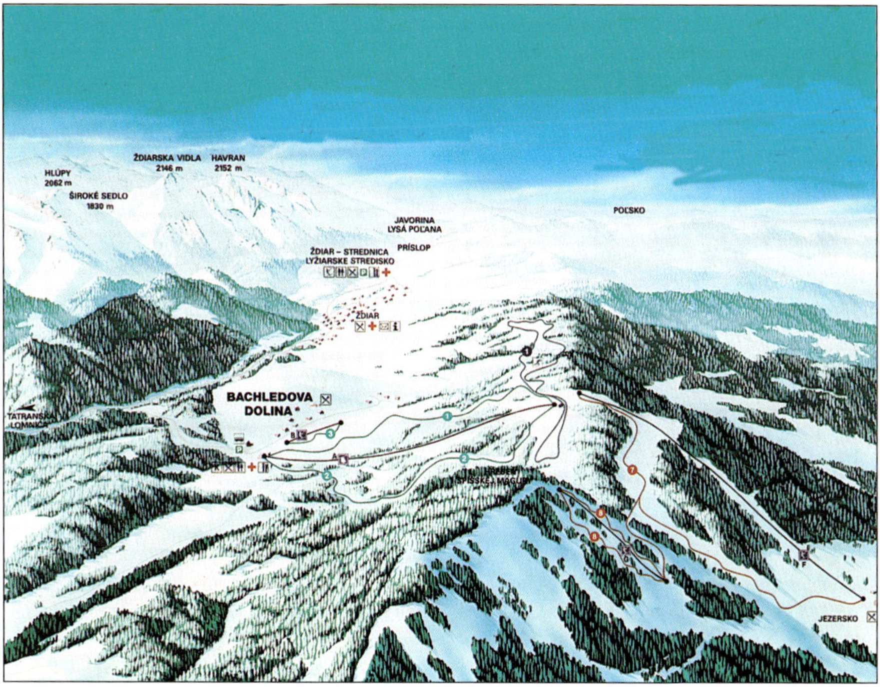

unique view of the panorama of the Belianske Tatry mountains over the typical community of Ždiar. Two of the marked footpaths crossing the main Magura ridge lead to Jezerské jazero lake, or to one of the Osturnianske lakes in the Zamagurie region. Summer tourists lodged in Ždiar prefer the slopes of Spišská Magura mountains as they offer the occasion to pick various forest fruit. They are famous for blue-coloured "carpets" of blackberries. In turn the winter in the Spišská Magura mountains means ideal conditions for cross-country skiing. Passes over the prolonged and rather flat Magura mountain ridges with slight different elevations are suitable also for less experienced skiers. Access to the main Magura ridge is facilitated by a **chair-lift** starting in the **Bachledova dolina valley**.

TATRANSKÁ KOTLINA (760 m, population 260) is the easternmost and simultaneously the lowest situated Tatra community. It lies under the eastern end of the ridge of the Belianske Tatry mountains, near the most pronounced curve of the Cesta Slobody road, 8 km of Ždiar and 10 km of Spišská Belá.

Tracing the origin of the name of Tatranská Kotlina one has to go well back into history, to the period preceding the origin of the community. The valley of Biela brook was always called Kotlina (Basin). However, it should be considered more of "a canyon" because it is a considerably tapered down part of the valley starting under Ždiar and ending below Tatranská Kotlina. The canyon of the Biela is squeezed between the slopes of the Bujačí vrch mountain (1,947 m) and Tokárňa (1,219 m) on the western side and Pálenica (1,175 m) on eastern side. There are two nature reserves here, both of them established in 1991 and both closed to the public. Closer to Tatranská Kotlina is the nature reserve of Pálenica extending over an area of 2,951 ha. It enshrines thermophile relic plant communities with numerous endemites and karst formations. Further in the north is the nature reserve of Skalka. In an area of 36.2 ha a natural structure of forest growths with abundant endemites are conserved. Tatranská Kotlina originated thanks to the opening of the Belianska jaskyňa cave in 1882. The founders of the community also intended to facilitate an easier access to the area of the Belianske Tatry mountains to the public. Before that there was the gamekeeper's house and a mill on the road of Lendak to Ždiar. In 1874 the Pole Kardoliňski founded here a settlement called Kardolin where the local stone-masons produced mill stones and cement. The community of Tatranská Kotlina was founded by the owner of the local land, the town of Spišská Belá. The first building of 1882 was a simple shelter for the guard of the Belianska jaskyňa cave, Ján Kohút. Nevertheless, the 1883 summer tourist season was opened by the community with a new restaurant and two hostels with 15 rooms. Before 1900 another 31 houses sprung up with 254 guest rooms for 370 guests. The well-to-do inhabitants of Tatranská Kotlina owned 13 villas. The entrance to the community had a decorated gate bearing a slogan that read "Barlangliget" (The Cave Paradise) which became the first official name of the holiday resort. The Germans living in the Spiš region changed it to Höhlenheim (The Cave Home). Finally, the name Kotlina used by the local Slovak population was widely used. The guide books sometimes cited the name Belianske Spa, because Kotlina also took up the function of a spa. In the centre of the community there was the **Kúpeľný dom** providing patients with water-cures and for a time advanced physical therapy in the form of gymnastics. The local Kasíno had a hall with catering facilities for 500 guests. The restaurant was occasionally used as a theatre. During the First World War Kotlina was a place where soldiers from the front recovered. After the war the town Spišská Belá sold the community to a businessman called Oldřich, who quickly passed it to a pharmacist by the name of Ctibor Zelený. He specialised in therapy of tuberculosis while serving also to the poorer patients covered by social security. The sanatorium of Dr. Zelený was called in the inter-war period "the railwaymen's sanatorium". After the Second World War the buildings were expanded and modernised and today they serve to the patients as a **Specialised Therapeutic Institute of Respiratory Disorders**. Tourists can find accommodation in the local **hostel Limba**.

Also the trip to Veľké Biele pleso lake, the final destination of the green-marked footpath, is interesting. The **Šumivý prameň spring** in a forest environment and 855 metres above sea level is the first stop. Near the place Čierna voda a blue-marked path separates and leads to the Kežmarské žľaby troughs. The green-marked path continues by moderately ascending serpentines to the easily accessible **Dolina Siedmich prameňov valley**. This comparably small Tatra valley is preferred by the botanists and lovers of the Tatra flora. Amid a beautiful limestone landscape one often runs into botanical excursions organised by the TANAP researchers or museum employees. This is often referred to as a natural botanical garden. Due to the limestone basis and the relative closeness of the valley that was not affected by glaciation, many rare endemic plant species grow here.

Erysimum wahlenbergii:

Along the footpath in the Dolina Siedmich prameňov valley a valuable Tatra endemite grows – Erysimum wahlenbergii. This plant, the name of which commemorates the Swedish botanist Göran Wahlenberg, (1780-1851) is one meter high. Its yellow flowers are similar to those of wild radish. This species occurs only in the Tatras, although a similar plant grows in the Austrian Alps.

An option for a short rest though without taking refreshment is offered by the **chata Plesnivec cottage** (1,209 m). It is the only cottage in the Belianske Tatry mountains and closed to the public since 1955. It is used by the employees of TANAP as a research base and stands on the site of a hut of the gold miner Drechsler of Austria, built as early as the mid-18th century. Before 1930 tourists used a shepherd's hut in the dolina Siedmich prameňov valley. The cottage standing there now was built by Tibor Gresch of Spišská Belá in 1932 and was confiscated by the government after the Second World War.

Tourists are particularly attracted by the Dolina Siedmich prameňov valley ending in an amphitheatre of snow white limestone rock faces called **Skalné vráta**. The footpath traverses the southern side of the Bujačí vrch mountain into the neighbouring Dolina Kežmarská Biela voda valley and heads to the end of the valley divided by several glacial cirques. After crossing the Napajadlo brook in the valley of Predné Meďodoly the path ascends through dwarf pine forest and across the threshold of the dolina Bielych plies valley bearing the curious name: Jerusalem. The landscape of the **Dolina Bielych plies valley** lying at the end of a valley system of the Kežmarská Biela voda is impressive and was frequently visited by shepherds and gold miners in the past. Under the cone-shaped Jahňací štít peak there are several lakes. The largest of them is Veľké Biele pleso lake and until recently there was the Kežmarská chata cottage on its shore.

Right: Belianska jaskyňa cave

It was built by soldiers commanded by general Votruba and that was the reason why it was initially called Votrubova cottage. In the autumn of 1942 it was pulled down and on same site a spacious two-storey cottage was built and called the **Kežmarská chata cottage**. In 1974 it was opened only for a couple of years when it was destroyed by fire. So far it has not been restored. Near the Veľké Biele pleso lake starts the longest Tatra footpath, the famous magistrála (see page 73). There are several options how to conclude the tour. Besides the return to Tatranská Kotlina by the same track one can continue along the main Tatra tourist path to the cottage at Zelené pleso lake and further to Kežmarské Žľaby troughs, or otherwise to Tatranské Matliare (see page 116)

Tourists are often interested in the **Belianska jaskyňa cave**. It is the only one accessible to public in the Tatras and situated in the northern slope of the Kobylí vrch mountain above the community of Tatranská Kotlina. The cave entrance is at an altitude of 885 metres above sea level. It was discovered by treasure-seekers in 1718 even though it is presumed that it was used as a dwelling for pre-historic people. The desire for wealth also led Michal Scholtz underground who confirmed his visit to the cave by a signature and date on the wall of the cavity called the Music Hall in the lower part of the cave. The discovery was kept a secret until August 5, 1881 when a forester named Július Husz, whilst hunting with one Johan Britz, noticed an opening between two rotten trees where a freezing draught was drawing. Equipped with a light and ropes they descended through the opening to a wall called Parnas in the Dome of the Discoverers. After this couple of speleologists another followed who discovered additional cave spaces. Thanks to their initiative the cave was opened to the public a year after its discovery. In spite of it being a rather tiring adventure and at the same time comparably dangerous, some 600 sightseers visited it in about three months.

Electric light in the Belianska jaskyňa cave:

The Belianska jaskyňa cave was well cared after by the citizens of Spišská Belá, whose efforts brought the introduction of electric light into the cave, and thus, on November 29, 1896, 165 bulbs were switched on. It was only twelve years after the discovery of the electric bulb by T. A. Edison. Electric power was supplied to the cave by a small power station built on the Biela brook. The entrance fee, then amounting to 80 groschen, was increased to one gulden and eighty groschen and three group visits were organised daily. The guide was obliged to make a tour around the cave even though there may have been only one visitor. At present sightseeing around the cave consists of a 1,001m long track and the visitor can see more than a half of the 1,752 m of discovered cave corridors.

PODSPÁDY (912 m, population 50) is a small Tatra community lying on the cross-roads of the Cesta slobody road and the Javorinka brook. They are situated 7 km of Ždiar and the 5.5 km of the boundary crossing into Poland in Lysá Poľana.

The name of the community (Podspády freely translated means "lying under steep slopes") illustrates its position between the steep northern slopes of the Muráň mountain (1,890 m) and the south-western slopes of the Repisko mountain (1,259 m). The name in Hungarian Zugó and the German Rausch are presumably connected with the ever-sounding roar of the Javorinka torrent. The contemporary community has sprung up around the gamekeeper's cottage built in the mid-19th century by the family of Horváth of Plaveč. Shortly after it was accompanied by a saw mill and in the years 1922-1936 a 13 km suspended cable lift transported the wood to and from the community of Lendak. It was used until a regular paved road leading to Podspády was constructed. At present in Podspády there are the **buildings of the TANAP administration, a saw mill, the hostel Muráň and an artistic wood-carving workshop**.

There are also two nature reserves in the vicinity of Podspády. The **nature reserve of Grapa** is situated on the slope of the highest mountain of the Spišská Magura mountain range, Repisko. It was established in 1991 on an area of 40.9 ha, with the aim of protecting a valuable forest growth with natural wood species. The **nature reserve of Goliasová** lies on the flank of the Spišská Magura mountains on the southern slopes of the Príslop mountain (1,214 m). It was declared a reserve in 1991 over an area of 27.3 ha and consists of variegated mosaics of natural forestation with numerous rare plants and animal species. Both reserves are closed to public.

Right: The wooden church in Tatranská Javorina

Sheep on the Muráň mountain:

The shape of the last but one peak on the ridge of the Belianske Tatry mountains is called Muráň (2,151 m) and is very interesting because it is reminiscent of a large table. As the top plain is limited on all sides by steep rocky walls it is difficult to believe that in the past shepherds brought up there their flocks to graze. Old records say that they used ropes and ladders to carry up approximately 80 to 100 sheep one by one. They left the animals there for several weeks alone, only supplying them from time to time with lumps of salt. If some of the sheep suddenly decided to return to the enclosure it usually fell into the abyss below. The shepherds prevented such unnecessary losses by planting pines on the edges of the plain, but the flock continued to diminish and became prey for hungry eagles.

TATRANSKÁ JAVORINA (1,000 m, population 150) is a small community amid huge forests in the northern foothills of the High Tatras. It is situated where the Javorová dolina valley opens to the shallow Podtatranská brázda furrow. Tatranská Javorina is 11 km from Ždiar and 2.5 km of the boundary crosses into Poland at Lysá Poľana.

The community's name originates first of all because of the original composition of the wood species of the local forests (Javorina = maple tree growth).

The maples of the Tatras:

Maple must have been a frequent tree in the extensive forest growths on the northern limestone slopes of the northern Tatras, and the "maple" nomenclature was carried over by the shepherds, poachers and wood workers over the northern Tatra forks and valleys where meets the Javorová dolina valley, the Javorinka brook and the Javorový štít peak. The names were also passed on to the original man made buildings. This is how the new settlement in the Javorová dolina valley became Javorina and the local estate gained the attribute of "javorinský". Even the part of the mountain range between the Bielovodská dolina valley and the Belianske Tatry mountains was called the Javorínske Tatras for some time after the First World War. The maple trees, however, have progressively disappeared from the Javorina territory, having been burnt down for the smelting works or processed into paperboard.

Javorina originated in a place where there was once only a seasonally inhabited farm of Lendak estate and a sheep enclosure. The enclosure was used by the shepherds guarding the flocks of sheep, herds of heifers, cows and horses belonging to the nearby sub Tatra communities which grazed on the surrounding grassy hills. In 1759 the owner of the Lendak estate, František Horváth, of Plaveč founded a hammer-mill and several modest houses for the smelters, colliers and railwaymen who represented the nucleus of a small community. The hammer-mill of Javorina employed initially seasonal workers from the nearby community of Jurgov, but later the iron-founders of southern Spiš, Morava and Silesia, even of Bohemia came here in pursuit of jobs. Through a marriage contract the property of the Horváth family passed later to the noble family of Solomon. At this time, however, the Javorina smelting-works had become unprofitable, as the local deposits of iron ore became exhausted, added to which in the nearby Polish district of Zakopane a competing iron-works had sprung up. Therefore, the new owners decided to change the smelting-works into an outlet for the manufacture of paper board.

The rebellion of Javorina:

The Solomons acquired together with the Jurgov and Javorina estates an unsolved problem of ownership. The local users of the communal land refused to pay to the new owners the cost of leasing the land which hitherto they had used freely without any restrictions. When the court of justice did not resolve the dispute tempers became heated and in May 1877 the discontented and angry local people rebelled against the authorities, represented by a special segregation commission delegated to Javorina. The commission came accompanied by 75 soldiers lead by two officers from Kežmarok. The villagers escaped to the mountains to guard the enclosures and the weeping village women tried to restrain the soldiers. The disobedient village mayor eventually had to be carried out on the shoulders of one of the soldiers to the valley to take part in the segregation of the Javorina lots. The rebellion finished by the end of June luckily without a bloodshed. Fifteen rebels were imprisoned over the affray and the enclosures and sheds on the Javorina hills and Tatra slopes were finally pulled down.

Left: Hohenlohe castle

The year 1879 was a significant one for the Javorina people. A member of the Prussian royal family, Duke Christian Kraft Hohenlohe (1848-1926), became the new owner of the Javorina Tatras. He purchased the land around Javorina for a fee of 500,000 *zlaté* and put additional investments into urgent regeneration of the land devastated by inconsiderate logging and grazing. The reconstructed forests became a part of a newly founded reserve closed off to the shepherds, and without a caretaker's permit, also to tourists. The introduction of game was protected by the foresters or jäger. Some interesting experiments were carried out in the closed forest lots but without any permanent effect. One such failure was the growing of some foreign species of wood in the Tatra environment. The imported seedlings of West Norwegian pine, Chinese billberry, Japanese larch and American varieties of ash tree were not able to adapt to the Tatra conditions. The enthusiastic Duke was not successful either in the acclimatisation of some exotic animal species, which is why there are no examples of any Sinai capricorns, American bisons or Caucassus deer in the Tatras. The Duke of Hohenlohe, however, also cared after the community. He built here a hunting castle, a building housing the management of the Duke's forests and estate, and some other houses for the forest administration employees. By the end of the 19th century the Duke also built the **wooden church of St. Anna**, the traditional patron of the forest worker. It is curious that the main sponsor of the Catholic church was a Protestant. Duke Hohenlohe spent the last years of his life in Tatranská Javorina and after his death in 1926 he was buried in the communal cemetery as he always wished, side by side with his great love, Otília Lubraniec-Dambska. Beside the Duke's family there is also a grave of the well-known Tatra landscape painter Jaroslav Votruba in the Javorina cemetery. The heir of the Duke's estates, August Hohenlohe, inherited the property but not the love of the forests of his famous predecessor. Moreover, he was not a good manager either and he solved his financial problems by selling his property to the government.

The Duke of Hohenlohe:

The Duke of Hohenlohe was a contradictory personality. A lot has been written or told on his character, good and bad, the stories agreeing with each other in only one point: he was a passionate hunter. The testimonies of his enemies associate the name of the Duke with bloody massacres of wild game in safari style and the unlimited shooting of all animals that happened to cross his path. He was also a proud aristocrat only caring for the collection of trophies to display later in the big world hunting fairs. But favourable biographers offer a more flattering picture of the human qualities of the Prussian Duke. They characterise him as a good manager who administered his Javorina estate with great sensibility and German pedantry. They say that he did not allow hunting in its large enclosure during the first ten years not to disturb the fragile balance of the restored Tatra nature. In spite of his undoubtedly strong hunting passion Hohenlohe seems to have preferred the preservation of game instead of chaotic and cruel killing. For instance he had a bakery in Javorina which made a bran bread only for the game. As a result of this rather generous attention, there were in the territory of the Javorina enclosure 600 chamois, 1,200 deer, 24 bisons and 150 capricorns in 1912.

In 1958 an employee of the TANAP research station, Hugo Oppitz, founded an experimental seed plantation of limba pine west of the Javorina community. The products of the plantation are the limba seeds necessary for the reconstruction of the limba pine growths in the area of the upper timber line in the Tatras. Limba tree wood was much more used in the past than today and has an aroma similar to the wood of the famous Lebanese cedar tree, used for making furniture, wooden tools and wood-carved products. The limba shoots contain etheric oil, an important ingredient for effective medicines used against different ailments. The limba tree nuts were a favourite delicacy of the local people. A new **hotel Poľana** has stood on the meadow above the village since 1977. This luxuriously equipped and decorated hotel was used by the top Communist party officials and today it is also used by the central state administration bodies for special, representative occasions.

A bear's visit to Javorina:

In the past it was not rare to meet a bear in the woods of Javorina. Fom time to time a hungry bear would set out on a longer walk and roamed among the Javorina huts, and as the people say, one of them even let himself in. This started a great deal of commotion and screaming by the farmer Plučinský. Curious villagers gathered around his house where an excited and stammering neighbour told them that right in his guest room a venerable old she-bear was sitting at the table. The villagers, deliberating what to do, finally threw a cat into the room through an open window. As the frightened cat faced the bear it started towards the half-open door and escaped. The bear followed it and stamping the ground disappeared into a spruce growth. The alarmed villagers calmed down only after the bear's steps finally died away in the discreet murmur of the thick Javorina woods.

Trips to the northern part of the Tatras are quite different to the classic hiking tours in the south. Secluded valleys are visited by people looking for the majestic silence and sublime tranquillity of the area. In turn the tourists who do not like long ascents to high mountains of the distant ends of extremely long valleys try to avoid them. Such is also the **Javorová dolina valley**. The green-marked path leaves Tatranská Javorina which ascends along a 12.5 km long glacial valley up to its conclusion. The path then leads mostly through the forest – through isolated alpine meadows providing fine views of the group of Ľadový štít peak (2,267 m) in the main Tatra ridge. On the western side of the valley the massive fork of the **Široká mountain** (2,210 m) is something to be admired. Limestone, in the High Tatras rather than seldom occurring rock, is the base of several caves. Entering the dwarf pine forest huge northern faces of the peaks of the Javorová suddenly appear. The path goes on ascending over the threshold to the terrace of the **Žabie Javorové pleso lake** at a sea level altitude of 1,886 m. The lake is the largest (area 1.67 ha) and also the deepest (16 m) of the 11 lakes in the Javorová dolina valley. The most demanding is the final part of the ascent to the **Sedielko saddle** (2,372 m). The track steeply ascends by serpentines up to the highest saddle, accessible to tourists, before reaching the Malá Studená dolina valley. There is the possibility to return to Sedielko by the same way to Tatranská Javorina (about 4 hours' walk) or to go on further around the Téryho chata cottage to Hrebienok (3 hours away) and to finish successfully the entire passage over the High Tatras in a transversal direction.

Tourists also enjoy a trip to the Zadné Meďodoly valley. The entire route coincides with the old poachers' path used for the traffic of goods

from Old Hungary to Poland. They preferred it because the pass over the Kopské sedlo saddle is the easiest one, overcoming the main Tatra ridge in its eastern part. The first section of the track leads from Tatranská Javorina to Poľana under the Muráň mountain along the green-marked path. Passing the cottage of the TANAP administration there is a blue-marked path turning left, taking the tourist to the **Zadné Meďodoly valley**. The entry to the valley leads over a rocky canyon called Bránka. In the north a limestone-dolomite ridge of the Belianske Tatry mountains towers. The name of the valley (Meďodoly = copper mines) says that in the past copper was extracted here. Besides the miners shepherds also liked to come here with their flocks of sheep and cattle herds. The ascent to the **Kopské sedlo saddle** (1,750 m) can be done by a path traversing several troughs and ribs sloping down from the ridge of the Belianske Tatry mountains. In a broad grassy saddle one can enjoy a wonderful view of the cliff tops of the Belianske and Vysoké Tatry mountains. Passing by the saddle the blue-marked path descends to the Dolina Bielych plies valley (see page124.) and continues along the valley of Kežmarská Biela voda to the Tatranské Matliare mountains.

Left: The ridge of the Belianske Tatry mountains
Right: The snow-covered Belianske Tatry mountains

Lysá poľana (970 m) is the last community on the Cesta Slobody road, in the direction to Poland. It lies 13 km of Ždiar in a place where the Bielovodská dolina valley opens to the Podtatranská brázda furrow. The mighty Biela voda brook in Poland's Bialka divides the community into two parts – the Slovak Lysá Poľana and the Polish Łysa Polana. They are connected by a bridge and a border crossing in one.

The origin of the name should be sought on the Polish side where there is the 1,119 metres high hill of Łysa Skalka. The small community has only the administration buildings of the TANAP and the TNP, two, today abandoned old customs offices and a new one common for both, Polish and Slovak sides opened in 1962 at the occasion of the world ski championship in Polish Zakopane. The landscape under Lysá Poľana on the western side of the Skorušiak mountain (979 m) is covered by thick woods and has two **nature reserves** – **Čikovská and Pavlová**. Both of them were established in 1991. Čikovská over an area of 6.20 ha was principally created to protect the peat bog plant cultures growing on the top of the mountain, and Pavlová, with an area of 58.5 ha, is an attempt to conserve the rare north-type plants of waterlogged soils and peat bogs. Both reserves are closed to the public.

A good hiking opportunity is the **national nature reserve Bielovodská dolina valley**. The Polish physician and writer Tadeusz Zelenski-Boy called the Bielovodská dolina valley "a matchless one". This largest Tatra valley belongs indeed to the most attractive parts of the Tatras. The lower reaches of the glacial trough offers an occasion for pleasant and comfortable walks in a most peaceful natural setting where spruce woods alternate with fresh green mountain meadows. The final reward is the beautiful panoramic view of the grey silhouette of the Tatra peaks usually presented in all picture guides books of the Tatra mountains.

More demanding tourists will certainly choose the pass over the High Tatras across the Polish mountain ridge. The blue-marked path is a part of the longest and most exacting transversal pass over the mountain range. The huge Bielovodská dolina valley provides exquisite high-moun-

tain scenery seen of both sides. The path follows the torrent of the Biela voda. It alternatively crosses the forest and forest meadows. On an meadow under the Vysoká mountain the path passes by a point where a hunter's cottage, built back in the 19th century by the Javorina estate owner Aladár Solomon, used to stand. Its following proprietor Duke Hohenlohe changed it to a gamekeeper's lodge. In 1923 it burnt down. Three years later a nearby small hostel also fell victim to fire. Long lasting debates over the issue of a new cottage in the Bielovodská dolina valley ended with a victory for the conservationists who claimed that a cottage in this valley would be a disturbing element bringing about undesirable civilisation to the wild Tatra valley. The part of the route near Poľana under the Vysoká mountain provides impressive views of the rocky face of the Mlynár mountain (2,170 m) with the most difficult climbing tracks in the Tatra mountains. Rather difficult to ascend is the threshold of the Kačacia dolina valley with a wonderful 15 metres high **Hviezdoslavov vodopád waterfall**. It is also called the Kačací vodopád waterfall. The **Kačacia dolina valley** is undoubtedly one of the most beautiful valleys in the Tatras. Its beauty is enhanced by a high rocky background of the northern faces between the Ganek and Litvorov štít peaks. Its name (Kačací = duck) is derived from a gold miners' legend about a golden duck that laid a big golden egg once a year precisely in the time of the summer solstice. The gold miners tried, though unsuccessfully, to find the egg. The footpath passes by the Kačacia dolina valley and traverses to the neighbouring **Litvorova dolina valley** with an eponymously named lake and peak above the valley. On the left side it passes by the higher situated **Zamrznuté pleso lake**. The water table of the lake is in a cool shadow of the northern faces of the Tatra mountain ridge at an altitude of 2,047 metres above sea level. It was the reason why the lake named Zamrznuté (= frozen). The cross-roads above the lake offers a choice of a shorter and a longer pass to the southern side of the High Tatras. The shorter route leads along a green-marked footpath across the **Poľský hrebeň saddle** (2,200 m) to the Velická dolina valley (see page 102). The longer one continues by a blue-marked path to the **Prielom saddle** (2,288 m) which ends in the Veľká Studená dolina valley (see page 115).

ORAVA

Námestovo and its environs

The tourist centre of the Upper Orava region, called Biela Orava (White Orava) is the district city of Námestovo (614 m, population 8,000). Its wonderful location on the north-western bank of the Orava Dam has made it a much sought after holiday resort, especially for waterside recreation.

Námestovo, a Wallachian-peasant community, originated in 1557 as a result of the efforts of the Orava Castle landlord, František Thurzo who granted the role of "sholtys" or mayor to Ondrej Rando. Námestovo became a serf community of the Orava estate whereupon it was administered by hereditary mayors. The Thurzo family founded here an Evangelic parish and Námestovo was not only a market centre of this part of Orava but also a centre of religious life. Anti-Hapsburg rebellions affected Námestovo in 1671 when the leader of one them, squire Gašpar Pika settled here. He won the support of the people and the local priest Štefan Bocko, and they even conquered Orava Castle, after which the imperial army intervened and repressed the revolt. Twenty five of the Orava mayors, including Gašpar Pika were impaled on stakes and left to die a slow and painful death. After the 18th century Námestovo became the centre of the anti-reformation movement and also numerous Jews came to live here. The old trade road leading across Námestovo to Poland's Żywec, and the right to trade linen acquired by the town in 1776, helped its development. Linen manufacture and trade contributed to the progressive change of what was originally a farming community augmented by the Austro-Old Hungarian ruler Maria Theresa in 1776 when she granted the town a municipal market privilege. Námestovo obtained the right to run four annual fairs and a weekly market on Thursdays, which became the most popular in the Orava region. The linen-makers, tanners, leather-processing craftsmen and furriers from Námestovo were especially in great demand. One of the most important sources of income for the citizens of Námestovo in the course of the 18th and 19th centuries was also linen and textile trade, pre-

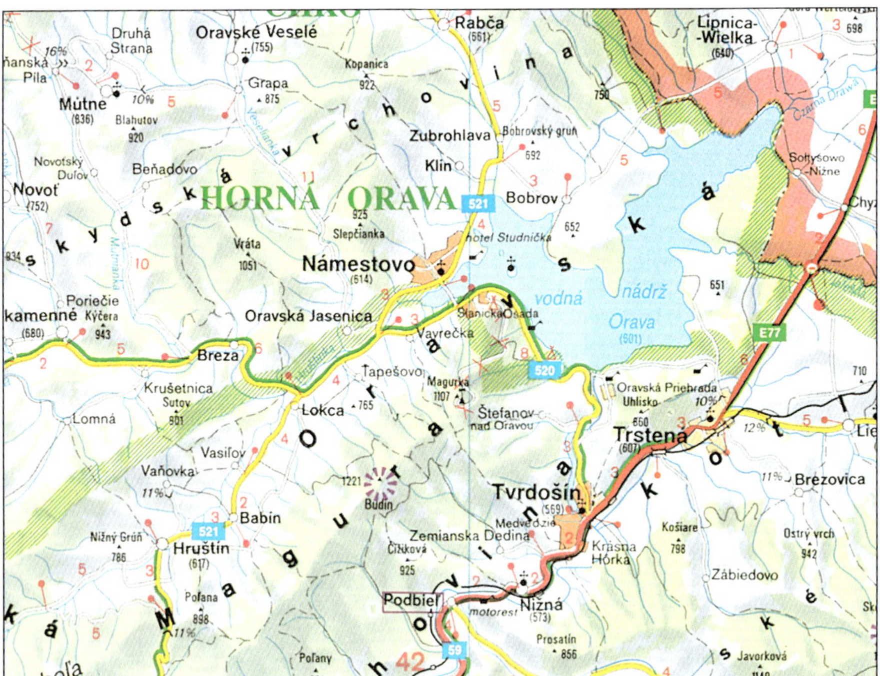

ceded by the growing of flax and hemp, which was typical female work, whereas men did linen weaving. Progressively the ornamentation of home-made linen with distinctive blue-print patterns, using mostly plant motifs, was created. In 1775 dyeing and mangling workshops were established where the linen was first mangled and afterwards manually printed with indigo. Throughout almost two centuries the blue-print linen cloth was typical for the decoration of Orava folk costumes.

The Association of Linen Manufacturers:

In 1884 the Industrial Association of the Upper Orava Linen Producers was founded. It associated almost two hundred members of the large-scale producers (owners of mangling and dyeing workshops), peddlers of linen, individually trading weavers, dyers and printers. The Association purchased the linen from the weavers, stored it and then exported and sold it all over Old Hungary, Croatia, Transylvania, Serbia, Rumania, Bulgaria, Turkey, Egypt, amongst other countries. Linen trade was permitted only to the members of the Association, some of whom left with their carts in the spring and returned at Christmas time. In the mid-18th century there were 37 linen traders in Námestovo, thirteen of them transported their goods on horses and 14 on their backs, in knapsacks. Among the wealthiest linen traders in Námestovo were the brothers Murín, who dispatched up to 30 carts fully-loaded with linen yearly. A different category was that of the peddlers. They were mostly poor farmers or landless villagers wandering about the country and offering their linen accompanied by small products. These wanderers had little means for purchasing good quality linen but sold it, nonetheless, at a certain profit. Peddlers in Orava disappeared only in the mid-20th century.

The decline of home-produced linen came at the period of the First World War, when it was drastically replaced by the manufacture and industrial production of textiles. Námestovo was then also one of the centres of Slovak intellectual and literary life. Here lived and worked for instance the poets P. O. Hviezdoslav and S. H. Vajanský, the publisher M. Hamuljak, the historian Š. Mišík and others.

The city was considerably damaged by fire in 1943 with the resistance fighting during the Second World War, when almost 60% of the houses were demolished. The socialist era completely changed the appearance and nature of the city. The development of industry and the construction of the Orava Dam offered the city opportunities in the form of travel and tourism and its importance has considerably grown since then.

The Orava Sea:

The Orava Dam was created by the artificial blocking of the river Orava in order to prevent frequent floods. The fist proposal of the construction of a dam emerged as early as in 1730 and its model is still deposited in the Museum of Orava Castle. The following project of an iron-concrete dam dates back to 1870 though, as with many others afterwards, it was not realised. The project of 1940-1941, however, was carried out, but the complex geological conditions, floods, the war and lack of experienced experts were the reasons why the construction took fourteen years to complete. When it was filled by water in 1954 the communities of Ústie nad Oravou, Slanica, Osada, Oravské Hámre, Ľavkov and the lower parts of Námestvo and Bobrov completely disappeared under the water table. Of all the flooded communities only the top of a mountain over Slanica sticks out in the form of a small island, called Slanický ostrov or Ostrov umenia (Island of Arts) with a church from the 18th century. The dam is fed by the waters of the Slovak Biela Orava and Polish Čierna Orava rivers. The area of the lake is 35 km^2, the mean depth is 15 meters and the maximum depth near the dam wall is 38 meters.

The Orava dam became an important holiday and sport centre with lodging, catering facilities and the usual services to the holiday-makers. Sport and recreation facilities are concentrated on southern shore of the water reservoir in two centres: **Slanická osada** and the **hotel Goral**. Numerous restaurants, hostels, hotels, two car-camping sites, sport facilities and sport equipment rental services contribute to the satisfaction of visitors. The summer tourist season starts in the middle of June and ends in September. There is also the possibility of a sight-seeing tour by boat. There are four boats with regular departures every day during the summer season.

A favourite point in the reservoir is the **nature reserve Slanický ostrov island**, which used to be the Slanica community. The first reference to it as *Zlavycha* dates back to 1564, whose inhabitants

were also linen-makers trading linen all over Old Hungary. Before its flooding in 1952, 850 people lived there. The church standing in the island is the Roman-Catholic **church of Ascension of the St. Cross** built in 1766-1769 first as a Baroque chapel. The chapel was reconstructed in 1843 in Classicist style into a church with two towers and a "locksmith's" chapel. The Baroque inventory of the church is deposited in the Orava Gallery, the church in turn shelters a permanent exposition of folk art. There are folk sculpture, works of arts and paintings by the female painter Matilda Čechová and collections from the Orava Gallery. In the exterior of the church a stone-masonry collection of the region is displayed and in a nearby tomb of the Klinovský family a small historical exposition concerning the flooded communities is installed. The bronze life size statue of A. Bernolák (1762-1813), the first codifier of the Slovak language, born in Slanica, stands on a pillar nearby.

Left: Námestovo
Right: The church on Slanický island

Slanický ostrov – Oravská Priehrada
(The Orava Dam), tel.: 0846/52 24 01
Opening hours: June-September daily 9:00-17:00h

The city itself has the Roman-Catholic **church of St. Šimon and Júda**, built between 1656 to 1659 as an Evangelical church. It was enlarged in the first quarter of the 19th century and later repeatedly renewed. In the interior the altars, the pulpit from the 19th century and a painting of the Madonna in the style of an icon from 1758, a wooden cross from 1818, and the reconstructed **tomb** of the Murín family, one of the wealthiest in Námestovo in the 19th century, are of interest. The secular monuments include Classicist wooden and brick **houses of linen-makers** forming a row in a street that used to be the most busy part of the city in the 18th and 19th centuries. Symbols of the Slovak National Revivalist movement are the **statue and a commemorating board of P. O. Hviezdoslav** and the **tomb** of M. Hamuljak at the local cemetery.

North-east of Námestovo, close to the Orava Dam are the three communities of **KLIN** (640 m, population 1,850), **ZUBROHLAVA** (624 m,

population 1,750) and **BOBROV** (610 m, population 1,450). Klin originated in the second half of the 16th century pursuing the Wallachian right. It belonged to the Orava estate and it was administered by hereditary mayors. It was repeatedly depopulated in the 17th century reaching somewhat more intense growth in the 18th century. The villagers were widely known as makers of high quality linen, especially the family of Skyčák. Other frequent activities were farming, cattle and sheep keeping, logging, rafting and shingle production. Several typical brick **houses of linen-makers** are preserved in the centre of the village, which date to the second half of the 18th and the beginning of the 19th centuries. In the yards of these houses the dyer's mangling and drying workshops operated. The houses are typical specimens of the Upper Orava building craft of well-to-do linen families and keep to Classicist patterns. The sacral monuments of the community include the Classicist Roman-Catholic **church of St. Anton**, built in the first third of the 19th century and a **chapel** with a round ground plan from 1900. Another place of interest is the national **nature reserve of Klinské rašelinisko** (The Peat Bog of Klin) extending over an area of 9.23 ha and situated between the city of Námestovo and Klin. It is the mountain type of peat bog with occurrences of specific forms of plant and animal life typical for waterlogged areas.

The neighbouring community of Zubrohlava also originated in the second half of the 16th century pursuing the Wallachian right and its history is similar to that of Klin. It belonged to the Orava estate and was administered by hereditary mayors. The inhabitants were mostly farmers and linenmakers (the family of Tomaštík were among the best known of them), supplementary crafts included lime burning and basket-making, and the village also had a large dyer's shop, fulling mill, sawmill and a brick-yard. The past glory of linenmaking can be recalled in the **houses of the craftsmen** of the second half of the 18th and beginning of the 19th centuries with their Classicist facades. The Baroque Roman-Catholic **church of St. Peter and Pavol** from 1761 is the only sacral monument in Zubrohlava, which has been gradually altered during the course of the 20th century.

Only a few kilometres southward is the community of Bobrov, which was founded in the mid-16th century pursuing the Wallachian right and belonged to Orava Castle. It was administered by hereditary mayors and the population made their living from farming, trading in oxen, stone-masonry, but mostly linen-making of which the families of Kompaník, Vlošák, Odrobiniak were most prominent. Bobrov was even promoted to the status of a town at the beginning of the 19th century when the population was higher than it is today. In the years between 1849 to 1867 the town was the seat of district administration and later a constituency seat. The most typical craft guild in Bobrov in the last century was that of the dyers' who owned several mangling and dyeing workshops. After the First World War *pogroms* (attacks against the Jewish people) worsened the tense situation on the Polish-Slovak border, and during the Second World War the community was severely damaged. Bobrov has attracted the attention of the public at the present time for its excellent weight-lifters which participate annually in international competitions in weight-lifting (O Štít Bobrova – Prize of the Bobrov Shield). There are remarkable Classicist **houses of linen-makers** standing in the centre of the community bearing testimony to the wealthy past. The most important sacral building is the local Baroque Roman-Catholic **church of St. Jakub** built in 1753, later reconstructed and expanded with a lateral **chapel**. Another interesting monument is the **Calvary** with a central chapel from 1894 depicting Christ stopping on the Way to the Cross. The sculptures on the edge of the road are of the end of the 18th and beginning of the 19th centuries.

Several villages lie south of Námestovo on the road to Oravský Podzámok. **ORAVSKÁ JASENICA** (630 m, population 1,400), **VAVREČKA** (648 m, population 1,100), and **ŤAPEŠOVO** (680 m, population 550) are in the extreme north.

Oravská Jasenica was founded in the second half of the 16th century and the first written record of it is from 1588. It belonged to the Wallachian-peasant villages of the Orava estate. It was depopulated and deserted in the 17th century and also in the years between 1739 to 1742 when the black plague swept all life out of the area. Later it was resettled and in 1782 a the village brewery was referred to in old documents. The local people made a living mainly out of farming or linen-making and trade. In 1789 Martin Hamuljak, the organiser of Slovak cultural life in the first half of the 19th century, was born here. His activities are commemorated with a plaque placed in the local school. Among the sacral monuments are the Roman-Catholic **church of Conversion of Christ the Lord** of mid-19th century and a **Trinity Pillar**, a work of folk masonry of 1836.

Vavrečka originated around 1600 under the name Sigmondka. It belonged to the Orava estate. Its inhabitants were active in farming, linen-making and linen trade, logging and the manufacture of wooden plates and tools. The village was also repeatedly sacked and destroyed during the 17th century. The oldest historical monument here is the Late Baroque **chapel** near the cemetery, built in 1830. The Neo Romanesque Roman-Catholic **church of St. Anna** built in 1932 is among the more recent buildings.

Further to the south lies the village of Ťapešovo which originated in 1580 pursuing the Wallachian right. It too belonged to the Orava estate and was administered by hereditary mayors. The local people made their living from farming and cattle keeping. The most important monument is the **chapel** of 1830 with its folk Baroque sculptures from the second half of the 18th century.

Continuing further south, up to the confluence of the Hruštínka and Biela Orava rivers, along the north-eastern slopes of the Oravská Magura mountains, the visitor reaches **LOKCA** (655 m, population 2,050). The village originated in the mid-16th century by Wallachian right and the first reference to it dates back to 1554. It also belonged to the Orava estate and was administered by hereditary mayors. Lokca, as an important point of the colonisation of the two river basins, Hrušínska and Biela Orava, was also the centre of crafts. It was often attacked and sacked by invading armies. Besides farming and sheep keeping its people were involved in logging, weaving, and the manufacture of sheep bells. The village has an original Renaissance Roman-Catholic **church of the Holiest Trinity** from 1665, expanded and rebuilt in the Baroque style in the 18th century. Also the Baroque **stone pillar of St. Ján Nepomucký** of 1751 is of interest.

South of Lokca lies the smaller village of **VASIĽOV** (650 m, population 750) which likewise originated in the mid-16th century pursuing

Right: A workshop of a wood-cutter in Orava

the Wallachian right, and similar to all the Upper Orava villages it belonged to the Orava estate and was administered by hereditary mayors until 1763. The villagers made their living from farming and an additional source of income was obtained by shingle-making, sawmilling, cloth and carpet manufacture. The religious life of the village exists around the **chapel of the Virgin Mary** built after World War II, and stone crosses in the cemetery with relieves of saints from the 19th century, the work of the local stone-masons.

Neighbouring **BABÍN** (680 m, population 1,350) was for the first time referred to in 1564 as a Wallachian community of the Orava estate. In the 17th century it was plundered several times and the Black Plague in 1739 also took its toll, and in 1934 most of the village was destroyed by fire. Traditionally the villagers worked in sheep and cattle farming as well as wood crafts. Among the religious monuments is the Roman-Catholic **church of the Holy Spirit** built in 1933 and designed by the architect M. M. Harminc. Its interior contains some parts of a wooden church that existed here from 1666 to 1930, and which were subsequently moved when the old church was pulled down. A Classicist chapel from the first half of the 19th century and **stone crosses** at the cemetery with relief ornamentation from the 19th century are among the sacral monuments.

The largest community of this part of White Orava is **HRUŠTÍN** (697 m, population 3,100) and located near the aforementioned villages. It originated in 1580 through Wallachian colonisation and belonged to the Orava estate. Although it was several times sacked in the 17th century, the 18th century brought about the development of crafts and trade. It was known for the manufacture of wooden tools and linen making. A distillery and brewery also contributed to additional income, but primarily the villagers traded in sheep, oxen, cheese, and linen and were good hunters. The village suffered intense emigration to the USA before the First World War, and its history is preserved in the form of several houses built in the original folk style typical for the Orava region. The most important sacral monument is the Roman-Catholic **church of St. Ján the Baptist**, built in 1820 with an interior dating from the end of 19th century. The **chapel of St. Anna** dating from 1800, **statues of St. Florián and St. Ján Nepomucký**, as well as the **Trinity Pillar** and a **crucifix** standing by the road to Oravský Podzámok, depict the religious life of the village. An erstwhile, independent village called **Vaňovka** now forms part of Hruštín, which was founded in 1600. It too has a remarkable Roman-Catholic church from 1833. The interior is created in folk style, and the folk art work of the statue of St. Ján Nepomucký dates from the same year.

Tvrdošín and its environs

The administrative centre of the Upper Orava region has been recently established in the district town of **TVRDOŠÍN** (575 m, population 9,500). It lies in the valley of the river Orava, on the dividing line of the Oravská Magura and the Skorušinské vrchy mountains. Its startegic location, from a transport and communications aspect, leading across from Orava to Poland, has determined the nature and significance of the town.

Tvrdošín was mentioned for the first time in 1265 in an act of the Old Hungarian king Belo IV as Toardosina, a customs point for the Old-Hungarian–Polish trade relations when salt, lead and linen was transported through the town. Also a fort belonging to the Orava estate probably existed there. Tvrdošín obtained the privilege of a royal city from king Ľudovít I in 1369. The inhabitants were allowed to elect their mayor, to run fairs, and to trade with foreigners, they were exempt of duties and tolls throughout the territory of Old Hungary. The town preserved its freedoms and privileges also in the 15th century, but the precariousness of the political situation in the 16th caused the gradual decline of the customs office in Tvrdošín and a growing dependence on the Orava Castle landlords, especially of Juraj Thurzo and his descendants.

Life in Tvrdošín in 1625:

In 1625 112 families lived in the town, who though exempt of serf duties had to pay to the landlord 750 guldens in cash, plus 1 ox, 100 ducks, 50 geese, 400 eggs and 25 partridges. They were obliged to render a gift to the landlord of Orava estate, to mark certain occasions, be ready to repair or to defend the castle, and to hand in 200 fish, as well as sheep and honey tithes, annually. The inn-keepers were allowed to tap beer all the year round, but the tapping of wine was permitted only during the fairs. The tavern of the landlord, however, sold wine all the year. The town ran three fairs a year and weekly markets were held on Mondays.

The period of anti-Hapsburg rebellions in the 17th century, and the presence of the Polish-Lithuanian troops of Jan Sobieski in 1683, caused

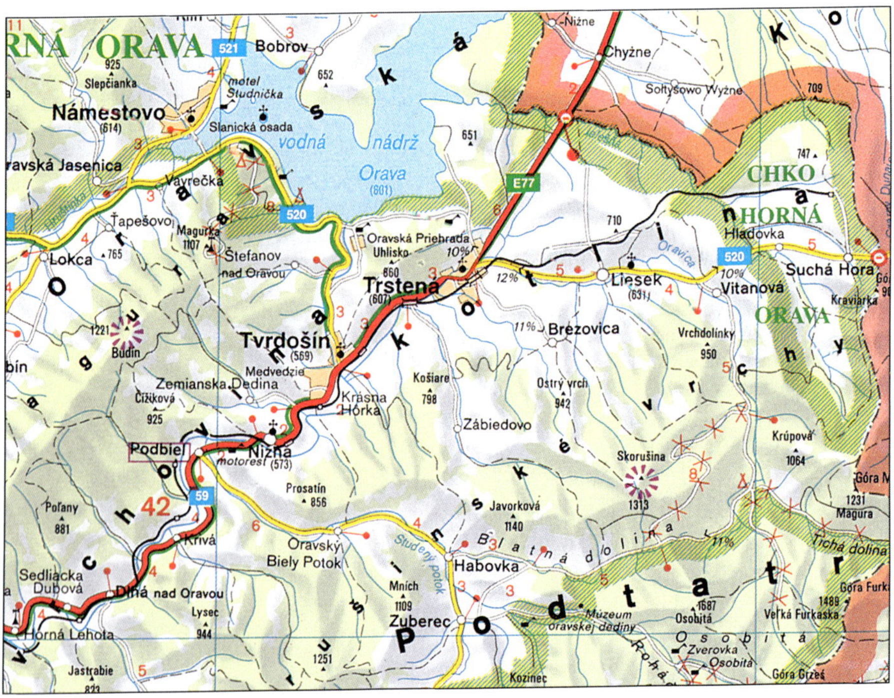

enormous damage to Tvrdošín. Life settled down in the 18th century and the people made their living by farming and cattle breeding, and craftwork was booming. Besides pottery, also brewery, stonemasonry, and the manufacture of linen were typical for Tvrdošín. In the vicinity of the town abundant flax was cultivated and linen was made almost in every household. Skilled traders purchased and sold the linen in big amounts. In the 19th century Tvrdošín, with almost two thousand inhabitants, became the seat of the Upper Orava district, actively employed in wood manufacture, tannery, dyeing and button manufacturing. Several money institutions and a sawmill originated after the First World War. The period after the Second World War was the one of intense promotion and development and today Tvrdošín is the cultural and administrative centre of the Upper Orava region. The pride of Tvrdošín and the oldest preserved building is the Gothic wooden Roman-Catholic **All Saints church** situated in the local cemetery. Its origins date back to the second half of the 15th century and it was rebuilt in Renaissance style in the 17th. The Baroque altar from the end of the 17th century, with the painting of All Saints, dominates the interior of the church. Formerly, there was a low Gothic altar of which one wing, with the paintings of St. Peter and St. Ján the Baptist was preserved. The original central part of the altar, a painting of Bemoaning the Death of Christ from the 15th century was moved in 1919 to a museum in Budapest. The interior of the church was finished in the mid-17th century. Viewing the church, especially the paintings of the Apostles, the Late Renaissance pulpit with figures of the Evangelists from 1654, and a painting of St. Juraj mounted on a horse fighting a dragon (a distemper painting on wood from 1653) will draw the attention of any visitor. The wonderful dome paintings (a sky with stars, angels and a panelled ceiling) complement the Gothic mysticism of the space. Highly artistic and expert reconstruction and restoration of the church was awarded a prize by EUROPA NOSTRA in 1993 and the church itself, as a **national cultural monument**, was included in the list of European cultural heritage. Among other important monuments in Tvrdošín is another Roman-Catholic church, the **St. Trinity church** built in 1766-1770 on the site of older foundations. The Late Baroque **Lady's Pillar** of the end of the 18th century, standing in front of the church, and a Baroque **chapel** from 1815 complete the list of sacral monuments. Among the secular ones the **municipal house**, built around 1811 in the square and several **curias, public buildings and the houses of linen-makers**, commemorating the lively trade and craft activities in the second half of the 19th century, are worth mentioning. However, the final destination for the many visitors to the town, is the municipal quarter called Medvedzie, and especially the **Gallery of Mária Medvecká** – a permanent exposition of the Orava Gallery. It is a biographic exposition of the paintings of this remarkable painter who was born and grew up in Medvedzie, and after a period of sojourn came back to work in Orava. The building of the curia where the exposition is installed dates back to the 19th century. The exposition with 261 artistic works occupies 583 m² and shows Mária Medvecká's (1914-1987) paintings of the landscape of Orava, including still life, portraits, floral and figural compositions.

Galéria Márie Medveckej (The Gallery of Mária Medvecká) tel.: 0847/32 27 93
Opening hours: Tue-Sun 9:00-12:00h and 13:00-17:00h

Part of Tvrdošín also includes the present day suburbs of **Krásna Hôrka** and **Medvedzie**, which were independent communities in the past. Archaeological discoveries from the Lower Bronze Age prove that a pre-historic settlement once existed there. Krásna Hôrka originated at the beginning of the 15th century through Wallachian colonisation being a serf community of the Orava estate. Its population made their living by lining-making, glass manufacturing, trading in stone-masonry and seasonal work in the lower parts of Old Hungary. The Baroque **chapel**, the **belfry** and the **Lady's Pillar** recall the deep religiosity of the local population. Neighbouring Medvedzie originated in 1355 as a squire community which later belonged to the Medvecký family. Their origins are well preserved in the architecture of the Classicist curias from the end of the 18th and the beginning of the 19th centuries.

The bears of Medvedzie:

One of the legends concerning the origin of the name of Medvedzie (medveď = bear) refers to the 9th century's Messengers of Faith – the brothers Constantin and Methodius of Thesallonike who wandered over the Great Moravian Empire and also visited the region of Orava. Pagan priests,

called žreci, dominated religious life and practices at the time and forced the people to sacrifice various gifts to the pagan gods. When the priests learnt the news about the arrival of the new Faith Messengers, they disguised themselves as bears knowing how much people feared them. One day during a feast in Tvrdošín the brothers of Thesallonike were preaching the Holy Script to the villagers when suddenly several bears appeared in the square. The audience became very frightened but Constantin and Methodious discovered the trick of the priests and changed them into real bears. Only one of them was eventually saved from this fate after he apologised to the saints. The brothers allowed him to build a wooden house near Tvrdošín, where he later lived. After some time a village arose there which was called Medvedzie.

Among the places of interest near Tvrdošín is **Oravice** (see page 51), although being 23 km from the city it was for three centuries connected to it.

Left: The wooden church in Tvrdošín

The not too distant water reservoir of the Orava Dam offers recreation and water sport facilities, and ski enthusiasts can use a ski lift and a downhill track at Bučník mountain.

TRSTENÁ (607 m, population 7,100) lies in the lower part of the Oravica stream, only several kilometers north of Tvrdošín, its eternal rival in the battle for the prominent position in Upper Orava region.

Trstená was founded in 1371 by German settlers as a market town under the name of *Bingenstadt*. It possessed the privileges of sword, hunting, fishing, scales, public baths and market. Later it adopted the name Trstená because of the abundant occurrences of peat bogs and cane (tŕstie = cane) around the town. In 1424 the Old Hungarian king Sigismond of Luxembourg freed it from paying the customs duty but it remained serf town of the Orava estate. It was administered by elected mayors, mostly members of the Trstenský family. Some of the lords of Orava Castle tried to deny the status of city to Trstená and occasionally it was referred to as a villa though at the beginning of the 17th century it was definitely adjudicated the term of oppidum (town). Though it was an agricultural community in the 17th century craftwork was developing rapidly. The Old Hungarian king Matej II granted it the privilege of four fairs a year and Trstená became an important centre of crafts and trade. The guilds of fur-makers, potters, boot-makers and carpenters and the storehouse of salt, workshop for the dyeing and ironing of linen are mentioned in records relating to the town. The guild of pottery manufactured a broad assortment of products which became famous abroad. Trstená ceramics were remarkable for their distinctive design, decoration and the very technology of its manufacturing. The development of crafts and trade went on into the 18th and 19th centuries and there even was a petroleum refinery in Trstená. By the end of the 19th century the population of Trstená amounted to almost 2,400 and the town became the seat of the district. Education and schooling also became deeply rooted traditions. A municipal Latin school existed there as early as in the 16th century and in the second half of the 19th century Trstená became famous for its local secondary school, where a renowned Slovak poet, of Polish origin, Hugolín Gavlovič (1712-1787) and the author and journalist A. H. Krčméry (1822-1891) were active. At present the school bears the name of an important Slovak linguist and a Prague university teacher – Martin Hattala (1821-1903). A significant monument in the town is the Roman-Catholic **church of St. Martin**. Originally a Gothic church, probably from the 14th century, it was altered in 1641 into the Renaissance style and a century later it became Baroque. It is surrounded by a wall with an entrance gate adorned by two sculptures and a sun-dial. In the spacious main square another Roman-Catholic **St. Juraj church** and a **Franciscan monastery** can be seen. Both Baroque buildings are from the 18th century and they close the southern side of the square. Extremely valuable are also the stone pillars – the **Pillar of St. Ján Nepomucký** in front of the church of St. Juraj and the **Pillar of St. Florián** in front of the parish office (the oldest stone sculpture in Orava). Two **chapels** and a **rectory** from 1743 complement the sacral monuments of Trstená.

Another part of Trstená, what was formerly an independent community called **Ústie nad Priehradou** (600 m), originated in the first half of the 16th century pursuing the Wallachian privilege. It was a serf community of the Orava estate administered by hereditary mayors. Its people were active in agriculture and sheep keeping, linen manufacturing and rafting. Among the historical curiosities of the community is a preserved identity card of a linen-maker obtained by the mayor Juraj Bulla in 1728 – it is the oldest document of the privilege related to linen-making. In the years between 1947 to 1953 the community was flooded and a valley dam was constructed on its site. A new community, its namesake, was built on the shore of the dam with a school in its centre. The destiny of the surrounding localities **Osada** and **Oravské Hámre** were very similar. The first was founded in 1600, again pursuing Wallachian privilege, belonged to the Orava estate and was administered by hereditary mayors. The somewhat younger community of Oravské Hámre was founded between 1607 to 1615 when Juraj Thurzo allowed the brothers Hámorník to extract iron and to build a smelting plant there. Iron was extracted and processed until the 19th century and linen-making was another craft popular in the community. Both Osada and Oravské Hámre disappeared when the dam was constructed and the population was moved to southern Slovakia.

The road ends south-east of Trstená at **BREZOVICA** (700 m, population 1,200). The community lies on the northern foothills of the Skorušinské vrchy mountains, about five kilometres from Trstená. It was founded in 1580 by the Thurzos and settled by the people of Trstená pursuing the Wallachian privilege. It also belonged to the Orava estate and was administered by the hereditary mayors. In 1683 it was destroyed by the Polish-Lithuanian troops and only at the end of the 17th century was it re-colonised. The local population made their living from farming, cattle-keeping, flux cultivation and the manufacture of mill stones. The craft of stone-masonry preserved until the mid-20th century. The only preserved examples of the old architecture are several **log houses** and a Roman-Catholic **church of the Virgin Mary** built between 1883-1884. The church stands along the green-marked and comfortable tourist route leading from Trstená across Brezovica to the Skorušinské vrchy mountains. After a mild ascent beyond the village and below the ski lift the first aim is the round top of the **Javorinky mountain** (1,123 m). Its south-western slopes are cloaked by pastures, and the north-western slopes are covered by forests providing shelter for numerous deer and boars. The green path continues further along the ridge south-eastward and ends up at the highest top of the Skorušinské vrchy mountains – **Skorušiná** (1,314 m). With the exception of the top and north-western slopes it is covered by spruce forest and it offers some attractive views of the Roháče mountains.

Trstená is usually the last stop for tourists before entering Poland. The most frequented border crossing, Trstená-Chyżne, is situated on the main Orava road, several kilometres north of Trstená. However, the Polish and Slovak citizens also use the Suchá Hora-Chochołów border crossing being the quickest way to the Polish town of Zakopane.

The first community lying on the route is **LIESEK** (631 m, population 2,300). It was founded by František Thurzo in 1558 on the land of Čimhová that used to belong to the Plathy family. Thurzo annexed it to the Orava estate. In the 17th century, at the time of hunger and plundering by armies, the community was almost depopulated. The new population, however, became skilled craftsmen and woodworkers, who also made a living from farming, sheep keeping, linen and the salt trade. After the First World War many emigrated because of unemployment. During the Second World War almost 85% of the houses were burned down and nothing remained of the original architecture. The only monument here is the Baroque

Roman-Catholic **church of St. Michal the Archangel** built in 1818 and reconstructed at the beginning of the 20th century.

Neighbouring **ČIMHOVÁ** (644 m, population 600) is an older locality and was founded in 1438. It belonged to the Plathy family who received it under the name *Chemechova* from the Old Hungarian king Albrecht II. The family was continuously in dispute with the owners of the Orava estate over questions of religion and possessions. In the 17th century Čimhová became the centre of re-Catholicism in Orava. While the Thurzos, owners of the Orava estate pursued the principle of "cuio regio, eius religio" (religion of the ruler) supported Protestantism, the Catholic priest Ján Sczechovicz, who came here from Poland's Ratulov, promoted the Catholic religion in Upper Orava. In 1645 a Roman-Catholic parish was founded in Čimhová and the people gradually became Catholics. The usual economic activities of the local people were linen production, weaving and basket making. Today the preserved old **log houses** and **brick buildings** from the 19th century can be seen. The Roman-Catholic Late Baroque **church of St. Imrich** from 1775 is remarkable for the ornamental sculptures of St. Štefan and St. Imrich placed in the main altar.

Several kilometers from Čimhová, on the bank of the river Oravica, lies **VITANOVÁ** (700 m, population 1,200), a community founded in 1550 pursuing the Wallachian privilege. It too belonged to the Orava estate. In the past iron ore was extracted here, but suffered from military plundering in the 17th century and several natural disasters, namely floods. During the First Czechoslovak Republic there existed saw mills, a fulling mill and blacksmith's furnace. Several **log houses**, the **Lady's Pillar** and the **sculpture of St. Róch** are the architectural monuments which still remain here. Vitanová is reached by road connecting Oravice (see page 51) a well-known and frequented resort during the summer and winter season.

Next to the Polish border lies **HLADOVKA** (756 m, population 900). It originated by the end of the 16th century pursuing the Wallachian right and it belonged to the Orava estate. It was mentioned in historical sources for the first time in 1598 as *Jeleszna*, after a nearby brook. Its present name (hlad = hunger) reveals that life was not easy for its population and hunger was common in the cottages of the farmers and craftsmen (mostly linen-makers, wood carvers and weavers). The community was annexed to Poland between the years 1920-1924. The only cultural and historical monument from the past is the Roman-Catholic **church of Ascension of the Virgin Mary** built in 1800-1808.

The last community before reaching the Slovak-Polish border crossing is **SUCHÁ HORA** (790 m, population 1,200). It originated in the mid-16th century pursuing the Wallachian right and as with the neighbouring communities it belonged to the Orava estate with administration by hereditary mayors. Its name (suchá hora = dry mountain) suggests that the barren soil did not yield enough produce to sustain the local people. Some of the villagers found additional income from pottery, whilst others emigrated abroad. In the years 1920-1924 it belonged to Poland. The customs of the local people are well preserved by the local folk group, who also present what is called the **Goral alternative** in folk costumes. The preserved **folk architecture** represented by the log houses give a true picture of the past life to the visitor. The sacral monuments in Sucha horá are a Baroque **stone cross** of 1861 and **sculptures of St. Florián** and **St. Ján Nepomucký** next to the Roman-Catholic **church of Christ the King**.

On the road from Trstená to Tvrdošín there is a turn off which leads to **ZÁBIEDOVO** (670 m, population 750) another small community situated in the northern slopes of the Skorušinské vrchy mountains. The origin of the community *Zawydov* is documented by the acts of 1567 when it was colonised after the Wallachian right. It belonged to the Orava estate and was administered by hereditary mayors. Part of the locality is the former independent community of **Hámričky** founded in 1607. The inhabitants of Zábiedovo were mainly farmers, whereas those of Hámričky produced iron for the lords of Orava Castle, the latter being annexed to Zábiedovo in 1870. The most important monuments here are the Roman-Catholic **church of Divine Jesus' Heart** of 1931 and the **Lady's Pillar** dating from the mid-19th century.

In the eastern part of the Oravská Magura mountains on the Tvrdošín road to the Orava Dam is **ŠTEFANOV NAD ORAVOU** (570 m, population 550). This community originated in 1968 by joining two separate villages of Horný and Dolný Štefanov. Dolný Štefanov was founded in the sec-

Right: A view of the Tatras

ond half of the 14th century when the Old Hungarian king Ľudovít I donated the land to Mikuláš, son of Folkus and Mikuláš, son of Ján. The community was owned in the 15th century by the family of Kubínyi and later by their relatives, while the people made their living from farming and additional resources were obtained from basket-making, weaving and carpentry. Štefanov nad Oravou has two Roman-Catholic churches, of **St. Constantin and Methodius** and **Visitation of the Virgin Mary**. Its surroundings today offer many options for summer recreation, such as bathing, water sport and hiking in the Oravská Magura mountains. A green-marked footpath, starting from the village leads to the main Magura ridge, where there are several routes either south or northward.

The larger village of **NIŽNÁ** (573 m, population 4,000) lies south of Tvrdošín, in the valley of the river Orava. While the southern part of the community, on the left bank of the river, is situated under the Skorušinské vrchy mountains, the northern part is under the slopes of the Ostražica mountain (765 m) belonging to the Oravská vrchovina mountain range. Archaeological discoveries of bronze objects from the Younger Bronze Age and a Hallstatt fort on Ostražica reveal traces of a settlement of Púchov culture to remind us of the remote past of this territory.

The castle on Ostražica mountain:

The wooden castle on the Ostražica mountain existed probably since the end of the Lower Bronze Age until the turn of that era. And one of the Orava legends tells what ill fate befell it. Once upon a time there was a powerful and rich, though rather capricious lord who often gave feasts. A poor old woman, accompanied by children, came once to his door when the master of the castle was feasting with his friends and begged him to give her some food. The amused lord sent her a basketful of stones. When the old woman saw the "gift" she pronounced a terrible curse: "Let stones like these cover your castle!" Whereupon the castle immediately fell into pieces leaving only a heap of stones. The legend says that every seventy seven years music and singing can be heard at the top of the hill.

The first written reference to Nižná as *Nissne Wes* is from 1420. It was probably settled by the people of Tvrdošín. Like almost all villages

around it belonged to the Orava Castle and it was administered by hereditary mayors. The population were farmers, living off flax and sheep, wool, cloth-making and rafting. In 1785 a paper mill, the property of the lords of Orava Castle originated here. The paper mill was leased to the Pánik family for almost one hundred years. Many historical documents and acts of northern Slovakia were written precisely on paper coming of Pánik's workshop. Besides the paper mill, a brewery, a fulling machine and an iron works, called Františkova huta existed here in the 19th century. The contemporary century brought industrialization to Nižná, and it is known to Slovaks mainly as the place where TV sets are made. The most important monument of Nižná is an originally Gothic Roman-Catholic **church of St. Gál** built between 1614-1620. By the end of the 17th century it was enclosed by a protecting wall and in 1715 it was styled in the Baroque. Among the most valuable items in the church are the golden chalice of Kraków (1570), two bells from 1629 and a painting of the Annunciation from the beginning of the 19th century. Visitors will be certainly intrigued by the **group of statues of St. Johns** from 1825 made of sandstone and located in the garden of the rectory. The local **cemetery** with Classicist tombstones from the beginning of the 19th century is also of interest.

The independent community of **Zemianska Dedina**, was also a part of Nižná, founded in 1355 by the squire family of Revicky of Revišné. It used to be a squire farming area and its original name was *Hodosin*. Although there also existed a distillery, a sawmill and advanced weaving crafts, in the 19th and 20th centuries, a lack of work still urged the local people to emigrate abroad. Religious life is symbolised by a Baroque **chapel** from the second half of the 18th century located above the community.

The surroundings of Nižná offer a variety of options for rest and recreation. Down-hill skiers can find here two ski lifts and a ski slope under Prasatín (856 m) equipped with artificial lighting, whilst cross-country skiers can enjoy ski running tracks over the Skorušinské vrchy mountains. There is a renowned moto-cross area in Rúbanka,

Left: The architecture of the Orava region

a shooting range and an in-door swimming pool which makes for an above-average equipped sport centre in Nižná.

Not far away from Nižná, at the mouth of the Studený potok brook which runs from the Roháč area to the Orava river is a typical Orava village called **PODBIEL** (555 m, population 1,200). The main road passing the village diverges to the Roháče mountains and this is the reason why annually thousands of motorists come through. Archaeological findings from the Hallstatt period and Púchov culture prove that the location of the community was important in pre-historic times. Its name was derived from the Biel hill, eventually the Biela skala rock (750 m) where there was a castle in the Middle Ages, and legend has it that there was also a Knights' Templar monastery here. At present the Biela skala rock is a protected nature locality with occurrences of valuable geologic, geomorphic, archaeological and botanic phenomena. The community itself was referred to for the first time in 1556 as *Podbella*, pertaining to the Orava estate. The people hereabouts were active in cattle and sheep rearing, and in the 18th century there was also a sawmill, fulling machines and a brewery. In 1803 three iron ore mines were built and in 1836 a smelting plant was also constructed, though it closed in 1864. Although the ore extracted here was comparably rich in iron the products made from it were too fragile and of sub standard quality. The industrial nature of the community, however, was maintained into the 20th century, with a strong workers' movement and a powerful local Communist Party organisation.

At the present visitors focus their interest mainly upon the locality called **Bobrova roľa** where there is a compound of original **log houses** built in the 19th and early 20th centuries and declared in 1977 a **monument reserve**, consisting of 74 two and three-roomed precious examples of folk architecture built on high base walls, covered by shingle roofs and adorned with typical ornamentation. The old iron industry is exemplified by the ruins of the iron-mills of 1836 standing at the entry to the Studená dolina valley, on the left hand side of the road to Zuberec. In the hall of the iron mill a partially preserved blast furnace can also be seen. The sacral monuments in Bobrova roľa are represented by the Baroque Roman-Catholic **church of Visitation of the Virgin Mary** built in 1781, which was restored at the beginning of the 20th century and a stone **Trinity Pillar** from 1870 near the local cemetery.

Dolný Kubín
and its environs

The centre of the Lower Orava region is the city of **DOLNÝ KUBÍN** (486 m, population 19,600). It extends over both banks of the river Orava in the southwestern part of the Oravská vrchovina highlands, not far away from its boundary with the Oravská Magura mountains. In this region are the former independent villages of Beňova Lehota, Bziny, Kňažia, Malý Bysterec and Veľký Bysterec, Medzihradné, Mokraď, Srňacie and Záskalie.

Archaeological finds suggest the existence of ancient traditions on the settlement of the contemporary urban territory and its immediate environs. Numerous finds are of the Younger Bronze Age, at the time of the cemetery of urns of the people belonging to Lusatian culture. On the nearby Trniny hill (739 m) a fortified elevated settlement of the people of Púchov has also been discovered. It is well-known for the unique finds of gold and silver barbarian coins dating back to the turn of the eras. The continuous settlement of the locality is also proven by a hill fort of the Great Moravia time. The name Kubín (Kolbin) appears for the first time in a document dating back to 1325. The community originated on the territory of the Orava estate in the 14th century and the historical sources of the time quote frequent property contentions of the inhabitants of Dolný Kubín and Vyšný Kubín. In the 15th and 16th centuries there were only several houses in the community and its inhabitants were "eternal serfs" – permanently bound to the land without the right of free movement. A distinct change in their life came in 1632 when the principal administrator of the estate, Gaspar Illesházy, exempted them from their duties and granted them the status of citizens. The landlords of the Orava castle brought here their clerks and tradesmen, partially also of German nationality which changed the original agricultural nature of the village. In 1632 Dolny Kubín was promoted to a town and a year after it obtained the rights to hold four annual fairs and weekly markets of the Old Hungarian king Ferdinand II. Since 1683 the town was the seat of the Orava county. The promising economic development of Dolny Kubín was inter-

economic development of Dolny Kubín was interrupted in the second half of the 17th century, especially during the devastating presence of the Polish-Lithuanian troops moving to Vienna to help out against the Turks. By the beginning of the 18th century the life of the town and the villages surrounding it progressively acquired normal features. In 1715 there were living in Dolný Kubín about 340 inhabitants, and there existed a guild of shoe-makers and tailors, and the local population made their living by farming and trade in cheese, bakery products, flax and distilled beverages.

The beer, wine and spirits of Kubín:

In the 17th century the town was allowed to tap its own beer, however, the sale of wine was permitted only at the fairs – a fortnight before and a fortnight after the fairs. The privilege of tapping beer was called frajung. In the 18th century when there were five fairs held in the town, the permission to sell wine was extended over five months. The restriction did not, of course, concern the manorial wine, and the manorial tavern served wine all the year round. The town leased the manorial tavern with uninterrupted sale since the mid-18th century but it was becoming ever more difficult to find lessees as no taverner was willing to sell the manorial wine. The municipal wine in turn was well marketed and in 1768 there were five prosperous taverners in the town. As the life of the majority of population was hard and monotonous, daily visits to taverns were on the programme of every male who wanted to escape the toil and weary reality of their lives. On account of this many of them lost not only their health but also large and small fortunes. Since the 18th century Dolný Kubín became attractive for the Jews who rented the taverns and the right to sell spirits. The Jewish taverners first bought the spirits from the local producers, but later they distilled it themselves. Their natural gift for economic activities and the drinking habit of the people brought them enormous profits. For decades the people of the region associated in their minds the two notions: the tavern and the Jew.

Extensive reconstruction of Dolný Kubín was initiated after a fire in 1834. Its square acquired a typical urban character. The town as an economic and trading centre of the Orava region (with numerous trades, food producing plants, an iron-plant, saw-mill, mill, printers, money institutes, and a business school) also became the centre of the Slovak national life in the region. Numerous personalities of Slovak culture and enlightenment were active here: Vavrinec Čaplovič, founder of the library and the Society of Scholars, who donated to the Orava county his library of 45 thousand volumes, (1778-1853), Pavol Országh Hviezdoslav, the most important of all Slovak poets, (1849-1921), Janko Matuška, poet and writer whose poem *Nad Tatrou sa blýska, hromy divo bijú* (The Lightnings and Thunders over the Tatras...) became the Slovak national anthem (1821-1877), Andrej Radlinský, one of the founders of Matica slovenská and of the St. Vojtech Society (1817-1879), the poet, Theo Herkeľ Florin (1908-1973), physician and writer Ladislav Nádaši-Jégé (1866-1940), among others. The economic and cultural progress of the city continued also in the 20th century but in the 1930's it was hampered by big economic crisis and general unemployment. Many solved their difficult situation by emigration, above all to America. After the Second World War and the territorial reorganization in 1960, Dolný Kubín became again the most important administrative, economic and cultural centre of the entire Orava region. At present it is the entry gate to all of Orava's attractive corners offering itself numerous options for leisure and sport.

The oldest cultural and historical monument here is the Roman-Catholic **church of St. Katarína** (1) with a Gothic wall and tower from the 14th century, reconstructed in Neo-Gothic style in 1885-1886. In its interior is a Late-Gothic winged altar of the beginning of the 16th century and a Renaissance epitaph of the family Zmeškal from 1622 which are most interesting. The basic urbanistic Middle Age monument is **Hviezdoslavovo námestie** (the Square of Hviezdoslav). It is the result of almost two hundred years' construction with numerous Renaissance and Baroque burgher houses. The dominant building of the square is **Župný dom** (2) (the County House) of the last third of the 17th century. A two storeyed house with a central arcade yard was built in Baroque style and later reconstructed. On its facade a coat-of-arms of Orava of the 18th century can be seen. Nowadays it is the seat of **Oravská galéria** (Gallery of Orava) with permanent expositions of old, folk and modern arts related to Orava. Regular expositions of art works and discussions with the authors are organised here.

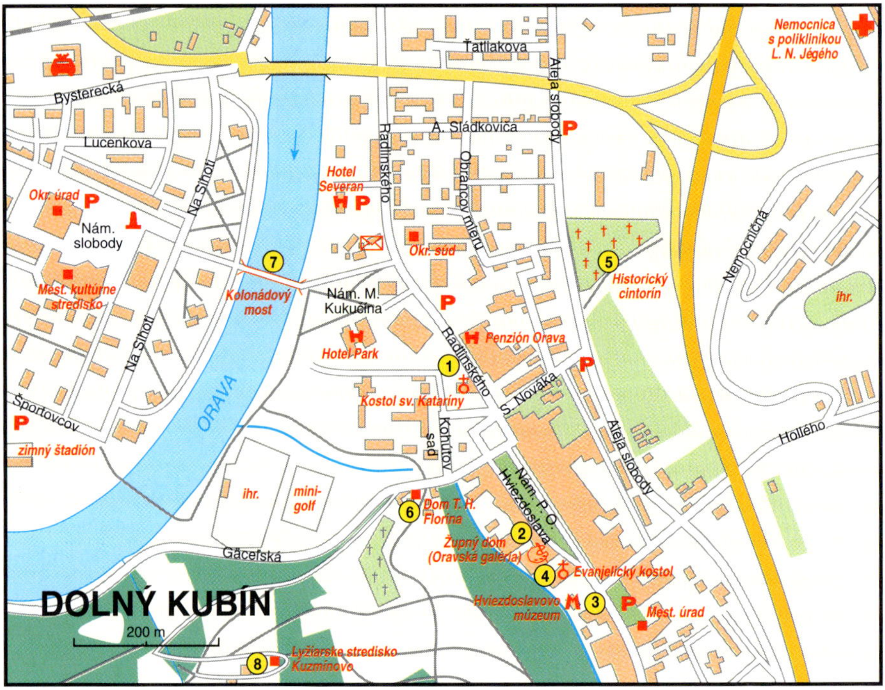

Oravská galéria, tel.: 0845/86 32 12
Opening hours: Tue-Sun 10:00-17:00h

In upper part the square is **Hviezdoslavovo múzeum** (3) (Museum of Hviezdoslav). The building of the Museum was built at the beginning of the 20th century as a library for V. Čaplovič, whose book collections are there until now. There is also a literary museum of P. O. Hviezdoslav commemorating the life and artistic work of this genius of Slovak poetry. In front of the Museum stands the **statue of P. O. Hviezdoslav** by F. Štefunko. Opposite is the house of the poet where he lived, worked and died. The facade of the building bears a **commemorative board**.

P. O. Hviezdoslav Múzeum, tel. 0845/86 47 80
Opening hours: Tue-Sun 7:30-16:00h

Next to the Museum is an **Evangelic church** (4) built in the years 1893-1894 as designed by B. Bulla. It stands on the site of the original church damaged by fire. Among the sacral monuments is also the nearby historical **cemetery** (5) with the tombs of important figures of the Slovak nation. As far as the secular buildings are concerned visitors should pay attention to the reconstructed **house of T. H. Florin** (6). It was originally a house of a dyer occupied later by this globetrotter active in cultural life. The basement of the house is made of stones and the upper part of the house is partially made of bricks and wooden logs. At present it is used by the Orava Museum for its expositions.

Dom T. H. Florina (House of T. H. Florin),
tel.: 0845/86 25 07
Opening hours: Tue-Sun 8:30-16:00h

An admired object of the contemporary Dolný Kubín is the wooden **column bridge** (7) over the river Orava connecting the old part of the city with the local part Bysterec. Fans of skiing will appreciate the modern **ski centre Kuzmínovo** (8) almost at the centre of the city. This "ski paradise" offers to the visitor a 900 m long ski track with three lifts, artificial snow and night illumination.

Right: Dolný Kubín square

There is a ski school for small children, hiring service of ski equipment and other services. Catering and lodging contribute to the unforgettable experience of night skiing.

Dolny Kubín is also an ideal starting point to the most beautiful parts of the **Oravská Magura** mountain range. In the railway station starts a yellow-marked footpath which passes the local part Záskalie and continues along the paved field road across the meadows and a forest to the cottage at the **Kubínska hoľa mountain** (1,346 m). The cottage is approximately 1,000 m south below the ridge of the Oravská Magura mountains and is the cross-roads of several hiking routes. The most frequently visited mountain of Oravská Magura is the Kubínska Hoľa mountain accessible by a yellow-marked tourist path, beginning steeply then later becoming a moderate slope up to the shallow saddle at the ridge of the Kubínska Hoľa. Its huge, denuded massive ridge offers some admirable panoramic views. The grassy surface of the mountain is covered by flowers throughout the vegetation season. On the northern slopes diverse swamp plant communities grow, and the spot called Puchmajerovej jazierko (Puchmajerová's lake) is a protected locality for its peat vegetation and its unique micro-fauna. But Kubínska hoľa is rather more visited in winter as a ski resort. Lovers of cross-country skiing prefer the ridge of the Kubínska hoľa mountain, while down-hill skiers concentrate in the area with five ski lifts on the southern slopes of the mountain. An ideal walk on skis is the one to nearby **Minčol** (1,396 m), the highest mountain within the mountain range. Because of its well-preserved spruce-beach-fir forest, bordered with primeval forestation it was declared a **national nature reserve**. Especially in winter time when the trees acquire bizarre shapes as a result of fierce northern winds, a walk to Minčol can be a wonderful experience. The return trip from the cottage on Kubínska Hoľa is possible following the green-marked route leading across the wood and along the down-hill ski track, continuing over the saddle up to the hill Trniny, a well known archaeological locality, the name of which is derived from thorny shrubs that used to cover the hill in the past. From there it is only a short walk to the river Orava and the city centre.

North-east of Dolny Kubín, next to the main road communication heading to the Polish border and on the bank of the river Orava is the small community of **MEDZIBRODIE NAD ORAVOU** (514 m, population 400). Historical acts mention it as *Medzbrode*, a serf community of the Orava estate. As its name suggests, (brod = ford), suggests there used to be a ford here which the community cared for. However, after a great flood in 1813, the community was moved to the opposite bank, where it now exists. The river played an important role in the life of the villagers as it provided them with work and sustenance. The local people were busy in wood floating, the building of rafts and of course, farming. As there was also a quarry here the manufacture of paving stones was also one of the local occupations. In the 1960's, north of the community a big metallurgical plant was constructed, where the majority of population of Medzibrodie now work.

Nevertheless, the most attractive locality for the tourists is the nearby community of **ORAVSKÝ PODZÁMOK** (520 m, population 1,300), lying only several kilometers north of Medzibrodie on the river Orava, under impressive cliffs. The area of the community was inhabited as early as the Younger Bronze Age, an era to which the cremation graves are dated. A decisive role in its past was played by the castle built on the cliff, at the top of which a settlement of the Púchov culture was discovered. Though the castle was mentioned as early as in the 13th century, the village under it originated later. It developed from the castle community founded by the family of Thurzo in the mid-16th century. It was first inhabited by the castle servants, clerks and the craftsmen. In the 17th century it had a toll gate, saw mill, a brewery, a mill and carried out the making of gunpowder. There was also an agile trade and social life, and several crafts thrived. The population at the beginning of the 18th century and the end of the 19th oscillated between 100 and 400. In the 20th century, however, the community partially lost of some its economic importance but one of the most interesting landmarks of northern Slovakia, the **Orava Castle,** still attracts thousands of tourists every year.

Construction of the castle, much like others in Slovakia was created on the site of old wooden forts after the Tartar invasion in 1241. This boundary fort was built above all because of the need to protect the northern boundary of the Old Hungarian state and an important trade road to Poland. It soon became the administrative centre of the Orava region. The first written reference to Orava Castle as *castrum Arva* is dated to 1267, as the property of the Old Hungarian king Belo IV. Succeeding owners changed and it was alternatively possessed by the king and rich Old Hungarian aristocrats. In 1370 it became a county castle and the seat of the Orava Castle estate which included almost the whole of Orava. The lords of the castle were also hereditary counts until 1713. Among the best known owners from the 13th to 19th centuries, besides the kings, were count Donč, Matúč Čák Trenčiansky, Stibor of Stiboríc, Ján of Dubovec amongst others. All of them more or less rebuilt the castle. Originally it was built in the Romanesque and Gothic styles and later altered in Renaissance and Neo-Gothic styles. It consists of several buildings copying the shape of the castle rock. The buildings of the upper, central and lower castle were built progressively before the end of the 17th century. In the 13th and 14th centuries the upper castle existed on the top of the rock, while the central castle was actually a fortified foot part of the castle. Extensive building adjustments were made by the Old Hungarian king Matej Korvín by the end of the 15th century, who ordered the construction of a palace in the central castle near the castle wall. In the first half of the 16th century Ján Dubovec continued in the reconstruction of the upper castle and built also a palace for living in the central part of the castle, fortified the walls and had the contemporary second castle gate with loopholes and drawbridge made. In 1556 the Castle fell into the hands of the Thurzos' who were the authors of the most extensive reconstruction of the castle's history. Frantisek Thurzo reconstructed in the years 1556-1561 the decaying upper castle, and finished the work in the central and lower castle, namely Thurzo's Palace. His son Juraj finished the fortifications and adjustments and Orava castle acquired its present form in 1611.

The Thurzos':

The family of Thurzo belonged to the richest Old Hungarian families since the 15th century. Their fortune and power derived from the copper mines near Banská Bystrica. They joined then with the most important industrial and financial figures of Europe, the Fuggers' of Augsburg, Germany and created a common and highly profitable en-

Right: Orava Castle

terprise trading in copper. As a primary trade route lead from Banská Bystrica to Orava and further into Poland and Germany, passing the all important Orava castle, it is little wonder that it aroused the interest of the Thurzos', namely František. One of the folk legends asserts that František decided to purchase the castle after an argument between Thurzo and the castle Lady of Hričov, whom he incarcerated in the basement of Hričov castle where she later died. Thurzo did not recover his peace of mind in the Castle of Bytča and after marrying the rich Lady Barbora he left for Orava. He rebuilt and repaired the castle but his beloved wife died. Though he married again, bad luck did not abandon him as his daughter drowned in the castle well. Thurzo believed that her death was a punishment for the deeds committed in Hričov. Thurzo died in hallucinations and horrid recollections of Lady Hričov. His son Juraj, an Old Hungarian paladin also settled down in Orava Castle mainly, so it is rumoured, because of good hunting and fishing possibilities offered by the local natural setting. Hunting in the woods of the nearby village of Krivá he once sent a basketful of beautiful and tasty apples to his wife Alžbeta. When he was later fighting against the Turks his wife sent him fruit from the same apple trees of Krivá far to the Lower Land (the southern part of the Old Hungarian Empire). Legend has it that they made him feel so strong that he defeated the Turks. When he came back home he ordered the picking of all the apples around Krivá, but they never gave fruit again and Thurzo's greed for happiness and delight was punished.

After the Thurzos' died out the castle was owned by several landlords who did not take much care of it. The biggest disaster affected the castle in 1800 when it burnt down, and became useless. Only at the end of the 19th century did Jozef Pálffy make a partial attempt to reconstruct it, though the most extensive reconstruction was made after the Second World War. Today the Castle is a remarkable compound of buildings of the lower, central and upper castles with palaces, fortifications and towers. Visitors are intrigued by the three entrance gates communicated by a tunnel, under which there is a dungeon. In the Castle itself **Oravské múzeum** (the Orava Museum) was established with a numerous series of expositions. In the oldest part of the upper castle an archaeological exposition documenting the oldest history of the Orava settlement is installed including the finds of the golden and silver coins, and evidence of a remote Slavic settlement. Natural history is represented in the bottom floors of the central castle with samples of fauna and flora of the Roháče mountains, the Orava Dam and the Oravská kotlina basin. In the upper floor of the central castle an ethnographic exposition is placed. It displays the typical tools, garments and products of the rural people, describes their customs, their way of life and work. Historical exposition consists of a group of medieval and Renaissance buildings with their original furniture. The rooms with the furniture from a particular era, medieval arms and the dungeon with the torture chamber are open to the public which makes it possible for visitors to delve into the past and appreciate both its bright and dark sides.

Oravský hrad – Oravské múzeum
(The Orava Castle)
tel.: 0845/89 31 93
Opening hours: November 1,-April, 30 only in advance announced visits, May, September, October, Tue-Sun 9:00-16:30h, June 1,- August 30, daily 9:00-17:30h.

Of the remaining cultural and historical monuments in Oravský Podzámok the Late-Baroque building of the former **prefecture** of 1797 with a Neo-Classicist facade in the square is worth attention. Also the building of the old **post office** of the first third of the 19th century with Classicist facade, is interesting. The most important sacral monument is the Roman-Catholic **church of St. Ján Nepomucký** from the beginning of the 19th century. A part of Oravský Podzámok is the former independent community of Dolná Lehota. It originated in the 15th century as part of the castle manor of the Orava estate. Its inhabitants were exempt of hard toil and the community was administered from the very beginning by elected mayors. The only cultural monument of the local part of Dolná Lehota is the **chapel of the Virgin Mary** from the beginning of the 19th century, situated at the centre of the community.

Two kilometres to the east and up the river stream, near the main Orava road and railway communications is the village of **HORNÁ LEHOTA** (534 m, population 550). This community was for the first time mentioned in historical acts in 1420 as *Lehotha*. First it belonged to the Orava estate and in 1587 it was donated by the Thurzos' to Ján Abaffy. The family Abaffy constructed here two manor houses, one of them was preserved, the other turned to ruins. The community was populated mostly in the 18th century. A century later it had even more than 700 inhabitants, busy in farming and pottery, in the 20th century also embroidery and cloth weaving handicrafts were popular. The Baroque **manor house**, later reconstructed in Classicist style, is the pride of the community. After an ambitious reconstruction it is used nowadays as a motel with a stylish restaurant and a tavern that should satisfy the most particular clientele. Among the sacral monuments a Roman-Catholic **church of the Holiest Trinity** predominates. Originally a Renaissance building from the beginning of the 17th century it was restored in the 18th century into a Baroque style. In the interior of the church a Renaissance wooden painted dome and wooden paintings from between 1671 and 1691 are of interest.

The nearby community of **SEDLIACKA DUBOVÁ** (530 m, population 500) is probably the oldest community in the vicinity and was settled as early as the early Hallstatt period. It was quoted in the historical acts for the first time in 1397 as a serf community of the Orava estate with hereditary village mayors called *Dubowa*. It fell into decay and was abandoned during the fights of the rebellious aristocracy against the crown and after restoration it was again damaged in 1808 by a great flood. It suffered destruction also in the Second World War. The most important monument of the community is the Neo-Gothic Roman-Catholic **church of St. Michal Archangel**, built in 1880-1886.

Until the 16th century a part of Sedliacka Dubová was also what is now an independent community **DLHÁ NAD ORAVOU** (527 m, population 1400). It was mentioned in historical acts for the first time in 1420 as *Dluha Luka*. It belonged to the Orava estate and administered by the hereditary mayors also after its independence. In 1683 it was sacked by the Polish-Lithuanian troops, but by the beginning of the 19th century its population rose to more than 1,000. The people of

Right: The hammer mill in Podbiel

the village lived by farming, cattle keeping, cheese trading and various crafts. There were three sawmills, blacksmith's hearths, advanced weaving and basket-making. A good quality linen was made here in the 19th century. After the First World War the economic growth of the community was severely affected by emigration and fires in 1930 and 1962. The fires damaged several objects of folk architecture. The Roman-Catholic **church of St. Ladislav** in the Baroque and Classicist styles built in 1811 as a chapel and expanded later is the dominant building.

More to the north-east the community of **KRIVÁ** (545 m, population 764) developed similar to some other communities nearby from a castle manor estate founded in the mid-16th century. It was mentioned for the first time in historical acts as *Krywa* in 1575. As a serf community of the Orava estate under the administration of the hereditary mayors, it decayed during the wars of the aristocracy against the crown. Later is was known for its pottery all over the region of Orava. The local people were also busy in weaving and basket-making. But at the time of the First Czechoslovak Republic many of them had to emigrate. Old folk architecture is represented by several **log houses and farm buildings** and a wooden **mill** of 1898. The Roman-Catholic Neo-Romanesque **church of St. Jozef**, built in 1926 and a Baroque **chapel** of the beginning of the 19th century are of much interest as well.

Several kilometres south and south-east of these communities, lying along the principal Orava road and the river Orava, at the dividing point of the Orava hills, Choč and Skorušinské vrchy mountainns are several other small communities.

The community **CHLEBNICE** (594 m, population 1,500) was founded pursuing the Wallachian privilege in the mid-16th century presumably by the settlers of nearby Dlhá. Historical acts quoted it for the first time in 1564 as *Chlewnica*. It also belonged to the Orava estate and it was administered by hereditary mayors. The local population subsisted on farming, sheep-keeping, linen and tobacco trading, and later trading in flax and iron products. They were also known for producing top quality cheese. At the time of the First Czechoslovak Republic the glass manufacture and cooperage became popular crafts. Fires in 1929 and 1932, however, caused great damage in the community and among other things a valuable wooden church of 1753 was consumed by the fire. Several **log houses** from the 19th century are preserved. Sacral monuments are represented by the Roman-Catholic Baroque **church of the Virgin Mary's Ascension**, built in 1753, later expanded and adjusted, as well as the 19th century **chapel**.

The nearby communities of **PRIBIŠ** (643 m, population 500), **PUCOV** (591 m, population 700) and **POKRYVÁČ** (640 m, population 200) also originated in the 16th century pursuing the Wallachian privilege. They belonged to the Orava estate and were first administered by hereditary village mayors. When the Theresian land and duties register was introduced the mayors were elected. The population suffered greatly during the wars, when Pokryváč and Pucov were totally destroyed. Farming, cattle and sheep keeping were accompanied by trade in food products, stonemasonry (preserved until the 20th century in Pokryváč and Pribiš), weaving and making wooden products were the most common occupations of the local people. The best preserved cultural and historical monuments are mostly the sacral buildings such as the Roman-Catholic Baroque **church of St. Katarína** from 1780 and a **chapel** of the first half of the 19th century and a **stone cross** from 1808 in Pribiš. Pucov boasts a Roman-Catholic Classicist **church of St. Andrej** with preserved folk wood carvings, built in 1805. There are excellent conditions for skiing and tourism around these communities.

Going to the south under the slopes of the Choč mountains are the communities of **MALATINÁ** (803 m, population 850), **OSÁDKA** (670 m, population 150) and **LEŠTINY** (586 m, population 220).

Malatiná originated by the beginning of the 14th century on the road from Liptov to Orava. Historical documents quoted it for the first time in 1313 under the name *Malocharyta* as a serf community of the Starhrad castle in the Liptov region. Later it belonged to several Liptov and Orava landlords. Its relatively elevated position above sea level was the cause of several "frozen" years (1716, 1776, etc.) when famine thinned the population. The people of Malatiná were mostly busy in farming, though at the beginning of the 19th century also iron ore was extracted here for a short time. The community's life was severely affected by massive emigration in the time of the First Czechoslovak Republic. The most important monument here is the Roman-Catholic Classicist **church of All Saints** of 1804. Malatiná is the starting point for trips to the **Sestrčská dolina valley**, also called Malatínska, once a usual route when passing from the Liptov to the Orava region (see page 187).

Not far away from Malatiná is the village of Osádka, quoted in historical documents for the fist time in 1381 as de *Superiore Leszina* or *Vyšné Lešiny*. Before 1548 it belonged to the family of Zmeškal, clerks of the Orava estate, to whom it was donated by the Old Hungarian king Ferdinand I. The population lived off cattle and sheep keeping, while at the beginning of the 20th century it was also producing home-made cloth and carpet manufacturing was also common. **Log houses** of the 19th century are preserved in Osádka and also the **log belfry** in the cemetery is of interest.

West of Osádka, on the northern foothills of Veľký Choč mountain is the village of Leštiny. It originated at the beginning of the 14th century as a serf community of the Orava estate and it is quoted by historical sources in 1381 as *Dolné Leštiny*. It was donated together with Osádka to the family of Zmeškal in 1548. In the past it used to be a larger community, the population in the 18th century was higher than at present. The people lived by traditional farming, specialising in bull breeding. Several important figures of Slovak cultural life stayed or lived for some time in the community (V. Čaplovič, P. O. Hviezdoslav amongst others) and from the 18th century on there existed here a school well-known for its enlightened, open and patriotic teaching. The whole area is a cultural monument. The most important monument in the community is the wooden Evangelic **church** of 1688 with wooden belfry. Its origin is connected with an anti-Hapsburg resistance, when the Austro-Hungarian emperor Leopold I issued legal articles permitting the Protestants to build two churches in each county after the defeat of Thököly's rebellion, (henceforth referred to as articled churches). The lavishly painted interior of the church is from the 17th and 18th centuries. Visitors are attracted especially by the main altar from the beginning of the 18th century, church pews with coats of arms, Renaissance baptistery of the 17th century, a copy of the burial flag of J. Zmeškal and an epitaph of M. Meško of 1753.

The wooden church and the bull:

The building of the articled church in Leštiny was not simple as the landlords of Orava Castle did not want to consent to it. The owners of the community, the family of Zmeškal intervened on behalf of the villagers but in vain. Finally the local people decided to build the church outside of the village and without permission. However, 25 years after the building was started the authorities finally permitted the building of two churches in the Orava region and the people of Leštiny did not waste any time, and so they took the church to pieces and moved it to the village. The rumour about the beautiful wooden church spread and attracted people from other villages. One day the church was attacked by robbers. The villagers led by the owner of the village, Zmeškal, bravely defended the church when one of the peasants let loose the most violent bull in the village. All villagers safely shut themselves in the church and the robbers who were outside were confronted by the bull. Consequently they had to retreat and to give

Right: The wooden church in Leštiny

up their plan to sack the church. Since then there is a bull in the coat of arms of the family Zmeškal as a token of gratitude for the protection it gave them.

An important secular building in Leštiny is the Late-Baroque **manor house of the Zmeškals'** from the end of the 18th century, rebuilt in Classicist style in 1840, and a **curia** of the 17th century, rebuilt in the first third of the 19th century.

West of Leštiny, under the Veľký Choč mountain and the cliffs of Ostrá and Tupá skala lies **VYŠNÝ KUBÍN** (525 m, population 500). The territory of the community was settled in remote historical times. In the valley of the Jasenová potok brook the urn cemetery of the Lusatian culture of the Younger Bronze Age neighbouring with a hill fort on Tupá skala rock was discovered. The hill fort was situated 300 metres above the community, its area was 200×400 metres and it was fortified by a massive rampart (8-12 m high and 380 m long). In the same vicinity the cemetery of the Hallstatt era was also found. On the Ostrá skala rock was another similar fortified settlement of the Hallstatt and La Téne periods. Further discoveries proved continuous Slavic settlements on the Ostrá skala rock up until the 13th century. The beginnings of the community Vyšný Kubín are linked to the year 1325, when one of the richest Old Hungarian aristocrats, Donč – the head of the Orava county administration and a castellan – donated the land of Vyšný Kubín (*Falseu Kolbin*) changing it for Liptovská Revúca for the descendants of Hudkont of Liptov, of which the aristocratic families of Kubínyi and Meško derive their origins. In 1355 the Old Hungarian king Ľudovít I separated the community from the Orava estate and finally adjudicated it to the families of Kubínyi and Meško. The community reached its present population in the 18th century. Farming, work in the local sawmill, blacksmithing and the three mills were the usual occupations of the local people. During the Second World War there were active strong partisan groups here and one of them camped above the community. Numerous important personalities of Slovak culture were born or lived in Vyšný Kubín: the poet P. O. Hviezdoslav, the writer A. V. Gazda, the teacher A. Medzihradský, the book collector A. Čaplovič, the female writer M. Figuli amongst others. P. O. Hviez-

doslav is here commemorated by a **monument** at the site of the house where he was born, as the house itself was burnt down. In the community are several **squire houses** and **log buildings** from the 18th and 19th centuries. The **Kubínyis' manor house** from the end of the 18th century, rebuilt in the second half of the 19th, the Classicist **squire curia** from the 19th century and an original Renaissance **manor house** from the 17th century, later rebuilt in Classicist style represent the squire traditions of the community. The spiritual life of Vyšný Kubín is symbolised by the Roman-Catholic **church of the Holiest Trinity**, built on Late-Gothic foundations from the end of the 15th century. It was later rebuilt and altered. The Late-Baroque main altar with the Gothic sculpture of the Holiest Trinity from the 15th century and a squire's tombstone from 1792 in the interior of the church are of interest.

In Vyšný Kubín begins a tourist path to the highest mountain of the Chočské vrchy mountains – **Veľký Choč** (1,611 metres). The green route continues by first crossing the community by a field road from where there is a magnificent view of the panorama of Ostrá and the Tupá skala rocks, which are protected rock areas. As the road continues across the forest the tour becomes a lot more toilsome ascending to Veľký Choč and passing the spruce forests and mountain meadows. In the alpine meadow called Drapáč the footpath crosses the red-marked route starting in Jasenová. The paths separate from each other for a while and eventually meet at the top of the Veľký Choč mountain. The mountain is covered by forests, prevailingly spruce and in the highest parts the only continuous growth of dwarf pines in the whole mountain range can be seen. Because of the well-preserved forests, at places almost virgin, and the rocks with rare species of flora the area has become the **national nature reserve**. A wonderful open panoramic view comprises all the mountain ranges of northern Slovakia. Descent is possible to Liptov or to Orava by several footpaths. Going to Orava is a comparably steep descent which ends either in Vyšný Kubín or in **JASENOVÁ** (537 m, population 400), situated more southward, and in

Left: The northerly slopes of the Chočské vrchy mountains

VALASKÁ DUBOVÁ (649 m, population 750). Jasenová was founded in the first half of the 14th century by the squires of Liptov and it was for the first time mentioned in the historical acts as *Jessen*. In the 16th century the landlords of Orava castle sent here the serfs to settle the community and as a result the community was partially settled by serfs and partially by squires. Similar to other nearby communities it dilapidated during the continuous wars between the aristocrats against the ruler but the life here was shortly after renewed. The population at the beginning of the 19th century was much in excess of the present time. Although the local people were above all farmers, popular activity was also distillery. The most famous native of the community, besides the founder of the Orava library V. Čaplovič, was the writer M. Kukučín (1860-1928). His **native house**, a typical Lower Orava homestead from the mid-19th century still exists in the community. An exposition installed in four rooms of the house commemorates by written and picture documents the life and work of the famous writer. The house is furnished with typical wooden furniture and its exterior is likewise an example of Orava wooden architecture.

Rodný dom M. Kukučína
(The native house of M. Kukučín), tel.: 0845/86 20 56
Openning hours: At call

Among other artistic monuments is the Classicist **manor house** of 1830 with its medieval balcony, four columns and a tympanon. The Evangelic Classicist **church** of 1836 with an interesting altar decorated by the picture of the Last Supper, a pulpit and baptistery also from 1836 represent the sacral monuments.

Nearby Valaská Dubová is the southernmost village of Orava in the border of the region contiguous with Liptov. It was mentioned for the first time as *Dubova* in 1322 in an act by count Donč, owner of the Orava estate. Later it belonged to the Likava estate, but in the mid-16th century passed under the rule of Orava Castle. Originally it was a Wallachian community. Its privileges were confirmed, for instance by the act of the Old Hungarian king Matej Korvín in 1474 containing the list of the duties for the people in Dubová connected with the protection of the trade roads against robbers.

The capture of Jánošík:

A position on the foothills of the Chočské vrchy mountains and at the passage of the important trade route from Orava to Liptov were the principal factors that predetermined Valaská Dubová as the place preferred by robbers. The robbers were a variety of people. Some were compelled to rob because of poverty, others were driven by hate against the lords and their inhuman treatment towards their lesser mortals. There were also some vicious individuals who simply relished human suffering. Among their victims were also the poorest villagers. The people of Dubová were merciless towards such robbers. But Dubová entered Slovak history mainly by capturing the Slovak national hero, Juraj Jánošík (Jurko) who robbed the rich to give to the poor. His capture took place in 1713 in a local wooden tavern. The taverner betrayed Jánošík to the landlord's armed servants. Poor Jurko, who meantime had lost his magic waist belt which kept him strong, had no chance against the servants much superior in number. The legend recounts that an old woman threw a fistful of peas under his feet. And Jurko slipped, and fell to the ground and the servants captured him. Later he was tried in court and sentenced to death by hanging from his ribcage.

The old folk traditions of Jánošík's capture is commemorated in the local tavern, a simple brick building built at the beginning in the 19th century on the site of its wooden antecedent. The board placed on its facade in 1930 reminds us of the sad event. The people of Dubová besides catching the robbers lived by farming the area's rocky and barren soil and trading in tobacco. The community used to have more inhabitants in the 19th century than in the present day. In 1933 the village was burnt down (133 houses and 2 mills were destroyed by fire) but after the Second World War it was thriving again. Valaská Dubová is the starting point for tourists heading to the Veľký Choč mountain. The most important sacral building in the community is the Roman-Catholic Neo-Romanesque **church of St. Michal Archangel**, built between 1866-1872. The main altar with the painting of St. Michal Archangel is from the end of the 19th century and the wall paintings by J. Hanula are from 1904.

LIPTOV

Ružomberok and its environs

The centre of the Lower Liptov region, that is the westernmost part of the Liptov Basin, is the district city of **RUŽOMBEROK** (494 m, population 30,650). It extends almost exclusively along the left bank of the river Váh and both banks of its tributary, the Revúca. Its location on the eastern foothills of the Veľká Fatra mountains, the north-western slopes of the Nízke Tatry mountains and the nearby south-western slopes of the Chočské vrchy mountains, creates the city's unique background – its three sides are enclosed by the mountains and the eastern side is open to the Liptovská kotlina basin. The fact that the city lies on the cross-roads of an ancient trade route leading form the Central Slovakian mining towns to Poland and the road along the river Váh from Košice and Spiš to Žilina, and further to Silesia, has strongly influenced its economic and cultural development.

The favourable position of Ružomberok has always attracted people long before the present era. In the city's territory numerous archaeological finds prove the existence of ancient settlements (discoveries of a Bronze Age axe, fortifications of Lusatian culture from the Younger Bronze Age, and Roman and old Slavic settlements). The Slovak settlement at the lower reaches of the river Revúca, in the territory of the present city, was for the first time referred to in 1233 as *terra possessio Reuche*. The settlement of the area in that period is also documented by the existence of a church in the last third of the 13th century. A new incentive for the development of the settlement was the arrival of German settlers at the beginning of the 14th century. The Germans founded here a new settlement called *Rosenberg* (Rose Mount) allegedly because of an abundance of rose shrubs on mount Hôrka, (today the site of the historical square and town hall), where the settlement was built and progressively dominated over the original Slavic settlement. In 1318 the head of the Žilina district administration, Donč, granted the settlement municipal privileges (the election of the mayor and priest, free use of the contiguous lands and exemption

from fees at the local market place) written down by the Estergom Archbishop. Gradually around the town the communities of Černová, Biely potok, Vlkolínec and Ludrová originated. In 1314 Ružomberok obtained extended municipal privileges from the Old Hungarian king Karol Róbert – such as exemption from the legal power of the head of the province, free fishing and hunting rights in the land adjacent to the town, the mining of gold, silver and copper, and exact delimitation of the city's territory. The growth of the city stopped in 1390 when the Old Hungarian king Sigismod of Luxembourg donated the city to the head of the Liptov province seated at Likava Castle so that Ružomberok became a serf town of the Likava estate. It was not entitled to build the town walls and it lacked the right of storage. A significant event in the social development of the town was the invasion of the Hussite troops and the occupation of Likava Castle and its estate in the years 1431-1433. Although the Hussites caused a lot of economic damage, they changed the German character of the town and reinforced the Slavic component. While in the 14th and the beginning of the 15th century the administration of the town was in the hands of the German colonists, during and after the Hussite movement it gradually passed to the Slovak population. The use of the German languages gave way to 'Slovakized' Czech, as proved by the preserved municipal document of 1527.

After the battle at Mohács Ružomberok developed as an agricultural town. The usual occupations of its population, besides farming, were the keeping of cattle and sheep and logging. The privilege of weekly markets and two annual fairs (from 1525) expanded by the Old Hungarian king Ferdinand III by another two fairs, helped the promotion of crafts and trade. Consequently, Ružomberok became and important market town of the Liptov region. In 1625 the town was the second largest Liptov settlement after Ľupča, and it possessed three mills, a sawmill, three breweries and numerous crafts existed here. By the end of the 16th century the craftsmen were organised into guilds. From 1578 there is a reference to the shoemakers' guild, ten years later the guild of tailors, cloth-makers and button-makers, and even later guilds were established amongst the blacksmiths, locksmiths, boot makers, butchers and coopers. But the most important role in the history of the crafts in Ružomberok was played by paper manufacturing, a symbol of the city which is preserved until the present day.

The paper mill in Ružomberok:

Although paper was used in Slovakia since the 14th century, its production in this country started only in the 16th. The Liptov region had ideal conditions for such production and progressively paper mills in Liptovský Michal, Ružomberok and Palúdzka were opened. The best known of these was the paper mill in Ružomberok situated on the banks of the river Revúca, today called Biely Potok, which provided a torrent of clear water endowing the paper with a pure white colour and serving as a driving force for milling the cloth – the basic raw material made of flax was a condition of primary importance. Though reference to the paper mill dates back to 1721 it was undoubtedly founded before that – at the turn of the 17th and 18th centuries. This is confirmed by the watermark – a rose – the trade mark of the manufacturers of Ružomberok which existed in the beginning of the 18th century. The paper mill was owned by the city and rented to the manufacturers at a yearly rate. In mid-18th century it had two rooms and a kitchen where the glue was also cooked. The technical equipment consisted of paper shredders, processing the cloth, and a beater. The shredders and the beater were driven by a water wheel. The building of the paper mill was originally constructed of wood and only at the beginning of the 19th century the brick buildings of the paper mill were built. The paper mill worked practically until 1847 when the general decline of the manufacture of paper gave way to the better and more economic machine paper production.

The landlords of the Likava estate in the 17th and 18th century considerably limited the city's privileges and whimsically increased its duties and fees. The city was incessantly in dispute with the landlords and the Liptov heads of the province and at the end of the 18th century these city disputes came to a head in the four streets of what is now the municipal section. The city's dependent position on the Likava estate ended only in 1848, the year of the onset of its growth. It was triggered by the construction of the railway track from Košice to Bohunice. The first train stopped in Ružomberok on December 8, 1871 in early hours of the morning. Ružomberok became one of the centres of Slovak economic enterprises associated under the Slovak, and later, the Popular Bank. By the end of the 19th century a big textile factory (in its time the biggest in Old Hungary), two pulp mills, a machine paper mill, a brick-yard, a matches manufacturing plant, a printing plant, and a

world famous plant producing the typical Slovak sheep cheese *bryndza* were founded here. Ružomberok was at the time also the centre of intellectual life amongst Slovaks. The journal *Hlas* (Voice) representing the Czech-Slovak trends and inclinations existing among the entrepreneurs in the field of big investment was edited here. A. Hlinka, a politician and fighter for the rights of the Slovaks and their autonomist movement, was also concentrated here. The spiritual and cultural development of Ružomberok was first of all based in the schools, which played a very important role in the city at this time. As early as in the 16th century there existed here the Evangelic Latin school for the children of the aristocracy and in 1729 a Catholic piarist secondary school also emerged. Among the most famous students of the latter were, for instance, A. Bernolák (the first codifier of the Slovak language), D. Makovický (the personal physician of the Russian writer L. N. Tolstoi), A. Hlinka, amongst others. The flourishing industry in the city also called for the establishment of vocational training for young people and that was the reason why the paper industry and textile schools were founded here and soon gained a national reputation. At the beginning of the 20th century the workers' and trade union movements were also gaining in importance and their most conspicuous manifestation came after the end of the First World War. The founding congress of the Marxist left was held in the city (as a follow-up to the congress held in Ľubochňa) and also the supreme bodies of the Communist Party and trade union organisation were seated here. Ružomberok became in the period of the First Czechoslovak Republic one of the most significant economic and political centres of Slovakia. Its importance grew in time from the existence of the Slovak state (1936-1945), when it was the military centre in the region. Simultaneously the resistance and anti-Nazi movement grew and the city suffered a lot in 1944 from German occupation. The Socialist era brought about further economic and cultural development for Ružomberok which is today and important industrial and cultural centre in northern Slovakia.

The best place to begin sightseeing in the city is the upper part called **námestie A. Hlinku** (the square of A. Hlinka), originally a quarter where the first German settlers arrived and founded the settlement Rosenberg. The "upper" part of the city is actually a copy of fort hills, common to other medieval cities. Because of the preserved **craftsmen's** and **burgher houses** in an original street structure from the 18th century, and numerous sacral and secular monuments, it was declared a monument reserve. Among the most valuable is the Late-Gothic Roman-Catholic **church of St. Ondrej**, (2) built in 1585 in the eastern part of the square on the site of a former Gothic church. However, a Neo-Romanesque reconstruction of the church in 1902 considerably changed its original appearance. The interior of the church is particularly interesting for its various wood-carvings art works and paintings, especially the Gothic babtistry from the beginning of the 16th century. And it also houses in its tower the oldest bell in the Liptov region called Andreas from 1506. Next to the church a part of the **old fortifications** are preserved and together with Tmavé schody (the Dark Stairs) it creates an impressive silhouette of the church. The secular landmark dominanting the square is the **town hall** (1) which stands beside the church. It was built in 1897 in Neo-Renaissance style. In its southern part there used to be a Roman-Catholic parsonage where A. Hlinka spent a part of

Left: The St. Ondrej church in Ružomberok

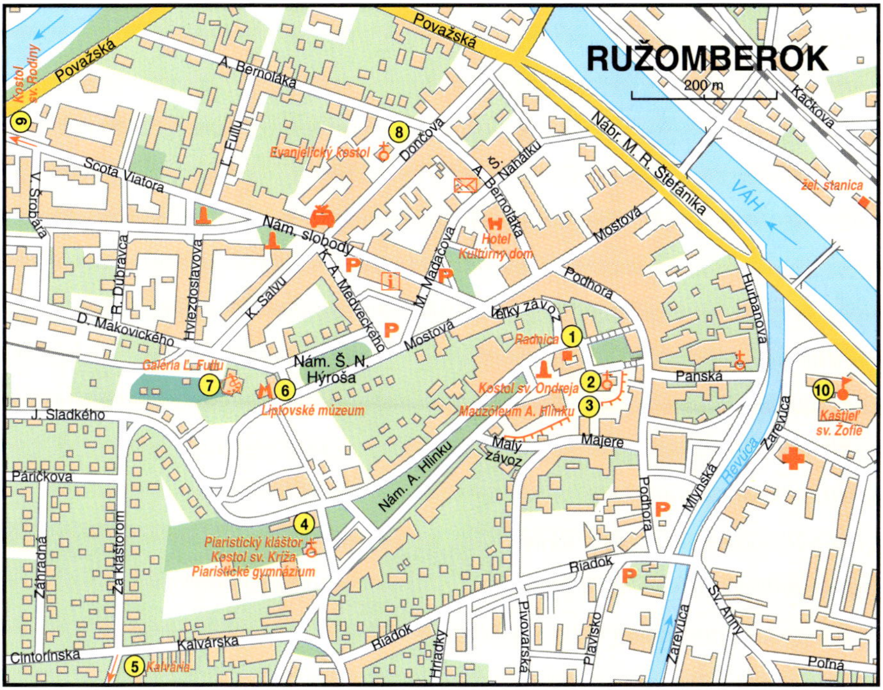

his life. His presence in the city is commemorated in the **mausoleum of A. Hlinka** (3) located next to the southern nave of the St. Ondrej church and set in the area of Veľké schody (the Big Stairs) with numerous balustrades. Other unique monuments in this part (4) of the square are the **Lady's Pillar** of 1858 standing in front of the town hall, and at the opposite, western end of the square is a **piarist monastery**, the Roman-Catholic **church of St. Cross** and the buildings of the **piarist secondary school**. The piarist monastery from the years between 1730-1735 was originally a Baroque building later reconstructed and expanded by the Jesuits. The monasterial church of St. Cross was built in 1806 and the baptistery and art work called the Good Pastor is from the same time. The piarist school was founded by count Löwenburg in 1727 and the Emperor Charles VI approved its foundation by his act of 1729 when the tuition actually began. The tradition of schooling in Ružomberok is also symbolised by the building of a former girls' school, the opening of which coincided with the arrival of the Merciful Sisters of the Order of St. Vincent in 1885. Beyond the square of A. Hlinka is another remarkable architectural monument – the **Calvary** (5). It is the only Liptov calvary and consists of the chapels of the Way of the Cross with 14 stations from the years 1858-1859 and a church from 1873.

After seeing the upper part of the city visitors usually proceed to the lower part using one of the staircases (for instance the Dark, Big, Rose or Monastic Stairs) which emphasise the charm of the upper part of the city. A favourite old town street is called Podhora – the oldest street in the city, including several **burgher houses**. Of these there are the houses of the family of Makovický, the house of the family of Houdek, which later became the seat of the Slovak Bank, and the **houses of the aristocracy** (the palace of Š. Rakovský, the chairman of the Hungarian Parliament and prime minister, in the second half of the 19th century) all of which document the architectural nature of Ružomberok in the 19th and 20th centuries. The nearby **Jewish synagogue** of 1880 bears witness to the diverse religious and ethnic essence of the city in the past. One of the liveliest streets of the city is Mostova street (Bridge Street) which indeed symbolises the city's link between history and the present, which leads from the river Váh and once served as a passage to Likava and its castle. An imposing building in the middle of the pedestri-

an zone is the one of the former **Ľudová banka** (Popular Bank) of 1807. The traditions of the workers' movement are represented by the building of the former **Robotnícky dom** (the Workers' House), the seat of the Slovak Communists and trade unionists after the First World War. Opposite this is the extensive multi-purpose building of **Kultúrny dom** (House of Culture), the centre of theatrical and cultural life of the city in the 20th century. Mostova street ends in the square with a large park, and the building of **Liptovské múzeum** (The Liptov Museum) (6). It was founded as an institution of the Liptov Museum Society and the museum now houses objects and documents of natural history, with branches all over the Liptov region. In this building can be seen archaeological finds, historical expositions from the feudal period, artefacts testifying to the activity of the craftsmen's guilds in Liptov, an ethnological exposition, sacral art, the history of paper manufacturing in the region, as well as an exhibition documenting the life and work of A. Hlinka.

Left: Vlkolínec

Liptovské múzeum (The Liptov Museum), tel.: 0848/32 24 68
Opening hours: Sept. 1-May 1, Mon-Fri 8:00-16:00h, Sat-Sun 9:00-13:00h, June 1-Aug. 31, Mon-Fri 9:00-17:00h, Sat-Sun 9:00-16:00h.

Not far away from the Museum is the building of the **Gallery of Ľudovít Fulla** (7) which contains the lifetime work of this internationally known Slovak painter and illustrator Ľ. Fulla (1902-1980). This impressive architectural gallery built in 1969 is the work of architect Š. Hatala. The visitor can also see, besides Fulla's paintings, his flat and studio.

Galéria Ľudovíta Fullu, tel.: 0848/32 48 67
Opening hours: daily Tue-Sun 10:00-17:00h.

Several **end of cetury buildings**, the Evangelic **church** (8) of 1926 and the Roman-Catholic "workers'" **church of the Holy Family** (9) (also called Fabrický) built in 1921 prevailingly for the employees of cotton manufacture are of interest. Also of fairly historically importance is a building which stands near the confluence of the rivers Revúca and Váh called the **mansion of St. Žofia** (10). The purpose of this originally Gothic medieval building was that of a fort and it was first referred to as *castellum* in 1397. It has been reconstructed many times and in the Middle Ages it was used as a luxurious "hostel" for the guests of the Likava Castle landlords. The mansion provided shelter to the Old Hungarian king Sigismond of Luxembourg, the Polish king Ján Kazimír, the Transylvanian prince Ján Bethlen, amongst others. Important negotiations took place here and in 1622 after pulling down the Likava Castle the mansion even became the seat of the Likava landlords. The assembly of the Liptov county held its sessions here, and at various times has been the seat of the court of justice, a prison, and also the elections of the Ružomberok mayors were held here. At the beginning of the 20th century, at the time of the most aggressive Magyarisation the "trials of Ružomberok" were held here against the supporters of the Slovak patriotic movement. Presently its five buildings (70 rooms) and two court yards are under reconstruction.

Another important feature of the city, from an historical point of view, are the communities located outside of the centre, which developed individually in the past, but have, nevertheless, depended not only on the Likava landlords but also on the city administration. The areas of Biely Potok, Vlkolínec. Černová and Hrboltová joined them in 1981. Another community called *Villa Ludrova* in 1876 once existed here, but since 1953 it became part of the community of Ludrová, lying east of Ružomberok. **Biely Potok** is in the southern part of the city along the road to the Donovaly mountains, mentioned for the first time in 1329. Its most important object of interest is the Roman-Catholic **church of St. Vendelín**, built in 1902. Biely Kostol is the salient point for the community of **Vlkolínec – a monument reserve of folk architecture** lying on southern foothill of the Sidorovo mountain. This extraordinary and remarkable oasis of folk architecture was included in 1993 in the List of the World Cultural and Nature Heritage of UNESCO. It is the place where time has stopped and one of the most frequently visited Slovak localities. The community was first referred to in 1376. It remained untouched by modern construction and represents a unique urbanistic compound of original folk buildings. Vlkolínec is a typical example of a two-line street pattern with long yards. Roughly in its centre the community divides into a street leading to the Baroque-Classicist brick Roman-Catholic **church of the Virgin Mary's Visitation** (1) of 1875 and a street heading along a more steeper terrain to the foothills of the Sidorovo mountain (1,099 m). At the division

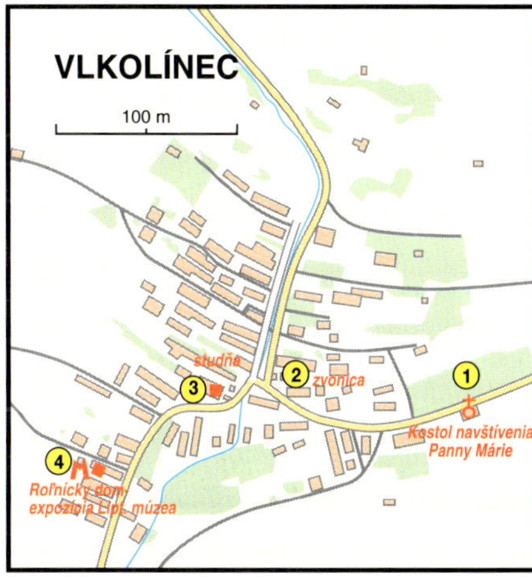

of the streets stand the two most frequently photographed objects – a log two-storey **belfry** (2) from 1770 on a stone stand and a **log well** (3) from 1860. Amongst the protected buildings in the community are 45 log houses with farm yards, which consist mostly of three-roomed houses with an entrance chamber in the centre. The houses are covered by shingle saddle roofs and behind them are the farmsteads and stables. A typical example of a house in Vlkolínec is the **farmers' house** (4) – a detached outdoor part of the expositions of the Liptov Museum. The house was built in 1886 and opened to public in 1991. Its well preserved original interior and furnishing provide a true picture of the way of life of its ancient inhabitants from the end of the 19th and beginning of the 20th century.

Roľnícky dom Vlkolínec
(The Farmers' house in Vlkolínec), tel.: 0848/32 24 68
Opening hours: May-Sept. daily 9:00-18:00h

The remaining protected objects in the monument reserve are still inhabited, therefore the visitor can see only the exterior of the houses. Through the middle of the community flows a brook which together with the surrounding nature, terraced fields and hay huts enhances the impressive scenery of this gem of Slovak folk architecture.

Part of Ružomberok is also **Černová**, which lies in the west and was referred to for the first time in 1376. The village has a Neo-Gothic Roman-Catholic **church of the Virgin of the Rosary** from 1907, the construction and consecration of which were connected with tragic events.

The tragedy of Černová:

Events in Černová also involve the aforementioned activist A. Hlinka, who was born here and initiated the construction of the church. The catholic priest A. Hlinka (1864-1938) was one of the prominent representatives of the fight for Slovak national freedom under the Austro-Hungarian empire. In 1906 he ran for candidacy as the Slovak deputy in the Parliamentary elections. As a punishment Bishop Párvy stripped him of his rector's office and his rights as a priest. However, when the building of the Černová church was finished the villagers demanded that their priest, Hlinka should be the one who should consecrate the new church. The bishop refused and sent other priests chosen by him to do the job. The villagers responded by blocking the road in an attempt to prevent the incoming official coaches from reaching the church. This show of defiance terribly irritated the Hungarian police who opened fire on the perpetrators of the blockade. Consequently 15 villager were killed in the conflict. A year later the Hungarian authorities staged the "Trial of Černová" against the protagonists of the rebellion sending forty of them to prison.

The tragedy is today commemorated by the **Monument of the Victims of the Černová Tragedy** at the local cemetery and a **commemorative board** marking the location of the conflict. The life and work of A. Hlinka is also commemorated by a plaque at the place of his native house. Other places of interest include a Classicist **chapel** from the beginning of the 19th century with a wood carving of St. Trinity by A. Belopotocký. The neighbouring community **Hrboltová** is the last municipal quarter of Ružomberok. The first written reference to it dates back to 1474 and in the past it belonged to the Likava estate. What is remarkable here is the **St. Katarína of Alexandria church** from the 13th century with an interesting stone statue of the Virgin Mary (mid-19th century). It was rebuilt and expanded in 1827.

The environs of Ružomberok offers lovers of nature some excellent trips. There are three wonderful Slovak mountain ranges within reach: the Low Tatras, the Veľká Fatra and the Chočské vrchy mountains. The starting point for the Low Tatras is in the local municipal part of Biely Potok with a tourist footpath marked in green leading to the Borovinsko mountain (866 m) with enchanting scenery and views of Lower Liptov which continues to the peaks of Ostrý (1,066 m) and Veľký Brankov (1,134 m). At the foothills of the latter is the **protected Brankovský vodopád waterfall** which falls from a height of 55 m. Though the ridge tour from Ostrý to Brankov is not among the typical ones in the Low Tatras, as it is rather comfortable and not too demanding, it provides wonderful views, for instance, of the wide grasslands on Brankov and the higher situated Low Tatra and Fatra mountain tops. A **commemorative board** placed at the top of the Ostrý recalls the dogged fighting that took place in this locality during the Slovak National Uprising against the German occupying forces in 1944.

Visitors to Ružomberok generally concentrate on the Veľká Fatra mountain range and the massive **Malinné** (1,209 m). Under the top of Malinné is one of the most frequented ski resort throughout Slovakia. Its big advantage is that it has easy and comfortable access from the Hrabovo valley by a cabin lift to the Májekova chata cottage, where there are safe ski tracks with four ski lifts available for skiers of all levels. Summer tourists prefer the ascent by foot, or otherwise they choose the red-marked footpath passing the Veľká Skala (908 m) and the Sidorovo (1,099 m) mountains to the Malina Hotel and continue by a blue-marked path. At the eastern foothills of the Sidorovo mountain is a conspicuous rocky formation, the phenomenal and **protected landscape of Krkavá skala**, a rock with a group of pines atop.

In the north of Ružomberok are the Chočské vrchy mountains, that likewise offer beautiful corners for tourists. One of the most attractive views of the city's panorama is from the Čebrať mountain (1,054 m) and the Predný Čebrať mountain (945 m) accessible by a red-marked path from the city.

The red-marked path also leads to the neighbouring community of **LIKAVKA** (520 m, population 3,000) located on the right bank of the river Váh, in the valley of the Likavka brook below which is the ruins of once famous Likava Castle. An important road linking Lower Liptov with Orava passes the village.

Likavka is among one of the oldest Liptov communities. Although the precise date of its origin is not known, it is supposed that it was founded as early as in the 11th or 12th century. A cemetery of Púchov culture and a post-Great Moravian settlement were discovered at the top of the castle hill suggesting an early settlement on the territory. In the 14th

---

Right: The St. Martin church in Martinček

century the community received additional settlers by Wallachian colonisation and fell into a serfdom connected to the **Likavský hrad castle**. Hence its history is closely connected with that of the Castle. The Castle was referred to for the first time in 1315 when the Old Hungarian king Karol Róbert donated it to Dvonč, the head of the province of Zvolen, for his devoted service. Its construction started probably at the beginning of the 14th century with the intention to have a guarding point over the passage across the river Váh and the trade route from the Váh Basin to Orava and further to Poland. A military guarding service and the administration of the royal properties in Lower Liptov were seated here. In the years between 1431--1434 the castle fell into the hands of the Hussite troops and after their expulsion king Sigismond of Luxembourg donated the castle to Ján Hunyadi. When, in 1474, Liptov Castle was destroyed it later became the centre of administration for the region of the Central Liptov. Its following owners expanded it serving the purposes of the time. At the beginning of the 14th century there was the upper Gothic castle with a chapel, which the Hunyadis' then progressively rebuilt and expanded the original nucleus of the castle building. In the mid-16th century the family of Pekry rebuilt the upper castle in Renaissance style and in the first half of the 17th century the Ilesshazys' finished the Renaissance-Baroque fortification of the first courtyard. In the second half of the 17th century the Thökölys' eventually finished the entire fortification system though it was of no use as it did not prevent the disaster at the beginning of the 18th century when the retreating troops of František Rákoczi completely pulled down the castle in 1707.

The life of the Likavka people was in hands and at the service of the owners of the Likava estate, performing their duties, engaged in farming, weaving, basket-making, wood carving and above all, rafting. Likavka was famous for its rafters on the river Váh and later with the development of manufacturing and industrial production new jobs were provided in Ružomberok. During the Second World War the local people actively participated in the Uprising against the Nazis with fatal consequences. In the locality of Kramariská pod Chočom, the Nazis executed 11 patriots and the event is commemorated by the **monument** erected in memory the victims. The most important sacral monument in the community is the Neo-Gothic Roman-Catholic **church of St.**

Juraj built in 1880. Folk traditions are held in the community in the form of a **children's folk festival** regularly held in an amphitheatre under the castle.

The neighbouring and somewhat higher situated community of **MARTINČEK** (598m, population 400) lying at the northern foothills of the Mních mountain (The Monk) also has an interesting history, where on its summit a remarkable system of ramparts, representing an extensive set of fortifications of the people of Lusatian culture in Liptov, was discovered. A collective discovery of Liptov swords from the Younger Bronze Age is a unique testimony of the settlement which has continued ever since. The community was for the first time referred to in an undated act of the Old Hungarian king Ladislav IV (1272-1299) and it was probably founded around the **church of St. Martin** (from which the community took its name). The Early-Gothic Roman-Catholic church was built around 1260 and in the second half of the 14th century it was expanded by a tower and a vestry. In the 18th century reconstruction it acquired Baroque features and in interior a part of the original frescoes have been preserved. The church is not only of local significance, but also important for the entire Lower Liptov region. The massive **Mních mountain** (696 m) by its form and appearance is also typical for this part of the Liptov region. **Skalná päsť** (The Rocky Fist) also called Jánošík's Fist, and is the subject of numerous myths which will certainly interest the visitor. It is a 6m high and 4 m wide rocky formation of dolomitic limestone amazingly similar to the human fist, hence its name A walk over the Mních mountain can end in the **Liskovská jaskyňa cave (national nature reserve)** at the eastern protuberance of Mních. The cave originated because of the activity of the river Váh and it has a labyrinth of corridors with several entrances. As it has always been easily accessible its ornamentation have been considerably eroded. Its total length is 2,120 m and it is closed to the public at present. It became famous for its archaeological finds, consisting of the skull of a primitive man and other human remains. It is highly probable that it was continuously settled since the Younger Stone Age up to the La Téne period.

The cannibals of Liskov:

One hundred years ago in the Liskovská jaskyňa cave some longitudinally broken human marrow bones were found. The place is presumed to be the one where a severe conflict between two tribes occurred several hundred years ago, whereafter the victors eventually ate their victims. The bones of approximately 48 people testify to what was probably the greatest cannibal "feast" in the history of the Central Europe.

Near the cave lies the community of **LISKOVÁ** (189 m, population 2,100). It was mentioned for the first time in 1252. In the past it was among the largest communities of the Likava estate. In the 18th century its population amounted to almost 1,000 who were engaged in farming, rafting, linen and cloth weaving, carpet-making and the knitting of laces. Many worked in the local quarry and brewery, referred to for the first time in 1625. The community became famous as the birthplace of Dr. Vavro Šrobár, the first minister for the administration of Slovakia during the First Czechoslovak Republic, a writer and patriot, whose life story can be read on a **commemorative board** on the site of the house in which he lived. The tragedies of the Second World War also visited Lisková when the Nazis executed here 23 people accused of participating in the Slovak National Uprising. The dominating building in the community is the Roman-Catholic **church of the Lord's Conversion** with a Baroque tower built in the years 1935-1936. The tower ending in an onion-shaped dome, is preserved from the original Gothic church and in 1803 it was rebuilt.

TURÍK (500 m, population 200), now an independent community, has until recently belonged to Lisková. It originated in the administrative territory of the community of Liptovská Teplá and it was referred to for the first time in 1278. Later it belonged to squire Turánsky's family, who received it as a present from the king for his loyal service as a royal messenger to Poland. The local population made their living from farming and were the first people in Liptov who introduced the idea of the co-operatives. The community includes also two smaller communities, Turíček and Vlčia jama, known in the past for its mill and a carriers' inn where almost all passengers used to stop. As for the monuments, the visitor will find here a **manor house**, originally built in the Baroque style in the 18th century, and the Roman-Catholic **church of the Visitation of the Virgin Mary** from 1798 with a wooden superstructured tower from the end of the 19th century.

On the right bank of the river Váh is the community of **LIPTOVSKÁ TEPLÁ** (510, population

Right: Lúčky waterfall

900). It developed from one of the oldest Liptov communities and it was referred to as early as in 1264. It belonged to the estate of the Liptovský Starhrad Castle and later to the Likava Castle. From the 18th century it was a squire's town given the privilege of fairs. Its population was engaged in farming, wood processing and rafting. The most important sacral monument of the community is the Roman-Catholic **church of St. Filip and St. Jakub** with some Early-Gothic parts from the end of the 13th century. In the 16th century it was rebuilt and in the 17th fortified. Its valuable Gothic details and frescoes are preserved up to the present day. The secular monuments are dominated by an originally Late-Renaissance **manor house** of the second half of the 17th century its style changed to Baroque in the 18th. Another **manor house** (Classicist from 1830) is also in the local part of **Madočany** made famous by a 14th century forger of historical acts, Ján Literát, executed in 1390 in Liptovská St. Mara.

In the territory of Liptovská Teplá originated today the independent community of **IVACHNOVÁ** (508 m population 450), for the first time mentioned in 1298 as the land belonging to Ivanko. Later it was owned by the royal family and since the second half of the 16th century by the squire family Rády. It was a farming community often destroyed by floods, but has preserved its agricultural character until the present time.

Visitors of this part of Liptov usually make the point of visiting the spa of **LÚČKY** (598, population 1,700) situated under the impressing massive mountain of Veľký Choč. Its lower part consists of the old village and the upper part is the location of the spa. The settlement has been in existence since the Younger Stone Age. The Younger Bronze Age is documented by a collection of bronze vessels from this period. It was referred to for the first time in 1287 and used to belong to the Likava estate. Its population made their living from sheep raising, fishing and work in quarries. The most important sacral monument in the community is the Roman-Catholic Classicist **church of St. Cross Ascension** of 1824, that together with the old rectory and school form a common compound. But Lúčky is above all a **spa**. Mineral springs are known here from 1761 when the squire Adam Turanský built here the first spa building. The fame about the healing effects of the local spring spread rapidly, bringing the spa abundant visitors even as early as in 1777. In the years 1820 to 1824 the spa expanded, but in the second half of the 19th century it gradually declined. Its importance grew again only after the Second World War when new therapeutic facilities were built and the overall standard of therapy improved, and the spa has since then become important for the cure of gynaecological ailments. The decisive healing element here is the plaster-earthy carbonic mineral water of the spa spring with a water temperature of 32°C. The therapeutic procedures in the swimming pools and bath tubs are accompanied by rehabilitating exercises and physical therapy. The patients have the privilege of enjoying unique natural scenery and their walks often end in either of the two protected natural rarities: the **Lúčanský vodopád waterfall** – a cascading waterfall with water falling from a height of 12 m in two little lakes, and the **Lúčanské travertines** formed by two rocky walls (a well-known paleonthological and archaeological locality).

Tourists will certainly enjoy the occasion to ascend the majestic **Veľký Choč mountain** (1,611 m) – the highest summit of the Chočské vrchy mountains. The ascent is rather demanding, especially its first part is steep and tiresome. It starts in a forested valley steeply passing later into meadows called

Žimerová. The aesthetics of the green grassland contrasts here by the steep cliffs of the Veľký and Malý Choč mountains that usually are the aim of the high mountain hiking tour (see page 156).

Lúčky neighbours with **KALAMENY** (568 m, population 450). It originated in 1264 in the territory of Liptovská Teplá. The land was obtained by the squire Kelemen giving the name also to the community. The local people were farmers and shepherds. The history of the community is closely linked to that of the **Liptovský hrad castle**, ruins of which are accessible following a yellow-marked path. Liptovský castle also called Sielnický on Sestrč mountain (1,000 m) belongs to the highest situated castles in the Central Europe. It was built in 1262 above an old trade route leading across the Sestrč valley and communicating the regions of Liptov and Orava with Poland. But even before that a Halstatt fort existed here proven by the finds of bronze objects relevant to the period. The castle passed in 1313 from the hands of the "lord of the Váh and the Tatras", an Old Hungarian magnate Matúš Čák Trenčiansky to the ownership of the head of the Zvolen province, Dvonč and in 1340 it became the seat of provincial administration for the Liptov region. At the beginning of the 15th century it was repeatedly damaged by the fighting caused by king Sigismound of Luxembourg and later by those of the Hussites. Although the family Pongrác had the Castle repaired in 1447, the Old Hungarian king Matej Korvín ordered it to be demolished in his revenge against the former owner Komorovský who conspired against him. Today only one wall remains and a basement is overgrown by weeds.

Several kilometres south, on the right bank of the river Váh is **BEŠEŇOVÁ** (512 m, population 400). The territory of the community was settled since Neolithic times, by people of linear ceramic culture. And later by a continuous Aeneolithic settlement (people of a culture of fluted ceramics) and in the Bronze Age (with collective discoveries of bronze objects, and a cemetery of Lusatian culture) which all proved the advantages of this location for living even since ancient times. The community probably developed in the second half of the 12th century of the one formed by the royal border guards, called Pečenehs. Other sources quote in 1279 a community under the

Left: The manor house in Bešeňová
Right: The thermal swimming-pool in Bešeňová

name Marcelová, later renamed after the squire Bešeň's family. Since the 15th century the community had two names – Marcelová, later Mitošiny – for the western part of the community around the manor house and Bešeňová for the rest of the community. It previously belonged to the Liptovský Starý Hrad Castle, then in the 15th century to the Likava estate and from the 17th century to the family of Dvornik. The villagers were above all farmers, and other worked in local distilleries. The community is today one of the most visited of the Liptov villages, because of its cultural monuments and nature. The Renaissance-Baroque **manor house** with towers dates back to the first half of the 17th century. It was rebuilt by the family Dvornik and 'Baroquised' in the second third of the 18th century. At present, although it is in private hands, there are still collections at the **Liptov Museum** documenting the history of hunting, ways of hunting and development of hunting organisations.

Poľovnícke múzeum Bešeňová
(Hunting Museum Bešeňová) tel.: 0848/32 24 68
Opening hours: May-Sept. Tue – Sun, 9:00-18:00h.

The most important monument of the community is the **chapel of the Holiest Trinity** dating from 1890. However, most visitors come above all because of the **thermal swimming pool** built on the site of thermal healing water springs from a depth of 1,980 m and reaching a temperature as much as 62°C. In five swimming pools the water temperature is between 30-40°C depending on the season. These mineral spring are proven to be beneficial to human health, as well as a stay in the hot the water in winter months amid the snowed landscape. The **protected nature area Bešeňovské travertíny** north of the community is also interesting. Its area is 3.18 ha and consists of older travertine formations called the Travertine Field.

The nearby community of **POTOK** (554 m, population 120) was for the first time referred to in 1273 in relation to the Liptov Castle. A well-known medieval trade route connecting the castles of Zvolen, Liptov and Orava once passed through the community, which once belonged to the local squires Potocký and Kubínyi. At the turn of the 18th and 19th centuries it was burned down and only several houses escaped the fire. It has preserved its agricultural character until the present time.

Beside Bešeňová, on the other end of the motorway, is **LIPTOVSKÝ MICHAL** (526 m, population 250). Again evidence of a settlement by the people of fluted ceramics culture, people of Lusatian culture and a Slavic settlement of the time of Great Moravia suggest ideal living conditions, that have existed here for centuries. The first reference to the community dates back to 1331. But it probably originated a century earlier as the existence of church from 1294 suggests. The community developed from the serfs of the church and in the past, in spite of low population it was known for the production of paper (a paper mill was built here in 1606 and belonged to the former town of Partizánska Ľupča which was the oldest one in the Liptov region) and it was also known for iron smelting. It belonged to the rectory in Liptovská Teplá and since the end of the 18th century to the family of Rády. Its most important monument is the Roman-Catholic, originally Gothic **church of St. Michal**, built in the 13th century. The church was rebuilt in the second half of the 19th century though the Gothic arches, windows and portals have been preserved. The current interior is prevailingly in the Baroque style dominated by the main altar with a painting of St. Michal by J. Hanula. An interesting item of the exterior is a wooden **belfry** of the 17th century, originally built as the gate to the enclosure of the church yard. Also the **Trinity Pillar** of 1823 connected with the following anecdote is of interest.

How the villagers lost the Trinity Pillar:

While in Michal several sacral monuments existed, Bešeňova had none, and that was the subject of frequent jokes and mockery. Once the rafters of Michal and Bešeňová came back home from Budapest on foot and on the way those of them from Bešeňová collected gifts of charity for the building of a Trinity Pillar hiding it before their colleagues of Michal. But because along the route there were numerous taverns and the wine was good, the rafters of Bešeňová not wanting to lag behind their colleagues of Michal in drinking, spent all their collected money. This is how they won the nickname "trojičkári" (the Trinity handlers).

Returning to Ružomberok, there are several communities in the Liptovská kotlina basin, particularly in the part within the Low Tatra. The easternmost of them is **SLIAČE** (550 m, population 3,800) consisting of three localities: Nižný, Stredný and Vyšný Sliač. In Vyšný Sliač an Aeneolithic elevated settlement of the people of fluted ceramic culture was discovered, along with bronze Liptov swords and a burnt-burial place of the Halstatt period. Nižný and Stredný Sliač were referred to as early as in 1251 as the property of the Premonstratesian monastery seated in Kláštor pod Znievom. Vyšný Sliač probably originated only in the first quarter of the 16th century when the three communities were connected into one with a common mayor. Interesting enough is that the community elected its mayors and pretended to be a town even though it did not possess any municipal privileges. At the beginning of the 17th century Sliače was the largest community in Liptov with various crafts and guilds. Cattle handling, work in the brewery and several mills were the common occupations. In the 18th century Sliače became a serf town with a market and fair privileges. Besides their crafts the local population made their living from farming and sheep keeping. The shepherds of Sliač were highly estimated experts hired by the surrounding villages and cattle raising was also connected with the production of cheese and practical utensils. As there was a shortage of jobs in the second half of the 19th and early 20th century the population left en masse for seasonal jobs in the south or emigrated overseas. Strikes by the local wood workers and carriers in the thirties of the 20th century were also commonplace. After the Second World War the community prospered as the population found work in nearby Ružomberok. Sliače preserved its traditions and folk customs, which inspired artists of all kinds, and are promoted by the **local folk ensemble** up to the present time. The dominant building in the village is the originally Gothic Roman-Catholic **church of St. Šimon and Júda** built in 1334. The tower and the defensive wall are from the 17th century. In the first half of the 18th century the church the style of the church was changed to Baroque by reconstruction and in 1830 it was expanded. In the interior of the church are the original Gothic wall paintings from the 14th and 15th centuries, as well as numerous architectural details (the arch, portals, windows and bars). The main altar is adorned by a Late-Gothic board painting of Madonna dated 1517. The lateral Late-Gothic wing altars are from the early 16th century, the pulpit is from the 17th century and baptistery is 18th century. Lovers of folk architecture will find here log white-painted **granaries** and a **wooden belfry** from the beginning of the 19th century. The **protected nature area Mofetový prameň Spring** near Vyšný Sliač

Right: The St. Michal church in Liptovský Michal

with thermal, slightly hydrogen monosulphide mineral water, and travertine deposits are also worth visiting.

West of Sliače along the main road connecting with Ružomberok lies **ŠTIAVNIČKA** (497 m, population 500). In the territory of this community the traces of a settlement by the people of Púchov culture of the La Téne and Roman eras were found. The community itself was later documented in 1505 and developed on the territory belonging to the community of Štiavnica with a variety of different owners. The local population were mostly farmers or worked as agricultural hands. Today with its urban fabric it progressively has become a part of the city of Ružomberok. South of Štiavnička in the immediate neighbourhood is its older "brother" **LIPTOVSKÁ ŠTIAVNICA** (560 m, population 800). The settlement of this community is also connected with the people of Púchov culture, the remains of which are represented by a fort in the locality of Lúčny Hríb, south of the community. The community was referred to for the first time in 1300. It belonged to the squire Štiavnický's family, and from the 16th century to the family of Rakovský and some of its smaller parts also to other squire families. By the end of the 18th century is had almost the same population as at present. The people were always prevailingly engaged in farming and their occupation has virtually not changed with the exception of the some individuals who have found jobs in industry in Ružomberok. There used to be two **manor houses** here. Only the remains of the older of them (from 1640) are preserved, as it was damaged during the Second World War. The more recent Late-Renaissance **manor house** from the 17th century was conserved and in 1880 it was expanded to include four towers.

South-west of the community where the Ludrovská dolina valley ends in the Liptovská kotlina basin, is the community of **LUDROVÁ** (565 m, population 950) first referred to in 1461. The owners of its eastern part belonged to rural noble families and it was called Zemianska Ludrová, its western part, *Villa Ludrova*, documented in 1376, belonged to Ružomberok. The population of both parts of the community, now joined into one, were active in farming and craftwork. A fairly developed weaving craft thrived above all in the western part of the community. The most important building here from a historical point of view is the Gothic Roman-Catholic **All Saints church** from the last third of the 13th century, built on a low hill among the fields. It was expanded by the late 15th century and in 1843

the southern nave was built. The church is protected by Late-Renaissance defensive walls with battlements. The wall paintings in its interior representing the individual scenes of Christ's life are from the early 15th century. Within in the community is another Roman-Catholic **All Saints church** built on the site of an older wooden church in 1825. This single-nave Classicist building together with the **chapel of St. Ján Nepomucký** complements the sacral monuments of the community. However, lovers of nature usually merely pass the community on their way to the Ludrovská dolina valley and go on tracking to the Salatín mountain (1,630 m). The red-marked route, comparably comfortable at the beginning but quite demanding towards the end offers some interesting views of karst phenomena (small narrows, caves, sinkholes, sinking streams) and rare flora species. Its upper parts, in turn, opens up wonderful views of the surrounding landscape. Salatín is accessible from Ludrová also following the green-marked pathway which, in combination with the previously described route, is among the most beautiful tracking routes in the Nízke Tatry mountains.

Liptovský Mikuláš
and its environs

The administrative, cultural, economic and travel centre of the central Liptov region is the city of **LIPTOVSKÝ MIKULÁŠ** (577 m, population 33,600) stretching mostly on the right bank of the river Váh and in the middle of the Liptovská kotlina basin. Its situation on the eastern bank of the water dam Liptovská Mara and the nearby tops of the Low Tatras, the Západné Tatry mountains, and the Chočské vrchy mountains have directly predetermined this city to become one of the most important tourist centres in Slovakia.

The territory of the present city was already settled in the Bronze Age as documented by the finds of what is called the bronze treasure of Ondrašová (a set of 12 bronze objects) about 3,000 years old. A settlement of people of Lusatian culture, the discovery of a mill stone of the La Téne period and Celtic coins point to the continuous settlement of this territory that culminated in a Slavic settlement. The best known remains of the Slavs is the ruins of an old Romanesque chapel and cemetery from the 12th century and also an Early Gothic St. Mikuláš church of the last third of the 13th century, which was visited by the people of Vrbice, Okoličné, Palúdzka, Ploštín and Bobrovec. Liptovský Mikuláš was first referred to in 1286 when the Old Hungarian king Ladislav IV conferred the ownership of the St. Mikuláš property to Mikuláš and Andrej, the sons of Serafín. They and their descendants, the family of Pongrácz of Ondrašová owned it for many centuries after that. The Pongráczs' obtained in the mid-14th century municipal privileges with the right to weekly markets. The promotion of trade and crafts was intense especially after 1442 when the family achieved also the right to run two annual fairs. The initiative of the owners of the town was mainly based on the fear of its powerful neighbour, the privileged Vrbica which belonged to the landlords of the royal castle in Liptovský Hrádok. In 1443 the Pongráczs' fortified the church of St. Mikuláš and built a curia enhancing the role of the fortified

town. In spite of frequent disputes with the neighbouring town, Vrbica and the quarrels of the Pongráczs' with the Polish aristocrat Peter Komorovsky, who obtained in the second half of the 15th century a half of the town, the town was developing and by the end of the century it became the most important trade point of central Liptov. The first guilds (shoe-makers) were founded here as early as the 16th century, and in the town lived numerous noble and squire families and the local people owned the rights to the mill, meat distribution, the tapping of spirits and other beverages. In the 17th century Liptovský Mikuláš was a medium-size town with thriving crafts (blacksmiths, furriers, shoe-makers, boot-makers, butchers, millers, etc.). The reformation adopted by the Pongráczs' was also beneficial to the local people. In the years 1631 to 1637 an important Evangelical priest Juraj Tranovský, author of the collection of religious songs Cithara Sanctorum, known also under the name Tranoscius was active in the town. In 1677 the town became the seat of the Liptov province and provincial assemblies were held here regularly together with the sessions of the provincial court of justice. Certainly a great deal of Slovaks are aware of the session of 1713 which sentenced to death the robber Juraj Jánošík who later became a Slovak folk hero. He was hung to death by his ribcage.

Juraj Jánošík:

Perhaps the most famous robber in all Old Hungary was born in 1688 in the north-western Slovakian village of Terchová. He spent his childhood in a local peasant environment and when he was 18 he enlisted himself into the army of František Rákoczy. After their defeat by the imperial army at a battle near Trenčín, Jánošík paradoxically served in the guarding squad of the emperor (1709), and as a guardian of the prisoners at the Castle of Bytča he met a prisoner, a robber captain from Kysuce, by the name of Tomáš Uhorčík. Juraj's parents later bought out their son from military service whereupon he returned to his native village. He did not stay long because after Uhorčík escaped from prison he joined his band of outlaws taking an oath on September 29. However, Uhorčík married by the beginning of 1712, changed his name to Martin Mravec, and procured himself a tavern in the town of Klenovec and became an honourable citizen. Jánošík was consequently elected the captain of the robbers. After a year though in February 1713 he was captured in a tavern in Klenová together with Mravec. This time Jánošík did not escape prison in the manor house of Vranov (today part of Liptovský Mikuláš) as he had done before from the prison of Hrachov. And after a trial and torture he was executed in Liptovský Mikuláš on 18 March 1713. A month later Mravec, alias Uhorčík, suffered the same fate. During his short "career" as a robber Jánošík accomplished numerous robberies and he must have been an extraordinarily dangerous individual as only the biggest rebels were condemned to execution by hook hanging. Who knows what else he would have been able to perpetrate if he had lived longer? In spite of this Juraj Jánošík became Slovakia's national folk hero and a legend in his own right which has been reflected in many literary, artistic and dramatic works.

The development of the city went on apace into the 18th century. Its citizens were exempt from paying tolls, and the number of crafts in the city grew (tailors, bakers, cabinet makers, carpenters etc.) and the prominent position among the guilds was occupied by that of the tanners and furriers – the famous tanners of Liptovský Mikuláš. Rich craftsmen and tradesmen built sumptuous houses which changed the face of the city. An important part of the economic life of the city was also made by the Jews who moved here from Moravia in the first third of the 18th century. They traded in spirits, wood, leather and textiles. Their solvency manifested itself in the purchase and repair of numerous houses and with their help the Pongráczs' were able to finish the construction of the city's square. In the first half of the 19th century Liptovský Mikuláš became the centre of Slovak cultural and national life (the first Slovak public library in 1829 opened here, the first Slovak amateur theatre in 1930, the cultural association Tatrín in 1844) culminating in 1848 by *The Appeals of the Slovak Nation* – the first political Programme of Slovaks declaring themselves an independent nation. The main figures of the cultural and political life in Mikuláš in the mid-19th century included the

publisher, librarian and playwright Gašpar Fejérpataky-Belopotocký (1794-1874), the priest and politician Michal Miloslav Hodža (1811-1870), the poet Janko Kráľ (1822-1876), the poet and columnist Ján Francisci (1822-1905), amongst others.

A decisive effect on the development of the city was that of the railway track, Košice-Bohumín, constructed in the second half of the 19th century as a basic incentive for the promotion of industry. The guilds, however, were not able to follow the modern trends of production anymore and new factories were founded in the city (textile plants, a chemical factory, distillery and a spirit refinery). The city became known as the most important centre of tannery in the upper part of Old Hungary.

Tanneries in Mikuláš:

This craft enjoyed a long history in the city. Its growth was based not only on human talent and skill but above all on the favourable natural conditions: the soft water of the Západné Tatry mountains, plenty of spruce bark and expanded cattle husbandry. The tanners of Mikuláš separated themselves from the guild of shoe-makers back in the 13th century and created one of their own. They processed the animal hides and produced furs and other objects for everyday consumption. They travelled a lot to keep pace with the world trends in their craft by visiting factories in Western Europe and the American continent (often in disguise) in order to learn new techniques in the craft. No wonder then that by the late 19th century there were some of the most recent leather processing facilities in Old Hungary. In 1892 the production of artificial leather also started here and its quality had no equal in the world. Modern factories were owned by the Slovak families of Stodola, Pálka, and Žuffo, who influenced also the national and social life in the city. Their patriotism connected with pragmatic and economic Europeism, and with friendly relations with the Czech nation was the germ of future social and political relations in the decades to come.

Left: The square in Liptovský Mikuláš

The industrial boom also brought about the workers' movement which was particularly well organised in the city. The workers presented themselves in numerous manifestations, namely the folk assembly of May 1, 1918 when they protested against the war, required improvements of their social situation and expressed support for the idea of the common state of the Slovaks and the Czechs. After the Second World War Liptovský Mikuláš became the seat of a large sub Tatra province and preserved its status of social and cultural revival until 1958. From the econom ic point of view the city and its industry during the First Czechoslovak Republic more or less stagnated, some tanneries were closed which was followed by increased unemployment. The Second World War cruelly stigmatised the life of the local people. The numerous members of the Jewish community in the city were deprived of their properties and citizenship and deported from the city. Two years later Liptovský Mikuláš became the centre of the Slovak National Uprising and anti-Nazi resistance. On September 4, 1944 it was occupied by the German troops and the liberation battles in April 1945 caused numerous deaths. After the war the development of industry, and travelling prospects shot up and Liptovský Mikuláš quickly changed into an industrial and tourist centre of the Liptov and sub Tatra regions.

Probably the most obvious sightseeing tour should start at the **Námestie osloboditeľov** (Liberators' Square), an historical nucleus of the city, the formation of which started in the 14th century. In its southern part is the dominating and oldest building, the Roman-Catholic **church of St. Mikuláš** (1). Originally a Gothic church it was built on the site of an older chapel in 1280. The Pongráczs' fortified the church and added little shops creating a compound of market halls. In the second half of the 15th century the church was expanded into the Gothic style and in the 18th century reconstructed in Baroque. The last adjustments were made during the Second World War the fortifying wall was removed. In the interior of the church the stained glass windows, glass paintings by J. Alexy and J. and M. Želibský (1943), the arch paintings of the Triumph by J. Hanula and J. Škorvánek (1903) and medieval architectural details will intrigue any visitor. The Neo-Gothic main altar of St. Mikuláš with the original painted lateral wings of the early 16th century, the lateral altars of the Virgin Mary of 1480 and the Host of Altar (1520), will also please the visitor's eye, as well as the stone baptistery in the form of a chalice of the 14th century with a worked brass cover from the 17th century is of great historical value. In the opposite end of the square is another famous monument of the city, the former house of the province – **Župný dom** (2), which is today the seat of the district office. Construction of the Late-Baroque building was started in 1713 and in the 18th century it was expanded and altered into the Classicist style. The last alteration in 1907 gave it its present face. In the late 17th and early 18th century the seat of the provincial administration was in the **Illésházy's curia** located at the western end of the square. Originally it was a Renaissance building characterised by a heavy triple arcade. In 1713 the legendary Slovak robber captain Juraj Jánošík was tried here. It was rebuilt in the second half of the 19th century and the beginning of the 20th century and at present it is the residence of the **Múzeum Janka Kráľa** (3) (Museum of Janko Kráľ). It originated in 1955 and bears the name of an important Slovak poet of the period of revolutionary Romanticism. Collections of the Museum contain mainly the items documenting the literary traditions and the history of the city. Among the numerous artefacts, especially the Bronze treasure found in Ondrašová, the plastic work of art of St. Mikuláš from the 18th century, the genealogical tree of the Pongrácz family, objects and historical acts of the guilds, a tanner's workshop, interiors of the houses of the local important figures, collections related to the legend of Jánošík and to the Jewish community's history are of interest. Part of the exposition are also items related to the **Tatrín** association and **Appeals of the Slovak Nation** (in the building of old Evangelical rectory where the priest, patriot and politician M. M. Hodža lived and worked); an exposition concerning the work and life of **Martin Rázus and Mária Rázusová-Martáková**, a couple of important Slovak writers (in their native house - the municipal part, Vrbica).

Múzeum Janka Kráľa (Museum of Janko Kráľ),
Námestie osloboditeľov 31,
tel.: 0849/52 25 54
Opening hours:
Tue-Fri 9:00-16:00h, Sat-Sun 10:00-17:00h.

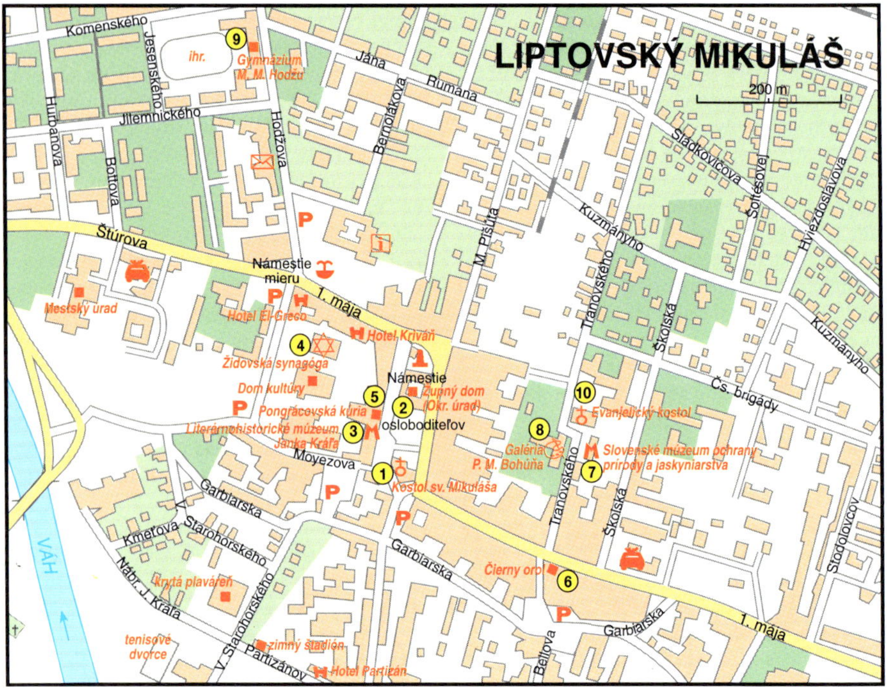

Stará evanjelická fara (The Old Evangelical Rectory), Tranovského 8, tel.: 0849/52 25 46
Opening hours: Tue-Fri 8:00-14:00h, Sat-Sun visits should be arranged in advance

Rodný dom Rázusovcov (The house of the Rázus's), Vrbická 312, tel.: 0849/52 25 54
Opening hours: Mon-Fri 8:00-15:00h, visits should be arranged in advance

Right beside the Museum of Janko Kráľ stands the oldest secular building of the town and the seat of the wealthiest family in Mikuláš, the **Pongrácz curia** (5). Its origin dates back to the mid-15th century and it is remarkable for its irregular shape and the remains of the fortifications in the northern side of the yard. The central square of the city is skirted by a row of **burgher houses**, the majority of which had been built in Renaissance style, and restored after fires in the late 19th century. South-east of the square several **houses of tanners and dyers** built in 19th century are preserved. In the street of 1. mája is a **national cultural monument**, the building called **Čierny orol** (6) (Black Eagle) where the first cultural events in the town were held. Later its name was changed to the Workers' House where in 1918 the first popular assembly was held, an occasion when the Slovaks declared their social and national requests. Today it houses the exposition of the **Liptov Museum** of Ružomberok.

Čierny orol, Ulica 1. mája, tel.: 0843/32 24 69
Opening hours: Tue-Fri 8:00-16:00h, Sat-Sun 9:00-13:00h, Mon 7:30-15:30h

Near Čierny orol in the building of a former Jesuit monastery is the seat of the **Slovenské múzeum ochrany prírody a jaskyniarstva** (7) (The Slovak Museum of Nature Conservation and Speleology) opened in 1930. In this Baroque-Classicist building are collections testifying the natural wealth of Slovakia and its protection, with especial regard to caves and minerals.

Slovenské múzeum ochrany prírody a jaskyniarstva, Školská 4, tel.: 0849/52 20 61
Opening hours: April 1-October 31, Mon-Fri 8:00-16:30, Sat-Sun 9:00-16:30, November 1-March 31, Mon-Fri 8:00-16:30

Right: The water slalom area

Next to the central square is the **Gallery of Peter Michal Bohúň** (8). It was founded in 1955 and offers, besides the life-long work of the painter P. M. Bohúň (1822-1879), some older works of Slovak fine art from the 15th-18th century and the works of Slovak painters and sculptors from the 19th and 20th centuries.

Galéria Petra Michala Bohúňa,
Tranovského 2, tel.: 0849/52 27 58
Opening hours: Tue-Sun 9:00-17:00h.

Among the most important secular cultural-historical monuments in the city centre are the monumental buildings of the grammar school **Gymnázium** (9) built in the years 1914-1916 and of **Tranoscius**, a publishing and book trading association founded in 1889. Sacral monuments in the central part of the city include the Roman-Catholic church of St. Mikuláš and the Classicist Evangelical **church** (10), with Neo-Romanesque facade, built in the years 1783-1785.

A part of the city also contains the originally independent communities of **Vrbica**, Okoličné, Palúdzka, and Liptovská Ondrašová. The most important of them was Vrbica, lying south-east of the city centre, first mentioned in 1267. Its municipal rights were even older than those of Liptovský Mikuláš and the people of Vrbica were known as good craftsmen, above all the tanners and rafters. The town declined in the 17th century to the level of the surrounding serf communities and in 1923 it even lost its independence. As a consequence of urbanisation it was almost completely pulled down in the 1960's and the 1970's and the village houses gave way to high tenement blocks. At the southern edge, and on bank of the river Váh, sprang up a modern **water slalom area**, the nursery of many a champion. The most recent of them being Michal Martikán the gold medal winner of the Atlanta Olympic Games in 1996. Of the ancient monuments of Vrbice only the Baroque-Classicist Evangelical **church** preserved (originally a tabernacle of 1785 it was expanded into a church in 1841) and the **native house** of the poet Martin Rázus (1888-1937) and the female writer Mária Rázusová-Martáková (1905-1964).

Okoličné, an eastern quarter of Liptovský Mikuláš, has more monuments to interest the visitor. The first written reference to the community is from 1248. It used to belong to the

family Okoličányi until the abolition of serfdom and they built here in the 15th century a Franciscan church with a monastery. The Roman-Catholic **church of St. Peter of Alkantara** and the Franciscan **monastery** form an architecturally enclosed compound belonging to the largest Gothic buildings in the region. They were built in the years between 1480-1492 and were reconstructed by the end of the 17th century. The Late-Gothic church was restored in 1904. Its interior is interesting for its main Baroque altar with its work of art of the Annunciation, the lateral Baroque altars from the 18th century, a Baroque pulpit and carved pews from 1700, a stone Classicist baptistery from the second half of the 18th century, and the Late-Gothic statues of St. Barbora and St. Katarína by Maestro Pavol of Levoča from 1510. Next to the church is also an original Renaissance two-storey **manor house** of the Okoličányis' from the first half of the 17th century, which was later restyled in Baroque fashion. The past glory of Okoličné is reminded to us by several **curias** of the 18th-19th centuries. Okoličné absorbed the surrounding communities of **Stošice** and **Vitálišovce** lying in the north-east and all three were joined to Liptovský Mikuláš in 1971.

The city has also grown north-westward, south-westward and south-eastward absorbing some more of the nearby communities. One of them is **Liptovská Ondrašová** first mentioned in 1286. It belonged to the family of Pongrácz and there are several squire **curias** preserved from the 17th -19th centuries. The religious life of the villagers is represented by the Gothic Roman-Catholic **church** from 1911, a **chapel** of the Pongráczs' from the mid-19th and an Evangelical **church** from the present century.

Palúdzka also boasts of many architectural monuments. It lies west of the city centre, on the opposite bank of the river. First mentioned in 1273, it belonged until 1884 to the squire family Palugyay and in 1960 it was annexed to Liptovský Mikuláš. Its landmark is above all the Classicist **manor house** of the Palugyays' built in the second half of the 18th century and the former **granary** from the mid-19th century. This wonderfully restored building today houses a restaurant and the Bocian hotel and its attractiveness is enhanced by the neigbouring **Vranovský kaštieľ** (The Vranov manor house) where in 1713 Juraj Jánošík was imprisoned. Quite recently the in-house exposition, entitled "Jánošík's Tradition", was moved to the Museum of Janko Kráľ in Liptovský Mikuláš. Today this folk hero is commemorated by a statue built in 1985 by the sculptor L. Pollák which is erected in front of the manor house. Among the sacral monuments of Palúdzka are the Baroque-Classicist Roman-Catholic **church of St. John Evangelist**, built in 1854, the Evangelical **church** from 1941 and the **chapel of Ján Nepomucký** from 1856 built on the site of an old Gothic church.

A part of Liptovský Mikuláš also consists of the formerly independent communities lying south of the city centre. At the foothills of the Low Tatras are the municipal districts of **Ploštín** and **Iľanovo**. The area of Ploštín was settled in the Lower Bronze Age, with the first written record dating from 1263. From the 15th century it also consisted of the estate of Liptovský Hrádok and its inhabitants were known as skilled craftsmen (bricklayers, linen-makers), carriers and sheep breeders. Neigh-bouring Iľanovo was likewise included in the Liptovský Hrádok estate and its population lived off similar activities. Above all the bricklayer's trade gave them much sought after employment.

On the road from Palúdzka to Partizánska Ľupča are the municipalities of **Benice**, **Andice**, and **Čemice**. Benice is documented in a reference from 1317 and it belonged to the family of Benický. Andice was first referred to in 1267 and in the past belonged to various squire families. The first written reference to Čemice is from 1299 and it belonged to the family of Čemický. Among the preserved monuments in these municipalities is a Classicist **curia** from the early 19th century in Benice and an originally Rococo **manor house** from the mid-18th century in Čemice, later reconstructed and altered.

The most frequented tourist route in the environs of Liptovský Mikuláš is the one to the Demänovská dolina valley along which are two other municipalities, **Bodice** and **Demänová**. Bodice was mentioned in 1314 and of its various owners the best known is the family of Bodický. The community has a Roman-Catholic, **St. Ladislav church**, from 1860. In front of the church allegedly the oldest **protected limes** of the region grow. Not far away is a **protected study area** called **Bodický rybník** representing a typical alluvial landscape with a variety of tree greenery and bird nesting area. Neighbouring Demänová, documented in 1299, belonged in the past to several squire families and the villagers extracted iron ore in the Demänovská dolina valley in the 17th and 18th centuries. Later the typical occupations here were tannery and linen-making. Nowadays they are engaged mostly in travel and tourism as the **Demänovská dolina valley** has become one of the most favourite tourist and ski resorts in Slovakia.

Since 1964 all existing tourist interests in the valley are concentrated in the self-governing village of **DEMÄNOVSKÁ DOLINA** (820 m, population 200). It consists of five small communities: **Tri studničky** in its lower part, **Jaskyne**, **Repiská**, and **Lúčky** in the central area and **Jasná** in the upper part of the valley. The settlement of Demänovská dolina valley, above all its caves, was documented since primeval times, as proved by numerous archae-

Right: Jaskyňa Slobody cave

ological finds, especially in the Okno cave. Although it was deserted over the last two millennia, life returned here. At some places ore was extracted, there were some shepherds' and loggers' huts, and later after the First World War the first bungalows and weekend cottages were built here. The discovery and opening of the caves, the paved roads, and the construction of ski facilities meant a rapid growth in the popularity of the valley which is among the best known Slovak holiday and sport resorts. Its geomorphologic diversity, rich flora and fauna and friendly climate have also contributed to its popularity among tourists. Over an area of 837 ha extends the **national nature reserve**, the lower part of which is formed by a canyon-like valley of limestone and dolomites. The upper part of the valley has a granite base with a glacier surface (the **Vrbické pleso lake**, the **national nature reserve** is on one of the moraines) and with a compound of smaller valleys. It is drained by the streams Zadná voda and Demänovka, creating with their sinkholes a unique underground system: the **Demänovské jaskyne Caves**.

The Caves of Demänová:

Although the caves are known since very remote times, the oldest written reference to them is from 1299. However, they became famous only after 1723 when the Slovak polyhistorian Matej Bel published their description. The caves are a result of a chemical process, whereby the water's condensation and the stream Demänovka created nine layers of caves in the limestone rock. The unique cave system consists of 21 km of corridors with two sections open to the public: Demänovská ľadová jaskyňa (Demänovská Ice Cave) and Demänovská jaskyňa Slobody (Demänovská Cave of Freedom). The connecting space between them is the Demänovská jaskyňa mieru (Demänovská Cave of Peace) currently under preparation to be opened for the public. The circuit will be 2 km long and includes a magnificent interplay of colours (the pale pink stalactite waterfall and the green-blue of the lakes) will certainly offer a wonderful display. Among the caves not accessible to the public are the most interesting ones such as the Okno cave (the highest situated one), the Beníkova jaskyňa cave (with terraced lakes), and the Zbojnícka jaskyňa cave with a stalactite waterfall.

The most beautiful and most popular cave, not only in this region, but all over Slovakia is the **Demänovská jaskyňa Slobody**. It was discovered in 1921 and opened to the public in 1924. It consists of six floors and in the lowest of them flows the Demänovka stream. Its total length is more than 7 km, although the tourist circuit is shorter, about 2 km. The entrance to the cave, to which visitors are carried by a chair lift, is at an altitude of 870 m. Abundant drip-stone ornamentation, with many lakes attracts many tourists and is the most frequently visited Slovak cave. Also the nearby **Demänovská ľadová jaskyňa**, one of first such caves known around the world, is most attractive. Though the first reference to it is from 1299 it was opened to the public only in the 1880's. It has four floors with a total length of 1.7 km. The entrance is at an altitude of 840 m with the tourist circuit being 700 m long. Especially charming is its lower part called "the freezer" with icicles and ice waterfalls.

Left: The wooden church in Svätý kríž
Right: Interior of the wooden church in Svätý kríž

Demänovská jaskyňa Slobody,
Demänovská dolina, tel.: 0849/916 73
Opening hours: Sept. 16-May 15, Tue-Sun 9:00-15:00h, May 16-Sept. 15, Tue-Sun 9:00-16:00h, August Mon-Sun 9:00-17:00h.

Demänovská ľadová jaskyňa,
Podbreziny 197, tel.: 0849/75 91 76
Opening hours: 16 Sept. 16-May 15, Tue-Sun 9:00-15:00h, May 16-Sept.15, Tue-Sun 9:00-15:00h, June, July Mon-Sun 9:00-16:00h.

The Demänovská dolina valley offers lovers of hiking **ten marked routes** and a **thick network of footpaths** suitable also for more leisurely walkers. In the lower part of the valley the paths lead across forests and deep canyons interspersed with steep cliffs, contrasted by the upper part which is dominated by dwarf pine forests and alpine meadows. The majority of the routes are connected into circuits. Tourists in good physical condition almost always use the occasion to ascend to some of the Low Tatra peaks, like **Chopok** (2,024 m) or **Ďumbier** (2,043 m) providing them with a superb view of almost half of Slovakia. Skiers are well familiar with the community of Jasná situated at the lower station of the lift to Chopok. A number of funiculars, ski-lifts, and tracks in the localities of **Záhradky**, **Otupné**, and **Chopok-sever** provide skiers with excellent conditions for their much loved sport. Comfortable lodging of all categories and catering facilities have made Jasná an internationally renown ski resort, providing the most modern standards.

Near the opening of the Demänovská dolina valley to the Liptovská kotlina basin, at the foothills of Siná mountain is the small village of **PAVČINA LEHOTA** (700 m, population 350). Above it, in a locality called Na Jame (1,438 m) one of the highest situated forts in Slovakia was discovered. It used to belong to the people of Púchov culture. The community itself originated in the territory of the community of Bodice and was first referred to in 1365. It progressively belonged to the families of Bodický, Palugyay and Okoličányi. The villagers were farmers and obtained additional income from home-made linen, the manufacturing of sheep bells and sackcloth-making. Of the original architecture a wooden **belfry** from 1883 is

preserved here. North of the community on the flood plain of the Demänovka stream is the **nature reserve of Jelšie** with protected species of elm trees.

The westward located community of **LAZISKO** (660 m, population 450) likewise belongs to one of the smaller Liptov communities. It was first referred to in 1352 as the property of the family Okoličányi and a sawmill, water mill and some traces left by the extraction of antimony have been found here. The inhabitants were mostly farmers, shepherds and weavers and in the 20th century emerged construction and factory workers in the adjoining towns.

The history of the community **SVÄTÝ KRÍŽ** (630 m, population 600) is similar. It is documented in 1277 when the king Ladislav IV exchanged it for the community of Nedožery in the Turiec region because gold had been found in its territory. It belonged to the family of Okoličányi and the local population were farmers and weavers. Both communities are known to the locals for the **wooden articled Evangelical church**. One of the largest wooden buildings in the Central Europe was moved here in the years between 1974-1982 from Paludza and it stands on the boundary between the territories of Svätý Kríž and Lazisko.

Reformation and articled churches:

The ideas of the Reformation quickly spread all over Old Hungary in the 16th century and the majority of the population readily adopted the new ideology. The only exceptions in Slovakia were the large cities like Bratislava, Nitra and Trnava which became the centre of Old Hungarian Catholicism. Protestantism had a definite impact in the Liptov region by the beginning of the 17th century. The absolutist regime discriminating the Protestants in Austro-Hungarian empire was simultaneously getting stronger and fought against the new religion. It was no accident that the 17th century was the period of the Rebellions of the Estates and much unrest. One of the boldest was Thököly's rebellion in 1678, which although defeated, compelled king Leopold to grant some freedom to the Protestants. In 1681 a legal article allowing the building of two Evangelical churches in some districts of Old Hungary was adopted at a parliamentary session in the Hungarian town of Sopron. The construction of what was called articled churches was permitted only at the edge of the communities, off the municipal limits, but they were not allowed to have towers with bells and their entrance doors had to be turned away from the communities. For the construction of such churches no stones or iron parts could be used. Consequently they were built of wood and the joining material was also wood. The wooden church in Paludza, today part of Liptovský Mikuláš was built in 1693, and as the number of Evangelics was continuously growing in 1774, the carpenter Jozef Land rebuilt and expanded it. It was a remarkable work of art of a carpenter who did not use any project designs (he could not read or write and relied only on his experience) and yet he finished it in an incredible eight months. The wooden belfry was built independently in 1781 after the Toleration Patent was issued by Emperor Joseph I. Construction of the water dam of Liptovská Mara and the subsequent flooding of Paludza were the reasons why the church was moved and rebuilt between the communities of Svätý Kríž and Lazisko.

The ground plan of the church is in the shape of a 43 metre-long cross, admitting almost 6,000 people. The Baroque wooden furnishing has an arousing emotional impact, together with the remarkable wooden Baroque altar from 1693 with the painting of Christ's Transformation. Also the pulpit standing on log foundations supported, as if by a Baroque angel, is both visually and acoustically unique. The altar and the pulpit were made by the wood-carver J. Lerch of Kežmarok. The two-storeyed choir emporia in the interior of the church are adorned by Biblical paintings and along with a big chandelier of Venetian glass create a charming atmosphere. A harmonious part of the church is also an independently standing wooden tower serving as a belfry. Its original bells from the end of the 18th century were confiscated during the First World War and the bells that replaced them (Belief, Hope, and Love) are from 1822. Of the sacral monuments of the community there is also the Classicist Roman-Catholic **church of St. Kríž** from 1819 built with the use of the building materials taken from the older Gothic church destroyed in early 18th century. The way of life of the squires in the community is testified by the Classicist curia from the first half of the 19th century.

North of the road from Liptovský Mikuláš to Partizánska Ľupča are two villages: **GALOVANY** (580 m, population 200) and **GÔTOVANY** (595 m, population 350). The first of these developed in the 13th century in the territory of the community of Paludza. It belonged to several squire families but the village bears the name of the first of them, Ján Galo. Neighbouring Gôtovany was first mentioned in 1368 and in the past belonged mostly to the Gouth family. Its locality of Fiačice is even documented from 1267. The people of both villages made their living from farming and cattle raising.

Continuing further from Ľupča, south of the main road, is the community of **ĽUBEĽA** (612 m, population 1,150). It originated by merging two communities, Kráľovská and Zemianska Ľubeľa which existed independently since the 14th century. Somewhat older of the two is Kráľovská Ľubeľa with written evidence from the year 1278, following which part of its property was acquired by several squire families, who helped develop its close neighbourhood. The local peasants obtained additional income from the extraction of antimony and iron ore, and in the valley of Kľačianka even some gold was found. Mining activities were maintained in the community until the 20th century, when many people left to pursue work in the mines located in the districts deeper in the South.

Ľubeľa is almost joined with two other communities at the foothills of the Low Tatras: **DÚBRAVA** (636 m, population 1,350) and **LIPTOVSKÉ KĽAČANY** (672 m, population 300). Both of them also boast of a tradition of mining. Dúbrava is the older, first being referred to in 1372. It originated in a clearing amid an oak forest. It used to belong to the squires of Ráztoky and later also to other squire families. Liptovské Kľačany was first referred to in 1474. It was founded in the territory of Ľubeľa and belonged to the squire family Fejérpataky. Also the old community of St. Alžbeta founded around an old church of the same name

Right: The St. Matúš the Apostle church

built by the Liptov head of the district Dvonč in 1339, became progressively a part of Liptovské Kľačany. Today on the site of an old Gothic church (of which two paintings of St. Alžbeta and St. Barbora and a bell from 1612 are preserved) stands the Roman-Catholic **church of St. Alžbeta**. It was built without a tower in the years 1878-1879. The principal landmark of contiguous Dúbrava is the Roman-Catholic **church of St. Andrej the Apostle** from the late 13th century, which was originally Early-Gothic. It was rebuilt in the Renaissance style and fortified in the 17th century. Between the 18th and 20th centuries it was gradually restored. In the interior of the church the remains of Gothic wall paintings and architectural details are preserved, but the majority of the interior furnishing are in the Baroque style from the mid-18th century.

Almost ten kilometres long the **Krížska dolina valley** with the Paludžanka brook leads from Dúbrava to the Low Tatra mountain chain. Parallel to it runs an unmarked but comfortable footpath starting in Liptovské Kľačany and ending at Ľupčianska Magura mountain (1,315 m) that offers splendid views of the whole Liptov region, including the nearby village of **MALATÍNY** (580 m, population 150). It originated on the banks of the stream of the same name documented in 1263 in connection with the delimitation of the territory of the community of Partizánska Ľupča. In the 14th century there were the separate communities of Nižný, Stredný and Horný Malatín (Lower, Central and Upper Malatín) referred to by the collective name of Tri Malatíny. The area of the communities used to belong to several squire families and the largest share was owned by the family of Malatínsky. The population of these latterly merged three communities were occupied in farming, weaving, tannery and basket making.

Historically more important is the nearby community of **PARTIZÁNSKA ĽUPČA** (568 m, population 1,300) the oldest and once the most famous town of the Liptov region. Its territory was settled in the Lower Bronze Age and though the first written reference is only from 1252, the community undoubtedly existed much earlier. Around the 13th century "guests settlers" were invited to settle here. They were burghers from Krupina and Banská Štiavnica, mostly Germans who came here to look for gold, silver, and antimony. The first privilege of Ľupča is from 1270 when the Old Hungarian king Štefan V granted extensive privileges of a municipal nature to Ľupča: the free election of a mayor with legal executive powers, exemption of the legal power of the head of the province administration, exemption of tolls in the territory of the Zvolen province, the right to extract gold, silver, copper, to fish and organise weekly markets. In the 14th-16th century Ľupča (called Nemecká Ľupča from the 14th century on) was the most important town in Liptov. The occupation of the Hussites of the Likava Castle during the 15th century meant that the town was partially "Slovakized" (the municipal book was written in Slovak). The town bubbled with lively trade as the merchants of Ľupča were known as good tradesmen, dealing in linen and woolcloth which they sold in all the important market places throughout Old Hungary. Though the main occupation of the population was still farming, part of them were living from mining whilst others worked in crafts. In the 16th and 17th centuries the guilds of tailors, blacksmiths, knife-makers, furriers, boot-makers, cloth-makers, and button makers were founded in the town and later also the guilds of millers, butchers, coopers and boiler-makers originated.

Liptov cheese:

Most visitors to any foreign country in the world can sufficiently perceive the spirit of that country after tasting one of its typical meals. Slovakia's typical meal are the dumplings flavoured by the regionally famous Liptov cheese called bryndza. The genuine bryndza is a soft cheese made of full-fat sheep milk, and the best cheese is made in May. It is filled into wooden receptacles called "gelety" used for the storing and transporting of bryndza. The coopers of Ľupča were regarded as the best experts in making these vessels, which were made of spruce wood in capacities of 0.5 to 50 kg. The wooden parts were joined with willow rings. The artisans worked individually and sold their products through agents. For instance, in the early 20th century there were almost 80 producers of these vessels active in Ľupča and traders purchased their products from them usually once a week. There also existed in Ľupča in the 18th-19th century a guild of coopers with clients as far a field as Vienna. Good quality bryndza was transported on rafts to the lowland town of Sereď where it was taken in carts to Vienna. The genuine bryndza of Liptov was also supplied to the Emperor's family.

Although Ľupča originated and developed as a town on royal ground it never obtained the privileges of a free royal town and did not free itself from the Liptov and Likava Castles. The citizens of Ľupča were obliged to fulfil the obligations, in the 17th century, as those of the remaining serf communities in the Liptov province (duties, working the lord's fields, cartage, rafting and the repairs of the castle, etc.) The buying out of the duties at the second half of the 17th century provided an impulse to the promotion for trade and crafts. Numerous mills, smelting plants and even a municipal bath, along with a popular tavern, where famous Liptov squires congregated, are mentioned in the documents of the time. Other guilds also sprang up (carpenters, rope-makers, strap-makers, hat-makers, saddle-makers, etc.) reaching a total number of 21 guilds altogether. However, in the 19th century when the guilds became obsolete and were not able to compete with industry, the town started to decline. The population reached its peak in 1828 (exceeding the present number three-fold) and since the mid-19th century there has been a decreasing trend in its numbers. In that time the mining activities began to progressively disappear and a big part of the population moved out of the town. The fact that Ľupča was situated off the Košice-Bohumín railway track, the main developmental stimulus of late 19th century, certainly contributed to its decline. After the First World War the local population lived mainly off farming and forestry work, in which the local business was based (coopery, saw mills, etc.) The people in the region were also very actively involved in the Slovak national resistance during the Second World War, especially the communities of Železné and Magurka which were the centres of the partisan movement, which is the reason why Ľupča gained its present attribute of Partizánska.

In Partizánska Ľupča several architectural monuments commemorating the history of this famous town are conserved. In the centre is a rectangular **square**, formerly the site of the once famous cattle markets, with a stable ground plan originating from the 14th century. The square is skirted by former Renaissance **burgher houses** which acquired in the course of the 18th and 19th centuries their present appearance. Visitors will today be attracted mainly to the re-built Renaissance tavern with its fin-de-siécle facade, the very place where the "history of the town was written". As the location of the town did not require the construction of municipal fortifications the defensive function was fulfilled by the fortified Roman-Catholic **church of St. Matúš the Apostle** which has strong loopholed walls. A tower was also added, one of the highest in northern Slovakia. The compound was modified in the Baroque style in the 18th century. The most valuable item in the interior of the church is the Renaissance-Baroque, original main altar is from 1620, today located behind the Neo-Gothic main altar. It has firm and movable wings ornamented by scenes of the life of Christ in

Right: Liptovská Mara

Protestant iconography as at that time it was used by Protestant worshippers. The very first and original Gothic main altar from the 15th century is deposited in the Slovak National Gallery in Bratislava. The second Roman-Catholic church, originally the Gothic **church of the Virgin Mary of Seven Grievances,** is at the local cemetery. It was built in 1263, expanded in the 17th and reconstructed in Baroque style in the 18th and 19th centuries. Sacral monuments of the community also include the Evangelical Neo-Classicist **church** built in 1887 on the site of an older church from 1783. In its interior is a painting of the Crucification of Christ by P. Bohúň.

Partizánska Ľupča is also the starting point for tourist trips to the almost 20 km long **Ľupčianska dolina valley** remarkable for its continuous natural forests and abundance of game. There are several gamekeeper's lodges and hunting cottages in the area. The valley has numerous lateral branch routes, of which the most favourite is the Ďurková (blue-marked path) leading from a place called Tajcha, with traces of a valley water reservoir, once used for floating the timber to the small mountain community of **Magurka** (1,036 m). This old community originated in the 14th century around the gold, silver and later antimony and iron ore mines. Here there are the remains of a ruined ore screening facility called bašovňa, pits, heaps of waste rock and a network of roads, which is today used by tourists. Its remoteness was the reason why during the war numerous partisan squads encamped here. Three marked paths lead from Magurka to the main ridge of the Low Tatras. Tourists who lodge at Magurská Cottage frequently visit the nearby community of **Železné** (970 m) accessible by a green-marked footpath. There used to be a **climatic spa** in the community in the 19th century used as a summer residence by writers, poets and artists. Among its regular guests was the famous Slovak poet P. O. Hviezdoslav who translated Shakespeare's texts here. Today, besides the mineral water spring, there is also a children's sanatorium.

North-east of Partizánska Ľupča, on the opposite side of the railway track and motorway, stretches the largest summer holiday resort in the

region – the water reservoir of **Liptovská Mara**. The reservoir, namesake of one of the flooded communities was built in the years 1970-1975. As far as the volume of water is concerned, it holds the largest in Slovakia (the maximum volume of water in the reservoir is 360 mill m^3) and the area of the water table is 21.6 km^2. The length of the dam is 1,225 m, its height is 45 m and its foundations are 270 m wide. The dam was built above all because of the flood risk on the river Váh and also for the production of power. A part of this large dam also contains a smaller one, the Bešeňovská reservoir, serving for the pumping of water into the main reservoir. Construction of the dam meant the flooding of the communities of Dechtáre, Liptovská Mara, Liptovská Sielnica, Paludza, Parížovce, Ráztoky, Sokolče, Vrbie, and a section of Bobrovník and Liptovský Trnovec. A part of the population built new houses on the shores of the lake, but most of them moved to flats in Liptovský Mikuláš and Ružomberok. The dam water also engulfed numerous cultural and historical monuments, though the most important ones were moved to the Museum of Liptov Village in Pribylina. The flooded communities played quite an important role in the history of the region and their ancient settlement points to the suitable living conditions in the territory.

Left: Havránok

Liptovská Mara – the community:

Historically speaking the most remarkable community was Liptovská Mara, an important archaeological locality. Numerous finds from the Lower Bronze Age, Iron Age and La Téne periods evoke the image of its remote, Pre-Slavic past, when it was one of the most significant Celtic cult centres on the territory of Slovakia. The disclosure of stone barriers, palisade walls, tower gates, crude Celtic sacrificial altars and Celtic imitations of ancient coins in the locality of Havránok invoke the importance and the culture of the place. Also finds dating from the period of the existence of Great Moravia settlements are unique. The Slavs made use of the Celtic fortifications with palisades, a ditch and a tower in Havránok and the traces of them (ceramics, ear rings) were also found in other places in the territory of the community of Liptovská Mara. Its original name Svätá Mara derived from the Early-Gothic church from the late 13th century. On its site an older sacral building from the 11th-12th century probably existed. The church presumably fulfilled the function of a centre for Church administration in the Liptov region. Around it a community progressively developed and from the 14th century until 1582 it served as the place of regular meetings of the Liptov aristocracy. Its remote past, however, has been submerged in the waves of the dam over a water table of which only the tower of the old church can be seen. The most valuable items and monuments were moved to Pribylina.

The locality **Havránok** is at the present time an **open-air archaeological museum** and a **natural cultural monument**. A part of the exposition are reconstructions of Celtic buildings and a medieval castle.

Archeologické múzeum, (Archaeological Museum)
tel.: 0848/32 24 69
Opening hours: June 1- Sept. 30, daily 9:00-18:00h.

The water dam Liptovská Mara and its environs today offer a variety of leisure activities connected with water sports and hiking in the Chočské vrchy mountains and the Západné Tatry mountains. A tour around Liptovská Mara can start under the castle wall of the village **VLACHY** (528 m, population 600). Although the first written reference to the community is from 1262 its name reveals the traces of the origin of its founders, who were Walloons from the Belgian-French boundary regions who settled here by the late 12th century when they probably assisted in the construction of the Liptov Castle and the Early-Gothic churches in the region. One of them, Gallicus became later the only owner of extensive land and his duty was to carry out military service for the king in Liptov Castle. The community then was inherited by his descendants and several squire families. Part of the village also consists of the smaller communities of **Krmeš** and **Vlašky** with a similar squire past. Vlašky was connected with Vlachy since the Middle Ages by a wooden bridge over the river Váh and this north-south route across Liptov was in the past an important road, alongside which there was a drinking trough for the horse-driven mail carriages. The inhabitants of three communities were mainly farmers and rafters with additional crafts like linen, wool-cloth and carpet weaving. The squire families left an originally Renaissance, later "Baroquised" **manor house**, from the 16th century in Vlachy and a Baroque-Classicist **manor house** in Vlašky from the 18th century. There is also a sacral building in the form of a *fin-de-siécle* **chapel** from 1930.

The community **BOBROVNÍK** (568 m, population 150) lying on the western bank of Liptovská Mara has an interesting origin. The village was founded in the 12th century, remarkable for its abundant occurrence of beavers (beaver in Slovak is "bobor") and it belonged to what was called the servicing communities of the royal guards, or beaver hunters. Gradually it developed into a squire village inhabited mostly by farmers. In the mid-19th century it absorbed the smaller communities of Hliník, Tvarožná, Nežitovce, and Sestrč flooded in the 1970's with the advent of the dam. The best known among them was the community of Sestrč, mainly because of the carriers' tavern visited by every carrier passing by on his way from Liptov to Orava.

This road passed also **BUKOVINA** (590 m population 510) situated at the foothills of Chočské vrchy mountains. Its name ("buk" meaning beach tree) suggests that it was erected in a place covered by beach forests in the Middle Ages. It belonged to the squire family of Bukovinský. Later it joined the communities of Podhradie, Jánošovce, and Dušany and became one. The farming character of the community can be imagined by the restored **farmstead** of the 19th century in Dušany, administered by the Liptov Museum. The medieval road continued from Bukovina past Liptov Castle, (see page 168) across the **Sestrčská dolina valley** along a brook of the same name. A walk over the valley rimmed by limestone rocks with relic pine and spruce forests, connected with an ascent to the castle ruins, is a pleasant and refreshing trip and a perfect escape from the civilised world. Parallel to it only several kilometres to the east between the mountain ridge of Pravnáč (1,206 m) and Lomné (1,278 m), connected by green-marked footpath stretches the **Dolina Liptovskej Anny valley**. The name of the valley derives from the community of **LIPTOVSKÁ ANNA** (660 m, population 100) lying in its southern extreme which opens up into the Liptovská kotlina basin. Together with the neighbouring community of **IŽIPOVCE** (605 m, population 100) both settlements represent the Central Liptov type of small village of squire origin active in farming. They originated in the 14th century and the only monument is the **ruins** of an Early-Gothic church from the 14th century consecrated to St. Anna.

The most attractive community for tourists is **PROSIEK** (600 m, population 200) situated more to the east, the territory of which was settled as early as in the Lower Bronze Age (as documented by the Aeneolithic finds and a settlement from the Roman period in the Prosiecka dolina valley as well the Hallstatt, La Téne and Slavic settlements at the foothills of Hrádok). The community probably originated in the 13th century and was built by the inhabitants of the nearby community of Sielnica. It used to belong to various squire families, similar to the communities of Vyšný and Nižný Zádiel, which were also eventually flooded by the creation of the Liptovská Mara dam. Only the former Renaissance **manor house** from the late 16th century, rebuilt in Classicist style in the first half of

the 19th century is preserved. The sacral monument of the community is the Roman-Catholic **church of St. Alžbeta the Widow**, originally built as a Gothic chapel at the beginning of the 14th century. Later it was altered and rebuilt into a church and in 1880 it acquired a Neo-Classicist facade.

But the community is generally known as a starting point for a trip to one of the most beautiful and most visited Slovak valleys – the **Prosiecka dolina valley**. This karst valley almost 4 km long is deeply embedded between the massive mountains of Lomné and Prosečné (1,372 m). Through the valley leads a blue-marked **educational path** with several wooden panels bearing details on geologic, geomorphic, and pedologic facts concerning the valley and the local fauna and flora. It starts at the entry to the valley consisting of a rock called Vráta (The Gate) above which the Prosečianka brook springs. In its central part the valley widens to a grassy clearing called Polhora on the sides of which are a group of cliffs called Medveď (the Bear), Sova (the Owl), Ťava (the Camel), Jánošík, etc., waterfalls and caves. At the beginning of its upper part the valley branches out to a little valley called Červené piesky with an imposing 15 m high waterfall and the canyons of Nižný and Vyšný Sraz, which are the most attractive sections of the valley. Their steepness and wildness will most certainly impress any visitor, who will conclude the ascent, and the experience, by the use of ladders. The Prosiecka dolina valley is a **national nature reserve** with occurrences of several rare and protected plant species.

Beyond the upper end of the valley is a grassy plain called Svorad crossed by a blue-marked path heading to the community of **VEĽKÉ BOROVÉ** (828 m, population 100) Together with another two communities, **MALÉ BOROVÉ** (850 m, population 250) and **HUTY** (789 m, population 220) this place indeed represents an oasis of peace and silence set in the heart of some wonderful nature. They are situated in a relatively forgotten corner, isolated from traffic and the distant settlements. They are, however, holiday communities which originated in the 16th century when the Goral population of the Upper Orava region settled here around a glass smelting plant. They used to belong to several squire families and the local population, besides glass manufacturing, lived off farming, sheep raising and the manufacture of utensils used by the shepherds. From the 18th century the inhabitants of Borové and Huty were known as peddling glaziers wandering all over Old Hungary. Among the preserved monuments are two Roman-Catholic churches, of which the Classicist **Promotion of St. Cross church** in Veľké Borové, built in 1823, is the older. It was built on the site of an older wooden church and in the years between 1800-1890 it was rebuilt in Neo-Classicist style. The other more recent Neo-Gothic **church of Lord's Conversion** in Huty was built in 1894.

Veľké Borové and Huty are popular as a tourist base for trips to the **national nature reserve Kvačianska dolina valley**. This canyon-type valley deeply cut into the dolomite and limestone rock between the Čierna hora (1,098 m) and Ostré (1,128 m) mountains runs parallel to the Prosiecka dolina valley. Both

Left: The entrance to the Prosiecka dolina valley
Right: A mill in the Kvačianska dolina valley

create a well-known one-day tourist circuit. The Kvačianska dolina valley has an **educational path** with numerous stops. There used to exist an old road in the valley leading along the bottom and it served as the only communication for the communities of Veľké Borové and Huty with the rest of the world. The landmark in the upper part of the valley is called **Oblazy** – a unique and ancient **wooden water mill**, and another attractive place is Roháč, a rocky promontory in the lower part of the valley and the highest point on the old road. In 1860 a **stone cross** was built here and the place provides wonderful views of the entire canyon.

At the point where the Kvačianska dolina valley opens up to the Liptovská kotlina basin is the community that gave the name to the valley – **KVAČANY** (610 m, population 570). The first reference to the community is from 1379. It used to belong to several squire families and the population made their living from farming, wood processing and sheep keeping. They suffered a lot during the Second World War when many were executed by the German troops for the assistance they provided to the partisans and some were also deported to concentration camps. The events are commemorated by two **commemorative boards**. The main building of the community is the former Gothic Roman-Catholic **church of St. Katarína of Alexandria** from the early 14th century. The church was rebuilt in the 16th century in Renaissance style and a tower with fortifications was added. Of the numerous remarkable architectural and artistic details the Gothic wall painting of the first half of the 15th century is of especial interest. A part of Kvačany is the formerly independent community of **Dlhá Lúka** where an Early-Renaissance **manor house** from the 16th century is preserved.

Motorists travelling from Liptov to the Zuberec region usually use the interesting and picturesque road passing the community of **LIPTOVSKÉ MATIAŠOVCE** (655 m, population 300). This community originated by the merging of the communities of Nižné and Vyšné Matiašovce, the territory of which was settled as early as in the Hallstatt and Roman periods. Its name is derived of the one of the first settlers, Matej, in the 13th century. The

communities belonged to squire families and the majority of the property belonged to the family of Matiašovský. The religious past of the local farmers is realised in an impressingly fortified Renaissance-Baroque, Roman-Catholic **St. Ladislav church** from the early 16th century. The Baroque fortifications with loopholes and corner bastions, as well as parts of the interior (main altar, lateral altar, Pietas, baptistery, pulpit, epitaph of the family Matiašovský, etc.) are from the 17th century.

The community is the starting point of tourist trips to the westernmost valley of the Západné Tatry mountains – the **Suchá dolina valley**. The valley represents a frontier between the Západné Tatry mountains and the Chočské vrchy mountains and it has several lateral branches. In its lower part is the **jaskyňa Dúpnica cave** (with the remains of a settlement from the Roman period) and besides several water springs in its upper part there are also waterfalls.

Left: The church in Liptovské Matiašovce

South of Liptovské Matiašovce, on the bank of the water reservoir is the community of **LIPTOVSKÁ SIELNICA** (562 m, population 450), a great part of which was flooded by the reservoir. The community has probably existed as early as the 11th century and is one of the oldest villages in Liptov. After the 15th century it developed as a squire town under the administration of the Liptov and later Likava Castles. In spite of the fact that the lords of Likava did not support the independent development of the town, there existed crafts (tannery, coopery), flax and hop were also grown, beer was brewed, linen made and there was a lively trade. The population by the end of the 19th century was double the present figure. Even though the crafts still existed in the 20th century, the economic importance of the community gradually decreased and in the 1970's it was flooded by the Liptovská Mara dam. The dam water also covered parts of the community called Brnice and Parížovce, as well as the most important cultural-historical monuments of the community – the Late-Gothic Roman-Catholic church from the second half of the 13th century (later Baroquised) and an Evangelical church from 1783. The most valuable architectural and artistic items of the Late-Gothic church were in time moved to the Liptov open air museum in Pribylina. The people who lived in the flooded community built their new houses north of their original homes.

The most important summer holiday resort on the shores of the Liptovská Mara dam is the community of **LIPTOVSKÝ TRNOVEC** (570 m, population 550). The first written reference to the community is from 1265 though there is no doubt that it existed long before this time. The place must have been attractive for settlers as archaeological finds from the Bronze Age and Iron Age document their existence from these periods. Trnovec used to belong to royal property and the Old Hungarian kings were generous with their privileges (allowing a market and fair in 1429, the exemption of tolls in 1480). In the 16th century it became the property of the Likava estate and although it tried to preserve its privileges it never freed itself of serfdom. In spite of this crafts thrived (dyers and linen-makers), and there was a saw mill, brewery and distillery; also some of the inhabitants were farmers, loggers and rafters. The most interesting monuments within and around the community include a **pillory** from the 17th century, **brick houses** and a **belfry** from the mid-19th century. There is a Classicist Roman-Catholic **Holy Spirit church** from 1820 built on the site of a medieval church and an Evangelical **church** from 1925 that replaced an old temple. Even though a part of the population works in industry and agriculture, Liptovský Trnovec is frequently referred to in connection with travel and tourism. A modern **car camping place** at the shore of the reservoir is visited by lovers of water sports. A nearby beach, the renting of sport equipment and excellent conditions for yachting and wind-surfing are the assets of this sought after holiday centre, offering also a good base for trips to the Chočské vrchy mountains and the Západné Tatry mountains.

In the immediate vicinity of Liptovský Mikuláš, towards the north and north-east are several small communities. The first of them is **TRSTENÉ** (639 m, population 200). The community developed in the first half of the 13th century and belonged to the squire family of Trstenský. By the end of the 13th century a Late-Romanesque church was built here, one of the oldest in Liptov. On its foundations the Roman-Catholic **church of All Saints** stands today, rebuilt in 1830. Next to it is a **belfry** from the 17th century.

The nearby community of **VETERNÁ PORUBA** (820 m, population 350) originated in the 14th century on the estate of the family of Okoličányi, to whom it belonged until 1848. The community of St. Štefan also used to be a part of it, but it was destroyed in 1719 by an ice-fall. Up until the middle of the 20th century the local people were engaged in home-made linen carpets and shepherds' utensils.

Along the road from Liptovský Mikuláš to Liptovský Hrádok is **BEŇADIKOVÁ** (615, population 450). It originated as a seat of squire Beňadik in the 14th century and later it belonged to several squire families as testified by the two **curias** from the mid-17th and 19th centuries which are preserved here. Neighbouring **LIPTOVSKÝ ONDREJ** (690 m, population 450) originated like Beňadiková in the territory of Uhorská Ves, though somewhat earlier in the 13th century. In this period a parsonage with a church existed here and the name of its patron is perpetuated in the name of the community. It belonged to the small squire villages mostly inhabited by farmers, as the community has a **mill** from the 17th century. The heritage of the local squires is the originally Renaissance **manor house** from the 17th century with preserved arcade in the court yard. A fire in 1709 left only fragments of the original Gothic Roman-Catholic **church of St. Andrej the Apostle** from the 13th century. The burned down remains were mostly pulled down and the church was rebuilt again. However, three layers of 13th, 14th and 15th century original wall paintings were preserved.

Liptovský Ondrej is practically connected with another community **JAKUBOVANY** (715, population 550) first referred to in a written document in 1474. It belonged to the squire villages, owned by several families and has preserved its agricultural character until the present time.

More to the north is located **KONSKÁ** (745 m, population 250) which was first referred to in 1357 and also belonged to squire families. Although in the 20th century the people tried to extract coal in the area, they lived mostly from farming and cattle husbandry. In the environs of both of these aforementioned communities are several **holiday facilities** serving the visitors of the Západné Tatry mountains during winter and summer.

Fans of skiing or of water sport and swimming prefer to depart from Liptovský Mikuláš heading to the south-east to visit the ski resort in Závažná Poruba or the thermal swimming pools in Liptovský Ján.

The community of **ZÁVAŽNÁ PORUBA** (634 m, population 1250) lies at the foothills of the Low Tatra mountain Poludnica (1,549 m). The first reference to it is from 1377. It used to belong to the family of Szentiványi (St. John) and the population lived from producing linen and cloth weaving and basket-making. Of the sacral monuments the Neo-Gothic Evangelic **church** of 1933 and the Classicist Roman-Catholic **chapel of St. Lukáš the Evangelist** from 1837 with the tower from the beginning of the 20th century are the most important ones. The community became well-known among skiers and winter sport fans mainly because of its ski and cross-country tracks situated south of the community. The entire area is known under the name of **Opalisko** and offers ski tracks and

ski lifts for the keenest of sporty visitors. In turn, the summer visitor can undertake an ascent from Opalisko to Poludnica by a yellow-marked footpath. Lovers of bathing and swimming, however, prefer Liptovský Ján.

Going to Ján they will cross the village of **UHORSKÁ VES** (611 m, population 450) the name (Uhorská means Old Hungarian) is derived from the fact that here used to exist the Old Hungarian frontier, and trade road guards were moved here by the rulers probably at the beginning of the 12th century. The community, first referred to in 1230, is the first documented community in the Liptov region. It used to belong to the family Szentiványi. The local people lived off agriculture, rafting, wood processing and the production of home-made linen. Among the most interesting buildings in the community are the **municipal** and **fire brigade house** built in 1937 after a project by M. M. Harminec.

Left: A natural swimming pool in Liptovský Ján
Right: Jánska dolina valley

The final aim for most visitors though is **LIPTOVSKÝ JÁN** (654 m, population 800). The oldest written reference to the community is from 1327 and it belonged to the Szentiványis' until the abolishment of serfdom. The main occupation of the local people was farming and many were bricklayers travelling in pursuit of jobs all over the Old Hungarian territory, especially from the mid-19th century onwards. In the same period iron ore was extracted here and the local thermal water springs gave origin to a small spa where gynaecological and rheumatic ailments were cured. This activity was renewed in the years between 1927-1929. At the present time there is an area of summer thermal **swimming pools** south of the community and an **in-door swimming pool** making use of the thermal water spring called Rudolf with a temperature of 28.5°C. Also a natural pool utilised for hip-bathing is available. The local springs are conducive for skin therapy and female diseases.

Liptovský Ján has preserved its nature of being a former squire community until the present day. There is a number of **curias** and

manor houses in the community built in Renaissance, Baroque and Classicist styles. Their ground plans are mostly L or U-shaped, others are in the shape of a block. Although the principal ones were rebuilt in the 19th century, it is still possible to recognise in their facades or interiors the remnants of grafitto ornaments, Renaissance domes and Classicist pillars. The best know of them is the **manor house** with a **spa building** built in 17th century, later rebuilt in Classicist style. The community is dominated by the former Gothic Roman-Catholic **church of St. Ján the Baptist** built in 1380. In the 17th century a fortifying wall was built around the church, and in the 18th century it was remade in Baroque style and later a tower was added to it. In the interior of the church are impressive Gothic domes, the main Baroque altar from the 17th century and the tombstone of the Szentiványis' of the first half of the 16th century. Other sacral monuments in the community include the Evangelical **church** built in 1785, and rebuilt after a fire in 1907.

Liptovský Ján is the point of departure for the **Jánska dolina valley**, one of the longest valleys in the Low Tatras. It is crossed by a blue-marked footpath leading to the Chata hrdinov SNP cottage (The Cottage of the Heroes of the Slovak National Uprising) lying under the highest point of the Low Tatras, Ďumbier (2,043 m). Out of the valley several hiking tracks depart offering on their way an opportunity to admire variegated flora, karst phenomena, sinkholes, water springs, caves and abysses in the area. The best known is the 1.5 km long Stanišovská jaskyňa cave and the deepest Slovak cave jaskyňa Záskočie (-267 m). Numerous ski lifts, downhill tracks and cross-country ski tracks are the reasons why Liptovský Ján has became so popular as a summer and winter holiday resort.

Liptovský Hrádok
and its environs

LIPTOVSKÝ HRÁDOK (637 m, population 8,600), is the tourist and economic centre of the region of Horný Liptov and is situated under the northern protuberances of the Nízke Tatry mountains and at the confluence of the Belá and Váh rivers.

A pre-historic settlement, of what is today the area of the town, is documented by the finds left here by the people of Lusatian culture. A predecessor of the town was the community, Belsko, existing as early as in the 13th century. Although it disappeared later, the continuity of the settlement of this territory was maintained by the castle Hrádok built on a small hill near the river Belá.

A castle and a woman:

Though several versions of a story narrating the origin of the castle exist, one thing is certain: The first reference to the castle is from 1341 as novum castrum. The castle, made of stone, was built by the head of the Zvolen province, Donč, at the beginning of the 14th century when the land of several squires was confiscated beforehand. Their protests in the Ostrigom canonry were made in vain. Donč was a confidential friend of the Old Hungarian king Karol Róbert and belonged to the most influential figures in Old Hungary. A castle was built on a five meter high limestone rock. Even though it was protected by fortifications and a water ditch it was very vulnerable as was proved by numerous sieges and destruction. It belonged to military buildings guarding an important trade route along the river Váh. One of the legends testify that the castle was connected by underground passages to the fortifications near Liptovský Ján and even with the castle Liptovský hrad. Later it became the seat of administration of the castle estate, the property of the Old Hungarian kings until the mid-15th century and later it was owned by donation or by the forfeiting of several landlords (for instance, the families Zápoľský, Thurzo, Ballas and others). The reconstruction of the castle is attributed to a woman – Magdaléna Zayová. There is a Slovak proverb which says: the devil sends a woman where he himself cannot get to. In other words, the deed impossible for men was

done by Magdaléna. Even though it is true that she outlived three husbands (the castle owners) she kept her energy, as well as the castle and her fourth husband. She completely restored the castle in Renaissance style and added to it a Renaissance manor house. The final effect makes the impression that the old castle remained in the courtyard of the new one. After her death, probably more lamentated by her subjects than by her husbands, the owners of the castle changed hands periodically, belonging either to the rebellious nobility or to the imperial owners. The castle was heavily damaged during the Rebellions of the Estates at the turn of the 17th and 18th century. After a fire in 1803 only the manor house was restored as it was the seat of the administration of the estate in Likava and Hrádok. Further repairs to the building included an ethnographic museum completed in the 20th century but which is again in need of restoration.

The community of Liptovský Hrádok originated in the early 18th century near a location where salt, copper and iron were stored. Forest workers and state clerks founded here a community called Mravník which later developed into an important market place of the Horný Liptov region. In the second half of the 18th century numerous manufacturing, including wood production and forestry (sawmills, raft ports, etc.) were founded here and shaped the economic life of the region. In 1768 even a forestry school was opened here by Franz Wissner von Morgenstern, a forestry prefect of the estate. It was the only school of its kind in Old Hungary to teach in the Slovak, German, Latin, and Hungarian languages. Tuition was based on a previously prepared "forest catechism". Also the newly established iron and smelting works which together with the forest-technical buildings laid down the foundations of the town, and have joined the prospering and rapidly growing wood-processing plants.

Hámor, maša *and the armament works:*

In 1792 the people of Hrádok built a hammermill, processing copper ore and a blast furnace called maša. The copper ore and forged copper plates were transported by rafts down the river Váh. Iron ore was weighed in a weighing station and also processed in a blast furnace. About 70 experts from Germany brought here for their expertise participated in the production of iron. They belonged to a group of royal workers who were dressed in uniforms with a complementary salary. As the iron produced here was of top quality, an armament works was built in Liptovský Hrádok in 1804 to 1805 where rifles, pistols and carbines were made. Yearly about 24 thousand pieces of good quality armaments were produced here.

The community which assumed the name of the local castle, had by the end of the 18th century been promoted to a town, with market and fair rights from 1805. This little town simultaneously became the basis for rafting on the river Váh. Half-rafts that were later joined to proper rafts near Ružomberok were made here, goods (iron, salt, copper, cheese) was transported on the Váh and even up stream on the river Danube to Vienna. Other new plants and works originated and finally Liptovský Hrádok became the centre of the Slovak wood processing industry. In 1851 a forest office which assumed the administration of the properties was established and in the locality Na Maši, a blast furnace and workshop producing wood, wool and wooden pipes was formerly opened in the mid-19th century. An important event in the life of the local population was the construction of the Košice-Bohumín railway track in the 1870's. Consequently a new social group was born – the railwaymen. They participated, together with workers and bricklayers in the workers' movement instigating strikes that resulted in the partial improvement of their social situation. Liptovský Hrádok was also the centre of anti-Nazi resistance in the region of Horný Liptov and the place of numerous operations by partisans. After the liberation, the renovation of the town started and a new electrotechnical plant was opened here. The revival of the tradition of wood-processing brought further industrial promotion. The symbols of wood and hammer are reflected also in the coat of arms of the town. Its very favourable position near the Nízke Tatry mountains, at the confluence of two rivers, together with an attractive natural setting have, in addition, predestined Liptovský Hrádok to become a centre of water sports and tourism.

As far as the secular, cultural and historical monuments are concerned, besides the **Gothic castle compound** from the 14th century and the Renaissance **manor house**, with fortifications from the 17th century, there is also the **belfry** and **weighing station** from 1792 which have been preserved. These are located in the area called Podjaková between Liptovský Hrádok and Kráľova Lehota. The prismoid building of the bel-

fry has a Baroque-Classicist facade and a castellated copula. The building of the weighing station is oblong in shape with a space for passing carts and the weighing process. The history of the town is reminded by the Classicist **single-floor houses** of the 18th and the first half of the 19th centuries rimmed by a **protected lime alley** and a Classicist building of the former **school of forestry**. Sacral monuments include the Classicist Roman-Catholic **church of the Visitation of the Virgin Mary** from 1790 with original interior from the same time. The victims of anti-Nazi resistance and the two world wars are immortalised by **commemorative boards** and a **monument to the war dead**.

In the immediate vicinity of the castle is a park called **Hradocké arborétum, a protected study area** of 7.2 hectares with numerous foreign wood species. Also the **nature reserve Balvan pri Maši** situated east of the town on the left bank of the river Váh is worth seeing. It is the remains of a rocky limestone terrace.

Left: Liptovský Hrádok castle

Part of the town is also the municipal locality north-east of the centre, originally an independent community, called **Dovalovo**. It was probably founded in the 13th century around an Early-Gothic church and it belonged to the castle Hrádok estate. Its inhabitants were mostly farmers and carters, and they also made their living by lime burning, carpentry and bricklaying. Until almost the second half of the 20th century it was also the home of the manufacturing of linen, wool cloth, carpets and utensils used in sheep-keeping. Dovalovo is dominated by the Early-Gothic Roman-Catholic **St. Martin church** from the second half of the 13th century. In 1610 it was restored in Renaissance style and later altered in Baroque and Classicist styles. In the Baroque interior of the church an Early-Gothic window and fragments of Gothic wall paintings are preserved. The original Late-Gothic parts of the altars are deposited in museums in the towns of Martin and Budapest. Sacral buildings include the Classicist **Evangelical church** from 1857 with valuable paintings of Christ on Mount of Olives and of Martin Luther by Peter Bohúň.

Moving on from Liptovský Hrádok, passing Dovalovo in north-easterly direction, one arrives at **LIPTOVSKÁ KOKAVA** (787 m, population 1,150). The community was built by the serfs of Dovalovo probably in the first half of the 15th century. A century later though it did not exist and had to be repopulated again by the late 16th century. It is one of the youngest villages around Liptovský Hrádok. Because of favourable natural conditions, the population lived mainly from agriculture, sheep raising, logging, colliery, cartage, and home made linen up until the Second World War. There used to exist also an iron hammer-mill in the community. The main architectural monuments include the Classicist Roman-Catholic **church of St. Šimon and Júda** with Baroque interior (built in 1830 on the site of an older wooden church) and a Neo-Romanesque **Evangelical church** from 1923. In the territory of the community is also a **nature reserve Machy**, a locality with peat communities over an area of almost 26 hectares.

At the northern edge of Liptovský Hrádok there are four communities. Closest to the town is **LIPTOVSKÝ PETER** (681 m, population 1,400). It was for the first time referred to in 1286 and bears the name of the patron saint of the local Gothic church. In 1363 the community, belonging to the family of Szentiványi was granted market privileges and since then it developed as a squire townlet. Later it was repeatedly destroyed and fell to the level of a serf village. Besides agriculture, the local population lived off local crafts and the men were bricklayers. For instance, every fifth man in the community was a bricklayer in the second half of the 19th century. It is no accident that Liptovský Peter was the first village to have all its houses made of bricks in the Liptov region. As the old Gothic church completely disappeared, the only sacral monuments are the **Evangelical church** of 1940 standing on the site of an older church and a **belfry** of 1850.

Nearby Liptovský Peter, in a north-westerly direction is the community of **JAMNÍK** (695 m, population 400). It was first mentioned in 1346 and as its name suggests (jama means hole) that it actually originated in a hole. Legend has it that there were large holes in Jamník used by the local people to catch game. This squire community belonged to the squires of Podtureň until as late as 1848. The local population were mostly farmers; sheep-keeping was another common occupation and since the end of the 19th century they were also good bricklayers as proved by the Classicist and fin-de-siécle houses from the late 19th century. Supplementing occupations were linen weaving and the manufacturing of utensils used in sheep-keeping. The only sacral monument here is the **Evangelical church** of 1907. There used to exist a community called Sv. Duch in the territory of Jamník but it disappeared in 1709 during the battles between rebels and the imperial troops.

VAVRIŠOVO (712 m, population 500), a community situated east of Jamník, was first referred to in 1346. It bears the name of its first owner Vavrinec, an ancestor of the squires of Podtureň. The community has suffered a lot during the Rebellions of Estates in the 17th and 18th centuries. It was completely destroyed in a battle between the Rákoczi's rebellious troops and the imperial army that took place in the territory in 1709.

The Battle of Švihrov:

This battle is one of the last in the history of anti-Hapsburg rebellions in which the rebels were successful in their fight against the imperial troops. It was preceded by a bitter defeat of the rebels by the imperial troops commanded by General Heister near Trenčín in 1708. The imperial troops then occupied almost the whole region of Liptov and the defeated rebels had to withdraw to the distant Spiš region. As the leader of the rebels Rákoczi prepared a new charge in Liptov, the imperial general A. Thollet was going to use then an unusual method of defence. He built a military defensive line (earthen ramparts with rotundas and stellar formations) from Liptovský Hrádok passing Liptovský Peter, Vavrišovo up to the foothills of the Západné Tatry mountains and simultaneously he fortified the villages. Near the river Belá are still some traces of trenches to be seen. The battle of Švihrov (so called because it took place at the alpine meadow of Švihrová near Vavrišovo) started on August 4, 1709. The rebels (artillery, infantry, and cavalry counting in total about ten thousand men) first conquered all the surrounding villages and the imperial army (about a thousand men of cavalry and infantry) with the mortally wounded general Thollet had to retreat to the fortifications in Švihrová. The infantry inflicted enormous losses and their capitulation was only a matter of time. However, in the night of August 9 the commanders of the rebels ordered an incomprehensible retreat and practically fled from a victorious battle. Whether it was the incompetence of the commanders, mistaken estimates of the enemy's number or the bad morale of the men, nobody knows, and it is still a subject of conjecture. The fact is that after the "victorious" battle the morale of Rákoczi's rebellious troops totally collapsed.

Life in Vavrišovo after its restoration acquired again a normal pace and the local people lived off agriculture, crafts and masonry. Bricklayers are particularly mentioned since the mid-19th century in connection with Vavrišovo, as they belonged to the most numerous groups in the building sites in Budapest and other Old Hungarian towns. There are even references from 1910 that out of 842 inhabitants of the community 192 were bricklayers. Similar to the surrounding communities the bricklayers of Vavrišovo founded a supporting association that defended their interests in relation to employers and helped the poorest members. The villagers actively participated also in anti-Nazi resistance and supported partisans which operated around the village.

There is a couple of sacral monuments in the village – a Neo-Romanesque **Evangelical church** from 1884 (the tower is from 1928) and a Neo-Classicist **Baptist church** from 1888.

The community of **PODTUREŇ** (615 m, population 450) boasts of a rich pre-historic, as well as medieval history. The community, now hidden behind a big motorway bridge (the longest one in Slovakia, more than 1 km long), lies north-west of Liptovský Hrádok. Its territory was settled as early as the Aenaeolitic period and then in the Bronze, La Téne, Roman and Slavic eras, proven by the finds from the settlements, including channelled ceramics, Lusatian culture, a Celtic fort and a Slavic settlement. The name of the community is derived from the word *turňa* meaning tower, which used to stand here probably in the 12th century followed by a church. The first written reference to the village is from 1345 and it belonged to the squires of Podtureň, who owned it until 1848. It developed as a squire agricultural village, where the people occasionally also assumed other activities: crafts like stone-masonry, bricklaying and linen weaving. Examples of the once rich and thriving squire life in the community are two original Renaissance **manor houses** from the 17th century, rebuilt in Baroque style in the 18th century. The somewhat younger building is that of the Classicist **curia** of 1845.

Right: The Tatra mountains

A part of Liptovský Hrádok used to be **LIPTOVSKÁ PORÚBKA** (647 m, population 1,000), today an independent village. It lies on the south-eastern boundary of the town. It developed in the 14th century on the land of the family of Szentiványi (Szentiványi means Saint John).

The squires of Szentiványi:

In the 16th and 17th centuries the number of squire families living in the Liptov region increased as a consequence of later resettling and flights from the Turks. The old families and the newcomers consisted of the members of various nationalities and their language of communication was mostly Latin or Hungarian. The old squire families derived their origins also from the Czech and Polish ancestors but as their interests were in Old Hungary they progressively adopted the Hungarian language as well. Such was the case of one of the oldest and most important squire families living in Liptov – the family of Szentiványi of Liptovský Ján. They derived their origins from the Czech aristocrat Hauk Polka who received an extensive estate in Liptov from the Old Hungarian king Ondrej II as a donation in the 13th century. They used though, the name Szentiványi. What is interesting about this family is that they did not portion their immense property and administrated it together as a family estate. They owned numerous communities situated on the left bank of the river Váh. The administration of the property was headed by an elected manager, most frequently a family member and the most important matters were dealt with at family sessions. The income was rendered by the forests, the lease of mills, taverns, farmsteads, land and mines. The net profit was annually distributed according to an established key. Their activity can be thus be characterised as "the gem of a family joint stock company" later to be realised during the severe Slovak privatisation in the 1990's.

The people of Porúbka in the past were farmers, rafters, basket-makers and since the 18th century many of them were employed in the wood or iron processing workshops in Hrádok. During the Second World War they were engaged in the illegal partisan movement and the community belonged to one of the main Liptov centres of anti-Nazi resistance. The village is dominated by the **Evangelical church** of 1918 built together with Evangelical parsonage and designed by the architect M. M. Harminc.

Lovers of comfortable walks will certainly appreciate the red-marked **footpath bound for Smrekovica mountain** (1,277 metres). The path proceeds from the community over wonderful meadows and a thin forest and the ascent to Smrekovica becomes slightly steep only in one section. This tourist walk can be combined with a descent to the Jánska dolina valley by a red-marked path.

Only a few kilometres eastward near the confluence of Biely Váh and Čierny Váh rivers is the village of **KRÁĽOVA LEHOTA** (741 m, population 700). It developed in the mid-14th century on land belonging to the Old Hungarian king after whom it is named (King's Time). Later it belonged to the squire family of Lehotský and gradually by division of the property, to several families of their descendants – minor squires. The local population lived by farming and on the rivers (they were excellent fishermen and rafters), later on the mines with deposits of iron ore, the railway and copper hammer-mill provided them with additional resources. There existed also a narrow-gauged railway from Litovský Hrádok to Liptovská Teplička part of which is under reconstruction at the present time. During the Second World War the environs of the community belonged to the most exposed areas as it is situated in a strategic place on the cross-roads of the Liptov route bound for the Pohronie region. Several attacks of partisan squads took place here in which many civilians were killed.

Among the monuments preserved in the community certainly several **manor houses** and **curias** are of interest as they document its squire past. All eight single-floor Classicist curias are remarkable for the simple architecture from the 19th century. Also two Classicist manor houses are of the same period, while one of them was built on older foundations. Secular architectural monuments include the late 19th century **villa** of the local citizen, the architect A. Stróbel imitating a Gothic castle with towers. Sacral monuments are dominated by the Neo-Gothic Evangelical church of 1894 built on the site of an older building.

Kráľova Lehota provides an entry gate to the 35 kilometre long **valley of Čierny Váh**, the longest one in the mountain range of the Nízke Tatry mountains. The river Čierny Váh springs from under the Kráľova hoľa mountain, at an altitude of 1,680 metres above sea level. In the valley there are two foresters' communities, Svarín and

Čierny Váh, known above all because of the water power station built on the river, the highest situated one in Slovakia. The valley of Čierny Váh valley together with its smaller lateral valleys are part of the National Park of the Low Tatras and for its aesthetic landscape assets it is frequented by tourists wishing to find the rest and solitude in the mountains.

East of Liptovský Hrádok and south of the motorway bound for Poprad lies the famous community of **HYBE** (690 m, population 1,650). It probably originated in the 12th century and its name is derived from that of the Hybica brook. Its existence was recorded in 1239 when the Old Hungarian king Belo IV annexed it again to the royal property. The famous period in the history of Hybe started in the mid-13th century with the arrival of German families from the Spiš region and in 1265 they obtained municipal privileges following the example of the town Krupina. Hybe was originally a mining community and the local miners extracted gold in the Bocianska dolina valley until the mid 15th century. Since Hybe acquired the municipal rights it was referred to as a privileged royal town in historical acts. The people of Hybe were entitled to vote for their mayor and priest, and they were exempted from duties at the local market, and were allowed to use their delimited territory amongst other things. Nevertheless, in the 14th century they fell under the administration of the head of the province of Liptov becoming a part of his property and its existence continued in a form of a serf townlet. A more rapid promotion was stimulated by additional privileges of the Old Hungarian king Sigismond of Luxembourg who granted the town a market right in 1396 and a fair right in 1423, and the people of Hybe were exempted from paying tolls in Lučivná and Dovalovo. This was an incentive for the development of trade and crafts (smith's, wheelwright's, shoe-maker's, and pottery) and Hybe progressively lost the character of a mining centre. It was also related to the limited and low-yielding deposits of ore and comparably high duty fees for mining in the neighbouring community of Boca. The town started to decay in the 16th century also because its original

Left: The All Saints church in Hybe

privileges were gradually cut and the pressure of the landlords of Hrádok Castle increased. The town suffered a lot as a consequence of anti-Hapsburg Estate rebellions as the enemy troops who passed through the country repeatedly damaged the property of Hybe. It was also one of the reasons why robbery as a manifestation of the resistance on the side of serfs grew more predominant.

Pacho of Hybe and the witches of Liptov:

One of the legend Hybe boasts of is a famous figure – the robber Pacho (a film was also made of the story). The protagonist and his adventures were mostly invented, though based on a true story as robbery was indeed a popular activity in the 17th century. As the manifestation of resistance of the serfs to the growing oppression by the landlords went too far, the landlords fled to other provinces of Slovakia or concentrated themselves in the castle of Liptovský Hrádok. Numerous trials with the robbers in the Court of justice were held, but the witchcraft processes won the biggest popularity. The Court of Justice of the Liptov county at the time put on trial several cases of women and condemned them for witchcraft and conspiracy with the devil. Before they were ultimately condemned, the Court of Justice subjected them to a water trial. They were compelled to enter deep water and the ones that did not get drowned were considered guilty and executed. In other words they could prove their innocence only by drowning.

When the mining activity in Hybe faded away, the town lived by agriculture and local crafts. In the 18th century the people dedicated themselves to various crafts, such as carpentry, boot-making, textile dyeing, tannery, mining, coopery, and the production of juniper brandy of an excellent quality. The 19th century was characterised by the activity of the local bricklayers and stone-masons who exported their skills also beyond the frontiers of Slovakia (namely to Budapest). There is a famous novel *A thousand year old bee* by the contemporary Slovak writer Peter Jaroš giving credit to the period with great mastery and art, describing the life of the Slovak bricklayers. Many of the crafts preserved up to the mid-20th century and find examples in the local population even today.

Hybe has preserved a strong sense of tradition. The local school was referred to as early as in 1563. The theatre performances held regularly in the village, as well as several libraries date to the second half of the 19th century. Many figures of Slovak culture were born or lived here: the poet J. Grajchman (1822-1897), the writer B. Klein-Tesnoskalský (1853-1841), the writer D. Chrobák (1907-1951) amongst others. Their activity in the community is recalled by various **tombstones** and **commemorative boards**. The ground plan of the village has a typical "colonisation" layout. An oblong square is in the middle of the community and the streets depart from its corners. The main street runs parallel to one of its sides. The square is rimmed by brick houses prevailingly of the 19th century that substituted the original ground floor wooden houses. Their appearance, as well as the composition of the square evoke the atmosphere existing in the town a hundred years ago. Among the sacral monuments the Roman-Catholic **All Saints church** standing in the centre of the square is of especial interest. It was originally an Early-Gothic church built around 1300. Its fortifications are from the 17th century. The church was later rebuilt in the Baroque-Classicist style and in 1824 a tower was added to it. Its interior is dominated by the main Late-Baroque altar of the mid-18th century. Another sacral building is the Evangelical church built in the years between 1822-1826 on the site of the former wooden articled church from which also some interior parts (altar, pulpit and baptistery) were installed.

A well-known community, mainly because of its folk traditions is neighbouring **VÝCHODNÁ** (775 m, population 2,350). It originated on a extensive piece of land, first mentioned as a meadow called *Vichodna* in 1269. In the last third of the 13th century a community first belonging to the royal estates and later to the landlords of Liptovský Hrádok developed here. More settlers from Eastern Slovakia came here in the 15th century and the population was given by the Hrádok landlords what was called the Wallachian right (i.e. instead of working on the landlord's land they paid duties in kind and money). They made their living by farming, cattle and sheep-raising and wood processing. Sheep raising and the production of a quality cheese called bryndza made the villagers famous as they sold their products to almost all Slovak towns. From the 18th century rafting and cartage were occupations that provided for additional income. Later some of the villagers found jobs as railway workers and in the surrounding industrial firms.

The religious present and the past of the community is represented by two churches. The Roman-Catholic **St. Štefan the First Martyr church** which is the older, is from the 15th century. Origi-

nally it was Gothic and in the 19th century it was rebuilt in Classicist style. The **Evangelical church** was built in the years 1926-1927 on the site of an older church based on the design of the architect M. M. Harminc. Interesting secular buildings are represented by several houses of wooden folk architecture.

However, Východná is best known for its **folk festival** organised here annually since 1953. The local **natural amphitheatre** situated alongside the main road to Poprad is the pride of the village. The first weekend of July every year the national exhibition of the best folk ensembles under the title Folkórny festival Východná come here. Often renowned ensembles and individuals from abroad are invited to attend. No wonder then that the festival in Východná is a member of CIOFF, the international association of folk festivals which are among the best events of their kind in the world. The amphitheatre with its wooden sculptures and regular expositions and accompanying events enhances the atmosphere of the festival. The community maintains its traditions also by the local **folk ensemble** and **folk handicrafts** (embroidery, wood-carving, weaving, etc.)

Left: A Folk festival in Východná
Right: Važecká jaskyňa cave

A typical community of the Liptov region and an important ethnographic locality is also **VAŽEC** (792 m, population 2,400). It originated by the colonisation of the valley of the Biely Váh river, donated in 1269 to count Bogomír. Even though it was first referred to in 1286 the community was founded before that. The first hereditary mayor was Gerhard and later the community belonged to three branches of Bogomír's descendants: the Szentiványis', Smrečányis', and Baans'. Važec was one of the largest villages in Liptov in the 17th century. The local population were occupied in agriculture, cattle and sheep-raising, forestry work. Wood was extracted and sold, shingles were made and all the raw material and the products were transported by the local carters and rafters to the surrounding market towns. After 1871 many villagers found jobs as railway workers. The occupations of the people of Važec did not practically change until the first half of the 20th century. In 1931 almost the entire village burnt down and it was restored to its present appearance with the contribution of the state and wide public support.

Among the monuments of the community is the originally Gothic Roman-Catholic **church of St. Anton the Hermit** from the late 13th century. In 1738 it was altered into Baroque style and in 1910 it was completely reconstructed. Its interior (main altar, lateral altars, pulpit) are in Baroque-Rococo style; of the original decoration the Gothic Madonna from the early 15th century is preserved. The community also has a Neo-Gothic **Evangelical church** from 1892 built on the site of an older church from 1783. The interior of both churches was partially ornamented by an important Czech painter called Jan Hála.

The painters of Važec:

Važec with its natural scenery, wooden peasant houses and distinctive people was highly attractive for artists. It inspired the painters like P. Bohúň, P. Socháň, M. Benka, K. Plicka, J. Hála and even a married couple of English artists, the Stokes'. It was through the paintings of these artists that Važec became one of the most famous Slovak villages, a symbol of traditional rural life and culture. Especially the Stokes' and Jan Hála actually fell in love with the landscape and created some original paintings of the architecture and the people of Važec either in work or leisure, in hard and good times. Particularly valuable are the paintings of wooden houses, because after a fire in 1931 the majority of them burnt down and only a few examples remained. The picturesque beauty of Važec and its people fascinated the Czech painter Jan Hála so much that he stayed there permanently and found a new home in his beloved Važec.

Eloquent evidence of the life and work of this painter is all gathered in the **commemorative house of Jan Hála**. It is a house-gallery where he lived and painted in the years between 1923-1959 and contains about 60 paintings. All of them depict the wooden houses, folk costumes and the village life. An original peasant wooden house with authentic interior furnishing is the part of the exposition.

Pamätný dom Jana Hálu
(The commemorative house of Jan Hála), tel.: 0849/291421
Opening hours: Tue-Sun 12:00-16:00h

The most visited landmark of Važec is the national nature reserve the **Važecká jaskyňa cave**

situated in the southern edge of the community. Although the local population knew of it for a long time its hidden parts were discovered by a local native A. A. Húska in 1922. It was partially opened to the public in 1928 and it can be seen in length (235 metres) since 1954. The Cave originated in a limestone rock through the activity of condensation and the water of the Biely Váh river. Remarkable is its drip-stone ornamentation of various colours and the underground little lakes. The Važecká jaskyňa cave is one of the best known in Europe for the discovery of the bones of the cave bear *Ursus speleaus* that lived here about 15,000 years ago. Its bones are to be seen mainly in the alluviums of a passage called Kostnica (Deposit of Bones). Children especially appreciate the scene with the bones and huddle up to their parents when the lights are turned off for greater effect.

Važecká jaskyňa, tel.: 0849/29 41 71
Opening hours: April 1 to May 15 and September 16 to October 31, Tue-Sun 9:00-14:00h, May 16-31 and September 1-15, Tue-Sun 9:00-15:00h, June, July, August Mon-Sun 9:00-17:00h

SPIŠ

Stará Ľubovňa
and its environs

STARÁ ĽUBOVŇA (548 m, population 15,800) lies together with Poprad and Kežmarok on the principal settlement axis of north-western Spiš, represented by the river Poprad. It is 46 km from the town of Poprad and 64 km from the capital of the province, Prešov. The boundary crossing between Slovakia and Poland is 16 kilometres north from Stará Ľubovňa in the community of Mníšek nad Popradom.

The spur between the river Poprad and its right side tributary Jakubianka was settled as early as in older Stone Age. The oldest archaeological finds excavated from the clay of the river terrace point to a similar historical era, evidenced by the better known artefacts found in the Aksamitka Cave near Haligovce. Proof of a long sequence of settlements in Ľubovňa were gathered by archaeologists, showing few interruptions since the Palaeolithic period to the early Middle Ages. However, the first three centuries of the town's history are covered by a veil of ignorance. The oldest written reference mentioning Ľubovňa exists in a part of the historical documents belonging to the nearby community of Podolínec. The act of 1292 declares that the village mayor, Henrik of Podolínec, obtained some new privileges from the king, beside other established duties for the people of Hniezdne and Ľubovňa, such as assisting in the construction of the fortification of Podolínec. When shortly after the construction of Ľubovňa Castle was finished they were much less dependent on the protection of the Podolínec fortification and the town developed with more freedom.

Stará Ľubovňa received town privileges gradually. The greater part of them was granted in 1364 by king Ľudovít I who promoted it to a royal town, which meant an exemption of the jurisdictions of Podolínec and the Ľubovňa Castle. The inhabitants of the town enjoyed the Magdeburg privilege i.e. the right to elect their own town council and their mayor, to organise the annual fairs, to tap beer, to catch fish in the river

Poprad and to try its citizens in court. Besides this they were also exempt from paying some taxes. The town continues to flourish after 1412 when it was included among the 16 Spiš towns given by king Sigismond to the Polish crown as a guarantee on a loan.

The early arrival of tourism:

The forfeiting of the Spiš towns brought to Stará Ľubovňa something which is today called a touristic boom. When Ľubovňa Castle became the seat of the mayor of the forfeited Spiš towns, many diplomatic negotiations between the Old Hungarian and Polish authorities took place concerning the return of the unfortunate forfeit. Services to the royal negotiators and their courtiers enhanced the level of the local crafts and their guilds. The weavers, shoemakers, high-boot makers, tailors, furriers and butchers enjoyed an unusually high demand for their services. Above all the merchants and shopkeepers profited in the years of the forfeit taking part in seven annual fairs in Ľubovňa. At the end of the period there was also a mint established in the town, a sign of economic and social expansion. This part of the history of Stará Ľubovňa is very convincingly described in the historical novel by Jozef Nižnánsky Spišské tajomstvo (The Secret of the Spiš Region).

The final return of the towns to the lap of Old Hungary in the time of queen Mary Theresa did not favour Stará Ľubovňa. When a province of 16 Spiš town was established in 1778 the centre was located to Spišská Nová Ves and Stará Ľubovňa lost its privileged position dropping down to the level of the rest of the towns in the region. Later the impact of the industrial revolution came to the town at the beginning of the 20th century, firstly with the founding of a tannery co-operative followed by two printing houses. Further industrialisation of Stará Ľubovňa came only after the Second World War when three industrial firms were set in operation. The year 1966 is especially important for the town as it obtained a railway connection to Orlov. In 1968 Stará Ľubovňa became again, after eight years, a district town.

The centre of Stará Ľubovňa is the **square of St. Mikuláš** with a rectangular ground plan. It originated in 1346 by reconstructing an older spindle-shaped square. Brick buildings arose after the fire of 1556 that destroyed the older wooden houses. The majority of the contemporary houses in the square originated in the 17th and 18th century and underwent reconstruction which gave them Classicist, nouveau end-of-century façades. The most important building of the square besides the church is the arcade house of **Provinčný dom** (no. 12) (1) once the seat of the governor of the forfeited Spiš towns. This Renaissance house was reconstructed in 1639 and partially altered at the beginning of the 20th century, and is where the Tourist Information Centre is seated today. Attention should be paid to the Roman-Catholic **church of St. Mikuláš**, (2) built around the year 1280. It is very probable that it is located on the site of an older, perhaps wooden church of the local parish. Extensive reconstruction was made in the second half of the 17th century. In the prevailingly Baroque interior of the church some older artistic works can be seen. The most valuable of which are the Late-Gothic baptistery of the 16th century, the Late-Gothic tomb slabs of the so-called "marmon" marble from the nearby quarry and a Gothic sculpture of the **Madonna of Ľubovňa** on a lateral altar.

On a limestone cliff over the local part called Podsadek stands **Ľubovniansky hrad castle**. It originated at the turn of the 13th and 14th centuries as part of the system of boundary castles. Besides the protection of the former Polish-Old Hungarian border its task was to secure the important trade route passing along the Poprad valley to Poland, and for some time it also functioned as a customs point. It was mentioned in the historical documents for the first time in 1311 as a part of royal property. In 1412 a historical meeting of the Old Hungarian ruler Sigismond of Luxembourg with the Polish king Vladislav II took place here, when they signed a peace and mutual assistance treaty. It is possible that the offer of the forfeit which brought to Ľubovňa Castle such an exceptional position originated here. The castle remained the property of the Old Hungarian king but the captain of the castle fulfilled an important function of an administrator of the forfeited Spiš towns, of which there were 29 in all. The estate of the castle also contained 14 communities, several manors and a brewery. After an extensive fire in 1557 Ľubovňa Castle obtained through reconstruction a more modern look with advanced artillery facilities and more comfortable housing.

After the return of the Spiš towns to Old Hungary the role of the castle diminished and the castle itself fell into decay. Before that, however, in 1772 it was also shortly owned by the Tzar of Russia involved in the division of Poland. Attempts to restore the life in the castle by their new owners were not too successful, and the last lord of the castle, the Polish noble Ján Zamoysky, abandoned it in 1944, whereafter he moved to Spain with his noble spouse, the Princess Isabel, niece of the Spanish king.

The regal visitors to Ľubovňa Castle:

The importance of the Ľubovňa Castle is proven by a long list of noble personages who visited it. Out of the rulers they were, for instance, the Old Hungarian kings Karol Róbert (1314), Sigismond of Luxembourg (1396 and 1412), and Ján Albrecht (1449), the Old Hungarian queen Mary (1392) and the Polish kings Vladislav II (1412 and 1419), Ján Kazimír (1656), and Ján Sobieski, who came here for a short visit after a victorious campaign against the Turks in 1683. We can also include Móric Beňovský as he later became the king of Madagascar. Though in his case it was not exactly a visit because the famous traveller and adventurer was involuntarily staying in the castle prison. In the years between 1655 to 1661 the solid walls of the Ľubovňa Castle provided a temporary hiding place to the Polish coronation jewels when they were deposited here by the then lord of the castle, Juraj, of the Lubomirski family of princes, to protect them against the Swedes.

The present appearance of the castle is a mixture of several building styles beginning with the Romanesque and ending in Baroque. The system of inner fortification consists of four courtyards. The oldest part of the castle are the remains of a round defensive tower and a contiguous Gothic palace. Also the palace of the Lubomírski family of the 17th century was in ruins before it was successfully reconstructed and the castle museum collections were installed. In 1991 the castle chapel was reconstructed and again consecrated which today holds regular

Left: Ľubovniansky hrad castle

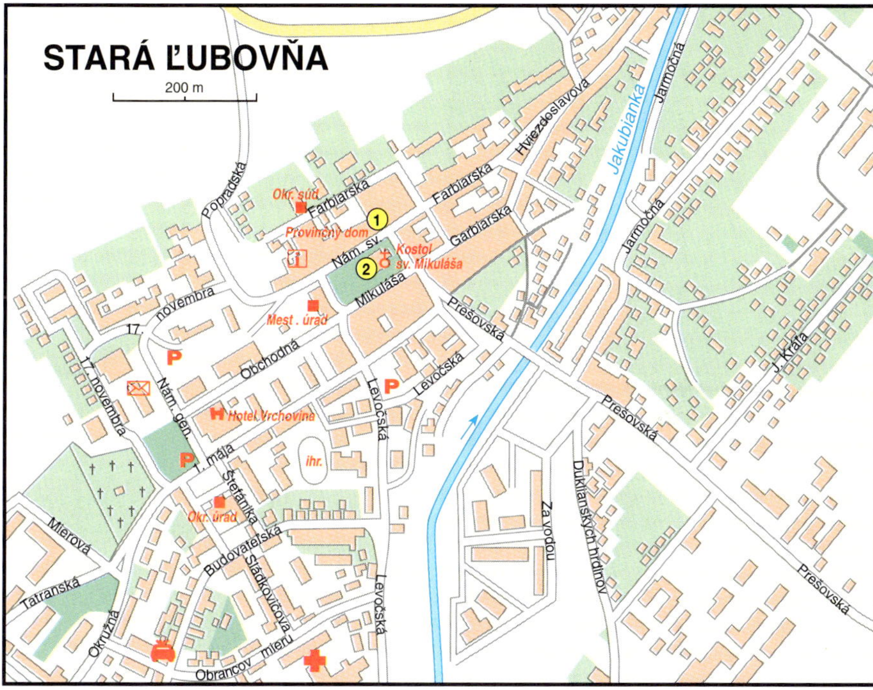

services. In the castle well in the second courtyard the bodies of dead partisans were buried in 1944. Ľubovňa Castle is open to the public (see times below). The castle **museum** contains a series of collections entitled the History of the Castle, the Forfeit of the Spiš Cities, Crafts and Guilds, Historical Furniture, and Sacral Art. An independent collection is represented by an **open air folk architecture museum** in the area at the foot of the castle, which consists of a set of folk buildings collected in the surrounding villages forming, along with the castle, a unique and impressing composition. The group of country houses provides a picturesque settlement around the castle. The most valuable item is the **wooden Greek-Catholic church of Matisová** of 1833. The wooden church is consecrated to St. Michal Archangel.

Múzeum Ľubovniansky hrad
(Museum of the Ľubovňa Castle), tel.: 0963/22 030,
Opening hours:
May 1- September 30, daily 9:00-17:30h,
October 1 – April 30, daily except on feastdays and Sundays 10:00-15:00h.

An interesting trip in this area is the one to **Oslí vrch mountain** (859 m). A red-marked foot path leads from Stará Ľubovňa which heads north-east, known from recent history as the path of the Polish war couriers. The first stop on the route is Ľubovňa Castle itself. The moderately ascending path then continues from the castle in the same direction, passing alternatively a meadow and forest landscape up to Oslí mountain. The view from its rounded top is one of the most rewarding in the Ľubovnianska vrchovina highland. On its northern side is a rich spring. At the top of Oslí mountain four footpaths meet. The red-marked footpath of the Polish couriers goes on further along the long mountain ridge following the meandering river Poprad and ends near the Sulinský water spring. The blue-marked path heads from Oslí mountain, westward towards the Vabec saddle, where some buses returning to Stará Ľubovňa stop, providing a quick and comfortable return to the town. The third option on how to finish the trip is by a walk which first follows the yellow and then the green-marked path around the **Marmon** cliff. In the local quarry the so-called "marmon marble" – a reddish decora-

tive limestone similar to marble – was extracted in past. There are several caves around the cliffs. The trip is also pleasant in winter when one can make it on cross-country skis.

The route of trip to Jarabinský canyon starts in Stará Ľubovňa. The first part leads up the valley of the Pasterník brook to the **Vabec saddle** (744 m). The saddle is on the main ridge of the Ľubovnianska vrchovina highlands. It is an excellent location if you want to get a splendid and complete view of the High Tatras. From there the path winds around the ridges surrounding the community heading to the one of the most interesting natural places, the **Jarabinský prielom gorge**. The local brook, which cuts deeply into the belt of cliffs, creates here a unique 200 m long gorge. The stream of five cascades has created beautiful giant pots, called by the local people "baďury", some of which are 5 m in diameter with a depth up to 2 m. The passage over the gorge is very exacting and it cannot be accomplished without entering the water. Shoes alone are of no use whatsoever, so one needs high rubber boots or wellingtons. The footpath avoids the most difficult parts. It deviates from the gorge before it ends in the quarry and heads towards the community of Jarabina. The quarry is known for its abundant occurrence of amonites.

Left: Jarabinský prielom gorge
Right: The pilgrims chapel in Zvir

In the lateral valley of the Ľubovnianka brook, 8 km south-east of Stará Ľubovňa is the **Ľubovnianske kúpele** (the Ľubovňa spa, 580 m). They were established in the 19th century making use of four local mineral water springs efficiently used in therapy of digestive ailments. The attractiveness of the spa was enhanced by a park after the French tradition and it used to be a favourite resort for patients coming from Budapest. The spa closed during the Second World War, but in the after-war years it changed to a comfortable holiday resort of over-regional importance. Nowadays it is a large and modern trade union hotel with in-door swimming pool and several cottages belonging to private owners or to firms. In a valley above the spa community three ski lifts are available for skiing during the winter season. The local **educational path** with six rest stops explains to the tourist the history of the area and its natural landmarks. The path crosses the park which boasts of numerous rare and valuable species of trees. Visitors can see there four specimens of Pyrenean pine, the only ones in Slovakia, as well as the remarkable and huge white pines.

North-west of Stará Ľubovňa are three small communities: Kamienka, Jarabina and Litmanová. Originally they were settled by shepherds who besides their houses also built unusual seasonally utilised buildings called locally "majdány". These were shepherds' huts where the shepherds moved with their families and animals in the summer and are preserved in the territory of Kamienka. A "majdán" from Litmanová was included in the open air ethnographic museum near Ľubovňa Castle.

KAMIENKA (585 m population 1,445) is the largest community on the road between Ľubovňa castle and Červený Kláštor, and lies in the valley of the brook bearing the same name, 8.5 km from Stará Ľubovňa. It is one of the oldest communities in the region. Historians suppose that it existed as early as before the 12th century, and its name appeared in old documents in 1342 as *Villa Lapidis* (Stone village). Half a century later the Slavic form *Kemenyk* was used proving the arrival of the Slavic population which participated in the Wallachian colonisation. Kamienka belonged for a long time to the estate of Ľubovňa Castle and later it became famous for the tinker's trade. In the second half of the 19th century a great part of the Kamienka population emigrated to America. The local Greek-Catholic **church of the Apostles St. Peter and Pavol** dates back to 1790, near to which grows an especially old specimen of maple. It is about 300 years old and 21 m high. In the local cemetery there are four valuable willow trees, specimens of white willow (*Salix alba L.*) and on the slope on the easternmost side of the Pieniny mountains, Vysoká (1,013 m) there exists a unique type of forest with an abundance of yew trees. Kamienka is a place for the annual meeting of the Ruthenian and Ukraine minorities living in Slovakia during the **national folk feast**. The principal artistic events are held in the natural amphitheatre taking an audience of as much as 3,500. A part of the feast is usually an exposition of the works of Ruthenian and Ukrainian artists.

Neigbouring **JARABINA** (587 m, population 826) is an agricultural community in the valley of Malý Lipník brook, 5 km from Stará Ľubovňa. It was founded in 14th century during the Wallachian colonisation by the Ruthenian people and was mentioned for the first time in 1329. Its population made their living from agriculture and the tinker trade. Nearby the community is a large limestone quarry and next to it a **protected nature area**, the well-known **Jarabinský prielom gorge** mentioned above.

LITMANOVÁ, (679 m, population 652) is a small boundary community and the highest situated one in the region of Ľubovňa. It lies at the foothill of the highest mountain of the Ľubovnianska vrchovina highlands, the Eliášovka (1,023 m), 10 km from the town district. It originated in the 15th century and its inhabitants were occupied in agriculture, namely cattle husbandry. At present the locals mostly work in Stará Ľubovňa. The immediate environs of the area will impress any admirer of landscape beauty and the white limestone cliffs will also attract the attention of tourists. The brook passing the community was declared a **nature reserve** under the name **Litmanovský potok brook** for its perfectly preserved shoals of fish.

The apparition of the Virgin Mary:

The community of Litmanová became famous because of the alleged apparition of the Virgin Mary which appeared before two girls in a place called Zvir. In commemoration of the event a Christian pilgrimage is held here, which is the reason why Litmanová is the most visited village in northern Slovakia. Tens of thousands of Catholics throughout Slovakia and from abroad come to a log chapel on the southern slope of the Eliášovka mountain to take part in an open air service and to listen to the words of the Virgin Mary pronounced by the girl-visionaries.

West of Stará Ľubovňa on the bank of the river Poprad is the village of **HNIEZDNE** (539 m, population 1,360). It was mentioned for the first time as early as the second half of the 13th century under the name *Gnezdna*. Its founder was the village mayor Mikuláš together with the settlers of the Sholtys colonisation arising from the German privilege. Originally an agricultural community it changed to a town populated mainly by tradesmen and craftsmen. Hviezdne once

belonged to the 16 forfeited Spiš towns administered by the Polish village mayor of Ľubovňa Castle, and was until 1946 inhabited mostly by Germans. The urban past of what is now a village is evidenced by a pattern of 17th and 18th century **burgher houses** standing in a spindle-shaped square and built in the Late-Renaissance and Baroque styles. Hviezdne and its neighbouring community of **FORBASY** (535 m, population 370) is rich in sulphurous mineral water springs.

The same mineral water springs made famous the neighbouring town **VYŠNÉ RUŽBACHY** (617 m, population 1,170). It is situated in a lateral valley of the left tributary of the Poprad river, on the south-eastern foothills of the Spišská Magura mountains and about 3 km from the main road from Poprad to Stará Ľubovňa. The assets of the microclimate near the mineral water springs were already well known by the pre-historic people of the Paleolithic period, traces of which were found in the local travertine quarries. The settlement was mentioned for the first time in historical acts from 1329 as *Nova Rusunbach*. The name Ružbachy is of German origin and is derived from the German words for booming (*raschen*) and brook (*bach*). The curing effects of the earthy carbonate mineral water springs were also well known in the Middle Ages and the first spa was founded there. The captain of Šariš castle, Juraj Wernher, mentioned its existence in a document in 1549. In the past the spa was a favourite place for the Polish and Old Hungarian aristocracy. In 1882 it was purchased and modernised by count Zamoyski. Today there is not much preserved of the old architecture in Vyšné Ružbachy. The urban buildings with shingle roofs and gables facing the street were typical for the community and yet in spite of the great changes it has undergone its inhabitants have conserved their beautiful folk costumes and Goral dialect. The local Roman-Catholic **church** is consecrated to the **Purification of the Virgin Mary** and was built in Baroque style in the second half of the 18th century. Besides this there are 8 chapels around the town. An historically valuable building is the original town hall of 1682.

Left: The Vyšné Ružbachy spa

At present Vyšné Ružbachy is one of the most important **spa** and tourist centres in Slovakia, with nine types of mineral water springs of hydrocarbonate and calcareous-magnesian. The water temperature inside the springs is about 22°C. The most productive spring, **Izabela**, fills a 50×50m outdoor swimming pool. At the centre of the swimming pool there is a small round island with greenery. A part of the spa consists of therapeutic pools with mineral waters, tube baths, a sauna, gymnasium and massage rooms. The patients of Vyšné Ružbachy are predominantly adults suffering from neurosis, psychosis, climacteric syndrome, locomotion disturbances, bronchitis and oncological symptoms. The spa guests mostly concentrate towards the therapeutic houses of Travertín, Dukla and Kriváň, all surrounded by a charming forest-park, and tourist accommodation can be found in the hotels Kráter and Magura. The spa Vyšné Ružbachy is open all the year round. In the summer season, besides swimming and bathing, hiking trips to the forest of the Spišská Magura mountains are a favourite pastime. In winter there are ideal conditions for down-hill skiing as there are four modern ski lifts.

One of the principal attractions of Vyšné Ružbachy is the local **travertine quarry**. In the past travertine, as a decorative stone, was extracted here, but in 1964 the stonemasons were replaced by artists who changed the quarry into an interesting open air gallery of sculptures. Every year during the **International Sculpture Symposium** national and foreign artists meet here to create some common works from the noble and mouldable travertine of Ružbachy. Their artistic works remain in the quarry to be admired amid this impressing natural sculptural gallery.

The craters in Ružbachy:

The craters in Ružbachy have nothing to do with volcanos and volcanic eruptions. They originated by the sinking of the local travertine hills that precipitated around the mineral water springs rich in calcium. There are four large and several smaller travertine craters. The best known is the one called Kráter, which is the largest travertine lake in Slovakia with a diameter of 20 m and a depth of 2-3 m. The other travertine craters in Ružbachy are dry. Among them is one called the Kaplnkový kráter, named so because there is a chapel on its edge ("kaplnka" meaning chapel). Its dimensions 51×32 m and a depth of 4.5 m make it the largest formation of its kind in Slovakia. The Smerdžonka crater releases carbon dioxide and that is the reason why it is also called the Hole of Death.

NIŽNÉ RUŽBACHY (555 m, population 650) lies in the centre of the Ružbachy Gate at the tapering of the Poprad valley between the Popradská and Ľubovnianska kotlina basins. It is 11 km from Stará Ľubovňa and the nearest town is Podolínec situated about 5 km south-west. The community originated at the end of the 13th century. Between 1286 and 1288 a brook with the same name was mentioned. The old acts quote its original name Staré Ružbachy in 1303, and the villagers were famous cattle handlers in the past. Among the most valuable local monuments is the originally Early Gothic Roman-Catholic **church of St. Katarína** of 13th century, later reconstructed in the Baroque style. There is also an interesting technical monument, a **paper mill**, and next to the village on the bank of the river Poprad is a group of cottages called **Ružbašská Miľava**.

The pearl of the Spiš region is its north-western corner, called Zamagurie. It is one of the most attractive territories of Slovakia with a centre in **SPIŠSKÁ STARÁ VES** (505 m, population 2,300). The town is near the state borderline with Poland above the point where the Rieka brook joins the Dunajec river. The district town of Kežmarok is 37 km away and the seat of the neighbouring district of Stará Ľubovňa 34 km. As for the size of the population Spišská Stará Ves is the third smallest town in Slovakia.

The origin of Spišská Stará Ves is indebted to the village mayor Frydrich of Huncovce. In 1308 he obtained from master Kakaš permission to found a village on the bank of the Prinitz brook (the older name of the Rieka brook). The village originated at the place, or near the older community quoted in old acts as *Antiqua Villa* or Old Village. The place was called in the past *Katzengrund* – the German word for The Land of Cats. In other Spiš towns the oldest settled land lots had similar names, for instance *Kazwinkel* – the German for The Cat Corner, in Levoča. The neighbouring Polish village is still called Kacwin. The contemporary name of the town contains two historical data: The attribute "Stará" (old) expresses the antiquity of the village and one of the oldest parishes in the region. The word

"Ves" (village) was usually included in the names of settlements that were used as market stops on the trade roads. In 1377 Spišská Stará Ves was adjudicated to the Carthusian order, seated in Lechnice, after their prior Ján personally presented himself to king Karol Róbert, following which the generous ruler gave it to the order as an "eternal alms". Even though it was a serf village it was quite prosperous, especially amongst the tradesmen and the linen dealers. The village people exploited the position of their community which was located on an ancient trade road. The merchants travelling between Spišská Belá and Nowy Targ gladly exposed their goods in Spišská Stará Ves in the weekly and annually held markets, as they did not have to pay the toll. Economic prosperity culminated in 1399 when king Sigismond endowed the community with town privileges similar to those held by towns on the other side of the Magura mountains. Less favourable for Spišská Nová Ves was the 15th century as it was affected by the political tension between the Old Hungarian and Polish crowns. The fact that the tension did not end in armed conflict was a great deal owed to the town of Spišská Nová Ves, which twice offered its hospitability to the negotiating parties: First on November 11, 1411 when the representatives sent by the Old Hungarian king Sigismond and the Polish king Vladislav met there and several weeks later when both kings came. Half a century later the royal envoys of both crowns met there again to conclude peace on February 21, 1474, this time between king Matej Korvín and Kazímír Jagelovsky. The town did not escape war during "two graceful rides" in 1431 and 1433 when it was attacked by the Hussite troops coming from Poland to Spiš and who consequently burned down Spišská Stará Ves. The town's decay became visible after 1563. Carthusians in the Červený Kameň estate were replaced by secular owners who deprived what was until then a prosperous town of some of its privileges. The situation improved only in 1655 when after the request of the landlord Ladislav Rákoczi, emperor Ferdinand III consented again to the weekly markets and annual fairs even with an attribute of

Left: Zamagurie

"for eternity". The 18th century brought a lot of distress to the population of Spišská Stará Ves, when the plague of 1710 was survived only by one farmer and several servants. Two years later the town was burnt to ashes. Another four catastrophic fires followed one after the other in the years 1746 to 1760. During the last of them all the houses fell victim to the fire, and the dome of the church tumbled down and its five tower bells smelted.

After the revolution of 1948 which also touched the region of Zamagurie a new Magura district, with the main seat in Spišská Stará Ves, was established. The duty and the right of the town was to administer 33 communities in the Zamagurie region. The situation changed after the First World War when the town passed over to Polish territory during the Polish-Czechoslovak territorial dispute. After the Peace Conference of July 28, 1920, 13 communities were adjudicated to Poland and the reduced district of Spišská Stará Ves became the smallest in Czechoslovakia. Spišská Stará Ves has not been a district town since 1960. Socialist industrialisation created two industrial plants here which completely changed its agricultural character.

Dreaming of a railway:

Spišská Stará Ves, Bojnice and Modra are three Slovak towns lacking a railway. It is a curiosity that in Spišská Stará Ves a factory was founded under the name Vagónka (railway car manufacturing plant), yet construction of a railway to the Zamagurie region was seriously considered. In 1876 a project for a railway track between Spišská Belá and Nowy Targ was prepared. In 1892 the deputy Ján Bobula obtained permission to construct the track Podolínec-Nedeca passing Hniezdne, Kamienka, Veľký Lipník, Červený Kláštor and Spišská Stará Ves. A year later the project was pushed aside by a competing project for a track communicating Ždiar, Podspády and Jurgov, in which the owner of the Javorina woods, Duke Hohenlohe was highly interested. But the plans remained only plans and the prospect of a view from a train over the beautiful Zamagurie landscape remained only dream.

Spišská Stará Ves will soon be able to boast of being the native place of a Catholic saint. At present the canonisation of a member of the Discalced Augustinian Order, Friar Alojz Mária Chmeľ, born in this town on October 17, 1913 is underway. He died on August 16, 1939 in Rome, where he is also buried. The most important sacral monument of the town is the Roman-Catholic **church of the Virgin Mary's Ascension**, built in the second half of the 14th century. After a fire in 1760 it was reconstructed acquiring Baroque features and the damaged tower was shortened and strengthened by pillars. Only some details remained Gothic. The main altar of 1765 is made in the Late-Baroque style. Among the secular monuments the **manor house Na tridsiatku** is of most interest, which was built in the 18th century. Originally a Baroque-Classicist building it was repaired in the Neo-Classicist style in 1860.

The localities of **Majere** and **Lysá nad Dunajcom** (formerly called *Kalenberg*) lying right in the valley of the river Dunajec, though not particularly suitable for settling because of frequent flooding, also belong to the town. In 1786 the settlement of these communities was completed by the German colonists from Würtenberg. In Lysá na Dunajcom is a **border crossing** with lively cross-boundary contacts.

South-east of Spišská Stará Ves is the tiny community of **HAVKA** (630 m, population 50). It was founded by the Carthusian order of Červený Kláštor in the 14th century. In 1786 it was likewise colonised by Germans from Würtenberg who were mostly farmers and loggers.

Neighbouring **MATIAŠOVCE** (556 m, population 760) is another village in the valley of the Rieka brook, 3 km south of Spišská Stará Ves. The community originated in the 14th century during the second wave of the Sholtys colonisation. It was already mentioned in old acts in 1326 under the name *Mathyasuagasa*. The population of the community was active in agriculture, sheep keeping and logging. The Roman-Catholic **church of St. Peter and Pavol the Apostles** in the community is probably the oldest sacral building in Zamagurie with numerous Early-Gothic features which have been preserved. This originally Gothic church dates from 1300, and was later several times rebuilt and "Baroquised".

Further down to the south and situated on an ancient trade road is the community of **SPIŠSKÉ HANUŠOVCE** (614 m, population 667). Historians assert that the community is also extremely old with its origin dating back to 1236. The first known village mayor of Spišské Hanušovce was Henrik jr. of Kežmarok who was charged by the friars of Lendak to clear the woodland on the bank of "Prinitz" (today the Rieka brook) and to found a village there. Acts of 1344 quote the name Henus giving origin to the Slavic version of the name Hanuš or Hanušovce. The community was bought in 1732 from the Lendak friars by the family of Spielenberg. The population was, just like in all surrounding villages, basically agricultural, breeding sheep and logging. The most important monument of Spišské Hanušovce, the Baroque Roman-Catholic **church of St. Andrej the Apostle** was built in 1763. Its architecture contains some slight elements of a Gothic church of the 14th century, such as the walled up Gothic window in the western wall. In the first half of the 19th century a Classicist **manor house** was built in Spišské Hanušovce with a typanum in the centre of the main facade, mirror domes in the rooms, and an attic roof.

Neighbouring **ZÁLESIE** (690 m, population 90) originated much later. It was founded only in 1636 during the Sholtys colonisation, taking advantage of the Wallachian privilege. It remained for long time a serf community of the Nedecký hrad castle. Traditional occupations of the people were farming and logging. The most important monument in Zálesie (formerly called Gibeľ), is the **chapel of the Virgin Mary and St. Joseph** which was built on the site of an older church from which a Rococo-Classicist painting of the **Holy Family** from the end of 18th century was moved to the chapel. The community has preserved relatively many of its **old log houses** with wooden shingle roofs.

The highest situated community in the valley of the Rieka brook is **REĽOV** (728 m, population 340). It is 13 km from Spišská Stará Ves and 4 km from the Magura saddle (949 m). Reľov originated as a community of German shepherds in the 13th century and was first mentioned in historical acts of 1344. The local people were engaged in farming, sheep raising and logging. In 1568 a Czech glass blower, Ján Gruber, the founder of the squire family Reľovský, settled in the community. He bought from the Carthusians for himself and his descendants the office of the village mayor in Reľov together with the local glass smelting works. Gruber's descendants held the office until the 18th century. The Roman-Catholic **church of the Ascension of the St. Cross** was built after 1787 and the older Renaissance chapel was included into the ground plan of the church.

In the valley of the Jezerský brook is the small community of **JEZERSKO** (720 m, population 100). Its name is related to the nearby lake and was founded in 1610 by Polish refugees on the land of the landlords of Nedece castle. The former community populated by loggers and farmers eventually became a holiday resort. The church of Jezersko originated in 1895. Near the upper end of the village is the **Jezersko ski resort**, which has two ski lifts. The longer of them meets, at the main ridge of the Spišská Magura mountains, the lift which connects with the Bachledova dolina valley near Ždiar. In a lateral valley under the main ridge of the Spišská Magura mountains is the **nature reserve** of the **Jezerské jazero lake**, established as such in 1967, and covers an area of 48.58 hectares. A huge landslide lowered the main ridge above the lake by 30 m shifting it at the same time to the south by another 100 m. The lake is surrounded by a thick spruce forest.

The spirit of the lake:

According to one legend a shepherd set out to the lake in the Magura mountains to drown two little puppies. When the green water table closed over the poor little dogs, the shepherd began to return to his sheep. But when he set off he noticed with great astonishment that the lake followed him. He began to run up the hill hoping that the water would not chase him up the slope. In desperation the shepherd climbed a very high spruce, but the lake, however was quickly on top of the tree and easily lifted the spruce out of its roots. The unfortunate shepherd fell into the water and drowned just like the two puppies. Superstitious villagers believe that it was the spirit of the lake that killed the shepherd. There is another legend which regards the spirit of the lake as that of an "ecologist". When a miller from Jezersko tried to take more water from the lake for his mill and dug out a channel, the angry spirit appeared in front of the miller and under the threat of inundating the whole Zamagurie region ordered him to cover the channel with earth.

Right: A Goral band

On the way from Spišské Hanušovce to the west is **VEĽKÁ FRANKOVÁ** (664 m, population 360). It lies in the valley of the Frankovský potok brook, joining below the village the Osturniansky brook and under the name of Kacwianka enters Polish territory where it ends as a tributary of the Dunajec. Franková originated during the Sholtys colonisation taking advantage of the German privilege in 1296. It acquired its name after its founder, the village mayor Michal Frank of Vlková. Both villages the Malá Franková and the Veľká Franková used to belong to the Carthusians of Červený Kláštor and since the 19th century to the Prešov episcopate. The main source of living of the local people was always agriculture and forestry work. The most important monument in the community is the Roman-Catholic **church of St. Mikuláš the Bishop**, built in 1784 in the Classicist style. Part of the building has several valuable Baroque and Rococo features such as the wooden cross over the church door, baptistery and paintings on wood, from end of the 18th century. Near the church is a small wooden belfry.

Sholtys colonisation:

Sholtys colonisation of Spiš proceeded in two waves. Most of the Zamagurie communities originated during the Sholtys colonisation pursuing the German privilege in the 13th and 14th centuries. Settlers were mainly the inhabitants of the Spiš towns and German colonists. Polish settlers were invited here by the friars of the Lendak's monastery. The organisers of the colonisation were the Sholtys who concluded the tenant contracts with the owners of the land, as far as Zamagurie is concerned, with the noble families of Spišský Hrhov, and Brezovice. After the Sholtys colonisation there still remained a lot of uncultivated land covered by forests, which is the reason why the second wave of colonisation was necessary. In the 16th century the existing communities were completed and new ones founded, such as Stráňany. In this period the first Ruthenians arrived in Zamagurie. The conclusion of the settling of Zamagurie took place during the Kopanitze colonisation in the 17th century. Further division of the territory created the communities of Osturňa, Jezersko, Malá Franková Hágy and Zálesie.

MALÁ FRANKOVÁ (750 m, population 170) is the northernmost situated community in Zamagurie. The village lies in upper part of the valley of the Frankovský potok brook above Veľká Franková. It originated during the Kopanitze colonisation before 1611 and was settled by the Polish Gorals. The people lived off agriculture, sheep breeding and forestry work. Among the most interesting landmarks is the wooden **chapel of St. Jozef** built in the 20th century. The altar of the chapel is much older dating back to the 18th century.

Continuing westward the visitor arrives at **OSTURŇA**, (717 m, population 450), a typical Goral village in a wide valley of the Osturniansky potok brook. It is probably the longest village extending over the banks of a brook in Slovakia, measuring 7 km. Osturňa was founded around 1590 on the land of the Nedece castle, during the Sholtys colonisation, resulting from the Wallachian privilege. The population was actively involved in farming and forestry. The community has an Orthodox **church, St. Michal the Archangel**, built in 1796 in the Classicist style and rebuilt in 1937 and again reconstructed ten years later in 1947. Of historical value is the Rococo pulpit from the 18th century, however, there are many original buildings preserved in the community and protected as a **folk architectural monument reserve**.

There are several natural lakes around Osturňa blocked by landslides with numerous rare varieties of plants, typical for swamps. In the north of the village is the **nature reserve of the Veľké Osturnianske jazero lake** stretching over an area of 48.8 hectares, including also lake Jarušovo jazero. The **nature reserve Malé jazerá lakes** covering an area of 7.06 ha lies in the neighbouring valley next to the mountain ridge. Here one encounters the Rusnákovo and Opondkovo lakes. Unfortunately, all lakes north of Osturňa are gradually disappearing, slowly being absorbed by the surrounding vegetation and peat. The **nature reserve of Jazero** on an area of 14.4 hectares is situated on the opposite slope of the valley of the main ridge of the Spišská Magura mountains which protects the lake, called by the local people Donkovo jazero, from the process of vegetation overgrowth.

The Gorals and the Goral language:

The Gorals represent a special ethnicity inhabiting the communities in the Slovak-Polish border area in the Spiš, Orava and Kysuce regions and in some villages of the former Orava and Spiš counties, adjudicated to Poland in 1920. The Gorals differ from the rest of the population namely by their language, almost unintelligible to most Slovaks. The Goral dialect originated through a mixture of the Spiš, Orava and Polish dialects. It contains many words of what is referred to as Subcarpathian dialects. Within this rich dialect occur words expressing some notions or activities connected with sheep-keeping that do not occur in the Slovak lowland dialects, such as bryndza (sheep cheese), žinčica (sheep's whey), putňa (tub), košiar (sheep enclosure), krpce (simple kind of footwear). The strongest influence on the Goral dialect was the long-lasting Slovak-Polish linguistic contact. Also the Ukrainians, Ruthenians, Hungarians and Rumanians contributed to the Goral vocabulary. Authentic Gorals can be met, above all, in the villages of Zamagurie, in Ždiar, Lendak, Vyšné Ružbachy and in the upper Orava region.

Right: Červený Kláštor and Trzy Korony

The most important tourist centre of Zamagurie is **ČERVENÝ KLÁŠTOR** (465 m, population 240) which lies on the road between Spišská Stará Ves (8 km) and Stará Ľubovňa (25 km). The discovery of fragments of thin-wall ceramics indicate that this particular territory was settled in the Younger Bronze Age. In 1319 master Kakaš donated the community of Lechnica to the friars of Skala (today Kláštorisko) who built in the nearby valley of St. Anton a **Carthusian monastery**. Some historians suggest that there was a monastery of the Benedictine order before this time. Because the buildings of the monastery were built of red bricks the people began to call it Červený Kláštor (the Red Monastery). Soon a village sprung up around the monastery mentioned in historical acts of 1344 under the name Uyvagas (New village). In 1360 the construction of a monastic church was initiated, as the Lechnice estate gradually expanded by adding new lands and properties. In the mid-16th century the monks owned 12 communities in Zamagurie, as well as manors lying between Franková and Veľká Lesná. In 1563 the monastery was closed by Emperor Ferdinand and the Carthusians were obliged to move out of Červený Kláštor after 243 years.

The Order of the Carthusians:

The hermit order of Carthusians was founded in 1084 by Bruno of Cologne who built the Grande Chartreuse monastery near Grenoble in France. The order quickly spread and in the 14th century 109 Carthusian monasteries existed all over Europe. The Carthusians belonged to the strictest hermitic orders. They lived in complete seclusion in the monastic community, keeping an eternal silence, fasting, engaged in prayers and meditations. The architecture of the monastery of Lechnice was altered to this way of life, within its centre was a church with a yard and small houses for the monks. The church service was the only occasion of gathering amongst this silent monastic community. One of the activities of the monks in their seclusion was the copying and illustration of the book of codexes. Two codexes from the Lechnice monasteries are deposited in the University Library of Budapest, one is owned by the Jagelovská library in Kraków.

Carthusian friars were, due to the animosity of the Emperor, replaced by secular proprietors.

In 1563 the former monastery was acquired by Gašpar Magóczy, the count of Tolno whose name is quoted in the oldest known list of communal lands of the Červený Kláštor estate, which changed hands quite frequently. Between 1608 to 1612 Štefan Thökoly, the landlord of the Kežmarok Castle, was one of them. In 1704 Červený Kláštor after 142 years became again a church property, when bishop Ladislav Maťašovský, suffering from a serious illness, donated Camaldolese Order of the Monte Corona Congregation. The monks of the order who came from Toscany in Italy repaired and rebuilt the monastic buildings in the Baroque style and added to it a church tower. They also founded there probably the oldest pharmacy in Slovakia. Because of the contribution of the enlightened Father Romuald Hadbavný (1714-1780) the monastery of the Camaldolese Order ultimately became an important cultural and national centre in the region. Hadbavný participated in the first translation of the Holy Script into the Slovak language in 1750 and a compilation of the Latin-Slovak dictionary in 1763. This voluminous work of 942 pages contained also a brief grammar of the Slovak language, which could be considered the first attempt to codify the Slovak language.

Father Cyprián:

The most famous friar of Červený Kláštor was undoubtedly Father Cyprián (1724-1775) whose real name was František Ignác Jaschke. He came to Červený Kláštor in 1756 from his native Silesia. He was known for his scholarly propensity and as such he earned various nicknames, such as "the doctor of a thousand sciences" or "the flying monk". He possessed extraordinary knowledge about medicine, pharmacy, chemistry and botany. He was also engaged in writing scientific books, fiction and a collection of folk literature. But perhaps his herbarium, created in the years 1765-1771, is his best known achievement. While collecting the plants he undertook long walks, not only to the Pieniny mountains, but also further afield, above all to the Belianske Tatra mountains. This valuable book, bound in leather contains in the first part 272 pressed plants on 97 pages with denominations

in Latin, Greek, German and the local Goral language. The second part of the herbarium consists of 36 pages of notes on the medicinal use of plants, a description of the symptoms of ailments, and the curative properties of plants. The prevailing part of the text is in German. The herbarium appeared in the collections of the Carpathian Museum in Poprad in 1883 and later it was moved to the TANAP Museum in Tatranská Lomnica. Its restoration is at present in the hands of the scientists of the National Slovak Museum in Bratislava. One of the legends surrounding Father Cyprián is that he became the Slovak follower of Leonardo da Vinci from Tuscany. Another is that Father Cyprián constructed a flying machine and used it in his flight from the top of the Pieniny mountain, Trzy Korony, to land on the shore of the Morskie Oko lake in the Polish Tatras. This is why the astonished witnesses of his flight called Cyprián the flying monk. But such experiments were viewed with a jaundiced eye by the church authorities, who believed that flying was the privilege of fowl and insects. Consequently, the diabolic flying machine was burnt down in the main square of Spišská Belá and Father Cyprián was exiled to life-long seclusion in the monastery.

But such stories are unproven of course. Historical sources certify only the fact that the free-thinking Father Cyprián actually fell into disgrace with the Holy Inquisition. His biographers suppose that he died in 1774 chained to the wall of the basement of Pannohalma Abbey.

The national cultural monument of Červený Kláštor is a unique cultural and historical relic set in the wonderful natural environment of Pieniny under the majestic mountain Tri koruny. The monastery was successfully restored in the years 1956-1966. The best building, from an architectural point of view, is the Gothic **church of St. Anton** from the end of the 14th century with one nave of unusual length restored in the Baroque style. The cross-shaped rib dome of the nave has six fields, and the chapels have lateral Late-Gothic saddle portals. There is an organ brought here from the monastic church in Nižná Šebastová. The main altar is in the Baroque style, built in 1745. The **monastic buildings** are next to the church. In the Baroque building some older Gothic features are recognisable. The remains of the Late-Gothic paintings on the walls of the monastic refectory date back to 1520. In the building of the former monastery is a **museum** with ethnographic, pharmaceutical and historical collections.

Museum Červený Kláštor, tel.: 0964/2353
Opening hours: Tue-Sat 8:00-17:00h, Sun 8:00-13:00h

In front of the entrance to the monastery is a park declared the **protected area of Pieninské lipy** in 1972. It protects 19 old and valuable lime trees. There is a hydrogen sulphide water spring of the Glauber type in Červený Kláštor yielding 6 litres per minute, which in the past was utilized by the Smierdžonka spa. The community is the seat of administration of the National Park of Pieniny. The most important sports event in Červený Kláštor is the **International Pieniny Water Slalom**, a competition held annually since 1954. The biggest attraction for tourists though, is raft-

Left: Rafts on the Dunajec

ing on the Dunajec river on wooden rafts. About 38 thousand tourists annually pass down the Dunajec river on Polish and Slovak rafts.

PIENAP:

The Polish authorities declared the Park Narodowy in Pieniny a reserved area in 1930, and two years later the Slovaks established their part of the Pieniny natural reserve in 1932. The contemporary Pieninský Národný Park (PIENAP) was established on January 16, 1967 on an area of 2,125 hectares. Of its total area forests represent 928 ha while the rest is unique agricultural landscape with small fields, green meadows and pastures adorned in summer with stacks of a sweet smelling newly mown hay, typical for Zamagurie. PIENAP is rich in rare species of plants with several local endemites. A part of the variegated fauna are 766 species of butterflies, 99 species of molluscs and more than 200 species of vertebrates. In the cliffs or forest pathways one can, for instance, meet a lynx or see an otter hunting in the water in the Dunajec river.

The principal cultural event in Červený Kláštor is the **Folk Festival of Zamagurie**, which has been organised annually in July since 1976. The preface to the event is a passage down the Dunajec river on rafts, followed by a programme which takes place in an open-air amphitheatre before an audience of 7,000 people. It is situated on a beautiful green meadow with the familiar silhouette of the Trzy Korony mountain in the background. Over the two-day event tens of folk ensembles and artists from Zamagurie and other regions perform on the stage.

A trip to the canyon of the Dunajec is one of the most beautiful in Slovakia. It starts in Červený Kláštor, continues on to the mouth of the Lesnícky potok brook and follows for quite a long while along the right bank of the meandering Dunajec. The red-marked pathway leads along the well-known Pieninská cesta road that used to connect in the 19th century Červený Kláštor with the Polish spa of Szczawnica. In this part the road passes over the national **nature reserve of Prielom Dunajca** declared as such in 1967, on an area of 362.47 hectares. Thirteen stops along the **educational footpath** provides tourists with more information about the reserve, and much of its terrain is connected with romantic folk legends.

The legends of Pieniny:

At the entrance to the canyon there is a tapered place of the bed of the Dunajec called Jánošíkov skok (Jánošík's Jump). The river is 12 m deep here and the river bed is 10 m wide. According to an old legend Jánošík (the Slovak Robin Hood) selected his followers on their ability to jump across the river at this point. If he were alive today Jánošík would have either to have remained alone or would have been forced to choose another river, as the present record in long jumping is less than the 10 m wide of the Dunajec. At the third bend of the Dunajec the towering rocks of Holice (828 m) can be seen on the slope. The name, Sedem mníchov (Seven Monks) as they are known is also related to folk legend. Folk identified seven human characters who changed into rocks while trying to reach, with not altogether honest intentions, a nun, the silhouette of which can be seen on the Polish side of the river on the rocky face of Facimiech. At the end of the canyon under the Osobitá skala rock is the karstic water spring Storočná voda (A Hundred Year Old Water) that does not freeze in winter. The story goes that the one who drinks of it will live for a hundred years.

The second section of the trip follows the blue-marked path across the **nature reserve Prielom of Lesnický potok brook – Kače** established as such in 1967 on an area of 25.53 hectares, which in its narrowest part is almost 300 m deep, on the right hand tributary of the Dunajec, locked in vertical dark grey limestone cliffs. Looking from Lesnica on the right hand side is the rock Vylízaná skala and on the left is Osobitá skala. The mountain called Kača (704 m) above the canyon offers a magnificent view of the cliffy landscape of Pieniny. The trip eventually ends in Lesnica.

Hiking along the ridge of the Haligovské skaly rocks is also another favourite trek. Starting from Červený Kláštor walkers take the red-marked footpath leading along the conspicuous cliffy crest of Haligovské skaly. The path crosses the brook of Lipník and ascends by serpentines to the saddle over Huta from where one has a splendid view of the Trzy korony mountain (982 m) and the meandering river of the Dunajec. Passing around the forest landscape the path opens again into wide meadows on the top of the Plašná mountain (889 m). The round top of the mountain

provides a view of the cliffs of the Haligovské skaly rocks, the small community of Haligovce squatting under the row of rocks and the very long valley of the Lesnícky potok brook. In the background, behind the back of the Spišská Magura mountains, covered by forests a dramatic silhoutte of the Tatras can be seen. The **national nature reserve of Haligovské skaly rocks** was established in 1967 on an area of 80.80 ha. Impressive limestone cliffs with grey rocky towers and walls are more than 300 m above the Lipník brook. The karst forms on the surface are modest but the underground karst is more interesting. The **Aksamitka Cave,** at an altitude of 753 m, called in the past Mlečna džura, is known more for the occurrence of a rare species of bats and some valuable traces of an Older Stone Age settlement than for its drip-stone decoration. The discovery of a broken tip made from a reindeer's antler is so far the oldest proof of a settlement in Zamagurie. In 1874 it was the first proven Paleolithic find in Old Hungary. As early as the 18th century people took out of the cave bones of unknown animals and the story goes that Juraj Bohuš, a teacher at a college in Kežmarok, compiled a dragon's skeleton of the collection. As the immediate environs of the cave were considerably damaged, the access path for tourists is closed. The Zbojnícka brána gate, a spacious opening in a limestone rock is another interesting landmark. The end of the trip, when the path descends to the community of Veľký Lipník, rewards the hiker with generous views of the surrounding landscape.

Left: Haligovské skaly rocks

South of Červený Kláštor is **LECHNICA** (490 m, population 280), a community which originated at the end of the 13th century. In 1319 master Kakaš donated it to the nuns of the Carthusian order who intended to build here a church and a monastery. The population lived by farming, sheep breeding and forestry work. The most important monument of the community is the Roman-Catholic **church of St. Jodok**. It originated in the 19th century by reconstructing an Early-Gothic building from the 14th century.

HALIGOVCE (530 m, population 650) is the first community on the road from Červený Kláštor passing by Podolínec to Stará Ľubovňa. The village spreads along the left lateral valley of the Lipník brook. Haligovce were founded in the 14th century and colonised by hamlets along the Lesnícky potok brook on the lands of the Görgey family. The ancient names of the hamlets are still used today (Dox, Jeruše, Pienkalovka, Bednáre, and Paluby). The community's name was quoted for the first time in 1338. In the past the population made their living from logging, breeding, natural oil production, linen weaving and lime burning. There used to exist in the locality "Na mogily" in the Middle Ages a community called **St. Peter**, which disappeared in the 14th century, with only the remains of stone walls and ceramics left.

In the spring of 1443, near Czorstyn, on the bank of the Dunajec river the Hussite troops gathered in a fortified camp to undertake armed attacks to the surrounding countries. Since then for two decades Zamagurie experienced fighting, led by King Albert's widow, by the Hussite army of Ján Jiskra of Brandýs. After her son Ladislav Pohrobek ascended to the Old Hungarian throne in 1453 the Jiskra's troops had to abandon Old Hungary. Part of them, led by commander Peter

Aksamit, refused to subdue to the king's decision and to leave Spiš. Aksamit obtained support from several landlords, took possession of several castles and built several fortified camps, such as the one in Haligovce built in 1485. The event is commemorated in the name of a karst hollow in the Haligovské skaly rocks, the Aksamitka Cave.

The legend of the Aksamitka Cave:

The legendary commander of the Hussite troops, Peter Aksamit, refused to obey Ján Jiskra and decided to sack and rob in the Spiš region and in the surrounding counties. Legend has it that at the end of his life he decided to do penance and sat down in a cave in the Haligovské skaly rocks and wept. Every tear that fell from of his eyes changed to a drip stone. Ever since then the cave bears his name.

VEĽKÁ LESNÁ (605 m, population 420) lies in the valley of the Lesniansky potok brook 2 km above Haligovce. The road passing the village crosses the main ridge of the Spišská Magura mountains at the Toporecké sedlo saddle (802 m) continues to the community of Toporec near Podolínec. The older name of the community was Richwald. Veľká Lesná was founded during the Sholtys colonisation pursuing the German privilege in the 14th century. Its inhabitants were farmers, shepherds and loggers. The local glass works disappeared the same as the medieval village Svätá Margita in the place called Margoričani. The most important monument in the community is the **church of St. Ján the Baptist** built in Early-Gothic style at the beginning of the 14th century. The interior and southern Gothic portal are adorned with Renaissance wall paintings from the 16th century. Near the church a huge protected **lime tree** grows. Its age is estimated at between 350 to 400 years old, is 29m high and the circumference of its trunk is 6.20 m.

Continuing eastward from Červený Kláštor one arrives at the community of **VEĽKÝ LIPNÍK** (580 m, population 990). The first colonists came here during period of the Sholtys colonisation in the 14th century, the second wave of new settlers arrived in 1567 during the Wallachian colonisation. In the past there were two communities, Starý (Horný) and Nový Lipník. The inhabitants were farmers and shepherds, some of whom manufactured and sold linen. The community has a Baroque-Classicist Roman-Catholic **church of St. Michal Archangel** built in 1794 and reconstructed in 1930. The tower of the church ends in a cupola in the Old Russian style. On the flanks of the nave, above the presbytery, are small Baroque roof towers. The **Ikonostas** placed on the main alter dates back to the beginning of the 20th century. This valuable work of art is included in the list of the national cultural monuments.

Eastward of Lipník is the village of **STRÁŇANY** (640 m, population 230). It is the highest situated village of the valley of the Lipník brook on the road between Červený Kláštor (11 km) and Stará Ľubovňa (14 km). The community originated in the 15th century near an older manor house that used to belong to the landlord of Nedeca Castle. The population lived off farming and forestry work. The historical acts mentioned the name of the community for the first time in 1439. Stráňany is situated on the western edge of the enclave of Ruthenian ethnicity living in the north-east of Slovakia. Its ethnic and religious past is commemorated by the Greek-Catholic **church of the Virgin Mary** built in 1857 in the Classicist style.

In the north is situated **LESNICA** (492 m, population 480) which lies in a small lateral valley modelled by the Lesniansky potok brook ending in the Dunajec canyon. It connects with Veľký Lipník by a 6 km log road passing the saddle in the ridge of Haligovské skaly rocks. Villagers can now, however, use a **new border crossing for pedestrians** to the Polish spa town of Szczawnica. The community is the first one in Zamagurie mentioned in historical documents (in 1497). In the Middle Ages there use to be a glass works near the community. Later Lesnica belonged to the Lechnice monastery. In the years 1938 and 1939 it belonged temporarily to Poland. The community has a Roman-Catholic **church of St. Michal the Archangel** from the first half of the 17th century and is a Renaissance variation of an older church. In the main altar is a painting of St. Michal the Archangel from the mid-18th century.

Kežmarok and its environs

KEŽMAROK (630 m, population 17,000) lying in the middle of three district towns on the river Poprad, (15 km from Poprad and 3 km from Stará Ľubovňa) is one of Slovakia's most historical towns, dating back to the Upper Stone Age.

Over the years, extensive archaeological research of Kežmarok Castle has disclosed many rare objects and details concerning its past, especially from the time of Púchov culture at the turn of the millenium, rendering proof of a Slavic settlement in the territory from the time of the Great Moravian Empire up to the 13th century. The medieval town of Kežmarok was preceded by three independent communities with their own rector's churches and cemeteries. The oldest church of St. Michal stood on a hill on the left bank of the river Poprad and belonged to the community of the royal boundary guards. The second community was probably called Sti Petri and Pauli and was inhabited by Slavic fishermen. It originated around a chapel that later expanded to a the rector's church of St. Kríž which still exists. The third community lay near the church of St. Alžbeta, which archaeologists discovered near Kežmarok Castle. This community was first mentioned in an historical act of 1251 in which the Old Hungarian king Belo IV donated "the community of Saxons near the church of St. Alžbeta" to the Premonstratesian order of Turiec. Medieval Kežmarok originated by the merging of the main communities in one municipality. In 1269 it obtained proper municipal self-administration and up to 1348 it was protected by municipal walls. The communities of St. Michal and St. Alžbeta did not survive a devastating raid by the Hussites in 1433 which destroyed the local rector's churches and left the barely half-century old monastery in ruins.

The origin of the name of Kežmarok has been subject to numerous studies, in Latin and German, but it is thought that the German expression for cheese seems the most justified explanation. Records from 1329 refers to the Latin names of the town, *forum Caseorum*, *Caseoforum* or *Caseopolis*, which clearly suggest that there was cheese sold at the local market. Closer to the contemporary name of the town is the German translation *Käsmark* i.e. cheese market. This name, however,

Käsmark i.e. cheese market.

mutated into *Kaisermark*, meaning an imperial market or imperial town. This is the way in which the citizens of Kežmarok tried to express their loyalty to Emperor Ferdinand of Hapsburg by supporting his claim for the Old Hungarian crown with Ján Zápoľský in 1528.

Kežmarok confirmed its economic and political position in the first half of the 15th century with additional privileges. The citizens were exempted from custom duty (1412), toll duty, throughout Poland (1440) and the thirtieth part duty throughout the territory of Old Hungary (1464). Furthermore, they were allowed to run the annual fairs (1419), and obtained the privilege of storage (1435), the privilege of beheading (1438) and after 1463 they were allowed to use the municipal coat of arms and seal. On the downside of the economic development of the town was the on-going and often bloody disputes with the people of Levoča and the landlords of the newly built Kežmarok Castle. The conquering and plundering of Kežmarok by the Hussite troops in 1433 showed that the municipal fortifications were imperfect and vulnerable. As the enclosure of the whole town within huge walls was financially not viable, the alternative of constructing a well-fortified municipal castle, offering protection not only to the lords of the castle but also to the citizens, was adopted. Ironically, the castle from the very beginning of its existence did not protect its citizens, but instead became a threat to them. The mistrust which existed between the castle and the townspeople was proven by the fact that the head of the Spiš region, Imrich Zápoľský, constructed fierce castle fortifications with loopholes and a moat also on the side facing the town. The animosity culminated at the time when the family of Thököly moved into the castle which was stormed by the discontented citizens. The failure of their attack led them to be forced to sign a declaration admitting Šebastián Thököly as their landlord and giving up their citizens' rights of a free royal town.

The Thökölys' of Kežmarok:

The Thökölys' ruled the castle and the town of Kežmarok for over four generations. The last, and certainly the most famous of them, was Imrich Thököly, the leader of one of the most extensive anti-Hapsburg rebellions in Old Hungary during the 17th and early 18th centuries. After the bloody suppression of Thököly's rebellion its leader, also called the King of Rebels, was compelled to flee to Turkey where he finally died in 1705. His body though was returned to Kežmarok in 1906 and deposited in the mausoleum of Imrich Thököly, built next to the new Evangelical church.

In 1651 Imrich Thököly, under the weight of the Vienna Agreement, gave up the ownership of the town for a compensation of 210 thousand guldens. Four years later the emperor Ferdinand III confirmed the past privileges of Kežmarok and included it in the list of free royal towns. In 1720 the citizens of Kežmarok became the owners of the municipal castle by means of additional purchase and at the same time joined the big feudal owners by the purchase of 20 serf towns and communities, and even of some highly productive vineyards in the south of the country.

The hundred years' war:

Kežmarok and Levoča were for centuries the richest towns in the Spiš region. But their prosperity soon pushed them into the situation of being two cocks on one scrap heap. Both towns longed for domination over the transit trade between Old Hungary and Poland and that could not be achieved without an important municipal privilege – the right to store. Levoča obtained it back in 1321 and at the same time endeavored to prevent its rival from reaching the same right. But the people of Kežmarok, thanks to a trick, were able to stop the small carriages of merchants coming from Poland and Silesia. In 1434 they wrote to king Sigismond a petition for confirmation of all municipal privileges allegedly stolen by the Hussites They also included in the list the right of storage which the king confirmed. Anyway, the old dispute between Levoča and Kežmarok lost none of its original intensity, and consequently it was nicknamed "the hundred years' war". This long lasting war between the two hostile towns gradually divided the whole region of Spiš into two camps. The forfeited towns and communities supported Kežmarok, but the supreme instance in the country, the Old Hungarian ruler himself had decided in favour of Levoča repeatedly in the years 1544 and 1558. The inhabitants of Kežmarok had to accept the will of the crown and to give up the important right of storage, without complaint.

The further growth of Kežmarok benefited by the return of the Polish forfeit, and the favourable economic development of the town,

by the end of the 17th century, is documented by the existence of 21 guilds. In 1715 up to 263 workshops of 51 different trades and crafts were active in the town. The first factory in Kežmarok, mechanical flax weaving manufacture, founded in 1860, only followed in the long tradition of wool and linen making in Kežmarok, goods which were made famous and sold as far as Greece and Albania. In 1884 another factory was built for flax processing, and in 1901 also cloth-production plant. Today this rich tradition in textile production is maintained by the firm of Tatraľan Kežmarok. Construction of the Bohumín-Košice railway track meant rapid development for the towns of Poprad and Spišská Nová Ves, pushing into the background Levoča and Kežmarok. The first train came to Kežmarok in 1889 by a newly constructed track from Poprad. Up to 1960 Kežmarok was the seat of district administration, a status which it regained following the implementation of the new territorial-administrative divisions of the Slovak Republic in 1996.

Left: Kežmarok castle

Along with Levoča, Kežmarok represents the most extensive and most compact compound of cultural and historical monuments in the region of Spiš, declared in 1950 a **municipal monument reserve**. Sightseeing in the town requires at least a good half day. The historical core of Kežmarok has a triangular ground plan squeezed into the spur between the river Poprad and the Ľubica brook. The walk over the town can start at the building of the town-hall: **Kežmarská radnica** (1) or at the Town Hall of Kežmarok dominates the **Hlavné námestie** (**The Main Square**). The first town hall on the site was built in 1461 by maestro Juraj of Spišská Sobota in the Gothic style. It should have been called a new town hall as the original town hall that stood at the Starý trh (Old Market) was burned down by the Hussites. After the new town hall was damaged by fire in 1515, the mayor had the seat of his office built at the same place, in what was then the most recent Renaissance style. In 1799 the town hall was made higher by another floor and equipped with a tower which is today one of the main landmarks of the town. As a matter of fact, it is a copy of the monasterial church tower of St. Peter in Salzburg, Austria. Not far

away from the town hall is the Classicist building of **municipal redoubt** (2) that originated in 1818 on the foundations of a former guard tower. The two oldest streets in Kežmarok start from the town hall, one heading to the north and other north-east. Both are skirted by ancient **burgher houses**, some of which have preserved high shingle roofs with double shingled cornices on the front gable. The best conserved Gothic-Renaissance houses at Hradné námestie (Castle Square) are from the first half of the 16th century. Also the **craftsmen's houses** of the tanners, in Garbiarska street, are very interesting.

Hradná street leads eventually to the **Hradné námestie square**, which is dominated by the **Kežmarský hrad or Kežmarok castle** (3). The urban compound of the castle originated in 1462 on the site of the medieval community of St. Alžbeta and the Knights' of the Cross of the Holy Grave monastery. Built originally by Imrich and Ján Zápoľský in the Gothic style, they laid much stress on the defensive nature of the castle building including thick walls and massive bastions. The castle gained its contemporary Renaissance form after extensive rebuilding, proceeding in various stages in the years 1572, 1575, 1883, and 1624. The last phase was completed by Šebastián Thököly, the founder of the famous family, who invited renowned Italian stone-masons, bricklayers and painters to change the original stronghold into a representative family mansion. The buildings in the castle courtyard were equipped with Renaissance arcades, and its sumptuous halls were adorned with wall paintings, and the interior of the castle chapel was renewed in Early-Baroque style. After 1720 Kežmarok castle was used by the town for various purposes, and sometimes even as a place of storage.

The historical deed of the Lady of the Castle:

Curiosity and courage were properties the noble princess Beata Laská of Kežmarok Castle certainly possessed. Otherwise she would never have set out on a trip accompanied by several burghers from Kežmarok to the not too distant Snow Mountains (today called the Tatras) in 1565. When the princess returned three days later, after having visited Zelené pleso lake, her angry husband was waiting for her at the gate of the castle. The lord of the castle, Albert Laský, immediately and without hesi-

tation, pronounced over his emancipated wife a surprisingly cruel resolution: That she should be interned in the strongest tower where she passed six long years in extremely hard conditions. The only mercy for the unfortunate princess were two small windows, one overlooking her beloved Snow Mountains, and the other through which she was given food. Beata Laská was released from prison only by the new landlord of the castle, Ján Rueber. Allegedly completely insane she was transferred to Košice where she died soon after. Some assert that Albert Laský used the occasion to get rid of his twenty year older wife to enjoy her immense fortune. The journey of Beata Laská to the mountains was considered immoral in the 16th century, today it represents the first known tourist trip to the High Tatras.

In 1931 the first exposition of the **Museum of Kežmarok** was opened in a part of the castle compound. After general repairs to the castle between 1962 to 1985 its collections were expanded. Visitors today can see the following expositions: The Ancient and Medieval settlement of Kežmarok; the Development of Kežmarok from the 13th century to the mid-19th century; the Shooting Association of Kežmarok; the Association of Physicians and Pharmacists of the Spiš Region; the Life and Work of Dr. Vojtech Alexander; Historical Portraits, and finally Kežmarok and the High Tatras. Besides this there is an independent **exposition of housing culture** with interiors of Spiš burgher houses in the 18th and 19th centuries, in the Hlavné námestie square, which is open to the public.

Left: The interior of the wooden church in Kežmarok

Múzeum v Kežmarku, Hradné námestie 42,
tel.: 0968/52 26 18
Opening hours: June-Sept., Tue-Sun 9:00-17:30h,
Oct.-May, Tue-Fri 8:00 16:30h.

The late Gothic Roman-Catholic **church of St. Cross** (4) is enclosed within the space of the fork formed by the main streets. It was built in the 14th century on the site of an older Romanesque chapel. Because of its dimensions it is one of the largest hall churches in Slovakia. The church tower was adapted in Renaissance style in the 16th century. There are wood carvings by artists who belonged to the circle around Maestro Pavol of Levoča. The church neighbours with a Renaissance **belfry** (5) of 1568, which is the oldest and certainly one of the most beautiful in the Spiš region. The pride of Kežmarok is the Protestant **wooden articled church** (6) included in the list of national cultural monuments. Because of the edict of 1681 the Protestants of Kežmarok were obliged to build their church out of town. Thus, they chose a place near the Vyšná brána (Upper Gate) where there used to stand an inn which was later rebuilt into a school. This Protestant church was built in 1688 next to an older sacral stone building from 1593, which today is a sacristy. The building of the church was sponsored and helped by fellow Protestants from Scandinavia and Germany. This unique wooden building made of yew and red spruce wood was built without using a single metal component, and its ground plan is in the form of a Greek cross. The Baroque interior of the church is also made of wood. Its architects were the carpenter Mütterman and the wood carver Lerch of Kežmarok. Of immense artistic value is also the church organ with wooden pipes made in 1719 by Vavrinec Čajkovský. In 1898 the Protestants were granted a new **church** (7) designed by the architect Theofil Hansen and built in a decorative Neo-

Byzantine style. Next to the articled church is a building which is also included among the national cultural monuments, namely the **Lutheran Lyceé** (8), built in 1775 with the approval of the ruler Maria Theresa herself. At present it is the home of an exposition of the literary traditions of the former lyceé placed here after a general reconstruction in 1975. It also contains the largest school library in Central Europe with about 150 thousand volumes, four thousand of them concerning Slovakia. A visit to Kežmarok can be concluded by a climb up the **Jeruzalemský vrch mountain** at the eastern end of the town. It offers an excellent view of Kežmarok skirted by the charming frame of the Tatras' silhouette.

The Tatras, Kežmarok and the lycée:

In a long list of the discoverers and admirers of the Tatra mountains the names of people somehow linked to Kežmarok very often appear. Besides the lady Beata Laská, who won for her trip to the Biela voda Valley in 1565 the title of "the first Tatra tourist" another citizen of Kežmarok, David Fröllich, undertook the first historically proved ascent to a Tatra peak. It was also from Kežmarok that the scholarly professors of the Kežmarok Lyceé, Juraj Bucholtz the junior, Juraj Bohuš and Kristián Generisch, and the enlightened priest and enthusiastic nature historian, Tomáš Mauksch, set out for the pioneer trips to the Tatras. Also in the lyceé at Kežmarok originated the famous adventure book of travel "Simplicissimus hungaricus seu dacianus", which contains an exciting description of a trip by a group of students to the High Tatras. The account was allegedly written by an anonymous student sometime in the second half of the 17th century. The Lutheran Lyceé in Kežmarok had the character of a modern academy, and because of the financial support from the city it attracted excellent teachers and students throughout Central Europe. An extensive list of the graduates who later found positions in various fields of science and culture proves the quality of the Kežmarok lyceé, amongst them important Slovak poets, writers and playwrights, such as Pavol Jozef Šafárik, Samo and Ján Chalúpka, Janko Kráľ, Jonáš Záborský, Ivan Stodola, Janko Jesenský, and Martin Rázus. In the years between 1865 to 1870 an extraordinarily talented student by the name of Pavol Országh studied at the Kežmarok lyceé, who later adopted the artistic name Hviezdoslav and became the greatest Slovak poet of all time.

MALÝ SLAVKOV lies off the main roads, 3 km west of the centre of the city. It is crossed by the Slavkovský potok brook originating in the Skalnatá Valley in the Tatras. Its original Slovak name meaning "forfeit" was mentioned for the first time in 1251. On a hill overlooking the community is the burial site where 49 Levoča citizens died in 1531 in fights with the people of Kežmarok, proof indeed that the struggle for power between the two cities was not limited to innocent verbal disputes or judicial conflicts.

The main road between Kežmarok and Poprad passes two larger communities. The first of them is **HUNCOVCE** (639 m, population 2,000) lying on the right bank of the river Poprad, 5 km from Kežmarok. The present name of the village originates from its main practical function. In 1308 it was quoted as *villa Canis* or the Village of Dogs, although the Latin name for the village gave origin to the German *Hundsdorf*, more similar to its present name. The densely forested territory administered by Huncovce which extends up to the Tatra peaks, was in the Middle Ages, a favourite hunting ground for the local nobility, including that of the king, which provided the local people with the employment of tending the lords' hunting dogs. The serfs also made their living by farming, linen weaving, trade and crafts. The most valuable monument in the area is the Roman-Catholic **church of St. Cross** from the 13th century, of which only the tower has been preserved from the original Romanesque building. Other parts of the church were altered in the 14th and 15th centuries by Gothic reconstruction and other adjustments. The Evangelic **church** in the community was built in 1859 in Late-Classicist style. The local **curia** originated in the second half of the 18th century.

The Jewish community in Huncovce:

In the 18th and 19th centuries the most numerous Jewish population throughout the Spiš region resided in Huncovce. During the rule of Jozef II at the end of the 18th century a higher Jewish school was established here for the education of future rabbis. One of them, Eliser Horovicz, was invited to Frankfurt in Germany as a main rabbi. However, the Jewish community in Huncovce was considerably reduced in number in the years of the Second World War. Many Jews who had to leave involuntarily never returned to Huncovce, leaving behind a synagogue, built in 1821.

VEĽKÁ LOMNICA (639 m, population 3,300) is a large community lying near the confluence of the Studený potok brook and the river Poprad, at the cross-roads to Poprad (9 km), Kežmarok (6 km) and Tatranská Lomnica (9 km). The remains of the primeval fort on the hill called Burchbrich bears testimony to a very old settlement in the territory. It was for the first time referred to in 1257. Mostly farming people, the local population obtained additional income through tannery, shoe-making and linen-making. Deserving of special attention in Veľká Lomnica is the Roman-Catholic **church of St. Katarína of Alexandria**. Originally a Late-Romanesque building it was built before the end of the 13th century and rebuilt in 1412 in Gothic form. In its sacristy unique medieval wall paintings from the 14th century were found and in 1992 it was declared a national cultural monument. They depict scenes of the legend of St. Ladislav fighting against the Tartars. The Evangelic **church** in Veľká Lomnica was built in 1785 by František Bartel of Spišská Nová Ves, however, its tower was built much later in 1908. In the community are two **manor houses** and a **curia**.

At the foreground of the Tatras, west from the main road Poprad-Stará Ľubovňa lie another four communities belonging to the district of Kežmarok. **STARÁ LESNÁ** (736 m, population 750) is situated at the left bank of the Studený potok brook about 4 km from Veľká Lomnica and 5 km from Tatranská Lomnica. Its name suggests that it originated at the territory covered by continuous (les = forest) forestation. If was first referred to in 1292 and belonged to the family of Berzeviczy practically since its origin, until the eventual abolition of serfdom. The local population made their living from flax cultivation and the manufacturing of linen. In addition to which they were renowned chamois hunters. The predominant feature in the community is the **church of St. Peter and Pavol the Apostles**. Originally Early Gothic the church was later "Baroquised" and around 1600 a Renaissance **belfry** was added to the church. The Evangelic **church** here was built in 1821 in the Classicist style.

STRÁNE POD TATRAMI (700 m, population 900) is accessible by a secondary road from Kežmarok and the distance from this district town is 5 km. The community originated near an urban estate on a territory that originally belonged to the cadaster of Kežmarok. In 1438 it was mentioned under the name of Forwerk. Its present name has been used since 1848 and before that it was called Folvarky. Traditionally the main occupation of the local people was farming. The local Roman-Catholic **church of St. Martin the Bishop** was built in the late 13th century in Early Gothic style and later several times reconstructed. There is in the community also an Evangelic **church** from 1802 in the Classicist style.

MLYNČEKY (680 m, population 500) lies on the bank of the Kežmarská Biela voda brook, 5 km north-west from Kežmarok. The name of the community (mlynček = small mill) clearly suggests that there once existed medieval mills built by the citizens of Kežmarok. However, the established community originated only later, in the course of the 18th century, and grew larger in the 19th by the progressive building of the houses for the immigrants who arrived mostly from the Zamagurie region. Mlynčeky actually belonged to Kežmarok until the Second World War and was granted the statute of an independent community only in 1956. In this "young" community there is also a small **Roman-Catholic church**, consecrated in 1970. Mlynčeky benefits from its ideal position, being close to the High Tatras growing progressively into a popular holiday destination.

The last of the four communities mentioned here, **RAKÚSY** (704 m, population 1,500) is also on a secondary road communication between Kežmarok (5.5 km) and Tatranská Kotlina (6 km). The history of the community dates back to the 13th century, and was partly owned by Kežmarok city, while the rest belonged to small landowners. In the first written reference it is quoted as Rokus, obviously derived from the name Rochus. The population of Rakúsy lived off farming, but today many of them work in the Tatra hotels. Of the numerous local **squire curias** only one has been preserved up to the present day. It is Classicist, dating from the mid-19th century. The Roman-Catholic **church of St. Martin the Bishop** was built in 1883 in a pseudo-Gothic style on the site of the foundations of an older Gothic church. The Classicist Evangelic **church** in Rakúsy was built in 1797 and the tower was added to it a century later.

In the triangle between Tatranská Kotlina, Spišská Belá and Podolínec there are six sub Tatra communities.

Right: Lendak girls

Nearest to the Tatras is the comparatively large Goral community called **LENDAK** (749 m, population 4,100). Being 3 km from Tatranská Kotlina it originated on the estate of the Bercevicz family in the mid-13th century. It is quoted in the oldest known document of 1288 as Landok. In 1313 it was acquired by the monks of the Knights of the Cross of the Holy Grave order in exchange for the properties in Chmeľov whereafter they built a monastery. It disappeared in 1593 upon the sale of the order's property to the family of Horváth-Palocsay of Plaveč. The people of Lendak made their living through farming, but they also produced linen, burnt lime and raised sheep. The wooden utensils used for the processing of sheep milk are still made in Lendak and the local artisans are known for their beautifully carved wooden mugs. Lendak was stricken by an extensive fire in 1946 which subsequently destroyed two thirds of the houses. The ruins of a 17th century **manor house** originated after the rebuilding of a Gothic monastery. However, the most important monument in the community is the original Gothic Roman-Catholic **church of St. Mikuláš the Bishop**. It was built in the 14th century on the foundations of an even older church. The main late Gothic wing altar was made in 1500.

The neighbouring village of **VÝBORNÁ** (706 m, population 700) is situated approximately halfway from Lendak to Slovenská Ves, under the southern slopes of the Partizánska mountain (937 m) which was founded by German colonists in the mid-13th century. The name *Viborna* first ocurred in 1463, which refers to the local mineral spring water which is said to be of excellent taste (výborná = excellent). The population of this serf community which served the Bercevicz family were engaged in farming and linen weaving. There are two churches in Výborná: the Roman-Catholic **church of St. Uršula**, which was built in the 14th century in the Gothic style, and later rebuilt several times. It has a rare wooden Renaissance ceiling supported by two carved twisting pillars. The wooden panels are decorated by paintings on religious themes. The other Classicist Evangelic church dates from 1833.

The nearby village of **SLOVENSKÁ VES** (650 m, population 1,700) originated on an old trade route and is the first settlement on the road from Spišká Belá (4 km) to Spišská Stará Ves (26 km). It is also the last community before the ascent of the road to the Magura Saddle (949 m). The former serfs of Slovenská Ves served several landlords most of whom were farmers and loggers. Seasonally they also wove and bleached linen. Special attention should be paid to the Roman-Catholic **church of the Virgin Mary's Purification** from the second half of the 14th century. A part of the main altar is the valuable Late Gothic **statue of Madonna** made around 1510 in the workshop of Maestro Pavol of Levoča, which is now a national cultural monument. The **Lady' Pillar** was transferred to Slovenská Ves from Ruskinovce. Out of the numerous **curias** in the community only one, dating from the late 18th century, has been preserved up to the present day, which is presently a schoolhouse. The area also boasts some wonderful protected **ash trees**.

VOJŇANY (668 m, population 200) is a small village at the southern foothills of the Spišská Magura mountains and was probably settled in the remote past. This originally medieval serf community was founded by one of the ancestors of the Görgey family in 1256, but its first written reference dates only from 1296. The local Roman-Catholic **church of St. Katarína of Alexan-**

dria is from the first half of the 14th century, an original Gothic building which underwent only minor adjustments. The valuable interior Early-Gothic cabinet altar made in 1300 was moved to the Slovak National Gallery in Bratislava. The Evangelic **church** in the community was built in 1871.

The Olympus of the Spiš Region:

The mountain Vojnianska at the southern edge of Spišská Magura mountains is the subject of numerous legends. This isolated mountain of interesting shape, 930 m high was used as a place of worship by the ancient inhabitants of the area. After one of early-Christian legends St. Vojtech stopped here and christened a man named Eden some time in the 10th century.

PODHORANY (598 m, population 1,000) is 1 km from the main road between Spišská Nová Ves and Podolínec, heading towards Vojňany. The oldest reference to the place dates from 1297, and until the abolition of serfdom Podhorany belonged to the family of Görgey. The earliest settlers lived off farming and the dyeing of linen. The **church of St. Martin** in Podhorany is from the early 15th century. Later a Renaissance attic tower was added to it. Podhorany's Evangelical church was built in 1806.

TOPOREC (527 m, population 1,500) lies 4.5 km west of Podolínec on a secondary road bound for the Zamagurie region. In the area administered by the community two original separate settlements are distinguishable even today. Old Toporec existed before the 13th century on the site of the present locality called Pustovec. New Toporec, which today represents the present village was founded in the 13th century. Toporec had close links with the old noble Görgey family who owned it since its origins, and until the abolition of serfdom. The Görgeys' founded here in 1630 a school for aristocratic children, and Latin, Greek and their mother tongue was taught to them for all of thirty years. The people of Toporec were, besides farming, also busy in making linen, haulage and distilling. In 1900 an Association of Distillers was founded. Toporec was also widely known for its excellent cheese. The Roman-Catholic **church of St. Filip and Jakub juniors the Apostles** in Toporec was built in 1326 and later several times rebuilt. Besides the church is the Renaissance **tomb of the Görgey family** from 1600, whilst the local **manor house** is from 1794. In the community of **Pustovec**, under the Toporecké Saddle grow two protected **lime trees** which are amongst the biggest and oldest in Slovakia.

PODOLÍNEC (570 m, population 3,100) is an ancient Spiš town lying on the main road from Spišská Belá (10 km) to Stará Ľubovňa (14 km). The original Slavonic community, on the site of present day Podolínec, was destroyed by the Tartar hordes in the years between 1241 and 1244. The oldest written reference to Podolínec dates to the period before the Tartar invasion when the boundary between Old Hungary and Poland had not yet been clearly established. The Act of 1235 comments upon the dispute over the tithe of Podolínec, between the Ostrigom and Kraków Abbeys over which the Pope himself intervened. It was probably his resolution that included Podolínec into the territory of Old Hungary of the Arpads. The rebuilding of the community destroyed by the Tartars became a matter not only

Left: Municipal fortification in Podolínec

for the German immigrants, as in the case of most of the Spiš towns and communities, but also for the immigrants from Poland. The sphere of Polish influence in this area was strong and the people of Podolínec made corresponding use of it. They benefited from its advantageous location on the old trade route from Poprad to Kraków and the navigable river Poprad. The merchants transported various goods on the river which were widely sold in the countries around the Baltic Sea. In the north especially weaving products and knives, with beautifully ornamented handles, produced in Podolínec were taken. Podolínec rapidly grew into a town obtaining some municipal privileges as early as1292 and was self governing after the Magdeburg right, having the right to mill, storage, and a right to fortify its limits. The municipal walls were used also by the people of the surrounding villages, including Hniezdne and Stará Ľubovňa. In 1412 thanks to its promotion to a free royal town, Podolínec reached the same status as Levoča or Kežmarok. However, in the same year the Old Hungarian king, Sigismond of Luxembourg, forfeited Podolínec to the Polish king Vladislav and it remained so until 1772. The people of Podolínec did not mind, though, as they enjoyed double privileges, Polish and Old Hungarian, attaining an extraordinarily favourable position among the forfeited Spiš towns. In 1642 a Piarist order came to Podolínec and built a monastery and a church in the north-eastern part of the town. The compound of the monastery became an important centre of education and culture in the Spiš region, as it had a secondary level school and a library. The earlier chapters of the history of the town are not so successful and glorious. The town missed out on the progress and the trends of development brought about by the industrial revolution and the urbanisation process, in the course of the 19th and 20th centuries, and sank to the level of small provincial town lacking any important industry or necessary urban infrastructure.

The lost castle of Podolínec:

Few of us know that Podolínec used to have its own municipal castle such as in nearly Kežmarok. Its existence is documented by various sources of the 15th to 18th century. Historians associate the origin of the castle in Podolínec with a secret royal secretary called Imrich Perényi, owner of Podolínec at the beginning of the 15th century. In 1409 king Sigismod permitted him to build within the municipal walls a castle or a small stronghold. In spite of the fact that the king took away the town from Perényi a year after, the people of Podolínec continued with the construction of the castle. And three decades later the walls of Podolínec castle were so strong as to allegedly resisted the attacks of the troops of Jan Jiskra of Brandýs. In the 18th century the castle lost its defensive function and gradually fell into decay. Its ruins were there until the late 19th century but later the castle completely disappeared under the pressure of new constructions. They say that the lost castle of Podolínec should be looked for under the building of the town hall.

Fading out of economic growth, precisely at the time when many other Slovak towns greatly changed their original appearance, meant that Podolínec remained has it had done since the 16th and 17th centuries of the Renaissance period, and in 1990 was thus declared a **municipal monument** reserve. Its ground plan is compact, typical for the Middle Ages, squeezed into a well-preserved municipal fortification. The network of streets inside the walls was formed along with the growth of the medieval Gothic Podolínec. In the centre of the town is a picturesque square made of a widening out main street. At the middle of the square is the **church of the Virgin Mary's Ascension** of later 13th century. Original one-nave Gothic building was later enlarged by an additional building of two lateral chapels and repeatedly adjusted. In the presbytery of the church are unique Gothic **wall paintings** in several layers of the years 1380-1430. They depict various biblical motifs. A part of the main altar is the Gothic **statue of Madonna** made around 1360. In 1659 a nice Renaissance **belfry** was built beside the church with a rare bell of 1392. The square is skirted by the row of Renaissance **burgher houses**. Most of them originated in early 17th century. Special attention deserves the **house no. 15** built in the 15th century. At the southern edge of the square building of the **town hall** of 1903 when it originated by rebuilding an older object, very probably a part of the disappeared castle of Podolínec. At the northern suburb of the town is a monumental building of the **Piaristic church and monastery**. The monastery compound was built in the years 1647 to 1651 in Renaissance style. The twin monasterial towers with Baroque onion-like roofs originated by building adjustment in 1762. Today it is an inseparable part of the town's beautiful silhouette. The best place for the view of which is the eastern end, i.e. the road bound for Lomnička. At the eastern edge of the monasterial compound are the best preserved sections of **castle wall with bastions**. On the facade of the building is the **commemorative board of Július Krúdy**, a Hungarian writer, who studied at the local Piaristic school in late 19th century. He is an author of well-known literary work: The Ghost of Podolínec that appeared also as a film. Interesting enough is the fact that the oldest building monument of Podolínec, the **chapel** of the 13th century, is situated out of its boundaries, at the local cemetery.

LOMNIČKA (617 m, population 1,100) lies in the valley of Lomnický potok brook, 3 km east from Podolínec. The community was founded by the Görgeys' who became its owners. The first reference to it is from 1294. The population of Lomničky traditionally made their living by farming and by the 18th century a linen bleaching workshop existed here. A great part of Lomnička was burned down in the years 1813-1887. After the displacement of the German population in 1945 the immigrants of the surrounding villages settled in Lomnička. Today it has a prevailingly Roma population. The originally Early-Gothic Roman-Catholic **church of St. Katarína of Alexandria** was built in Lomnička around 1300. It was rebuilt in Classicist style in the 19th century. The Gothic sculpture of Christ on the Cross of 1520 is attributed to Maestro Pavol of Levoča. The local rectory is adorned by the **statue of Madonna** of the first half of the 15th century. Lomnička also boasts of the **house of the lady-writer Terézia Vansová** (1857-1942) who was the daughter of the local Evangelic priest Ján Vansa. She lived here in the years 1875-1882. In her memory a national artistic competition was held here annually.

In the valley of Holumnický potok brook joining the river Poprad are three Spiš communities.

The first of them, **HOLUMNICA** (593 m, population 700) is located 5 km from Podolínec. It was first mentioned in 1293 and in the course of history it was a serfdom of the families Bezeviczy, Ujházy and Görgey. The population's typical occupations were farming, linen weaving and bleaching. Until the Second World War the villagers also manufactured shingles. At the upper end of the village are the ruins of **Holumnica Castle**. Originally a Gothic-Renaissance building of the late 15th and early 16th centuries it had a square ground plan. In the centre of the community stands a Renaissance **manor house** from the 17th century. The Roman-Catholic **church of St. Katarína** originated in the 19th century by the rebuilding of an older Gothic church. Holomnica has also an Evangelic **church** built in the years 1796-1797 which served the German part of the population who left before the arrival of the Red Army in 1945. Not far away form the turn off to the main road to Holomnica there used to stand a remarkable wooden and roofed bridge over the river Poprad.

JURSKÉ (647 m, population 600) lies only 4 km from Holumnica. It was founded by the Görgey family in the 13th century. Again the original village folk almost exclusively made their living through farming, but by the early 20th century there existed a cloth mill and a press for oil production. The local Roman-Catholic **church of St. Juraj** has Early Gothic foundations from the 13th century. It was rebuilt and domed in the 17th century with a tower added later. Of the sacral monuments in the village there is also an Evangelic **church** from 1865 of typical classicist architecture.

The neighbouring **IHĽANY** (706 m, population 1,100) is the highest situated community in the Holumnická valley and lies 3 km from Jurské. It originated by the merging of Majerka and Stotince in 1960. The common name of this community is derived from the mountain nearby called Ihla (1,283 m) in the Levočské vrchy hills. **Majerka** has probably developed from the former estate, and became a serf community of the town of Ľubica. **Stotince** originated in the last third of the 13th century, and in the 16th century it was settled by the colonists from Ukraine invited by the landlord Laský of Kežmarok. The population of both communities were farmers and shingle-makers. In Majerka stands the Roman-Catholic **church of St. Martin the Bishop**, an rebuilding of an older medieval church. The Evangelic church was built in 1787. Stotince has an Orthodox **church of St. Michal the Archangel** from the last third of the 13th century.

BUŠOVCE (594 m, population 300) is a community on the main road from Spišská Belá (4 km) to Podolínec (6 km). The area administered by the community is rich in archaeological finds

Right: Huncovce and the Tatras

that document its almost continuous settlement since the Older Stone Age. The earlier community originated on the territory of a forest called Stragar donated by king Ladislav IV to the ancestors of the Sváby family. The community as a rectory seat was referred to for the first time in an act of 1345 under the name Bussundorf. The inhabitants of Bušovce made their living from agriculture and linen weaving and bleaching and at its most productive period produced around 25 thousand meters of fine linen. Until 1940 a distillery operated here. There are two churches in Bušovče. The most important of these is the Roman-Catholic **church of St. Vavrinec the Deacon**. Originally a Gothic building from the 14th century it was "baroquised" in the 17th century. A Late Gothic statue of Madonna from 1400, in style are very much like the works of Maestro Pavol of Levoča. The local Evangelic **church** was built in 1818.

The community of **KRÍŽOVÁ VES** (624 m, population 1,500) lies off the main road on the right bank of the river Poprad, 3 km from Spišská Belá and was founded by the Berzeviczy family. The first reference to the community dates from 1290. In 1312 it was joined to Lendak and both communities became the property of the Knights of the Cross of the Holy Grave order. Later a part of the community was owned by Kežmarok. Its population mostly lived off farming and cartage. Besides which they also worked in the woods. A landmark of the community is the local Roman-Catholic **church of Lord's Birth** built in the Gothic style at the end of the 13th century and contains some valuable **wall paintings**. On the slope of the cemetery stands a brick Classicist **belfry**. In Krížová Ves one can see also a wooden Lutheran **tabernacle**. Two local Renaissance **manor houses** of the 16th and 17th centuries have been joined into one.

In the neighbouring town **SPIŠSKÁ BELÁ** (625 m, population 5,800) four important road communications meet: from Kežmarok (7 km), Stará Ľubovňa (30 km) and Lysá Poľana (31 km). As the archaeological findings have proven it, the territory of Spišská Belá was settled in the Older Stone Age, Bronze and Iron Ages. The oldest document mentioning the existence of Spišská Belá is the act of the Old Hungarian

king Belo IV from 1263 by which the ruler invited the German colonists to Old Hungary with the aim of restoration and resettlement of the area devastated by the Tartars. The town acquired through a donation from king Štefan V in 1271 its first municipal rights and quickly became one of the richest towns organised by the Association of the Spiš Saxons. The Polish forfeit in the years 1412 to 1772 did no harm to the town and its inhabitants and craftwork and trading continued to thrive especially after the town received the important right to hold two annual fairs. There lived in Spišská about 225 craftsmen in 1752 – tanners, furriers, shoe-makers, boot-makers and linen-makers. The high quality flax linen made here was exported as far as to Turkey. In the 18th and 19th centuries Spišská Belá became the largest sheep-raising centre on the southern part of the Tatras. Its flocks could graze on extensive pastures of the Belianske Tatra mountains, over clearings of an area of 12 km². The shepherds annually drove there the flocks amounting to as much as 2,200 sheep and 300 oxen, heifers and horses.

Left: The church and belfry in Spišská Belá

The fights for the Tatra clearings:

When in 1310 the boundaries of the areas administered by the Spiš communities were laid, after the order of king Karol Róbert, the villagers of Spišská Belá received a nice chunk of land. Their biggest area reached far north up to the high ridges of the mountains known since very early times as the Belianske Tatras. In spite of the generosity of the royal surveyors the people of Spišská Belá were not content and often entered bloody disputes with the neighbouring communities concerning the Tatra mountain pastures. In 1701 the villagers of Belá began one such argument because of the meadow called Rakúska poľana on the southern side of the Bujačí vrch mountain was also claimed by the people of Kežmarok and Rakúsy. The fighting parties were separated only by the arrival of the imperial troops and the dispute was transferred to a court of justice. The judge finally pronounced a Solomon's resolution: the meadow was marked by a big stone bearing the letters K-R-B announcing that the meadow shall be in future used by the people of Kežmarok, Rakúsy, and Belá.

Industry in Spišská Belá started comparably early in its development. In 1778 the canning factories and a distillery producing the famous borovička of Belá were founded. The local smelting shop worked with the iron ore traded within the town. In the 19th century a saw mill, starch producing shop and a tobacco factory, today the most important industrial firm in the town, joined the list. In 1895 Spišská Belá was connected by railway with Poprad.

The oldest, originally Late Renaissance and Baroque **burgher houses** in the centre of the town are from the 17th and 18th centuries. At the core of the spindle shaped square stand three buildings. The Roman-Catholic **church of St. Anton the Hermit** is the main dominant monument in the town. Of the original Late Romanesque building dating back to 1264 only the peripheral walls and the western portal are left. The interior of the church is recent, pseudo-historical. The valuable painted boards of the main altar ended up before the First World War in the collections of the Budapest Museum of Szépmüvészeti. They depict the scenes of the legend about St. Anton the Hermit, a patron of the town. The authorship of the paintings is attributed to the so-called maestro of St. Anton's legends, a colleague of Maestro Pavol of Levoča. In the neigbourhood of the church a Renaissance **belfry** of the late 16th century stands. On the opposite side of the church is the **Museum of J. M. Petzval**. The museum was opened to the public in 1964 in the former school building, where on January 6, 1807 the outstanding discoverer, mathematician and physicist Jozef Maximilián Petzval was born. Besides the documents about the creative life of this famous Belá citizen the museum displays more than 600 artefacts illustrating the history of world photographic optics. There is also a famous daguerreotype apparatus with a revolutionary Petzval's lens that brought to its discoverer a world wide reputation. Petzval's lens, based in the principle of greater illumination, reduced the exposure time of thirty minutes to a mere thirty seconds. In several European cities streets bear the discoverer's name and there is even a crater on the moon which is named after him.

Museum of J. M. Petzval,
Petzvalova 3, tel.: 0968/913 07
Opening hours: Mon-Fri 8:00-17:00h

A typical feature of the medieval Spišská Belá were the barns standing close to each other, acting as a kind of municipal fortification. Many of the defensive walls in Spišská Belá have been preserved until today.

East of the town lies the former **Belianske kúpele spa**. It originated in the 17th century on the local sulphur water springs. In the 18th century, in addition to the traditional baths, mud therapy was added making use of nearby sources of pit, which was accompanied by the drinking of herb tea made from the Tatra dwarf pine. Belianske spa was renowned for treating rheumatism and skin diseases. They were closed after the Second World War and today the area is used for recreation and leisure.

The local part of Spišská Belá – **Strážky** (635 m) is on the left bank of the river Poprad on the main road between Kežmarok (5 km) and Spišská Belá (2 km). The name of the area (stráž = guards) suggests that there used to live the guards of the Polish-Old Hungarian border, who were subjects of the king. When the frontier was settled down in the 13th century the guarding mission of Strážky lost its purpose and its population from then on dedicated itself to cultivation of flax. The list of the owners of this serf community contains several noble names. In the 15th century a rich Silesian family from Warkotsch moved to the community and chose Strážky for their family seat. Following the example of nearby Kežmarok castle they too built a strong Gothic castle in the middle of the community. The castle allegedly stands on the site of what once used to be a Knights Templar monastery. After the battle at Mohács the family of Warkotsch lost its political influence as well as its Old Hungarian property. This was the reason why in 1556 the hero of the Turkish wars Marek Horváth-Stansith moved to the empty castle in Strážky. The new owner of an important Croatian noble family gradually rebuilt the Gothic castle into a Renaissance manor house providing more comfort. In 1588 the Marek's son Gregor Horváth Stansith founded a humanistic school in the family estate and in the years from1618 to 1628 continued in the reconstruction of the castle which has given it more or less its contemporary form. In 1862 the baron Eduard Mednyánszky moved to the Strážsky manor house, bringing his ten year old son Ladislav, who later became a famous painter. This artist of European ranking during his stays at the family seat at the foothills of the Tatras created several of his wonderful landscapes containing some original social elements. In 1885 his father baron Eduard left us a valuable library containing 6411 volumes.

A school for young aristocrats:

Gregor Horváth-Stansith born in Strážky after having graduated from the Paduan University taught at the University of Wittenberg, Germany. Brought up in the spirit of the Italian and German humanism he founded after his return to Slovakia a Latin school for the offsprings of the Old Hungarian noble families. He developed a school based on a university model at his family's seat in Strážky Castle, and at the time reconstructed it into a comfortable Renaissance manor house. He invited some excellent teachers from abroad and he himself lectured rhetorics and ethics to his students. The first rector of Stážky college was Egid Hunnious, Professor of Theology of Wittenberg University. The school disappeared in 1711 and the centre of Spiš education and scholarship moved to the Kežmarok lycée.

Strážky today represents a complete compound of cultural and historical monuments, declared in 1970 a **natural cultural monument**. The **manor house in Strážky** is a gem of Renaissance architecture in Slovakia. It was built progressively in the years 1556 to 1628 on the site of an older stronghold or fortified monastery from the 12th century. The original three-winged building was completed after a fire in 1708 creating a typical square-shaped ground plan with a square inner courtyard. The charm of the manor house is enhanced by an English park from the 19th century. Besides a precious library there are paintings by Ladislav Mednyánszky and a valuable Stibor stone coat of arms from the Beckov Castle. The manor house is administered by the Slovak National Gallery.

Manor house Strážky,
Mednyánszkeho 25, tel.: 0968/58 13 12
Opening hours: Mon-Fri 10:00-17:00h.

Opposite the manor house stands the Roman-Catholic **church of St. Anna**, which was built in Gothic style by the end of the 15th century. At the western wall of the church nave are some wall paintings from the early 16th century representing the Passion cycle and illusive architecture. Three precious Gothic wing altars were probably made in the workshop of the Levoča maestros, one of them is even made by maestro Pavol himself. The most valuable artistic works of the interior of the church were included into the collections of the Slovak National Gallery in Bratislava. Near the church a Renaissance belfry is adorned by an original grafitto ornamentation of the facade. The bells in the **belfry** were made in the years 1517, 1588, and 1642.

The community of **ĽUBICA** (636 m, population 500) lies 2 km east of the centre of Kežmarok near its namesake brook flowing from the Levočské vrchy hills. Kežmarok and Ľubica are today one settlement. The old name of the community quoted in 1251 testifies to the Slavonic origin of its settlers. After the Tartar invasion Ľubica was resettled by Saxon colonists who soon after had a dispute with the old Slavonic settlers. The dispute had to be settled by king Štefan V himself who issued an act delimiting the duties and rights of both parties. This in fact meant municipal privileges, allowing them to elect their magistrate, establish fields and pastures in cleared forests, to hunt and fish and to extract minerals and metals. In 1364 Ľubica was also granted the right to hold weekly markets and after 1656 to invite merchants to three big annual fairs. The active local population created numerous crafts, above all home cloth making. The guild of the local cloth-makers was one of the first established in the Spiš region and it is referred to in the acts of 1480. Culture and education was in the hands of the local Evangelic school founded in the second half of the 16th century. In 1830, the local Catholic rectory was established, whose library after a half-century of existence counted up to 2,279 items. Economic decline came in 1876 the same as in Kežmarok. Kežmarok, however, succeeded in preserving its municipal rights while Ľubica finally became an agricultural community.

Examples of the past glory of the town are today the originally Renaissance **burgher houses** and three valuable sacral buildings. The nucleus is formed by a triangle square with an Evangelic **church** built in 1786. In Ľubica are another two ancient Roman-Catholic churches from the 13th century. Even in spite of repeated reconstruction there are some Romanesque elements recognisable in the architecture of the **church of the Virgin Mary's Assumption**. The pride of the church is the **statue of Madonna** by the famous maestro Pavol of Levoča. In the **Holy Spirit church** there used to be valuable Gothic altars, but they were carried away to Budapest before the First World War and never returned to Ľubica. The altars are replaced by copies today. Another landmark of Ľubica is the **plague pillar** built by the magistrate of the forfeited Spiš towns, Teodor Ľubomírsky, in commemoration of the victims of the plague in the years 1710-1711.

In the valley of the Ľubica brook are the sulphurous water springs which gave origin to the Ľubické kúpele spa founded in 1718. They are now a part of the military training field of Javorina and are closed to the public. Ľubica was the birth place of David Fröllich (1595-1648) an important mathematician and physicist known for the first description of a mountaineering trip to the Tatras.

In the valley of Tvarožniansky potok brook, southeast from Ľubica are three communities.

The first of them, **TVAROŽNÁ** (676 m, population 500) originated at the boundary between the Poprad Basin and the Levočské vrchy hills. It

Right: A blacksmith's craft

was first referred to as early as 1268 and belonged to the Association of the Saxons living in Spiš. The name appeared for the first time much later, in 1786, after the expiration of the Polish forfeit of the Spiš towns. The inhabitants kept horses and sheep, grew and processed flax. After the departure of the Saxons the settlers of Ruskovce and Dvorce came to live in Tvarožná. There are several original burgher houses preserved in the community from the 17th-19th centuries. The local Roman-Catholic **church of St. Matej the Apostle** from the 13th century was several times rebuilt. The Saxons in the village had also an Evangelic **church** from 1778, in addition to a Baroque **pillar** with a statue of the Immaculation made of sandstone from 1730.

More to the south is located the village of **VLKOVCE** (825 m, population 400) founded after the Turkish invasion with its first reference dated in 1268. Its original name contains an older Slavonic word for wolf vilg, as the forests around the community were probably full of wolf packs. From 1317 on the community belonged to the Association of the Saxons. In the 15th century it became a serfdom given as a forfeit to the city of Levoča lying on the opposite side of the mountain ridge of the Levočské hills. The villagers made their living from farming, cartage and shingle-making.

HRADISKO (840 m, population 100) is the highest situated community of the district of Kežmarok. It extends on the western edge of the Levoča Plains, south of the Levočské hills. It was mentioned for the first time in 1264 as a serfdom belonging to the city of Levoča. Its present name derives from 1773, however the Roman- Catholic **church of Ascension of St. Cross** in Hradisko is modern, built between 1937-1944.

One of the few footpaths for tourists begins in the region of the Levočské Hills. A red-marked path runs eastward along the main European water divide. It passes through meadows to the mountain of **Brezová** (948 m) offering a charming view of the High Tatras over the Poprad Basin. Excellent vistas are also to the south into the basin of the river Hornád. Below the Ostrá mountain a green-marked pathway turns southeast and descends to the very centre of Levoča. Before reaching the city one can enjoy a nice view from this aspect. A red-marked footpath continues to the east and to the Levočská dolina valley, then further across the Levoča Plains to Oľšavica at the southeastern edge of the Levočké hills. The path passes alongside the **nature monument of Kohlwald**. The lime trees of Kohlwald were the dating point for the generation of Slovak patriots who supported their leader Ľudovít Štúr active in Levoča between 1844-1848.

On the ancient road connecting Kežmarok with Spišský Štvrtok and Levoča are more communities. **VRBOV** (662 m, population 1,200) lies in the valley of the Vrbovský potok brook, 7 km south of Kežmarok. The first written reference to the village dates from 1251. The name Werbew proves that it was a Slavonic settlement before the Tartar invasion. Vrbov was granted municipal privileges in the 13th century and later it was included in the forfeit of the Spiš towns to Poland. The inhabitants of this prosperous little town made their living via farming, distillery and linen trade. Vrbov has a precious Late Romanesque Roman-Catholic **church of St. Servác** built in the second half of the 13th century and was "baroquised" through reconstruction in the 17th century. In 1644 a Renaissance **belfry** was attached to it. The Evangelic **church** has stood in Vrbové since 1784.

Vrbov attracted tourists mainly because of its **holiday resort** established south of the communi-

ty. At the beginning there were only ponds around the Vrbovský potok brook, but following the discovery of a generous thermal water source in 1981 it soon had a system of thermal swimming pools. These pools are filled with thermal water of a temperature of 56°C blended of course to acceptable bathing temperature.

VLKOVÁ (670 m, population 600), is a community situated more to the south and is 12 km from Kežmarok and the first reference to it was in a donation act by king Ladislav IV in 1278. It was acquired by the ancestors of the Berzeviczy family. The population of this serfdom lived primarily off farming, however, in the years from 1880 to 1887 there was also a small pottery in the community. Vlková has a Roman-Catholic **church of the Virgin Mary's Annunciation**. This Baroque building was built in 1779 on the site of an older church from 1408 and has a Gothic wing altar from 1480. There are also two manor houses in the community. The older **manor house** was built in the 17th century, originally in Renaissance style and later rebuilt, whilst the second **manor house** dates from 1764 and is done in Late Baroque style. Miss Babetta von Wieland, a descendant of the last landlord family of Vlková, was admired by the outstanding Slovak playwright Ján Chalupka, the author of the well known literary work Kocúrkovo, who used to come to visit her from Kežmarok. The small community of **Levkovce**, first mentioned in 1306, belonged to Vlková since 1895.

The village of **ABRAHÁMOVCE** (713 m, population 200) similar to Levkovce, is also one of the so-called lancer communities. It was referred to firstly in 1286 as Abraham, probably the name of its founder. The villagers occupied themselves with farming, haulage and basket-making. There is an interesting **church** by the name of **St. Šimon and Júda** in Abrahámovce. Originally a Gothic building from the first half of the 14th century it was later repeatedly rebuilt. The paintings adorning the main altar from the late 15th century are from the workshops of the painters in Spišká Kapitula. Also the Gothic altar plaster art works from the 14th century are valuable specimens. In 1859 the little nearby village of **Pikovce** was adjoined to Abrahámovce.

ŽAKOVCE lying west of Vrbov (671 m, population 600) is among one of the oldest Spiš communities, as it was first mentioned as early as 1209. After the Tartar invasion it was settled by the German colonists who made use of their mining rights, which allowed them to extract copper and mercury. Žakovce was first included in the Province of 24 Spiš towns, and later became a serf town of the Spiš Castle. It was owned by the family of Thurzo and later by that of the Csáky family. The local landlords left here a Late Baroque **manor house** from the 18th century, and the villagers were made their living from farming and linen manufacturing. After the departure of the Germans in 1945 Žakovce were resettled by the immigrants of Blažov. Besides the manor house another important and valuable monument in the community is the Roman-Catholic **church of St. Mikuláš the Bishop**. Originally a Gothic church from 1300 it acquired its contemporary Baroque form in the 18th century. The local Evangelic **church** was built in 1793.

LEft: The thermal swimming pool in Vrbovo

Poprad and its environs

POPRAD (672 m, population 55,500) lies south-east of the basin and on both sides of the river Poprad. It is the main entrance "gate" to the High Tatras. Annually tens of thousands of tourists of Slovakia and abroad pour in through the local airport, railways and roads to continue to Starý Smokovec or other Tatra communities.

The plains of the glacier-river terraces which meander along the river Poprad were settled in ancient times, proven by collective discoveries of Liptov type of swords from the Lower Bronze Age. Medieval Poprad was probably founded before the Tartar invasion. The oldest Slavic community was strengthened by the German colonists invited here by the king in the mid-13th century. The present name of Poprad appears in the oldest known act of 1256. After 12 years a younger historical document quotes a different name: villa Theutonicalis perhaps attached to the community by Saxon immigrants. Initially Poprad did not develop as quickly as the neighbouring Veľká and Spišská Sobota communities. In spite of its favourable geographic situation Poprad only slowly changed from a farming community to a town of craftwork and trade. In the years between 1412-1772 it was included among 13 Spiš towns given as a forfeit to the Polish crown. In the period of the first municipal integration Poprad merged with Veľká, Stráže, Majerovce and Spišská Sobota into a free association of five Upper Spiš towns, the wealthiest of which was Spišská Sobota. Only in the 18th century did Poprad economically catch up with its contemporary towns. The first factor that contributed to the change was a delayed granting of market rights to Poprad. These weekly markets assisted the promotion of crafts. Copper-engravers producing various objects of copper extracted in the nearby mines were typical for Poprad. The principal driving force of the dynamic development of the town was finally the Košice-Bohumín railway track built in 1871. When on December 8, 1871 the first train whirled into a decorated Poprad railway station, built in the meadows between the town and Veľká, the situation suddenly changed. The route of the Spiš section of the all important Transcarpathian railway tracks promoted Poprad to a pre-eminent position and the town correspondingly made use of it. The dynamic growth of the town,

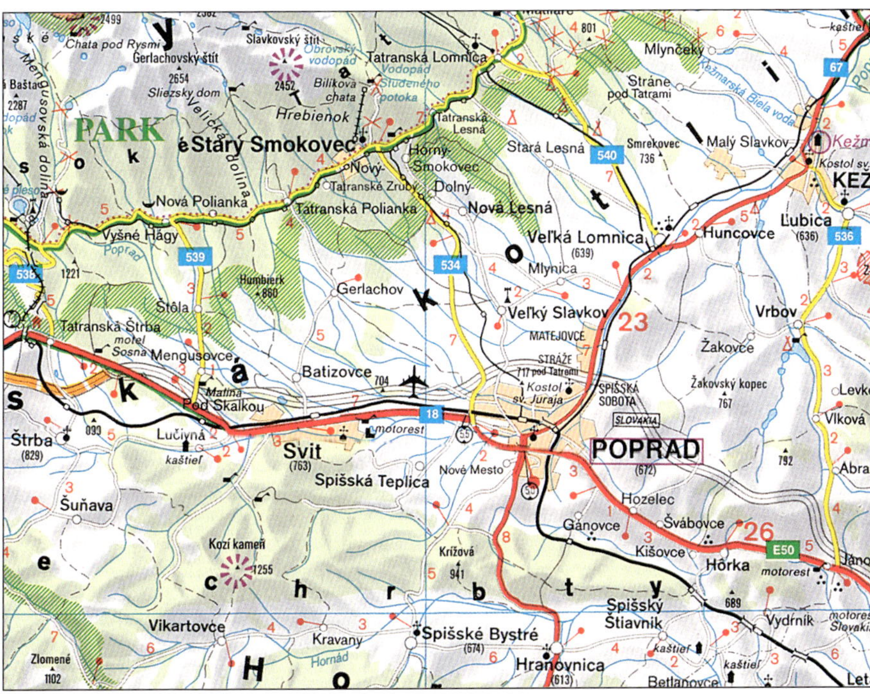

to the detriment of Spišská Sobota and Veľká, gradually changed the hundreds of years' hierarchy of the settlements in the Upper Spiš region. Former small manufacturers developed into factories with the machine production of textile, paper and pulp. Later the industrial base of the town was widened by the establishment of a brewery, power station, brickyard, starch manufacture and additional smaller firms. After the First World War a plant producing railway cars was founded in Poprad (Tatravagónka) and in its present form it represents the most important industry in the city. The growing interest of the tourists in the Tatras geared up intense cultural and social life in the city. And the administrative position of Poprad was strengthened in the inter-war period when in the years 1923-1932 several district administration offices were moved here from Spišská Sobota and Poprad became the centre of an extensive sub Tatra district. In spite of the evident economic boom, Poprad's population amounted to only 4,000 in 1940. After the Second World War the number grew more than ten-fold as a result of the annexing of the neighbouring small towns, and above all because of the migration of the rural population into the city offering more jobs, concluding with the gradual integration of the five towns. Continuously growing, Poprad first swallowed its greatest rivals Spišská Sobota and Veľká, then in 1960 Stráže pod Tatrami were absorbed and the creation of the present "Large Poprad" was completed by annexing Matejovce in 1974. Poprad today with its large population is the largest city in the sub Tatra region, ranking tenth in the national scale.

Left: The Námestie sv. Egídia square in Poprad

The airport for the Tatras:

The right to built an airport for the Tatra region was fought over by several applicants. The originators of the 1922 project, of what was called a spa airline, communicating the spa centres in Western Czechia through Prague, Brno, Piešťany, the Tatra mountains up to Uzhgorod, chose to situate it in a meadow near Veľká Lomnica. This, however, was not altogether approved by the Poprad people who preferred to see the new airport on another meadow, near Veľká. However, Liptov was also actively involved and

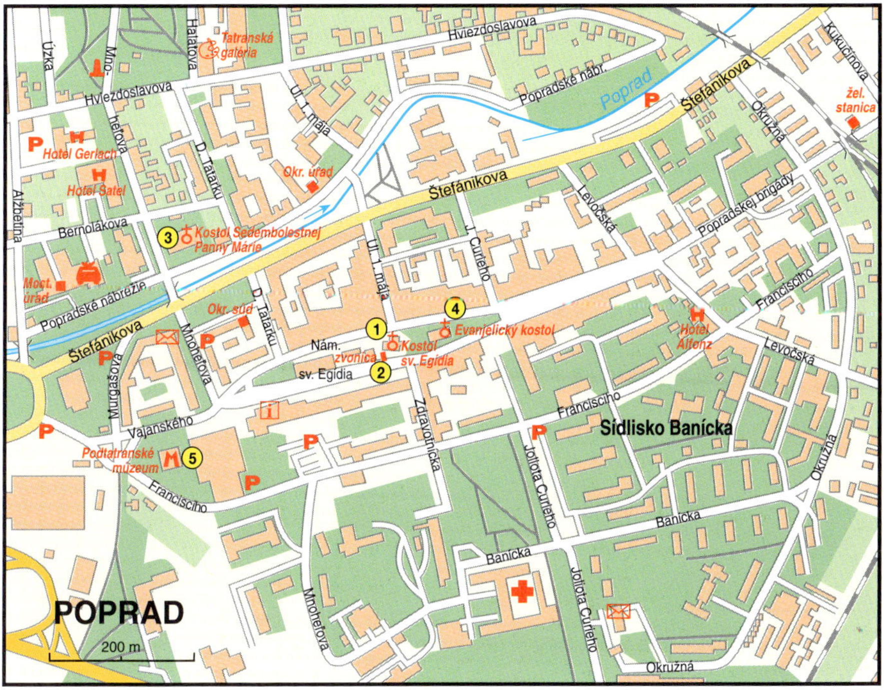

offered two localities for the airport: Važec and Palúdzka. The circle of active participants grew larger in 1935 by Štrbské Pleso where, pursuing a curious project by Teodor Sauter, hydroplanes were expected to land on the actual water table of the high-mountain lake. Finally a businessman by the name of Baťa of Zlín entered the competition personally who clinched the deal for Veľká, next to his shoe factory in Svit. The first plane under the neutral name of TATRY landed here in 1940. It was a two-motored Folker Wulf 58. Today the airport is used not only by regular inland and international air transport but also by the helicopters of Horská služba (the Mountain Rescue Service).

The historical centre of Poprad is concentrated into the space around the spindle-shaped **square of St. Egidius**. The square is rimmed by a row of prevailingly Baroque and Classicist **burgher houses** from the 18th and 19th centuries. The city has an Early-Gothic Roman-Catholic **church of St. Egidius** (1) from the late 13th. The local people know it as "the old church". In its interior the medieval wall paintings from the first half of the 15th century are preserved. One of the paintings by an unknown artist depicts the panorama of the Tatra peaks within a Biblical scene of Christ's resurrection. It is probably the oldest artistic picture of the Tatras. Alongside the old church stands a Renaissance **belfry** (2) from 1658. At present there is in Poprad a new Roman-Catholic **the Virgin Mary of Seven Grievances church** (3) built during the Second World War and the Classicist Evangelical **church** (4) was built in the years 1829-1834. The Poprad synagogue is from 1830. Visitors to Poprad should not forget to visit the **Podtatranské múzeum** (5) which offers an abundant information about the region. The museum, belonging to the oldest in Slovakia was founded in 1886 thanks to the generous support of the local patron David Husz (1813-1889) who built the oldest tourist base in Poprad known as Husz's Park. A part of the exposition of Podtatranské múzeum is located in Spišská Sobota.

Podtatranské múzeum, Vajanského 4/72
tel.: 092/72 18 74
Opening hours: Tue-Sun 9:00-16:00h

Podtatranské múzeum, Spišská Sobota,
tel.: 092/72 13 23
Opening hours: Mon-Sun 9:00-16:00h

The municipal part of **Veľká** lies in the northern end of Veľký Poprad (first stop on the Tatra tram). In its territory of the traces of settlements from the Lower Stone Ages have been found. Existence of the community is documented by an act of 1269. The oldest name of the community Veľká ("veľká" meaning big) is often associated with the unusual size of its adjacent land that in the past stretched along the Velický potok brook as far as the Velická dolina valley in the High Tatras. Veľká was prosperous and in the 15th century it was a wealthy little town. Its inhabitants were farmers and craftsmen. The local crafts included the dyeing of blue-printed linen and the art of wood-carving. By the end of the 19th century in Veľká a workshop of the Sub Tatra Association of Domestic Industry producing souvenirs originated. The medieval community Veľká grew around a wide square crossed by the Velický potok brook. In the eastern side of the square stands a fortified Early-Gothic Roman-Catholic **church of St. Ján the Evangelist**. Its oldest part is from the mid-13th century. A part of the prevailingly Baroque interior of the church is a valuable Gothic bronze baptistery from 1439 attributed to maestro J. Weygel of Spišská Nová Ves. Near the church is the **Lady's Pillar** with the statue of Immaculate of the first third of the 18th century. The Evangelical **church** built in 1817 has a ground plan of an isosceles cross. The community **synagogue** is of the same period. The square is rimmed by original **burgher houses** in Baroque or Classicist style, but there are also Late-Renaissance buildings of the 17th century here.

Left: A view of Poprad

Spišská Sobota was for centuries the wealthiest of the five Upper Spiš towns. From 1945 it has represented one of the municipal parts of large Poprad. The first reference to is the act of king Belo IV of 1256 as one of the boundary towns under the name Forum sabatthe, i.e. the Saturday fair. After the Tartar invasion the population increased because of the influx of German colonists. The privileges endowed to the Saxon immigrants by the king contributed enormously to the growth of Spišská Sobota and it quickly joined the important towns in the Spiš region, namely Levoča and Kežmarok. The people of Spišská Sobota had the right to run weekly markets on Saturdays since 1380 and in 1567 also the right to two annual fairs was given. Destructive fires in the years 1545, 1682 and 1775, though resulting in vast damage, also provided the opportunity to modernise the housing. Spišská Sobota lacked any municipal walls and its defences were provided by the back walls of the buildings connected into a continuous row. During Bethlen's rebellion this provisional defensive system was rebuilt and fortified, and expanded by four municipal gates built at the point where two main roads departed out of the town. The Poprad Gate was pulled down only in 1870. The period of culminating prosperity for the town were the 17th and 18th centuries when the craftsmen joined in guilds. There were for instance the following guilds: bakers, butchers, shoe-makers, boot-makers, furriers, and button-makers. The cultural progress of Spišská Sobota is documented by the fact that it possessed the only book shop in the region for some time. The economic growth of the town reached a standstill in the 19th and 20th centuries. Its past rivalry with Poprad finally ended in favour of its economically stronger south-western neighbour.

Spišská Sobota represents one of the best preserved medieval urban units in Slovakia declared in 1953 a **municipal monument reserve**. Its core is a triangle-shaped square bordered by a row of burgher houses built on narrow medieval plots. There are two-floor arcade type drive-through houses, including hallways. The ground floor served for living, the second floor was occupied by workshops and stores. The typical trait of the burgher houses in Spišská Sobota are high shingled roofs with massive shingled cornices. They can be seen, for instance, on the houses of the tanners at the north-eastern end of the square. Most of the burgher houses in this town were built in the period between the 15th to the 17th centuries in Gothic and Renaissance styles and later into the Baroque. Special attentions should be paid to several Gothic burgher houses from the second half of the 15th century, some of them only slightly altered by later alterations of style (for instance nos.16 and 25). In the centre of the square, besides the rectory church, belfry and the town hall a small butcher's shop once existed in the 19th century. The Roman-Catholic **church of St. Juraj** (1) built be-

fore 1273 in Late-Romanesque style, was rebuilt in Gothic style in 1464 and at the beginning of the 16th century it was enlarged by the St. Anna chapel. In the 18th century a Baroque southern hallway was also added to it. The Late-Gothic wing altars of St. Juraj and St. Anton were installed in the years between 1503 to1520 in the workshop of Maestro Pavol of Levoča. The creation of the board paintings on both altars is attributed to the author of the legends of St. Anton. Near the church stands a Renaissance **belfry** (2) from 1598 and a Baroque statue of Immaculation from 1772. In a small park nearby a corn gauge can be seen as a single memory of the famous markets held in Spišská Sobota. The isolated building of the **town hall** (3) was originally a Late-Baroque palace dating from the last third of the 18th century. The Evangelical **church** (4) was included into the row of houses around the square in 1777 and its interior includes a valuable altar painting of Christ on the Mount of Olives by Jozef Czauczik from 1852. In the back part of the building of the parsonage, built between 1638-1674 one can see the 17th century fortification of Spišská Sobota. The town is the birth place of several important figures. The well-known Baroque sculptor Ján Brokoff (1652-1718) was born here, and an important architect and author of several Tatra hotels, Gideon Majunke (1848-1928) lived here. Zuzana Henshová, wife of the famous traveller Móric Beňovský, who became the king of Madagascar in the 18th century, was the daughter of a Spišská Sobota butcher.

A chronicle of Spišská Sobota:

The towns of Spiš have minutely recorded all events in their chronicles, which at the present time are an excellent source of information about their history. The oldest preserved chronicle is that of Spišská Sobota from the mid-15th century written by an anonymous author. It records many important historical events of the 10th century up until 1457, containing a copy of the Spiš law controlling the life of all towns and communities in the region.

The territory of Poprad's local area **Matejovce** was settled, judging by the archaeological finds, in the Lower Bronze Age. The medieval settlement is first referred to in 1251. In the years between 1412-772 Matejovce, together with other Spiš towns, came under Polish sovereignty and the villagers earned their living from linen weaving, distillery and farming. In the 18th century they also successfully traded in vinegar and beer. In 1845 the local citizen K. A. Sholz founded here a workshop manufacturing metal horse combs which later developed into enamel works producing kitchen pots. Since 1968 there is in Matejovce a washing machine producing plant called Tatramat, today a part of the Whirlpool concern. The most significant monument of Matejovce is the Roman-Catholic **church of St. Štefan the King**. It was built in the first half of the 14th century in Gothic style and later "Baroquised". The most valuable part of its interior is the Gothic wing altar of St. Štefan and Imrich dating back to the period around 1450. The altar board paintings are the work of a Spiš painter of European origin known under the name of Maestro of Matejovce. Near the church is a Renaissance **belfry** from the 17th century which later underwent Classicist alterations, containing a precious Gothic bell. There is also a Gothic **Lady's Pillar** with the statue of the Immaculate Conception from 1728. The Evangelical **church** was built in Classicist style in 1785.

The part of Poprad called **Stráže pod Tatrami** probably originated as a guarding community

Left: Burgher houses in Spišská Sobota
Right: The altar in the St. Juraj church

at the territory administered by Spišská Sobota in the second half of the 13th century. The first written reference to the community is from 1300. The contemporary name of the community ("stráže" means guards), expressing the primary function of the settlement, appeared in a document from 1786. The inhabitants of this agricultural community which later developed into one of the Spiš towns made their living mainly from craftworks, a distillery, a brewery and by linen weaving. This small town, however, was doomed to live in the shadow of the surrounding wealthier neighbours, Matejovce and Spišská Sobota. The original street and urban structures which consist of **burgher houses** from the 15th to 18th centuries are preserved until the present days. Also a Baroque **granary** from the 17th century and the Roman-Catholic **church of Ján the Baptist** from the 14th century deserve attention. Of the original Gothic church only the tower and surrounding walls are preserved, whereas the remaining parts are the result of Baroque reconstruction in 1777. Near the church stands a sandstone **Lady's Pillar** with a Baroque statue of Immaculation from a period around 1730 and the local Classicist Evangelical **church** is from 1784.

South of Poprad in a pleasant setting of a forest park is the holiday and spa community of **Kvetnica**. The first buildings standing near the municipal forester's cottage were built by the Old Hungarian Carpathian Association in 1875. The arrival of the first spa physician Dr. Aladár Kern in 1892 created the opening of the climatic spa in Kvetnica, which still today serves patients suffering from respiratory diseases. On the site of what was once a forester's house, the biggest building in the community, there is now the Jubilejný pavilón sanatorium.

SPIŠSKÁ TEPLICA (704 m, population 1,700) is a small village lying off the main road between Poprad (4 km) and Svit. It was first mentioned in 1280 and used to belong to the serf communities of the Cistercian abbey in Spišský Štiavnik, although archaeological discoveries have proved the existence of a Bronze Age settlement. In 1530 Spišská Teplica was forfeited to the town of Levoča. Its last landlord was the bishop of Spiš. It used to be a prosperous community especially because of the right to run weekly markets. From 1755 the villagers were entitled to invite merchants also to two annual fairs. Samuel Spillenberg, a citizen of Levoča, founded here a paper mill, producing paper in the years between 1613 to1885, also the growing and trading in vegetables which was a prosperous occupation. Spišská Teplica has a comparably new Roman-Catholic **church of the Holiest Trinity** built in 1837 on the site of a demolished Gothic church from the 14th century. Its interior is interesting, especially for a valuable statue of the Madonna from the 14th century. Another interesting building in the community is a **burgher house** from the 18th century.

SVIT (763 m, population 7,500) is the youngest of the sub Tatra towns, and following Starý Smokovec the second highest situated town in Slovakia. Svit lies on the left bank of the river Poprad, only 9 km from the district city. In terms of recent history, in 1934 the Moravian company Baťa bought waterlogged meadows, called Štokava in the town of Veľká, to erect a modern plant producing synthetic fabric also providing houses for its workers. The contemporary name of this youngest sub Tatra settlement has been used since 1937. Svit became administratively independent in 1946 and in 1962 it acquired the status of a town. The nationalised chemical works was divided after 1945 into two independent plants – Tatrasvit and Chemosvit. The town is typical for its red brick "**Baťa houses**" which exemplify the sofisticated social policy of its original owner, the businessman Baťa.

South of Svit lies a sport and leisure centre for skiers called Lopušná dolina valley equipped with ski-lifts and tourist accommodation facilities.

LUČIVNÁ (767 m, population 800) lies on a subsidiary road between Svit (4 km) and Štrba (5 km). The oldest written reference to the community is from 1321. The beautiful setting of the community attracted the attention of the Old Hungarian king Matej Korvín, who built here a hunting manor house. The local landowners later reconstructed it into a curia. There was once also a toll house on the trade route between the Spiš and Liptov region, and later also a post station was built beside it. Medieval Lučivná was a serf community of the Cistercian abbey in Spišský Štiavnik. The main source of living of the local population was sheep keeping, cartage and lime burning, and the sheep cheese of Lučivná was always considered the best in the region. In the early 18th century the community became the property of the family of Várady-Szatmáry, who built a **climatic spa** north of the community in 1872. After the First World War the spa was purchased by the workers' insurance company and they established here a children centre for tuberculosis therapy. Later in 1937 another modern, clinic specialising in children's therapy, was built in Lučivná. Today Lučivná has available three sanatoriums with 330 beds for non-specific respiratory diseases and children's allergies.

The landmarks of the community are two churches, that originated almost at the same time and both of which are in the Classicist style. The Roman-Catholic **church of St. Martin the Bishop** was built in 1814 and the Evangelical church was opened for worshippers a year later. In its altar the painting of the Good Pastor by P. M. Bohúň can be seen. There is also an originally Renaissance manor house from early 17th century, which was rebuilt in the 19th century. A direct view of the High Tatras is obstructed by the hill called Bôrik. On its southern slope the **nature reserve of Bôrik** was established in 1991, protecting the rare plants which grow on the limestone and dolomite rocks.

The community of **ŠTRBA** (829 m, population 3,800) is located off the main road of Žilina to Poprad (16 km). The main European waterway is divided between the Baltic and Black Seas and crosses the lands adjacent to the community. Štrba originated in the 13th century on an extensive territory cloaked by forests owned by count Bogomír of Liptov. The oldest written reference to it is from 1280, and the ancient name of the community *Chorba* is associated with its location in a gap between the High and Low Tatra mountain ranges. The founder and the first hereditary mayor of Štrba, called Hotta, colonised the village with shepherds living around it. The community then belonged to the squire families of Szentiváni, Szmrecsáni and Bánov (three lines of count Bogomír's descendants). The people of this erstwhile serf community made their living from logging, sheep and cattle raising, burning coal and lime. They also made good quality sheep cheese and fur coats. From the end of the 16th century part of the population worked in the local saw mill. Later the villagers found new jobs in the construction of the Košice-Bohumín railway track 1871 which skirted the northern edge of the community and then the new Tatra community near Štrbské pleso lake. In difference to the other communities the older of the two churches in Štrba is the Evangelical one, which was built in 1784. The Classicist Roman-Catholic **church of St. Ondrej the Apostle** was built in 1844 on the site of a demolished medieval church from the 13th century. In the locality of Šoldov which is a part of the community used to stand a Romanesque abbey, which disappeared in the course of the 14th century. The last references to the ruins of the abbey appeared in the documents of the 19th century. Štrba was the place where Miloš Janoška (1884-1963), the author of the oldest Slovak tourist guide book to the High Tatras, lived and worked as a local teacher.

The community of **Tatranská Štrba** with the highest located railway station for rapid trains also belongs to Štrba. It is connected to the Štrbské Pleso by a rack railway. West of Štrba is the **nature reserve of Pastierske**. It was established in 1986 on an area of 2.93 hectares with the aim to protect the hygrophilous plant culture amongst other species of precious plants.

ŠUŇAVA (871 m, population 1,800) is one of the highest located sub Tatra communities, which lies 20 km from Poprad. It originated by the merging of the two communities of Vyšná and Nižná Šuňava in 1974. Vyšná Šuňava originated on the territory donated to count Bogomír of Liptov in 1269. Initially it was the property of the Carthusian monastery in Letanovce, and later it passed to another Carthusian monastery in remote Zamagurian region of Lechnica and finally it belonged to the Jesuits and a Religious Fund. The people here lived by farming and by working in the woods. The Roman-Catholic **church of St. Mikuláš the Bishop** in the community was built in 1832. The interior is older, predominantly in the Baroque style. The community of Nižná Šuňava was founded by the family of Szentiványi. The first reference to the community dates back to 1346. In the 15th century it belonged to the Cistercian abbey in Spišký Štiavnik and its last owner was the Religious Fund. The local Roman-Catholic **All Saints church** was built in Late-Baroque style in 1765.

In the forefront of the High Tatras, within a triangle between Štrba, Poprad and Veľká Lomnica are the seven sub Tatra communities which belong to the district of Poprad. Their territories in the past reached as far as the High Tatras which is why today they also include the valleys of Mengusovská, Štôlska, Batizovská, and Slavkovská dolina and the peaks of Gerlachovský and Batizovský štít.

Right: Easter in Šuňava

The community **MENGUSOVCE** (825 m, population 500) lies near the main road connecting Svit with Tatranská Štrba, 13 km from Poprad. It probably originated in the 13th century, though the first written reference to the community is from 1398. Mengusovce belonged for a long time to the Abbey of Štiavnica, and in the 16th century it was acquired by Albert Lasky and afterwards by the family Máriássy. The villagers were well-known trough-makers. Besides which they were busy in farming, namely cattle keeping. The local **St. Tomáš the Apostle church** is very valuable building. It was built in the second third of the 13th century in Early-Gothic style and rebuilt in the 17th century. Part of it is a precious Early-Gothic baptistery and wooden ceiling with paintings from the 18th century. The Classicist Evangelical **church** is from 1840. In the lower end of the village is a **log water mill** from the 18th century.

The small community of **ŠTÔLA** (840 m, population 500) lies 2 kilometres above Mengusovce to which it belonged until 1870. A forested area at the foothills of the High Tatras was donated by king Belo IV in 1279 to various nobles in order to have it settled. After Batizovce, Gerlachov and Mengusovce were founded, and colonisation also reached the forests at the left bank of the river Poprad it was once called *Stoly*. Historians associate the old name with the miners' expression *štôly* (in German *Stollen*) meaning pits, as there probably was some mining activity in here in the Middle Ages. On a clearing a spacious stone Benedictine monastery was built in 1314, but the monks did not stay for long under the Tatras. In the Christmas of 1318 the Archbishop of Ostrigom sent another group of Benedictines to the Spiš region who brought new life to the abandoned monastery. The monks lived on the support of the local aristocracy. Due to the fact that count Eberlauf of Spišská Sobota donated an uncultivated piece of land to the Benedictines around the monastery a new community today called Štôla originated. The monastery was burned down in 1526 and what remained the family of Máriássy used for the building of a manor house and an Evangelical rectory in Batizovce. The people of Štôla made their living from farming, sheep keeping and logging. And later in the 18th century they also sustained themselves by limba oil production. In 1938 the communities

were connected by a road from Vyšné Hágy creating the way for the origin of a new role – that of a holiday resort. Several tourist facilities were constructed above the community and many villagers are now employed in travel and tourism. There has been an Evangelical **church** in the community since 1870 with an altar painting made by the outstanding Slovak painter Peter Bohúň.

The nearby community of **BATIZOVCE** (756 m, population 1,900) is on a side road off Svit (2 km) to Tatranská Polianka (6 km). The community was founded by count Botyz, who was donated an extensive forest Chetene in 1264 by the king Belo IV, and fifteen years later he ordered his people to clear and settle it. Batizovce was originally a serf community belonging to the family of Máriássy. Its people lived by farming, coal burning, pottery and linen weaving, and in 1794 a linen bleaching plant was built in the community. In the 1930's the Baťa works were opened in the newly founded town of Svit and many villagers found jobs in the factory. The local brick-yard serving the construction of Svit was in production until 1965. The local Roman-Catholic **All Saints church** built in the mid-13th century in Romanesque style is worthy of attention. The prevailingly Baroque interior of the church is from the 18th century. The later Evangelical **church** in Batizovce is Classicist and built in 1791. Part of the altar is a valuable painting of Christ's Resurrection by Jozef Czauczik in 1814. An independently standing **belfry** also belongs to the church. There are two **manor houses** in the community, the older manor house of the 16th century was originally built in Renaissance style with later architectural alterations and the later Baroque manor house from 1756. Batizovce can boast of a special folk tradition with typical folk costumes, songs and dances, carrying on from the old folk artists who made fancy ornamental wooden coffers in the past, as well as remarkable embroidery and Easter eggs adorned by using a special scraping-out technique adding verses and plant motifs. The important nature historian and expert of the Tatras called Juraj Buchholtz Senior (1643-1725) lived in Batizovce.

Left: The landscape below the Tatra mountains

Three kilometres north of Batizovce is the small community of **GERLACHOV** (791 m, population 700). It is known especially because of giving its name to the highest of all Tatra peaks. It originated on an area covered by forests, a Máriássy property. The first reference to the community as Gerlahfalvya is from 1326. Its name commemorates the mayor Gerlach from Spišská Sobota. It was one of the first communities of the Tatra gold miners as shown by the two miners' hammers in its coat of arms. Besides searching for gold the people of Gerlachov lived by raising sheep, the production of limba oil and linen. In 1876 the community was almost entirely burnt down. To Gerlachov also belongs the Tatra community of Tatranská Polianka and the highest located Tatra mountain hotel Sliezsky dom in the Velická dolina valley. Of the Gothic Roman-Catholic **church of the Promotion of St. Cross** from the 13th century only the ruins, the tower, and the remains of the nave and foundations are left. The Classicist Evangelical **church** was built in 1800 and a century later it was rebuilt.

The community of **VEĽKÝ SLAVKOV** (677 m, population 1,100) is 5 km north of Poprad, where a tram runs between Poprad and Starý Smokovec. Numerous archaeological finds in the neighbourhood of the community bear witness to its medieval settlement dating back to the 13th century. A document of 1251 mentions it as part of the Turčiansky monastery estate. The community was colonised by Germans including it into the Association of the Spiš Saxons. In 1465 it became the property of Spiš Castle and simultaneously offered as a Polish forfeit along with other Spiš towns and communities. The inhabitants of Veľký Slavkov made their living by farming, sheep raising, linen weaving, charcoal burning and distillery. When the Germans left after the Second World War, families from twenty Slovak villages moved in. The Roman-Catholic **church of St. Andrej the Apostle** was built in the 13th century in Early-Gothic style and later it was altered in a variety of other styles. The largest reconstruction took place after an extensive fire in 1861. However, two original Gothic altars from this church are on display in the National Museum in Budapest. The Baroque-Classicist Evangelical **church** was built in 1788.

Further north is the community of **NOVÁ LESNÁ** (747 m, population 1,200) which was settled as early as in Lower Stone Age proven by the finds of channelled ceramics. The first reference to the community dates back to 1315 and was founded by the Berzeviczys' who owned a large part of the village until the abolition of serfdom. The people lived off the cultivation of flax and cartage. At present it functions as a typical as a holiday resort. The Roman-Catholic **church of Lord's Annunciation** in Nová Lesná was built in the second half of the 13th century in Early-Gothic style and in 1815 it was rebuilt in Classicist style. Another ecclesiastical church is the Classicist Evangelical **church** of 1792, restored after the fire in 1859. In Nová Lesná a teacher called Ján Still (1805-1890) lived here and was among the best experts of the Tatras and was also one of the first mountain guides accompanying the tourist to the Gerlachovský štít peak.

The sub Tatra community of **MLYNICA** (688 m, population 300) lies off the main road 6 km north of Poprad. It originated probably after the Tartar invasion by German colonisation. The first reference to it is from 1268. In 1465 Mlynica became a serf community of the Spiš Castle, and its last landlord was a member of the Csáky family. The people living here in the past were mostly farmers and linen weavers. As the name of the community suggests ("mlyn" means mill) there used to be several grain mills in the community. The Roman-Catholic **church of St. Margita of Antiochia** built in the mid-13th century is one of the most precious ones in the sub Tatra region. In spite of repeated reconstruction its older features are recognisable in its architecture. The main altar consecrated to the patroness saint originated in 1515 and is allegedly created by the Maestro Pavol of Levoča. The former Evange-lical church of Mlynica was used as a granary after the departure of the German citizens. In 1997 it was granted a new and interesting function when the members of the Veteran Club of Poprad restored it and established here a remarkable Auto-moto múzeum. Besides the collection of the material documenting the motor history, the founders of the Museum also established here a symbolic cemetery commemorating the victims of traffic accidents where recently a plaque dedicated to the late politician Alexander Dubček was included.

Auto-moto múzeum, Mlynica, tel.: 092/45 54 77
Opening hours: Tue-Sun 10:00-17:00h

The community of **GÁNOVCE** (650 m, population 800) is 5 km from Poprad and is well connected by road and railway. Gánovce is known for its unique archaeological finds, especially the famous travertine cast of the brain of a Neanderthal man (see page 29). The medieval history of Gánovce dates back to the early 14th century. In an act of 1317 among the owners of the community is one Bazilius, son of Gaan who is quoted as giving his name to the community. Gánovce belonged to the territory of the Spiš lancers. The more recent history of the community is connected with the **spa** which prospered in the second half of the 19th century and where digestive ailments were cured.

The Gánovce spa:

The therapeutic effects of the hot calcium hydrogen sulphate mineral springs were know by even the most ancient inhabitants of Gánovce. The description of the local mineral water by Juraj Wernher confirms that a spa existed here as early as in 1549. The old wooden spa community was pulled down by its new owner Augustín Korponay which were eventually replaced by modern balneological pavilions. But the low yield of the original mineral water spring did not allow for further expansion of the spa. Fortunately in 1876 a renowned mining expert and drilling technique pioneer, Viliam Zsigmondy, arrived in Gánovce and it was his idea to open a drilling bore here in April 1877. After two years and seven months the drilling works were prematurely stopped at a depth of 183 m as the thermal acidulous water was flowing out at a rate of 13.5l/sec. allowing the owner of the spa to use it as a swimming pool. Today, however, the Gánovce spa is closed.

Among the monuments in Gánovce the Early-Gothic Roman-Catholic **church of St. Michal the Archangel** built in the second half of the 13th century is of interest. In the presbytery and nave of the church some precious wall paintings from the 14th century can be seen, which represent a Christological cycle of the saints. The Gothic bell from the 14th century is also of considerable value. The Classicist **curia** in Gánovce is from the mid-19th century. A natural landmark of Gánovce are the travertine hills declared in 1985 as a protected nature formation. Since 1924 also the small community of Filice has become a part of Gánovce. Its existence is proved by an act of 1256 documenting the donation of the community by king Belo IV to the squire family of Filicko. Later it was divided between several landowners.

Right: The travertine of Gánovce

The main road in Poprad towards the eastern frontier of the district crosses four communities. Travelling towards Poprad the first of them is **HOZELEC** (695 m, population 700). The first reference to the community dates back to 1280, but it is probably older as it belongs to what was called the lancer villages. Hozelec was owned by the family of Mariássy until the abolition of serfdom. The people dedicated themselves, besides farming to the manufacture of a very fine linen. The only landmark of the community is the Classicist curia from the early 19th century.

The community of **ŠVÁBOVCE** (639 m, population 900) which is almost connected to Hozelec also boasts of a famous history and was a settlement at least in the Lower Bronze Age. In the 10th to 12th century a Slavic fort used to exist here. This medieval community was founded in the first half of the 13th century and in 1268 it was referred to under the name villa Sweui. In 1294 it was acquired by the family of Šváby giving the community its name and in 1578 it was sold to the family of Horváth-Stanish. Since 1870 manganese ore was extracted near the community. In addition to mining the population dedicated themselves to farming, weaving and sheep-raising. The Roman-Catholic **church of St. Filip and Jakub the Junior** in Švábovce is very old and was built in the first half of the 13th century in Early-Gothic style and later reconstructed. In the presbytery and nave Gothic paintings from the 14th century can be seen. The Classicist Evangelical **church** was built in 1806. Near the community is the **nature reserve Švábovská stráň** established in 1993 on an area of 18.26 hectares. It is interesting for the abundant occurrence of the plant *Adonis vernalis*.

More to the east is located the community of **HÔRKA** (610 m, population 1,300) which is the largest of the four communities that emerged in the mid-19th century. Together with Hôrka there belonged here the former independent communities of Ondrej, Kišovce and Primovce. Hôrka was first mentioned in an act from 1347 and **Kišovce** in 1324 and the people who lived in these communities were miners. In **Ondrej** archaeologists disclosed valuable finds of the Lower Stone and Bronze Ages. The medieval *Sanctus Andreas* was first mentioned in 1317. One curiosity about this small community is that it used to be the seat of the district court of justice. In Ondrej is the Roman-Catholic **church of St. Ondrej** from the mid-16th century. Originally an Early-Gothic building it was reconstructed in the 18th century. The community **Primovce** originated before 1312 on the grounds which were sold by count Henryk to Primo in 1248, giving his name to the community. Primovce was just like the rest of the surrounding communities being also a lancers' village. East of the community are the **Primovské skaly** rocks declared a **nature reserve** in 1982 on an area of 7.61 hectares protecting rare species of plants.

More to the east is located **JÁNOVCE** (591 m, population 1,100) the last village of the Poprad district on the road from Poprad (12 km) to Spišský Štvrtok (2 km). This former lancer village is documented by an act in 1312. Later it was included into the property of the Spiš Canonry. The villagers were mostly farmers, but by the end of the 19th century many of its inhabitants emigrated. The former Late-Romanesque Roman-Catholic **church of St. Katarína of Alexandria** from the 13th century underwent several changes of style. However, an original interior Gothic board-painting from the wing altar created in 1491 has been preserved (which today is in the Slovak National Gallery in Bratislava). The painting of the Virgin Mary is attributed to maestro Martin of Spiš. In 1963 Jánovce merged with Machalovce, the oldest written reference to this community is in 1209. Čenčice, the neighbouring small community merged with Machalovce in the period during the First World War.

The Comitat X of the Spiš Lancers:

In the twelfth century a specific autonomous unit of communities, called the Comitat X of the Spiš Lancers, also called the Small County was founded. The oldest lancers in Spiš were probably Slovaks of the Gemer region invited by the ruler to protect the northern frontier of Old Hungary. The name reflects their obligation to supply one lancer for each fourth house in case of war or rebellion. In 1243 the Old Hungarian king Belo IV confirmed numerous privileges to the lancers. Among them were exemption of taxes and tolls throughout the Spiš region, he also granted them hereditary rights to the property and the right to elect the judge. The Comitat X of the Spiš Lancers had its own coat of arms and a seal. Almost thirty communities belonged to it in the 15th century. Its highest body was a congregation ruling by statute over the inner life of the autonomy. The congregation was for a long time seated in Spišský Štvrtok, and the county, as a self-governing unit, disappeared in 1803.

Spišská Nová Ves
and its environs

SPIŠSKÁ NOVÁ VES (470 m, population 39,000) is the metropolis of the southern part of the Spiš region. It lies on the rim of the Hornádska kotlina basin below the point where the river Hornád leaves its canyon over the edge of the karstic plains in the region called the Slovak Paradise.

Its favourable location on the plain of the Hornád river terrace most certainly attracted the ancient people of La Téne and the Great Moravian periods who left here some traces of their existence. The medieval town originated on this river terrace in the course of the 13th century. The name *villa Nova* (New Village) in an act of 1268 denoted a new community founded by German colonists beside an older Slavic community called *Iglov*. This small mining town created from these two communities preserved the original German name. Its initial development was stimulated by the privileges of the Saxons living in Spiš granted by king Štefan V in 1271 and extended later by king Karol Róbert. The most important right for Spišská Nová Ves was the right to mine and extract the ores that allowed its people to use the rich deposits of copper, iron and silver ores found there. The first smelting plants and hammer-mills originated in the town and its environs during the 14th century, though it culminated only in the 18th and the first half of the 19th centuries. Among the traditional crafts was also the practice of bell-casting.

The bell-casting workshop of maestro Konrád:
Among the first clients of the famous bell-casting workshop in Spišská Nová Ves was allegedly king Ľudovít I himself. In 1357 he ordered maestro Konrád Gaal to cast a bell for his favourite city Visegrad. The reward for a satisfactory job was indeed royal. Instead of the usual wages the ruler granted the bell-casting workshop extensive privileges. After the death of maestro Konrád the shop passed to an equally skilful craftsman Ján Weyge. It was he who cast the bell of the Maria church in Kraków and the bell called Urban in the tower of Spišská Kapitula (the Spiš Canonry). In the second half of the 15th century the workshop was in the

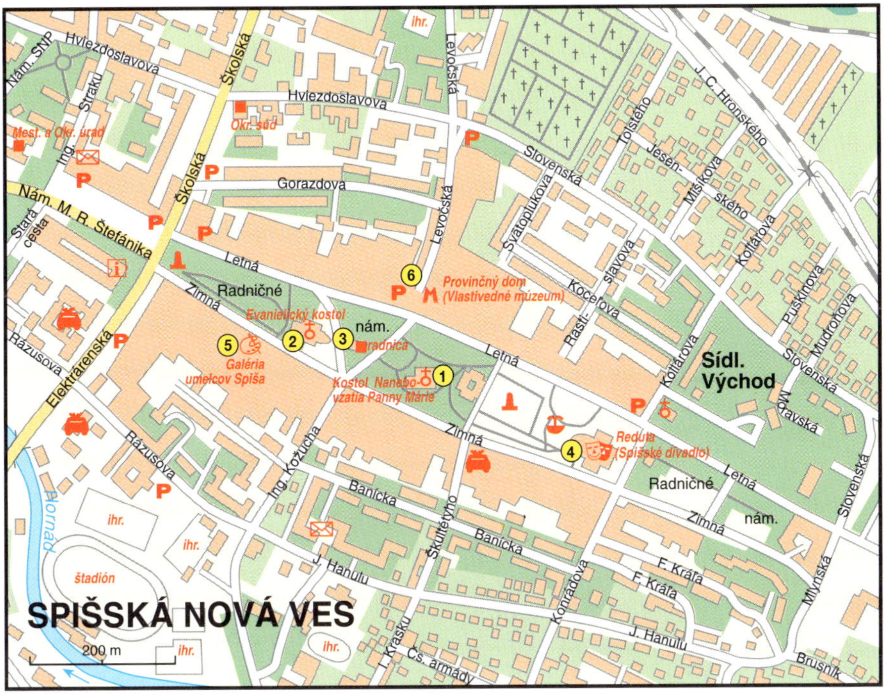

charge of maestro Ján Wagner who in addition to making bells created some precious Late-Gothic pulpits.

In the years 1412-1772 Spišská Nová Ves was included in the forfeit of the Spiš cities to the Polish ruler. In an atmosphere of certain anarchy, when the forfeited towns did not really belong either to Poland or to Old Hungary, Spišská Nová Ves gradually developed into one of the most important cities of the Spiš region. When it was promoted to the seat of a newly created province of sixteen Spiš towns in 1778, it became a serious competitor to Levoča, establishing its own identity. After 1871 the dynamic economic development of the city was stimulated by the Košice-Bohumín railway track. Numerous factories processing metals and wood, china and food items were founded in the town, and its rapid growth after the Second World War manifested itself in the construction of new municipal quarters and the up-dating of the industrial base was accompanied by a significant growth in population.

The historical core of Spišská Nová Ves consists of the spindle-shaped Radničné námestie (The Town Hall Square) tapering in the western end to Zimná street and in the eastern side to Letná street. Its most conspicuous building is that of the Roman-Catholic **church of the Virgin Mary's Ascension** (1). It was built in the second half of the 14th century on the site of an older church from the 13th century. In 1395 the still existing Gothic **chapel of St. Michal** was added to it. The later Gothic reconstruction in the course of the 15th century was necessary after damage caused by a fire in 1435 and an earthquake in 1441. Baroque adaptations were subsequently made in the years between 1742-1772. Its massive basilica with three naves and tower at 86 m is the highest in Slovakia. The last general repair of the church in 1954 removed some pseudo-stylish alterations made during the 19th century and revealed the Early-Renaissance paintings of the figures of the Evangelists painted in the years 1460-1470. The interior of the church has plenty of valuable works of the old masters. The most precious of them is the group of the Calvary made in the workshop of maestro Pavol of Levoča at the time around 1520 and the board paintings by maestro Martin painted in 1490. The Classicist Evangelical **church** (2) was built in 1790-1796 as an independently standing hall in the centre of the square. In its original interi-

or a precious altar painting of Jesus on the Mount of Olives by J. J. Stunder of 1797 is of considerable interest, as is the Classicist and detached building of the **town hall** (3) built in the years 1780-1820. Among the most important *fin-de-siécle* buildings in Slovakia is the building of **Reduta** (4) in Radničné square. It originated in the years 1890-1905 after a project by the architect K. Gerster. Numerous **burgher houses** skirting the square have a Gothic core from the 15th century, and in a house on Zimná St. is the dwelling of **Galéria umelcov Spiša** (5) (The Gallery of the Artists of Spiš Region) displaying many canvases, especially those of the renown native painter J. Hanula.

Galéria umelcov Spiša, Zimná St. 46, tel.: 0965/24 710
Opening hours: Tue-Fri 8:30-17:00h, Sat-Sun 8:00-12:00h

The conspicuous facade with rocaille ornamentation and allegorical reliefs of **provinčný dom** (6) (the Provincial House) on Letná St. no 50, a former seat of the provincial authorities, will certainly attract the attention of visitors. Today it functions as the **Vlastivedné múzeum** (the Museum of Natural History) with a variety of general historical, natural historical, artistic, musicological and ethnographic collections. In a house which stood on the site in the 15th century the armistice between Ján Jiskra of Brandýs and the Old Hungarian king Vladislav I was signed.

Vlastivedné múzeum, Letná 50, tel.: 0965/42 37 57
Opening hours: June-September Tue-Sun 8:00-17:00h, October-February Tue-Fri 8:00-16:00h, March-May Tue-Fri 8:00-17:00h, Sat 9:00-13:00h, Sun 13:00-17:00h

A favourite leisure area for the citizens of Spišská Nová Ves is the **forest-park Modrý vrch** which is a protected locality. The red-marked footpath heads to the chapel on mount Sansouci. At the top of the mount a beautiful panoramic view of the landscape of the southern part of Spiš awaits the vi-sitor. South of the city is the holiday resort of **Novoveská Huta**, once a climatic spa. Tourists may also enjoy the annual event held in Spišská Nová Ves in July, the **Spišské výstavné trhy** (Spiš Fair) a follow-up to the city's famous market tradition.

Left: The market in Spišská Nová Ves

Spišská Nová Ves is also the starting point for trips to the **national park of Slovenský raj** (The Slovak Paradise), a wonderful landscape where deep forests alternate with karst plains, canyons and caves. Many visitors like to visit the canyon of the river Hornád crossing it by the bridges hanging above the torrents of the river stream. The stone plateau Tomašovský výhľad offers a wonderful sight over the deep valleys of the Slovak Paradise, as well as the distant peaks of the High Tatras. Also the ascents by ladders placed in the deep rocky narrows of Suchá Belá or Veľký Sokol add to the experience of this beautiful natural location. In summer the deafening roar of the falling water contrasts to the silent winter solemnity of the frozen waterfalls all of which astonishes tourists. The karstic plains of Geravy and Glac are very pleasant for springtime walks over the meadows when in full bloom. Winter in turn is the time for skiers.

The most visited place in the southern part of the Slovak Paradise is the universally known **Dobšinská ľadová jaskyňa** or the Dobšinská Ice Cave.

The community of **SPIŠSKÝ ŠTVRTOK** (570 m, population 2,200) in the western part of the Hornádska kotlina basin is the place where the roads of Poprad, Kežmarok, Levoča, Hrabušice and Spišská Nová Ves meet. This advantageous situation was also exploited by the oldest fortified settlement at nearby Myšia hôrka about 3,500 years ago (see page 30). An original Slavic settlement complemented by German colonists after the Tartar invasions is referred to in the act of 1263. In the 14th century the community, thanks to the favourable position from the point of view of communications, developed into a small market town. However, it gradually submitted to the landlords of Spiš Castle and it was owned by them until the abolition of serfdom. In 1672 the Csákys' invited the Order of Minorites to build a monastery near the church in Spišský Štvrtok. In the 17th century the town lost its position as a significant settlement of the Comitat X of the Spiš Lancers and gradually sank to the level of neighbouring rural settlements. The most remarkable landmark of the community is the Roman-Catholic **St. Ladislav church** from the late 13th century, impressive for its Gothic architecture with additional Romanesque and Baroque features. In its interior is a precious 13th century Early-Gothic baptistery, and in the following century a **chapel of the Zápoľský family** was added to the church, built for the head of the Spiš province and an Old Hungarian paladin and his family. When it was completed, however, the owner deliberated about his burial place and decided to be eventually interred in another chapel, constructed near the cathedral of the Spiš Canonry. There is a precious Late-Gothic Pieta relief from the workshop of maestro Pavol of Levoča in the chapel. The Early-Baroque building of the former **monastery of Minorites** built in 1688 is today an asylum for old people.

SPIŠSKÝ ŠTIAVNIK (567 m, population 1,900)) extends along the bank of the river Hornád, 13 km west of Spišský Štvrtok. As early as in the 10th century there was a Benedictine monastery here giving origin to the community, first mentioned in 1446. After the Benedictines left, the monastery was occupied by the Cistercians, who came to Spiš from Wachoc abbey in Poland, invited by the owner of Spiš Castle, prince Koloman, son of king Ondrej II. The monks built in the community a Cistercian abbey, thereafter their property grew quickly finally expanding from Jánovce to Liptovská Teplička. The people living in this serf community made their living from farming and cattle raising, whilst the Cistercians possessed the local mill and ponds. The remains of the old pond dykes near the manor house are preserved until the present time. The abbey was sacked in 1530 by the feared robber-knight from Muráň, Matej Bašo and the heavily damaged monastery disappeared 13 years later. The Cistercian realm was invariably owned by a succession of owners. The village acquired its present form after a fire in 1906 which destroyed the majority of the houses. The local Roman-Catholic **church of the Virgin Mary** was built by the end of the 14th century in Gothic style and in Spišský Štiavnik rebuilt in Baroque style in the 18th. The Renaissance **manor house** stands on the left bank of the river, east of the community. It was probably built by the Thurzos' some time in the 16th century on the ruins of the former Cistercian monastery. The family of Thököly bestowed it a more respectable appearance and in the following century it served as a summer residence for the bishops of Spiš. It was twice reconstructed over the 19th century and its contemporary appearance is the result of the last reconstruction after a fire in 1925. The designer of the reconstruction project was the significant Slovak architect Dušan Jurkovič and since 1669 the **chapel of Annunciation of the Virgin Mary** has also belonged to the manor house. For its construction the original Gothic stone elements of the former Carthusian monastery in the Slovak Paradise were used and

visitors will certainly appreciate the altar painting of the Annuciation of the Virgin Mary of 1835 by J. Czauczik of Levoča.

Only two kilometres east of the monastery in Štiavnik is the former lancer community of **BETLANOVCE** (546 m, population 500) the birth place of the prominent Old Hungarian noble family Thurzo.

The Thurzos' of Betlanovce:

The Thurzo family were among the most important and wealthiest aristocrats in Old Hungary. Their ancestors were the squires of Betlanovce. They succeeded in ascending to the Old Hungarian high aristocracy because of their prosperous family business seated in Levoča, which concentrated on mining, smelting and metal trade. Together with the family of Fugger they led a trading company that acquired, for a certain time, a monopoly in the copper world market. Over the 16th and 17th centuries the Thurzos' enlarged their property by extensive lands in the Spiš, Orava and Považie regions including numerous castles, manor houses, towns and villages. For a long time they were also the hereditary heads of the provinces Spiš and Orava.

Behind the originally Gothic Roman-Catholic **church of St. Kozma and Damián** from the early 14th century stands the major building in the community – the Renaissance **manor house of Betlanovce**. It was built in the years 1564-1568 by Peter Faigel and his wife Elena Bobstová, for the rich Thurzo family. The manor house, with an impressive arched attic gable along the roof, represents the first Renaissance building of its type without fortification and bastions. On the nearby Zelená hora mountain (654 m) are the remnants of **Marcelov hrad** (Marcel's Castle) from the 13th century. In the first half of the 15th century this castle was the seat of the headquarters of the Hussites. Peter Aksamit used it as a base for his assaults. After they left the mayor of Levoča had it pulled down.

The city of **LEVOČA** is often considered the brightest jewel in the the Spiš crown. It lies near the northern edge of the Hornádska kotlina basin at the southern foothills of the Levočské vrchy mountains. The territory of Levoča was settled as early as the

Left: Spišský Štiavnik manor house

Lower Stone Age. In the time of the Great Moravia there existed an ancient Slavic fort here and the predecessors of medieval Levoča were several Slavic communities. In the second half of the 12th century they received the first German colonists, miners and poor landless people from Flanders. The original settlement structure was considerably changed by the Tartar invasions. On one of the sacked territories the first market town of the present city of Levoča originated. It was first mentioned in an act of 1249 as *Leucha*. The community, thriving from its advantageous position on the trade route Via Magna, rapidly grew into a town with numerous privileges. Shortly after, Levoča became the centre of German colonisation in the Spiš region and in 1271 it was even promoted to the capital of the Association of the Spiš Saxons, which eventually lost its influence and Levoča was declared a free royal town in 1323. The biggest impact on the economic development of the town was the right to store the goods imported from Poland, Silesia, Germany, and Russia, which it enjoyed until 1321. Later the priviledge was expanded to include goods from Old Hungary. The driving force of the Levoča's development was trade which gradually acquired an international dimension. The citizens of Levoča traded with Kraków, the Hanseatic towns and even with Venice. They mainly exported copper, iron, wax, leather, furs, corn, dried plums, and wine. The principal imported articles were salt, precious textiles, fish and spices. The craftsmen of Levoča produced not only for local consumption but also for the markets and fairs throughout Old Hungary and Poland. The most important guilds were those of the goldsmiths, coppersmiths and pewterers. In the 14th century Levoča in pursuing of the protection of its rights and privileges joined Košice, Prešov, Bardejov and Sabinov in an association of five Upper Old Hungarian towns called *Pentapolitana*. In the 15th century the economic boom was partially slowed down by the Hussite assaults into Old Hungary and the activities of the troops of Ján Jiskra in the Spiš region. The so-called two hundred years' war with its rival town Kežmarok (see page 223) did not favour its development either, and the first signs of its decline appeared in the 16th century, mainly because of the economic shift in inter-continental and overseas activities. The focus of European trade moved away from Levoča to the shores of the Atlantic after the discovery of the American continent. Trade and crafts also suffered from the disturbances typical for the 17th century brought about by the Turkish wars and the bloody Rebellions of the Estates. There is a curious historical novel and a film version, connected with the privileges of the honourable citizens of Levoča.

The land-gaining blood of the Levoča mayors:

The city itself had little available territory to realise its ambitions. In pursuit of its enlargement the city sent a delegation to king Karol Robert, reminding him of their assistance to him in beating the rebellious Matúš Čák, asking him for the land where their mayor bled to death. The king received the citizens of Levoča and his resolution was as follows: "Let the blood of the mayor of Levoča acquire land-gaining power". The sentence was added to the rights and privileges of the city and all the succeeding rulers confirmed it. The citizens used the act again when in 1700 the Spiš deputy head of the province, Pavol Görgeyi, shot and wounded the mayor of Levoča, Karol Kramler, during a New Year's hunt. Both were hunting on their respective lands when one of Görgeyi's favourite dogs entered the territory of Levoča where it was shot by the mayor. The deputy head of the province then shot and wounded the mayor and went home. The mayor's companions, instead of helping, raised him in their arms and carried his bleeding body over and around the Görgeyi's land which was due to be adjudicated to the city of Levoča. Later they carried home the dead body of the mayor and buried him without his right arm. Following Saxon custom his arm was cut away, embalmed and displayed in a glass cabinet in the town hall until his death would be revenged, and until that time all feasts were banned in the city and the citizens were obliged to wear black clothes. All these events are described by the writer Kálmán Mikszáth in his novel "The Black City" depicting an evocative atmosphere of this particular era giving the reader an imaginative insight into the life of the Levoča and Spiš people at the beginning of the 18th century.

The cultural and social life of the city actually advanced in the period of the onset of economic decline and Levoča became the regional centre of the Renaissance and humanism in Old Hungary. Since 1624 a Breuer book-printing shop existed in the city, and among its thousand or so volumes is the famous Comenius' work *Orbis Pictus* and a well-know Evangelical hymn-book by Tranoscius. Education and schooling thrived as well. The Jesuits obtained permission to found the first "gymnasium" in

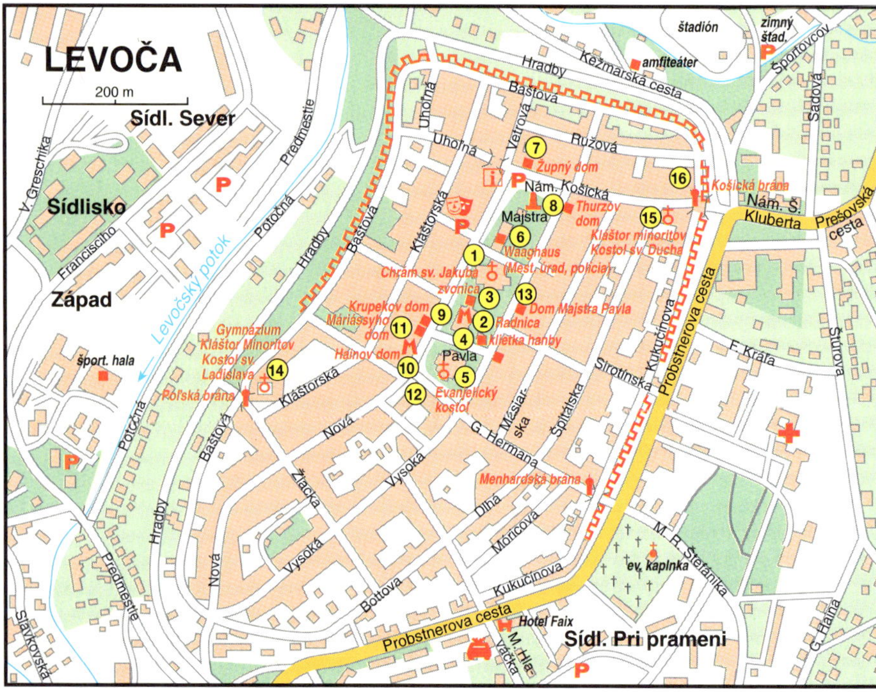

Levoča in 1672 from the emperor Leopold I. Besides other significant figures there is also the recognised physicist and astronomer Maximilian Hell who taught here. The local Evangelical lycée became an important centre of the Slovak national revival in the 19th century. In 1844 a group of thirteen students came here who left the lycée of Bratislava in protest against the official ban of the lectures of Ľudovít Štúr. It was in the Levoča lycée where the revolutionary song *The lightnings over the Tatras*..., later to become the national anthem of the Slovak Republic, was sung. Unfavourable modern developments which affected Levoča culminated in the construction of the Košice-Bohumín railway track, which avoided the city and the epicentre of southern Spiš moved to neighbouring Spišská Nová Ves. From 1996, almost after four decades, Levoča is again the seat of the district.

The **municipal monument reserve of Levoča** represents a complete set of important cultural and historical monuments bordered by oblong municipal walls. Gothic Levoča was entirely destroyed by an extensive fire in 1550. In the town hall precious documents were destroyed, some of which most certainly quoted the surname of maestro Pavol and other details respecting his life and the life of the city where he worked and lived. The restoration of the city destroyed by the fire gave it the Renaissance face which is preserved until the present time, observing the medieval ground plan with a rectangular street network from the year 1300. Examples of Baroque architecture are represented by the facades of some burgher houses. The focus of ancient Levoča is the large oblong square of Meastro Pavol -- **Námestie majstra Pavla**. In its centre two big three-nave churches and a town hall stand. The Roman-Catholic **St. Jakub church** (1) is one of the most important sacral buildings in Slovakia and is a national cultural monument. Originally Gothic it was built during the course of the 14th century on the site of an older church from 1280.

The Gothic St. Juraj chapel is of the same period. The church has undergone several alterations. The high slender tower of St. Jakub from the first half of the 19th century is the most distinct feature in the city's silhouette. Especially precious is the interior of the church, which is in fact a unique museum

Right: The main altar in the St. Jakub church

of medieval sacral art. The Late Gothic main **altar of St. Jakub** at a height of 18.60 m is the highest of its kind in the world. Made of lime wood in 1507-1518 in the workshop of Maestro Pavol of Levoča the carving, by the maestro himself, is of extraordinary high artistic value, whilst the board paintings are attributed to the painter Hans. Part of them are based in the patterns of the wood carvings of Lucas Cranach. The altar was exhibited in Montreal during the famous international EXPO'67 exhibition and achieved great acclaim there.

Majster Pavol of Levoča:

Majster Pavol (1455-?1530), considered the greatest medieval artist of Slovakia, lived for almost four decades in the creative atmosphere of Levoča. He was invited here around 1500 by the Thurzo family to lead the local wood-carving and painting workshop, whereupon he developed his exceptional talents under the tuition of the masters of Nuremberg and Kraków. The exceptional work of art of Majster Pavol is the outstanding wood-carving ornamentation of the Late-Gothic main altar of Levoča's St. Jakub church. Three main altar panels depicting the Madonna with child, St. Jakub and St. Ján the Apostle are the monumental pieces, and it is alleged that he included his self-portrait among the twelve statues of the Apostles in a wonderful composition of the Last Supper. However, Majster Pavol was not only a craftsman of genius but also a good tradesman and a respectable citizen of Levoča. The last record about him was found in the tax list of the citizens of Levoča of 1537.

There are another ten lateral altars in the church, six Late-Gothic, one Late-Renaissance and three Baroque ones. Also the collection of Gothic liturgical objects and a Baroque monstrance by the Levoča goldsmith Ján Szilassy is of immense value.

Kostol sv. Jakuba Apoštola (The church of St. Jakub the Apostle), Námestie Majstra Pavla, tel.: 0966/51 23 47
Opening hours: Tue-Sat 9:00-17:00h, Sun. 13:00-16:00h

The church neighbours with the arcaded building of the former **town hall** (2), built after the fire in 1550 and is one of the finest buildings of secular Renaissance architecture in Slovakia. It houses the collections of the **Spišské múzeum** (Museum of Spiš) dedicated to the history of the city.

Spišské múzeum,
Námestie Majstra Pavla, tel.: 0966/512 449
Opening hours: Tue-Sun 9:00-17:00h

Close to the town hall stands the Renaissance **belfry** (3). The **cage of opprobrium** (4) from the turn of the 16th and 17th centuries and was used in the past for the public humiliation of petty criminals. Today, together with the balcony of the town hall, it is the stage for historical theatre, especially for the performance of the White Lady of Levoča, a favourite summer show for visitors to the city.

The White Lady of Levoča:

The sad story about the White Lady of Levoča took place in the turbulent years of Levoča's siege by the emperor's troops in the early 18th century. The protagonist of the story, Júlia Géciová-Korponayová, saw her husband off to war after which she organised a ball in her house. In the festive confusion she stole a key of the gate to the city from the mayor of Levoča to let in the alien troops. The reason for her treacherous deed was her love for the commander of the emperor's soldiers, general Ján

Pálffy. However, later on she returned to the rebels, provoking the anger of her noble lover. Count Pálffy consequently imprisoned the unfortunate woman in the Castle of Červený Kameň where she was tortured and humiliated in all possible ways. Eventually her life ended in the Old Hungarian city of Rába where she was beheaded. The legend says that the spirit of Lady Júlia came back to her native city where she was seen walking on the city walls in a white gown, which gave her the name of the White Lady of Levoča.

The Classicist Evangelical **church** (5) was built in the years between 1825-1837 in the southern part of the square on the site of an older wooden church. The ground plan of the church is in the form of a Greek cross and it has a central dome. In the northern side of the square is a remarkable storehouse building – **Waaghouse** (6). It originated in 1588 as what was referred to as the building of the town scales. The merchants who came to Levoča in the past had to declare and store their goods at the store, which is today the municipal office. The neighbouring building of **Župný dom** (7) was built in the Empire style in the years between 1805-1831. It used to belong to one of the most representative buildings in Old Hungary and was the seat of the provincial office until 1922. The central square is skirted by more than 50 remarkable burgher and patrician houses, many of which carry the name of their former owners. Of especial interest is **Thurzo's house** (8), which acquired its Neo-Renaissance graffiti facade in 1904. Much older Renaissance facade paintings of the 16th century can be seen at the Late-Gothic **Krupek's house** (9). **Haln's house** (10) was temporarily the seat of the Evangelical lycée and was acquired by the Evangelical church as a donation from the son of Levoča's chronicler Gašpar Hain. Today it houses the exposition of Fine Art of Spiš, the Spišské Museum in Levoča.

Left: The cage of opprobium in Levoča
Right: Thurzo's house in Levoča

Spišské múzeum,
Námestie Majstra Pavla 40, tel.: 0966/51 27 86
Opening hours: Tue-Sun 9:00-17:00h

One of the most beautiful houses in Levoča is **Mariássy's house** (11) with an arcade courtyard. Similar arcade constructions used to surround the whole main square of Levoča before 1711. In a burgher house no. 36 the well-known **Breuer's printing office** (12) is seated. The famous wood carving workshop of Maestro Pavol has allegedly been located in the yard of **house no. 20** (13). An exposition of the Spišské Museum containing the material about the artist can be seen here.

Spišské múzeum,
Námestie Majstra Pavla 20, tel.: 0966/513 496
Opening hours: Tue-Sun 9:00-17:00h

In the side streets of Levoča another approximately 200 remarkable **burgher and craftsmen's houses** can be seen, many of which would grace any main square. In the neighbourhood of the Poľská brána Gate stands the former **old monastery of Minorites** and the **St. Ladislav church** (14). The monastic buildings were built into the town walls in the course of the 14th century. After 1671 the monastery was rebuilt by Jesuits in the Baroque style. After they left the monastery gradually fell into decay. On the site of one of the wings there emerged in the years 1913-1915 a gymnasium, which is an eclectic building. Near the Košická brána Gate is the **new monastery of Minorites** and the **St. Spirit church** (15) from 1753. The Baroque church has a well preserved original interior from the second half of the 18th century with frescos by the local painter O. I. Trtina. The decorator of the altar is the well-known painter J. Czauczik, a native of Levoča. The historical centre of Levoča is enclosed by the **town walls**. The oldest parts of the fortification originated back in the 13th century while the entire town was enclosed in 1410. The fortification consists of high inner and outer moat walls, with a water ditch which was two meters deep. The walls were fortified in several places by bastions and towers. There was an eastern **entrance gate** to the town called Menhardská and a southern one called Košická (16). A part of the southern fortification and the Dolná brána or Lower Gate were pulled down in the 19th century. Of the 2.5 km long original walls only about four fifths have been preserved. The Košická Gate has now been converted into a restaurant and the polygonal bastion near the new monastery of Minorites provides shelter to the museum of the blind. Today the unique artefacts of this museum are included in the **Múzeum špeciálneho školstva** (the Museum of Special Education) located in a burgher house on the Maestro Pavol square. The Museum is unique in Slovakia. It introduces the visitor to Levoča's long tradition in the area of assistance to the blind who have in this city a special school, printing office and a manufacturing co-operative.

Múzeum špeciálneho školstva,
Námestie Majstra Pavla, tel.: 0966/51 28 63
Opening hours: July-August Tue-Sun 8:00-16:00h
September-June Mon-Fri 8:00-16:00h

High above the town is **mount Mariánska hora** (781 m). Every year at the beginning of July Levoča becomes the meeting point of the largest pilgrimage in Slovakia. Ten of thousands of pilgrims in long queues ascend to the mount to render their gratitude to the Virgin Mary in the Neo-Gothic **church of the Virgin Mary's Visitation** from the beginning of the 20th century. In 1996 Pope John Paul II himself was one of the pilgrims. The **Levočská dolina valley** lying north of the town has several recreation and leisure amenities including ski tracks and ski lifts. In 1863 the Levoča spa originated here. The city also purchased a former wire making factory and converted it into a climatic spa. It closed after the Second World War.

SPIŠSKÝ HRHOV (481 m, population 900) is situated along the main road from Levoča to Spišské Podhradie. The community probably originated in the second half of the 12th century and the first written reference to it is from 1243. In 1278 a part of the village became the property of an old aristocratic family using the surname with origin in the name of the community – Görgey (alternation of consonants "g" and "h"). In this time two villages named Hrhov existed: Slovenský Hrhov acquired privileges pursuing purchasing rights in 1280. After the Tartar invasion the German colonists repopulated Nemecký (German) Hrhov. In the 14th century the Görgeys' owned also the whole land adjacent to the community and they always owned at least a part of its environs before the abolition of serfdom. In the period of the Reformation count Arnold de Gara founded a school for aristocrats, that existed in Spišský Hrhov until 1666. In the second half of the 19th century the Görgeys' property was sold to the family of Csáky who built here a distillery. The most important monuments of Spišský Hrhov are the village church and a manor house. The Roman-Catholic **church of St. Šimon and Júda** was built

in Early-Gothic style shortly after the Tartar invasion. Its prevailingly Baroque interior includes a precious painting of the Immaculate Conception by Jozef Czauczik from the period around 1830. The Neo-Baroque **manor house** from the second half of the 19th century was built for the count Viktor Csáky and designed by the Vienna architect H. Adam. This sumptuous building stands at the site of former family residence of the Görgeys'. Today it functions as an orphanage.

Since ancient times the heart of the Spiš region was the eastern edge of the Hornádska kotlina basin. The land was ruled from behind the walls of Spiš Castle by the heads of the region and the ecclesiastical life was organised in Spišská Kapitula (the Spiš Canonry) by the bishops, provosts, and canonists.

In a valley between these two centres of power the small town of **SPIŠSKÉ PODHRADIE** (435 m, population 3,500) originated probably as early as in the 11th century before the Tartar invasion. According to an act of 1174 this small foothill community settled by German colonists had its own church and a priest. Relation to the neighbouring Spišská Kapitula is expressed by the German name of the town *Kirchdorf* (Church village) still used at the time of the Second World War. A new wave of immigrants after the Tartar invasion helped the community towards rapid development and the acquisition of some municipal privileges (1321). In 1456 it obtained a market right, and in the 16th century the first craft guilds were founded. In 1671 an important trial took place in Spišské Podhradie the resolution of which drove the Evangelical priests out of 13 Spiš towns. By the late 19th century the town obtained a railway track joining the main Košice-Bohumín line, which stimulated the development of the local industry. Spišské Podhradie became famous for its travertine deposits and locally made tasty sausages.

The ground plan of medieval Spišské Podhradie was arranged in the form of a fork around the roads leading to Levoča, Prešov and Spišské Vlachy. The streets and squares of the town are skirted by originally Renaissance **burgher houses** sandwiched between houses of a later period. In the southern part of the Palešovo námestie square stands the Roman-Catholic **Birth of the Virgin Mary church**. Its contemporary Classicist form originated in 1829 on the site of a burnt down Gothic parsonage church of 1258. The most valuable items in its interior include the Gothic wing altar of St. Barbora from around 1500 and a Gothic baptistery made by Ján Weygel in the second half of the 15th century. The Baroque compound consisting of the **monastery of Charitable Brothers** and the **St. Ján of God church** originated in the years 1653-1658 by rebuilding of a medieval town spital of 1327 once administered by the Augustians. The monastic compound was later styled in the Baroque and adjusted for the purpose of the municipal workhouse, asylum and eventually a spital. On the main altar of the monastic church is a valuable altar painting of the Celebration of St. Ján of God by M. Speer dated 1737. The Classicist Evangelical **church** was built in the years 1799-1808. In the middle of the altar is a painting of Christ on the Mount of Olives by J. Czauczik from the period around 1835. In Mariánske square stands an originally Renaissance building of the old **town hall** from 1546 and the Baroque **Lady's Pillar** of 1726.

The **municipal monument reserve of Spišská Kapitula**, or the Spiš Canonry, extends on the hill west of Spišské Podhradie, administratively belong-

Left: St. Martin's cathedral in Spišská Kapitula

ing to the community. It acquired the position as being the ecclesiastical centre of the Spiš region way back in the 12th century. The religious setting evokes in the visitor a comparison of this small ecclesiastical townlet situated below the Spiš Castle to the Holy See. The primeval community preceding Spišská Kapitula developed in the 11th century in the neighbourhood of a fortified Benedictine monastery. The community and the monastery originated on an old road called *Via Magna* connecting the Spiš and Šariš regions. The provostship in Kapitula initiated its activity in 1198 and shortly after also the canonry was established here. Its destruction by the Tartars was soon followed by new construction and in 1245 the building of the cathedral was started and four years later the provost made use of the ruler's consent to build the provost palace. Numerous assaults of the ecclesiastical community at the end of the 13th century instigated the building of fortifications. A stone wall with bastions restricted the area of the medieval settlement which never achieved the characteristics of a town, but has been rather more a fort or clerical community divided in lots and adjudicated by the individual canonries. Since 1647 it was occupied by the Jesuits who built a monastery and gymnasium (secondary school) on the plot of the former workhouse. The gymnasium eventually moved together with Jesuits to Levoča in 1773. The provosts of Kapitula made a great effort to promote the provostship to a bishopric but always ran into strong resistance from the Ostrigom Archbishopric. Only in 1776 did Spišská Kapitula finally acquire the status of a bishopric the status of which it has kept until today.

The most important building of Spišská Kapitula is the Late-Romanesque **St. Martin's Cathedral** (1). It acquired its massive form of a three-nave building with two towers in the years between 1245-1275. In 1382 a Corpus Christi chapel was added to it, though it was replaced by the contemporary one in the years 1488-1493. This chapel of the family Zápoľský imitates the French chapel of Saint Chapelle. Baroque traits were erased by reconstruction in the years 1873-1889 in an attempt to give it a medieval character in line with the taste of the period of Romanticism. Also the main altar between the years 1470-1478 was modified at that time. The original lateral altars are more valuable, above all the altar of the Veneration of the Three Kings from around 1490 and the altar of the Death of the Virgin Mary created in the years 1477-1478. The stone sculpture of a lion *Leo Albus* from the second third of the 13th century belongs to the oldest of its kind in Slovakia. Also an untraditional secular wall painting of 1317 depicting the coronation of the Old Hungarian king Karol Róbert of Anjou is intriguing. The monstrance of 1740 by J. Szilassy is a national cultural monument. In front of the Cathedral stands the **statue of St. Ján Nepomucký** built in 1732. The **Bishop's Palace** (2) was built together with the Cathedral as a provost's palace, and from 1281 was the object of repeated Renaissance and Baroque reconstruction. A part of the palace is also a chapel. In the past there used to be a French park around the palace and its entrance was at the Clock Tower or **Hodinová veža** (3) from 1739. On the grounds of a former inn stands the building of the former **seminary** (4) from 1647. The original building of the Jesuit monastery was rebuilt in Classicist style for the needs of the seminary between 1810-1815. In 1943 a modern wing was added where future teachers studied. In the eastern part of the Spiš Canonry on narrow Gothic plots are the **canonries** of the Spiš canonists accessible only by one narrow lane. The **fortification** of this ecclesiastical townlet, with two entrance gates, was built in the 14th century and several times rebuilt. Its contemporary shape with two Late-Renaissance gates is from the second half of the 17th century, when Old Hungary was threatened by the Osman Realm. Fortunately, Spiš was spared the ignominy of Turkish occupation and other significant military assaults. The only exception was the penetration of a small Turkish squad into the Hnilická dolina valley and a failed siege of the mining town of Gelnica. In 1570 allegedly another Turkish squad reached the gates of Spišská Nová Ves, but historical sources do not quote the event and its probable consequences.

The eastern horizon of Spišské Podhradie is occupied by **Spiš Castle** standing on the land administered by the community of Žehra situated at the opposite side of the hill. As a **national cultural monument Spiš Castle**, with its area of more than 4 ha, and partially in ruins, is one of the largest castle compounds in Central Europe. In the period when the Spiš region was settled by the Celts there used to stand on the castle hill a mint where silver coins were made. According to legend it is probable that the present castle area was also inhabited by the Slavs at the time when a fort on the nearby Dreveník Hill existed.

The legend of Vesen and his sons:

A tribe of Old Slavs was brought here by the ruler Vesen. They paused next to a pair of conspicuous rocky hills standing in the centre of a broad undulant landscape. The two hills, were ideal places for the construction of new forts, which Vesen delegated to his two sons. Bystroň, one of his sons, started to construct his fort on the left hill and his twin brother Dragovit constructed his on the other hill. The cause of their later dispute was the beautiful Zorica, whom the brothers fought over. The fight was won by Bystroň and as a result the beautiful girl was to become his wife. However, Dragovit convinced Zorica to escape with him and the angry Bystroň burned down the brother's fort. Dragovit, however, managed to escape and his burned out fort on the hill Dreveník was never restored. In contrast, Bystroň's fort was rebuilt over the centuries to become the present day Spiš Castle.

Construction of the medieval castle on a travertine hill dates back to the beginning of the 12th century. The oldest written reference to the castle dates back to 1120. At the beginning it was a boundary fort placed at the northern frontier of an Early Feudal Old Hungarian state. Afterwards it became the seat of the head of the Spiš region for many centuries. At the centre of the Romanesque castle, built on the highest plain of the castle cliff, a massive round tower used to stand. It was replaced in the first third of the 13th century by another Red Tower and simultaneously the castle was expanded with a Romanesque palace. After the Tartar invasions the Old Hungarian king Belo IV granted the provost Matej of the Canonry to build a tower-shaped palace on the location of the present central court yard and a new castle chapel was also made for him. Spiš Castle resisted the Tartar assaults but the defensive system was, nevertheless, accordingly strengthened. During the building activity in the 13th century north Italian stone-masons were also involved. A new castle courtyard was built in the 14th century, and in the following century a small fort was built in this courtyard for the commander of the Hussite troops, Ján Jiskra. In the second half of the 15th century the reconstruction of the castle fell upon its new owner Štefan Zápoľský whose intention was to remake it into a representative aristocratic residence. He built a palace, a knight's hall and the chapel of St. Alžbeta. In one of the rooms of the castle his son Ján, later king of Old Hungary, was born. The last building works at the Upper Castle were constructed under the orders of the Thurzos' and the Csákys'. In 1780 the castle compound was destroyed by fire and the proud Spiš Castle gradually fell into ruin. Fragments of the interior furnishing were saved by moving them to a nearby manor house in Hodkovce. Some pieces enriched the collections of the manor house in Markušovce. The total decay of the castle was prevented only through the intervention of conservationists who in 1970 got down to the difficult job of preserving the walls and palaces threatened by the instability of its rocky base. Their enormous effort was rewarded when Spiš Castle was included in the **UNESCO list of monuments** belonging **to the world cultural heritage** in 1993. At present there are museum collections placed in the castle documenting its history, along with medieval arms and feudal jurisdiction.

Spišské múzeum, Spiš castle, tel.: 0966/81 13 66
Opening hours: May-September, Tue-Sun 9:00-17:00h

The landscape around the community of Spišské Podhradie can be seen comfortably by using the **tourist educational footpath Sivá Brada-Dreveník**, which has seven information boards along its route apprising the visitor about the seven travertine hills and the significant natural phenomenon of this part of the region. Its length is 14.5 km. The footpath starts at a mineral water spring in Sivá Brada, where drivers travelling by car along the main road from Poprad to Prešov frequently prefer

Right: Spišské Podhradie and the Spišský hrad castle

to stop. At the top of a low travertine hill stands a **pilgrim's chapel** of 1675. The hill is a fine example of a still "living" (in terminology of geologists) originating travertine form and has been a **nature reserve** from 1979. South of Sivá Brada is the the community **Baldovce**. The water of the local mineral spring is filled in bottles and sold as a favourite table water called *Baldovská*. The educational footpath heads eastward from Sivá brada towards the **nature monument of Jazierko na pažiti**, also a "living" travertine hill. The nearby **St. Ján Chapel** of 1776 offers a magnificent view of the cathedral Canonry and the Spiš Castle. The path then passes by the walls of the Spiš Canonry and beyond Spišské Podhradie it ascends to Spiš Castle standing on the highest travertine hill. Spiš Castle Hill (634 m) was in 1990 declared a nature monument along with the neighbouring Tertiary travertine hills of **Ostrá hora** and **Sobotisko**. The caves **Podhradská** and **Tmavá jaskyňa** lead into the rocks of the castle hill, which according to legend provided the castle people with a safe hiding place in the caves under the castle during the Tartar invasion. The largest travertine form in Slovakia is mount **Dreveník** (609 m) above the community Žehra, which entered in the list of **nature reserves** in 1953. The thickness of its travertines reaches in places as much as 100 m. The hill ends in plains originated at the end of the Tertiary period by the joining of several travertine hills. The edges of the hill have broken down as a consequence of weather and block sliding and form towers and gorges. The local people, endowed with imagination, attached interesting names to these bizarre rocky formations. One of the gorges is called Peklo (Hell) and the rocky city at the eastern edge is called Kamenný raj (The Rocky Paradise). On the western side of Dreveník are large travertine quarries where for centuries constructive and decorative material was extracted. Travertines are subject to karstification and it is the reason why the karst phenomena – sinkholes, dolines, fissures and small caves occur here. The educational footpath carries on along to the Baroque-Classicist **manor house in Hodkovce** from the 17th century where it eventually ends.

The community of **ŽEHRA** (442 m, population 1,300) is known for its precious local Roman-Catholic **Holy Spirit church** included in the list of **national cultural monuments**. A simple single-nave building with a square presbytery has kept its original Early-Gothic form until the present time. More recent is the vault of the church built in 1425 and the Baroque dome of the church tower. The interior of the ancient church contains unique medieval **wall paintings** originating in different stages since the third quarter of the 13th century to the first third of the 15th. The temple paintings in Žehrovce are remarkable for their artistic quality and unusual thematic diversity. They depict various Biblical stories and legends of the saints. The main altar is Early-Baroque dated 1656.

The community of **BIJACOVCE** (562 m, population 700) also deserves the attention of the visitor to the southern part of Spiš, which lies 4 km north-east of Spišské Podhradie, where there is a valuable Romanesque rotunda and a large Rococo-Classicist manor house built by the Csákys', after Spiš Castle was burned down in 1780.

SPIŠSKÉ VLACHY (389 m, population 3,400) is located 21 km east of Spišská Nová Ves near the place where the river Hornád leaves the Hornádska kotlina basin. The settlement of this territory is documented since the Upper Stone Age. The medieval history of the town goes back to the mid-13th century. Originally a Slav community it was repopulated after 1242 by colonists, according to some historical sources, Walloons. Others, however, assert that the colonists arrived from over the Alps, and were probably stone-masons from Italy invited to assist in the construction of Spiš Castle and the Spiš Canonry. Spišské Vlachy, after receiving the first privileges of the Old Hungarian king Belo IV in 1243, also acquired thirty years later other important royal resolutions exempting the town of the jurisdiction of the Spiš provost, and the community fell under the direct administration of the Estergom Archbishop. Until the 18th century copper ore was extracted here and carried to the local copper smelting plant. The traders and craftsmen of Vlachy benefited from the town's favourable position on the road from the Gemer region to Poland. As far as crafts are concerned, dyeing and stone masonry reached a considerable degree of mastery. Numerous men from Spišské Vlachy worked in the travertine quarry and the stone mason workshops in Dreveník. The 19th century was a period of stagnation. Only the construction of the Košice-Bohumín railway track in 1871 and jobs which became available in iron works in Krompachy prevented Spišské Vlachy from falling into deeper decay.

The spindle-shaped square is skirted by burgher houses, the oldest of which is from the 15th century. After a devastating fire in 1666 the appearance of the houses changed dramatically as the original gable roofs of the damaged medieval houses were replaced by saddle roofs. The square is dominated by the Roman Catholic **St. Ján the Baptist church**. Of the Romanesque buildings from around the middle of the 13th century very little is preserved. In 1434 the damaged church was pulled down and reconstructed in Late-Gothic style. Also the Late-Gothic baptistery is of the same period. Among the most precious items in its interior is a crucifix made in the workshop of Master Pavol of Levoča around 1520. Perhaps the most attractive building in the town is the former Gothic town hall from the 15th century situated in a fork which comprise the two main communications in the town. A part of this remarkable architectural monument serves today as the Roman- Catholic **church of the Ascension of the Virgin Mary**. Also the **Lady's pillar** with the statue of the Immaculation of 1728 stands in the square. In the southern part of the square an Evangelical **church** was built in 1787 and occupies the site of an original wooden Evangelical church destroyed by fire in 1727.

Once you are in Spišské Vlachy it is not far to **Plejsy**, an important ski resort near the town of Krompachy. It is very popular for its above-standard amenities. Due to its supplies of artificial snow and the high capacity of the ski lifts Plejsy can successfully compete with the best High Tatra ski resorts.

MARKUŠOVCE (445 m, population 2,900) is a community remarkable for its unusual concentration of historical monuments. It is situated on the bank of the river Hornád, 6 km east of Spišská Nová Ves. Markušovce originated some time at the beginning of the 12th century as a guarding village on the northern frontier of the early feudal Old Hungary. In an act of 1280 two communities are referred to, founded by an important aristocratic family called Máriássy who owned the community until the abolition of serfdom. They gradually built here a castle, several manor houses and curias. In 1663 a humanistic school for squires was founded here, unique in that the tuition was given in the Slovak language. The people of this serf community made their living from farming and many of them were

Right: Žehra – wall paintings

employed in the mines. In the western part of the community stands the **castle of Markušovce** built in 1284. In the 14th century a Gothic palace and fortification were added to it. The continuous quarrels of the lords of the castle with the city of Levoča and other Spiš towns wound up in the destruction of the castle in 1527, which the Máriássys' started to reconstruct eleven years later. Numerous branches of the family, however, moved to more comfortable manor houses and the abandoned castle gradually fell into ruination. The most representative building in the village is the manor house, built in 1643 by František Máriássy. The original form of a Renaissance fort with round towers at the corners was changed during extensive reconstruction in 1773 when it acquired a Rococo style. Shortly after, because of the expected arrival of emperor Josef II, the **summer residence Dardanely** was built in the garden. Even the most astute visitor will probably fail to realise that the lateral wings were finished only in the 1970's. The summer residence now houses the **Vlastivedné múzeum** or the Museum of Natural History containing, besides other objects of interest, an exposition of key musical instruments, a unique example being the "giraffe piano". An exhibition of historical furniture located in the building of manor house is under reconstruction at present.

Left: The manor house in Markušovce

Vlastivedné múzem, Letohrádok Dardanely,
tel.: 0965/49 82 12
Opening hours: June-August, Tue-Sun. 8:30-17:00h, May-October Tue-Fri and Sun 8:30-17:00h, the remaining months Mon-Fri 7:30-16:00h

Another two manor houses in Markušovce were built in the late 18th century in Baroque or Baroque-Classicist style. Originally a Late-Romanesque Roman-Catholic the **church of St. Michal the Archangel** is extremely old, built before 1280. A visit to Markušovce can be refreshed by a pleasant walk around the community. A yellow-marked footpath leads from the community to the **stone mushroom of Markušovce**. At its northern edge it passes by a geological exposure demonstrating the covering of the Mesozoic limestone by the sea sediments of the Palaeogenic sea. Both localities are nature monuments.

Turistická informačná kancelária – Slovakotour, Gäceľská 1, 026 01 **Dolný Kubín**
Tel.: 0824/186, 223 07, Fax: 0824/211 22

Kežmarská informačná kancelária, Hlavné námestie 46, 060 01 **Kežmarok**
Tel./Fax: 0968/40 47

Kultúrno informačné centrum, Nám. Majstra Pavla 58, 054 04 **Levoča**
Tel.: 0966/186, 51 37 63, Fax: 51 04 16

CK N – REISEN, Ul. SNP 324/12, 033 01 **Liptovský Hrádok**
Tel./Fax: 0844/22 31 75

Informačné centrum mesta Liptovský Mikuláš, Nám. Mieru 1, 031 01 **Liptovský Mikuláš**
Tel.: 0849/186, 51 44 49 Tel./Fax: 0849/5144 48, Tel./Fax/Mod.: 0849/224 18
e-mail: infolm@trynet.sk

INC, a.s. Námestovo, Nábrežie Oravskej priehrady, 029 01 **Námestovo**
Tel.: 0846/53 25 52, Tel./Fax: 0846/52 37 77

Popradská informačná agentúra, Nám. sv. Egídia 2950/114, 058 42 **Poprad**
Tel.: 0838/186, 72 17 00, Tel./Fax: 092/72 13 94

Kultúrne a informačné centrum, Madačova č. 3, 034 01 **Ružomberok**
Tel.: 0848/186, 32 10 96, Fax: 0848/32 32 16

Turistické informačné centrum, Nám. M. R. Štefánika 10, 052 01 **Spišská Nová Ves**
Tel.: 0965/186, 42 82 92, Fax: 0965/42 69 80

Informačné centrum mesta Stará Ľubovňa, Nám. sv. Mikuláša 12, 064 01 **Stará Ľubovňa**
Tel.: 0963/217 13, Fax: 0963/230 33

Tatranská informačná kancelária, Dom služieb, P. O. Box 7, 062 01 **Starý Smokovec**
Tel.: 0969/186, 42 34 40, Fax: 0969/42 31 27

CS TOUR, Trojičné námestie, 027 44 **Tvrdošín**
Tel.: 0847/186, 32 31 11

TIK Zuberec, č. d. 248, 027 32 **Zuberec**
Tel.: 0847/39 51 97, Fax: 0847/39 53 59

THE POLISH TATRAS

LOCATION

The Tatras are the highest mountain range of the whole Carpathian massif and accordingly the highest in Poland. They represent a natural barrier separating Poland from Slovakia. The part of the Tatras belonging to Poland constitutes a continuous state border. The northern rim of the mountain range is emphasised by the deep Rów Podtatrzanski (The Sub Tatra Furrow), enclosed in the north by the Pogórze Spisko-Gubałowskie mountain range. At the foothills of Giewont in the middle of the furrow is Zakopane, the main tourist centre of the Polish Tatras. North of the Tatras is the region called Podhale. It comprises the Rów Podtatrzanski, Pogórze Spisko-Gubałowskie mountain ranges and the extensive Kotlina Orawsko-Nowotarska basin. In its centre is the Kotlina Nowotarska basin. At several points in the Pogórze Spisko-Gubałowskie mountain range isolated limestone cliffs appear, the summits of the Pieninski Pas Skałkowy (the Pieniny cliff belt). All these rock formations are part of the Polish inner Carpathians, whereas in the north they border on to the outer Carpathians. The border between the two basic reliefs is very pronounced and easily identifiable. The Beskidy mountains are the northern limit of the described area.

All the above mentioned mountain ranges follow in the direction of geographical parallels and their borders are clearly distinct. The southernmost landmark is the highest peak of the Polish Tatras – Rysy (2,499 m) situated in 49°11, latitude north and 20°10, of longitude east. The northernmost part of the Nowotarska Kotlina basin extends up to the geographical parallel of 49°29, latitude north. The length of the region measured from north to south is almost 37 km. The distance between the westernmost point on the shore of the Orava Dam and the state border near Niedzica in the east reaches 50 km. The area is comprised of three historical regions: Podhale, Spisz and Orawa, the latter two being separated by the state border. The larger parts of Spisz and Orawa are in the Slovak part of the Tatras, the whole area, however, is situated within the Nowosącske Wojevództwo county.

Above: Giewont

THE NATURAL SETTING

GEOLOGY AND LANDFORMATIONS

The geological history of the High Tatras is almost 300 million years old. It is the time that elapsed since the moment when in this area boiling lava penetrated the Earth's crust and gradually it cooled down creating a granite massive deep under the Earth's surface. This is how the transformed rocks – gneiss and crystalline shales originated. Later this area was subject to further reshaping through erosion and denudation over the course of approximately 70 million years. By the end of the Palaeozoic age the process resulted in an extensive plain agreeing in the area of what are now the Tatras. The whole plain was flooded by the Mesozoic sea. The sea was more shallow in the northern part and deeper in south. Sediments of different thickness were deposited here. During the Lower Mesozoic era quartzose sandstone and various kinds of limestone originated at the bottom of the sea. The sea left here thick limestone sediments with skeletons of extinct animals. In the time of the Upper Mesozoic period strong tectonic movements, connected with alpine orogenic movements, occurred in the Tatras. As a consequence of this activity folded series of sediments were separated from their base and carried on further to the north. A series of nappes originated during the process. The Tatra crystalline rock was covered by the nappe of the Czerwone Wierchy mountains and in turn by the Giewont nappe, both of which were covered by the Krížna nappe. In the Tertiary age the area of the Tatras was flooded by the sea, leaving here conglomerates, sandstones, limestones and dolomites.

The Tatras represent a mosaic of various rock formations. The most important ones are the Palaeozoic rocks forming the crystalline core of the Tatras. The Tatry Wysokie (The High Tatras) mountains are made of granitoids, but the crystalline cores of the Zachodne (West) Tatry mountains are created mainly by the transformed rocks. The Choč nappes – Czerwone Wierchy and the Giewont are highly projected mountains over the upper timber line.

Right: The Valley of Five Polish Lakes

The sleeping knights:

It is said that here are knights sleeping in the Tatras waiting for the proper moment to go on fighting for the freedom of Poland. The biggest of them changed into a stone, the mountain Giewont, where he lies on his back with his head looking west. A shield is visible on his crossed arms. When Poland lives through bad times the knight tries to get up and fight for truth and freedom. The last time when it happened was in 1981 when warfare was declared in Poland. The stones and boulders that fell down from Giewont were proof that the warrior tried to get up. When the news reached Warsaw the arguing parties gathered around a table and peace was negotiated. Thus the knight calmed down and fell asleep again.

The forms of the Krížna neighbour in the north with the Tertiary sedimentary rocks, creating the **Rów Podtatrzański** and the **Pogórze Spisko-Gubałowskie**. Conglomerates, dolomitic sandstones and organic limestones can be found here. There are also classic sediments of the Podhale flysch made of sandstones and clayey shales. The Podhale flysch consists of three geological units, which are called the zakopiańskie, chochołowskie, and ostyskie layers. Enormous tectonic movements ripped open the flysch of the Podhale and a number of faults originated. Its northern border coincides with a belt of cliffs. Its single higher formations emerge from under younger forms in Stare Bystre, Szaflare and in a stone gate created by Kramnicę and Obłazowa. Further to the north the cliffs are denuded and represent the back of Branisko-Hombark, also called the **Pieniny** and the **Małe Pieniny mountains**. The cliff belt was subject to folding on three separate occasions, resulting in a huge difference in altitude within the belt and some of the isolated cliffs, accompanied by the disruption of the continuous layers.

The **Kotlina Orawsko-Nowotarska basin** is an extensive tectonic depression filled by younger sediments. There used to exist here a big lake in the Upper Tertiary period later filled by scree and earth of the Tatra and Beskidy mountains carried here by the rivers. It was prevailingly gravel and clay and their thickness reaches in places approximately 300 m in the Orawian part of the basin. These series were covered by the Quaternary forms. Their surface is slightly inclined to the north and channels the valley of the river Dunajec towards the slopes of the Beskidy mountains.

The Polish part of the Tatras comprises the northern fragments of the **Zachodne and Wysokie Tatry mountains**. The whole mountain range of the Belianske Tatry mountains is in the territory of Slovakia. The border between the Wysokie and Zachodne Tatry mountains stretches from the Przełęz Liliowy saddle to the northeast passing the valley of Sucha Woda. The distribution of the highest Tatra peaks geologically evolved mainly by the resistance of the rocks and the degree of uplifting and the mountainous character of the landscape occurred through the landforming processes, especially the Quaternary glaciers. Because of more intense uplifting of the Tatras in the south the highest peaks like Gerlach, Łomnica, Lodowy Szczyt, and Bystra are beyond the Polish border. The highest peak of the Polish Tatras is **Rysy** (2,499 m) which is made of granite. The highest Polish peak in the Zachodne Tatry mountains, Starobociański Wierch or Klin, is only 2,176 m high and is made of gneiss and crystalline shales. The highest summit situated out of the region is Krzesanica with its 2,133 m. It stands within the group of the Czerwone Wierchy mountains.

The effects of geological activity on some parts of the Tatra relief are very pronounced. The weak resistance of the Mesozoic formations made possible the origin of Borowieckie, Iwaniackie and Tomanowo saddles and the caves originated in the limestones and dolomites of the Zachodne Tatry mountains. Altogether we know about 650 such caves, the biggest of them being the Wielka Śnieźna cave, which is 776 m deep and its corridors are in total more than 15 km long. Unlike the Belianska jaskyňa cave situated in Belianske Tatry mountains in the Slovak territory, these caves either lack entirely the dripstone decoration, or at best it occurs only sporadically.

The rocky surface karst creates formations like chimneys, bastions and rocky needles which can be seen here the same as in the Slovak Tatras. The most beautiful examples of karst phenomena are in Dolina Małej Łaki valley, and the karst springs and caves are located in the valleys of Kościeliska, Bystra and Chochołowska. The geological creation, and above all the permeability of the base, caused the glaciers in the granite rock of the Polish Tatra mountains to be much longer than in the limstones of the Západné Tatry mountains. The glaciers in

Bielovodská dolina and in Mengusovská dolina valleys were 14 and 11.5 kilometres long respectively. The biggest glaciers in the West Tatra mountains were mostly on the Slovak side but they were always shorter than 10 kilometres.

The result of repeated glaciation of the Tatras altered the shape of most of the glaciated valleys. Consequently, the U-shaped valleys and lateral valleys originated so that their ends are placed higher than the bottom of the main valley – ideal conditions for the origin of waterfalls like the Wodogrzmoty Mickievicza waterfall. Also the origin of the deep glacier cirques, precipices and moraine ramparts in the bottoms and on the flanks of the valleys is bound up with the activity of such glaciers. Extreme weather conditions during the Quaternary period, caused by frost, led to the origin of the peaks, ridges, crests and numerous other rocky formations typical for an alpine system. By the end of the glacial period the surplus thaw water carried large amounts of rocky material to the foothills of the Tatras creating extensive alluvial cones at the bottom of the Orawsko-Nowotarska basin. Chunks of ice buried under the moraine gradually thawed and eventually created some of the Tatra lakes. This was how the Staw Smerczyński lake originated. The biggest and deepest Tatra lakes are in the glacier cirques.

The contemporary landforming processes are mainly caused by intense seasonal weather under the effect of sun radiation, frost and rain, which washes the eroded material down the slopes by way of avalanches or gradual collapse. Consequently, troughs were formed ending in a debris cones (in Polish piarg). These cones are slowly moving towards the lakes and gradually cover them. The results of this geological activity can be observed near the Morskie Oko lake and the Czarny Staw Gasienicow lake. Also the limestone rock faces of Pieniny mountains are subject to the effects of the weather, where the bottoms of the valleys show traces of lateral erosion. In cases of long term undercutting of the slopes imbalances can occur causing landslides. The formations and processes of this activity can be seen in the Pogórze Spisko-Gubałowskie mountains and on the left slopes of the Dunajec valley between

Left: Winter in Hala Gąsienicowa mountains

Climatic indices of selected weather stations in the Polish Tatras:

Station	Altitude above sea level *(in m)*	Annual total of precipitations *(in mm)*	Mean annual air temperature *(in °C)*
Nowy Targ	593	857	5,7
Poronin	778	975	4,7
Zakopane	844	1 129	4,9
Kuźnice	1 023	1 529	4,2
Myślenickie Turnie	1 360	1 563	3,4
Hala Gąsienicowa	1 520	1 610	2,4
Kasprowy vierch	1 991	1 817	– 0,8

Nowy Targ and Dębno. In some reaches of the rivers flowing across the Orawska-Nowotarska kotlina basins gravel accumulates and it is connected with a still lasting very slow movement.

CLIMATE

The Tatras create a distinct climatic barrier between Slovakia and Poland. The higher exposure of southern slopes to the sun and easier access of the warm air from the south cause considerable climatic differences between the Polish and the Slovak parts of the mountain range. This is the reason why there are different climatic zones on the southern and the northern sides of the Tatras.

The climate of the Tatras, however, is typical for mountainous regions, characterised by the zones of altitude which affect the basic elements like mean annual air temperature and mean annual precipitations. The mean annual air temperature in the Tatras changes accordingly with increased altitude from +6 °C in Kotlina Orawsko-Nowotarska basin to -4°C at the highest points. The annual difference of air temperature also correspondingly falls according to the variations in elevation, as well as the number of days of occurrences of frost. There are 50 days of frost at the foothills of the Tatras and more than 200 in the highest peaks. Another typical phenomenon in the Tatras and the Podhale region is the winter and spring inversions of temperature. That is the reason why the annual mean temperature in Zakopane is higher than in the lower situated town of Poronin. The precipitiation total on the Polish side is much higher than on the Slovak side. They are mostly snow precipitations. The number of days with snow cover increases from 100 in the basin to 290 in the highest peaks. The climatic frontier of permanent snow runs in the Polish Tatras at an altitude of 2,200 m and depending upon the morphological conditions it is probable that also some small glaciers might originate here.

In the same way the higher the altitude above the sea level the greater the prevalence of windy days. A particular wind, called in Polish *halny*, is a strong gusty southern wind also called fall-wind, which reaches the strength of a hurricane causing considerable damage to forests, especially in the higher tiers of vegetation.

In 1968 this wind caused such damage that traces of its devastation are still evident today. Halny is a warm wind which descends to the furrow of Rów Podtatrzański, which speeds up the snow-thawing process in winter and spring, besides which it negatively affects the psychic and physical condition of humans. It is especially dangerous for people suffering from heart diseases.

Halny wind:

"Put out the fire, put out the fire" shouted a Goral who was once walking the streets of old Zakopane when the halny wind came. As it approached the wind tore off the tops of the spruce trees, lifted the roof shingles and forced the smoke down the chimneys of the village huts. Because of the likely danger of fire (caused by sparks) it was necessary to extinguish every household fire. In the

The ten biggest lakes in the Polish Tatras

(in ha)

1.	Morskie Oko	34,9
2.	Wielki Staw	34,3
3.	Czarny Staw	20,6
4.	Czarny Staw Gąsienicowy	17,9
5.	Czarny Staw z Pięciu Stawów	12,7
6.	Przedni Staw	7,7
7.	Zadni Staw	6,4
8.	Zielony Staw	3,8
9.	Długi Staw	1,6
10.	Kurtkowiec	1,5

past the effects of the halny wind was a notorious cause of fire, which in some incidences destroyed an entire community.

Based on the mean annual temperature six climatic zones are distinguished in the Tatras, the coldest being at the highest points. Its lower frontier in the northern part of the Tatras, runs at an altitude of 2,200 m and in the southern part it is more than 100 m higher. The lower frontier of the next, moderately cold zone starts at an altitude of 1,800 (2,000 m on the Slovak side). The mean annual temperature of the cold zone oscillates between – 4 °C and – 2 °C and in the moderately cold zone it is between – 2 to 0 °C. The two lower situated climatic: the very cool and the cool are separated from each other by the upper timber line of the Polish Tatras at an altitude of 1,550 m. Above this height, at 1,850 m the mean annual air temperature shifts between 0 and +2 °C. In an area of cool zone, the lower limit of which runs at an altitude of 1,150 m, the temperature increases by 2 °C (2-4 °C). Moderately cool and moderately warm zones are situated lowest. The border between them runs at the altitude of 700 metres. Orawsko-Nowotarska kotlina basin for instance is situated in moderately warm zone. And as it is basin it retains frosts in winter and air temperatures are sometimes very low. The town Jabłonka lying in the basin was the place where the lowest temperature ever taken in Poland (almost –40 °C) was recorded.

Right: Morskie Oko lake

WATER

The lakes of the Tatras are the most picturesque part of the mountain range and therefore the final destination for many tourists. There are twenty such decorative lakes in the Polish part of the mountains. The biggest and the deepest of them fill the glacier cirques, the remnants of the Glacial period. The smaller and shallower lakes are in the area of moraines. Their water is partially mineralised with small amounts of phytoplankton. Fish are found only in Morskie Oko lake. The Tatra lakes are gradually silted by debris, largely caused by avalanches, or overgrown by plants. The lakes are supplied by the torrents and brooks that flow northward to the valleys. In the Zachodnie Tatry mountains, in an area with a frequent occurrence of carbonates, the brooks are fed by highly abundant karst springs. The best known are the Chochołowski and Olczyski springs, and the Bystra and Lodowe Źródlo springs in the Kościelska dolina valley.

The crystal clear water in the Tatras is one of their biggest assets. Thanks to abundant rainfall the highest run-off in one square kilometre in Poland is recorded here – it amounts to 30 litres per second, but does vary in the course of the year. The highest volumes are reached in May to October.

The argument over the Morskie Oko lake:

Some boundary areas of Poland and Old Hungary have been subject to numerous arguments as early as the 16th century. Also the valley of the Rybí potok brook and the Morskie Oko lake have been the object of much dispute. By the end of the 19th century argument turned into conflict between Wladyslaw Zamoysky, the owner of Zakopane estates and the Prussian prince Christian Hohenlohe, who bought a part of the Tatra lands. In 1901 an international arbitration was formed, whose task was to determine where the frontier between Old Hungary and southern Poland-Halič, which then belonged to Austria, should be drawn. The court of justice was chaired by the Swiss Johann Winkler. The court which sat in Graz, Austria, surveyed the disputed locality and determined on September 13, 1902 that the course of the frontier should run from the Rysy mountain, passing the Žabí hrebeň crest,

to the Rybí potok brook. This frontier still exists today. The Morskie Oko lake belonged to Halič, and 20 years later to Poland.

The Polish part of the Tatras lies in the draining area of the river Dunajec. The river Dunajec is the result of the confluence of the rivers Biały Dunajec, Czarny Dunajec and Białka and is the biggest Carpathian tributary of the river Wisła. European water divide separating the area feeding the Baltic sea from the one feeding the Black Sea passes the Orawsko-Nowotarska kotlina basin.

The Slovak Orava Dam also reaches the territory of Poland, and another water dam in the Kotlina Orawsko-Nowotarska basin is under construction in Czorsztyn. Its area will be 13 square kilometres. There is also a reservoir in Sromowce which regulates the water table of the Dunajec at its most beautiful point. The Dunajec passes the Pieniny mountains, through a picturesque canyon starting in Sromowce and ending in Szczawnica. The depth of the valley, in this 9 km long section, is in places as much as 500 m, and its width occasionally tapers to just over ten meters. This is where the Dunajec creates a natural boundary between Slovakia and Poland. An attraction for tourists is the navigation of rafts along the most interesting part of this admirable landscape, which starts in Sromowce in Poland and ends two hours later in Szczawnica.

SOILS, VEGETATION AND FAUNA

The Tatra and sub Tatra soils originated on different rocks. Alkaline soils developed on limestone and crystalline rocks and sandstone gave origin to the acid, calcium carbonate-free soils. Brown soils occur in a lower vegetation tier or zone under variegated forestation. Podzol type of soil is found in the upper vegetation tier with prevailing fir and spruce trees. Higher in the alpine and dwarf-pine tier the peat and gleyic soils occur, whilst rendzinas are usual to a limestone base. In the valleys and foothills of the Tatras sandy-gravelly soils are common. These soil layers are comparably barren and shallow throughout the whole Tatra region.

The vegetation in the Tatras is organised in clearly distinguishable vegetation tiers, which is the obvious result of climatic conditions and the northern exposure of the majority of the slopes. With increasing altitude above sea level the number of species of plants decline. For instance, the blooming plants of the lower tiers are represented by 665 species, while at an altitude of 2,000 m there remains only 200 of them and even higher, at 2,500 m only 16 of them occur. Besides the climate also the geological structure of the underlying rocks determines the variety of the plant species. Some plant communities prefer a limestone base others thrive on granite or siliceous rocks. Rare species occur on the debris cones, southerly exposed limestone rock faces, or in snow fields.

The lowest vegetation tier is sub-mountainous comprising the region lying out of the Tatras. It is mostly agricultural land. The whole of the Kotlina Orawsko-Nowotarska basin and a great part of the valleys of the Białka, Biały and Czarny Dunajec rivers belongs to this tier. Typical are the spruce-pine forests covering extensive alluvial cones and peat bogs in the area of the Czarny Dunajec and Orawa water divide. Some dwarf-pine forests can be found here. On the left bank of the river Biały Dunajec, north of Nowy Targ, a **peat bog forest reserve** called **Bór na Czerwonem** was established. Out of agricultural crops some species of oat, potato, rare barley, resistant to raw climatic conditions, are cultivated. No orchards or gardens exist here.

At an altitude between 700 to 1,200 m is the lower vegetation tier dominated by spruce trees, artificially planted here to replace the original beach-fir forests, alternating in places with maple trees. As a matter of fact the mixed forests in the region were cleared in the 19th century as the wood was used in metallurgical plants. The best preserved forests are in the valleys of Białego and Strążyska, where rainfall is more usual than snow in this vegetation tier. Snow cover lasts about 140 days a year.

The higher, upper vegetation tier reaches an altitude of 1,550 m creating natural spruce growths. Amount of snow prevails over the rainfall. The mean annual air temperature rises to 2 °C, and snow cover lasts here for 180 days. The upper timber line, running parallel to the limit of the upper vegetation tier, is much higher situated than in Beskidy mountains lying more in north. Along the upper timber line, next to the spruce trees, also grows birch and limba pine, under which are blueberries, mountain cranberries (*Vaccinium idaea*) and gentian.

The next vegetation tier, the one of dwarf pine, reaches an altitude of 1,800 m, and the mean annual temperature here drops to 0°C. Snow prevails over rainfall and the snow cover does not disappear for up to 215 days in a year. The typical plant species of this tier is dwarf-pine, and various grasses and lion's foot (*Leontopodium alpinum*) and gentian also occur here.

In the subalpine tier grow mainly the communities of high-mountain grasses, and the mean annual air temperature hardly ever reaches above – 2°C. Snow cover lasts 250 days in a year. The upper limit of this tier depends on the base rocks: granodiorites at an altitude of 2,300 m but on limestones it does not surpass an altitude of 2,000 m.

The alpine vegetation tier on the peaks is the last and highest tier in the Tatras, comprising only the granodiorites of the High Tatra mountains. The mean annual temperature reaches only – 4°C and snow cover continues for 300 days of the year in this vegetation tier. In spite of the extremely harsh climate about 120 species of plants grow here. On the rocky faces lichens occur and in the clefts and small open spaces grass can be seen.

In the Tatras, besides the common animal life found all over Poland, there are species typical for a high-mountain environment which is not found anywhere else. The biggest animal living in the Tatras is the bear, and the number of bears on the Polish side varies between 10 and 20 in number. They attack sheep in the summer and they have also adopted the habit of roaming around the tourist cottages looking for food. In the autumn they consume large amounts of blueberries and raspberries. They pass the winter sleeping in a den, usually a hole of an overturned tree. Also the typical mountain animal in the Tatras, the marmot, an extremely swift and gentle creature passes the winter sleeping. These rodents do not occur anywhere else in Poland except in the Tatras and have been a completely protected animal, along with the chamois, since 1868. There are about 150 chamois living in the Polish Tatras, which live in herds, which is the reason why they are usually seen in groups. However, the male of the species prefers a more solitary life and joins the herd only during the rutting season, lasting from September to the end of October. Other animals, which also live all over Poland are the wolf, the fox, the lynx and the deer.

Right: A narmot

The marmot:

This particular mammal, of the order of rodents, lives in Poland only in the Tatra region. It is rare to meet the animal as it passes the winter sleeping in deep burrows high over the upper timber line. Just like most things which are rare and inaccessible the marmot has also been the subject of numerous legends. One conviction is that its fat is the best medicine for all kinds of ailments, and because of this its very existence was threatened. As early as the 18th century a mass cull of marmots took place in the Tatras, and people flocked to the market of Czarny Dunajec to buy the magic marmot fat, which proved to be a very lucrative trade. But when the population of the marmot in the Tatras dramatically dropped, its hunt was prohibited in 1868. But poachers, of course, hunt the creature up to the present day. The absurd belief about the curing properties of the marmot fat is still maintained in some villages of the Podhale region.

Birds represent one of the most "visible" groups of fauna in the Tatras. Besides the regular varieties some extremely rare birds are found here. In the rocks the eagle (*Aquila chrysaetos*) and the falcon live. From 1976 the employees of the Tatra National Park reserve observed the nesting of one pair of eagles in this area. It is a very rare species in Poland, and again is a protected animal species. It is estimated that in the territory of Poland only about 15 pairs of eagles (the symbol of the country) nest. Falcons, on the other hand, visit the Tatras only occasionally and seldom nest here.

Several varieties of fish also live in the Tatra streams, trout being the most frequent, found as far afield as Morskie Oko, the only Tatra lake with natural fish life. The goby and grayling also live in the Tatra streams.

NATURE CONSERVATION AND THE PROTECTION OF THE LANDSCAPE

The unusual natural beauty and picturesque landscape were the primary reason why enlightened and sensitive people tried to enforce the legal protection of this wonderful corner of the Carpathians, as early as the 19th century. Their efforts ended in a total ban on the hunting of the marmot and chamois, issued in 1886, and enforced throughout the entire territory of the Tatras. In 1925 a Polish-Czechoslovak project of a **Tatra National Park** was worked out and realised after the war, and a governmental decree established officially the Tatra National Park in 1954. Its area is over 211 square kilometres and includes, besides the Polish Tatras, also some parts of the Pogórze Spisko-Gubałowske (Zgorzelisko and Głodówky regions). The headquarters of the Polish administration of the TPN is in Zakopane (Chałubiński street) which includes an interesting museum.

Another national park in the region is the **Pieniny National Park**, founded in 1932 by a decree from the Minister of Agriculture. Soon after, on the other side of the frontier, the Slovak nature reserve was created. The legal confirmation of the statutes of the national park was issued long after the war as it was approved by the government only in 1954. Its area extends over 23.3 square kilometres. Only a half of it belongs to the state. The second half consists of private or communal plots.

THE HISTORY AND POPULATION

The first people appeared in the territory of contemporary Poland by the end of the Glacial period. They were hunters who arrived to the Tatra mountains while chasing game and lived in caves in the cliff belt. The most eloquent traces of their stay in the Podhale region were found in a cave situated in Obłazowa, a rock near the village of Nowa Biała. The cave is almost 9 meters long and the entrance is seven meters above the bottom of the river Białka, where in 1985 archaeologists discovered here the remains of bones and tools, typical for the Lower Stone Age man. They were hidden under sediment covering the bottom of the cave.

The boomerang:
Among the finds that were found in the cave was a unique boomerang – the oldest example ever discovered – made from a mammoth's tusk. A perfect copy of this boomerang showed that it possessed all technicalities of a typical boomerang, which thrown by a skilled hand has a cutting flight action, although it does not return like the Australian version and was probably used for hunting purposes. Determining the age of the find, by what is called the C-14 method, scientists from the Oxford archaeological laboratory established its age as being more than 18,000 years old.

Further important information has also been rendered by the study of fossils. Any plant in a given terrain spreads its pollen and is capable of being preserved in sediment for many years. An analysis of the plant pollen concentrated in the peat bogs of Podhale proved that the first corn pollen appeared here 3,000 years ago. This means that the primeval nomadic people who originally lived by hunting and collecting crops changed the way of their life to a more settled one. The cultivation of soil and the cutting of corn thus began in Podhale some three thousand years ago, however, the fields they used must have been small amid the Carpathian primeval forest.

In the early Middle Ages the region of Podhale was covered by Carpathian primeval forests. In the Kotlina Orawsko-Nowotarska basin the individual waves of settlers (Poles coming from the north and Slovaks from the Spiš and Orava regions) met. The word Tatry appeared for the first time in an act by King Henrich IV in 1086, and the oldest references confirm the first inhabitants in the territory around the year 1234. It was then when King Henrich the Bearded granted count Teodor Cedro of Kraków the privilege to found settlements in the basin of the river Czarny Dunajec. The Bishop Wislaw of Kraków consented to the building of a church in Ludźmierz in the same year. The first Cistercian monks came to Ludźmierz from Jędrzejow, but did not remain for long and left for Szczyrzyc following the Tartar invasion in 1241. Later, but still in the 13th century another order of Templars came here from Miechow and founded a parish in Frydman, Łapsze and Krempachy. The region of Pieniny belonged then to the female order of Stary Sącz. Podhale was at that time the property of the king, and the Kotlina Orawsko-Nowotarska basin was owned by the family of Gryfit who began to establish villages in the area. A change was brought about by the 14th century, when intensive settlement during the rule of Kazimierz the Great brought about the origin of the villages around the Dunajec river. This was also the period when the first German settlers came from the south to Podhale, arriving here from Levoča, then the centre of the independent German province in the Spiš region. Traces of their colonisation are evident in the German names of the villages, such as Frydman, Waksmund, Grywald, Falsztyn or Czorsztyn. In 1342 King Kazimierz entrusted count Teodoryk of Nowy Targ to found a town pursuing the right of Magdeburg. The town of Nowy Targ, stretching along the state border fulfilled important administrative and commercial functions in the region.

The process of colonisation lost some of its dynamism in the 15th century but it also acquired new developments when Wallachians moved in from Orava and along the Carpathian ridge from the east. These east-European shepherd tribes were wandering in pursuit of better pastures for their flocks. Consequently pasturing and the related practices, techniques and customs gained more importance under the Tatras. The Wallachians introduced the construction of sheep dairy farms and the summer grazing of their cattle far from their villages. Podhale, itself, became a melting pot of various races, languages and customs. A special ethnic group, called the Gorals, was born here and their unique dialect, costumes and rituals, as well as their handicrafts, were their distinguishing features. Also in the regions of Podhale, Spisz and

Right: A room in a typical Goral house

Orawa settled peasants who fled from the feudal estates in other Carpathian regions, namely the region of Żywiec. They fled in search of freedom and found it in a boundary area of Podhale. Their rebellious spirit later played a significant role in various uprisings and protests.

In 1556 the Orava region fell into the hands of a rich owner called František Thurzo who was intensively settling the area. The migrants were prevailingly Wallachians who came here in the 16th century, as well as Poles from Żywiec, beyond the Babia Góra mountain. A big inflow of people also took place from the Lower Podhale and the valley of Skawy (Jordanów, Sucha, Maków). Eleven villages originated in Orava during the rule of the Thurzos in the 16th and early 17th century: Jabłonka, Bukowina, Podsarnie, Podwilk, Orawka, Piekielnik, Podszkle, Harkabuz, Zubrzyca, Lipnica and Chyzne. And in the Pieniny region there existed seven of them by the end of the 16th century: Kluszkowce, Wyzne Sromowce and Nizne Sromowšce, Szczawnica, Krośnica, Grywałd and Mizerna.

By the beginning of the 17th century the parish chronicle in Czarny Dunajec quotes for the first time the name of Zakopane. This old document of 1605 proves that there existed a community that later developed into a village and eventually became a town. The estates of Zakopane and Nowy Targ were then owned by a feared tyrant called Mikołaj Komorowski and the continual increase of duties and oppression caused numerous rebellions in the region of Podhale. In 1651 an armed uprising of Gorals, led by Kostka-Napiersky, and a fight of the peasants against the royal troops in 1670 are proof enough that the people of the region appreciated, above all else, their freedom ("šlebodu" in the Goral dialect), a characteristic which still exists today.

Various manufacturing activities were founded in Podhale in the 18th century. Alongside the existing mills, fulling mills and sawmill the first primitive metallurgical plants originated and were built in the Tatra valleys. The first of them sprung up in 1756 soon followed by other such enterprises.

Austria occupied and simultaneously annexed the estates of Nowy Targ, Czorsztyn and Sącz in September 1770. It was a year after the Austrians took possession of Spiš. The estates of Zakopane and some land in the Tatras were bought by Emmanuel Homolacs and he became the owner of the metallurgical plants in Kuźnice. Zakopane experi-

enced its big boom in the 19th century when the first tourists arrived in the Tatras. The population, until then busy in agriculture and cattle breeding, progressively started to realise the opportunity to gain some additional financial sources by letting out rooms. Thus, Zakopane soon became a fashionable tourist centre although it remained only a village until the end of the 19th century. The first train in the Polish Tatras arrived in Zakopane from Nowy Targ in 1899, replacing the tedium of travelling by horse driven coaches. But unfortunately the railway did not continue up to Szczawnica. The town competed with Krynicą spa in aspiration to become the most important spa in Poland but lacking the railway connection it had to give up the idea.

The size of the population in Zakopane as of January 1, 1901 was 4,452. It was the time when the first sanatoriums were built here, various social activities were organised and societies founded. Zakopane was the place where the first Congress of Podhale people was held in August 19-20, 1911. The events of the First World War did not seriously affect the life in this Tatra village. After Poland obtained its independence in 1918, which was also

The area and population of the towns and villages of the Podhale region in 1966:

Town or gmina	Area in square km	Number of villages	Population	Density of population
Nowy Targ	50	—	34 020	675
Zakopané	84	—	29 693	352
Szczawnica	88	—	7 289	83
Total towns	222	—	70 982	315
Biały Dunajec	36	4	6 191	174
Bukowina Tatrzańska	132	8	11 710	88
Czarny Dunajec	218	15	20 010	92
Czorsztyn	62	7	6 446	104
Jablonka	215	7	15 235	71
Kościelisko	136	3	7 517	55
Veľká Lipnica	66	2	5 215	79
Nižné Lapše	125	8	8 203	66
Nowy Targ	209	20	20 382	98
Poronin	84	7	9 770	107
Szaflary	54	7	9 349	172
Krościenko	57	5	6 411	112
Total gmins	1 394	93	126 439	90

celebrated in this region, a new territorial division adjudicated it to the county of Kraków.

The twentieth century has been a period of on-going dynamic development for Zakopane, Nowy Targ and the entire region. A rack-railway track to Gubałowka, and a funicular to the Kasprowy Wierch mountain, which continues to operate today, were built during the inter-war period. Also the tourist cottages and paths, such as the road to the Morskie Oko lake was constructed during this period. The tragic years of the Second World War brought much persecution and death for the Gorals, who responded by maintaining their fight for freedom and independence and keeping open the courier routes across the Tatras. Heavy fighting between the Polish partisans against the Nazis and resistance to the post-war regime took place here. The Tatras, Podhale, Spiš, Orava and Pieniny were represented by one district with its seat in Nowy Targ, which belonged to the county of Kraków.

After 1975 the region became one of the most attractive parts of Poland for tourists. Tourism also brought negative effects, such as the impact upon the environment which concerned the authorities of the Tatra National Park. In 1994 almost half of the 4.5 million tourists arrived by motorised vehicles, passing through the border in Łysa Polana. Consequently the biggest problem today is to find a balance between the economic benefits of tourism with those of nature conservation of this area of such natural beauty.

THE POLISH TATRAS

Zakopane
and its environs

The Tatra region comprises the Tatra moutain range, Rów Podtatrzański (the sub Tatra Furrow), and the Spisko-Gubałowskie mountain range. Its central point is Zakopane, a town with the highest altitude above sea level in Poland besides which the region also includes the following villages: Biały Dunajec, Poronin, Bukowina Tatrzańska, Kościelisko and several other communities situated in the Gubałow mountains.

ZAKOPANE (740 m, population 29,700) also called the capital of the Tatras and the winter tourist centre is the biggest town on both sides of the border, neighbouring with the arch of the Tatra mountains. The compact urban nucleus is concentrated at the bottom of Rów Zakopiański (the Zakopianski furrow) enclosed in the south by the limestone Tatras and in the north by the belt of the Gubałówka mountains. Zakopane compared to other Polish towns has the most elevated position above sea level. The centre of the town, at the cross-roads of Krupówki and Kościusku streets is at an altitude of 838 m above sea level. The town is connected by three main roads and a railway.

The first reference to Zakopane is from the end of the 15th century. The Polish king Štefan Bátory granted the village its first privileges. But no document exists to prove its actual existence, although historians are quite certain that four hundred years ago there existed on the territory of the sub Tatra furrow the first communities that gave origin to this town. The name Zakopane appeared for the first time in a document of 1616. The land where it existed was owned by Paweł Rubzdel, son of Jan of Maruszyna. The mayor of Nowy Targ, Mikoła Komorowski, referred to the "new community" lying between the Tatras and Gubałówka when surveying his properties in 1624. The most frequent surnames in the population were then Gaşienica, Topor, Bachleda and Jarząbek. The settlers were concentrated in the

surrounding forest meadows, in total fifty, in an area populated by more than 650 people. On April 20, 1630 king Zygmunt III Waza granted Jędrzej Jarząbek of Bańska the privilege to use some of the mountain meadows. But the original document about property rights was not preserved, as in the case of the document proving the right of settlement granted to the people by Michał Wişnoviecky in 1670. Consequently, only copies of the documents are available. The village grew in size over the years. The royal survey of the properties in 1765 recorded in Zakopane 37 farms and several mills. There were many treasure seekers at the time but they only found iron ore, a fact which also influenced the history of Zakopane. In 1756 in Kuźnice a smelting plant was built. The ore was extracted in the valley of Jaworzynka in the Kopa Magura and Mała Kopa Królowa mountains. A similar plant also sprang up in the Kościelska dolina valley.

In 1770 Austria occupied the whole estate of Nowy Targ and Zakopane became part of the Austro-Hungarian monarchy. The royal property (forests, land, and mining equipment) all fell into the hands of the imperial court. But the Goral people preserved their ownership rights. The smelting plant in Kužnice headed by Jakub Reichsdorfer was damaged and burnt down in 1794 by Tatra robbers who were on good terms with the Goral blacksmiths. Only at the beginning of the 19th century did Jan Vincent Homolacs of Moravia renew the plant. His son Emanuel bought from the imperial court in 1869 the whole of Zakopane's property along with a large portion of Tatra territory. The family of Homolacz ruled in Podhale until 1869. Then the property passed to the hands of various owners and the most popular of them, frequently mentioned in the chronicles, was Władysław Zamoysky. But the previous owners of Zakopane, the family of Homolacs, are remembered not only as important promoters of local development, but also for various scandals typical amongst aristocratic families of the era.

The unruly aristocracy:

The priest of the Zakopane parish deeply esteemed the heiress of the Homolacz family but could not put up with her second husband and two sons from the first marriage. Dislike for the young aristocrats was felt generally in the village as they were insolent and cynical and seduced the local girls and servants. Their mother had to change her maids after several months and their step-father was compelled to hush up the reproaches on the side of the girls of Zakopane and frequently had to settle their financial requests. The eloquence of some of the names of the local areas, such as Burdel (Brothel) and Pierdołówka (Fornicating place) suggests where the unruly young men brought their lovers. The new names of the lots in question situated along the road from Bystre to Olcza were entered also in the land register and remind future generations of the erotic plays that once took place there.

In 1854 a vicarage was established by an imperial decree in Zakopane and the construction of the first chapel was started. The first priest in Zakopane was Józef Stolarczyk who founded here the first parish school. The church was built near the community of Nawsie and was situated at the point where three roads met. The first of them headed to Kościelisko (today Kościeliska street). The second one led towards Kuźnice across an alpine meadow and the community of Krupowa Rola (today Krupówki). The road leading to Nowy Targ was replaced by Nowotarska street. This road was used for transporting the iron ore to Kraków. The return trip was used for carrying the citizens of Kraków to Zakopane who admired the Tatras and spread enthusiastic stories about them. In the second half of the 19th century the owners of the smelting plants became the wealthiest citizens of Zakopane. The plants provided a considerable source of income, also to the Gorals whose main occupation was cattle raising and field works, but their living standard was low anyway, evidenced by their eating habits.

The diet of the people in Zakopane:

The diet of the Gorals was very modest and starvation was not unusual. Głodówka and Nédzówka were especially among the communities where poverty of Podhale prevailed. Eggs were eaten only once a year – at Easter time. Two traditional meals were prepared: moskale, *(an oat pancake) with butter and an egg omelette. On festive days during the poorest years only gruel with milk was available. The women used to collect various herbs and grasses in the spring time and cooked* varmuz *a warm soup with a little milk*

Right: The old church in Zakopane

added to it. Butter was sold rather than eaten. The everyday food of the Gorals consisted of oats in various forms and in good years also potatoes were eaten. Mashed oats with its husks boiled in hot water was called kluska, bryja *or* zacierka *and when baked it became* moskal. *It was accompanied by a cup of milk, sheep whey or simply water. Occasionally cabbage, beet root and beans appeared on the table. In bad years there remained only herbs to be served. The diet was the same every day of the year.*

Later when the number of visitors grew, the original function of the Goral huts changed, as more buildings were constructed and used as pensions. One can find a reference to allegedly the first summer holiday-maker here, a professor from Jagielloński University, Jan Steczkowski. Accompanied by his wife and daughter he spent his holiday here every year from 1854. But the actual "discoverer" of the Tatras was Tytus Chałubińsky. The Tatra Association (Towarzystwo Tatrzańske) which started to organise tourism in the Tatras on a professional level was founded in 1873. By the end of the 19th century Zakopane became a climatic spa. On the slopes of Gubałówka, in an area enjoying the most sunshine in the Polish Tatras, sanatoriums for patients with lung disorders were built, and are open up to the present time.

Tytus Chałubiński:

Tytus Chałubiński was born in 1820 in Radomia and later studied medical science and botany in Vilnius and Wurzburg. He became famous as a physician in Warsaw. As a university professor he came to Zakopane for the first time in 1873, from which time he spent every summer in the Tatras and in 1887 he settled here for good. Chałubiński was the first to introduce the "trend" of hiring Goral mountain guides, when making trips of several days in the mountains. One such guide was the legendary Sabała a well-known and witty narrator, musician and poacher. The groups of tourists he accompanied were always gay and noisy. There was also a Goral band who travelled with them, which entertained the tourists around the camp fire until late in the night. These tourists also collected stones and minerals or interesting plants. Zakopane also became the seat of a weather station and Chałubiński further promoted the village so that it soon reached wide popularity.

He was also nicknamed "the discoverer of Zakopane", and supported the origin of lace-making and wood-carving centres existing in the village. He died at the age of 69 and is buried in Pęksowy Bryzek. Two monuments in Zakopane commemorate this character, the Tatra museum bears his surname and one of the Tatra saddles is called Wrota Chałubińskiego.

Zakopane became ever more popular even though it was still a mere village. Tourists as well as artists visited it. Villas were built here in a style typical for the region. The best known architect of the period was Stanisław Witkievicz, son of the painter and writer Ignacy Witkievicz. 1899 was the year when the steam railway was introduced to Zakopane and the same year fire destroyed the centre of Krupówki. One of the greatest Polish writers, Stefan Żeromski also spent some time in Zakopane during the First World War. He was active in founding liberation movements, the aim of which was to take over the rule of Poland. When on November 1, 1918 the Polish National Party originated, Żeromski became the president of what was called Rzeczpospolita Zakopiańska – the Republic of Zakopane. Zakopane obtained the privileges of a town in 1933 when its population amounted to 15 thousand. Between the wars the most important amenities for sport and tourism were built in the town, such as two stadiums, a funicular to the Kasprowy Wierch mountain and a rack-railway to Gubałówka. A ski-jump on Krokwa was opened in 1925. Due to its promotion Zakopane became the place where two world ski championships were held. In 1937, 55 thousand tourists visited Zakopane, however, the period of the Second World War resulted in very tragic circumstances for Zakopane. Resistance fighting against the occupying German army produced plenty of victims. Polish people fled from Nazi terror passing through Zakopane and the Tatras to Slovakia and Hungary. There were secret pathways and escape routes for the couriers of the Polish resistance. The after war time became a period of unlimited boom for the town. Numerous buildings, mostly owned by the government and public institutions seated in Warsaw, were established for recreation and leisure. Also big industrial firms built their cottages and hotels here. But the architecture of the newly built hotels did not respect the style traditional to Podhale. They were built without regard to the landscape and the conservation of the environment. The socialist era ended in Zakopane in 1989. At present the town is managed by a democratically elected self-government which puts great emphasis on the needs of the local people, and the preservation of nature is also a priority. Zakopane becomes ever more beautiful and attracts the growing number of tourists.

Present Zakopane stretches over an area of 8,435 hectares out of which 4,921 ha is in the Tatras. The urban fabric is concentrated around the old historic core situated in the sub-Tatra furrow. Its southern border coincides with the Tatras and the north is closed in by Gubałówka. The town lies in the river basin of Zakopianka and its tributaries. The oldest part of Zakopane is on both sides of **Kościelska street** with **Stary Kościół** (1) (the Old Church) and a **cemetery** (2) on **Pęksowy Brzyzek**.

The cemetery:

The trees in the old cemetery in Pęksowy Brzyzek look as if they bow towards the old tombs of famous Zakopane natives. This is the resting place of those who gave the town and the Polish culture some permanent values. The cemetery is often compared to two well-known Polish necropolises – Powązki in Warsaw and the Rakowicki cemetery in Kraków. The oldest graves date from 1850 and famous poets, painters and sculptors are buried here, side by side with old aristocratic families and famous sportsmen and priests.

In front of the gate to the cemetery there stands a small chapel protected by iron bars. According to local legend it was built in the early 19th century by Pawel Gąsienica using money obtained by robbery. The chapel is consecrated to two saints – St. Ondrej and St. Benedikt. The wooden **church** next to the chapel was built in 1847 by the carpenters of Zakopane and later it was expanded. The precious altars were made by a famous wood-carver in the 19th century, Wojciech Kułach Wavrzyńcok, a native of Gliczarow. As far as the modern elements in the interior of the church are concerned, the calvary stations painted on glass by Ewelina Pęnksowa deserve the visitor's attention. Numerous wooden houses and Goral farmsteads are preserved in Kościelska street, which represent the remnants of the old part of Zakopane. Two villas – **Koliba** and **Cicha** also deserve attention. Koliba houses the **Museum of Zakopane of St. Witkiewicz** (3).

Museum of Zakopane of St. Witkievicz in Koliba
Zakopane, Kościeliska st. 18, tel.: 018/20 13 602
Opening hours: Wed-Sun 9:00-16:00h

Walking around Zakopane the tourist will be certainly intrigued by the **houses of Gąsienica-Siecko** and **of J. K. Sabała**.

Jan Krzeptowski Sabała:

This extraordinary narrator, musician and poacher was born in 1809 into the family of Gaşienica-Krzeptowski. He never went to school and was illiterate, but he had great talents for trailing game and hunting. Due to his exuberant imagination he invented improbable stories about his accomplishments. Great writers living in Zakopane like Sienkiewicz, Witkiewicz, Tetmajer and Chałubiński recorded and later published his

Right: The St. Family church in Zakopane

narrations. Sabała never missed any big event taking place in Podhale including the war-time patriotic resistance. His participation in Chochołowski's uprising in the time of the Austro-Hungarian empire brought him imprisonment. The violin was his inseparable companion. Many Goral songs played by him were recorded and thanks to the composers Kolberg and Paderewski these melodies have survived up to the present day, and they are often played by folk ensembles. The name of this "bard" of Zakopane is used by many folk events as for example the festival of folk narrators called Sabałowe bajania or Sabałowe nutki. Sabała was a good companion and many famous visitors to the Tatras sought out his company. He was a living symbol of "Goralness", who lived for eighty five years and is buried in a cemetery on the Pęksowy Brzyzek hill.

The commercial centre of Zakopane is in Krupówki street and the adjacent lanes. There are many famous buildings which boast of their original history, favourite coffee houses, restaurants, fancy shops, tourist bureaux and the parish **church of the Holy Family** (4). This was until recently the biggest church in Zakopane. Its construction was started by the priest Solarczyk in the 1870's but finished only after his death. This stone church, in the Neo-Romanesque style, has no connection with the traditional local style, which is understandable if we realise that the project was designed by the Warsaw architect Józef Dziekoński. Only the interior of the church was designed by local architects and folk artists. The main altar, the work of the Kraków sculptor Kazimierz Wakulski is also not typical for the local style. On the other side of the street, after crossing the brook, there is a big wooden building of Technikum Bodowlanego (a medium level Building Institute). The previous occupant of the institute was the department for carpentry of the previously mentioned wood-carving school. The wood carving department of the ancient school gave origin to another famous school in Zakopane – Liceum Technik Plastycznych (the Fine Arts Lycée). On the cross-roads of the streets Krupówki and Kościuszka there are two hotels: **Giewont** and **Gazda**. Nearby stands the post office building and the tourist bureau Orbis neighbouring with the gallery of fine art. Going on up Krupówka one arrives at the favourite, pre-war hotel called **Morskie Oko**. The most frequently visited place in Krupówki is the **Cocktail bar**, mainly frequented by young people who like to come to sample its excellent pastries, cocktails and ice cream.

In the main street of Zakopane, Krupówki St. No. 10 seats the **Tatra Museum** (5). The first museum housing some rare specimens of Tatra nature was established in Kuźnice back in the time when the lands of Zakopane were owned by the Homolacz family. But the collection from this period did not preserve and a new exposition was established due to the efforts of doctor Tytus Chałubiński and it was opened to the public in 1888. The first administrator of the Museum was the local teacher Władisław Roszek. The existing building of the Museum was finished after a few years of construction, in 1920, but the first visitors entered it only two years later. Since then the Tatra Museum became the principal scientific and research institution in Podhale, all owing to its first director Juliusz Zborowski, an outstanding linguist and ethnographer. The museum was spared from any damage during the Second World War as it bore on its facade a

Goral ornament – "the goral swastyka" – slightly reminiscent of the infamous Nazi symbol. The visitor will find on display in the Museum a completely furnished Goral room from the 19th century, folk costumes and tools used for field work, sheep dairy farm, as well as household dishes. A permanent exposition giving information about Tatra nature is on the first floor of the building. It contains samples of rare plants and animals, and geological items.

The Tatra Museum of Dr. Tytus Chałubiński,
Krupówki St. No.10, tel.: 018/201 5205
Opening hours: daily except Mondays 9:00-16:00h

Also the **Muzeum Tatrzańskiego Parku Narodowego** (the Museum of the Tatra National Park) near the roundabout of B. Czech houses precious collections and a library concentrating on the literature of the High Tatras.

Left: The Tatra Museum in Zakopane

Museum of the Tatra National Park,
Chałubińskiego St. No. 42, tel.: 018/20 63 271
Opening hours: Mon-Sat 9:00-14:00h

In the area around Zakopane there are several communities which have a typical rural character and are only several kilometres distant from the town. One of them is called **Olcza**, and spreads along the lower bank of the Olczyski Potok brook. It was an independent village until the 18th century when it was then annexed to Zakopane. By the end of the 1980's the **church of Priests missionaries**, one of the most beautiful in Podhale was built here. Its design, though modern, includes the elements of the original architectural style of Zakopane perfectly harmonising with the rural setting.

The community of **Bystre** lies at the foot of the Nosal mountain on the right bank of the Bystra brook. About a kilometre from its centre, in the local part Jaszczurówka, stands the wooden **chapel of the Holiest Jesus' Heart** built in the years 1904-1908 as designed by Stanisław Witkiewicz. Another very precious historical monument in this part of Zakopane is the **church of Norbertarians** which originated on the site of the wooden chapel built by the monks in 1902. The church acquired its present appearance in 1959. In its interior some very precious statues and paintings on glass, made by the excellent folk artists of the Podhale region, can be seen. Bystre is very busy in winter time. On the Nosal mountain there is a ski slalom slope artificially lighted and if necessary can supply artificial snow. Its top is reached by a chair lift and below several ski lifts operate. Paragliding is possible in summer and in winter. On the other side of the road is the building of the **Rehabilitation Sanatorium for children** with its own surgery department. It was built before the First World War.

Kuźnice, lying in southern part of Zakopane, is today only a small Tatra community but its history, especially industrially speaking, is rather rich, as there used to be numerous smelting plants here. The sound of the hammers was regularly heard here from early morning until late night, and the machines produced various iron products which were later carried to Kraków, Lwow and even to Vienna. Once there was a big farmstead here which belonged to the owner of the iron works where the first tourists visiting the Tatra valleys and peaks found accommodation. Kuźnice is still a central point from which several routes to different parts of the Tatras start. Tourists can obtain basic information concerning these tourist routes in the booking offices located on the edge of the Tatra National Park which also sells maps and bulletins. The blue-marked footpath leads from Kuźnice to **Hala Gąsienicowa** passing Boczań and Skupniów Upłaz. The orange-marked route passes the **Dolina Jaworzynki** valley to Przełęcz między Kopami where it joins the blue-marked path. The green-marked path is reserved for more experienced tourists and it leads to the **Kasprowy Wierch** mountain. In Kuźnice begins a comfortable road leading to the cottage at an alpine meadow called Kalatówki, and continues following the blue path passing Kondratowa Polana to Giewont. There is also a **cabin funicular** commuting to Kasprowy Wierch. Near the bottom station of the funicular are the buildings of the oldest water works in Zakopane operating from 1908. Near the alley Przewodników Tatrzańskich is the **commemorative monument** erected in memory of the victims of the German occupation, the work of Władysław Hasior. One of the greatest attractions of Zakopane is the funicular to Kasprowy Wierch.

The funicular to Kasprowy Wierch:

Kasprowy Wierch (1,985 m) is the only place in the Tatras where nature created extraordinary conditions for down-hill skiing. In the east and north-west there are two enormous cirques in the crystalline body of the Kasprowy Wierch mountain – Gąsienicowy and Goryczkowy. They are situated above the upper timber line with slopes turned to the north and east, the ideal position for long lasting snow cover. The funicular was constructed following the design of Aleksander Bobkowski. It was opposed by various organisations of the state council for nature conservation but it was finally approved due to the fact that the promoter was the son-in-law of the then Polish president Ignacy Mościcki. Its construction started in 1935 and despite difficult terrain it was completed in an unusually short time. The first cabins began to commute on February 29, 1936. The route of the funicular consists of two parts. The central station is situated at Myślenicke Turne (1,352 m). The capacity of the funicular (which takes 35 people) is not sufficient to satisfy the demand, and the trip to the top station takes 20 minutes. The difference in elevation is 936 m. The lower station is at an altitude of 1,023 m above sea level and the top station is at an altitude of 1,959 m. The journey by the funicular is still one of the most attractive pastimes for tourists and holiday-makers in Zakopane. In spite of the inflated price it is almost impossible to get a ticket in the high season. Any proposed plans for modernisation and to increase the capacity of the funicular meet with stubborn resistance from the Tatra National Park administration and other ecological organisations.

In the north-western part of the town is Gubałówka the highest situated mountain area of Zakopane. The peak and ridge meadows of **Gubałówka** offer a splendid view of the Tatras and the Rów Zakopiański furrow. Especially impressive is the view of Giewont and the group of the Czerwone Wierchy mountains. Gubałówka is accessible by **rack-railway** (6). Its lower station is right beside the Zakopane market hall, in the historical centre of the town. The railway was opened in December 1938 before the ski world championships took place. The equipment of the railway was supplied by a Swiss firm. The railway car takes almost 100 people and the trip to the top over a distance of 1,300 m with an elevation of 300 m, takes only five minutes. Reclining chairs are let out to tourists who love the sun and sunbathing, whilst more active tourists can hire mountain bikes. Holiday-makers can have their photographs taken here in company of a bear, they can also hire a horse-driven coach, and if they have still any money left there is a big choice of souvenirs on offer. Three ski lifts and the possibility to hire snow scooters are other attractions here in winter. But the walks, for instance to the **Butorowy Wierch** mountain, are exceptional, especially when the weather is fine, from where the return trip to the town is possible by chair lift. One can also explore the opposite direction, passing Furmanową and Rafaczówka and ending up in the village of Ustup or Poronin.

The eastern part of the town is dominated by **Antalówka**, a broad elevated plain at an altitude of 940 m above sea level forming a water divide, separating the valley of Bystra from the valley of the Chycow potok brook. Here too is a beautiful view of the Tatras and the Rów Zakopiański. The **outdoor swimming pool** is another attraction for summer holiday-makers, with a water temperature of 28 degrees Celsius and its source is from a

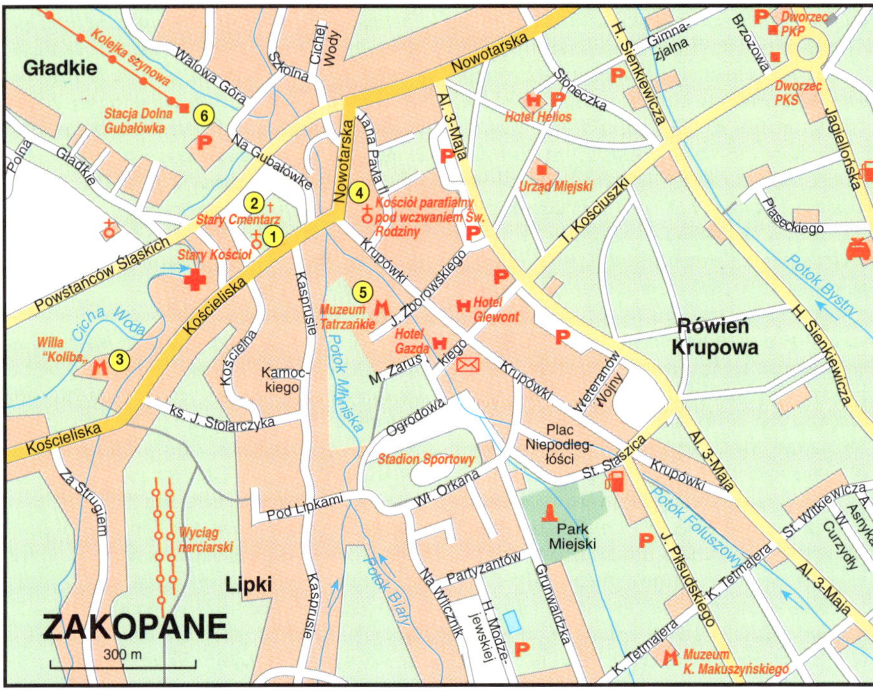

natural spring. Several ambitious projects for constructing a series of swimming pools in the area are under consideration, but prohibitive costs make them impossible at present. There is also the **station of nature conservation of the Polish Academy of Sciences** in **Antałówka** and several ski lifts to pleasantly occupy the winter visitor.

Skiing in Zakopane:

The area of Zakopane and Kasprowy Wierch is also nicknamed "the winter capital of Poland" or the "centre of ski sport". Its high altitude above sea level and the mountains, the great part of which is above the upper timber line, are the prerequisites for cross-country and down-hill skiing. The first skiers came here in the last years of the 19th century and the first pair of skis were brought to Zakopane by Stanisław Barabasz. Accompanied by M. Karłowicz and M. Zaruski he founded the ski section of the Tatra Association in 1907. Several years later the elite of Zakopane adopted the custom of making ski trips to Hala Gąsienicowa and Kalatówky. But a tragic event put an end to their rather noisy and hilarious excursions when one of the tourists, the outstanding Polish composer Mieczysław Kar-łowicz, became a victim of an avalanche on February 8, 1909 on the slopes of Mały Kośielec near Czarny Staw Gąsienicowy and died. The event speeded up the implementation of the idea to establish an organisation to help tourists in the Tatras caught in a similar situation. Following a scheme by M. Zaruski in 1909, the Tatra voluntary rescue service (Tatrzańkie Ochotnicye Pogotowie Ratunkowe – TOPR) was founded. However, the local people at first distrusted the "whims of the lords" and refused to get involved in rescue initiative. The first Goral to learn to ski was Klimek Bachleda, who became the first TOPR rescuer to die during a rescue operation.

The following years brought about a boom in skiing in the Tatras. In the inter-war period a funicular to Kasprowy Wierch and a rack-railway to Gubałówka were constructed for skiers, along with the **ski-jumps** below the Krokiew mountain. **Krokiew** (1,378 m) is one of the Tatra peaks covered by forest. The steep slopes of Krokiew mountain face northward towards Zakopane. The society Park Sportowy of Zakopane rented here a part of the slopes at the foothills of Krokiew in 1923. They intended to build here a ski-jump with criteria that would comply with the requests of international competitions. The plan was eventually realised and the first ski-jumping competition on Wielka Krokiew was organised in March 1925. The winner Stanisław Gąsienica Sieczka jumped what was a record then – 36 m. Over the years the ski-jump has been repeatedly modernised and today it is quite different from the one of seventy years ago. In the Continental Cup competition held in Zakopane, in 1996, the Slovenian Primoz Peterka established a new record on Wielka Krokiew at 132 metres. Experts have declared the ski-jump in Zakopane one of the safest. Moreover, it lacks any hideous towers or pre-running tracks that might spoil the natural landscape. The site bears the name of one of the best Polish ski-jumpers, the deceased Stanisław Marusarz who also administered for many years this ski-jump. Beside this there are also small and medium size ski-jumps and the whole compound represents the local cross-country skiing centre. It is the place where usually the start and finish of the running track is situated, but the stadium under Wielka Krokiew is also used for other events. In June 1997 for instance the biggest assembly of the population of Podhale was organised here when the Pope John Paul II visited Poland.

Chair lifts began to commute under the Kasprowy Wierch mountain in the Goryczkowa and Gąsienicova valleys after the Second World War and additional lifts were built in the direction towards the Butorowy Wierch and Nosal mountains. The authorities of the Tatra National Park, accompanied by numerous ecological organisations, have refused any further investments in the Tatras. However, there are still several "illegal" ski lifts in various parts of Zakopane: in Gubałówka, Antałówka and Krzeptówki. In Szmoszkowa Polana the alpine meadow next to the Kasprowy Hotel is a typically commercial four-seat chair lift. It takes more passengers but its track is too short, the slope too moderate, and the snow prevailingly artificial. Prices are also high and is used mostly as a favourite resort for rich beginners who normally stay in a smart hotel nearby. Tourists who prefer the more classic ski disciplines (such as cross-country skiing) can use the marked routes below the Regle, in Antałówka or Cyrhli. Cross-country skiing is possible also in the Tatra valleys of Kościeliska and Chochołówska.

Besides amateur skiing the top professional skiing is also promoted in Zakopane. The World Ski Championship of the FIS were held here three times and every year in February or March a traditional memorial event for Bronisław Czech and Helena Marusarzówna takes place here. The last day of the year belongs to the Ski Run on Sylvester Day. The ski competition under Nosal mountain for children aged between 3 and 9, called the Cup of Koziołka Matołka, is also very popular. The Championship of Poland in classic and alpine skiing (cross-country and down-hill ski disciplines) are mostly organised in Zakopane. Here is also the seat of several ski clubs. The best Polish skiers were either born in Zakopane or have lived there. Also the so far only Polish Olympic medal winner, Wojciech Fortuna, learnt his ski-jumping skills in Zakopane.

Among the most interesting trips starting in Zakopane is the one to **Gubałówka**, **Butorowy Wierch**, and **Krzeptówki**. The route is not demanding as the elevation can be taken by the rack-railway. Gubałówka encloses the Rów Zakopiański in the north. The geographical term Pogórze Gubałowskie (the Gubałowskie mountain range) derived from the one of its highest peaks the Gubałówka (1,120 m). It can be ascended by the rack-railway and then the track continues westward. Once on top the visitor can see typical buildings built here before the First World War. Similar houses can also be seen in Góra Parkowa in Krynica. In what was once a smart restaurant the traces of lavish interior decoration are still preserved. In a terrace in front of the restaurant stands the bronze statue that used to adorn the Polish pavilion in the World Expo in Paris. A bit further to the east is an iron cross from 1873 that Tytus Chałubiński had built in gratitude of the reconciliation of his relatives and an end to the negative passions within his family. The top of Gubałówka offers a beautiful panorama of the Tatras, and many tourists spend hours here admiring the snow covered peaks. The people of Gubałówka live off the tourist industry and their trading spirit has long been renowned.

How Vojto Plaza earned his living:

On the top of Gubałówka used to live in the past century Vojto Plaza, a big and lazy man. Vojto disliked any kind of work. He invented an unusual way how to earn his "cvancigers" – the currency then in use – by simply lying down! The

Gorals during this time were punished for offences by whipping, although they could rent a substitute person to be punished instead. This was the service Vojto Plaza of Gubałówka provided for money, charging half a cvanciger for twenty cane lashes. He was nicknamed by his fellow-villagers "Velka ric" (Big Bottom), which is a direct reference to the part of his body which saved him from starvation. For the value of one cvanciger, for instance, two hat-full of plums could be bought.

Travelling westward along the ridge of **Gubałówka** one arrives at the modest **chapel of the Virgin Mary of Perpetual Help** built in 1967 by the family of Bachleda-Księdzulorz. In the interior of the chapel is the statue of the Virgin Mary, a work of art by Antony Kenar, the outstanding sculptor from Zakopane,. The road continues to the large **alpine meadow of Pająkówka**. Here a wonderful view of the Tatras, the northern part of Pogórze Gubałowskie and the Beskidy mountains, closing the wide horizon in the north, opens in front of the tourist. Passing the crossroads one enters the forest and after a moderate ascent gets to the upper station of the **chair lift to the Burotowy Wierch** mountain. A 15 minutes ride by the lift exceeding an elevation of 280 m and at a distance of 1,600 m brings us to the lower station in the community of **Sobiczkowa**. Along the comfortable descent the constantly changing panorama offers a pleasant experience. Following the road Powstańców Śląskich one comes to the Szmoszkowa Polana alpine meadow and the **Kasprowy Hotel**, which is the biggest hotel in Zakopane. It was built in 18 months and opened in 1974. In total 522 clients can be accommodated in its smart single or double rooms or suites. Its facilities include an indoor swimming pool, sauna, restaurant, coffee bar and night bar. In summer tennis courts are available and in winter ski lifts are another option. Ubocz street near the hotel connecting with Kościeliska street is the one that leads to the centre of the city.

Another little demanding trip is the one to the **Dolina Strążyska valley**. The best way to start is under Wielka Krokiew going on by the Droga pod Reglami road heading westward. Several minutes later there is the entry to Dolina Białego valley with steep layers of dolomites and limestone. There is also a brook flowing along the narrow valley with an uneven bottom full of steps, small waterfalls with foaming water. Here there are the most beautiful oaks, firs, and spruce trees preserved in this valley, and occasionally limba pine can be seen here. The road heads from Dolina Białego to a small brook called Spadowiec. Do not miss the beautiful view of the waterfall from the bridge over the brook. Then follows a wide opened alpine meadow with a sheep dairy farm on its edge, where one can taste sheep whey and cheese. In winter this is the best place for the beginner skiers. Going further on one finally gets to the Dolina Strążyska valley praised by everyone as the most beautiful valley throughout Zakopane. It divides the forest adjacent to Giewont in the north. The perpendicular faces of this Tatra peak close the valley in the south. The highest peaks of the ridge Samkowa Czuba, Turnia Kiernia and Lysanki constitute its western limit and the east is bordered by the ridges of Grześkówki and Sarna Skała. Along the almost 3 km long valley leads a tourist path marked in red. The name of the valley is derived from the Goral word straga meaning a fenced place for the milking of sheep. Right at the beginning of the valley in the meadow Młyniska stands a game-keeper's lodge dating to the time of Władyslaw Zamoyski, the former owner of the Zakopane estates. Today it belongs to the Tatra National Park. The road passes an impressive beach-fir forest preserved from the 19th century when the majority of the forests fell victim to the logger's axe. There used to be mines and a smelting plant here. The economic centre used to exist in Polana Strążyska, an alpine meadow where cattle and sheep grazed. Of numerous sheep dairy farms only two are preserved up to the present time. The alpine meadow offers a captive view of the northern face of Giewont, whereas a yellow-marked path leads to the picturesque **waterfalls** called **Siklawica**. The brook Bacucha falls down the almost perpendicular dolomite rocks. The lower situated waterfall is, compared to the previous one, two metres higher, with a total height of 12 metres. On the return trip one can stop in Strążyska street, in the **villa Atma** where the famous Polish composer Karol Szymanowski spent the last years of his life. Today it is the seat of the **Museum of Karol Szymanowski** founded by the Warsaw musical society.

Right: The Pope in Zakopane

Museum of Karol Szymanowski,
Kasprusie St. tel.: 018/20 63 150
Opening hours: Tue-Thurs, Sat, Sun: 10:00-16:00h,

All day trips from Zakopane include the one to from Kuźnice to alpine meadow **Kalatówki**, to Kondratowa valley, and to Giewont. Kuźnice can be reached from various parts of the city – by bus, microbus or taxi. There is a ban on the entry of other personal cars. In a parking lot near the lower station of the funicular, which commutes to Kasprowy Wierch, starts the road heading to Kalatówki. The first part of the route is marked in blue. After about one kilometre appears the **monastery of Albert's sisters**. The **hermitage of St. Albert** (his civil name was Adam Chmielowski) and the **chapel of St. Cross of Albert's Brothers** are open to the public. This founder of the order of Albertinians, who was a talented painter, is one of the few Polish Saints to be recently canonised. After seeing the wooden buildings of the monastery visitors can set out by a paved road to Polana Kalatówki. On the left side there can be seen the remains of the Glacial period in the Tatras – a rampart of lateral moraine. The moraine divides this alpine meadow into two –the lower part (1,160 m-1,200 m) and the upper part (1,200 m-1,250 m). The meadow was all pasture land in the past with numerous sheep dairy farms and the first ski competition in the Tatras was held here in 1909. Suchy Żleb overlooking Kalatówki is the oldest slalom mountain in Zakopane. In its foothills, on a moraine, a wooden tourist cottage that used to belong to the Tatra Ski Society which organised the ski competitions, was built. In 1938 a big mountain hotel was built in its site with accommodation for 84 guests in single, double and triple bedded rooms. For the time being it is the most comfortable cottage in the Polish Tatras especially enjoyed by foreigners, providing a restaurant, two coffee bars, sauna and the opportunity for the renting of ski equipment. There are also two ski lifts near the hotel. Standing in front of the hotel one gets a panoramic view of the Kasprowy Wierch mountain. A path leading from the hotel joins the blue-marked tourist track is leading to another picturesque alpine meadow – **Polana Kondratowa**. In its northern edge stands a cottage. It originated in 1948 when it replaced a hostel originally built in 1910. It is at an altitude

of 1,333 m above sea level, it has a capacity of 28 beds, and is mostly used by tourists who continue by the blue-marked path further on to Giewont. The ascent is demanding and recommended only for the more experienced hikers, as there is an elevation of 600 m. Although Giewont is not the highest peak in the Polish Tatras, the ascent is one of the most dangerous, with no climbing recommended in winter or in summer when storms are expected.

Another all day trip from Zakopane is to Kasprowy Wierch mountain, alpine meadow Hala Gąsienicowa, to the lake Czarny Staw, and to Dolina Jaworzynki valley. **Kasprowy Wierch** (1,985 m) is accessible by a cabin lift from Kuźnice. Its upper station is on the southern slope of the mountain. The top of Kasprowy Wierch is built of granite and crystalline shales. Right beside the top is the **highest situated weather station** in Poland, built in 1938. If the weather is fine, one can observe almost the whole mountain range of the Western Tatras: the Tichá dolina valley (the Slovak part of it), the southern slopes of Giewont and also great part of the High Tatras, with Swinicą in the foreground can be seen. This is the place where various tourist tracks meet, some heading towards Zawrat and Swinicą, others to Czerwone Wierchy, to Myślenickie Turnie and the Dolina Cichą valley. The orange-marked path leads downward to the alpine meadow of **Hala Gąsienicowa**. The panoramic view of this wonderful glacier kettle with its many lakes can be admired from the terrace of the restaurant in the building of the funicular station. On the left side of a comfortable and broad footpath is the track of the chair lift which takes passengers from the bottom of the kettle up to the Kasprowy Wierch mountain. It is open only in winter for skiers. On the right side there are the sharp mountains of Swinicą, Mały Kościelec and Kościelec. A deep, easily distinguishable depression in the mountain crest between Swinicą and Beskid is the saddle of przełęz Liliowe (1,952 m) separating the Western Tatras from the High Tatras. Nearby is the **tourist cottage of Murowaniec** situated under the upper timber line. The cottage was completed in 1925 and has a capacity of 100 beds. It offers meals and

Left: Kasprowy Wierch mountain

a good resting place, especially when the weather suddenly changes, something all too frequent in the Tatras. Many tourists do not miss the visit to Czarny Staw Gąsienicowy, one of the most beautiful glacier lakes in the Tatras. It is accessible by a blue-marked tourist path passing by a modest monument erected to the Polish composer M. Karłowicz, at the place where he died under an avalanche. The area of the lake is 18 hectares and its maximum depth is 51 metres. The trout living in the lake was introduced here by the end of the 19th century. The lake is surrounded by an admirable rocky amphitheatre of the peaks of Żołta Turnia, Kozie Wierchy, Mały Kościelec and Kościelec. The more experienced walker can go on along the blue mark passing the Zawrat saddle to the **Dolina Pięciu Stawów Polskich** (The Valley of Five Polish Lakes). The best option then is to spend the night in the cottage near the first of the lakes and then decide upon one of the return trips to Zakopane. Those who do not choose the ascent to the Zawrat saddle can use the same route to go back to Hala Gąsienicowa and once they get to the Murowaniec cottage they can then take one of the options of descent to Kuźnice. One of them is the blue marked route passing the saddle Przełęcz między Kopami, the ridge Skupiniów Upłaz and Boczań. Another option is the descent following the orange marked route to the **Dolina Jaworzynki valley**. In the first way there is a lovely view of the picturesque valley of Dolina Olszyska where the water springing of Wywierzysko Olszyske can be heard; and the second option provides the opportunity to see the dry karstic valley with old sheep dairy farms. The first option is longer but much more moderate and comfortable.

Kościelisko
and its environs

KOŚCIELISKO (850 m, population 3,890) is a big village lying 5 km west of Zakopane. It consists of more than 20 communities dispersed over the slopes of the Pogórze Gubałowskie mountains and at the bottom of Rów Potatrzański furrow.

Four centuries ago there were only small groups of houses built on alpine meadows. The meadows were used by the people in Polish Podhale, and they finally settled and made their homes there. The first communities in the territory of the village originated in the 17th century. The early chronicles quote the names of the villages, such as Blachówka (1623), Spyrkówka (1623), or Kiera (1646). The settlers first cleared the forests and then built their houses and farmsteads. Their herds grazed in the Tatra meadows. In the 18th century new settlers arrived to the region who were not either shepherds or hunters. King Stanisław August invited here miners and colliers from Germany and the Slovak Spiš area who came to extract the iron ore deposited in the eastern slopes of the Ornak mountain in the upper part of the Dolina Kościeliska valley. The new settlers opened a mine there. The remains of it are still to be seen from the orange-marked tourist pathway leading from the cottage in the Ornaczańska alpine meadow to the saddle of Iwaniacka Przełez. The ore extracted here was carried to a smelting plant built in a place called Stare Kościelisko. The first ore smelting furnace was built in 1767 and was surrounded by other buildings – a mill, a tavern, houses of the colliers and their masters. Ore was extracted also from the Maturka mine in Stoły and two galleries in the saddle of Miętusi Przysłop. Today there is no building left in Kościelisko. The past prosperity of the place has disappeared without leaving any major traces of its earlier existence. There is though a stone **chapel** near the road called the Chapel of the Robbers (Zbójnicką) built by the miners. It is confirmed by their symbol over the entrance, of two crossed hammers. The tradition of robbers lives on here in the legends of Jánošík, the Slovak national hero (see page 173).

Jánošík in Poland:

Even though the name of this legendary robber is only too often mentioned in the Polish part of the

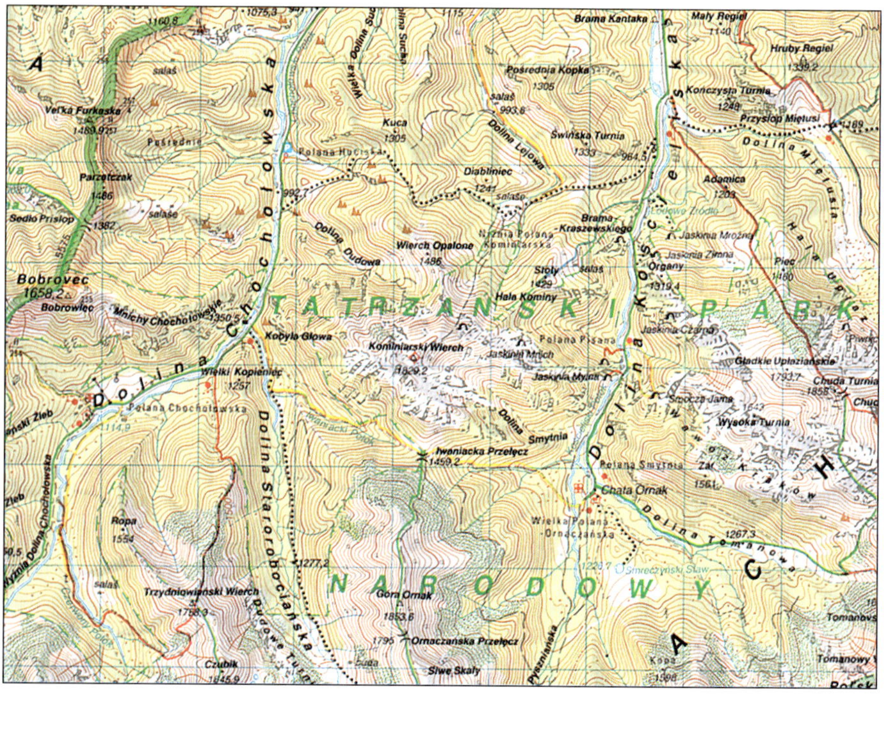

Tatra mountains (in the names of the restaurants and bars or pensions) one has to realise that he seldom visited these places. He lived and robbed almost exclusively in Slovakia, and again over a period of about two years. The film series on Jánošík, made by Polish TV, presenting Jánošík in Spisz or Pieniny, or even his marriage to Marína in a church in Polish Dębnie is mostly fiction. Also the successful Polish musical "Painted on Glass" based in Jánošík's life (with more than 500 performances in 1974 in the Slovak National Theatre), in spite of being set in the Polish Podhale, is little more than fictitious.

The visitor to Kościelisko valley who is a good observer will certainly notice the remnants of a rampart and a dyke which once conducted water to the mill. Luckily for Tatra's nature the mining activities did not last long in the valley. By the end of the 19th century the colliers left this narrow and shadowy valley and many of them moved to the sunny meadows on the Kościeliska Palenica and Butorowy Wierch mountains, north of the Tatras.

From 1790 the village of Kościelisko was a part of Zakopane, within which lived about 500 people. The Gorals from many settlements around Kościelisko visited the church in Zakopane even though it involved a 10 km walk. The first church of St. Kazimierz was built in Kościelisko only in 1916 and an independent parish was established even later, in 1932. The population grew in the meantime to one thousand. Many important figures from cultural and artistic circles associate their lives and work with this Tatra village. For instance, the authors Andrzej Stopka Nazimek and Stanisław Nędza Kubiniec were born here. Also the legendary Goral Jan Krzeptowski-Sabała lived here, as well as the Tatra robbers of the 19th century, the Matejowies, were born locally in Nędzówka. Its name (Poor Village) reflects the material situation of the population of Podhale in the 19th century. Poverty and starvation, especially in springtime were commonplace, which resulted in intense out migration to the Americas, and also to seek adventure and freedom. Some returned others stayed overseas for ever. However, new settlers under the Tatra peaks took their places, and so the population steadily grew. In 1970 there lived in Kościelisko about 3,000 inhabitants. New hotels, pensions and sanatoriums were built here the same as in Zakopane.

The centre of contemporary Kościelisko is in the settlement of **Szeligówka**. Here is also the oldest **church**, that of St. **Kazimierz**. But of most interest for tourists is two kilometres further southward the village of **Kiry**. Groups of tourists start hiking here to reach the most beautiful but also most frequented Tatra valley – **Dolina Kościeliską**. It runs from north to south over almost the whole of the Polish Western Tatras as its length is 9 kilometres. Anyone who wants to know the Tatras any time of the year and does not like tiresome tours should visit the Dolina Kościeliska valley. The trip usually starts in the community of Kiry. In summer there are horse driven coaches on offer and in winter sleds can be used. On the right side of the road is the **famous inn, Harnaś**, with a typical Goral atmosphere and offering interesting national food. The characteristic features of the valley are the tapered places called gates, and on the other side, extensive meadows. The first tapered area is called **Brama Kantaka**, and originated at the place where the Kościeliski Potok brook cuts the massive limestone. The same base rock is

Above: The old church in Koscielisko

found also on the peak of **Kończysta Turnia** seen on the left side. A broad alpine meadow called Wyznia Kira Miętusia was once frequented by shepherds and their flocks of sheep. But the only shepherds hut left here is today more of a tourist attraction then a real shepherd household. Passing the bridge over the brook the visitor arrives at an extensive alpine meadow full of furrows and little hills – **Stare Kościeliska**, a place where the smelters worked in the 19th century. Passing the southern edge of the meadow one can pass over the bridge to the spring of **Lodowe Żródło**. It is one of the most yielding karstic springs throughout the territory of the Tatras, with a capacity of 200-600 litres of water per second, cold in temperature, which does not rise above 5 °C. It is sourced by ground water from the territory around the south-easterly mountains of **Czerwone Wierchy**. The road leading over the valley and bound for the south crosses the narrow gate called **Bramą Kraszewskiego** called so after J. I. Kraszevski, famous Polish writer. In limestone and dolomite rocks beside the road are some caves. One of them, the **Jaskinia Mroźna** is open to the public. The next widened part of the valley is the meadow called Pisana. Here the routes of the coaches and sledges end and the rest of the tour is to be done on foot. After a while the traveller will come to the limestone peaks of Raptawickie Turnie towering over the Kościeliski potok brook. Six kilometres along the track is the **tourist cottage Ornak**. A place for a good meal and relaxation before setting on the last part of the tour, it was built between 1947-1949. Energetic hikers are recommended to continue by passing the saddle of Iwaniacka Przełęcz to the Dolina Chochołowska valley. But for others, who are not prepared for the steep ascent and the equally demanding descent are advised to go back to the village of Kiry following the same route along the Kościeliski potok brook. If there is enough time tourists can see the lake Smreczyński Staw, a half kilometre south-east of the Ornak cottage which is accessible by a black-marked tourist footpath starting near the cottage. Unforgettable impressions are also left by the walk over the canyon of Wąwóz Kraków. It is marked in orange and the track starts at the Pisana meadow. Tourists who like underground adventures should visit the Mrozna cave the entrance to which is next to the spring Lodowe Żródło.

Parallel to the Dolina Kościeliska valley going westward is the **Dolina Chochołowska valley**, the longest and biggest valley (10 km) in the Polish Tatras. Its water divide, closing the water basin of Chocholowski brook, runs at an altitude of 2,176 m (Starobociański Wierch). The trip to Dolina Chochołowska starts in **Siwa Polana** lying on the borders of the Tatra National Park, south-west of Kościelisko. Here there are old sheds and huts where the shepherds used to pass the winters with their flocks of sheep. In summer they even wandered up to the highest situated pastures. Until recently tourists could drive their cars as far as the Huciska meadow where there used to be a big parking lot. Nowadays the Gorals take the tourists there by horse driven carts. Polana Huciska is the second biggest alpine meadow in this part of the Tatras. Its name is derived from a small smelting plant that used to exist here in the 18th century. The meadow tapers down in its southern edge and creates a gate called **Niznia Chochołowska Brama**. Also the stop at the spring **Chochołowskie**

Left: Dolina Koşcieliska valley
Right: A Goral coach

Wywierzysko is very interesting, which is not a far off the road, and as with other Tatra springs it is also very cold. The valley gets wider with rising altitude and there are no karstic forms or springs – the rock base contains soft marls. Another rocky gate – the **Wyźnia Brama Chochołowska** is made of pale limestone easily inclined to karstification. An example of the process is the cave **Szczelina Chochołowska** with a total length of the corridors of more than 2,500 m. The road continues along the game-keeper´s lodge up to the Dolina Starobociańska valley. The short passage up to the saddle Iwaniacka Przełecz is marked in orange and its leads to the parallel valley of Kościelska. Continuing south-westward the road leads over the forests to an extensive alpine meadow called **Polana Chochołowska** with abundant shepherd huts. It is one of the most charming Tatra meadows throughout the region. In its south-western edge is a big cottage offering lodging for 100 people at any given time, built in 1953. A red-marked footpath starting near the cottage leads over the Dolina Jarząbcia valley to the Trzydniwiański Wierch mountain (1,758 m) and later an orange-marked one goes to the Grześ peak (1,653 m).

The return trip along the Chochołowski potok brook, north-westward, ends in the village **WITÓW** (800 m, population 1,539). The village belongs to the group of associated communities of Kościelisko and it is situated in the valley of the Czarny Dunajec river near the point where the Kościeliski brook (Kirowa Woda) joins the Chochołowski brook (Siwa Woda). The road leading from Zakopane and Kościelsko to the community of Czarny Dunajec forms the main communication axis of the valley. The western limits of the community's territory are close to the state border running along the mountain ridge from the **Magura Witowska** mountains to the north.

In 1620 the mayor of Nowy Targ Stanisław Witowski founded here a community bearing his name. The wonderful setting of the village attracts ever more tourists who long for pure air and silence. The natural setting is much nicer than in overcrowded Zakopane, however the village does not have many historical monuments left. The log **church of Matka Boska Szkaplerzna** was built in 1912 after the design of Jan Tarczałowicz. The modern interior decoration was made by the Zakopane sculptor Michał Gąsienica Szostak.

There is also an old **black-smith furnace** from the second half of the 19th century. Similar to neighbouring Chochołow there are also **old buildings** and **farmsteads** here, and old traditional crafts are kept alive in the village such as fur-making, wood-carving and embroidery. Witow is the seat of the forestry administration owning large forested areas in the Western Tatras. Visiting Witow tourists find themselves only 3 km from the border crossing to Slovakia, in Sucha Hora. The Slovak part of the Western Tatras, or the Západné Tatry mountains, is then best accessible from this place.

East of Witów is **DZIANISZ** (840 m, population 1,815), a small village stretching along the Dzianiski Potok brook, the right side tributary of the Czarny Dunajec. The village originated in the 17th century in a similar manner to neighbouring Witów. The population mainly made their living from agriculture and traditional wood-carving crafts. Today it is mostly involved in tourism offering accommodation in private houses like the majority of the villages in Podhale. Among the most valuable buildings in the village is the **belfry** of the turn of the 18th and 19th century. Visitors usually undertake a hiking tour along the ridge of Pogórze Gubałowskie rising east of the community, and it is crossed by a red-marked route called **szlak turistyczny Powstania Chochołowskiego** (the red route of the Chochołow Uprising). The most beautiful part of the track is between Chochołow and Bukowina Tatrzańska.

Left: A cottage in alpine meadow of Ornak

Bukovina Tatrzańska
and its environs

BUKOWINA TATRZAŃSKA (800 m, population 2,700) is a large village dispersed on the crests and slopes of the Bukowina mountain range, which forms part of the Pogórze Spisko-Gubałowskie mountain range with the highest peak, Cyhrla nad Białka – 1,158 m. The centre of the village is represented by the local part of Bukowina Klin from where the main roads to Białka Tatrzańska, to Łysa Polana, Poronin, and the minor roads to Gronkow, Gliczarow and Brzegów depart. Bukowina Tatrzańska originated in the 17th century and it bears the name of its first mayor, Kaspra Bukowiński. He was entrusted with the foundation of the village high above the base of the valleys by the mayor of Nowy Targ Tomasz Zamoyski in 1636. Bukowina is mentioned also in older documents, in relation to a dispute over the borders between Poland and Old Hungary in the years 1589-1625. The village originated through the Wallachian right. Extensive forests were administered by a game-keeper, whose house stood in the area which is now contemporary Bukowina Klin. The village used to belong to the Nowy Targ estate before the division of Poland. Later, in 1824, Bukowina, along with other villages in Podhale, became the property of the family of Homolacs. New workshops producing wooden shingles, mills, black-smith furnaces were built in the village in that time.

The game-keeper's files:

Tourists who visited Morskie Oko lake by the end of the 19th century usually passed Bukowina. The last house on the route was the game-keeper's lodge in Klin. The game-keeper, Franz Klein, was a very earnest man and he recorded the names of all tourists who stayed in his lodge on their way to the Tatras. His unique files were edited by the end of the 19th century by S. T. Razikowski. Among the list of names of his visitors are that of Archprince František Karol (1823) and later, in 1832, the famous Polish poet Seweryn Goszczyński who spent a night there.

Also the first mountain guides came from Bukowina. The best known of them was Józef Bigos, who guided the tourists in the Tatras in the years between 1833-1856. Bukowina was off the

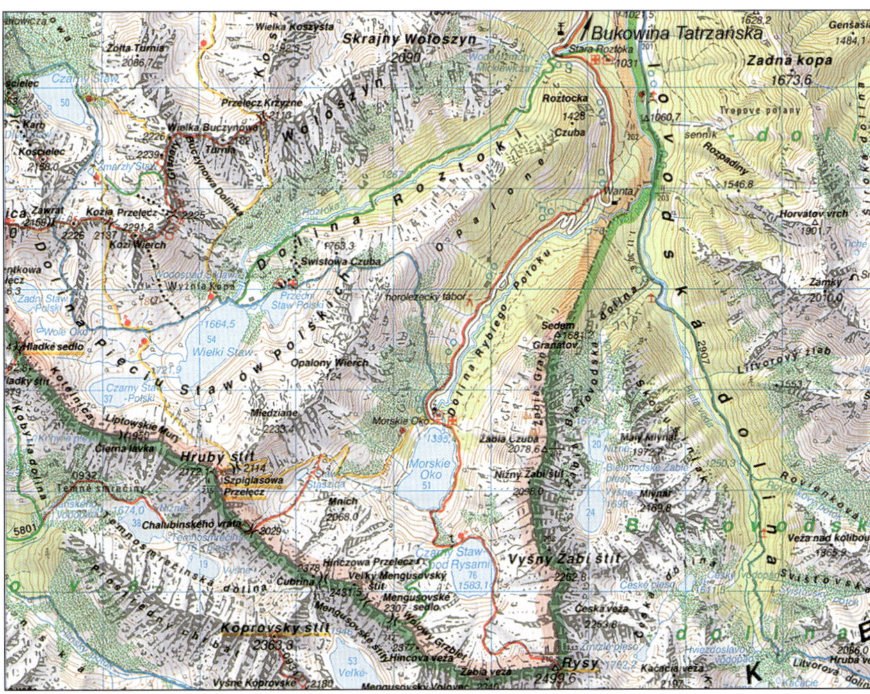

route from Poronin to Morskie Oko as it passed Klin and Głodówka, and the first guests arrived in Bukowina by the end of the 19th century. The priest Walenty Gadowksi built the first villa in Bukowina in 1900, and later the village rapidly grew during the inter-war period. The numbers of visitors also reflect some interesting data about the history of Bukowina. For instance, in 1923, 193 trippers visited Bukowina. Three years later their number grew to 1,941 and in the winter 1935 even to 3,354 persons. The Society of the Friends of Bukowina initiated an additional change in the name of Bukowina, to Bukowina Tatrzańska, which became valid from 1935. The building of what is called here the People's House is the most interesting secular monument in the community as it is probably the biggest wooden building in Poland. An important sacral monument is the **church** from the 19th century, built by Jędrzej Kramarz, also the designer of the interior wooden decoration. The altars and statues were removed in 1902 and today the church is a cultural monument. A new **church of the Holiest Heart of Jesus** consecrated in 1982 was built nearby. The religious life of the Bukowina people is connected not only with the churches but also with various significant events, one of which took place during the Second World War.

The rescuer of Bukowina:

In the Second World War there was a courier route connecting the occupied country with Western Europe leading across Bukowina. In the local church the statue of the Virgin Mary Jaworzyńska, was moved here from Rusinowa Polana and was hidden during the whole time of the occupation. In January 1945 the German troops, retreating before the Russian army stopped in Bukowina and the people prayed to the Virgin Mary for salvation as an attack of artillery and bombing was under preparation. But when the bombers approached the whole landscape was covered by a thick mist and the village was subsequently saved from the onslaught. To mark the occasion of moving the Virgin Mary's statue to Rusinowa Polana the grateful villagers organised a pilgrimage, repeated also in 1995, the 50th anniversary of the event.

Left: Białka gorge
Right: The Rysy mountain

Bukowina Tatrzańska is the favourite place for the people of Kraków, who come here to spend their holidays and weekends. Also the population of other cities prefer the silent rural atmosphere of Bukowina to the noisy and overcrowded Zakopane. Bukowina Tatrzańska is today a popular winter and summer holiday resort, but in winter the narrow village lanes leading to the ski lifts are full of cars. There are more than 20 ski lifts in Bukowina itself and every season one or two more are built. Moderate slopes and prices attract above all families with children and novice skiers. Bukowina, on the whole, represents a lively folk centre and the People's house organises folk events. In February the Goral carnival takes place, which includes competitions of Goral dances, songs and amateur theatre. August is the month when competitions of folk narrators is staged, the **Sabałowe Bajania**. The main attraction of the event is an all-night ball at a camp fire in the Dolina Niebieska valley, part of which is imitating the rituals of robbers. There are several folk ensembles and traditional products of leather and wool are still made here. Wood-carvers and artistic cabinet makers are well-known, glass painting and decorations are also typical handicrafts. In winter an event called kumoterki – races of horse driven sleds are held here.

The same as in the past, a popular trip is the one to the Morskie Oko lake. It starts in Bukowina Klin where there used to stand the game-keeper's lodge of Franz Klein, who used to put down the names of the tourists who were heading for the Morskie Oko, the most beautiful lake of the Tatras. The first part of the road to Polana Palenica lying south-west of Lysa Polana can be made by bus or car. Along the road is **Głodówka**, a place offering some wonderful landscape views. Anyone who stops here will never regret the experience, the view of the surrounding peaks of the High Tatras, of Zakopane squatting at the bottom of sub-Tatra furrow and the Gubałówka mountain over Zakopane is indeed rewarding. The road continues further to the south and ends by serpentines leading to the **Dolina Białka valley** where there is a border crossing in Łysa Polana. Several kilometres to the north starts the Tatra National Park. The road to Morskie Oko lake leads along the border crossing to a parking lot in the locality of Palenica Białczańska. From here one can go further on foot or by bicycle. Also the tram pulled by horses is recommended, as the walk on the paved road is long and tiresome and not so exciting. But the required effort ends at the waterfalls called **Wodogrzmoty Mickiewicza** with a fine view of the falling foamy water of the Roztoka brook. The end of the Białka valley is steep and the water falls down three cascades. The waterfalls were given their name by the Tatra Association in 1891 in commemoration of the famous Polish author Adam Mickiewicz, buried a year before in Wawelski castle in Kraków. Mountain guides explain to visitors that the landscape looked quite different here in the Quaternary period. A big glacier filled the Białki valley and reached as far as the road on which they stand. Following the disappearance of the glacier the steep slopes, enclosing the lateral valleys in a hanging position in relation to the main valley, were uncovered. The distinct U-shape of the Bielovodská dolina valley, a branch of the Białka valley, is visible from the curve over the forester's house of Wanta. The route of the Goral trams ends a little further southward on the **alpine meadow of Włosienica**. The rest of the track must be negotiated on foot, where the deep trough of **Żandarmeria**, remarkable for frequent avalanches, follows. In the 19th century one such avalanche destroyed the police station and the event gave the origin of the name of the trough. On the left side there are several small lakes and a rampart of moraine closing together with the rocky threshold of the bed of the

lake. The extraordinary beauty of the **lake Morskie Oko**, at an altitude of 1,400 m above sea level has been celebrated by many poets. Its area, though constantly diminishing, is still 34 hectares and its maximum depth is 51 metres. The walk around the lake takes about an hour. A nearby cottage offers the prospect of rest for the most tired visitor. The first cottage was built here in 1874, as the first tourist cottage ever in the Polish Tatras. The road was built in 1902 when the argument over Morskie Oko between Old Hungary and Poland was settled. Several years later the construction of a big cottage was started and was opened in 1908. Some visitors will certainly also like to see the lake **Czarny Staw pod Rysami** from where it is possible to see Morskie Oko below. The trip to Czarny Staw takes about one and a half hours. The return trip to the alpine meadow Palenica is possible taking the same route. A variation to the trip is also the visit to the cottage in Roztoka, which takes about ten minutes from the waterfalls of Mickiewicz. The cottage was built in 1876 as the second cottage in the Tatras, but it lasted only 37 years. The present cottage was built in 1913 and it has a regular clientele who always come back.

Left: The environs of Bukowina Tatrzańska

Bukowina Tatrzańska is at the present time a compound community, in Polish gmina consisting of eight villages. Three of them: Jurgów, Czarną Górę, and Rzepiska are described in the chapter on Spisz.

BIAŁKA TATRZAŃSKA (700 m, population 1,900) is situated in the valley of the river Białka near the road from Jurgów and Bukowina Tatrzańska to Nowy Targ. It is a typical village with one main street more than 5 km long. Its natural eastern border is represented by the river Białka, and in the west it is bordered by the slopes of the Pogórze Bukowińskie mountain range (also called Gliczarowskie) dropping in a moderate manner into the valley. The village was founded in 1636 pursuing the privilege granted by the Polish king Władysław IV. The local parish was established much later and it included the neighbouring villages and Bukowina. The **wooden church** was built in the centre of the village around 1700. Surrounded by a low stone wall and old trees this little church is a picturesque part of the landscape. A new **church** with a high tower was built on the other side of the road in 1921. Both churches are consecrated to St.

Szymon and Tadeusz. Białka Tatrzańska competes with Bukowina Tatrzańska for primacy among the ski resorts of the Spisko-Gubałowskie mountain range. New ski lifts were built here and the slopes are artificially lit and snowed if necessary, guaranteeing good ski conditions in any weather. Białka has several restaurants and self-catering facilities, where tourists can prepare their own hot meals.

BRZEGI (850 m, population 660) is a small village lying in one of the valleys of Pogórze Bukowińskie mountain range. It is not easy to find it because it is reached only by a narrow winding road deviating to the east from the main route, Bukowina Tatrzańska-Morskie Oko. The turn is only a kilometre from the cross-roads in Bukowina Klin. In the lower part of the village are the steep banks of the river Białka from which the name of the village is derived ("brzegi" means river banks). There are several old village huts here, roadside chapels and the **church of St. Anton of Padua**. There are also five ski lifts available in the winter season.

Two villages **GROŃ** (760 m, population 1,750) and **LEŚNICA** (660 m, population 1,550) belonging to the gmina of Bukowina Tatrzańska are situated in the northerly upper part of the Leśnica valley. Both villages are connected by a narrow but interesting road leading from Bukowina Tatrzańska to Nowy Targ. Leśnica is the older of the two. It was founded in 1610 and the first written reference to it is in 1635 when it belonged to the parish of Ostrowsko. The most important monument of both villages is the chapel in Groń standing on mountain of Kobylarzówka and dates back to 1776. There are active folk ensembles in both villages and the people proudly preserve their Goral traditions and wear regularly their regional costumes, even when there is no special occasion.

In the southern edge of the Polish Spisz, on the right bank of Białka is the border village of **JURGÓW** (760 m, population 850), 18 km away from Nowy Targ towards the south-east. This village, similar to all the Spisz villages, also had various owners in the past. It is a community of wood carvers, pottery makers, carpenters, weavers and cabinet makers. The production of farming tools and househould equipment also has a long tradition here. The oldest historical monument in Jurgów is the wooden **church** of 1670 that lost its original style because of repeated reconstruction. The walled **belfry** dates back to 1811. In the former mayor's house is now the **Muzeum Kultury Ludowej Spisza** (Museum of folk culture of Spisz)

Muzeum Kultury Ludowej Spisza
Zagroda Spiska – The mayor's house, Jurgów 215,
Opening hours: Wed-Sun 10:00-14:00h

Jurgów used to be the administrative seat of an extensive area comprising two Tatra valleys – Jaworowa and Biała Woda, where the shepherds of Jurgów brought their flocks. In the community of **Podokólne**, 2 km away from the village, is an **open-air museum of shepherdic culture** consisting of several sheep enclosures which are still in use. In the southern border of the territory belonging to the village, though on the Slovak side, is the **border crossing of Jurgów-Podspády** which serves only the local people. It is eventually going to be expanded and developed into an international border crossing to substitute the one in Łysa Polana.

Because Łysa Polana falls under the territory of the Tatra National Park its operation will be reduced to local use. Jurgów borders in the north on one of the best situated Spisz villages, **CZARNA GÓRA** (750 m, population 1,500). This village spreads along the southern and northern slopes of the mountain bearing the same name (903 m) with the steep slopes of the Białka valley disclosing layers of shale and sandstone. The wonderful panorama of the Tatras is seen from the southern slopes of the mountain and its northern side offers a view of the Kotlina Nowotarska basin and the Gorce mountain range. In the southernmost part of the community, near Białka, is a poor Gypsy community. The landmark of the village is the museum – **Zagroda Korkoszów** displaying a series of old tools, buildings and household utensils.

Zagroda Korkoszów (Museum of farming),
Czarna Góra, Za Górą St. 86, tel.: 018/26 77 879
Opening hours: Wed-Sun 10:00-16:00h

The small community of **Łysa Polana** is ten kilometres south of Bukowina Tatrzańska on an alpine meadow of the same name, where the houses are concentrated around the **border crossing** to Slovakia. The community lies at the bottom of the river Białka valley. On the left bank of the river near the bridge is a big building, constructed in Podhale style. It is the seat of **customs office** and of the **border guards**, with accompanying services for tourists, for instance, the **money exchange**. There are also **insurance companies** for both countries. In its neighbourhood is the forester's house, the property of the Tatra National Park. Several buildings are also on the right bank of the river belonging to Slovakia near the bus stop of the lines commuting to Poprad, Kežmarok and Tatranská Lomnica.

Poronin and its environs

PORONIN (720 m, population 3,850) is one of the largest communities of the Podhale region. It lies on the confluence of the brooks Poroniec and Zakopianka, which together form the river Biały Dunajec. The village stretches along the valleys of the brooks and partially along the foothills of the mountain ranges Gubałowskie and Bukowińskie.

The first settlers probably arrived here very early, as written references from the 13th century mention the land near Poroniec. Nevertheless, the existence of the village itself is confirmed at the time of the 16th century. Poronin belonged then to the village of Biały Dunajec and it became an independent community in 1624. Its first mayors were the Pawliks. At the beginning of the 19th century Poronin was better known than Zakopane. In one of the communities belonging to the village a simple iron smelting plant was built where scythes and sickles were made. The scythe has given the name to one of the parts of Poronin: Kośne Hamry ("kosa" meaning scythe). Poronin became known also as a holiday resort for Polish intellectuals and artists like the painters Jan Matejko and Leon Wyczółkowski, the poets and writers Władysław Orkan and Kazimierz Przewa-Tetmajer. Even V. I. Lenin lived here in the years 1912-1914, and a stylish museum dedicated to Lenin was established in the house of Podhale with a monument standing in front of it. After the political changes of 1989, however, the museum was changed into the cultural centre of the village and the monument was removed.

Today Poronin is an important junction point of the roads from Kraków and Nowy Targ. There are more roads leading to Zakopane, Bukowina Tatrzańska and the border crossing in Łysa Polana passing Poronin. The centre of the village is on the right bank of the river, east of the cross-roads and the railway station and is the seat of administration of the compound of the communities, gmina, which administers seven Goral communities. Nearby is a church and several public buildings. The first wooden church of St. Mary Magdalena, built in 1830, was burned down in 1915 and subsequently rebuilt on the same site. It was designed by the distinguished architect Franciszek Mączyński, and the main altar is the work of Mieczysław Starobier-

ski. The church was finally completed in 1926. Along the road to Bukowina, on the right hand side, is the parish cemetery notable for the several graves of the victims of Nazi terror. The recreation and sport area with a ski lift, a down-hill ski track, and a small ski-jump is situated under the steep slope of Galicowa Grapa (982 m).

Similar to many other Podhale villages Poronin carefully preserves its Goral nature. A typical feature of the Gorals is their traditional costumes which are worn by the local people, both the men and women, even today.

The Goral folk costume:

At the occasion of Pope John Paul's visit to Zakopane in 1997 about thirty thousand people dressed in Goral folk costumes gathered for his service in Wielką Krokwią – evidence of their strong traditions and the respect they hold for their ancestors. Goral costumes were once made in the village households, which they wove from flax and wool. The cloth was then passed to a fulling mill where a thick and dense fabric was produced. It was used for the special hats which were adorned with a row of white china shells. These hats are still an important accessory of the men's costume. The women wear linen head scarves, once home-made and printed in a variety of colours, and the same material is also used for their aprons and knee-length skirts. The patterns and colours of the costumes change according to the different regions. The women from Szczawnica and Krościenka wear green skirts and scarves, while the women of Ochotnica and Nowy Targ prefer a combination of yellow, red and blue. The people of Zakopane and the surrounding area choose more conspicuous colours with sophisticated patterns. Red prevails in Orawa, pale blue with a motif of big flowers in Spisz. The Goral men and women in general wear woollen socks and simple footwear. The beautiful male costume includes a leather belt with brass buckles and studs. The men's trousers are embroidered with ornaments and the type of ornament around the pockets, called parzenice, *distinguishes the different regions. Over a white shirt the men wear a reversible fur vest. The leather part of it usually has a decorative element made of small pieces of coloured leather and sewn with a white silk thread. For special occasions and on feast days Goral peasants wear a short coat called* sukmana. *It is sleeveless and worn loosely over the shoulders, bound by a ribbon around the neck. The embroidery on the coat should agree in colour and pattern with those on the trousers. The basic colour of the sukmana and trousers depends on the raw material of wool. The high mountain sheep have usually much whiter wool than the sheep grazing in the valleys, which is the reason why the clothes in Skalne Podhale were always paler than in other regions, where some aspects of the clothing might be brownish in colour. The ornamental elements on the male Goral costume represent the special way of imitating the vertical stripes on the sides of trousers of military uniforms. Parzenice have their origin in Liptov and Orava frequented by the royal troops who wore similar ornaments on their uniforms, including a feathered hat. This kind of ornamentation was also carried over to the Polish side of the Tatras – the Polish Gorals adorn their hats with feathers on special occasions.*

Left: View of the Tatras from Poronin
Right: A Goral family

BIAŁY DUNAJEC (660 m, population 4,410) is another of the old villages of Podhale situated on the bottom of the valley of the Biały Dunajec river, separating the Pogórze Gubałowskie mountain range in the west from the Pogórze Bukowińskie in the east. The southern neighbour of Biały Dunajec is Poronin and in the north it borders with Bańska Nizną. The busy road from Kraków to Zakopane is rimmed by a row of houses.

The first written reference to the community is from 1564 on the occasion of the survey of the royal properties in Poland. The right to construct the village was granted by the mayor of Nowy Targ to Jęndrzcj Pawlik, a peasant from Szaflary. He was also the founder of the family of mayors, the Pawlik. In the past Biały Dunajec was a small community the population of which lived off agriculture. It grew in size in the inter-war period, when two schools, a mill, and a paper-mill were built here. As far as historical monuments are concerned, the mayor's log **curia** of 1830 and the **huts** of the villagers deserve attention. The **cultural centre** of the village is very active and there are several regional **folk ensembles** associated with it. The community also organises folk competitions and festivals.

Geothermal energy:

The heating of the community, which is in the planning process, is indeed a remarkable scheme, as it will be based in the use of underground thermal springs, the ultimate aim of which is to protect the air from pollution, especially intense in the winter season. The energy will be used also for heating greenhouses, drying plants, ponds and swimming pools. The plan is being supervised by the Polish Academy of Sciences, the building of which is in the northern edge of the village on Jan Pawoł II street.

One of the many villages dispersed over the slopes of the Pogórze Gubałowskie mountain range is **NOWE BYSTRE** (780 m, population 1,150) stretching west of Poronin. The village is situated at the bottom of the valley of Bystry brook and some of its houses are on the northern slopes of the mountain range. The origin of the community dates back to the 17th century when it was a part of Rogoźnik also called Stare Bystre. Only after the division of the old settlement its name changed to Nowe Bystre. The population was originally active in agriculture and cattle raising, but modern times have brought about the advent and promotion of tourism and associated private enterprises. There are many opportunities for **lodging** in private houses and the standard varies accordingly. The oldest sacral monument of the community is the **church of St. Ján the Baptist** from the end of the 19th century.

Nowe Bystre belongs to the compound of the villages (gmina) of Poronin the same as **MURZASICHLE** (800 m, population 1,100), a village situated south-east of Poronin. The axis of the village is represented by the road connecting Poronin and Brzeziny – the easternmost part of Zakopane. The village is restricted by the Tatra National Park on three sides which reduces its possibility to expand. The first written record of the village is in 1630, describing it as a small shepherd settlement. Even though the population still maintains its agricultural activity, their main source of income is tourism. The range of private lodging in Murzasichle is wide, as the Tatras and Zakopane are nearby. The pride of the village is its beautiful log **church**.

East of Murzacichle is a small village called **MAŁE CICHE** (820 m, population 400). Originally it was a shepherd community belonging to Biały Dunajec. Today it is an independent village within the gmina of Poronin. It is situated on the bank of the Cichoviańska Woda brook, a confluence of two Tatra brooks, Sucha Woda and Filipczański potok. This village is also in close proximity to the Tatra National Park. True to its name ("ciche" means silent) the village is an ideal harbour of tranquillity and rest.

The more northerly located **GLICZARÓW** (760 m, population 950) lies in a narrow valley of the Bukowińskie (Gliczarowskie) mountain range near a brook which flows into Biały Dunajec. In the past it consisted of two parts: Gliczarów Dolny and Gliczarow Górny. The local people still make their living from agriculture and cattle raising, preserving original Goral **folk traditions**.

On the northern slopes of Pogórze Gubalowskie, along the westerly road from Poronin is the village of **ZĄB** (920 m, population 1,300). It is the **highest located community in Poland**. In the south it borders with the houses attached to Zakopane. The village originated in 1620 when the family of Zdanowski acquired the settlement from

Right: A shepherd from Podhale

the mayor of Nowy Targ, Stanisław Witowski. Mikołaj Komorovski, a well-known tyrant and owner of the estate of Zywiec, and later also the mayor of Nowy Targ, who forcibly obtained what was formerly an independent village. Ząb changed owners several times. The most important monument here is the **church of St. Anna**, and was built by Jan Ustupski of Zakopane with the assistance of the best carpenters in the Podhale region. Behind the church is a cemetery partially separated by a limba pine grove offering a charming view of the whole belt of the High Tatras. Due to the wonderful position of the village and its pure air it is being more frequently visited by tourists.

North of Ząb is the village of **BUSTRYK** (880 m, population 700) situated on the flanks of the Gubałowskie mountain range. In the north-west the valley of Szyposzowi Potok brook can be seen and in south-east the ridge of the mountain range drops down into the valley of the brook. The villagers still occupy themselves with agriculture and cattle raising, and in the surrounding fields and meadows numerous huts of former **sheep dairy farms** have been preserved. Life is not easy in this region and the **chapels** dispersed all around the area testify to the religious devotion of the local people.

Bustryk belongs to the group of villages headed by Poronin, the same as the more southerly lying village of **SUCHE** (740 m, population 1,150). It stretches over the valley of Suchy Potok brook, the left tributary of the Biały Dunajec river. Suche and Ząb have a common history. The village was founded in the same year and its original name was Jastrzębiec. Both villages, Ząb and Suche were practically one until the 1930's. The situation changed after the Second World War and today it is an independent community, though very close to Poronin. Its people have always been mostly farmers.

More to the north are situated the villages of **LESZCZYNY** (840 m, population 300) and **SIEROCKIE** (900 m, population 600), high in the Gubałowskie mountain range, and which belong to another gmina, that of Biały Dunajec. Both villages offer their hospitality to tourists at much lower prices than other villages in Podhale. The population are mostly farmers and a big part of them commute in pursuit of work to Zakopane or Nowy Targ.

NISKIE PODHALE

Nowy Targ
and its environs

Niskie or Low Podhale is a region which has its central point in the town of Nowy Targ. The most important communities of the region are situated on extensive terraces of the river Dunajec valley and in the lower and central reaches of the valleys of Czarny and Biały Dunajec. Here also belong several villages situated in the lowest positions on the southern slopes of the Gorci mountain range. Niskie Podhale is the historical name for the areas which represent the southernmost tip of Poland. The main administrative, economic and cultural centres of the region is the town of **NOWY TARG** (585 m, population 34,000). It lies in the centre of the Kotlina Nowotarska basin at the confluence of the rivers Biały and Czarny Dunajec. It is well connected by railway with Warsaw and Kraków. In addition, two roads meet here: one leading from the north to the south connecting Kraków with Zakopane and the other connects the east with the west (i.e. Krościenko and Szczawnica with Jabłonka and Chyzne). The airport of the Tatra aviation club in south-eastern part of the town is too small for public or commercial transport.

In the 13th century there existed here only a small settlement called Długie Pole, or Dunajec, on the territory of the present town and it belonged to the Order of Cistercians who had their monastery in Ludźmierz. In 1346 the Polish king Kazimier Wielki entrusted Ditrich Szyja, the mayor of Nowy Targ, to found a town on the basis of the Magdeburg right. The castle near the southern border of Poland fulfilled the function of what was an important customs community. The rapid development of the settlement was predetermined by its advantageous situation on a trade road leading from Silesia and Kraków to Old Hungary. The population was prevailingly Polish until the first half of the 15th century and later it became mixed with Germans. The presence of German ethnicity is still in evidence in the strange sounding names like Waksmund or Frydman, situated south-east of

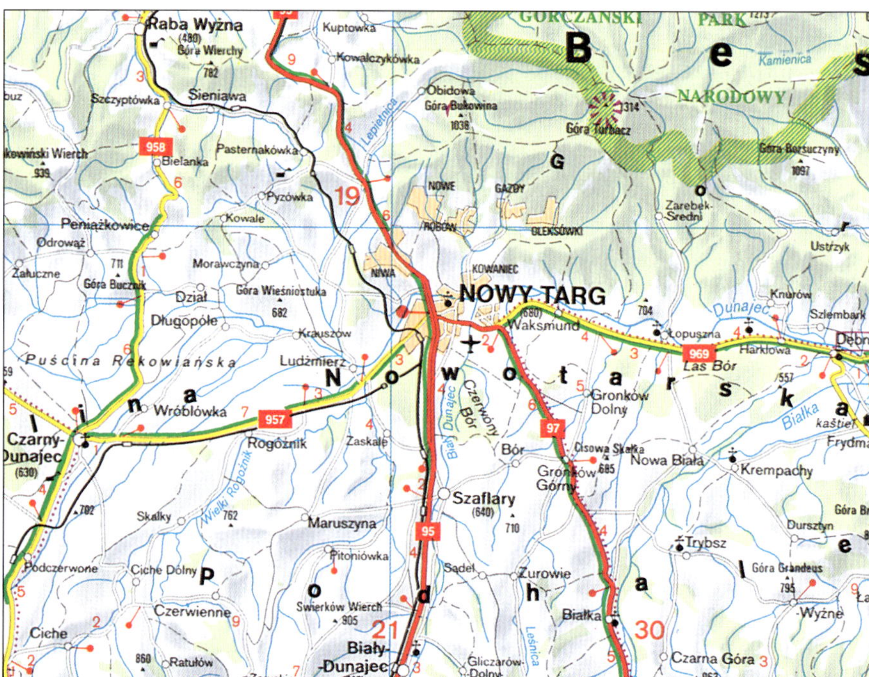

Nowy Targ. The name of the town (New Market) suggests its main function and was the trading centre of Podhale. Because of its good position it possessed from the 16th century the privilege to store salt and lead. It was also the centre of trade for Old Hungarian wine for many years. Nowy Targ had 96 houses in 1536 which increased to 179 a hundred years later. There were, for instance, five butchers, four bakers, three tailors, two furriers and representatives of many other crafts at the time. The owners of the estate of Nowy Targ frequently changed. The most important of them were the families of Ratułowski, Peniązko, Kazanowski, and Komorowski, the last of whom is remembered especially for his cruelty towards the subjects. Continually rising taxes and duties provoked protests amongst the peasants of the communities of Klikuszowa and Czarny Dunajec. Nowy Targ was conquered and entirely destroyed by the Swedes in 1655, and in the following century, in 1770, it fell into the hands of Austria. By the beginning of the 19th century the population in Nowy Targ amounted to almost 2,700 and half a century later it had swollen to 5,000 people. The end of the 19th century brought along an economic revival. New power plants were built, a brickyard and printing plant were all operating here and the overall appearance of the town improved. Nowy Targ entered the 20th century as the most important centre of economic and political life in the Podhale region. The National Democratic Party and the Polish People's Party were also active here. In 1904 the first secondary school in Podhale was opened in the town and it played a significant role in the patriotic education of its students. During the inter-war period the town gradually changed into a holiday resort. In 1938 its population amounted to 11,000, and during the grim years of Nazi occupation many inhabitants of Nowy Targ and its environs were involved in conspiracies against the Germans. After the Second World War the territory of the town expanded, with the opening of a big shoe factory, a new hospital and the construction of a new two-lane road which eased traffic congestion.

Nowy Targ has fulfilled an important administrative function since as early as the 14th century and was the seat of the mayor until the division of Poland. In the period when Halič obtained autonomy Nowy Targ was promoted to a district town. Also the year 1994 is important in the history of Nowy Targ as it then became the centre of the Euroregion Tatras, the secretariat of which is in the municipal cultural centre. The function of the town is still that of a supra-regional centre for the population of the Podhale region, with several medium level schools and many cultural institutions.

The Pope and Nowy Targ:

A unique historical event took place in the airport of Nowy Targ on June 8, 1979, when its people met the arrival of Pope John Paul II. It was the biggest ever religious assembly in Podhale and one of the biggest in all Poland. In 1996 the Pope accepted the title of Honorary Citizen of Nowy Targ granted to him by the municipal council. A year later the Pope again visited his beloved Podhale and this visit was again one of the greatest events of the year in Poland.

As in past centuries the town remains the centre of trade, and is a hive of activity on the market days of Thursday and Sunday when waves of Slovak shoppers cross the Tatra border to spend their money (see the town plan (1) for market place). There is still also a **customs office**, the employees of which serve the border crossings in Chyzne, Chochołow, Łysa Polana and Niedzice. Typical features of the town are the numerous **small private businesses** and **workshops** processing wool, hides and furs, as well as wooden and woollen souvenirs. There are also many excellent carpenters here renowned for building houses in the traditional style. Among the schools in the town the **lycée of S. Goszczyński** is the best known. Also the **music school** is more than fifty years old and it boasts of such famous students like Lucjan and Jerzy Kaszycki, Jan Kanty Pavlukievicz, and Janusz Stokłosa. There are also two university faculties – the **Academy of Economy** of Kraków and the **Business College** of Nowy Sącz. The town also abounds with many cultural institutions, like **the municipal cultural centre, the cultural house of youth, the house of culture of the cooperatives, a gallery of fine arts** and the **musical club called Dudek**, all of which promote the cultural traditions of the region. There are also several **folk ensembles** based in the town: Swarni, Mali Swarni, Hyrni and Turlicki.

As for the sacral monuments of the town, attention should be paid to the Baroque **church of St. Katarzyna** (3), the patron saint of the town, located in the centre and the wooden **church of St. Anna** (2) standing on the other bank of the Czarny

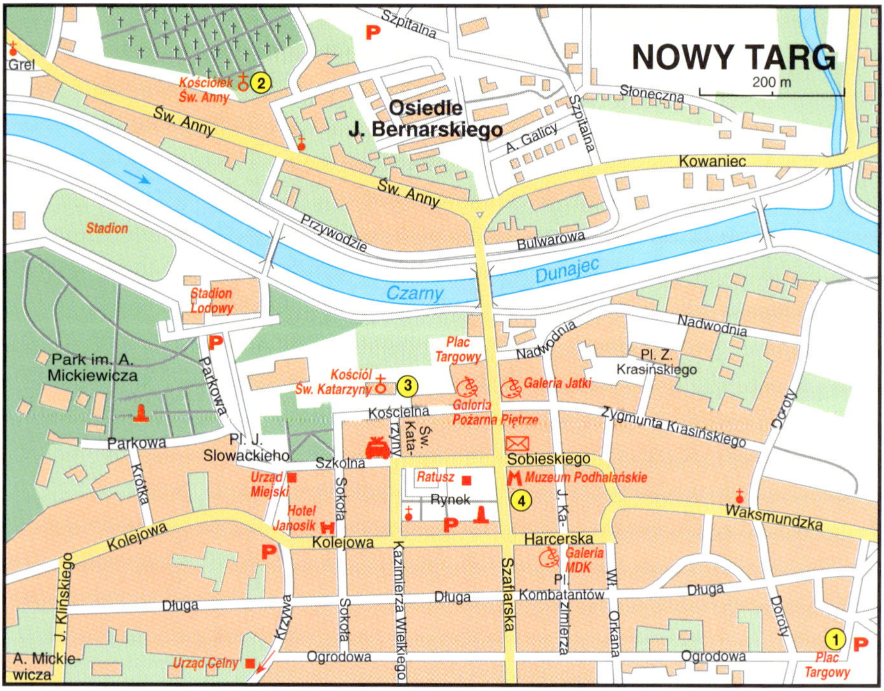

Dunajec river on a cemetery hill. It is constructed of red spruce wood and its origin dates back to the 13th century. It is also associated with an interesting legend.

The church of the robbers:

Once upon a time when there lived many robbers in the border area a local hermit convinced the robbers to start a new and honourable life. He also advised them to build a church as a way of asking for God's forgiveness, to which the robbers agreed. In a short time the local people heard the noise of falling trees and the sound of axes but they were afraid to go and see what was happening. In the meantime the church was acquiring its shape and one day there appeared in its altar a beautiful picture of St. Anna, allegedly stolen in Old Hungary. The robbers used to bring a priest every Friday to celebrate Mass in their church, and the robbers hanged their guns on the walls of the church as a token that they had given up their former discreditable life. On one occasion a merchant from Kraków got lost in the forest and ran into the church in the middle of forest, whereupon he prayed to St. Anna and shortly after found his way out of the forest. Only after this event did the local people learn about the existence of the church. They say this all happened back in 1219, as this is the year carved on the church arch.

The town has preserved its original medieval ground plan, where the streets depart from a square-shaped central square. There is a Neo-Classicist **town hall** standing in the main square called Rynek. It is the seat of the Museum Podhalańskie – **the Regional Museum of PTTK** (Polish tourist association) (4) which houses ethnographic collections. Another landmark in the square is the **statue of Władysław Orkan**, a renowned Polish writer, dedicated to the town by the Podhale Association in 1934.

Muzeum Podhalańskie
Ratusz, tel: 0187/26 62 377
Opening hours: Mon-Fri 9:00-14:00h

Nowy Targ possesses many **sport facilities**. Lawn tennis courts, playgrounds, in-door swimming pool and the ice stadium prove to be the most popular. In Kowaniec two ski lifts and a ski slope in Długa Polana, along with a small ski-jump, are provided for this nationally popular sport. The pride of the town is the local ice hockey club which won repeatedly the Polish national championship. The international **kayak track on the Dunajec river**, beginning in Nowy Targ, is well known by fans of this sport. Nowy Targ is the starting point to the nearby mountain range of **Gorce** and there is a tourist track to its highest peak, **Turbacz** (1,310 m). Every first Sunday in August a **Mass** is given here by Professor Józef Tischner for the "mountain people". Lovers of the mountains and the people living or working in the mountains come here to hear the Mass accompanied by singing and Goral music.

Nowy Targ is the administrative centre of the biggest compound of the communities in Podhale. It comprises 21 villages. In close vicinity to Nowy Targ, only four kilometres west of the city centre is **LUDŹMIERZ** (602 m, population 2,100). This village is one of the oldest in Podhale founded near Czarny Dunajec by the Cistercians in 1234. The Cistercians owned the village several centuries until finally it became the property of Adolf Tetmajer in the mid-19th century. His son Kazimierz Przerwa-Tetmajer, one of the greatest poets of Podhale, who was also a writer and author of literary works written in the Goral dialect, was born here in 1865. The pride of the community is also the Pseudo-Gothic **church of the Virgin Mary's Ascension** built in the years 1869-1877. In its interior is a **statue of the Virgin Mary with the Child** from the 15th century placed on the main Rococo altar, adored not only by the Podhale people, but also by the whole of southern Poland. To mark the occasion of the Virgin Mary's ascension the statue was crowned by Cardinal Stefan Wyszyński on August 15, 1963. Pope John Paul II also prayed at the foot of the statue on June 7, 1997. Most tourists also like to visit the **local cultural centres** where the works of contemporary folk artists are exhibited, such as embroidery, glass paintings, wood cuttings, folk costumes and musical instruments.

Ludźmierz neighbours with the much smaller village of **KRAUSZÓW** (600 m, population 650), which is actually one of the smallest communities around Nowy Targ. It is about 5 kilometres away from the city centre. The village is situated at the confluence of the Czarny Dunajec and Lepietnice rivers. It was first referred to in the same year as Ludźmierz, in 1234, when it was founded by the Cistercians. The village is surrounded by waterlogged fields which have caused problems to the local people for centuries and are still quite useless for agricultural purposes.

On the right side of Czarny Dunajec is the village of **DŁUGOPOLE** (620 m, population 500) which lies 8 kilometres west of Nowy Targ and like Krauszów it is surrounded by barren soil.

Along the road from Nowy Targ to Jabłonka, about 7 km from the centre of the town, is the village of **ROGOŹNIK** (640 m, population 850). This village, stretching along the Wielki Rogoźnik brook, is also one of the oldest villages of Podhale as it was founded in the same year (1234) as Ludźmierz and Krauszow by the Cistercians. The community owned a part of the forests in the West Tatras where there is an alpine meadow bearing the name of the village – Polana Rogoźnicka. South of the village is the **nature reserve of Skałka Rogoźnicka** which covers an area 0.26 hectares.

North of Nowy Targ is the village of **KLIKUSZOWA** (690 m, population 1,350) which is situated in the valley of Lepietnica, the river which springs under the Turbacz mountain in the Gorce mountain range. The village is 5 kilometres from Nowy Targ and it lies along the main road to Zakopane and Kraków. It was founded in 1389 on a trade road that used to lead over the Lepietnica valley heading towards Ludźmierz. Its history, however, is sadly remembered for the tragic events during the Second World War when the Nazis executed a group of insurgents in the local cemetery. The black-marked tourist footpath starting in the village leads to the **Bukowina Obidowska** mountain and other peaks of the Gorce mountain range. There is a quarry on the outskirts of the territories of both villages where limestone is extracted. The mountain ridge Kulakowy Wierch-Obidowa is south-west of the village and there are two ski lifts on its slopes.

Along the old road from Klikuszowa heading towards Ludźmierz is the village of **LASEK** (660 m, population 1,000) which lies in the Lepietnica valley and has a railway track commuting to Zakopane and Kraków. The local people make their living mainly from agriculture and cattle raising. The character of the adjacent villages **TRUTE** (640 m population 550), and **MORAVCZYNA** (650 m, population 650), and **PYZÓWKA** (700 m, population 850) is similar and are typical farming villages of the Podhale region, situated on the moderate slopes of Beskidy mountains. As the soil is mostly infertile, the landscape consists of spruce forests and pastures, suitable only for sheep raising. It has a long tradition in these parts and it is also connected with numerous stories and legends.

The shepherd Anjoł:

The shepherd Anjoł (Angel) was one of the most famous shepherds in the region. Born in the village of Obidowa he had a small farm on the Turbacz mountain, and in springtime, just like the other shepherds, he drove his flocks out to the meadows of the Gorce mountains. His position in the village was special, for he was esteemed for his wisdom and capability to cure any disease. But then all his sheep died of some unknown ailment, which he determined to be the cause of a spell that someone had cast on his animals. The only cure to the disaster, he believed, was to cut the head off one of the sheep so that the rest of them would revive. The only problem was how to find the right animal. But shepherd Anjoł eventually found it and cut its head off, so the dead sheep suddenly came back to life and jumped to their feet. Anjoł knew though, that the one who cast the spell would end in a similar manner. And indeed, the envious and vicious shepherd of Łopuszna, his neighbour, lost his head and died the very moment when Anjoł cut off his own sheep's head.

Nowy Targ neighbours in the east with the big village of **WAKSMUND** (575 m, population 2,200) stretching on both banks of the river Dunajec. It is one of the oldest communities in the Podhale region. The first name of the village *Wilcze Pole* was mentioned as early as in 1254. The later name of the village is linked to the German population which founded the village here and lived here for some time. The owners of Waksmund also possessed a part of the Tatras until 1860 as witnessed by the name of one of the alpine meadows – Polana Waksmudska. During the Second World War the village was the focus of fierce resistance against the Nazis. The present appearance of the village is marked by the construction of a dam on the river Dunajec.

East of Waksmud is **OSTROWSKO** (570m, population 1,200), 5 kilometres east of Nowy Targ and lies on the right bank of the river Dunajec near the main road from Krościenko to Nowy Sącz. According to historical sources it was founded by settlers who arrived from the north in the 13th century. In 1824 it was purchased, along with the surrounding communities, by Emanuel Homolacs. It became famous first of all for the skilfulness of its craftsmen, as brooms and baskets were made here in the inter-war period. Its most historical significance occurred after the war, when in 1947 the last battle took place in the village and the partisan leader, nicknamed Ogień, who was famous for his cruelty was caught and executed here. The place where this controversial figure was buried is still unknown. The **walled church** of 1927 is the most interesting cultural monument in the village remarkable for its interior wooden decoration, made by the local carpenter, cabinet-makers and woodcarvers.

Near Ostrowsko and the river Dunajec, along its left tributary Łopuszanka, is the village **ŁOPUSZNA** (560 m, population 1,300). It is 8 km from Nowy Targ. The village originated in 1406 on the terraces of the river Dunajec. It was owned in the past by various knights. In the 18th and 19th centuries it belonged to the families of Lisiecki and Tetmajer. The best known of the village owners was Leon Przewa-Tetmajer, a great patriot and participant in the November insurrection (in 1830 against the Tsar's Russia) where he met the poet Seweryn Goszczyński. The poet was living for some time with the family of Tetmajer and the village became an important patriotic and revolutionary centre in Podhale during the 19th century. The poet and writer L. Pzerwa-Tetmajer became one of the first to promote the beauty of the Tatras, and it was here where he wrote his "Diary of the Tatra Walks". The most important monument of the village is the log **curia** of 1784. It was built by the owner of the village Romuald Lisiecki and nowadays it is the biggest attraction in the village and houses the Museum of the Culture of Nobility.

Muzeum Kultury Szlacheckiej
(Museum of Culture of Nobility),
curia in Łopuszna, tel.: 018/265 39 69
Opening hours: Wed-Sun 10:00-16:00h

At the present time an open-air museum of Podhale architecture near the curia is under construction, and there is also a private **gallery** nearby. The most important building in the village is

Right: The Regional Museum in Nowy Targ

the repeatedly rebuilt **church** originating from the 16th century, which contains a precious triptych commemorating the coronation of the Virgin Mary from the second half of the 15th century. Besides the cultural and historical monuments Łopuszna boasts of a trout hatchery on the right bank of the river Dunajec. In the southern part of the village there is a ski lift and a blue-marked footpath leading to the Turbacz mountain.

Further eastward along the road to Krościenko is the small village of **DĘBNO** (540 m, population 800) which is situated on the right bank of the river Dunajec, 12 km away from Nowy Targ. Dębno was founded by the knight Urban by pursuing a privilege obtained in 1335 and it bears an oak (dęb in Polish) in its coat of arms. In the Middle Ages it used to belong to the estate of Czorsztyn. Dębno is the **reserve of folk architecture**. The most important building here is the oldest wooden church in the Podhale region, the **church of St. Michael the Archangel**. It was built in the years 1480-1490 and is decorated by a well-preserved **painting**. It is the only painting on wood from the late 15th century in Europe preserved in an original log sacral building. The painting contains 77 plant, animal, and geometrical motifs. The oldest item of the decoration of the church is the wooden cross from the early 15th century. Also the glockenspiel which consists of five metal plates (the longest of which issues the highest tone and the shortest produces the lowest tone) is very precious. Most attractive for tourists is certainly the **Czorztyńska dam** separated from the eastern part of the village by a high dyke.

On the other bank of the Dunajec, north of Dębno, there are the two little villages of **KNURÓW** (570 m, population 450) and **SZLEMBARK** (570 m, population 550). As with Dębno they belong to the group of villages administered by Nowy Targ. Of the two Szlembark is better known and was founded by the Order of the Clare nuns of Nowy Sącz. Both villages are set in wonderful nature, as if squatting below the slopes of the Gorce mountain range. There are several locations from where one gets a fine view of the Tatras and parts of Podhale region, favourite chosen landscapes of Polish painters.

West of Dębno and 10 km from Nowy Targ on the bank of the Dunajec lies **HARKLOWA** (545 m, population 450). On a high terrace in the southern part of the territory of this village is a

continuos forested canopy called **Harklowy Bór**. The oldest written reference mentions the village as a knight community called "Harthle" existing here probably as early as in 1325. In the past Harklowa belonged to the Czorsztyński estate. The local po-pulation made their living by sheep and cattle raising and agriculture, the same as the people of the neighbouring Podhale villages lying on the southern foothills of the Gorce and banks of the river Dunajec. Its history is well recorded in several folk legends which tell of some charismatic figures such as the "witch of Podhale".

The witch of Dunajec:

In the 19th century there used to live near the bridge over the Dunajec river a witch who was famous throughout Podhale. Young and very pretty she possessed curative powers and was also a fortune-teller. One day an unusual event stirred the sleepy life in the village when a horse belonging to one of the farmers strayed into an enclosure, and the gate closed behind him so that it could not get out. Several days of searching for the horse ended unsuccessfully. and the Gypsies camping nearby were suspected of stealing it. But one of the villagers advised the owner to ask the witch for assistance. She knew immediately and told the farmer where the horse was, whereupon he found the famished and thirsty horse just where she said it was. In the same way the witch also helped another farmer to find his lost pigs. But her life ended in a tragedy when one day she fell down the roof of her own cottage and died. Her special powers were unable to save her own life, but she became famous all over Podhale.

The most important sacral monument in the village is the local parish **church of the Holy Family**. It is from the turn of the 15th and 16th centuries and is famous for the painting of the Holy Family in its main altar. The best known secular building in the village is the squire **curia** of the 19th century. The outstanding Polish painter, Włodimierz Tetmajer, the brother of Kazimierz Przewa-Tetmajer, the great Polish poet and writer, was born here in 1861.

Left: A church in Dębno

In the valley of the Leśnica brook, on the right tributary of the Dunajec, flowing between Ostrowske and Łopuszna is **GRONKÓW** (580 m, population 1,450) which lies 6 km south-east of Nowy Targ, 6 km. Its houses are arranged in a long approximately 4 km long row, orientated in north-south direction.

Different ground plans exist for those villages north of the Czorsztyńska dam, for instance, **MANIOWY** (520 m, population 1,850) on the main road of Nowy Targ (18 km) towards Krościenko and Szczawnica. When the dam was built the old part of Maniowy disappeared. The village was subsequently moved from the bottom of the Dunajec valley to the southern slopes of the Gorce mountain range, where **Nowe Maniowy** emerged, but unfortunately, the new community did not preserve the old Goral style of architecture. The history of the old village dates back to 1326 when its was founded on the bank of the Dunajec neighbouring with the old Czorsztyn village about the same time. Maniowy had many precious and remarkable old buildings. There was a chapel made of red spruce wood from 1723, a 19th century curia and many peasant farmsteads. Unfortunately, these monuments do not exist anymore. The people today live in new houses arranged in regular streets. Compared to the monotony of the houses, the new **church** deserves attention for its height and interesting architecture, and there is a precious view of the Czorsztyńska dam of the Pieniny mountains and the Tatras when standing on the square in front of the church.

KLUSZKOWCE (500 m, population 1,450) stretches on the bank of the dam. The village running from the north to south is crossed by the main road connecting Nowy Targ with Krościenko, passing over Kluszkowce via a high viaduct. The exact date of the origin of the village is not known but it was probably founded in the 14th century. It used to belong for a long time to the Czorsztyński estate, and was stricken by fire in 1816 which destroyed almost the whole of the village. By the beginning of the 20th century Kluszkowce became a famous tourist centre. Also the dam has enhanced its attractiveness. The highest part of the village neighbours with the **mountain of Wdźar** built of andesites, at the foot of which there is a **monument** commemorating the Polish heroes who lost their lives during the Second World War. The place offers a wonderful view of the Nowotarska basin, the Pieniny and Gorce mountain ranges, even the Tatras if the weather is fine.

South of Nowy Targ is the village of **SZAFLARY** (650 m, population 3,200) which is near the Biały Dunajec river, on the main route of the road and railway connecting with Zakopane. The village probably originated in the 13th century under a small **castle** built on a limestone cliff called **Szaflarska Skałka**. The castle was pulled down in the time of king Luwik Węgierski, and was reconstructed in the 15th century and became the seat of the mayors of Nowy Targ. Then it gradually decayed, although the remains of the castle are preserved until the present time. An important sacral monument in the village is the **church of St. Andrej the Apostol** built in 1799. Szaflary is also an important economic centre of the Podhale region, and until recently it had the only ski manufacturing plant in Poland. There is also in the village the seat of regional administration, gmina, serving the group of surrounding villages.

The community of **ZASKALE** (640 m, population 1,100) neighbours in the north with Szaflary. The village is situated in the valley of the Rogoźniczek brook, the right tributary of Czarny Dunajec, 6 km south-west of Nowy Targ.

Nearby, is **MARUSZYNA** (660 m, population 1,750). It became famous as the birth place of Jan Rubzdel, who purchased the alpine meadow of Zakopane where he settled down and founded the famous family of Gąsienica.

The smallest of the group of villages, **BÓR** (630 m, population 450) neighbours in the east with Szaflary. It lies in the upper part of the Czerwony potok brook, on the left tributary of the river Leśnica.

South of Szaflary, next to the main road to Zakopane, is **BAŃSKA NIZNA** (820 m, population 900). The community lies on the left bank of Biały Dunajec, 8 km south of Nowy Targ and is widely known for its thermal springs used for heating the houses.

Within easy distance is **BAŃSKA WYŻNA** (820 m, population 900) which lies in the south and on the ridge and slopes of Świerkowy Wierch. Some of its houses are at an altitude of 900 m above sea level. One of the most picturesque **tourist tracks** passes the village. It starts in Szaflary, passes Bańska Wyzna and Sierockie and leads to the small community of Ząb – the highest situated village in Podhale.

SKRZYPNE (700 m, population 950) neighbours with Bańska Wyzna and Nizna in the west, lying in the valley of the Skrzypny brook. The other part of it, Skrzypne Górne, stretches along the above-mentioned tourist track.

One of the biggest and also one of the oldest villages in Podhale is **CZARNY DUNAJEC** (670 m, population 3,500), the seat of regional administration, *gmina*. It is located near the river Czarny Dunajec, 15 km south-west of Nowy Targ. The village originated in 1552 on the land that used to belong to the Cistercian monks of Ludźmierz. The peasants of Czarny Dunajec and the surrounding villages built here a church and the village became the centre of the parish. The people were active in farming and sheep raising. In the first half of the 19th century Czarny Dunajec was one of the wealthiest villages of Podhale. An infamous event in its history happened in 1846 when the population, agitated by the Old Hungarian authorities, took part in the fight against the Chochołow uprising. Czarny Dunajec had 552 houses and 2,445 inhabitants by the end of the 19th century, and their most common occupations were farming, cattle raising, weaving and peat extraction. There were weekly markets, three mills and five saw mills working in the village. However, Czarny Dunajec lost its municipal rights in 1934. The most important sacral building here is the **Holiest Trinity church** built in 1865. At present the village heads the group of 15 villages, all situated in the western part of Kotlina Nowotarska basin and in the eastern part of the Orawa basin. The natural landmark of Czarny Dunajec is the extensive **peat bogs** situated west of the centre, where the variegated flora and fauna is also quite unique.

The neighbouring community of **WRÓBLÓWKA** (650 m, population 550) is on the right bank of the Czarny Dunajec river, only 2 km north-east of Czarny Dunajec. Wróblówka has several **log houses and farmsteads** built and preserved in the old Podhale style.

Another village of the same gmina is **STARE BYSTRE** (630 m, population 1,650) stretching along the Wielki Rogoźnik brook. In the east it neighbours with Czarny Dunajec and its is 10 km away from Nowy Targ.

In the north of Czarny Dunajec is the old village of **PIENIĄŻKOWICE** (680 m, population 800) lying on the southern slopes of the Beskidy Orawskie mountains and surrounded by a continuous belt of forests. The settlement was founded by Jan Peniązko the mayor of Nowy Targ, by the end of the 16th century. The local population made their living by farming and cattle raising and the local farmers took their herds even to the Tatra pastures. In the 17th century they also had their sheep enclosures with huts in the Dolina Małej Łaki valley in the Zachodnie Tatry mountains. The architectural landmark of the community is a wooden **church** from the 19th century with numerous very old and precious works of art. They were gathered here from several log churches and chapels within the region which do not exist any more. The church bell of 1545 is the most precious item in the collection. Tourists visiting the village like to follow the blue-marked tourist path to **Żeleznicę**, one of the highest peaks of the Orawskie Beskidy mountains.

Right: The village of Nowe Maniowy

South of the village, on the border of the Kotlina Nowotarska basin, is the small village of **DZIAŁ** (650 m, population 500), 10 km away from Nowy Targ. A red-marked track passes the village to Ludźmierz and Szaflary.

ODROWĄŻ (660 m, population 900) also belongs to the administrative territory of Czarny Dunajec and is located in one of the valleys of Beskidy Orawskie. Its name has its origins in the coat of arms of its founders, the mayors of Nowy Targ, the noble family of Pieniązko. The coat of arms, called Odrową depicts a silver arrow on red background turned upwards and ending in the form of a moustache. This village also originated at the end of the 16th century. Of great interest to visitors is certainly the **St. Maria Magdalena church** built in the first half of the 19th century on the site of the original church dating back to the 17th century. Also numerous chapels built on the surrounding hills constitute the sacral monuments of the community.

From the road heading south one gets a wonderful view of the panorama of the Tatras and going west of Odrowąz, on the road to Piekielnik, is the last community lying north of Czarny Dunajec and belonging to the same gmina, **ZAŁUCZNE** (650 m, population 650).

South of Czarny Dunajec are several villages. The first of them is **PODCZERWONE** (720 m, population 950). The village was founded in 1605 on the left bank of Czarny Dunajec near the road to Zakopane. There used to be a railway track connecting the village with Nowy Targ but it was dismantled in the 1970's. A newly built church in the centre of the village is the main attraction for visitors.

Another village along the road heading south to Chochołow is **KONIÓWKA** (740 m, population 300), one of the smallest communities in this group of villages. It lies on the right bank of the river Czarny Dunajec. The most valuable monument preserved here is an old log **belfry** standing in the lower end of the village. There were in the past many belfries in Podhale which functioned as alarm bells in the event of emergencies like thunderstorms or other natural disasters, such as floods and fires. The rather **deep bed of the Czarny Dunajec** river attracts tourists who are fond of bathing.

In the southernmost part of the area of the Czarny Dunajec village lies **CHOCHOŁÓW** (740 m, population 1,100). This larger village is situated in the valley of the Czarny Dunajec river on the main road to Zakopane or to Czarny Dunajec heading out towards the border crossing with Slovakia – Suchá Hora. It originated in the 16th century and its first mayor was Bartołomiej Kluska also called Chochołowski, who was granted the mayor's right by king Zygmunt III in 1592. The same year the people of the village were allowed to bring their herds to the Tatra pastures, a privilege extended to another six villages. The biggest valley where the people of Chochołow pastured their livestock attributes its name to Chochołowka, just like many other local names in this part of the Zachodnie Tatry mountains. For example, the alpine meadow of Chochołowska or the Chochołowska Szczelina cave, the Chochłowski Potok brook and the Chochołowskie Wywierzysko spring, amongst others. A remarkable sacral monument in the community is the **church of St. Jacek** built in the second half of the 19th century. The village nowadays represents a living **open-air architectural museum**, as there are numerous old log Goral huts contributing to the typical appearance of this type of village. The oldest **Goral huts** are normally rather low with a rectangular ground plan. They are turned with their shorter wall to the road heading from the south to the north and their fronts face the warmer southern side. The log houses have steep, saddle-shaped shingle roofs. The front part of the house next to the road is intended as a living room and the back part is designed for farming purposes. The women always used to clean the walls of the log huts in the

spring time before Easter, using soap and water, and so the log huts preserve their light colour. In one of the houses standing in a rather untypical manner for this particular village – as its facade faces the street – seats the **Museum of the Uprising of Chochółow** (Muzem Powstania Chochołowskiego).

The Chochołów uprising:

The Gorals of Chochołów and adjacent villages argued for their rights to the lands in the Tatras, to the pastures and for logging in the forests, and these rights were granted to them by a royal privilege. The growing tensions between the Gorals and count Kajetan Borowski culminated in an armed uprising. It started on February 21, 1846 to coincide with a nation-wide uprising planned for the same day. But the national event was called off at the last moment of which the Gorals of Chochołow were unaware. At the beginning their uprising, led by the organist Jan Kanty Andrusikiewicz, and the priest Józef Kmietowicz was successful. They disarmed the boundary and custom station and destroyed the boundary poles. But after three days they were defeated by the army assisted by the Gorals of Czarny Dunajec in league with by the Austro-Hungarian authorities. Even to this day the people of Chochołów still cannot forgive the Gorals of Czarny Dunajec for what they consider to be an act of extreme treachery.

One of the longest and most densely populated villages of Podhale, belonging to the group of villages administered by Czarny Dunajec, is **CICHE** (700 m, population 2,800), which lies in the valley of Cichy Potok brook east of Chochołów. The Cichy brook, together with the Bystry brook form the beginning of the river Wielki Rogoznik, which is turn is the tributary of Czarny Dunajec. The oldest reference to the village dates from 1595, when Tomasz Miętusz of Czarny Dunajec, with the consent of king Zygmunt III, founded the first settlement here, which has a long history of shepherd traditions. The inhabitants of Ciche are still the owners of the meadows and forests in Zachodnie Tatry, mostly within the Chochołowska valley. The village of Ciche is

Left: The girls from the Tatras

14 km long and there are many preserved specimens here of traditional architecture, including precious and lavishly decorated **belfries** and a **chapel** from the 19th century. The people of Ciche are also famous for their wood carvings. Visitors follow the **red-marked footpath** leading to the top of Gubałówka and further to Poronin and Zakopane, or in a opposite direction to Chochołów.

In the east it neighbours with **RATUŁÓW** (640 m, population 1,900) lying in the valley of the Bystry brook. The lower part of the village is joined to one of the smaller settlements near Ratuł called Miętustwo, founded by the first mayor of Ciche, Tomasz Miętusz. The village was founded by Wojciech Ratułowski pursuing the privilege granted to him by king Zygmunt III in 1627. The local people have a long tradition of designing and making metal buckles and other metal accessories for Goral waist belts. One of the artisans, Andrzej Kubin-Opacian received various prizes in folk competitions and festivals for his work of art in this field. There used to live in the community also a well known folk narrator by the name of Władysław Przeworek. There are numerous precious specimens of wooden folk architecture like old **farmsteads** and **chapels** standing along the road and statues of various saints, and there is also a wonderful view of the Tatras from the village.

Similar panoramas can be admired also from the community of **CZIERWIENNE** (720 m, population 1,400) situated east of Ratułów. The wooden **belfry** is the most precious architectural monument in the village. In the community of **Bachledówka**, built on a hill between the villages of Ratułów and Czerwienne is a **monastery**, which is the most important sacral monument of this particular community. From here tourists can choose the green-marked footpath starting in Szaflary, passing Czerwienne and ending in Zakopane. Along this route picturesque crests and the elevation of Pogórze Gubałowskie provide the hiker with wonderful views of the Tatras and the Kotlina Nowotarska basin.

ORAWA

Jabłonka
and its environs

JABŁONKA (620 m, population 4,500) lies 26 km west of Nowy Targ, in the northern part of the Kotlina Orawska basin, near the river Czarną Orawa. It is the seat of administration of eight villages lying in the basins and on the slopes of Beskid. The borders of the administered territory coincide with the water divide delimiting two draining areas feeding the Black Sea and the Baltic Sea. The villages administered by Jabłonka form only a small part of the Polish territory where the water flows to the Black Sea.

Jabłonka like Lipnica Wielka, can make claim to having the highest number of inhabitants in the valley of Czarną Orawa. In the time of the Polish king Kazimierz Wielki (at end of the 14th century) there used to be a customs point on the site of the present village. The community originated later, in 1566, and belonged to the family of Jabłonski, and by 1659 there lived altogether 630 Catholics and 230 Protestants, two religious groups who were not entirely in harmony with each other. The Slovak and Polish languages, folk traditions and costumes survived the period of Magyarisation, which at the end of the 19th century, was an attempt by the Hungarian authorities to pressure ethnic groups to adopt the Hungarian language. The present population of the village is mixed and the Slovaks and the Poles coexist here quite peacefully. The Slovak minority has here its clubs and Slovak is taught as a foreign language in the local lycée. Besides this there is the basic school where all subjects are taught in the mother tongue of the Slovaks. There are some **folk ensembles** which are quite active as well.

Regular trade **markets** are held in Jabłonka every Wednesday when many shoppers arriving from the south visit the village. The original wooden Evangelical **church** does not exist any more, and the village has only one sacral building, the Roman-Catholic **church**, which is rather far from the centre of the community and built in 1817. It has a typical onion-shaped tower and sad-

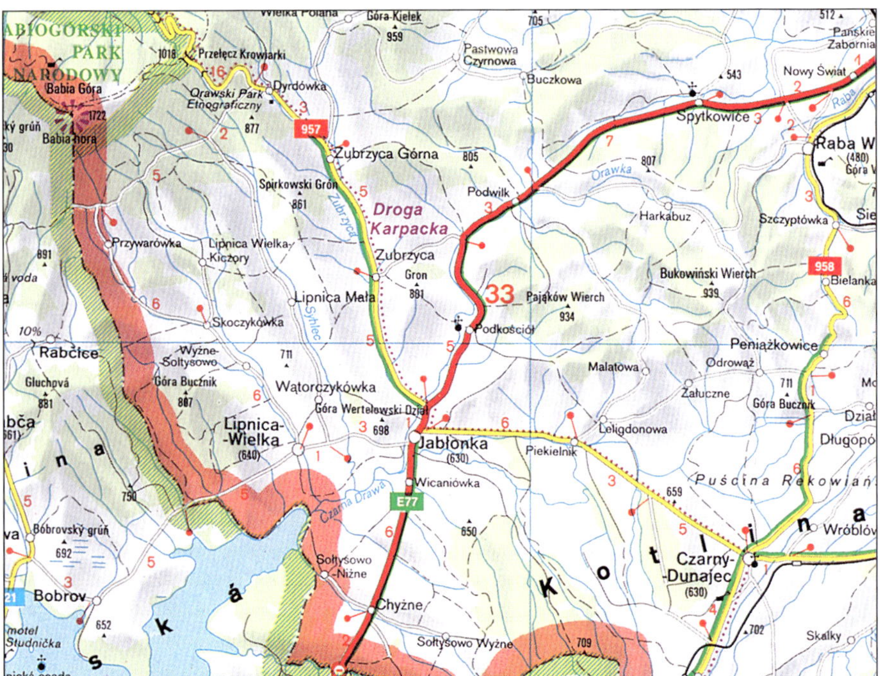

dle roof over the main nave with a small bell. These features are typical for many churches in the Orawa region, built by the end of the 18th century and the beginning of the 19th century.

The Polish part of Orawa:

The Polish part of Orawa occupies the Kotlina Orawska basin with the southern slopes of the belt of Babia Góra and Polica, which belongs to the Beskid Żiwiecky mountain range, as well as a big part of Orawski Beskid. The region stretches along the draining area of the Czarną Orawa river. In the Middle Ages two waves of settlements arrived here. The first of these were Slovaks who came here from the south, and were followed by Polish settlers spread from the north. By the beginning of the 16th century Polish refugees, mainly from the areas of Żywiec, Sącz and Podhale arrived here, and after the death of the Polish king Bolesław Chrobri Orawa was annexed to Old Hungary. Its northern region was returned to Poland in the 20th century. International treaties in 1920, concerning the alternation of the state border, adjudicated fifteen villages of Orawa to Poland and two of them, Sucha Góra and Głodówka, were given back to Slovakia in 1924. There are at present in Poland altogether thirteen Orawa villages: Chyzne, Jabłonka, Lipnica Mała, Lipnica Wielka, Piekielnik, Zubrzyca Dolna, Zubrzycza Górna, Orawka, Podwilk, Harakabuz, Podsarnie, Bukowina, and Podszkle. The administration of the villages is distributed into four gminas: Jabłonka, Czarny Dunajec, Lipnica Wielka, and Raba Wyzna.

The village of **CHYŻNE** (620 m, population 1,150) is also administered by Jabłonka and it stretches near the Chyzny Potok brook that flows into the Orava dam on the Slovak side of the border. Chyzne is 6 km away from Jabłonka and almost 33 km from Nowy Targ. An important road from Kraków, leading via Rabka to the **border crossing of Chyżne-Trstená** passes the village. This oldest and busiest border crossing between Poland and Slovakia is only two kilometres from the village and it is situated near the boundary brook of Jeleśna (659 m). Compared to other mountain border crossings to Slovakia it is the most accessible and it is open 24 hours, the main route for heavy trucks. Some villagers have found here permanent jobs.

East of Jabłonka is **PEKIELNIK** (630 m, population 2,100), a village situated on the border between the basins of Orawska and Nowotarska. Its southern part stretches along the main road from Jabłonka to Nowy Targ (21 km away). The village is crossed by a brook bearing the same name, the left tributary of Czarna Orawa. South of the village are the **peat bogs** called by the local people "the patrimony" as the lands were inherited from one generation to another. Interesting plant fossils and animal remains from ancient periods have been found here. Piekielnik, the same as other villages in the Orawa region originated as late as the 16th century, when the Old Hungarian aristocrat František Thurzo, seated in Slovak Orava castle, ordered the settlement of the area. There are several old **wooden buildings** preserved in the village and built in a style typical for the region, with what was called "wyzka" – a room upstairs where coal was stored. Also the Baroque stone statues in the local **St. Jakub church** are remarkable.

Near the main road from Chyzne to Kraków, north of Jablonka, is another village called **ORAWKA** (640 m, population 900). It lies in the valley of Czarna Orawa and was founded by Jerzy Wilga, the first mayor of the village, in 1585. In the mid-17th century, in 1650 to be precise, a parish comprising all the surrounding villages – Jabłonka, Lipnica Mała, Lipnica Wielka, Piekielnik, Zubrzyca Dolna, Zubrzyca Górna, and Podszkle was established here. The most valuable landmark of the period is the quaint wooden **church of St. John the Baptist** from 1651, one of the most valuable sacral monuments of wooden architecture in Podhale. Especially valuable are the wall paintings of 1711, part of the Baroque interior and representing the life of John Babtist. There is a walled house standing behind the church, once the seat of the customs office and later a salt store. In the **local cultural centre** a performance of **Christmas songs** is given annually. There is a wonderful view of the Tatras and Babia Góra from the village.

PODSZKLE (760 m, population 800) lying in the north-east and the neighbouring **BUKOWINA** form the northern edge of the Orawa regions, situated in the valley of the Bukoviński Strumień brook. In the 16th and 17th centuries refugees from the northern side of Babia Góra, Żywiec, Sucha and Wadowice settled here. The nobility of Orava castle tolerated the Polish settlers in the northern edge of the Old Hungarian

monarchy and allowed them to cultivate the land in northern Orawa. Cultural and historical monuments are represented here by the **St. Rozalia church** from the late 18th century and a wooden **belfry** covered with a shingle roof.

On the moderate slopes of Babia Góra and Polica turned to the Orawa basin is **ZUBRZYCA GÓRNA** (680 m, population 2,650). The village is 7 km south-west of Jabłonka and 30 km west of Nowy Targ. It was for the first time referred to in 1567 when the family of Moniak, with the consent of the nobleman Thurzo, started to build a mill, which later produced the famous linen of Zubrzyca in what was a poor shepherd community. Mateusz Moniak was even rewarded with a title in 1674 for his contribution to the economic development of the region. His grandson Stanisław Moniak built a wooden church in the village, which later was substituted by the walled **St. Michal the Archangel church**, a copy of the one in Jabłonka. The most valuable part of this Baroque building is the main altar fashioned by the wood carvers of Tyrol, who were especially invited for the task. But the most attractive part of Zubrzyca, and indeed throughout Orawa, is the open-air museum of folk architecture situated around the curia of the Moniak family.

Left: The Days of Slovak culture
Right: The interior of a house in Orawa

There are wooden houses and farmsteads and an old inn of the 18th century, moved here from Podwilk. It houses the gallery of folk arts, an office and the booking office of the museum. There is also a blacksmith's workshop, a fulling mill, a beehive, an oil plant and a sawmill. The pride of the museum are the beautiful specimens of old spruce, maple, poplar, oak and linden trees.

Orawski Park Etnograficzny
(Ethnographic Park of Orawa), tel. :018/265 27 09
Open daily from 8:00 to 15:00h

Zubrzyca Górna neighbours with **ZUBRZYCA DOLNA** (670 m, population 1,500) lying in the valley of the Zubrzyca brook, a tributary of Czarna Orawa in Jabłonka. The history of the village is tied to its twin, Zubrzyca Górna. Once upon a time both of them constituted one village with the administra-

tive seat located in Zubrzyca Górna. The new parish **church of Matka Boska Szkaplerzna** was built in the village in 1989. The village stretches along the road leading from Jabłonka over the mountain saddle of Krowiarki to Sucha, Zawoi and Makow.

West of Zubrzyca Dolna and at the foot of **Babia Góra**, the highest mountain in the Polish Carpathians, is **LIPNICA MAŁA** (640 m, population 2,900). It is built on both banks of the Syhlec brook which flows into the Orawa dam. The village was probably founded by the mayor, Jan Kral together with several settlers from the other side of Babia Góra and Żywiec, some time around 1608. The people of Lipnica Mała still maintain their old traditions and rituals. In the village can be seen some fine examples of wooden architecture with a typical window decoration often admired by tourists. The **church** and the **belfry**, the two most interesting cultural and historical monuments are from the 18th century. A **green-marked footpath** crossing the village leads to Babia Góra.

The last village belonging to the administration of Jabłonka is **PODWILK** (640 m, population 2,200) which lies near the confluence of the Orawka and Bukowiński Strumień brooks. The name of the village is derived from the one of its mayors, Wilczk, who founded the village in 1585. Later the family became the owners of the village. There used to exist an Evangelical church in the 17th century and later (1767) the Roman-Catholic **church of Matka Boska Częstochowska** was built on its site. The church was used as a model for another church built in Lipnica Wielka. A very valuable painting of the Virgin Częstochowska which used to hang in the local church until the Second World War was admired and worshipped by all Orawa people, but it was moved to Slovakia after the war.

LIPNICA WIELKA (650 m, population 5,300) is the biggest village in Orawa and also an administrative centre. It is 16 km long, situated in the valley of Lipnica brook that flows into the Orava dam. Like its neighbour, Lipnica Mała, it was founded in the early 17th century by the peasants who fled from the Żywiec area. The first mayor was Michał Śmietana Lipnicki. The Roman-Catholic **church of St. Lukas** and the parish date back to 1769. The destinies of two remarkable figures are connected with Lipnicá Wielka, the priest

Ferdynand Machay and Piotr Borowy. The first became senator of the Polish Republic and a patriot who promoted the annexation of Orawa and Spisz to Poland,and the priest, Machay, was one of the members of the delegation of Spisz and Orawa in the Peace Congress in Paris. He spent the last days of his life in Kraków as Canon of the beautiful cathedral of the Holiest Virgin Mary in the main square. Piotr Borowy was actively involved in the culture of Orawa. A bronze commemorative board placed in the church in Lipnica Wielka refers to him as an "Apostle of Orawa". The village is attractive mainly for its location next to Babia Góra, where deep forests with variegated vegetation are being increasingly visited by tourists. In the community of Przywarówka, situated closer to Babia Góra, the folk festivals which revive old shepherd traditions are organised in the meadows above the village every year on second of July. The village has also a **children's folk ensemble**, Orawianie.

HARKABUZ (800 m, population 500), is a village which in the past was called Orawką Górna and lies near the upper part of the Orawka brook in northern Orawa. It was founded by the Poles who fled from the estate of Mikołaj Zebrzydowski near Lanskorona and the present Kalwaria Zabrzydowska. The contemporary name of the village is in fact a mutation of the French name of a medieval shooting arm used by the infantry, and is one of the Orawa villages which comes under the administration of Raba Wyzna. Another is **PODSARNIE** (680m, population 750), formerly called Orawką Średnią which stretches on both banks of the Orawka brook below Harakąbuz. Its first mayor was a man called Sarna. Podsarnie was a boundary village of Old Hungary for many years and the seat of a customs point until the First World War. Both villages have wooden belfries from the 18th century.

Left: An Orawa woman

SPISZ

Łapsze Niżne
and its environs

At the foothills of the southern slopes of the mountain belt of Branisko-Hombark is the village of **ŁAPSZE NIŻNE** (580 m, population 1,400) which is situated on the bank of the Łapszanka brook and 19 km from Nowy Targ. The first unconfirmed reference to the village dates from 1274. It is probable that a parish founded by the Templar Order of Miechow, then owners of the local lands, probably existed in the locality at that time. In 1593 the villages became the property of the Horwath family.

The Polish part of Spiš :

The Polish part of Spiš, or in Polish language Spisz, represents an area of approximately 170 square kilometres enclosed in the south and the east by the state border, and in the north and west by the rivers Dunajec and Białka respectively. Poland lost the region, also called Spiskie Zamagurze, in the 14th century in favour of Old Hungary. The Old Hungarian rule and the immigration of the German settlers from Levoča in Slovakia has, over the course of time, created a remarkable blend of unusual customs, folk costumes and aspects of rural architecture quite unique to the region. Slovak, Polish, Hungarian, German and Wallachian and Russian influences coexisted here for many centuries. The seat of the rich Old Hungarian families, owners of the land in question, was in the castle of Niedzica and the population was prevailingly Polish and Slovak. The priests, however, were mostly Polish. Although the rule of Old Hungary over the territory lasted such a long time, the Hungarian language did not leave any traces in the local names or language. The most important event in the history of Spisz was what was called the "Spisz forfeit" in the 13th century. The Old Hungarian king Sigismond of Luxembourg changed sixteen towns and villages for a loan from the Polish king Władysław Jagielie in 1412. Part of the towns remained in Poland until as late as 1769. When Austria occupied Spisz the

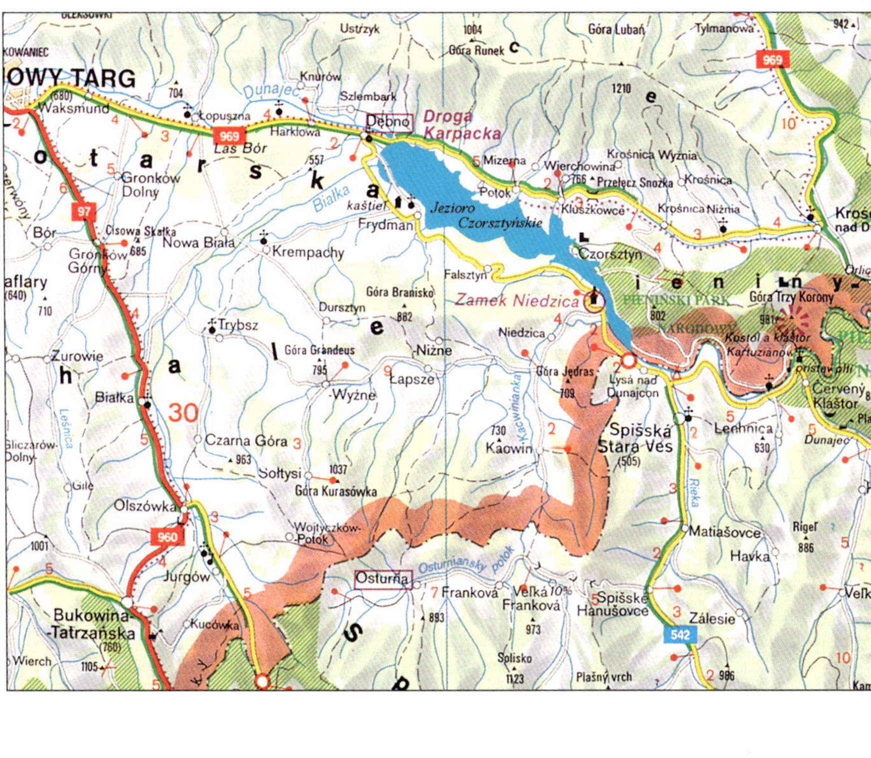

same year, and after the division of Poland, the border on Białka and Dunajec was abolished. Consequently the whole of Spiš fell into the hands of the Austro-Hungarian Empire for almost 150 years. Poland recovered the part of Spisz that belongs to it at present after the First World War.

Due to the support of the Templars the population remained faithful to the Catholic religion also during the Reformation period. An important year in the history of the village was 1846 when Polish insurgents started their march to Nowy Targ precisely from this village. Although serfdom was abolished here two years later, it existed in fact until the 1930's. The most important building in the community is the Gothic-Baroque **St. Kwiryn church** probably from the early 14th century, later rebuilt and reconstructed. A double Templar cross on the tower is preserved. The village plays now an important role in transboundary co-operation with Slovak towns and villages. For instance, the head of the administrative unit, *gmina* of Łapsze Nizne, Wendelin Haber was the chairman of Euroregion Tatry for one electoral period, now currently the vice-chairman of the organisation.

Neighbouring **ŁAPSZE WYŻNE** (620 m, population 900) is situated in the central part of the Zamagurze region, near the brook Łapszanka and about 17 km from Nowy Targ. The village was first mentioned in 1463 and belonged until the 16th century under the church and public administration of Łapsze Nizne. Ownership of the village changed, and as usual for other Spisz communities it was owned by the rich Old Hungarian families of Berzeviczy, Zapolay, Horwath and Salamon. The only Polish owners of the local estates were the family of Łaski. Łapsze Wyzne was settled in the 15th and 16th centuries by the Wallachian-Russian shepherds called locally "Rusnaci". Originally they adhered to the Orthodox Catholic religion and later converted to Roman Catholicism. It is very probable that there first existed an Orthodox Catholic church in the village, although there is evidence to suggest that in 1655 there was a very strong Catholic parish administrating six adjacent villages. Its first seat was probably in the former Orthodox church, abandoned by the "Rusnaci", although the cause of their abrupt departure is not altogether clear, and there exists hints of continuous conflicts and manifestations of intolerance of the original Polish population towards newcomers. Mixed marriages among Rusnaci and the indigenous population were not either concluded or tolerated here in difference from other villages such as Kacwin or Czarna Góra. Łapsze Wyzne emerged from the 18th century as an ethnically uniform community. In 1780 the **church of St. Piotr and Pawel**, the most beautiful specimen of the Rococo style in Polish Spisz was built here. The benefactor of the church was count Jan Ioanelli de Toluano from Niedzica castle and the construction was supervised by the priest Szymon Gorylowicz. After the First World War the village was adjudicated to Poland, yet some interesting **folk customs and traditions** observed during the main festive seasons, such as Christmas and Easter, are preserved here.

Near the state border, 5 km south-east of Łapsze Nizne is **KACWIN** (550 m, population 1,150). It lies in the valley of the brook of the same name, the source of which is in the other side of the border, in Slovakia. The oldest reference to the community is from 1320. The life of the local population is maintained by many old and typical Spisz houses, farmsteads and a two-hundred year old mill. The border position of Kacwin and inherent poverty forced the local people into smuggling during the 19th and 20th centuries. There is a Gothic **All Saints church** of the beginning of the 15th century which was later rebuilt in Baroque style. There is a **board** on the church wall which commemorates the soldiers passing the locality on their way back from the battle near Vienna in 1648. Three of them, two Poles and one Latvian, died here and are buried in the local cemetery. A big **waterfall** untypical for the Carpathians, in the centre of the village and near the church, is an interesting local natural landmark.

North of Łapsze Wyzne, on the south-west rim of the limestone mountain range of Branisko, far from the main communications and river valleys is **DURSZTYN** (700 m, population 450). Its beautiful location and wonderful view of the surrounding landscape made of Dursztyn the most visited one among the villages of Zamagurze. It is a very old village, confirmed in a reference to the community of *Durst* in an act of 1317. The documents of a later date, 1589, quote the full German-sounding name *Durchstain*. In the same year Olbracht Łaski sold the small community together

---

Right: The sheep farms in Jurgów

with the surrounding lands and other communities to an Old Hungarian gentleman by the name of György Horwath. The local people lived by breeding cattle and sheep. Writers in the 19th century who visited the village rendered a sad picture of the population of Dursztyn: "Unimaginable poverty, dirt, and very few children, they are either not born or they all die of hunger." However, the village has preserved its agricultural character until the present day, with **old wooden farmsteads**, and about 2 km of the centre from the eastern edge of the village there stands a group of sheds called **Jurgowskie Stajnie** (The stables of Jurgów). They originated in the time when sheep grazing was prohibited in Tatry Bielskie for the people of Jurgów, so that they purchased the surrounding pastures and farmsteads in 1902. Even today they provide shelter to the shepherds with big flocks in the "summer" season, which is from May to October. In 1994, for example, there were up to 900 sheep grazing here.

On the northern side of the Branisko mountain ranges and on the right side slopes of the Dunajec valley is the community of **FALSZTYN** (610 m, population 300). Its name is of German origin: Falkenstein in German means the "falcon stone". The first references to the community relates to the monastery that used to stand on the right bank of the Falsztyński Potok brook and was burnt down by Hussite troops in 1431. Later records date from 1535 mentioning Hieronym Łaski who began building a castle on the site of the present village, but the outcome of the construction is not known. Falsztyn belonged to the lords of Niedzica castle. The feudal system preserved here for a very long time as the people of Falsztyn were obliged to work on the lord's lands until 1926. A manor estate with houses and farmsteads, of the past owner family of Jungenfeld is preserved in the village. Nowadays it is attractive location for the Czorsztyn dam which filled the valley of Falsztyński brook with a picturesque **bay** near the village.

NIEDZICA (500 m, population 1,800) is a Spisz type of village with a beautiful situation in the valley of the Niedzieczanka brook, 25 km east of Nowy Targ. The first reference to the village dates back to 1320. Later records mention the dependence of the Niedzica church on Červený kláštor monastery. By the beginning of the 16th century the village belonged to the Polish family

of Łaski, though in 1589 is was again bought out by the Old Hungarian lords. The black page of the history of Niedzica and Spisz in general is that serfdom preserved here until as late as 1932. The life of the local population was hard and sustained by farming and sheep breeding. The oldest building in Niedzica is the **St. Bartłomiej church** from the 15th century, and was used by the Evangelicals between 1545-1640. During its reconstruction in 1991-1992 some unusually valuable fragments from the 14th century paintings were found in the presbytery.

But Niedzica is famous most of all for its **castle** built on a limestone rock, 2 km south of the centre. Its original name was Dunajec, which was quoted in the documents of 1325. It was constructed on a limestone cliff, towering on the right bank of the Dunajec river, which at the time belonged to the Old Hungarians. Much later the castle Czorsztyn was built on the opposite side of the river. The first owner of Niedzica castle was the Old Hungarian aristocrat Kokosz Berzeviczy. An important date in the history of the castle was the year 1412, when the messengers of the Polish king Władısław Jagiełłe handed over its loan to the messengers of the Old Hungarian king Sigismond of Luxembourg. The guarantee of the loan was accounted for by the Spisz towns and villages, but the Polish rule over the fort did not last long. The head of the Spisz province Emeryk Zapolya conquered the castle in 1470 and fortified its walls. His granddaughter, Barbara, was the first wife of the Polish king Zygmunt Stari whose brother Jan Zapolya, supported by the Polish nobility, became the king of Old Hungary. The family of Łaski received the province of Spisz stretching from Niedzica to Kežmarok as a token of the king's gratitude. But Hieronym Łaski was careless and eccentric with no interest in his properties, and eventually passed Niedzica estate to the Spisz prelate as a forfeit. The prelate converted to Protestant religion and married. His son Jan bought the remains of the Niedzice castle from the son of Hieronym Łaski, Olbracht, in 1589. This was how the castle after 60 years of Polish ownership passed again to an Old Hungarian owner. The castle was conquered twice by robbers, and by the end of the 18th century only

Left: The castle of Niedzica

ruins remained of it, but it was eventually rebuilt by its new owner, the family of Horwath. Mostly Ferdinand Horwath dedicated a lot of his energy to its repair and later organised balls and feasts in the castle. One of the guests in such a feast was the Polish poet Wincenty Pol, who described the experience in his book "Pictures of life and nature". By the early 19th century the castle became a part of the dowry of Ferdinand's daughter, Kornelia's, who married the Old Hungarian aristocrat Alexander Salamon. The family of Salamon lived in the castle until 1945 in spite of the fact that Zamagurze became Polish from 1920. There are numerous legends related to Niedzice castle, the most popular of them is the one about the Testament of the Incas.

The Testament of the Incas:

In the 18th century one of the relatives of the owners of Niedzica castle, Sebastian Berzeviczy, set out on a journey to Peru. He married there an Inca woman with royal origins. They had a daughter Umina who married Tupac Amaro, the last king of the Incas and gave birth to a son they named Antonio. After the last defeat of the Incas by the Spaniards and death of Tupac Amaro, Sebastian Berzeviczy returned to Europe accompanied by his daughter and grandson. He settled down, first in Kraków and later in Niedzica. But Umina was murdered and the accusation fell on the omnipresent Spanish inquisition. Little Antonio was adopted by Wacław Berzewiczy in the presence of the honourable ambassador of the Inca Council. The document of adoption was discovered in 1949 in the church of St. Cross in Kraków. Wacław, besides others, guaranteed by the document that he should keep the Inca testament secret until Antonio's maturity. The years passed by and young Antonio Incas Benesz married a Polish woman, Barbara Rubanowska, and gave no importance to the testament. But one of his distant relatives Andrzej Benesz who incidentally found the document mentioning the testament in the church of St. Cross in Kraków, started to look for it. The detailed description of the place where it was kept led him to Niedzice castle, whereupon he found a leaden tube which contained a handful of leather strings with mysterious knots – the Inca testament. The story, however, is surrounded by mystery as Andrzej Benesz died in a car crash and the relevant documents were irrevocably lost.

The castle that used to stand some 75 m above the water level of the Dunajec is still there, towering above the Czorsztyn dam. After thorough reconstruction it represents one of the most interesting buildings of the Polish Spisz. The lower part of the castle is nowadays called **Dom Pracy Twórczej Stowarzyszenia Hystoryków Sztuki** (The House of Creative Work of the Union of Art Historians) and a museum is located in the central and upper parts of the castle.

Museum of Niedzica – the Castle, tel.: 018/26 59 489
open daily 9:00-17:00h

NOWA BIAŁA (650 m, population 1,300) is nowadays the only village situated on the left bank of the river Białka, 10 km from Nowy Targ. The bed of this boundary river was on the west side of the village in the Middle Ages. It moved its course eastward after one of a series of floods thereby separating Nowa Biała from Spisz. By the beginning of the 16th century the village belonged to the Polish family of Łaski and then passed into the hands of the Old Hungarian family of Horwath in 1589. It used to be an important border point in the 16th century. The population is mixed and both Polish and Slovak is spoken here even today. However, the coexistence of the two nationalities was not always peaceful. For example, a conflict over what language should be used in church services arose, a conflict which amounted to nothing more serious than some fist fights but the church remained closed for ten years. Nowadays, the mass is celebrated in both languages. Besides the Polish basic school there is also the only basic school in Spisz with tuition in the Slovak language. The local walled Baroque **church** of 1728 has an impressive Rococo main altar and close to the village also stands the **chapel of St. Maria Magdalena** from the 18th century.

KREMPACHY (600 m, population 1,200) lies on the right bank of the Białka and it is situated 12 km south-east of Nowy Targ, neighbouring with Nowa Biała. The name of the village is derived from the German word Krummbach or "winding brook". The first written reference to the village is from 1439 though it was founded probably in the 14th century by the family of Berzeviczy. As with other villages belonging to the Niedzica estate it first belonged to the family of Łaski and later to Horwath. By the beginning of the 19th century there were 124 houses in Krempachy and it

was the biggest village in Polish Spisz. The old-fashioned ground plan with the main square, where the church and school stand is preserved to the present day. The **church of St. Martin** has a walled tower with an attic gable typical for churches in the Spisz region and quite different from the wooden churches of Podhale. The church was built in the 16th century and since then it has been repeatedly rebuilt and repaired. In the local school the Slovak language is taught as an optional language.

FRYDMAN (530 m, population 1,600) is the most interesting village of the Polish Spisz region. It lies in the Kotlina Nowotarska basin, 16 km east of Nowy Targ where the river Białka flows into the Czorsztyn dam. The first reference to the village is in 1320, when master Kokosz sold "terram Frydmanvagasa", or the land of Frydman, to his brother Jan. But the village was probably founded earlier, around 1308. The mayor Fridrich of Huncowce founded the village pursuing the German right. A famous native here was the local priest Jan Ratułowski, doctor of philosophy at the Jagielloński University. Frydman much like many other Carpathian villages was visited by the Polish king Jan Sobieski III who allegedly took part in a Mass celebrated in the local church on his way back from a battle near Vienna. When the Niedzica estate fell apart, Aladar Salamon became the new owner of the village. Also Michał Balara, writer and patriot, is among one of the important figures who was born or lived in Frydman. The village has numerous precious architectural monuments, like the walled Early-Gothic **church of St. Stanisław, the Bishop of Kraków** from the end of the 13th, as well as the **tower** and **belfry** of a later period. Next to the church is the **chapel of the Virgin Mary** with a unique wooden Rococo altar of St.Trinity. There is also a **manor house** standing in the centre of the village built by the Horwath family in the early 17th century. Also the 600 m long **wine cellars** situated under the castle and used for the storage of wine are interesting to visit. Frydman enjoyed the favourable position on the border for a long time and

Left: The view from Spisz
Right: A church in Frydman

thrived on trading in wine, Old Hungarian wine being the most important and sought after commodity.

In the western part of the Polish Spisz near the brook of Trybską Rzeką lies the community of **TRYBSZ** (640 m, population 800) which is 12 km south of Nowy Targ. The first reference to it is in 1439, and like many such communities it has an agricultural history. But because the land around could not sustain the local population many emigrated to America in the 19th century to find an alternative life. The most valuable architectural monument in the village is a **wooden church** built in 1567, with precious paintings adorning its log walls. These paintings were the work of the priest Jan Ratułowski who was inspired by the surrounding wonderful environment, as depicted in his Ascension of Virgin Mary, which includes a panorama of the Tatras in the background. Mountain landscapes are also clearly visible in other paintings, and are considered the oldest existing paintings of the Tatras in Poland. Another local, Ferenc Denes, who was born here in 1845, also dedicated his life to the Tatras and the Pieniny mountains as an explorer.

PIENINY

Szczawnica
and its environs

SZCZAWNICA (430 m, population 7,300) is one of the most picturesque spas in southern Poland. It lies in the valley of the Grancarek river which separates the Pieniny from the Beskidy mountains.

The Polish Pieniny mountains:

The mountains of Pieniny is the name to the central part of Pieniński Pas Skalkowi (the cliffs of Pieniny) divided by the picturesque canyon of Dunajec. Szczawnica and several adjacent villages on the rim of this little mountain group are quite different from the ones of Podhale region from the point of historical and geographical aspects. The area around the Pieniny mountains was owned by the Order of Clare nuns from Stary Sącz, and its beautiful landscape and mineral springs in Szczawnica and Krościenko have made the region one of the most visited corners of the Carpathians

The first written reference to the village is from the 15th century. At this time the Polish king Kazimierz Jagielończyk renewed the privilege of the use of three fields to Jan, the mayor of Szczawnica, and the right was confirmed in 1494. The first parish originated and the first church was built in Szczawnica in the 16th century. However, the most precious assets of this part of the Carpathians always were, and still are, the **mineral springs**, the main source of which are in the foot of a volcanic mountain called **Bryjarka**. Their existence was discovered centuries ago: A report under the title "The Report on Salty and Acid Mineral Springs in Szczawnica" was published in Warsaw in the 16th century. The community was divided in two parts at that time – Niznia and Wyznia Szczawnica. In 1777 Wiznia Szczawnica accounted for 104 houses where 527 people lived; whereas in the same year in Niznia only 223 lived. During Austro-Hungarian rule Szczawnica belonged to the estate of Nowy Targ. In 1828 the

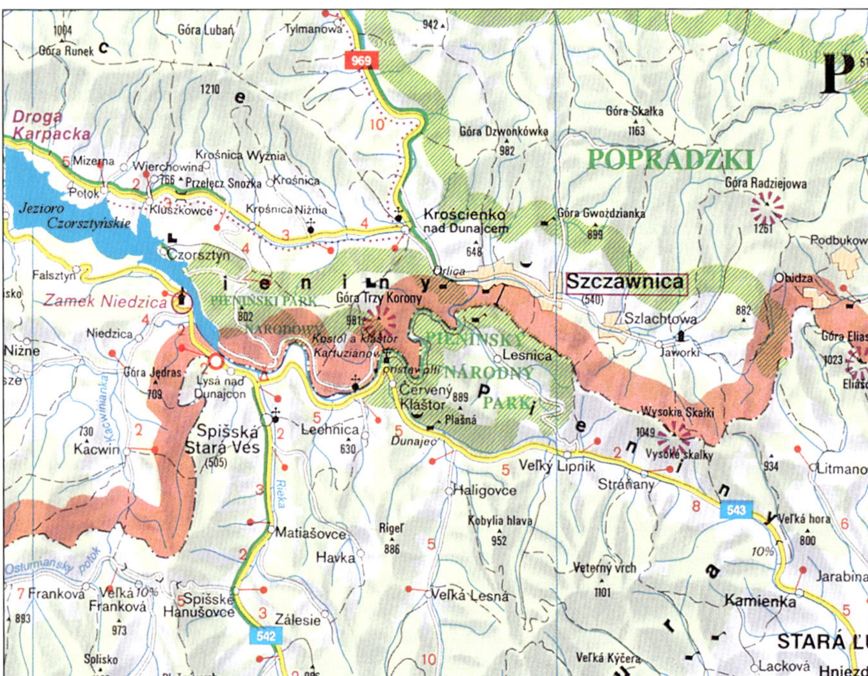

married couple of Stefan and Józefina Szalay of Old Hungary became the new owners of the community. This educated and enlightened couple wanted to change Szczawnica to a spa of European standards. Two principal springs were later named after them – Stefan and Józefina, and other springs received the names of their discoverers or of outstanding figures who visited the spa. But the one who most promoted the spa was the son of the couple, Józef, who founded the park, accessed all the springs and built the spa houses and villas. One of the original ideas of Józef Szalay was to decorate all the houses in the town with a coat of arms, therefore, the entrance doors to all the houses bear hearts, grapes, circles and other symbols painted on little boards. Szczawnica became a very popular spa mainly among the aristocractic and artistic community. Seasonally more than 1,000 visitors arrived here in the 19th century. Józef Szalay left the property of Szczawnica in his testament to the Akademia Umiejętnosti of Kraków. By the beginning of the 20th century the Kraków Academy, in spite of Szalay's testament, passed the Szczawnica property to count Stanicki of Nawojowa. Further modernisation of the spa was interrupted by the war and when it ended, Szczawnica had to compete with Krinicą, and failed. Railway, the basic dynamic element of progress in the Carpathian towns at the time, did not materialise here. Numerous specialised sanatoriums though were built in Szczawnica after the Second World War. For a short time Szczawnica and Krościenko were united into one town as ordered by the authorities in the years 1972 and 1982. Today Szczawnica is again an independent municipality with an active social and economic life. The town has a Neo-Gothic **church** built between 1882-1892, and the **spa buildings** are also interesting, which were built in the second half of the 19th century and surrounded by wonderful parks. The **Museum of Pieniny** provides sufficient information about the history, nature and ethnography of this region.

The Museum of Pieniny in Szczawnica,
Plac Dietla 7, tel.: 0817/26 22 258
Opening hours:
Tue-Sun 10:00-13:00h and 14:00-16:00h

A chair lift to the Palenica mountain was built recently, but the real attractiveness of the place is rafting down the Dunajec canyon, starting in Wyzne Sromowce. Szczawnica is the final destiny where the Goral rafts arrive after having passed the Dunajec canyon. Rafting down the Dunajec has been a unique experience for visitors for more than a hundred years. It is an enjoyable and completely safe adventure, but it was not always so. In 1895 the polish journalist Rehman described rafting down the Dunajec as follows:

Rafting down the Dunajec:

"Tourists are ushered to slim boats each made of a single log that are tied to pairs for better safety to in Wyznie and Niznie Sromowce and or in Červený Kláštor on the Slovak side. The trip on the rafts from Červený Kláštor to Szczawnica takes two or three hours. It is not altogether a safe trip as the current of the Dunajec is very strong particularly in this section. It twists the boat in the tapered bed first to one then to another side and carries it straight against the rocks bordering it. The rocks are either hidden close beneath the water line or jut out over it but they are a constant threat to the boat and the crew. Great skill and a clear mind are needed to pass the dangerous obstacles safely and though the local Gorals are experienced men, the loss of human lives and boats are not uncommon. But for the comfort of the readers we have to add that it mostly happens only if the rafters take too much vodka".

Lovers of long walks can set off on a trip to **Sokolica or Trzy Korony mountains**. In the opposite direction, up the valley of the river Grejcarek, is the route to the picturesque trough of Homole and the community of Jaworki. Winter tourists can use three ski tracks and more than 5 hectares of ski terrain around the Palenica and Szafranówka mountains. There are also numerous tracks for cross-country skiing and tourism.

KROŚCIENKO (444 m, population 3,400) is a small picturesque town lying at the foothills of the Pieniny mountains, near the mouth of the Krośnica brook to the Dunajec river. The oldest written reference to the town is entered in a church chronicle of 1354 but it was proved that the Polish king Kazimierz the Great granted the community municipal rights as early as 1348. The town began to progress only after another Polish king, Kazimierz Jagiellończyk, confirmed its former rights and privileges in 1485, after a fire that probably arose during the Polish-Old Hungarian war in 1474. Prosperity was brought to Krościenko by Jerzy of Pniew who bought it in 1522. The importance of the town grew again after 1569 when roy-

al privilege allowed it to hold two fairs a year. The year 1734 meant tragedy for the people when the soldiers of the Spisz mayor sacked and destroyed Krościenko, who also conquered the Czorsztyn castle and settled there, continuing to sack the surrounding settlements for another two years until they left in 1736. During the annexation of Poland the owners of Krościenko constantly changed. In 1822 it was bought by the family of Gross, and Henrik Gross, himself, promoted the local mineral springs and established the spa. But the spa could not compete with the one in Szczawnica and so it gradually lost some of its appeal. At the present it is a picturesque little town with additional tourist and recreational functions. The most precious monument in Krościenko is the **All Saints church** of 1665, built on the site of an older church with valuable frescoes of the 14th and 16th centuries. Also the altars carved in wood and a stone baptistery are of considerable artistic value. There are several **tourist footpaths** which cross the town: north to the **Lubań mountain** (1,210 m) in the Gorce mountain range, to the top of Dzwonkówka (982 m) in Beskidy Sądieckie mountain range and to the south, one of which ends at the most beautiful top of the Pieniny mountains – **Trzy Korony** (981 m) from where there is a beautiful view of the landscape below. There is also the seat of the Pieniny National Park in the town and the same building serves as a museum housing a collection of natural history.

Left: Rafts on the Dunajec

Museum of Nature History of the Pieniny National Park, Jagiellońska St. 107, tel.: 0187/262 3283
Opening hours Mon-Fri 8:30-13:30h

CZORSZTYN (510 m, population 300) situated beyond the canyon of the Dunajec is a small village, the oldest part of which does not exist any more. It was covered by the waters of the Czorsztyn dam and only the ruins of the castle towering over the water line remind the onlooker of the past grandeur of the place. The first reference to the community is dated 1348 when Czorsztyn was the seat of the royal customs station on the border with Old Hungary. The local people lived not only by farming and cattle raising but were also engaged in fishing in the Dunajec. Legends say that the local inn keepers supplied troutfish even to Warsaw castle. Czorsztyn was owned by the family of Drohojewski in the 19th century, and their curia used to stand close to the castle on the road leading to the valley of the Dunajec. The character of Czorsztyn gradually changed to that of a holiday resort and because of the growing number of tourists numerous villas and pensions were built here. Czorsztyn was a favourite place for famous Polish poets and writers, such as Władysław Orkan or Melchior Wańkowicz and the wife and daughters of the Polish president J. Piłsudski. Construction of the dam, however, changed the landscape, and the historical core of the town was submerged under water. There is, however, a plan to locate the most precious log buildings in an open-air museum in Kluszkowce. The new village originated in a former part of Czorsztyn, **Nadzamcze**. It is an administrative centre and its position on the shore of the lake, as well as some cultural and historical monuments, should soon make it an important tourist resort.

A remarkable historical monument here is the **castle ruins** on the mountain of Zamkowa Góra, which is 588 m above sea level and 38 m above the level of the dam. The famous chronicler of Polish history, Długosz, mentioned Czorsztyn castle as early as 1241, and it was allegedly the refuge of the Polish king Bolesław the Shy and his court during the Tartar invasion. It is proved that the castle did exist in the second half of the 13th century and its original name was Wronin. The German colonists of neighbouring Spisz gave it the new and strangely sounding name of Czorsztyn. During the reign of king Kazimierz the Great the original wooden castle was replaced by a stone substitute, which the king himself visited during his journeys to Old Hungary. Also king Władysław Jagiełło stayed in he castle hosted by the famous Polish knight Zawisz Czarny, the mayor of Spisz. The castle, however, began to decay in the 17th century.

Insurrection of Kostka Napierski:

The owners of the castle always oppressed the local population but especially so in the 17th century. It was no accident then that resistance and protest accumulated, even against the Polish king, culminating in an armed insurrection in 1651, when the peasants led by Kostka-Napierski conquered the castle of Czorsztyn. The leader of the insurrection invited all Goral people to join in the movement, but the rebellion was eventually defeated by the royal army commanded by the Spisz mayor Mikołaj Jordan. After the rebels were defeated three of their leaders were moved to Kraków where they were tortured and executed. Kostka Napierski was executed on a pole and the other two were quartered. This was the end of the most dramatic story of Czorsztyn castle.

The castle was repeatedly sieged, however, and eventually completely sacked in 1735. Lightning caused a fire that finally destroyed it in 1790.

Near Niedzice, on the left bank of the Dunajec and 2 kilometres from Niedzice castle is **SROMOWCE WYŻNE** (480 m, population 1,150). The name of the village derives from the name of the first mayor Szram. After one of the floods in 1334 when a big part of the village was destroyed the princess of Sącz ordered the division of the village into two parts, effectively creating two villages - Sromowce Wyzne and Sromowce Nizne. The influence of the Spisz region is evident here in the style of clothing and architecture, and the local dialect contains numerous Slovak and Hungarian elements. However, fires and floods destroyed the original architecture, as an example the **church** built in 1875 was the third one to be built after its two predecessors were burnt down. There is a recently constructed **water dam**, which in fact forms a part of the one in Czorsztyn.

SROMOWCE NIŻNE (455 m, population 950) lying near the Dunajec is a very old village. After the division of the original settlement this part played an important role in Polish-Old Hungarian relations of the 15th century. According to chronicles important Polish and Old Hungarian representatives met repeatedly in this community and in the Slovak Stará Ves lying on the opposite bank of the Dunajec.

Famous meetings in Sromowce:

In the swamps of Dunajec, called Równia Sromowka, two great kings – the Polish king Władysław Jagiełło and Sigismund of Luxembourg met in 1423. It was their second such meeting at the same venue. The first took place in 1412, when Władysław Jagiełło, inspired by victory in the battle near Grunwald handed to Sigismond a large amount of money as a forfeit for the Spisz towns and villages. The money was the ransom obtained by the Polish king of the crusaders who paid for their prisoners after the battle in Grunwald. Both these great men arrived at the meeting on horseback, greeted one another by raising their arms and then dismounted and hugged each other. Some chronicles assert though that later they reproached each other and demonstrated ill will in public later everything was explained and both set off on a trip to Levoča, to enjoy a festive Easter.

There is in the village a preserved 16th century wooden **church**, which is now closed, as a new one was built here in 1988. About 1.5 km away from the village is a stylish **cottage called Trzy Korony** situated in picturesque landscape between the Dunajec and the cliffs of three peaks. It can be used as a starting point for excursions to different areas of the Pieniny National Park.

On the northern side of the Pieniny mountains is the village of **GRYWAŁD** (530 m, population 1,550). It lies in the valley of the Wąski Potok brook flowing from Gorce and ending in Krośnica, on the left tributary of the Dunajec. The community was first mentioned in the 14th century. Its mayors, the family Grywałski, enjoyed various privileges (logging in the local

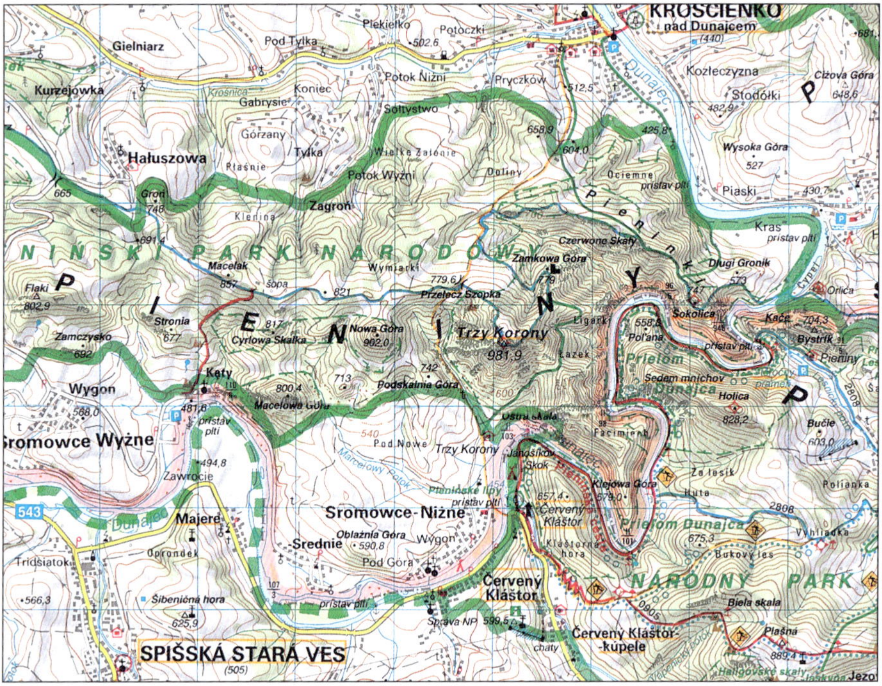

forests, milling and brewing). Historically, the local people lived by farming and craftwork and there are several cultural and historical monuments which have been preserved. The most valuable of them is the St. Martin church from the second half of the 15th century. As with the church in Dębno this is also a precious example of Polish Gothic wooden architecture. The renowned statue of the Madonna of Grywałd of 1618 was taken to safety abroad during the Second World War years. A green-marked footpath leads to the top of the Lubań mountain.

In the very centre of the Pieniny mountains, south of Grywald, is another small village called **HAŁUSZOWA** (620 m, population 300) which originated in 1608. Historically this community has always been extremely poor, due to its isolated location, however, the local people endeavoured to survive by farming with cow driven ploughs. Today, it has the character of a holiday community. From here there is a blue-marked pathway to the Trzy Korony mountain, a frequent destination for visitors to the Pieniny National park.

KROŚNICA (580 m, population 1,000) is situated near the mountain saddle of Snoszka beside the road from Nowy Targ to Krościenko which separates Pieniny from the Gorce mountains. The village originated probably in the late 15th century and bears the same name as the brook in this area. The visitors to Pieniny know that in its lower part a road cutting through the Pieniny National Park leads to the port for the rafts in Kąty.

Polskie Towarzystwo Turystyczno Krajoznawcze, ul. Krupówki 12, **Zakopane**
Tel.: 018/201 57 20

Koło Przewodników Tatrzańskich PTTK, ul. Krupówki 12, **Zakopane**
Tel.: 018/201 24 29, 201 58 48

Klub Wysokogórski, ul. Droga na Wierch 4, **Zakopane**
Tel.: 018/206 37 08

Centrum Informacji Turystycznej, ul. Kościuszki 17, **Zakopane**
Tel.: 018/ 201 22 11

Polskie Biuro Podróży Orbis, ul. Krupówki 22, **Zakopane**
Tel.: 018/ 201 48 12, 201 22 38

Tatry Biuro Turysticzne, ul. Chramcówki 35, **Zakopane**
Tel.: 018/201 40 00

Eurotatry Tourist, Jaszczurówka-Bory 15, **Zakopane**
Tel.: 018/201 59 23

Biuro Turystyczne Tatry, ul. Kościuszki 188, **Bukowina Tatrzańska**
Tel.: 018/207 72 93

Euroregion Tatry, Al.Tysiąclecia 37, **Nowy Targ**
Tel.: 018/266 99 81

Biuro Podróży Orbis, al. Kopernika 12, **Nowy Targ**
Tel.: 018/266 55 36

Biuro Podróży Gromada, Rynek 15, **Nowy Targ**
Tel.: 018/266 39 11

Biuro Podróży Ewmar, Rynek 21, **Nowy Targ**
Tel.: 018/266 72 88

Biuro Podróży Gorce PTTK, ul. Sobieskiego 2, **Nowy Targ**
Tel.: 018/266 31 12

Biuro Turystyczne Sport-Tour, ul. Krakowska 3, **Jabłonka**
Tel.: 018/265 21 95

Biuro Obsługi Ruchu Turystycznego PTTK, ul. Manifestu Lipcowego 1a, **Szczawnica**
Tel.: 018/262 23 32

Biuro Podróży Orbis, ul. Zawodzie 12c, **Szczawnica**
Tel.: 018/262 22 37

Biuro Usług Turystycznych Podhale-Tour, ul. Manifestu Lipcowego 14, **Szczawnica**
Tel.: 018/262 23 70

Biuro Turystyczne Pieniny, ul. Wygon 4a, **Szczawnica**
Tel.: 018/262 21 74

REGISTER

ABOUT THE AUTHORS:

RNDr. Daniel Kollár, CSc. is a social geographer currently employed in the Institute of Geography of the Slovak Academy of Sciences in Bratislava. He lectures social geography in the Faculty of Natural History at Comenius University in Bratislava. He is an author of several articles and publications (for example Slovakia – in pursuit of its beauties, Majcichov, a monograph of the community, Slovak-Austrian basin of the river Morava...) He is also a fan of sport, tourism and history.

RNDr. Ján Lacika, CSc. is a physical geographer and geomorphologist currently employed in the Institute of Geography of the Slovak Academy of Sciences in Bratislava. Being an avid traveller, he has been able to participate in several expeditions which have provided him with material for numerous scientific articles and newspaper reports. He is editor of the journal Geografia and author of text books on geography. He also enjoys photography, tourism and travel.

Roman Malarz, PhD. is a physical geographer and geomorphologist currently working in the Institute of geography of Wysza Szkola Pedagogiczna in Kraków. He lectures geomorphology and geographic interpretations of the aerial and space and aerial photography. Author of numerous articles and publications (for example, The region of Kraków, the Encyclopaedia of Poland...). He is a devotee of travel, tourism and photography.

DICTIONARY

áno – tak – yes
nie – nie – no
prosím – proszę – please
nech sa páči – proszę bardzo
Ďakujem. – Dziękuję. – Thank you.
Nemáte za čo. – Nie ma za co. – Not at all.
Prepáčte. – Przepraszam. – Excuse me.
dobre – dobre – well
Dobrú chuť. – Smacznego. – Good appetite.
Šťastnú cestu. – Szczęśliwej podróży. – Happy journey.
Ahoj. – Cześć.– Hello.
Dovidenia. – Do widzenia. – Good bye.
Dobré ráno. – Dzień dobry. – Good morning.
Dobrý deň. – Dzień dobry. – Good day.
Dobrý večer. – Dobry wieczór. – Good evening.
Dobrú noc. – Dobra noc.– Good night.
dnes – dzisiaj – today
včera – wczoraj – yesterday
zajtra – jutro – tomorrow
pozajtra – pojutrze – the day after tomorrow
teraz – teraz – now
potom – potem – afterwards
Ako sa máte? – Jak się Pan (i) ma? – How are you?
Choď preč! – Proszę odejść! – Leave me alone!
Pomoc! – Ratunku! – Help!

Cestovanie – W podróży – Travelling

tu – tutaj – here
tam – tam – there
naľavo – w lewo – to the left
napravo – w prawo – to the right
priamo – prosto– straight
Kde je ...? – Gdzie jest ...? – Where is?
Ako sa dostanem do ...? – Jak się dostać do ...? – How do I get to...
železnica – kolej – railway
nástupište – peron – platform
autobus – autobus– bus
vlak – pociąg – train
auto – samochod – car
pešo – pieszo – on foot
taxík – taksówka – taxi
lístok – bilet – ticket
spiatočný lístok – bilet powrotny – return ticket
železničná stanica – dworzec kolejowy – railway station
autobusová stanica – dworzec autobusowy – bus station
autobusová zastávka – przystanek autobusowy – bus stop
Ide do ...? – Czy on jedzie do ...? – Does it go to...?
Musím prestupovať? – Czy muszę się przesiadać? – Do I have to change?
Musím mať miestenku? – Czy muszę mieć rezerwację? – Do I have to have reservation?

Otázky a odpovede – Pytania i odpowiedzi – Questions and answers

Nerozumiem. – Nie rozumiem.– I do not understand.
Rozumiem. – Rozumiem. – I understand.
Hovorte pomalšie. – Proszę mówić powolí. – Speak slowly.
Ako sa to povie po slovensky? – Jak to się mówi po slowacku? – What is Slovak for...?
Mohli by ste mi to napísať? – Czy może mi to Pan (i) napísać? – Can you put it down for me?
čo – co – what
kde – gdzie – where
kedy – kiedy – when
prečo – dlaczego – why
Koľko to stojí? – Ile to kosztuje? – How much is it?
Máte voľné izby? – Czy są wolne pokoje? – Are there free rooms?
Chcem dvojposteľovú izbu. – Chciał bym pokój dwuoosobowy. – I want a double room.
na jednu noc – na jedną noc – for one night
so sprchou – z prysznicem – with shower
Sú tieto miesta voľné? – Czy te miesjca są wolne? – Are the places free?
Môžeme? – Czy możemy? – Can we?

Zaplatím prosím! – Chciał bym zapłacić!
– a bill, please
Máte...? – Czy ma pan(i)...? – do you have?
Nemáme. – Nie mamy. – we do not have
Máme. – Mamy. – we have

Nápisy – napisy – Notices

vchod – wejście – entry
východ – wyjście – exit
WC muži – toaleta męska – gentlemen (toilet)
WC ženy – toaleta damska – ladies (toilet)
otvorené – otwarte – open
zatvorené – zamknięte – closed
Pozor! – Uwaga! – beware!
Zákaz fajčiť! – Palenie wzbronione!– no smoking!
pasová kontrola – kontrola paszportów
– passport control
zákaz kúpania – zakaz kąpieli – no bathing!
vstup zakázaný – wstęp wzbroniony – no entry!
príchod – przyjazd – arrivals
odchod – odjazd – departures
colné prehlásenie – deklaracja celna
colná kontrola – odprawa celna – customs control
miestenka – miejsce siedzące

U lekára – U lekarza – at a physician's

lekár – lekarz – physician
prvá pomoc – pogotowie ratunkowe – first aid
nemocnica – szpital – hospital
lieky – lekarstwo – medicines
číslo prvej pomoci – telefon pogotowia
– first aid phone number
Tu cítim bolesť. – Tu mam bóle. – it hurts here
Som alergický na... – Jestem uczulony na...
– I am allergic to...
vysoký tlak – mam nadciśnienie
– a high blood pressure
Bolí ma hlava. – Mam bóle głowy.
– my head is aching

Polícia – Policja – Police

vodičský preukaz – prawo jazdy – a driver's licence
zelená karta – zielona karta – green card
pokuta – mandat, kara – a fine
Stratil som... – Zgubiłem... – I lost...
Niekto mi ukradol... – Ktoś mi ukradł...
– somebody has stolen my...
nebezpečenstvo – niebezpieczeństwo – danger
križovatka – skryżowanie – cross-roads
kruhový objazd – rondo – round-about
nehoda – wypadek – accident
havária auta – awaria samochodu – car crash

Čísla – Liczebniki – Numbers

jeden – jeden – 1
dva– dwa – 2
tri– trzy – 3
štyri– cztery – 4
päť– pięć – 5
šesť– sześć – 6
sedem– siedem – 7
osem– osiem – 8
deväť– dziewięć – 9
desať– dziesięć – 10
jedenásť– jedenaście – 11
dvanásť– dwanaście – 12
trinásť– trzynaście – 13
štrnásť– czternaście – 14
pätnásť– piętnaście – 15
šestnásť – szesnaście – 16
sedemnásť – siedemnaście – 17
osemnásť– osiemnaście – 18
devätnásť – dziewiętnaście – 19
dvadsať– dwadzieścia – 20
dvadsaťjeden– dwadzieścia jeden – 21
tridsať – trzydzieści – 30
štyridsať– czterdzieści – 40
päťdesiat– pięćdziesiąt – 50
šesťdesiat – sześćdziesiąt – 60
sedemdesiat – siedemdziesiąt – 70
osemdesiat– osiemdziesiąt – 80
deväťdesiat – dziewięćdziesiąt – 90
sto – sto – 100
stojeden – sto jeden – 101
dvesto– dwieście – 200
tristo – trzysta – 300
štyristo – czterysta – 400
päťsto – pięćset – 500
šesťsto – sześćset – 600
sedemsto – siedemset – 700
osemsto – osiemset – 800
deväťsto – dziewięćset – 900
tisíc – tysiąc – 1000

Dni týždňa – Dni tygodnia – The days of the week

pondelok – poniedziałek – Monday
utorok – wtorek – Tuesday
streda – środa – Wednesday
štvrtok – czwartek – Thursday
piatok – piątek – Friday
sobota – sobota – Saturday
nedeľa- niedziela – Sunday
deň – dzień – day
týždeň – tydzień – week
mesiac – miesiąc – month
rok – rok – year

Názvy mesiacov – Nazwy miesięcy – The names of the months

január – styczeń – January
február – luty – February
marec – marzec – March
apríl – kwiecień – April
máj – maj – May
jún – czerwiec – June
júl – lipiec – July
august – sierpień – August
september – wrzesień – September
október – październik – October
november – listopad – November
december – grudzień – December

Všeobecná terminológia – Terminologia ogólna – General vocabulary

aleja – aleja – alley
brána – brama – gate

chata – schronisko lub dom wiejski – cottage
cintorín – cmentarz– cemetery
divadlo – teatr – theatre
dolina – dolina – valley
dom – dom – house
dom kultúry – Dom kultury – house of culture
hrad – zamek – castle
hranica – granica – border
hora – góra – mountain
hostinec – gospoda – inn
jaskyňa – jaskinia – cave
jazero – jezioro– lake
kaplnka – kaplica – chapel
kaštieľ – dwór – manor house
katedrála – katedra – cathedral
kaviareň – kawiarnia – coffee house
kláštor – klasztor – monastery
kostol – kościół – church
kúpalisko – basen – swimming pool
kúpele – uzdrowisko – spa
lanovka – kolejka linowa lub linowo-szynowa – funicular
les – las – forest
mesto – miasto – town
nábrežie – nabreże – embankment
námestie – plac – square
ostrov – wyspa – island
pamätník – pomnik – monument
pamiatka – zabytek – monument
piváreň – piwiarnia – tavern
planina – płaskowyż – plain
pleso – górskie jezioro – mountain lake
prameň – źródło – mineral spring
prchliadka – zwiedzanie, oglądanie – sightseeing
radnica – ratusz – town hall
rieka – rzeka – river
reštaurácia – restauracja – restaurant
sad – park/sad – orchard
sedlo – przełęcz – mountain saddle
sieň – komnata, sala – hall
skanzen – skansen – open-air museum
slovenský – słowacki – Slovak
socha – rzeźba – statue
staré mesto – stare miasto – old town
štít – szczyt – peak
stĺp – kolumna, słup – column
štvrť – dzielnica – quarter
svätý – święty – saint
teplý prameň – uzdrowisko – thermal spring
trieda – aleja – avenue
ulica – ulica – street
veľvyslanectvo – ambasada – embassy
veža – wieża – tower
vináreň – winiarnia – wine cellar
vrch – wzgórze – mountain
vrchovina – wyżyna – highlands
výstava – wystawa – exposition, fair
výťah – winda – lift
záhrada – ogród – garden
zámok – zamek – castle
zvonica – dzwonnica

Gastronomický slovník – Słowniczek gastronomiczny – Basic vocabulary of gastronomy

borovička – jałowcówka – juniper spirit
čaj – herbata – tea
džús – sok – juice
likér – likier
káva – kawa – coffee
káva presso – kawa z ekspresu – coffee
malinovka – oranżada – lemonade
pálenka – wódka – spirit
pivo – piwo – beer
sódová voda – woda sodowa – soda
predjedlo – zakąska – hors-d'-oeuvre
polievka – zupa – soup
jedlo na objednávku – dania na zamówienie – ordered meals
hotové jedlá – dania gottowe, barowe – ready meals
hydina – drób – poultry
bezmäsité jedlá – dania jarskie meat-free meals
palacinky – naleśniki – pancakes
šampióny – pierczarki – mushrooms
bravčovina – wieprzowina – pork
hovädzina – wołowina – beef
teľacina – cielęcina – veal
jahňacina – jagnięcina – lamb
kačacie mäso – mięso z kaczki – duck
biftek – befsztyk – steak
sviečkovica – polędwica – sirloin
praženica – jajecznica – scrambled eggs
omeleta – omlet – omelette
volské oko – jajko sadzone – fried egg
bryndzové halušky – kluski z bryndzą – dumplings with "bryndza" cheese
párky – parówki – sausages
šunka – szynka – ham
saláma – salami – salami
múčne jedlá – potrawy mączne – cakes
žemľa – bułka – bun
čerstvá žemľa – świeża bułka – fresh bun
obložená žemľa – kanapka – garnished bun
knedľa – bułka gotowana na praze i krojona w plastry – dumpling
pirohy – pierogi – pies with filling
horčica – musztarda – mustard
klobása – kiełbasa – sausage
držky – flaczki – tripes
guláš – gulasz – goulash
ryža – ryż – rice
dusená ryža – duszony ryż – stewed rice
varené zemiaky – gotowane ziemniaki – boiled potatoes
zemiakový šalát s majonézou – salatka ziemniakowa z majonezem – potatoe salad
opekané zemiaky – smażone ziemniaki – baked potatoes
halušky – kluski – dumplings
hranolčeky – frytki – fried potatoes
paradajky – pomidory – tomatoes
cibuľa – cebula – onion
cesnak – czosnek – garlic

REFERENCES

ADAMEC, V., JEDLIČKOVÁ N. (1991): Slovensko. Turistický lexikon. Šport, Bratislava.

ADAMEC, V., ROUBAL, R. (1974): Vysoké Tatry – turistický sprievodca. Šport, Bratislava.

ANDRÁŠI, J., ANDRÁŠI, A. (1973): Tatranské vrcholy. Vysokohorský sprievodca. Šport, Bratislava.

ANDRÁŠI, J. (1988): Štrbské Pleso – Podbanské. Šport, Bratislava.

ANDRÁŠI, J. A KOL. (1985): Vysoké Tatry. Turistický sprievodca ČSSR. Šport, Bratislava.

BIAŁY, Z. (1987): Polski Spisz, Zeszyty Naukowe UJ, Prace Etnograficzne.

BOHUŠ, I. (1982): Osudy tatranských osád. Osveta, Bratislava.

BOHUŠ, I. (1988): Tatry očami Buchholtzovcov. Osveta, Martin.

BOHUŠ, I. (1996): Od A po Z o názvoch Vysokých Tatier. Štátne lesy TANAP-u, Tatranská Lomnica.

DŁUGOŁĘCKA L., PINKWART M., (1988): Zakopane. Przewodnik historyczny. Wyd. PTTK Kraj, Warszawa.

GÓRZ, B. A KOL. (1994): Studia nad przemianami Podhala, Wydawnictwo Naukowe WSP, Kraków.

HENCOVSKÝ, J. A KOL. (1990): Orava. Turistický sprievodca. Šport, Bratislava.

HLAVIENKA, J. (1986). Jubilejný zborník Literárno-historického múzea Janka Kráľa. Liptovský Mikuláš.

HOCHMUTH, Z. a kol. (1982): Nízke Tatry – západ. Turistický sprievodca ČSSR. Šport, Bratislava.

HOCHMUTH, Z. a kol. (1990): Chočské vrchy. Liptovská Mara. Turistický sprievodca. Šport, Bratislava.

HOCHMUTH, Z. (1984): Liptov. Turistický sprievodca. Šport, Bratislava.

HOUDEK, I., BOHUŠ, I. (1976): Osudy Tatier. Šport, Bratislava.

HUBA, P. (1993): Tvrdošín. Monografia. Vydavateľstvo Peter Huba.

HUBA, P. (1992): Námestovo. Monografia. Vydavateľstvo Peter Huba.

HUSOVSKÁ, Ľ. A KOL. (1994): Slovensko – prechádzka storočiami miest a mestečiek. Príroda, Bratislava.

KENDERA, R. (1993): Ružomberok. Prechádzky po kultúrnych pamiatkach. MÚ Ružomberok.

KONČEK, J. A KOL. (1974): Klíma Tatier. SAV, Bratislava.

KRÁSY SLOVENSKA, I – LXXIV.

KRIŽANOVÁ, E., PUŠKÁROVÁ, B. (1990): Hrady, zámky a kaštiele na Slovensku. Turistický lexikon. Šport, Bratislava.

LINHART, K. A KOL. (1982). Nízke Tatry – východná časť. Turistický sprievodca ČSSR. Šport, Bratislava.

MAZÚR, E., LUKNIŠ, M. (1978): Regionálne geomorfologické členenie SR. Geografický časopis, 30, 2, Bratislava.

MEDZIHRADSKÝ, V. (1982): Orava. Turistický sprievodca. Šport, Bratislava.

MIREK, Z., PIĘKOŚ-MIRKOWA H. (1993): Przyroda Kotliny Zakopiańskiej, TPN, Kraków – Zakopane.

MIREK, Z. (1996): Przyroda Tatrzańskiego Parku Narodowego, TPN, Kraków – Zakopane.

MOSKAŁA, E. (1980): Schroniska PTTK w Karpatach Polskich, Wyd. PTTK Kraj, Warszawa – Kraków.

NYKA, J. (1995): Pieniny (przewodnik), Wyd. Trawers, Warszawa.

PACL, J. (1972): Východisko Ždiar – Javorina. Šport, Bratislava.

PARYSCY Z. (1995): Wielka Encyklopedia Tatrzańska, Wydawnictwo Górskie, Poronin.

PINKWART, M. (1992): Przewodnik po Zakopanem, Wyd. Sport i Turystyka, Warszawa.

PODHALAŃSKI ZWIĄZEK GMIN (1997), System Perfekt, Bydgoszcz.

PODHALE I PIENINY – PRZEWODNIK DLA AKTYWNYCH (1997), GeoCenter Warszawa.

REHMAN, A. (1895): Karpaty opisane pod względem fizyczno-geograficznym, Lwów.

SLOVENSKO – SPRIEVODCA PO MÚZEÁCH A GALÉRIÁCH (1994), Slovenské národné múzeum, Bratislava.

SLOVENSKO – SPRÍSTUPNENÉ JASKYNE (1997), Knižné centrum, Žilina.

SŁOWNIK GEOGRAFICZNO-KRAJOZNAWCZY POLSKI (1983), PWN, Warszawa.

SZCZEPANIK, K. (1996): Zakopane (przewodnik), Wyd. PTTK Kraj, Warszawa.

STARÁ ĽUBOVŇA – KLENOT SEVERNÉHO SPIŠA (1993), Agentúra Vizual, Košice.

SÚPIS PAMIATOK NA SLOVENSKU (1969), Obzor, Bratislava.

ŠLACHTA, F. (1992): Ružomberok. Vydavateľstvo Osveta, Martin,

TKÁČ, V. (1993): Slovensko, Krajina kultúrnych podkladov. Optys, Opava.

TROCHIMIUK A., WROŃSKI P. A KOL. (1997): Podhale i Pieniny, Geo Center, Warszawa.

VLASTIVEDNÝ SLOVNÍK OBCÍ NA SLOVENSKU (1977), Veda, Bratislava.

VYSOKÉ TATRY, I – XXXVI

A - Autoopravovne (Car repair)

There is a network of car repair stations all over Slovakia and Poland, with one in every town providing general repairs and emergency services for virtually every model of vehicle. The opening hours during the tourist season are longer. Private workshops also offer, in smaller communities, a partial part-time service.

AUTOMONTI – Autoservis, Kamenná baňa 28, 060 01 Kežmarok, tel. 0968/52 20 40, 55 24 46, fax 0968/52 24 46
– Pneuservis, Kamenná baňa 28, 060 01 Kežmarok, tel.0968/52 20 40, 55 24 46, fax 0968/52 24 46
– Predajňa náhradných dielov, Kamenná baňa 28, 060 01 Kežmarok, tel.0968/52 20 40, 55 24 46, fax 0968/52 24 46
Autoservis Sarvaš, Garbiarska 905/4, 031 01 Liptovský Mikuláš, tel. 0849/52 61 29
Pneuservis Unigumm Citroën s.r.o., Ul. 1. Mája 161, 031 01 Liptovský Mikuláš, tel./fax 0849/51 44 02, 52 21 65
Pneuservis SEVYT, Komenského 18, 031 01 Liptovský Mikuláš, tel. 0849/522 501, 0945/32 37 59
Pneuservis a autoumyváreň, Ul. J. Alexyho 1988, 031 01 Liptovský Mikuláš, tel. 0849/205 80, 205 82, 0903/50 10 14
Autoservis LUNA (zn. Honda), Revolučná 3, 031 01 Liptovský Mikuláš, tel./fax 0849/51 43 47, 0903/50 16 86.

B – Bezpečnosť (Safety)

A network of police stations in the towns and bigger communities provides for the public order and safety of local citizens and visitors. In the event of any danger, loss, theft of personal belongings in the territory of the Slovak Republic call the phone number **158**. In the Polish part of the Tatras and the sub Tatra region call the emergency phone number **997**.

C – Cesty a cestovné doklady (Road and travel documents)

The road network in Slovakia and Poland is dense and well-maintained. It consists of motorways, primary and second class state roads, as well as side roads. For tourists in the Slovak sub Tatra region the motorway leading from Ružomberok to Hybe is relevant and the same is true for Kraków in Poland. Use of the motor ways is paid by purchasing a stamp at a price of 200 Sk which is sold in petrol stations.
Foreigners must possess and demonstrate a valid passport on entry to the Slovak Republic and the Polish Republic. Foreign drivers' licences and technical documents of motorcars are admitted in Slovakia and Poland, and an international green card of insurance is required at the point of entry. Visitors are recommended to possess also photocopies of the travel documents as it facilitates the provision of substitutes in the event of loss.

C – Cestovné kancelárie (Travel agencies)

Tourism and travel is serviced by a network of numerous travel agencies in every town and tourist resort offering attractive half-day, all-day and longer trips to the most interesting parts of northern Slovakia and southern Poland.

CK Krokus, Partizánska 677/18, 058 01 Poprad, tel. 092/72 31 11
Horizont, cestovná a obchodná agentúra, Ul. 1. mája 4, 058 01 Poprad tel. 092/644 11, 72 31 13
CK Ferrotour, VSŽ a.s., Námestie Sv. Egídia 87, 058 01 Poprad, tel./fax 092/637 75
CK Enos, spol. s.r.o., J. Curie 1, 058 01 Poprad, tel./fax 0969/42 20 93
CK Lerotour, Námestie Sv. Egídia 25, 058 01 Poprad, tel./fax 092/618 54
CK Tiptour, spol. s.r.o., P.O.BOX 30, 058 01 Poprad, tel. 092/72 31 25, 0905/30 04 00
CK Tatrania, ul. Mnoheľa 825/5, 058 01 Poprad, tel. 092/72 12 85, 652 50, fax 092/72 12 66
CK ADLER, Hviezdoslavova 3, 060 01 Kežmarok, tel./fax 0968/48 98

C – Colné predpisy (Customs provisions)

Custom-free import to Slovakia and Poland concerns items for personal use and consumption. Custom free export of items is permitted if their value does not exceed 3,000 Sk or 100 USD (only 1 litre of spirit and 2 litres of wine and 200 cigarettes per person are exempt from customs duty). Goods exceeding this limit are subject to custom surcharges. More detailed information on custom provisions are provided at every border crossing. Please read the leaflets updating the custom tariffs, or the list of the items with limited export or import duty.

Č – Čas (Time)

CET - Central European Time i.e. one hour ahead of Greenwich Mean Time is valid in Slovakia and Poland. Central European Summer Time is introduced for the summer season (six months) in the majority of European states, i.e. 2 hours ahead of the Greenwich time.

D – Doprava (Transport)

The best access to the Slovak Tatras by personal transport is from Ružomberok; the Polish Tatras are best accessible from Kraków. For the road border crossings between Slovakia and Poland see the section "Border Crossings". The biggest towns in Slovakia and Poland are connected to the Tatra holiday resorts by regular bus lines. The best and most frequented trains to the Slovak Tatras start in Bratislava and Košice, on the Polish side the best railway connection is from Kraków. Airline transportation is provided by the airport Poprad-Tatry.

D – Dopravné predpisy (Traffic rules)

All traffic signs agree with European standards. The wearing of safety belts is obligatory. In accordance with other countries there is a ban on the drinking of alcohol whilst driving. A speed limit of 60 km in the communities and 90 km outside the communities is to be observed. The speed limit on motorways and fast roads is 130 km/hour. Essential car equipment must include a first aid box, a tow rope, a warning triangle and a spare wheel. Children below 12 and pets must not sit in the front seats.

E – Elektrická energia (Electric power)

Electric installations are as a rule adjusted to 220V of alternate current (AC). Sockets corresponding to European standards are available for general use.

G – Gastronómia (Food)

The basics ingredients of Polish and Slovak food in the Tatra region in the past were usually milk, potatoes and cabbage, a combination of which was used for the preparation of simple and tasty meals (for instance, typical Slovak dumplings with salty sheep cheese or dumplings with stewed cabbage). Milk was drank natural or sour, milk products like whey, cottage cheese, cream and all kinds of cheeses were, and still are, very popular. Dumplings, in Slovak "halušky", with sheep cheese called "bryndza" garnished with fried bacon are the traditional Slovak national meal. However, at present Slovak and Polish cooking has acquired a European character with a higher meat consumption, and in the towns there is also foreign cuisine with the advent of international restaurants, including French, Chinese, Hungarian, Italian etc. The typical Slovak spirit is called "borovička" distilled from juniper fruit, other favourite Slovak spirits are plum brandy and "hriatô" (a mixture of spirit, honey and fried bacon). For the meals and drinks see page 344.)

H – Hraničné priechody (The border crossings)

The road border crossings:

- Barwinek–Vyšný Komárnik (24 hours)
- Piwniczna – Mníšek nad Popradom(24 hours)
- Niedzica – Lysá nad Dunajcom (8:00 – 22:00h, only for the citizens of Slovakia and Poland)
- Lysa Polana – Javorina (24 hours)
- Chyžne – Trstená (24 hours)
- Chochołów – Suchá Hora (8:00 – 22:00h, only for the citizens of Slovakia and Poland)
- Jurgów – Podspády (8:00 – 22:00h, only for the citizens of Slovakia and Poland)

The railway border crossings:

- Muszyna – Plaveč
- Zwardoň – Skalité

I – Informácie (Information)

Information on travel and tourism concerning the Tatra region is provided by some bureaux of travel information and promotion in certain areas (see INFO pages). Information concerning other regions is provided by the travel agencies (see page 346).

Publicity agency and graphic art studio Color Media,
Levočská 866, 058 01 Poprad, tel./fax 092/722 081, 477 116, 477 107
Design studio PROX T.E.C. s.r.o., Levočská 866, 058 01 Poprad, tel. 092/72 29 45, fax 092/72 23 58
Municipality of Kežmarok, Hlavné námestie 1, 060 01 Kežmarok, tel./fax 0968/52 26 21

J – Jazyk (Language)

Slovak is the official language in the territory of Slovakia, likewise Polish is the official language in the territory of Poland. The Slovak and Polish languages are mutually understandable both being Slavic tongues. In cities and popular tourist resorts and in the majority of hotels a reasonable level of German and English is spoken.

K – Kúpele (Spas)

Spas are located in the following communities: Lučivná, Lúčky, Starý Smokovec, Szczawnica, Štrbské pleso, Vyšné Ružbachy (see the register).

Beauty parlour Kleopatra, Hviezdoslavovo nám. 2, 058 01 Poprad, tel. 092/72 42 04

L – Lekárska pomoc (Medical care)

In all Polish and Slovak towns medical care is provided for in hospitals or clinics. Larger communities also have their medical centres. In the event of serious accidents or a sudden deterioration in health emergency services are available on phone number **155** in Slovakia and **999** in Poland. Before travelling to Slovakia or Poland health insurance enquiries are advisable.

Pharmacy "U ČIERNEHO ORLA", Sobotské nám. 1771/37, 058 01 Poprad, tel./fax 092/72 24 27

M – Mapy (Maps)

Whilst travelling around northern Slovakia and Southern Poland use a road map of Slovakia and Poland on a scale of 1:200 000, or a car atlas on a scale of 1: 400 000 available in book shops or road border crossings. For hiking in the Tatras, Slovak or Polish tourist maps in scales of 1:50 000 or 1:25 000 are recommended.

SLOVENSKÁ REPUBLIKA
lyžiarske strediská
skicentres • skizentren
ośródki narciarskie • síközpontok
1. VYDANIE
NOVINKA
2 HOHE TATRA STARÝ SMOKOVEC
1 : 25 000
WANDERKARTE
DEUTSCHE AUSGABE
112 WESTLICHE TATRA ROHÁČE
1 : 50 000
SKI UND WANDERKARTE
DEUTSCHE AUSGABE
112 ZÁPADNÉ TATRY ROHÁČE
1 : 50 000
TURISTICKÁ MAPA
3. VYDANIE
113 VYSOKÉ TATRY
1 : 50 000
TURISTICKÁ MAPA
5. VYDANIE
113 VYSOKÉ TATRY
1 : 50 000
LYŽIARSKA A TURISTICKÁ MAPA
3. VYDANIE
122 NÍZKE TATRY CHOPOK
1 : 50 000
TURISTICKÁ MAPA
3. VYDANIE
123 NÍZKE TATRY KRÁĽOVA HOLA
1 : 50 000
TURISTICKÁ MAPA
2. VYDANIE
VKÚ HARMANEC
VOJENSKÝ KARTOGRAFICKÝ ÚSTAV, š. p.
HARMANEC
Tel.: 00421-88-798247;-48
Fax: 00421-88-998153

N – Nákupy a suveníry (Shopping and souvenirs)

A great variety of traditional folk handicrafts and artistic products are available in numerous shops and retail stands all over the Tatras on both sides of the mountain range. As a rule they are open daily and in high season also late at night.

Souvenirs ORIENT, Hviezdoslavova 19, 060 01 Kežmarok, tel. 0968/52 26 86, 656 30

Bookshop alter ego, Hlavné nám. 3, 060 01 Kežmarok, tel./fax 0968/40 21, 52 54 31

Souvenirs MAGURA, Hlavné nám. 50, 060 01 Kežmarok tel. 0905/52 49 02, fax 0968/52 39 39

Shop PRAKTIK, Zdravotnícka 4, 058 01 Poprad, tel. 092/72 24 18

O – Otváracie hodiny (Opening hours)

Shops are open from 9:00 to 18:00h, some grocery shops open at 6:00h and close late at night. On Saturdays and Sundays the majority of shops close at 13:00h. Pharmacies open from 8:00 to 18:00h, and there is always one or two emergency pharmacies open during the night and during holidays. Banks open from 8:00 to 15:00h with a lunch break and are closed on Sundays and Saturdays. Banking automats are available. Museums open as a rule from 9:00 or 10:00h to 17:00h with closing days on Monday or Tuesday, with regional variation. See other opening hours included in other entries.

P – Parkovanie (Parking)

Parking in town centres is possible only in limited locations. In big cities parking cards are used. They must be made visible in the car and are sold in newspaper stands or tobacco shops. The parking of cars in prohibited places is subject to a fine amounting up to 500 Sk, or clamping and towing away.

P – Peniaze (Money)

The Slovak currency unit is the Slovak crown (1 Sk = 100 haliers). Bank notes are in the nominal value of 20, 50, 100, 200, 500, 1000, and 5000 Sk, the coins are in the nominal value of 10, 20, 50 haliers and 1, 2, 5, and 10 Sk. The Slovak crown is not a free exchangeable currency, and the exchange rate moderately oscillates. The import of foreign currency to Slovakia is optional and the export of the Slovak crown and foreign currency from Slovakia is limited. Banks, hotels, top restaurants, car rental shops and some retail shops mostly accept the majority of international credit cards. In towns and tourist centres the banking automats accept international cards, and cards issued by Slovak banks are available.

The Polish currency is the Polish zloty. Bank notes are in the nominal value of 10, 50, 100, 500, 1000, the coins are in the nominal value of 10, 20, 50 and 1, 2, 5, and 10 Zl. The Polish zloty is also not an exchangeable currency, the exchange rate moderately oscillates. The import of foreign currency to Poland is optional. Banks, hotels, top restaurants, car rental shops and some retail shops mostly accept the majority of international credit cards. In towns and tourist centres banking automats accept international cards and the cards issued by the domestic banks are also available.

P – Pohonné hmoty (Fuel)

The prices of petrol and motor oil are lower in Slovakia and Poland than the European average. All over the Slovak and Polish territories a dense network of petrol stations is available. In Slovakia the petrol SUPER (95), ŠPECIÁl (91), lead-free petrol Natural (95 and 98) and motor oil are sold. The export of fuel in an amount exceeding 10 litres is prohibited. In the towns and on the motorways and main roads some petrol stations are open 24 hours per day (see INFO pages)

Petrol station Benzinol, 031 01 Liptovský Mikuláš – Okoličné, tel. 0849/208 26

P – Pošta (Post offices)

Post offices are open Mon-Fri 8:00-18:00h, Saturdays they close at 13:00h. Some main offices and telegraph service in towns and tourist centres operate 24 hours per day.

R – Reštaurácie (Restaurants)

The opening hours in the majority of restaurants are generally from 10:00 to 22:00h in bigger towns and tourist centres night clubs exist (see INFO pages). Tipping roughly represents the percentage comparable to European countries, and where no service charge is included in the bill a tip generally expresses the recognition of the service.

Reštaurácia Panda, Zdravotnícka 4, 058 01 Poprad, tel./092/629 02

S – Sviatky (The state holidays)

The state holidays of the Slovak Republic:

- January 1 – Declaration of the Slovak Republic
- July 5 – The Day of the Slovak Messengers of Faith - Constantine and Method
- August 29 – The Anniversary of the Slovak National Uprising
- September 1 – The Day of the Slovak Constitution

The days of rest (in addition to Sundays and Saturdays)

- January 6 – Three Magi day
- Good Friday
- Easter Monday
- May 1 – May Day
- 8. máj – Victory over Fascism Day
- September 15 – The Virgin Mary of Seven Grievances
- November 1 – All Saints' Day
- December 24 – Christmas
- December 25 – The First Christmas Holiday
- December 26 – The Second Christmas Holiday

The state holidays of the Polish Republic:

- January 1 – New Year's Day
- 3. máj – Constitution of the Polish Republic Day
- 15. august – The Polish Army Day
- 11. november – Independence Day

Rest days:

- January 6 – Three Magi day
- Good Friday
- Easter Monday
- May 1 – May Day
- November 1 – All Saints' Day
- December 24 – Christmas
- December 25 – The First Christmas Holiday
- December 26 – The Second Christmas Holiday

T – Taxi

Taxi services are available in all towns and tourist centres in Slovakia and Poland.
The tourist tariff per 1km within the municipal limits is approx. 20 Sk or 2 Zl

U – Ubytovanie (Accommodation)

Accommodation in the hotels, motels, pensions, car camps and in private houses is available through the travel agencies (see page 346). Every town and tourist centre in Slovakia and Poland have sufficient lodging facilities (see INFO pages). Four categories of hotels exist: one, two, three and four star hotels, which correspond to level and price. In the mountain and sub-mountain regions of the Slovak and Polish Tatras private owners in most of the small communities offer accommodation in well-equipped and comfortable houses or individual cottages.

Hotel Štart, Pod Lesom 24, 060 01 Kežmarok, tel./fax 0968/52 29 16
Hotel TATRAN, Firma Pišta, 059 52 Veľká Lomnica tel./fax 0968/611 34
Hotel POPRAD, Partizánska 677/18, 058 01 Poprad tel. 092/72 12 51
Hotel Smokovec, 062 01 Starý Smokovec 25, tel. 0969/42 51 98, fax 0969/42 51 95
Hotel PRIMULA s.r.o., č. 373, 027 32 Zuberec, tel. 0847/39 50 01, tel./fax 0847/39 51 79
Club Hotel OLYMPIA, Partizánska ul., 058 01 Poprad, tel. 092/657 55, fax 092/72 41 83 – 27 beds
Penzión Alena, Ľubická 4, 060 01 Kežmarok, tel./fax 0968/42 81, 52 24 50
Penzión u Barborky, Pod bránou 4, 058 01 Poprad tel. 092/625 45 – 15 beds
Penzión na terase, Boženy Nemcovej 955/1, 058 01 Poprad, tel. 092/72 30 67 – 10 beds
Penzión Svätý Juraj, Sobotské nám. 29, 058 01 Poprad, tel./fax 092/72 30 65, 72 14 11, 0905/34 27 33 – 20 beds
Penzión NONSTOP, Bodice 101, 031 01 Liptovský Mikuláš, tel. 0905/27 25 38, tel./fax 0849/52 92 05 – 12 beds
Penzión Čierny Grúň, 059 40 Liptovská Teplička, tel. 092/961 16 – 24 beds
Penzión Dagmar, Sobotské námestie č.1731/8, 058 01 Poprad-Spišská Sobota, tel. 092/73 13 44, fax 092/612 36

Embassies and consular representations

Particular embassies and consular representations in Slovakia are as follows:

- Czech Republic – Ul. 29. augusta 5, Bratislava, tel. 07/5361204
- France – Hlavné nám. 7, Bratislava, tel. 07/5335725
- Hungary – Sedlárska 3, Bratislava, tel. 07/5330541
- Germany – Hviezdoslavovo nám. 10, Bratislava, tel. 07/5319640
- **Poland – Jančova 6, Bratislava, tel. 07/580 34 12**
- Austria – Ventúrska 10, Bratislava, tel. 07/5332985
- Russia – Godrova 4, Bratislava, tel. 07/5313468
- Italy – Červeňova 19, Bratislava, tel. 07/5312585
- Ukraine – Radvanská 35, Bratislava, tel. 07/5312651
- United Kingdom – Panská 16, Bratislava, tel. 07/5319632
- U.S.A. – Hviezdoslavovo nám. 4, Bratislava, tel. 07/5330096

Addresses of some of the diplomatic representations seated in Poland are as follows:

- Czech Republic – Ul.. Koszykowa 18, Warszawa, tel. 022/628 72 21
- France – Ul. Piękna 1, Warszawa, tel. 022/628 84 01
- Hungary – Ul. Chopina 2, Warszawa, tel. 022/628 44 51
- **Slovak Republic –** Ul. Litewska 6, Warszawa, tel. 022/628 40 51
- Germany – Ul. Dąbrowiecka 30, Warszawa, tel. 022/617 30 11
- Austria – Ul. Gagarina 34, Warszawa, tel. 022/41 00 81
- Russia – Ul. Belwederska 49, Warszawa, tel. 022/621 34 53
- Italy – Pl. Dąbrowskiego 6, Warszawa, tel. 022/826 34 71
- Ukraine – Al. Szucha 7, Warszawa, tel. 022/625 01 27
- United Kingdom – Al. Róz 1, Warszawa, tel. 022/628 10 01
- U.S.A. – Al. Ujazdowskie 29/31, Warszawa, tel. 022/625 01 27

Z – Zmenárne a banky (Foreign exchange)

In all towns and tourist centres a network of state-owned and private foreign exchange establishments are available. The opening hours on work days are as a rule from 8:00 to 16:00h, in bigger centres some of them open also on holidays or open longer hours. The use of the foreign exchange service at border crossings when entering Slovakia or Poland, and banking automats placed next to some banks in the biggest Slovak towns and holiday centres, are recommended.

For your personal safety the exchange of foreign currencies in the banks and exchange points found in all hotels, tourist agencies and shops is recommended. Producing a bank receipt also the reverse purchase of the previously exchanged currency is possible.

Istrobanka a.s., Partizánska 18, 058 01 Poprad, tel. 092/627 91, fax 092/72 12 43
Poľnobanka a.s. Bratislava, filiálka Poprad, ul. Karpatská 3056/15, 058 01 Poprad, tel. 092/72 27 70, fax 092/72 11 65

IMPORTANT!

- in hotels, public institutions, travel agencies and banks English, German, and to a limited extent, French and Italian are spoken
- change your money in banks and official foreign exchange points only, never in the street
- do not leave your money, cameras and valuable objects in a parked car
- do not carry on you large sums of money
- leave your money, jewellery and valuable objects in a hotel locker
- when taking a taxi observe whether the taximete is on or ask for a receipt beforehand
- if possible, park your car in guarded parking lot
- upon leaving the country the Slovak banks, Tatr Banka and VÚB admit the reverse purchase of Slovak currency, providing you show your passport and original receipt.

Map scales

Scale of the map in pages 132, 138, 146, 158, 172, 194, 204, 222, 239, 252, 310, 322 a 327 is 1 : 250 000

Scale of the map in pages 92, 77 a 110 is 1 : 25 000

Scale of the map in pages 43, 52, 55, 64, 67, 75, 89, 105, 119, 283, 296, 301 a 338 is 1 : 75 000

Explanations to the town plans

objekt popísaný v texte • object described in the text

hrad • castle

kostol • church

kaplnka • chapel

verejné budovy • public building

pamätník • monument

fontána • fountain

vežovitá stavba • tower building

divadlo • theatre

múzeum • museum

galéria • picture gallery

nemocnica • hospital

informácie • information

pošta • post-office

hotel • hotel

polícia • policestation

benzínová čerpacia stanica • filling station

parkovisko • parking area

cintorín • cemetery

ŽSR

We respect the past
We are aware of the present
We care about the future

General management
Klemensova 8, 813 61 Bratislava
Tel.: 07 - 204 44 11, 32 52 42
Fax: 07 - 36 22 96

Information bureaux of the Railways

KOŠICE	Tel.: 095 - 622 37 00, 613 11 11
ZVOLEN	Tel.: 0855 - 243 93
ŽILINA	Tel.: 089 - 62 22 26 (62 30 43)
BRATISLAVA	Tel.: 07 - 204 44 84, 49 82 75

Nature and intelligence

DAJAMA VYDAVATEĽSTVO

like each other!